T0330332

Global Securitisation and CDOs

Wiley Finance Series

Global Securitisation and CDOs

John Deacon

John Wiley & Sons, Ltd

Published 2004 John Wiley & Sons Ltd, The Atrium, Southern Gate, Chichester,
West Sussex PO19 8SQ, England

Telephone (+44) 1243 779777

Reprinted June 2004, February 2007

Email (for orders and customer service enquiries): cs-books@wiley.co.uk
Visit our Home Page on www.wileyeurope.com or www.wiley.com

This publication is designed to provide accurate and authoritative information in regard to
the subject matter covered. It is sold on the understanding that the Publisher is not engaged
in rendering professional services. If professional advice or other expert assistance is required,
the services of a competent professional should be sought.

Other Wiley Editorial Offices

John Wiley & Sons Inc., 111 River Street, Hoboken, NJ 07030, USA

Jossey-Bass, 989 Market Street, San Francisco, CA 94103-1741, USA

Wiley-VCH Verlag GmbH, Boschstr. 12, D-69469 Weinheim, Germany

John Wiley & Sons Australia Ltd, 33 Park Road, Milton, Queensland 4064, Australia

John Wiley & Sons (Asia) Pte Ltd, 2 Clementi Loop #02-01, Jin Xing Distripark, Singapore 129809

John Wiley & Sons Canada Ltd, 22 Worcester Road, Etobicoke, Ontario, Canada M9W 1L1

Wiley also publishes its books in a variety of electronic formats. Some content that appears in print may not
be available in electronic books.

Library of Congress Cataloging-in-Publication Data

Deacon, John, 1969–
      Global securitisation and CDOs / John Deacon.
          p. cm. — (Wiley finance series)
      Includes bibliographical references and index.
      ISBN 0-470-86987-9 (cloth)
      1. Asset-backed financing. 2. Debt. I. Title. II. Series.
   HG4028.A84D43 2003
   658.15′26—dc22   2003020789

British Library Cataloguing in Publication Data

A catalogue record for this book is available from the British Library

ISBN 13: 978-0-470-86987-1 (Hb)

The information contained in this publication should not be relied on as professional advice and should not be
regarded as a substitute for detailed advice in individual cases. No responsibility for any loss occasioned to
any person acting or refraining from action as a result of material in this publication is accepted by the editors,
author or publishers. If advice concerning individual problems or other expert assistance is required, the
service of a competent professional adviser should be sought.

Typeset in 10/12pt Times by Originator, Gt Yarmouth, Norfolk

This book is printed on acid-free paper responsibly manufactured from sustainable forestry
in which at least two trees are planted for each one used for paper production.

Contents

Preface

In recent years, against a backdrop of volatile equity markets and minimal M&A activity, the fixed income markets have assumed ever greater importance in global financing.

This book considers two of the fastest growing areas of the credit markets – the securitisation markets and the sister markets in credit derivatives and synthetic products. Both of these areas are relatively young, and are growing and developing fast amidst an increased focus on fixed income products in investment banking.

Combined here are a detailed overview of global securitisation, asset-backed and CDO structures, and an extensive analysis of synthetic and credit derivative structures, the new Basel Capital Accord, developments in worldwide accounting standards and details of 52 global markets ranging from the US, the UK and Europe, to Asia, Latin America and Australasia.

Over the last few years, global macro events have included:

- Introduction of the euro in Europe.
- The "dotcom" boom and bust.
- Heavy falls in global equity markets and an increase in the importance of the fixed income markets.
- Significant disruption in the corporate bond markets with fallout from Enron, WorldCom and other accounting scandals.
- 9/11, the Iraq War, and SARS.

These events have led to significant market volatility – not just in the equities market, but also in the debt markets. However, they have also given rise to significant growth opportunities for the ABS market. Historically ABS has flourished, if not as a counter-cyclical product, at least as a product that thrives in adversity.

The market was given birth in the savings and loan crisis in the US, and has since overcome recessions, adverse regulatory environments, currency crises and inherent complexity to emerge all the stronger. For each road-block thrown in the way of the development of the market, a new solution arrives which often leads to significant new growth – for example, the very difficulties being experienced in the German economy at present led to the weight thrown behind the announcement in April 2003 of a "true sale initiative" joint venture between the leading lights of the German financial community to develop securitisation by the financial sector.

In the US, securitisation is stable and mature. In Europe, the market is still growing rapidly but no longer has the patchy feel of a few years ago. The investor base is widening and information flow is improving. The Asian market is still more fragmented, but regulators are putting frameworks in place to develop the product.

In just the last five or six years, the accelerating pace of developments has included:

- New ABS laws or regulations of one form or another in France, Germany, Greece, Italy, Japan, Korea, Malaysia, the Philippines, Portugal, Singapore, South Africa, Spain, Sweden, Taiwan, and the UK.
- Inauguration and growth of the European covered bond markets in France, Ireland, Luxembourg, and the UK.
- REIT regulations or proposals in Hong Kong, Japan, Singapore, and Taiwan.
- Announcement of the German true sale initiative leading to an impetus to securitise.
- Ramping up of ABS issuance at Mortgage Corporations in Hong Kong, Korea, Japan, Malaysia, and Thailand.
- Sale of non-performing loan parcels in China, the Czech Republic, Indonesia, Italy, Japan, Korea, and Thailand.
- New pan-European directives on insolvency, accounting, withholding tax and securities regulation.
- Growth in the use of credit derivatives and guidelines from Australia, Hong Kong, Germany, Japan, Singapore, and the UK.
- ISDA credit derivative documentation and definitions.
- New accounting rules for ABS and for off-balance-sheet vehicles in the US and the EU.
- Increasing importance of International Accounting Standards.
- ABS bank capital guidelines published in Germany, Malaysia, the Philippines, Singapore, and the UK.
- New Basel Capital Accord proposals on regulatory capital.

About the Author

John Deacon is Executive Director and Head of Debt Principal Finance at UBS in London where he focuses on asset-backed investment opportunities for the Euro 3 billion Brooklands Synthetic CDO series originated by UBS Principal Finance in London since 2001.

He is also a co-founder of the ThorABS asset-backed securities website (www. ThorABS.com).

Prior to joining UBS he was Head of Principal Finance at Greenwich NatWest, where he was responsible for the acquisition and restructuring of performing and non-performing assets for the balance sheet of the bank.

Mr Deacon has worked as a securitisation, principal finance and derivatives specialist in the European and Asian markets and as an investor, issuer, investment banker and lawyer in London, Paris and Hong Kong. He has extensive global securitisation and principal finance experience from transactions in France, Hong Kong, Indonesia, Italy, Spain, Thailand and the UK and structuring in Germany, Japan, Korea, the Netherlands, Singapore, Sweden and the Philippines, for products as diverse as:

- Principal finance
- Whole business
- Synthetics
- Credit derivatives
- Structured derivatives
- Bond repackagings
- CDO structures
- Commercial paper conduits
- Asset-backed MTN programmes
- Non-performing loans
- Commercial mortgages
- Residential mortgages
- Auto leases and hire purchase contracts
- Trade receivables
- Multi-family residential real estate
- Commercial real estate
- Nuclear moratorium credits
- PFI receivables

Mr Deacon qualified as a lawyer at Clifford Chance. He is a Solicitor of the Supreme Court in England and Wales, a Solicitor of the Supreme Court in Hong Kong and an ACIB and has written articles for the International Securitisation Report and for the International Securitization & Structured Finance Report. He has spoken at seminars and workshops for securitisation and credit derivatives industry professionals organised by Euromoney, AIC Conferences, ICC and Futures & Options World.

1

Introduction

1.1 FORMS OF SECURITISATION

1.1.1 What is securitisation?

Securitisation is the process of converting cash flows arising from underlying assets or debts (receivables) due to the originator (the entity which created the receivables) into a smoothed repayment stream, thus enabling the originator to raise asset-backed finance through a loan or an issue of debt securities – generically known as asset-backed securities or ABS – which is limited recourse in nature to the credit of the receivables rather than that of the originator as a whole, and with the finance being self-liquidating in nature.

Deals are normally structured by a transfer of receivables from the originator to a newly established company known as a special purpose vehicle (or SPV), in a way designed to separate the receivables from the insolvency risk of the originator, and referred to as a "true sale". The SPV then issues ABS and transfers the proceeds to the originator by way of purchase price for the receivables. The purchase proceeds are normally less than the face value of the receivables, with some residual risk on the receivables being retained by the originator as a form of "credit enhancement" for the ABS issue (e.g. by way of a holding of subordinated notes issued by the SPV). The originator will also retain rights to receive from the SPV any profit realised on the receivables after repayment of the ABS issue. See Figure 1.1.

As most ABS are rated by one or more credit rating agencies for sale to investors, the securitisation structuring process is driven by the requirements which the rating agencies have in order to assign particular rating levels to the ABS issued.

This example deal structure does, however, disguise the fact that securitisation is a conceptual tool rather than a rigid form of structure, and multiple different developments and off-shoots of the core product have been seen, as discussed below.

The assets or cash flows that can be securitised vary widely. The market began with the securitisation of the contracted future payments due under long-term consumer financing contracts – chiefly mortgages. From here, it has rapidly developed into the securitisation of shorter-term financing assets such as credit card or auto loan receivables and into commercial or corporate assets such as real estate and lease cash flows.

The broadest classification of securities in the global asset-backed markets is into:

- ABS (asset-backed securities)
- CDOs (collateralised debt obligations)
- CMBS (commercial mortgage-backed securities)
- RMBS (residential mortgage-backed securities)

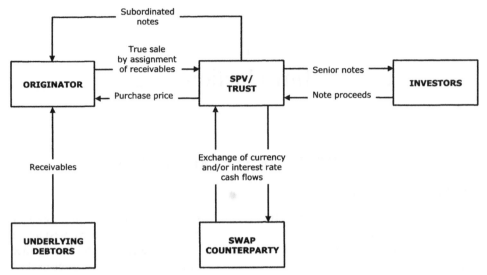

Figure 1.1   Paradigm securitisation structure

Of these, the main classes of securities in the pure securitisation markets today are:

- Commercial ABS (including EETCs)
- Consumer ABS (including credit cards and consumer loans)
- CMBS
- Non-performing loans or NPLs
- RMBS.

In addition, one further class of assets is typically financed through the use of commercial paper (CP) conduits rather than in the long-term markets:

- Trade receivables.

Other types of product overlap with securitisation to a greater or lesser extent, blurring the distinction between the pure securitisation markets and other asset-backed bond markets:

- CDOs
- Covered bonds and Pfandbriefe
- Future flows
- REITs
- Repackagings
- Synthetics
- Whole business.

Some of these (such as CDOs) are treated as separate, parallel markets, with their own characteristics. Some (such as repackagings) are more private, and typically do not feature in deal tables. Yet others – such as whole business and future flows – utilise techniques that are more hybrid than pure securitisation, introducing elements of corporate credit risk, or flexing the assumption that ABS are indeed truly backed by specific assets.

1.1.2 Securitisation off-shoots

- **CDOs**   Structures which divide chiefly into CLO or CBO trades, where a whole portfolio of loans or debt securities (respectively) is repackaged to investors. CDO is used as generic terminology for both CLOs and CBOs. The CLO structure was used over the late 1990s by a number of banks to remove loans from their capital adequacy balance sheet following the seminal US$5 bn Rose Funding sub-participation structure established by NatWest Markets in November 1996, and has been used more recently in Japan. Arbitrage CBO structures have grown significantly since the mid-1990s.
- **Covered bonds and Pfandbriefe**   These instruments began life as the German Pfandbrief, an instrument that is effectively senior secured debt over a ring-fenced but revolving pool of mortgages or public sector debt. They have become known as covered bonds as the infrastructure for their use has developed in other European countries.
- **Future flows**   These are partially asset-backed transactions, in which funding is made by means of an advance that exceeds the current level of receivables available, and risk is therefore taken on the future generation of business by the originator. This technique has been extensively used in countries with a low sovereign rating ceiling, to securitise payments due in major currencies from highly rated debtors in other countries, in order to raise debt rated above the sovereign ceiling. Consequently, the technique is mostly used in Latin America and Asia for securitisation of export flows or cross-border payments, such as the series of participation certificates arranged for Telefonos de Mexico ("Telmex") in the late 1980s participating in receivables due under an international telecoms line usage agreement between Telmex and AT&T, and the more recent securitisations of oil and gas export receivables arranged for PDVSA, Pemex and Petrobras.
- **REITs**   These are vehicles set up under specific legislation, originally in the US but now also in Japan and Singapore, with further development planned across Asia, to invest in real estate. REITs acquire real estate investments and issue classes of debt secured over their assets.
- **Repackaging**   These are structures for the repackaging of debt, in which the "receivables" are already in the form of a loan or a debt security. These may use a debt issuance programme (such as an MTN programme) as a means of funding, to allow for rapidity and ease of issuance. The key difference from CDOs is that repackagings generally only repackage a single asset or a low number of underlying assets, rather than a portfolio of assets.
- **Synthetics**   These are structures that use credit derivatives to effect a synthetic transfer of risk (and do not by themselves effect a true sale transfer of assets out of the insolvency risk of the originator). They are frequently combined with the use of high-grade collateral to ensure isolation from the originator's insolvency risk, and are being used increasingly for CDO transactions, as well as for CMBS and RMBS deals. They are explored in more detail in Chapter 7. In the case of some CDOs, the underlying assets may themselves be in the form of credit derivatives.

- **Whole business** These are structures that securitise the whole business, or general operating cash flows, of a corporate entity. As a form of secured corporate debt, they form a cross-over between the corporate bond markets and the asset-backed bond markets, and are explored in more detail in Chapter 8. These structures are gaining prominence in Europe and Asia following their use as an acquisition financing technique in the UK.

A further area of finance which frequently overlaps with securitisation is that of private finance initiative (PFI) transactions, the name given in the UK to structures designed to enable governments to free up capital, or reduce capital commitments, by raising private sector finance to acquire government capital assets or for the completion of projects, with the government then making payment for the provision of services by the private sector.

Such transactions are often intended to be treated for accounting purposes as a payment by the government for the provision of services, rather than a borrowing by the government. They have been used extensively in the UK for development projects for public sector facilities, and in Italy for large-scale divestment of government assets such as real estate and welfare contributions.

1.2 RATIONALE FOR SECURITISATION

The rationale for securitisation varies widely from company to company. Some of the more frequently cited reasons for undertaking a securitisation are:

- **Return on capital** In cases where the originator is a regulated entity for capital adequacy purposes, finance can be raised which is outside the regulatory balance sheet, as the essence of the transaction is to replace receivables with cash, which carries a zero risk weighting for capital adequacy purposes. Consequently, the originator can release capital that would otherwise have to be held against the risk of default on the assets. For non-regulated originators, there is a corresponding boost to return on capital resulting from a reduced equity requirement.
- **Balance sheet management** Securitisation can be used to monetise assets on the balance sheet of the originator, without the originator being forced to sell them outright. The original form of the receivables (for example, a mortgage or an auto loan) cannot be readily marketed, save to another company in the same line of business or a factoring company, and is therefore relatively illiquid. Securitisation enables the creation of more liquid ABS instruments, which may help to enable the company to survive a short-term liquidity crisis, or simply help them to avoid selling assets outright at the wrong point in the economic cycle.
- **Off-balance-sheet funding** Securitisation can be used to extend the balance sheet of the originator, as the finance raised will not appear, in whole or in part, as an additional item on the balance sheet of the originator in its statutory accounts or consolidated accounts, and the assets securitised will be removed in whole or in part from the balance sheet. This is fresh additional finance for the business, or if all or part of the proceeds are used to pay down existing debt, this will enable it to reduce its gearing. Also, it may rely on any reduction in its gearing in order to raise future bank finance on better terms.

- **Funding diversification** The ABS markets have their own investor base, some or all of which may not be current investors in the business of the originator, whether due to unfamiliarity with the originator, or credit concerns on the originator. Issuing in the ABS markets enables the originator to access this new base of investors and expand their current funding sources.
- **Bank liquidity** A significant new use has been to increase the liquidity of assets on the balance sheet of a financial institution originator (enabling compliance with bank liquidity ratios), due to the acceptance of certain instruments as repo collateral (for example, the June 1998 announcement from the Bank of Spain that mortgage-backed securities and asset-backed securities would be eligible for repo with the European Central Bank, and the activities in Hong Kong of the HKMC which guarantees mortgage-backed securities re-acquired by the originator of the mortgages, offering beneficial capital treatment and the ability to re-discount the securities with the HKMA for liquidity purposes).
- **Cost of funds** The segregation of receivables from the insolvency risk of the originator will enable funds to be raised which are not linked to credit risk on the originator. For an originator that is perceived as a bad credit risk, or has a low credit rating, this should serve to improve the all-in cost of funds to the originator, or the amount of finance that can be raised.
- **Strategic profile** If the originator has not previously issued in the capital markets, it may be an unknown name to capital market investors, and a securitisation process attracting a high credit rating may enable the originator to launch itself in the capital markets successfully through ABS issuance and achieve a good reputation, enabling further issuance on a full recourse non-asset-backed basis.
- **Matched funding** The use of capital markets instruments enables matched funding to be raised, with the tenor of the ABS issue matching the tenor of the receivables (although due to prepayments on the receivables, the weighted average life of the instruments is likely to be significantly less than their tenor, unless substitution or replenishment of receivables is permitted).
- **Tenor** The use of matched funding in turn means that the ABS issued can (for example, in the case of mortgage assets) be 20- or 25-year committed finance, exceeding the maximum term funding usually available from bank lenders.
- **Transfer of risk** The transfer of the receivables also has the effect of transferring the risk of losses on the receivables due to defaults or delinquencies, leaving the originator with the risk of loss only on that portion of the risk that is retained by the originator (e.g. as credit enhancement for the ABS issued).
- **Systems** It has also been perceived that the analysis of the originator's systems, underwriting procedures and day-to-day administration that is required for the transaction may actually prove beneficial for the originator subsequently in terms of ongoing business efficiency.

Consequently, the elements of any particular securitisation transaction will depend very much on the form of the receivables and the legal and regulatory regimes applicable in the jurisdiction or jurisdictions of the origination of the receivables, the type of originator (corporate, financial institution, governmental entity, fund, etc.) as well as the main goals for the transaction (cost of funds, freeing regulatory capital, reducing gearing, etc.).

1.2.1 Securitisation by corporates

The extensive use of securitisation by corporates has been criticised in cases where the corporate has unsecured debt outstanding as well as securitised debt.

As the securitised debt is effectively senior secured debt limited in repayment to certain assets, increasing issuance of securitisation implies that an increasing proportion of the company's assets are pledged to securitisation investors, with only the residual equity value of the securitisation pools and unsecuritised assets available to unsecured creditors. Consequently, the credit quality (and potentially, credit rating) of the corporate's unsecured debt will suffer.

This is not an issue if the corporate undertakes a whole business deal, as the structure will not permit other unsecured debt of the issuer to be outstanding alongside the deal, unless it is subordinated and cannot trigger a default on the securitisation – a product that is unlikely to be available in the market other than from the corporate's parent, as it is essentially equity.

1.3   GLOBAL ABS MARKETS

As described in section 1.1, there are a variety of products that may or may not be classed as ABS for the purposes of measuring the size of the market. Likewise, certain specific sectors – such as the issuance of Agencies in the US (which carry the implicit support of the US Treasury), or the issue of domestic securities in less-developed markets (which are typically not structured or rated to the same standards as international cross-border issuance) – may be included or excluded. Consequently, any measure is bound to be approximate in nature, and Figure 1.2 shows growth in cross-border new issuance only, excluding US Agencies.

As can be seen from Figure 1.2, the US is the clear leader of the market in terms of size and development. However, issuance in Europe has shown significant growth in recent years and, more importantly, has become an accepted means of financing operations. The slow development of the market in Europe was a result of a perception that securitisation was a financing method of last resort – something that was used by companies who were unable to raise finance by any other means. Consequently, it acquired a stigma that has only faded with time as more and more companies have decided to utilise it.

Issuance in Japan and Australia has also grown significantly in recent years, with Japan mostly financing consumer loans and commercial leases, while Australia has been predominantly an RMBS market. It remains clear that ABS issuance in both Europe and Asia is growing at a rapid rate, with further record-breaking issuance projected over 2004.

Figure 1.3 illustrates the global new issuance split among different asset classes (again, excluding domestic issuance and Agencies). This understates the extent to which RMBS dominate the global asset class tables, showing only 32.7% of total new issuance in 2002 against 42.3% for consumer ABS, given the exclusion of the massive level of issuance in the US Agencies market. This understatement of the importance of RMBS is likely to continue to be the case with the development of covered bond technology in the UK and across Europe, which may supplant some

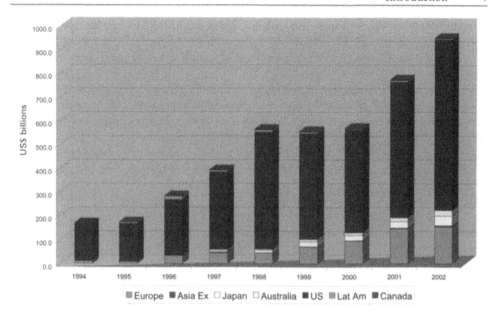

Figure 1.2 Global asset-backed annual new issuance by country; source www.ThorABS.com

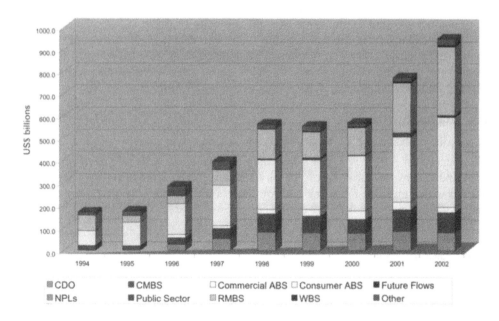

Figure 1.3 Global asset-backed annual new issuance by asset class; source www.ThorABS.com

pure RMBS issuance. Although the global importance of RMBS has been reflected in Japan more recently, as the RMBS sector has grown significantly, it has not to date been reflected in the rest of Asia, which is mostly dominated by short-term consumer asset deals.

A promising start to the Asian mortgage markets in Hong Kong, which saw private cross-border issuance from 1994 onwards, slowed following the Asian crisis and the start-up of the government-sponsored Hong Kong Mortgage Corporation (the latter leading to HKMC-sponsored programme issuance instead).

Despite this, RMBS still dominates global tables – second only to consumer ABS (which includes the US auto and credit cards market, as well as other forms of consumer finance).

CDOs and CMBS have steady global levels of issuance, although the dominance of the US markets understates the rapid growth in these sectors in Europe (see section 1.3.4 below).

1.3.1   US

The modern-day securitisation market began in the US and developed out of the market for mortgage-backed Ginnie Mae paper. US investment banks set up mortgage trading departments in the 1970s to deal in Ginnie Mae paper. The first private mortgage-backed securities issues for Bank of America began in 1977.

The impact of the rise of short-term interest rates in the US in October 1979 (which increased the cost of funds of the Savings and Loans – or "thrifts" – beyond their income receipts on mortgages largely bearing fixed long-term rates of interest), and the subsequent tax relief for thrifts passed in September 1981, gave a huge impetus to the market in trading of whole mortgage loans by providing that losses on the sale of mortgage assets by the thrifts could be amortised over the life of the loan and could be set against tax paid by the thrift over the previous 10 years.

The debt expansion in the US over the 1980s also added to the development of the securitisation market. The first non-mortgage backed deals were launched in 1985. The US market is significantly larger and more liquid than other global securitisation markets, and new issuance of ABS product rose significantly in 2002.

1.3.2   Canada

Canada has a large and developed domestic securitisation market, which has historically focused on ABCP issuance rather than term issuance. Offshore development has been hindered by withholding tax on payments overseas, although it was anticipated that this would improve following renegotiation of the Canada–US double tax treaty to remove withholding tax, opening up the US investor base for Canadian deals. Issuance in 2002 was up 2% on 2001.

1.3.3   Latin America

Transactions to date in Central and South America have largely centred on future flows style transactions, accounting for some 60% of issuance in 2002. Issuance has been dominated by the large future flows programmes for national oil companies – PDVSA in Venezuela, Pemex in Mexico and Petrobras in Brazil. The significant shift in geographic issuance over the course of 2000 (in 1999 Mexico accounted for 59% of issuance and Venezuela for 19%, while in 2001 Brazil accounted for 61%) has centred on the levels of issuance under these programmes.

The region has been dogged by economic and political volatility, which has created difficulties for transactions in some jurisdictions – notably Argentina, following exchange rate devaluation from January 2002 onwards. As a result, the level of cross-border issuance has dropped, while the level of domestic issuance has risen.

1.3.4 Europe

Europe has seen tremendous growth in new issuance of ABS since the introduction of the Euro in January 1999. Starting from a flat base in 1998, the market grew by 55% in 1999, 36% in 2000 and 55% in 2001. Growth was lower, at 5%, in 2002 (primarily due to a slowdown in the CDO market following negative performance trends) but issuance in the first half of 2003 once again proved to be impressive, with the market significantly ahead of 2002. Figure 1.4 illustrates the new issue split by country across Europe.

The surge in issuance has been primarily due to the bulk standardised issuance of the UK mortgage lenders, and the uplift in usage of securitisation in Italy:

- Despite the Eurostat ruling of July 2002 (see Chapter 10, section 10.4), the Italian government has continued to use securitisation extensively to transfer assets off its public sector balance sheet via the SCIP, INPS and INAIL transactions.
- Banks and financial institutions in Italy have increased their issuance significantly, now undertaking RMBS and lease deals as well as NPL deals.

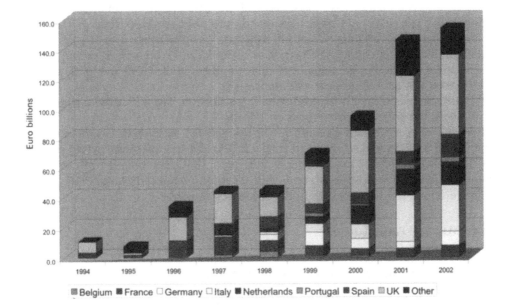

Figure 1.4 European asset-backed annual new issuance by country; source www.ThorABS.com

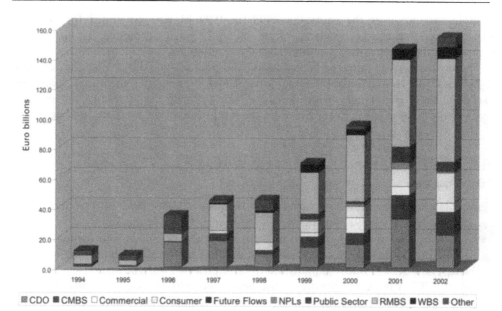

Figure 1.5 European asset-backed annual new issuance by asset class; source www.ThorABS. com

- CMBS issuance has risen Europe-wide, with bank conduit issuance, and corporates looking to outsource real estate ownership and management for reinvestment in core businesses.

These supply-side trends have been assisted by strong investor interest in Euro-denominated securities, and more recently by the positive value trend in the Euro currency. Despite exceptionally difficult corporate credit markets over the latter half of 2002, and challenges to the ABS market on several fronts – accounting concerns, new Basel Capital proposals, and a high level of downgrades in the CDO and WBS markets – the market has proved resilient and innovative.

Product split has varied from jurisdiction to jurisdiction. The UK covers a wide range of products, but with a primary focus on RMBS.

Italy has seen significant issuance in the commercial lease sector (combining real estate, auto and equipment leases in single deals), and has also seen hybrid RMBS/ CMBS deals that include small business mortgages. Italy also leads the way in public sector financing through securitisation, with the multi-billion INPS and SCIP deals.

Figure 1.5 shows the asset split in European new issuance.

1.3.5 Asia and Australasia

Asia has undergone significant changes over the past few years, between the Asian financial and currency crisis, a global slowdown that hurt export levels, and the more recent terrorist and SARS concerns. The cost of currency hedging is still a factor in considering cross-border issuance, although several Asian sovereigns have now regained their investment grade sovereign ceilings. Much of the new cross-border issuance has been assisted by monoline insurance wraps. Despite these issues, the flexibility of securitisation has proved durable, leading to significant new issue growth in Japan in particular of 23% in 2001 and 55% in 2002.

Japan remains the dominating factor in the Asian cross-border market – accounting for some 59% of cross-border issuance in 2002, with Australia accounting for 33% and Korea for 5%.

Figure 1.6 shows Japanese new issuance.

Domestic issuance has become a significant factor in Korea, with around US$33 bn in 2001 and around $18.5 bn in 2002, and if domestic Korean issuance is added into the cross-border Asian totals, Korea would account for some 24% of the Asian market.

The Australian market has developed primarily around residential mortgage-backed product, with a preponderance of highly rated tranches, due to the use of pool insurance from AAA- or AA-rated entities to cover most mortgages. Significant drivers for the market in Asia include:

- A Korean consumer credit boom, which has led to a surge in credit card transactions;
- The development of CMBS and CDO technology in Singapore and Malaysia, which are some of the more promising jurisdictions for product development;
- Continued problems in the Japanese financial sector, which are driving a revival in the CDO market in Japan – this time in the form of synthetics rather than balance sheet CLOs.

Asia remains a region of promise for whole business technology, due to favourable insolvency regimes, which have similar provisions to the UK.

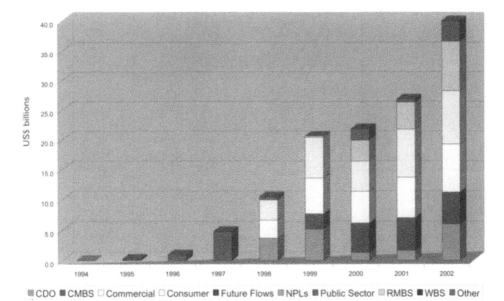

▓CDO ▪CMBS ☐Commercial ☐Consumer ▪Future Flows ▓NPLs ▪Public Sector ▓RMBS ▪WBS ▪Other

Figure 1.6 Japanese asset-backed annual new issuance by asset class; source www.ThorABS. com

2
Rating and Credit Structure

2.1 RATING AGENCIES

In a bank-funded asset-backed finance transaction dependent on the performance of certain receivables to effect repayment, it may be that each bank will perform its own analysis of the cash flows likely to arise from the underlying receivables in order to determine if there is sufficient likelihood of them being paid on time. In the main part, however, the securitisation market has developed on the basis of the disintermediation of banks, with most investors being capital markets investors – the majority of securitisations are funded either through an issuance of long-term debt instruments (typically floating rate notes or bonds) or through the issuance of short-term commercial paper.

In this regard, the credit rating agencies play an important role through the use of benchmark credit ratings that give a determination of the appropriate credit risk and pricing for a particular transaction, and reduce the due diligence burden on investors. Most investors have historically preferred to buy paper with high investment grade ratings, with issuance of AAA paper being the most common. The market has, however, expanded to encompass investor appetite for higher yielding products that are further down the credit spectrum, and issuance of AA, A and BBB tranches is commonplace. Sub-investment grade tranches of BB and lower are rarer due to the limited demand for these classes, although appetite is increasing here as well. The main international rating agencies are:

- Standard & Poor's
- Moody's Investors Service
- Fitch Ratings (Fitch is a result of the 1997 merger between Fitch of the US and IBCA of Europe, and the March 2000 acquisition of Duff & Phelps Credit Rating Co.).

The rating agencies adopt varying approaches to determine the appropriate credit ratings for a transaction and degree of credit enhancement by analysis of historic performance data on the receivables, and comparative market data obtained from extensive records and research over the years. See section 2.1.11 below.

2.1.1 Outcome of ratings process and tranching

The ratings process serves to provide a view on the required level of credit enhancement (and other structural enhancements) to achieve particular different rating levels for a transaction. For example, the output could be required credit enhancement of 7% below AAA, 4% below AA, 3% below A and 2% below BBB. This implies that, taking into account the rating scenarios considered by the agencies as being equivalent to AAA stresses, the deal suffers losses of 7% or less using a "probability of default" approach (see section 2.1.3), which are then fully covered by the credit enhancement.

For a pool of Euro 100m, this would then enable division of the deal into tranches of:

- Class A Euro 93m notes (rated AAA)
- Class B Euro 3m notes (rated AA)
- Class C Euro 1m notes (rated A)
- Class D Euro 1m notes (rated BBB)
- Class E Euro 2m notes (unrated first loss piece retained by the originator).

Tranching a deal into senior and subordinate note classes is only one method of achieving the necessary credit enhancement levels; other credit enhancement mechanisms are dealt with in more detail in section 2.2.

2.1.2   Components of rating assessment

Aside from the analysis of the receivables constituting the securitised pool, there are a number of other risks and features of a transaction that the rating agencies will consider in granting a credit rating for a transaction. These may be less relevant in a bank-funded securitisation as the banks may perform their own due diligence on the receivables in the company and thus limit the role of the credit rating agencies. Consequently, in such a transaction it is more likely that commercial negotiations between the parties will lead to a compromise wherein the lending banks take some of the other risks of the transaction (often including certain risks on the originator) in addition to the pure credit risk on the receivables. Many of these transactions will therefore be a form of hybrid transaction: part securitisation and part secured financing.

Chief among other risks and features that the rating agencies will consider are:

- Eligibility criteria for the replenishment or substitution of new receivables into the pool in order to ensure that the quality of the portfolio cannot be reduced over time by the addition of lower quality assets (see section 4.2);
- Liquidity risk (see section 2.2.4);
- Currency risk (see section 2.3);
- True sale (or other ring-fencing) in order to ensure that the receivables are isolated from the credit risk of the originator (see Chapter 3, section 3.1);
- Bankruptcy remoteness of the SPV, in order to ensure that the receivables are isolated from the credit risk of the SPV (see Chapter 3, section 3.2);
- Taxation issues (see Chapter 3, section 3.10).

In order to ensure that the analysis of the likelihood of investors being paid in full and on time (as indicated by the underlying rating based on the relevant level of credit enhancement) is not prejudiced by external risk factors such as liquidity risk or currency risk, the rating agencies will seek to isolate and remove these risks, typically by requiring that each risk in turn is taken by a third party. In this regard the rating agencies may use the weak link approach in analysing the additional risks which these other parties introduce into the structure. This would require the rating agencies to examine the credit rating of each "link" in the payment chain and will award the transaction a credit rating equal to that of the weakest "link". Thus an entity that takes one of the external risks, as well as any entity that holds the cash collected from the receivables or undertakes a payment obligation that is necessary to ensure timely payment to investors, should be a suitably rated entity (that is, have a rating equal to or higher than that sought for the funding instruments themselves). This includes the swap counterparty for any hedging transactions with the SPV, any entity providing liquidity funding, any guarantor providing a wrap of the obligations of the SPV (such as a monoline insurer) and any account bank holding receivables collections, unless they are carved out from the rating awarded (as is the case with a swap independent rating).

In some cases (for example, a risk of a particular taxation treatment being given), complete removal of a risk may not be possible or commercially viable, in which case the rating agencies may, depending on the nature of the risk in question, be prepared to either size additional credit enhancement or reserves to cover that risk, or rely on a fully reasoned legal opinion from transaction legal counsel as to why the risk in question is sufficiently remote that the rating analysis should be unaffected.

If part of the credit enhancement for the receivables is a guarantee or insurance policy written by a monoline insurer, typically at least two investment grade or higher shadow ratings from Standard & Poor's and Moody's will be required without the policy being taken into account, as a requirement of the credit rating agencies in their ongoing assessment of the monoline insurer's own credit rating based on the risks that it has guaranteed/insured. If the monoline is not AAA rated, a non-investment grade (that is, a speculative grade) shadow rating may be acceptable.

2.1.3 Meaning of credit ratings

Ratings given by a credit-rating agency reflect the degree of credit risk on an entity, either generally or in relation to a particular obligation.

For Standard & Poor's this reflects the capacity of the entity to pay interest and principal on the relevant obligation or obligations on a timely basis, or the "probability of default" on the senior debt. Consequently, at the simplest level, the anticipated loss on the pool over the life of the transaction equates to the amount of credit enhancement required to be present in the transaction, as the probability of losses exceeding this level is equal to the "probability of default" on the senior debt. Debt raised against the senior portion of the pool over and above the credit enhancement level will therefore be rated in accordance with the requested rating level, subject to analysis of the other features of the structure.

Moody's uses a more hybrid approach, which is not based on the risk that the senior investors will not receive their entire principal and interest on time, but leans more towards an "expected loss" approach that reflects the amount that investors may lose over the life of the deal, or the degree of investment risk inherent in the obligation (thus reflecting both default probability and degree of loss). Consequently, the level of credit enhancement equates to the amount which, when subtracted from the assumed loss severity on default, reduces the expected loss level to that of the requested rating level.

Fitch gives more weighting to the probability of default approach at the senior (investment grade) levels, but considers losses as well, most particularly at DDD rating levels, where recoveries are a more significant input.

The difference in these approaches can be illustrated by considering the consequences of a pure "probability of default" approach (or "frequency-only" approach, referring to the frequency of default on the rated debt) for a pool where, in the vast majority of scenarios, losses over the life of a deal are an amount of X or less. Consequently, the probability of a loss over and above X (and hence the possibility of a default occurring on the senior debt if the credit enhancement amount is set at X) is less than the threshold for an AAA rating. If however, the minority scenario occurs and the senior bonds default, the ratings do not describe the amount that the investor can expect to lose. There is the possibility that the scenario where losses could exceed the level of credit enhancement is an Armageddon scenario where losses are significantly in excess of the credit enhancement level.

By way of contrast, a pure "expected loss" approach would seek to classify ratings on the basis of the likelihood of the investment proving to be a good investment (solely in credit loss terms – rating agencies do not assess fair pricing), by having either a very small chance of default with a higher potential loss on such a default occurring, or by having a larger chance of default, but the likelihood of an extremely small loss if such a default did occur.

This means that the expected loss approach entails a greater degree of analysis of the ability of the transaction structure to manage and withstand an extreme defaulted scenario, and still go through the full recovery process of realising return for investors; hence an increased focus on servicing and enforcement, and on the ability to locate a substitute servicer if the originator becomes insolvent and is removed as servicer.

Another consequence of this approach is that, while debt under a pure "frequency-only" approach can be tranched relatively easily based on the probability of losses exceeding certain different levels in certain stress scenarios, the rating on tranches of debt under an "expected loss" approach is itself affected by the tranching process. Use of multiple tranches does not affect the possibility of losses on the collateral exceeding certain levels. It does, however, mean that losses are more concentrated into the lower tranches, than in a scenario where there is a simple senior and equity tranche split, where all losses above the equity tranche are shared equally by senior noteholders, rather than being concentrated in mezzanine noteholders (to the benefit of senior noteholders, but the detriment of mezzanine noteholders). In some cases this may give rise to arbitrage opportunities between the different rating agencies due to the different approaches they adopt.

The basic analytical approach may be coloured by the nature of the obligation being rated; for example, ratings of subordinate obligations reflect the basic corporate credit, notched down to reflect a lower recovery rate, while secured senior obligations would be notched up to reflect a superior recovery rate.

2.1.4 Rating symbols

The main credit rating symbols of each of the three main agencies are set out below. Rating symbols or classifications are also given in a number of other different areas, including assessments of the financial strength of banks, the capabilities of receivables servicing companies, and so on. Certain subscripts can be attached to ratings to indicate their application, or to indicate other warning factors to be aware of other than pure credit risk. For example Standard & Poor's uses the following:

r Implies that some market or other non-credit risk exists (such as FX risk);
m Indicates a money market fund rating;

f   Indicates a bond fund rating;

pi Indicates a public information rating (which is based solely on information in the public domain concerning a company such as published financial statements).

Ratings on senior secured obligations are generally one notch higher than those on senior unsecured obligations. Ratings on subordinated obligations are generally one or more notches below those on senior unsecured obligations.

2.1.5   Standard & Poor's

Long-term debt

AAA   Extremely strong capacity for timely payment
AA   Very strong capacity for timely payment
A   Strong capacity but may be susceptible to adverse economic changes
BBB   Adequate capacity but susceptible to adverse economic changes. Lowest investment grade rating
BB   Speculative but less vulnerable to adverse conditions. Speculative grade
B   Speculative and more vulnerable to adverse conditions
CCC   Currently vulnerable; dependent on favourable business, financial and economic conditions
CC   Currently highly vulnerable
SD, D Selective or general default.

"+" or "−" may be appended to a long-term rating to denote relative status within categories AA to CCC.

Short-term debt

A1+   Extremely strong capacity for timely payment; equivalent to AAA to A+
A1   Strong capacity for timely payment; equivalent to A+ to A−
A2   Satisfactory capacity for timely payment; equivalent to A to BBB
A3   Adequate capacity for timely payment; equivalent to BBB to BBB−
B   Speculative and vulnerable. Speculative grades; equivalent to BB+ to BB−
C   Currently vulnerable and dependent on favourable business, financial and economic conditions. Speculative grades; equivalent to B+ to C
SD, D Selective or general default.

2.1.6   Moody's

Long-term debt

Aaa   Best quality; principal and interest are secure
Aa   High quality; margins of protection not as large
A   Principal and interest adequately secure
Baa   Interest and principal security appears adequate but certain protective elements may be lacking. Lowest investment grade rating; has some speculative characteristics
Ba   Moderate protection of principal and interest; speculative grade

B   Small assurance of principal and interest.
Caa Poor security; present elements of danger
Ca   Highly speculative; often in default
C   Extremely poor.

"1"(+), "2" (neutral) or "3"(−) may be appended to denote relative status within categories Aa to Caa.

Short-term debt

P1   Superior ability to pay; equivalent to Aaa to A3
P2   Strong ability to pay; equivalent to A2 to Baa2
P3   Acceptable ability to pay; equivalent to Baa2 to Baa3
Not prime   Equivalent to sub-investment grades.

2.1.7   Fitch

Long-term debt

AAA Extremely strong capacity for timely payment
AA   Very strong capacity for timely payment
A   Strong capacity for timely payment but may be vulnerable to changes in economic conditions
BBB Adequate capacity but more likely to be impaired by adverse economic conditions. Lowest investment grade rating
BB   Possibility of credit risk developing. Speculative grade
B   Significant credit risk; capacity for payment depends on favourable economic conditions
CCC Default is real possibility; capacity dependent on favourable economic conditions
CC   Default appears probable
C   Default is imminent
DDD Default, actual or imminent; highest potential recovery
DD   Default, actual or imminent; c. 50–90% recovery
D   Default, actual or imminent; likely less than 50% recovery.

"+" or "−" may be appended to a long-term rating to denote relative status within categories AA to CCC.

Short-term debt

F1+ Exceptionally strong capacity for timely payment; equivalent to AAA to AA−
F1   Strong capacity for timely payment; equivalent to AA− to A
F2   Satisfactory capacity for timely payment; equivalent to A to BBB+
F3   Adequate capacity for timely payment; equivalent to BBB to BBB−
B   Minimal capacity for timely payment; vulnerable to adverse changes in economic conditions. Speculative grades; equivalent to sub-investment grades

C   Default is real possibility; capacity dependent on favourable economic conditions

D   Default, actual or imminent.

2.1.8 Change in ratings

A rating speaks as at the time it is given – it does not state or imply that circumstances will remain the same in the future and, consequently, it does not state or imply that the rating agencies will not reconsider the rating in the future if the position changes. This can be seen in the significant level of rating downgrades in the CDO market in 2002. In this respect, the position is the same as for corporate and sovereign ratings – witness the significant downgrades suffered by the south-east Asian countries during the 1997 and 1998 Asian crisis, and their subsequent upgrades as the worst of the crisis passed in 1999.

This means that generally, change of law (or change of tax) risk is not considered when rating a deal – although the rating agencies will take announced and planned changes into account.

The other significant point to bear in mind with regard to sovereign ratings is that movements in the rating of a sovereign after a deal has closed may affect the rating of the deal itself, even where there has been no deterioration in the credit or structure of the deal itself. See section 2.1.18. This was seen on Asian securitisations during the crisis (except for those with external support such as monoline guarantees).

2.1.9 Assumptions in rating process

The rating agencies will generally assume that the parties to a transaction will comply with their contractual obligations as set out in the documentation, and that representations and warranties given by the parties in the documentation are correct and that there is no fraud present in a transaction. These assumptions are made from necessity, due to the impossibility of rating the transaction on any other basis.

2.1.10 Rating analysis

Attempts are increasingly being made to standardise the credit assessment process in the wider market, with the internal credit ratings of banks, and the attempt (particularly in the credit derivatives field) to benchmark deals and issuers. This has also featured increasingly in portfolio assessment, with attempts to formulate the value at risk on an instrument, position or portfolio. Value at risk (VAR) is designed to reflect the maximum amount that could be lost on such instrument, position or portfolio: (i) over a certain holding period; (ii) at a certain confidence interval; and (iii) based on a data set extracted over a certain period. A VAR model usually reflects loss due to market price movements (the value at risk due to market risk), but may reflect potential loss due to worsening credit standing of the instrument obligor or counterparty (the value at risk due to credit risk).

In each case, models are based on trends in the value of the instrument in question, and are usually created: (a) by a historic mapping of prices and marking different percentiles; (b) by a standard deviation model on historical data (a covariance, volatility or parametric model); (c) by a Monte Carlo simulation; or (d) by a stress test of current market conditions. Each of these approaches has its own issues, with the result that no single standardised approach has yet appeared. Problems cited with each of these approaches are that: (a) is time consuming, (b) assumes a log-normal distribution without significant skew (i.e. tilt of the distribution to one side or the other) or kurtosis (i.e. the thickness of the distribution tails – thin tails are platykurtic, fat tails are leptokurtic), (c) is complex and time consuming to calculate, and (d) is arbitrary in nature.

2.1.11 General rating approaches

The same issue applies to the rating analysis carried out by credit-rating agencies on transactions, with the result that different methods of credit assessment are used, both by different rating agencies and for different asset classes (depending on the features of the asset, the data available for the transaction, and the particular view taken by the agency in question of the deal). In some cases more than one method of assessment may be used.

For portfolios with a large number of consumer debtors (a minimum of 300, but in practice around 5000–10 000+ for mortgages, 20 000+ for auto or consumer loans, and considerably more for credit cards) or a constantly changing profile (such as trade receivables), the general analytical approaches are as follows:

- **Actuarial or portfolio basis** Where a portfolio has reasonable distributed risk characteristics about a central default profile (whether on a flat, decreasing or increasing trend), with limited concentration in any one debtor, and limited correlation between defaults of the various debtors, this approach enables anticipated defaults and losses over time to be plotted on the basis of historic information. This approach is carried out on a static pool basis, by looking at the performance of multiple individual pools of receivables over time, as well as on a dynamic pool basis. Where static pool data is not available, the same level of statistical analysis is not permitted, which may mean that more "worst case" assumptions are likely to be made, potentially resulting in higher levels of credit enhancement. Comparisons are made to other pools of the same kind which have been analysed previously, and any spikes in default or delinquency levels are analysed.
- **Benchmarking** An extension of the actuarial approach, benchmarking is used for some products (for example, mortgages), where there is a significant amount of observed data over time, such that the rating agencies will have determined the characteristics of a hypothetical benchmark pool which will have a certain level of defaults and losses, and require a certain level of credit enhancement. In such a case, the actual pool is compared against the benchmark to determine areas where there are differences between the two, and the benchmark default or loss levels are adjusted accordingly.
- **Loan-by-loan analysis** This approach determines a default probability and a loss severity percentage separately for each asset in the portfolio off the basis of benchmarking information reflecting the characteristics of the asset. The product of these figures is the base credit enhancement percentage for that loan, and the weighted

average of the credit enhancement figures for each loan gives the base credit enhancement figure for the pool as a whole.

For portfolios with a smaller number (a minimum of 10, but in practice typically 50–100+) of (typically corporate or rated) debtors (such as CLO or CBO transactions), the general analytical approaches are as follows:

- **Single event**   The single event approach uses the rating of each asset in the pool to determine a weighted average credit rating for the pool. This weighted average rating is then used as a benchmark for the default probability across the pool. The product of this probability, and of standardised loss figures for different asset types, is used to calculate credit enhancement across the pool.
- **Binomial expansion**   This approach enables an estimation of expected loss to be made in all possible scenarios and is designed to be more accurate than the single event model. The pool is regarded as being composed of a certain number of homogeneous assets (i.e. each of the same credit rating – equal to the weighted average credit rating on the pool – and the same par value) reflecting the diversity, or number of uncorrelated assets, in the pool. Each possible scenario is modelled (one default, two default, etc.) to determine the resultant expected loss. The loss in each scenario is then weighted by the probability of that scenario occurring (as computed using the binomial formula), and the resultant weighted losses are summed. Where the pool consists of a number of sub-pools each of which are relatively homogeneous, the binomial expansion may be applied separately to each of them with a subsequent expansion between the sub-pools – this method may also be applied where the credit risk in the pool is significantly concentrated in one or two debtors which constitute more than 10% of the pool, but the remainder of the pool is more diversified.
- **Monte Carlo**   This approach creates a simulation of a large number (several thousand) of random scenarios with different default characteristics to determine the expected loss in each case. These expected losses are then combined.

For portfolios where there are a small number of debtors, the approach is generally limited to:

- **Weak link approach**   This approach is often used where there are less than 10 debtors, and a more distributed risk profile is considered unlikely to be achieved. In such a case, the rating of the pool may be capped at the lowest rating of each of the individual debtors in the pool (unless the concentration can be split out, enabling the remainder of the pool to be separately analysed for credit risk).

Other modelling approaches may be used for whole business transactions, or transactions based around the residual value of assets (such as ship or aircraft).

2.1.12   Notching

In rating CDO transactions, the rating agencies can usually look through to ratings on the underlying assets – either from themselves or other rating agencies for CBOs, or from bank internal scoring systems for CLOs. Credit can then be given to these underlying ratings in constructing a binomial expansion or Monte Carlo type model.

There are discrepancies in the manner in which the rating agencies will apply ratings of the other rating agencies on the underlying assets. Fitch will often regard the underlying rating of another agency as the same level in their own rating scale, whereas Standard & Poor's and Moody's will notch down ratings from the other agencies, and in some cases will ignore the rating completely and require that the asset in question be rated by them.

2.1.13 Data factors

In considering pool data, key data factors relating to the levels of default probability are such as:

- Seasoning
- LTV
- Underwriting (e.g. whether the borrowers are prime or sub-prime, and whether the underwriting criteria are rigidly adhered to)
- Debt-to-income levels
- Diversification/concentration (concentrations of 2% or more in smaller portfolios are typically not favoured)
- Geographic and industry concentration/diversity of the debtors (for example, diversity helps to avoid a catastrophic loss in the result of a significant event to any particular region such as the bankruptcy of a major employer, an earthquake (e.g. the Kobe earthquake) or other natural disaster, or economic events such as a regional tax change leading to a loss of economic status and activity in a region over time)
- The levels of arrears on the pool, and the trend in the level (upward or downward over time).

Important data factors when considering loss severity are such as:

- Property (or other relevant asset) market value decline
- Local property (or other relevant asset) market liquidity
- LTV
- Enforcement expenses.

These factors will also be considered in setting the eligibility criteria for the replenishment or substitution of new assets into the portfolio (see Chapter 4, section 4.2).

2.1.14 Stress testing

For each method of analysis, a cash flow model is built (either by the rating agency or by the lead manager institution, depending on the requirements of the rating agency) to illustrate the projected liability-side structure for the transaction, and taking into account:

- Timing and amount of defaults on the asset-side cash flows, and
- Timing and amount of recoveries on these defaults,

as indicated by the rating agencies.

Different stress test scenarios are run on the model, to determine what effect each of the stresses has upon the ability of the structure to continue to make payments on the securities to be rated. These scenarios typically assume the occurrence of adverse future conditions such as a general economic recession (which would operate to depress property market prices and recovery levels, and to increase default levels). The severity of these adverse assumptions will vary depending upon the level of credit rating that has been requested – more severe conditions are assumed for a AAA rating than for a BBB rating. The cash flow model is run at different levels of interest rates and prepayment rates in order to provide an indication of the default performance of the securities to be rated in these different scenarios, and the consequent final required level of credit enhancement which must be provided over the life of the deal, in order for the requested rating to be awarded over the relevant note class sizes.

2.1.15 Liquidity

As well as assessing the absolute credit of a pool, the rating cash flow model helps to determine any requirements for liquidity facilities to cover short-term shortfalls in cash. In a typical mortgage deal, the liquidity facility is likely to be around 3% of the note balance. In a whole business deal, the facility is likely to be designed to cover 18 to 24 months of debt service.

2.1.16 Procedure for obtaining a rating

Introducing a transaction to the rating agencies involves presenting:

- The originator company
- A termsheet of the intended transaction structure
- A data tape.

The rating agencies will typically want to see static pool data for different origination periods, developed monthly or quarterly over time. In addition, they will want to see historic dynamic pool data over time. Each of these will enable them to identify trends or changing factors in the performance of the pool which can be applied or extrapolated to assumptions on future performance. This should also enable isolation of seasonal variance – such as increased generation of credit card receivables over the Christmas period – from longer-term performance. The rating agencies will want to discuss the data content with the arranger and the originator in order to analyse any unusual features or significant characteristics.

Rating agencies are likely to require some degree of due diligence and verification of the originator and of the contents of the data tape. Data verification is usually carried out by a firm of auditors selected by the bank arranging the transaction. This is usually achieved with a data-sampling process comparing tape entries against the original loan files to either a 95% or a 99% confidence interval (depending on the requirements of the rating agencies in question) of a particular maximum error rate (generally around 2%). Assuming that the sample does not display more than a particular number of errors (dependent on the pool/sample size, confidence interval and error rate parameters), this should establish a 95% or 99% probability respectively that the error rate across the pool as a whole does not exceed that on the sample (this assumes a log normal distribution and is based on a mean observed deviation from the norm which enables

2 and 3 standard deviations to be plotted). Data errors in excess of the specified error rate levels may lead the rating agencies to make worst case assumptions about some areas of the pool data.

Diligence of the originator is usually carried out with site visits to inspect the originator's systems and discuss the business of the company and its industry position, to review financial projections, and to meet senior management. The agencies will wish to review credit and underwriting procedures in detail and track items through (a) the payment collection and enforcement systems and (b) the accounting and audit trail.

Following discussions on the transaction and the data with the rating agencies, the agencies will give their preliminary rating analysis with indicative credit enhancement levels. These levels will then be discussed and negotiated between the agencies, the arranger and the originator. A subsequent full rating process and rating committee will determine the final rating levels.

2.1.17   Corporate ratings

For corporate credit ratings, the ratings agencies may re-include certain debt or quasi-debt elements in forming a view on their rating. Thus, for example, the retained junior position in a securitisation may be "grossed-up" for rating purposes by also including the receivables pool and non-recourse debt issued against it, to reflect the true concentration of credit risk in the subordinate piece. Similarly, a debt equivalent amount may be calculated for operating leases by calculating the NPV of the minimum operating lease payments due.

2.1.18   Foreign and local currency sovereign ceilings

Another area of difference between the approaches of the different rating agencies is in the field of cross-border payments. Each of the agencies attribute "foreign currency" and "local currency" ratings to sovereign entities.

Foreign currency

Foreign currency sovereign ratings are generally lower than local currency sovereign ratings, due to the fact that they take into account the ability of the sovereign to access sufficient foreign currency to meet its local and offshore obligations. Foreign currency ratings often act as a ceiling on corporate or transaction ratings, as, in a scenario where the sovereign cannot access foreign currency, the ability of a corporate to access foreign currency is likely to be severely impeded due to the likelihood that transfer or convertibility restrictions will be placed on the domestic currency.

Standard & Poor's has permitted issuers in dollarised economies to issue in foreign currencies at ratings above the sovereign foreign currency rating since 1997.

On 7 June 2001, Moody's announced that it was relaxing the application of the sovereign foreign currency rating as a ceiling on ratings for corporate bond issuance from the relevant country. The new criteria look at whether the relevant government is likely, if it defaults, to impose a moratorium on the private sector as well or not (as well as the creditworthiness of the issuer and the ability of the issuer to access foreign exchange).

The easiest way around sovereign foreign currency ceilings for a corporate rating is to demonstrate significant international operations and non-domestic currency revenue streams, which can be accessed to make payment on non-domestic currency debt obligations regardless of domestic currency restrictions.

The equivalent route for a structured transaction is to put in place a swap or guarantee (such as a monoline insurance policy or a convertibility swap) with an entity based outside the domestic jurisdiction, and thus not subject to the relevant sovereign foreign currency rating (a favoured route in Asia has been to use the balance sheet of a multinational organisation such as the IFC). As long as the swap counterparty or guarantor is obliged to pay regardless of the imposition of transfer or convertibility restrictions, the transaction can then be rated as high as the rating of the swap counterparty or guarantor, and in excess of the sovereign foreign currency rating. An alternative used in future flows deals is to look at pools of export receivables which are payable by debtors outside the country of the originator. Provided that these can be trapped prior to entering the country of the originator, they may never become subject to the sovereign foreign currency ceiling in the first place.

Local currency

Local ratings reflect the ability of the sovereign to make payment of obligations due in their own currency. Due to control of the sovereign over the local currency, these obligations are generally significantly easier for the sovereign to meet, and local currency ratings are therefore almost always higher than foreign currency ratings.

The approach of the rating agencies differs significantly when considering sovereign local currency ratings. Fitch take the view that a local currency default by the sovereign does not provide the sovereign with an incentive to prevent local companies from making local currency payments (as opposed to a foreign currency default, where the sovereign may seek to prevent local companies from paying in foreign currency as part of broader exchange restrictions), and that it is consequently possible for a company or structured deal to have a local currency rating above that of the sovereign. Moody's have developed their own "local currency guidelines" for each country to reflect the risk of political disturbance or economic instability in the country as a whole. In most cases these guidelines will constitute the maximum level achievable for a structured transaction from that country. These levels are generally three to five notches higher than the local currency sovereign rating, with the result that a rating in excess of the local currency sovereign is possible. The toughest line on local currency ratings is taken by Standard & Poor's, who consider that default by the sovereign on its own currency indebtedness is, in practice, such a significant event that it would cause major disruption to the ability of other domestic operations to make payments on a timely basis. Even where an offshore swap or guarantee is used, this may not be sufficient to breach the ceiling of the local currency sovereign rating, where the payment offshore is dependent on receipt of local currency onshore (a swap which absorbs transfer or convertibility risk may nevertheless require that local currency is received by the swap counterparty, even if the currency cannot be converted or repatriated while the restrictions are in place).

2.2 CREDIT ENHANCEMENT AND LIQUIDITY

2.2.1 Credit enhancement

Defaults will form the foundation for sizing the degree of credit enhancement required by the rating agencies when assigning a particular credit rating to the credit risk on the receivables. The rating agencies will use the assumption that certain adverse market conditions materialise in order to stress test current rates of default and ascertain the effect on performance of the receivables. The higher the rating requested, the more stringent and demanding will be the assumed adverse market conditions.

An important further factor in credit assessment is the mitigatory effect provided by the potential realisable value of any property, vehicles or equipment which the receivables debtors are funding by contracting to pay the receivables (for example, a house for mortgage receivables or a car for auto loan receivables). This can be taken into account if the SPV has access to this value (due to the security interest in the assets, or the assets themselves, also being transferred to it) and this value can be protected by requiring the originator to ensure that insurance is maintained against the risk of degradation of the assets through fire, damage, etc. This is particularly important where sale or refinancing of the property or other assets actually forms a primary source of repayment for investors (for example, in some CMBS deals), in which case insurance policies may be required to be taken out with a suitably rated entity.

The resultant figure for losses suffered from a stressed level of defaults after taking a stressed level of collateral realisation into account will determine the required amount of credit enhancement to be provided in order for the transaction to be assigned the relevant credit rating.

Consideration may also need to be given to the foreign currency rating of the country in which the underlying debtors on the receivables are situated (see section 2.1.18 above).

2.2.2 Types of credit enhancement

The most common method of providing credit enhancement at the originator level consists of a first loss cover of the "excess spread" on the receivables (the gross spread earned on the receivables, less the cost of funds of the deal, expenses and credit losses), often backed by the deposit of excess spread in a reserve fund up to a certain level (although there may be rating agency limits on the amount of credit that will be given to a cash reserve that builds up over time from a low start).

This is followed by either overcollateralisation of receivables against the funding raised (with the difference constituting a deferred purchase price element due to the originator, which will be written off to the extent that the receivables do not perform) or by tranching the deal into different classes of senior and subordinated notes (with the most subordinate class of notes usually purchased by the originator). See section 2.1.1 above.

The overcollateralisation and deferred purchase price route has been considered suspect in some jurisdictions as it may potentially be regarded as a transaction at an undervalue, resulting in a risk of insolvency unwind of the true sale. The purchase of subordinated notes may in turn affect the capital adequacy treatment of the transaction, as bank regulators may require that subordinated notes be directly deducted from capital.

Due to ever-increasing concerns over the efficient use of capital, provision of credit enhancement will usually be structured in such a way that either:

- It can be sold in the market to ensure that the originator can entirely remove the need to hold capital against the securities; or
- The enhancement is funded from excess spread in the transaction, so that the originator is not required to hold capital.

Another increasingly popular way of realising extra proceeds in such a way that capital usage can be minimised, is to structure an IO (an "interest only" note that is a coupon entitlement formed by stripping part of the coupon from a note) at a senior level off the back of senior notes set with an above-market coupon. As the IO is paid from senior cash flows, the IO will receive a superior credit rating. The proceeds can be set against any capital that would otherwise be held against a junior piece. Although valuation of an IO is dependent on comfort as to the level of prepayments (given that valuation is likely to be based on an NPV of expected cash flows over different prepayment scenarios), it may still be saleable. Use of mortgage redemption certificates or bank loans which are limited recourse to the excess spread are other methods that may be used.

A similar alternative is to use the cash flow from the excess spread to "fast pay" the junior tranche, thus making the tranche more attractive and more marketable to third-party investors.

2.2.3 Insured transactions

Beyond these means of credit enhancement, it may be necessary to arrange further enhancement if the senior portion of the funding would still not have a sufficiently high credit rating for the intended sale to investors. This may involve a guarantee (or "wrap") given by a monoline insurer that amounts due to investors on the senior instruments will be paid in full and on time (generally speaking, monolines would not guarantee the amortisation profile of the securities, but simply payment of interest when due and principal in full on final legal maturity of the note issue). Other methods which have been used include a pool policy in mortgage securitisation transactions, whereby an entity would provide credit insurance across a pool of mortgages.

Insured deals came to attention in 2000, with the default of the Hollywood Funding 5 transaction. The Hollywood 5 deal was one of a sequence of Hollywood Fundings 1 to 6. Hollywood Funding 2 was insured by multiline insurer HIH Casualty and General Insurance, and reinsured by them in the market. They paid a claim on the policy, and tried to claim reimbursement from reinsurers, but reinsurers refused payment on the grounds that there had been misrepresentation and breach of warranty under the policy, which voided it.

The High Court in December 2000 and the Court of Appeal on 21 May 2001 affirmed the reinsurers' view that HIH did not have an absolute and unconditional obligation to make payment under the policy; the policy was subject to the normal defences of an insurance policy and, in particular, it was held to be a warranty of the policy that a particular number of films were to be made, which had not been met. On 20 February 2003, the House of Lords in *HIH Casualty and General Insurance Limited and Others v. Chase Manhattan Bank and Others (2003) HL* held that an insurer is able to contractually waive defences it could otherwise have to a claim, except for the defence of fraud.

One of the reinsurers (New Hampshire Insurance Co.) was a subsidiary of AIG. AIG wrapped Hollywood 4, 5 and 6 through its subsidiary Lexington Insurance Co. Following the High Court judgement in December 2000, a cash shortfall arose in Hollywood 5, and a claim was made on the Lexington policy for payment on 26 January 2001 (the next note payment date). The claim was disputed by Lexington, resulting in a downgrade of the bonds (previously rated AAA by Standard & Poor's) first to CCC and then to D. Standard & Poor's downgraded Hollywood 6 to CCC in January 2001 when Lexington disclaimed certain liabilities in relation to the policy for Hollywood 6, and also downgraded Hollywood 4 to BB on 30 March 2001.

A settlement of the deals was reached with investors in June 2003, amid continuing concerns in the market over the use of multiline insurers as financial insurance providers in asset-backed transactions – in particular, as to whether it is possible to structure these policies such that they do in practice constitute unconditional guarantees of the nature of a monoline wrap.

2.2.4 Liquidity support

In addition to credit risk, the receivables may carry a degree of liquidity risk. This risk is generally addressed by the provision of a liquidity facility by a suitably rated entity or by the use of a reserve fund. This risk is particularly evident in commercial-paper-funded conduit structures, given the inherently short-term nature of commercial paper, as rollover of the commercial paper must take place on a regular basis. Generally the rating agencies will expect 100% coverage of the maturing face value of the commercial paper by the liquidity facility, which can lead to discussions on the appropriate definition for the "borrowing base" for the facility (a dynamic figure which represents the amount available to be drawn on the facility at a particular point in time) in respect of "partially supported" conduits (conduits where the liquidity line does not provide a full credit wrap, and an assessment of credit risk on the underlying receivables is required).

In structures with the option to switch issuance from US commercial paper to Eurocommercial paper, a swingline facility may also be required to bridge the 2-day settlement gap between same day availability of funds against issuance in the US-CP market and spot availability of funds against issuance in the Euro-CP market.

2.3 HEDGING AND PREPAYMENT RISK

2.3.1 Currency risk/basis risk

Currency risk and/or basis risk may arise due to a mismatch between the currency of denomination or the basis of calculation of interest on the receivables, as against that applicable to the funding instruments issued to investors. These risks are typically passed to an entity under a derivatives or FX transaction, with the derivatives counterparty being a suitably rated entity, or guaranteed by a parent or other entity that is suitably rated.

Typically the hedging of currency risk and basis risk will depend on the nature of the receivables and the nature of the funding in question. For example, a securitisation of short-term trade receivables that is funded by the issuance of short-term commercial paper will most probably be hedged through spot and forward FX transactions, with the discount to face value of each issuance of commercial paper matching the discount to face value at which the receivables are purchased. A long-term bond issue backed by mortgage receivables is more likely to be hedged through a circus swap or (where the funding instruments were issued in the same currency as the underlying mortgage receivables) an interest rate swap, to exchange the interest basis on the mortgages (which will typically be a local prime bank lending rate) for the interest basis on the funding instruments (which will typically be a Euromarket interest basis such as LIBOR).

2.3.2 Transfer and convertibility risk

An area related to currency risk is the foreign currency rating of the country in which the receivables debtors are situated. Generally, the maximum credit rating which is achievable for receivables by the use of credit enhancement which is internal to the jurisdiction in question, is capped at the level of that country's foreign currency rating, due to the transfer risk of repatriating the receivables collections (see section 2.1.18 above). This may necessitate some form of external or offshore credit enhancement which clearly covers transfer or convertibility risk, such as a convertibility swap under which the swap provider agrees to receive collections onshore and make return payments offshore (passing the transfer risk to the swap provider) or a wrap from a monoline insurer (or some equivalent form of guarantee).

2.3.3 Prepayment risk

Payments of principal on the receivables are, in a pass-through structure (see "Amortisation structure" in section 4.3.2), passed to investors on each periodic payment date, effecting amortisation of the funding instruments. To the extent that faster than scheduled payments – prepayments – are received (for example, due to payment in full of a mortgage loan when a homeowner moves house), this gives investors two risks:

- **Prepayment risk**   Receipt of principal at par may cause a loss to investors if the instruments were trading above par when prepaid, and means that asset backed securities generally have negative convexity (see Chapter 4, section 4.4).
- **Reinvestment risk**   Early receipt of principal will speed up the amortisation profile and reduce the weighted average life of the funding instruments, meaning that the investor will need to reinvest in a new security. The investor is exposed to the risk that the yields or spreads that can be earned on reinvestment have fallen since the previous purchase.

Analysis of historic prepayment rates and underlying trends (the likelihood of people moving house for example, leading to their mortgage being prepaid in full from the sale proceeds) is therefore significant, with assumptions of different levels of constant pre-payment rate often made to analyse the effect on the weighted average life.

Other mechanisms may also be used to try to achieve greater certainty for investors as to when exactly they will receive their principal. These include structures where different tranches of securities are issued on a fast-pay, slow-pay basis (where principal receipts are applied first to the fast-pay tranche and second to the slow-pay tranche). This mechanism is not intended to subordinate the slow-pay notes, with fast-pay and slow-pay notes maintaining equal priority in the event that enforcement is required, but simply to narrow the expected variance range for the weighted average life for each tranche.

In many deals, substitution or replenishment of the receivables may be permitted, involving the use of principal receipts to purchase new receivables rather than to amortise funding. As well as offering more certainty to investors, this enables the originator to extend the term of the funding. This can have a noticeable impact on the all-in cost of a transaction, as a significant element of the cost of a transaction will be up-front structuring and advisory fees for professional advisers such as arrangers, lawyers, auditors, valuers, rating agencies, printers and so on. These will be greatly reduced when converted to an annual margin over the funding base if the term of the funding is extended, making the transaction more attractive to the originator.

Substitution and replenishment are not without complexities at the legal level, however, which can themselves increase legal and structuring fees for a transaction. Each further sale of receivables will need to achieve a true sale, which may require the periodic undertaking of solvency verification to ensure that the originator is still solvent when each sale is made. To try to simplify this position, some transactions will arrange a sale of current and future receivables, to take effect as and when the receivables arise.

Sales of further advances under an existing facility for which security has been given will need to be structured to be secured by the same security interest and in the same priority (using "tacking" to the original debt). This is particularly an issue for mortgage receivables, where the receivables debtor may sometimes have the right to require further advances (mandatory further advances) to be made.

2.3.4 Transaction reinvestment risk

Although, as outlined above, various structuring devices may be used to alleviate prepayment and reinvestment risk for investors, there is also a reinvestment risk arising within the transaction from prepayments which are made during an interest period. Once a prepayment is made, there is a commensurate loss of interest income, while expenses in the form of interest on the funding instruments will still accrue up to the end of the interest period. Redemption of instruments during an interest period would lead to administrative complexities in keeping investors appraised of the status of their investment and in making daily redemption payments through the network of paying agents appointed, as well as giving rise to the problem of break costs arising for investors.

The receipts may therefore be invested by one of the transaction parties to achieve a return and alleviate this problem; however, this will be subject to then current market rates, rather than the rates prevailing in the market when the transaction was first entered into. If market rates have declined significantly since the closing of the transaction, this may impact significantly on the return achievable. This issue may be addressed through entering into a guaranteed investment contract (GIC) at the start of the transaction. Whether a GIC or another form of investment is utilised, the rating agencies will require that the investment is in deposits of, or paper issued by, a suitably rated entity.

2.3.5 Derivatives and the ISDA Master

Most securitisation transactions contain some form of interest rate hedging and/or currency hedging to deal with currency risk and basis risk. In most cases however, the requirements for these derivatives will be somewhat different from the standard market for the products.

Swaps in most securitisations will amortise at an irregular rate to match the amortisation of the funding instruments from principal receipts on the receivables, as referred to in section 2.3.3. This may mean that the swap has to be executed as a corridor swap (which permits reduction of the swap notional in a range rather than on a fixed schedule) instead of as a plain circus swap. The element of uncertainty borne by investors will be priced in as a yield pick-up on the coupon they receive. The uncertainty borne by the swap counterparty is more difficult to price, as most counterparties will wish to have sufficient certainty as to the amortisation profile of a swap to be able to hedge receipts and payments over the life of the swap. The only perfect hedge for a securitisation swap is a back-to-back swap between the swap counterparty and the originator, and it will often be a requirement of the swap counterparty in a securitisation that the originator agree to enter into such a swap. This may raise issues for the accounting or capital treatment of the transaction if the swap is seen as recourse to the originator or if it is entered into at an off-market price. In some cases, a balance guaranteed swap (the notional of which matches that of the receivables pool) may be available at a price.

The requirements of the rating agencies will state that the swap counterparty should sign up to non-standard contractual terms as against the wider derivatives market (where trades are normally conducted on a relatively balanced position between the two parties to the trade). These are normally set by modification to the ISDA Master agreement, the standard derivatives market contract.

Derivative trades create exposure to the counterparty in the amount of any positive mark to market value at a point in time (this being the potential loss suffered if the counterparty defaults at such point). As these exposures can be two-way (i.e. positive and negative) on different trades entered into between the two parties (unlike a loan book), mechanisms which net these exposures against each other serve to reduce the exposure and the potential loss if the counterparty defaults, enabling more business to be transacted.

The ISDA is a master netting agreement, which is designed to provide a framework under which all exposures between two counterparties, in relation to trades entered into between them, can be netted and collateralised. Standard forms have been published in 1987, 1992 and 2002. The market has migrated from use of the 1987 Master to the 1992 Master, and is likely to introduce the 2002 Master over time.

Netting is achieved by the calculation of a single amount due (the "Early Termination Amount" under the 2002 Master, or the "Settlement Amount" under the 1992

Master) from one party to the other in respect of the future value of all trades entered into under the Master, following the occurrence of an Event of Default or an Early Termination Event. Collateral is provided for the net exposure by entering into a Credit Support Annex (or Deed) as a supplement to the ISDA Master, which requires one party to provide collateral to the other to reflect the amount that would be payable on termination of all trades under the ISDA Master.

The Settlement Amount under the 1992 ISDA Master was calculated using one of two methods specified in the ISDA at the choice of the parties – "Loss" or "Market Quotation".

The calculation of these amounts was the subject of a UK Court of Appeal decision in the case of *ANZ Banking Group v. Societe Generale* (decided by the Court of Appeal in 2000), in relation to the calculation of a loss amount suffered under the ambit of the "Loss" definition in the ISDA Master Agreement for a group of non-deliverable forward trades. The case concerned the loss suffered by SocGen when they paid a termination payment to ANZ on termination of their ISDA Master with ANZ following the Russian debt default in August 1998. SocGen could not claim under a hedge with a Russian counterparty due to the moratorium, and sought to reduce the payment to ANZ by the amount of the loss suffered by them in connection with the hedge. The Court of Appeal dismissed this reduction on the basis that losses sustained by a party to an ISDA as a result of the identity or particular circumstances of a hedge counterparty are not covered within the definition.

In *Peregrine Fixed Income Ltd v. Robinson Department Store plc*, decided on 18 May 2000, the Commercial Court was asked to consider the ISDA Master definition of Settlement Amount payable on termination, which provides that the Settlement Amount shall be: "Loss ... for each Terminated Transaction ... for which a Market Quotation cannot be determined or would not (in the reasonable belief of the party making the determination) produce a commercially reasonable result." The transaction provided for an ongoing one-way payment stream from Robinson to Peregrine. As Robinson was at that point undertaking a debt-equity swap, the quote for a person to step into Peregrine's shoes and assume the benefit of a payment stream from Robinson was much lower than the actual present value of that stream – thus the Market Quotation was much lower than actual Loss to Peregrine. The court held that it was unreasonable for Robinson (who was determining the payment) to ignore the much higher Loss figure, and also that there was nothing in the Loss definition in the ISDA Master which required that the creditworthiness of the parties be taken into account in determining the Loss.

The 2002 ISDA Master was published by ISDA on 8 January 2003 and is designed to simplify close-out mechanics, with a single method of determination of any Early Termination Amount (the "Close-Out Amount") rather than the choice of "Loss" or "Market Quotation" under the old 1992 ISDA Master. This moves away from the more widely defined Loss, and from the cumbersome and formal Market Quotation method. Instead the Close-Out Amount is based on the cost or gain in replacing the economic equivalent of the material terms of the terminated transactions and the parties' option rights in respect of the transactions. The parties may recognise associated hedge costs without duplication where it is commercially reasonable to do so. Relevant quotations, market data or internal sources may be used to assist in this process. The 2002 ISDA Master also includes a new Termination Event of "Force

Majeure" with a "Waiting Period" of 8 business days during which payments and deliveries are postponed, after which the transactions may be terminated. Other changes include the reduction of the Failure to Pay grace period from 3 business days to 1 business day.

As the SPV is, by definition, unlikely to enter into more trades in the future, the main rationale for the use of the ISDA Master in standard market trades (i.e. reducing aggregate exposure across many trades) does not exist. The ISDA Master is, however, still used to document trades with SPVs, due to its market standard nature. This necessitates the modification of several of its terms to meet rating agency requirements:

- Include limited recourse and non-petition language against the SPV.
- Reduce the potential for termination to very limited circumstances, due to the relatively small market for replacement swaps in specialist structured deals (if the swap is a total return swap or other instrument that provides some degree of credit wrap or subsidy to the SPV, this will be even more strongly the case). In particular, the ability of the swap counterparty to terminate the ISDA for breach by the SPV will be limited by removing most of the termination events and events of default as they relate to the SPV. This can be rationalised, as, due to the bankruptcy remote nature of the SPV, most of the potential termination events and events of default are highly unlikely to occur. Generally, those events in respect of which the rating agencies will allow the swap counterparty to terminate the swap are limited to:
  - failure to pay
  - bankruptcy
  - merger without assumption
  - illegality.
- No gross-up for imposition of withholding tax on payments made by the SPV should be required under the swap, unless it will have funds available for the purpose of making such payment.
- Gross-up for withholding tax on payments made by the swap counterparty should be required under the swap, unless the lack of obligation to gross-up is fully disclosed to investors in the offering circular.
- The swap counterparty should be obliged to provide collateral, or procure the transfer of the swap to a suitably rated entity, in the event that it is itself downgraded below certain trigger levels.
- The swap counterparty may only transfer the ISDA to a suitably rated entity.

Although not contained in the ISDA Master, the rating agencies will also focus on the ranking of any termination payment due to the swap counterparty under the swap in the priority of payments (see Chapter 4, section 4.3) for the transaction, and will generally only permit the following:

- Default by swap counterparty – swap counterparty ranks after notes.
- Default by SPV:
  - Swap counterparty may rank prior to the note class they are hedging for interest rate hedging.
  - Swap counterparty may rank pari passu with the note class they are hedging for currency hedging.

Chapter 13 provides detail on:

- General derivatives terminology such as options (including put and call, European and American, path-dependent, knock-in and knock-out and so on), futures, forwards, caps, collars, floors, swaps, netting (including novation netting, close-out netting and settlement netting).
- Some common options strategies such as straddle, strangle, butterfly and covered call, and also the fundamental factors influencing the value of options, namely: delta, gamma, theta and vega, together with the valuation by mark to market of swaps.

2.3.6 Credit derivatives

Derivatives are used extensively in the field of bond repackaging to completely transform cash flows, through the use of asset swaps, total return swaps or equity swaps. In the growing field of CDO transactions, derivatives may play a role in the genesis of the "receivables" themselves, which may be formed through the use of credit derivatives which transfer credit risk off the books of the originator, and which are then repackaged by the SPV.

Credit derivatives are designed to offer one party protection against the default of a third party "reference entity", by receipt of a payout from the counterparty on the derivative. The payout on credit derivatives may be determined:

- By the degree of widening of the spread of a particular reference obligation against a certain benchmark obligation (either by reference to yield or price) (such as a credit spread option);
- By the recovery value on a reference obligation following a particular credit event (such as payment default or insolvency) with regard to the reference entity (such as a credit default swap or a credit linked note); or
- By a combination of credit risks and market risks (such as a total return swap).

Credit derivatives can be funded (as with a credit-linked note, where the counterparty funds the full notional value up-front, and receives a reduced payout if a credit event occurs), or unfunded, as with a credit default swap. In this regard, funded credit derivatives do not bear the residual credit risk of the credit derivative counterparty pending funding by the counterparty of any required payout. Consequently, the issue of a credit linked note to an SPV, which is funded by a payment by the SPV up-front, may operate to effectively shift the risk of default by the reference entity to the SPV, without the issuer bearing credit risk on the SPV.

If this kind of risk transfer is recognised for capital adequacy purposes, then the resultant capital benefit for the issuer may be comparable to that achievable from a true sale. In many ways, this form of structure mimics that of a funded sub-participation (which may also benefit from favourable capital treatment), but also means that the issuer is a dependent rating in assessing the likelihood of payments to the SPV being made unless the deal structure is designed to address this.

The use of credit derivatives is examined in detail in Chapter 7.

Chapter 13 provides detail on terminology related to the modelling of credit risk as used for credit derivatives such as skew, kurtosis, VAR, Monte Carlo simulation, CreditMetrics, RiskMetrics, CreditRisk+ and correlation risk.

3
Deal Structure

The structure of a transaction is heavily influenced by the jurisdiction of the assets in question. Many of the differences seen are determined by local regulatory and taxation requirements, which are dealt with in more detail in Chapter 12.

3.1 RING-FENCING AND TRUE SALE

One of the key aspects of ensuring the marketability of the relevant debt securities or bank debt that will fund the securitisation is to enable the relevant rating agencies to analyse the credit risk of the relevant receivables free and clear of the credit risk of the entity that originated the receivables in question – such that the deal is delinked from the credit of the originator. Consequently, in the majority of fully asset-backed transactions, the creditworthiness of the originator is only of indirect concern in as far as it relates to the originator's ongoing obligation to act as servicer of the portfolio (in cases where there is no developed market for assuming the role of substitute servicer if the appointment of the originator as servicer be terminated, an entity may be appointed as back-up servicer, committing to take over the servicing role if no substitute can be found). This can enable the credit rating awarded to the funding instruments to exceed that of the originator itself. Instead, detailed historic performance data relating to the receivables themselves can be collated to enable an assessment of the credit risk attaching to the funding instruments.

In order to ensure that this treatment is available, a securitisation transaction will usually attempt to effect a "true sale" under the relevant legal regime relating to the receivables – terminology used to describe a sale of the receivables being securitised in a manner which ensures their isolation from the bankruptcy or insolvency of the originator. This usually consists of a sale of the receivables under the same law as the governing law of the receivables pursuant to a receivables sale agreement. The receivables sold will be subject to a warranty by the originator that they comply with certain eligibility criteria. Breach of this warranty will give rise to an obligation on the originator to repurchase the offending receivables.

Alternatively, a transfer of control over the securitised assets or business to a third party (e.g. a trustee) through a security interest, trust or other device (e.g. a secured loan) may be used. This may be referred to as "true control". The intention is to ensure that the securitisation noteholders can control the manner and timing of enforcement proceedings, and can obtain the benefit of the securitised assets in priority to other creditors.

Exactly how a true sale is effected will depend on the requirements of the legal system in question. For example, in some jurisdictions, to carry out a sale of receivables the seller must notify each of the debtors in question that the receivable owed by them has been sold; this requirement could be particularly onerous where there are a large number of debtors or the debtors change frequently (for example, in a trade receivables structure). Indeed, regardless of the administrative issues of giving notice to debtors, originators will almost invariably seek to avoid giving notice, as this may affect their ongoing business relationship with the debtors.

If the giving of notice cannot be avoided, a "two-tier" structure may be used, where an SPV is established as a subsidiary of the originator, but which is otherwise bankruptcy remote (see section 3.2). The transfer to this first SPV is notified to debtors, but as the SPV is a subsidiary of the originator, the impact on debtors is likely to be less significant. A second transfer is then undertaken (from the first SPV to a second independent SPV) which is not notified to debtors.

In some jurisdictions, notice may be given in a fairly innocuous form by way of a note on a periodic account statement, which may be relatively cheap and easy to carry out.

A refinement of the "two-tier" structure is used in the US (although not as a means of ameliorating the impact of notice requirements) with a transfer of the receivables to an SPV owned by the originator and then onward to a trust. This enables the first sale to be conducted without credit enhancement (with an SPV equity capitalised to the extent of the necessary credit enhancement) and thus achieve a true sale and a RAP sale for capital adequacy purposes (since no recourse to the regulated entity is allowed), while remaining in the originator's group for tax purposes, with the second leg of the sale achieving an accounting (GAAP) sale and being regarded as a loan for tax purposes (and thus not crystallising a capital gain due to disposal of the assets outside the group).

A similar structure has been used in other jurisdictions where the provision of credit enhancement by the originator to the SPV causes problems for a true sale analysis. Instead, the originator sells the receivables at face value to a first SPV, which then sells them on to a second SPV. The originator then purchases subordinated notes issued by, or provides another form of credit enhancement to, the second SPV.

In many jurisdictions, however, a single sale enables a legal true sale, an accounting sale and a regulatory sale, while a tax disposal may not necessarily give rise to any chargeable gain (for example, if the disposal is made at the face value of the receivables). Outside the US, use of two-tiered structures has therefore usually been restricted to establishing one onshore SPV and one offshore SPV in order to deal with other local law issues, such as the use of a Law 130 company in Italy which enables the originator to avoid the requirement to notify debtors of the transfer of receivables which it would otherwise be subject to, or the use of an onshore SPV in countries such as Thailand and Australia in order to avoid withholding tax being charged on receivables collections sold directly to an offshore entity.

The most common legal method used of effecting a ring-fencing of English law governed receivables is that of assignment with the alternative of novation used infrequently, as it entails obtaining the consent of each customer, and would operate to pass any obligations of the originator under the receivables contracts to the SPV. Most legal systems have an equivalent to the method of assignment. Certain factors, however – notification requirements for assignments in some jurisdictions, insolvency unwind risks (see below) and tax considerations (for example, transfer taxes on a sale of receivables or capital gains taxes on a disposal of the receivables by the originator) – have given rise to alternatives to a sale, such as subrogation, sub-participation, or a limited recourse loan with security. In each case, the method used to achieve a true sale or to otherwise isolate the cash flows from the receivables will have to address the risks set out below.

A key recent addition to the list of transfer mechanisms in England has been a declaration of trust over the receivables. A declaration of trust as a transfer mechanism had only been used to create a master trust style structure in credit card deals prior to the case of *Don King Productions Inc. v. Warren and others (1998)*. In the Don King case, the courts upheld the use of a declaration of trust over the benefit of various contracts despite certain of the contracts containing prohibitions on assignment by arguing that a declaration of trust is different in character from an assignment and that a clause prohibiting assignments is restricted to assignments and does not extend to declarations of trust (subject to an interpretation of the contract). The declaration of trust to circumvent transferability restrictions was first used in the Aurora CLO transaction for Sumitomo in April 1998. Since then, the FSA in the UK has published guidelines expressly recognising the use of a declaration of trust as a method of transferring assets off balance sheet for capital purposes. As a result of the potential to use this mechanism to circumvent prohibitions on assignment, and the flexibility of trusts to deal with revolving receivables pools and efficient profit extraction, trust structures have seen significant activity. Outside the UK (and especially in those jurisdictions where trusts are not recognised) it may not be possible to use this route, depending on consideration of the view likely to be taken by the local courts.

Insolvency unwind risk

Each jurisdiction has its own set of insolvency rules relating to an entity which is unable to pay its debts, which dictate circumstances in which a liquidator of the originator can attack transactions effected by the company on the basis that they prejudice other creditors in some way. Examples under English law arise under the Insolvency Act 1986 and include transactions at an undervalue, preferences, transactions defrauding creditors, the disclaimer of onerous property, the avoidance of transactions entered into after the start of winding-up and extortionate credit transactions. The circumstances of the transaction will need to be such that a sufficient degree of certainty can be achieved that no such insolvency regimes will lead to the unwinding of the transaction.

Recharacterisation risk

In many jurisdictions, there may be a risk of recharacterisation of the main receivables sale agreement such that the obligation and rights of the originator under this agreement will be considered at law to take the form of a loan backed by security of some description over the receivables, rather than an actual sale of the receivables as intended.

The disadvantage of a secured loan structure is two-fold. Firstly, on insolvency or near insolvency of the originator, automatic stay or moratorium regulations in the jurisdiction in question may prevent any kind of realisation of, or enforcement proceedings in relation to, the receivables (see under "Moratorium/automatic stay" below).

Secondly, in many jurisdictions there are detailed formalities, such as registration requirements, which may need to be complied with on the taking of a security interest. If these requirements are not met, this may render the supposed security interest invalid, leaving the purchaser of the receivables with simply an unsecured claim in the insolvency of the originator. In some jurisdictions (such as the US), it may be possible to undertake a protective registration filing to guard against this risk. In other jurisdictions, however (such as England), the mere fact of making such a filing may itself invite the analysis that the transaction is a secured loan rather than a sale. At the very least, this may then prejudice any intended off-balance-sheet treatment (see section 3.11).

Whether or not a transfer is recharacterised as a security interest will depend on the view of the courts in the relevant jurisdiction (usually the jurisdiction where the originator is incorporated, as this is typically where any action against the originator to wind up the originator and challenge the receivables transfer is most likely to be brought). In most jurisdictions, a variety of factors are considered when forming this view, such as:

- How the transfer is described, and whether such description is consistently applied throughout the deal documentation;
- Any right of the originator to re-acquire the assets which have been securitised;
- The level of risk and reward which remains with the originator in relation to profits or losses on the assets;
- In some cases, the form of recourse back to the originator (for example, whether recourse takes the form of a deferred purchase price, or a subordinated note).

Substantive consolidation risk

In some jurisdictions, notably the US, in circumstances where the assets and management of the SPV and the originator are not clearly segregated, the possibility exists that the court would apply the doctrine of substantive consolidation, effectively piercing the corporate veil that separates the SPV from the originator, and regarding the assets of the SPV as available to meet the claims of creditors of the originator in the insolvency of the originator. The risk is minimal under English law absent fraud.

It may also be necessary to address commingling risk if cash collections will still be paid to the originator after the sale, to prevent the collections being lost to investors on insolvency of the originator if they are commingled with other monies of the originator.

Moratorium/automatic stay

The jurisdiction in question may prevent any kind of enforcement proceedings in relation to the receivables. This is generally only relevant in relation to secured loan structures (or true sale structures recharacterised as secured loan structures), as the ownership of the assets has not passed to the SPV.

The US has particularly wide-ranging automatic stay provisions, which apply from the point at which a petition is filed for insolvency or Chapter 11 proceedings, and which prevent most secured creditor enforcement proceedings being undertaken. This may necessitate the interposition of a bankruptcy remote entity as the borrower in US secured loan structures.

In contrast to this, moratorium proceedings under English law are limited to a stay on enforcement by secured creditors from the commencement of administration proceedings. The effect of this is limited by the fact that any creditor with the benefit of a floating charge over the whole or substantially the whole of the originator's assets can appoint an administrative receiver, which will block the commencement of administration. However, the new Insolvency Act 2000 and Enterprise Act in the UK provide for a new regime for moratorium-style proceedings in the UK, and limit the use of administrative receivers, respectively. The limited application of moratorium proceedings in the UK has been one of the key reasons behind the growth of secured loan structures for CMBS and whole business deals in the UK.

In relation both to (a) secured loan structures, with limited recourse loans with security granted by an originator to isolate these three risks; and (b) the security interest that will be granted by the SPV over its assets in favour of investors, Chapter 13 describes the four main types of English law security over assets: namely mortgages, charges, pledges and liens. Generally speaking, only mortgages and charges are of particular relevance to a securitisation, as liens are created by operation of law rather than consensually pursuant to a contract, and pledges are only capable of being created over items capable of physical possession (which excludes intangibles such as receivables). Pledges may, however, be encountered in repackaging structures, as they are capable of creating effective security over negotiable instruments such as bearer promissory notes. Even in such a case a charge is generally preferred, as a pledge may be cancelled if the note is delivered back into the possession of the pledgor. Their use is therefore found most often in repackagings of notes originating from a civil law jurisdiction, or held through a clearing system in such a jurisdiction (such as Euroclear), as civil law systems advocate different forms of security. In particular, civil law systems may not recognise a floating charge, which is often used under English law as a round-up charge over all assets of the originator in favour of the SPV (for a secured loan structure) or of the SPV in favour of investors (for most structures). As noted above, this form of charge will also prevent the appointment of an administrator and the onset of administration proceedings (which would give rise to a moratorium as noted above, preventing enforcement of the security).

In a secured loan arrangement, if the security is over an asset that is actually to be the source of principal repayment to investors (absent refinancing by the originator), consideration will need to be given to the length of time that will be required to effect enforcement and realise cash.

3.1.1 Negative pledges

A further issue of relevance in considering a secured loan is the potential existence of negative pledge clauses in the originator's current loan or capital markets documentation. Negative pledges are often found in unsecured loans and usually consist of an undertaking not to create security over assets of the originator without seeking the consent of the relevant lender, or granting the lender equally ranking security (usually, except for certain permitted arrangements relating to the originator's day-to-day business). Capital markets negative pledges may in some cases be less restrictive and only limit the ability of the originator to create security for a subsequent issue of debt instruments. A related provision to the negative pledge is the undertaking by the originator often found in loan agreements that it will not dispose of assets whose value exceeds a certain amount, or a certain percentage of the value of its total assets, without receiving market value for them.

This provision may prevent a true sale transaction if the market value proviso is missing. The presence or absence of one or other of these clauses, and the precise limitations they impose, may lead to an intended secured loan transaction being structured as a true sale, or vice versa.

3.1.2 Set-off

The use of a transfer method that does not involve giving notice to the receivables debtors of the transfer (such as a "silent" or non-notified equitable assignment under English law) has certain consequences in most jurisdictions. Chief among these is that unless and until the debtor is notified of the transfer, the debtor may have a continuing right of set-off, which will enable it to apply any amounts owed to it by the originator in satisfaction of the amounts the debtor owes on the receivables. The most obvious example of this is a customer who applies amounts it has on deposit with the originator to discharge its mortgage with the originator. Since the SPV has only purchased the mortgage, any reduction in the amounts due under the mortgage operates as a direct reduction of the assets of the SPV.

The risk may also arise where the originator has undertaken to maintain goods provided to the customer (for example, in relation to equipment leased to the customer) where the customer may withhold payment if maintenance is not in fact provided. It may also arise under statutory protections for consumers (for example, in the UK, under s. 75 Consumer Credit Act 1974, a customer purchasing goods on credit, for example on a credit card, can claim the same defences against the card issuer that it could maintain against the seller if the goods are defective).

The simplest device for structuring around this risk is to exclude from the receivables being securitised any receivables where there is a risk of set-off or maintenance obligations, backed up by a warranty from the originator that no such set-off rights exist. This may not be feasible where receivables that are subject to such a risk constitute a large part of the portfolio.

It is often possible in many legal jurisdictions to obtain a waiver of set-off rights from the debtor which is legally effective in excluding their normal ability to set-off, although a reciprocal waiver may be required from the originator if there is local legislation requiring fair dealings with consumers (such as the Unfair Contract Terms Act 1977 or the Unfair Terms in Consumer Contracts Regulations 1999 in the UK). Unless such waivers are included as a matter of course in the standard documentation of the originator, this may require the replacement of the originator's standard forms, or the obtaining of signed waivers from each individual debtor.

A further alternative for deposit set-off (which again requires a fundamental business decision by the originator) is to have all deposit-taking activities undertaken by a different corporate entity from the originator. This will usually operate to prevent the debtor setting the deposit against the receivable, as set-off typically requires amounts to be owed from and to the same legal entities.

If set-off cannot be wholly excluded, then a cash deposit or a guarantee or indemnity from a suitably rated entity equal to the maximum potential set-off may be required. An indemnity from the originator will generally be required in any event, but will only be acceptable by itself if the originator is a suitably rated entity, or a wrap of the undertaking is provided by a suitably rated entity.

3.2   SPVS AND TRUSTS

The purchaser of the receivables is typically referred to as a special purpose vehicle, special purpose company or special purpose entity (abbreviated respectively to SPV, SPC or SPE). This SPV will be established to be "bankruptcy remote" – in other words, at extremely limited risk of being declared bankrupt or insolvent – where possible so that, having isolated the receivables from the insolvency risk of the originator, there is no additional credit risk analysis required on the purchaser.

Bankruptcy remoteness is ensured through a combination of key elements, including:

- Establishing the SPV in a zero or low tax jurisdiction, or in a jurisdiction where the taxation can be fixed and agreed with taxation authorities at a set figure, so that there are no potential claims for taxation payments from local tax authorities. This will prevent the tax authorities from being able to wind the company up for non-payment of tax. Any residual tax amount due can be reserved for by maintaining a cash reserve in the securitisation structure.
- Ensuring that the SPV has no preferential debt claims against it by ensuring it has no employees or VAT liabilities. This entails sub-contracting all functions, and is one of the reasons for the complexity of securitisation structures. Service agreements are required for all functions associated with the SPV, with different parties contracted for each service. The most significant of these services is generally the servicing of the receivables portfolio (i.e. the collection and enforcement of the receivables) and cash management to ensure the correct application of cash received to different parties in accordance with the priority of payments (see Chapter 4, section 4.3). This is generally undertaken by the originator acting as servicer (although if the originator is not a financial institution, a separate cash manager may be retained for cash management functions). The contractual structure of the relations between the SPV and the other parties to a transaction is illustrated in Figure 3.1.
- Requiring all creditors of the SPV pursuant to the securitisation to sign a written undertaking agreeing that their claims have limited recourse solely to cash that is available for payment of their claims in accordance with the order of payment priorities set out in the servicing agreement or other contractual documentation relating to the securitisation cash flows (see Chapter 4, section 4.3) and that any amounts outstanding after application of all proceeds within the SPV will be extinguished (but see section 3.10 with regard to use of such language in UK transactions), and that they will not take any action to enforce payment of amounts due to them or attempt the winding up of the SPV (so-called "non-petition" language) until the main investors are paid off in full.
- Prohibiting the SPV from undertaking business or incurring debts other than under the transaction in question – the SPV will undertake not to engage in any business or enter into any contractual obligations save for those that relate to the securitisation itself.
- Ensuring that there is no risk of substantive consolidation of the SPV with the originator or any other party by:
  - Providing independent directors and shareholders for the SPV. The provision of independent directors should be structured to avoid any consolidation concerns

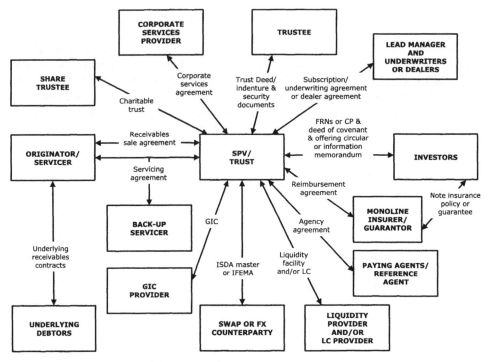

Figure 3.1   Main parties and documentation structure

> that might arise on the provision of any indemnity to the directors of the SPV against the risk of a technical insolvency of the SPV;
>
> – Having the SPV take the form of an "orphan company" whose shares are held by a trustee on charitable trust or on some other kind of purpose trust. In addition to precluding the possibility of the shareholders attempting to wind up the SPV, or use it to undertake other activities or business that could prejudice its bankruptcy remote nature, having independent shareholders serves to further reduce the risk of substantive consolidation (see section 3.1) of the SPV and the originator, and to avoid any concerns as to accounting or capital consolidation of the SPV on the balance sheet of the originator or arranger;

● Limiting the scope of the objects of the company set out in its memorandum of association to undertaking the transaction in question.

By ensuring that the SPV is bankruptcy remote, a need is created for service providers – including SPV managers and other servicers. A corporate services provider will normally be engaged to provide independent directors and shareholders for the SPV.

3.2.1   Choice of jurisdiction

Aside from bankruptcy remoteness issues on tax, the choice of jurisdiction for incorporation of an SPV will be influenced by local regulatory requirements – generally those related to the transfer or true sale of assets. For example, Law 130 in Italy provides for simpler transfer requirements for receivables if the purchaser is a Law 130 company (an Italian SPV). For this reason, onshore SPVs (i.e. SPVs located in the same jurisdiction as the assets) are used in many deals, despite the often more complex taxation treatment that follows from this. This is particularly the case for residential or commercial-mortgage-backed deals, due to restrictions or transfer complexities on the transfer of interests in land.

Securities laws requirements relating to the issuance of the desired funding instruments are also relevant to the choice of jurisdiction. Some jurisdictions may impose minimum duration requirements (often 2 or 3 years) as to trading records or profitability for companies that intend to issue listed instruments. As the SPV will be newly established and designed to generate only a nominal profit, any such requirements may be problematic. A brief summary of some of the most popular offshore jurisdictions for establishing SPVs is set out in section 3.3 and section 3.4.

Chapter 13 provides detail on:

- Various forms of UK corporation, such as registered companies, statutory companies, public companies, private companies, companies limited by shares, companies limited by guarantee and unlimited companies, as well as company groups, holding companies, parent companies and subsidiaries;
- UK company capacity and governance, under memorandum of association, articles of association, objects, annual general meeting, extraordinary general meeting, and other terminology such as resolutions, written resolutions, special resolutions, ordinary resolutions, elective resolutions and extraordinary resolutions;
- The capital structure of UK companies, under authorised share capital, issued share capital, reduction of capital, maintenance of capital, class rights, preference shares, ordinary shares, pre-emption, dividends and distribution;
- General accounting terms for UK corporates, under financial year, statutory accounts, consolidated accounts, parent undertaking and subsidiary undertaking.

3.2.2   Alternatives to SPV companies

In some transactions, the receivables are purchased by a trust, or purchased by an SPV and held by a trust. This is commonly used as a method of dividing up the receivables into shares in an "undivided interest" structure, so that the trust will hold one share for the SPV and another share for the originator. This is often the most convenient method of allocating shares where the quantity of receivables generated varies significantly from one period to the next, so that the SPV obtains an interest in a fixed amount of the receivables, which varies as a percentage of the total amount of receivables each period (a "floating allocation percentage"). This is often used for credit card transactions.

Undivided interest structures may also be used where receivables cannot easily be identified individually within a portfolio, making it difficult to transfer the desired receivables at law so that instead an undivided interest in the entire portfolio is transferred. Under English law, such a structure is at risk of not transferring a proprietary interest in the receivables, unless there is an express trust over the entire portfolio such that the share transferred to the SPV can be regarded as an interest in a tenancy in common of the whole portfolio.

Use of a trust may have US accounting or tax benefits (see sections 3.10 and 3.11); a trust may have fiscal transparency in the UK if it constitutes a bare trust. A trust may, however, be subject to adverse tax or regulatory treatment in the UK if it is considered to be a collective investment scheme.

In some jurisdictions (for example, Belgium and France), the form of local onshore SPV that has been provided for by legislation takes the form of a kind of fund or unit trust, which issues participating "units" to investors based on its asset portfolio, and is managed by a management company.

3.3 OFFSHORE CENTRES

Offshore financial centres (i.e. centres outside the local country) are extensively used in securitisation and repackaging transactions due to the tax efficiencies that they offer in structuring transactions. Securitisations are structurally designed to isolate the securitised assets from the originator without adding incremental costs to the collection of the assets. Generally the most problematic issue in the efficient management and collection of the assets is tax; mainly in the form of withholding tax on the underlying assets acquired, transfer taxes on sale of the assets (such as stamp duty), corporation tax and withholding tax on bonds or other financing issues (see section 3.10).

The first two are typically dealt with domestically, with structuring via an onshore SPV or a bank, or in some other way designed to minimise the tax. Where an onshore SPV is used, there may be no requirement to establish an offshore SPV as well, and corporation tax and bond level withholding tax issues may only be relevant at the onshore level.

However, an offshore SPV may be needed as well as an onshore SPV as a bond issuing vehicle where securities laws restrict the onshore company from issuing securities or prescribe a particular style or method of issuance or tie the issue down with withholding taxes. In some cases, use of an onshore SPV at all may be difficult due to concerns as to the tax treatment or bankruptcy remoteness of an onshore SPV, and the deal may simply be structured with an offshore SPV. This is most commonly the case for repackagings, where the underlying assets are generally free of withholding tax and transfer taxes, being in the form of securities.

Offshore centres divide into two camps:

- Low tax or liberalised centres (such as Ireland, Luxembourg or the Netherlands); and
- "Tax haven" centres (for example, centres in the Caribbean and the Channel Islands).

Liberalised centres are often used to take advantage of double taxation treaties (with the Netherlands and Ireland being the most popular), as most tax haven jurisdictions do not have these treaties. Most deals in the international ABS markets which do not need to take advantage of double tax treaties have used the offshore centres of the Cayman Islands or Jersey as key jurisdictions for establishing SPVs. Cayman has been used extensively for trades closed in the US and Asia, and Jersey and the Cayman Islands have both been used for trades closed in Europe.

3.3.1 Reasons for choice of jurisdiction

The choice of jurisdiction in which to establish an offshore SPV will be driven by:

- Tax issues – as noted in section 3.2, the SPV will often be established in a jurisdiction where either there is zero taxation, or where taxation can be fixed and agreed with taxation authorities at a set figure so that this amount of cash can be maintained as a cash reserve in the securitisation structure;
- Securities laws – again as noted in section 3.2, some jurisdictions may impose minimum duration requirements (often 2 or 3 years) as to trading records or profitability for companies that intend to issue listed instruments (or, for that matter, minimum capital requirements);
- Given the involvement of the rating agencies in most transactions, a premium is placed upon jurisdictions with a sufficiently certain, established and flexible legal system, which can address any rating issues on insolvency, limited recourse, nonpetition, etc.;
- Political stability.

Consequently, jurisdictions that have limited or no withholding tax and corporation tax, as well as sufficiently liberal securities laws and stable government, are the main choices for establishing an offshore SPV that can finance the transaction efficiently without tax leakage.

3.3.2 Use of different jurisdictions

Each jurisdiction has its own forms of corporation – however, there are generally three types of corporation used in most tax haven jurisdictions:

- An onshore company (which is tax resident and operating in the tax haven);
- An exempt company (otherwise known as a brass-plate company; this company does not have an established place of business in the tax haven and operates entirely offshore); and
- An international business company (this was first set up in the BVI in 1984, and is taxed locally at a nominal rate, which can permit profits to be repatriated or held offshore without incurring tax liabilities under onshore rules on controlled foreign companies, and so on).

One thing that most offshore jurisdictions have in common is the relative speed and simplicity with which companies can be established. Typically, offshore jurisdictions are well-geared to the provision of directorial and secretarial service functions, and can provide registered offices. Usually a company can be established in a matter of a few days, and generally within a week (if required, it is sometimes possible to establish companies overnight). Also, most offshore centres have extremely streamlined processes and requirements for filing annual returns and other ongoing corporate documentation compared to onshore jurisdictions.

Consequently, the most expensive item for the establishment is generally the costs of the local legal advisers or agents for the establishment of the company and for advice on the manner in which local laws in the jurisdiction of the SPV affect the transaction in general.

Required minimum share capital is generally nominal in most jurisdictions, although a certain level may be required to put the company on a more solid footing, and a certain level of fee or profit should be allowed for to create a legitimate benefit to the SPV (as a separate legal entity from the originator or the arranger) of entering into a securitisation transaction in the first place. Although the share capital is an expense of the deal in economic terms and as such will be borne ultimately by the originator in cost terms, it may need to be paid into the SPV indirectly via the services provider that provides the directors to the SPV in order to avoid an analysis that the originator is putting equity into the SPV and is thus the owner of the SPV.

3.3.3 New developments

Tax havens have come under fire from OECD countries for the distortions they may introduce into the international financial system as an available agent of tax evasion, and for the levels of drug trafficking, money laundering and other illegal activities that pass through them.

In 1998, the OECD reported on the effect of tax competition without commensurate financial regulation and monitoring, and sufficient information transparency and exchange, and announced plans for sanctions on tax haven jurisdictions.

On 26 June 2000, the OECD Forum on Harmful Tax Practices published a list of 38 offshore centres on which it threatened to impose economic sanctions if they did not commit to information exchange on financial affairs within 1 year. Of the more widely used jurisdictions for securitisation, Bermuda, the Cayman Islands, Delaware, Ireland, Labuan, Luxembourg, Mauritius and the Netherlands are not on the list, while the British Virgin Islands and Jersey are (as are, among others, Guernsey, the Isle of Man, Liechtenstein, Liberia, Monaco and Panama).

The action planned by the OECD received limited support from the US until a compromise was reached in June 2001, which was conditioned on the action of the OECD not imposing restrictions on the manner in which the tax havens structured their tax policies and which pushed back implementation until December 2001.

The final OECD list was published on 18 April 2002, and only contained seven remaining uncooperative jurisdictions; the other 31 jurisdictions had made commitments to transparency and exchange of information. The seven jurisdictions identified as uncooperative were:

- Andorra
- The Principality of Liechtenstein
- Liberia
- The Principality of Monaco
- The Republic of the Marshall Islands
- The Republic of Nauru
- The Republic of Vanuatu.

The Republic of Vanuatu was removed from the list on 20 May 2003.

Following the terrorist attack of 11 September 2001, the US made demands on the implementation of anti-terrorist laws and the freezing of bank accounts of suspected terrorists. This also gave impetus to the list of countries that do not comply with recommendations on money laundering that had been put forward by the Financial Action Task force (the FATF).

3.4   COMMONLY USED OFFSHORE JURISDICTIONS

3.4.1   Bermuda

The legal system in Bermuda is a common law system largely following English law. Companies may be set up either as a local company (where they are trading locally) or as an exempted company (where they are trading offshore). Exempted companies can obtain an undertaking against tax being imposed. Bermuda has been particularly used for the establishment of insurance companies.

Tax treatment

Stamp/Registration/etc.   No stamp duty except in relation to property in Bermuda.
Withholding tax   No withholding tax.
Profits tax   No profits tax.

Regulatory approvals

The approval of the Bermuda Monetary Authority is required for the establishment of a Bermuda exempted company.

3.4.2   British Virgin Islands

The BVI is the single most popular jurisdiction for the establishment of offshore companies in the world, due to the simplicity of its incorporation requirements, but has not been used for securitisation transactions as much as some other jurisdictions. In 1984 the BVI was the first jurisdiction to introduce the concept of the International Business Company or IBC. BVI law is a common law system largely following English law.

Tax treatment

Stamp/Registration/etc.   IBCs are exempt from stamp duty.
Profits tax   IBCs are exempt from profits tax.

3.4.3   Cayman Islands

Cayman Islands law is a common law system largely following English law. The Cayman Islands is probably the single most popular jurisdiction for the establishment of SPVs for securitisation transactions, due to the high level of availability of directorial services and the transaction friendly legal regime. Companies are either ordinary companies (which carry on business in the Cayman Islands), non-resident ordinary companies (which do not carry on business in the Cayman Islands) or exempted companies (which may not carry on business in the Cayman Islands and may not offer securities to the public in the Cayman Islands). An exempted company can obtain a 20-year undertaking from the Governor in Council that taxes imposed in the future will not apply to the SPV.

Ring-fencing and true sale

Moratorium/automatic stay   There are no moratorium or administration proceedings in the Cayman Islands.

Tax treatment

Stamp/Registration/etc.   Nominal, except for stamp on the transfer of real estate in the Cayman Islands.
Withholding tax   No withholding tax.
Profits tax   No profits tax.
VAT   No VAT.
Other tax issues   No other relevant taxes.

Other issues

Since the Companies Amendment Law of 1987, payment of dividends may be made out of any share premium account (in addition to payment made out of distributable profits as usual), provided that the company is solvent.

Limited duration entities may be established, which assists US pass-through fiscal transparency analysis.

Purpose trusts (which do not need to have an identifiable beneficiary or group of beneficiaries) were introduced under the Special Trust (Alternative Regime) Law 1997, establishing the legality of a non-charitable purpose trust (as an alternative to the typical charitable trust used in securitisations, which is the only permissible trust without an identifiable beneficiary under English law).

3.4.4   Delaware

The State of Delaware, on the eastern seaboard of the US, is often used as a jurisdiction to establish US commercial paper conduit issuers. Delaware has sophisticated and up-to-date companies laws, and the certainty and flexibility in its legislation has made it a leading jurisdiction for the establishment of SPVs for ABS deals in the US.

Tax treatment

Profits tax   Conduit vehicles are usually set up in Delaware as corporations with limited liability, which are not subject to state profits tax in Delaware to the extent that they do not carry on a trade in Delaware.

3.4.5 Ireland

Ireland has become a focus for the establishment of SPVs for use in transactions involving assets originated in certain jurisdictions, due to:

- The favourable tax regime applying to Irish securitisation SPVs (in particular companies which operate in the International Financial Services Centre (or IFSC) (which is located in the Dublin Docklands));
- The fact that Ireland is within the EU and benefits from EU regulatory approval under passport directives; and
- The network of double tax treaties Ireland is party to (unlike many tax haven jurisdictions) – for example, the treaty with Korea providing for a reduction in cross-border withholding tax on interest payments.

See Ireland in Chapter 12 for more details.

3.4.6 Jersey

Jersey law is a common law system largely following English law. Companies may be set up as an ordinary company, an exempt company or an International Business Company (IBC). IBCs are intended to benefit from controlled foreign company legislation under which profits already taxed in one country may be exempt from tax on repatriation to a parent in another country.

Jersey intends to remove exempt company status by 2008 in order to meet EU requirements, and to move instead to a 0% tax regime for SPVs (which is under discussion with the EU).

Securities laws

Exempt companies and IBCs may not offer securities to the public in Jersey.

Tax treatment

Withholding tax   Tax resident companies may pay interest gross out of non-Jersey source income that is not received in Jersey. Exempt companies are free of withholding tax.
Profits tax   Companies that are incorporated in Jersey, or are managed and controlled in Jersey, are regarded as tax resident in Jersey and are liable to pay profits tax at 20%, unless they are exempt companies or IBCs. Exempt companies are free of Jersey profits tax except on profits of a trade carried out in Jersey. IBCs are liable to pay tax in Jersey on profits from international activities at a declining rate from 2% down to 0.5%, and on profits from other activities at 30%.
VAT   No VAT.

Regulatory approvals

Consent from the Jersey Financial Services Commission is required for any issue of securities or circulation of a prospectus by a company incorporated in Jersey (including an exempt company). Approvals can generally be obtained within 2 weeks. Care may be needed to ensure that an SPV issuing notes with a right to participate in profits is not considered to be a collective investment fund, which would subject it to further regulation.

Other issues

Purpose trusts (which do not need to have an identifiable beneficiary or group of beneficiaries) were introduced under the Trusts (Amendment No. 3) (Jersey) Law with effect from 1996, establishing the legality of a non-charitable purpose trust (as an alternative to the typical charitable trust used in securitisations, which is the only permissible trust without an identifiable beneficiary under English law). Generally, an audit will be required for a Jersey company, although a structure without auditors is permitted in some cases.

3.4.7 Labuan

Labuan, situated off the north coast of Borneo, is a territory of Malaysia and was established as an International Offshore Financial Centre (IOFC) in 1990. As such, it enjoys certain benefits in dealings with Malaysia.

Tax treatment

Withholding tax   No withholding tax. A Labuan SPV is treated as Malaysian resident for the purpose of withholding tax on interest payment offshore from Malaysia, and would thus be able to receive payment free of withholding.
Profits tax   Companies may agree a fixed nominal tax payment.
VAT   None.
Other tax issues   Has double tax treaties.

3.4.8 Luxembourg

Luxembourg has been favoured as a jurisdiction for repackaging vehicles, and for the establishment of offshore banks and deposits. See Luxembourg in Chapter 12 for more details.

3.4.9 Mauritius

Mauritius is a financial centre off the east coast of Africa and Madagascar, in the Indian Ocean. Mauritius has a hybrid legal system, with a Civil Code based on elements of French law, but an English-style law of trusts. Mauritius has been favoured as a jurisdiction for incorporation of SPVs due to its extensive double tax treaty network. Companies may be set up as offshore companies or international companies.

Tax treatment

Withholding tax   No withholding tax.

Profits tax   International companies pay no profits tax. Offshore companies established prior to 1 July 1998 had the flexibility to opt not to pay profits tax, or to pay profits tax at different rates up to 35%. Offshore companies established since then are liable to tax at 15%, but a tax credit for 90% of this can be obtained.

Other tax issues   Mauritius has an extensive range of double tax treaties. The tax treaty with India has been particularly used by offshore investors, as it permits a company resident in Mauritius (for these purposes a company that is liable to tax in Mauritius – which can include an offshore company that elects to pay a nominal rate of tax – can be resident in Mauritius) to repatriate capital gains to Mauritius free of Indian capital gains tax (although the Indian authorities have recently attempted to attack the use of this provision). The treaty with the People's Republic of China reduces withholding tax on interest to 10%. The tax treaties with Luxembourg, South Africa and Singapore provide for withholding tax on interest payments to be reduced to zero.

Regulatory approvals

Offshore companies must obtain an offshore certificate from the Mauritius Offshore Business Activities Authority (MOBAA).

Other issues

Audited accounts must be prepared.

3.4.10   The Netherlands

The Netherlands has long been a focus for the establishment of finance subsidiaries, due to its favourable tax and withholding tax regime. It has been used in a number of securitisation, and particularly repackaging, transactions, due to:

- The ability to obtain rulings as to the amount of tax payable by the SPV from time to time;
- The fact that the Netherlands is within the EU and benefits from EU regulatory approval under passport directives; and
- The network of double tax treaties to which the Netherlands is party (unlike many tax haven jurisdictions).

See The Netherlands in Chapter 12 for more details.

3.5   BONDS AND CP FUNDING

The investor market for asset-backed securities is largest and most sophisticated in the US (see Chapter 1, section 1.3). Consequently, many particularly innovative or unusual transactions, or especially large transactions, are marketed to US investors.

It is, however, the case that the securities laws regime in the US contains various onerous requirements, pursuant to the Securities Act, the Exchange Act and the TEFRA taxation requirements. Consequently, many offerings are structured to circumvent the registration requirements of the SEC in the US. Placement is often made only to sophisticated US investors such as QIBs under the Rule 144A safe harbour, and using exemptions from the investment company provisions, with the remaining securities sold offshore pursuant to the Regulation S safe harbour. (See section 3.7.1 for more details.)

Generally speaking, asset-backed instruments offer a yield pick-up over ordinary capital markets paper due to the uncertainty surrounding the estimated weighted average life of the instruments and the related prepayment risk. Given the robust nature of securitisation structures approved by the rating agencies, investors have generally been willing to accept this risk in return for being offered paper at a favourable yield.

An analysis of different types of negotiable instrument is covered in Chapter 13, including promissory notes, bills of exchange and cheques as well as FRNs and forms of bond, such as foreign bonds, Eurobonds, and domestic bonds.

The choice of short-term commercial paper as a funding instrument, as against longer-term bonds or FRNs, will most often be determined by the nature of the receivables in question (in other words whether they are short-term or long-term assets), although "mismatched" transactions have been closed, such as short-term trade receivables funded by a long-term bond issue, and conduit or SIV structures where long-term lease receivables or bonds are funded by short-term commercial paper. In addition, a mismatch structure of sorts is typically used for assets such as credit card receivables (which have no legal maturity date in any event), to allow replenishment over an initial revolving period, and amortisation over a run-off period. Many US mortgage securitisations are funded with fixed rate bonds in order to match fixed rate underlying mortgages. Most mortgage deals in the UK and Hong Kong are funded with floating rate instruments such as FRNs, as the majority of UK and Hong Kong mortgages bear a floating rate of interest.

Other factors that may be relevant would relate to the desire to achieve, or avoid, publicity for the transaction. Commercial paper is typically privately placed with little disclosure of the nature of the receivables, whereas most US or Eurobond issues are SEC-registered, or listed on an international exchange such as London or Luxembourg, with the transaction documentation thus becoming publicly available.

Also, the originator of the transaction may prefer to issue commercial paper as the discount rate charged on commercial paper is generally lower than the interest rate on long-term securities, often achieving a rate below LIBOR in a positive yield curve environment.

The need for commercial paper issuers to establish a reputation and a certain critical mass, and to provide investors with the ability to rollover their investment, has led to the creation of commercial paper conduits. These consist of an SPV that will purchase receivables from a number of different originators and package them together to back the commercial paper it has issued. In some cases, these conduits will simply deal in short-term trade receivables from a number of originators. In other cases, the receivables packaged will be wide-ranging in nature, from short- or long-term consumer receivables to bonds or other capital market instruments. Many of these conduits issue commercial paper in the US commercial paper market due to the depth of liquidity in the asset-backed sector. Some, however, will fund in the Eurocommercial paper market instead, or will have the ability to switch from one market to another in order to arbitrage commercial paper rates over time.

CP conduits are increasingly being used for a larger variety of funding solutions that require a form of revolving facility. Conduits can make use of a CP tranche side-by-side with a bond tranche in order to take some of the prepayment risk or volatility risk out of the residual structure (for example, as a CP companion tranche to a bond PAC tranche).

3.6 SECURITIES LAWS

Securities laws relevant to an offering are generally centred around the country of origin of the issuer or underlying assets. However:

- The US regulates securities offerings world wide.
- Many offerings to European investors are marketed and sold through the City of London.
- The EU is rapidly consolidating securities laws across Europe.

Consequently, US, UK and EU securities laws are relevant to many international offerings even where the securitised assets originate elsewhere.

US securities laws have a global reach, in contrast to most other national securities laws, which tend to have local reach only. Securities restrictions will, however, also need to be complied with in any other jurisdictions where the securities are to be offered or sold, with the inclusion of selling restrictions (which consist of undertakings to be given by the issuer and the syndicate of underwriters as to the manner in which they will offer or distribute the securities) in the subscription agreement or underwriting agreement for the securities.

In particular, given the position of London as the centre of the Euromarkets, any Euromarket offering is likely to take place through London and may need to comply with UK selling restrictions. Selling restrictions are generally intended to regulate the circumstances in which any kind of public offering (such as an offer to the public in the UK) may be made. Stabilisation and other requirements of the FSA as to the contents of any information memorandum or offering circular may also need to be met.

3.7 US SECURITIES LAWS

The US regulates securities offerings via legislation which applies to impose penalties on offerings world wide. The main areas of relevance are:

- Securities laws (primarily the Securities Act of 1933) designed to protect the US public;
- Taxation provisions (under TEFRA) designed to prevent tax evasion by US citizens; and
- Investment company provisions (under the Investment Company Act of 1940).

3.7.1 Securities Act of 1933

The Securities Act of 1933 of the US governs offerings of securities by any "means or instruments of transportation or communication in interstate commerce or of the mails" (s. 5) and consisting of requirements which are intended to compel adequate disclosure of all those facts that are material to making an informed investment decision. Any securities offering on issue or resale that falls within s. 5 and is not exempted by the Securities Act or by other provisions of the Securities and Exchange Commission from registration must be preceded by a registration statement; s. 11(a) and s. 12(2) provide for liability for misstatements and omissions in registration statements and in prospectuses respectively.

Exceptions from registration are available for offerings within s. 5. These are normally relied on even where there is no clear US connection, since s. 5 is so wide-ranging. The main exemptions on issue are:

(a) For an offer of exempt securities (e.g. commercial paper offered under s. 3(a)(3), and securities issued or guaranteed by US banks under s. 3(a)(2)).
(b) For an offering of securities falling under Rule 903 of Regulation S (a regulation of the SEC under the Securities Act), which was introduced in 1990, and which defined the broad scope of, and clarified previous uncertainty over, SEC registration requirements. It provides for safe harbours from the requirement to register securities, either on issue, or on resale, of the securities. An offering is considered to be made "on issue" if it is made during the distribution period; i.e. it is made by the issuer (or an affiliate) or a distributor (or an affiliate) (distributors are defined as "any underwriter, dealer, or other person who participates, pursuant to a contractual arrangement, in the distribution of the securities"). The distribution period cannot end before the end of any relevant restricted period (see below), and is considered to extend indefinitely in relation to any underwriter of the issue unless and until the underwriter sells its initial allotment of securities. The safe harbours and categories are:

Issuer safe harbour   An issuer safe harbour under Rule 903 within which no registration is required. The safe harbour is not available where the securities offer is "part of a plan or scheme to avoid the registration requirements" of the Securities Act, there exists an understanding the securities will "flow back" to the US, or any distributor "knows or is reckless in not knowing" that any purchaser or distributor will not meet the Regulation S general and particular requirements.

To gain the Regulation S issuer safe harbour, the general requirements are that the issuer and others affiliated with an offering must:

(1) Ensure that the securities are offered in an "offshore transaction" (i.e. they are not offered to "US persons" such as US corporations, partnerships and individuals and the buy order is originated with a buyer outside the US or on the floor of a non-US exchange);
(2) Avoid "directed selling efforts" in the US (activities intended to, or that could reasonably result in, the conditioning of the US market for the securities); and
(3) Follow offering restrictions set out in the offer documentation.

The Regulation S particular requirements to gain the issuer safe harbour relate to each combination of issue and issuer within one of three categories:

- *Category 1* (issues backed by the full faith and credit of a foreign government, issues by a non-US issuer with no SUSMI (substantial US market interest) in such securities, issues directed to a single non-US country, issues pursuant to non-US employee benefit plans): no particular requirements.

- *Category 2* (issues by issuers who report under the Exchange Act (excluding issues of equity securities by a US reporting issuer from 17 February 1998), issues of debt securities by a non-US issuer with SUSMI in such securities): a distributor must offer or sell the securities only in accordance with a registration exemption, in any sale to another distributor or dealer the purchaser must be informed that they are subject to these same selling restrictions, no sale within 40 days (for debt) or 1 year (for equity) of the first offer of the securities (the "restricted period") (or otherwise falling within the distribution period – see above) must be for the benefit of a US person, and the securities must state that they have not been registered and may not be offered or sold in the US or to a US person save under a registration exemption.
- *Category 3* (other issues): the requirements are as for Category 2, save that, in addition, during the restricted period the securities are required to be "locked-up" in the form of a global note, only being allowed to be released into definitives after such period and upon certification of non-US beneficial ownership, or acquisition of US beneficial ownership under a registration exemption.

Use of the Regulation S issuer safe harbour, where there is an immediate resale of the securities into the US as seasoned securities after the end of any issuer safe harbour restricted period, is a practice frowned upon by the SEC in their release of 27 June 1995 as potentially forming a scheme to avoid registration requirements (depending on the circumstances). In a 1997 release, the SEC mooted increasing the restricted period for equity sales to 2 years.

(c) A private placement under s. 4(2) of the Securities Act, "transactions by an issuer [of securities] not involving any public offering". Purchasers must acquire the securities for investment purposes and without a view towards distributing them in order for the issuer to claim exemption from the Securities Act registration requirements. In order for the private (i.e. non-distributed) nature of the transaction not to be open to question it is usually considered necessary to: use large note denominations, offer to a limited number of potential purchasers, offer to purchasers who are experienced investors (typically sophisticated institutions), and offer subject to resale restrictions (which are often legended on the notes); confirmation of agreement to such restrictions being obtained in a "non-distribution letter". Typically, the restrictions would only allow resales in accordance with Rule 904 of Regulation S (see below), Rule 144 or Rule 144A. Regulation D, a safe harbour under s. 4(2), is often relied on rather than s. 4(2) itself, since it is hard to monitor compliance with s. 4(2).

(d) A Regulation D placement (a safe harbour under s. 4(2)). An SEC safe harbour within the s. 4(2) Securities Act exemption from registration on issue for private placements. Compliance with the Regulation D requirements ensures obtaining the issue exemption. Regulation D requires that no general solicitation or advertising of the offering occurs and that purchasers are not acquiring the securities with a view to distributing them (in order to comply with which resale restrictions, legends on the securities and "non-distribution letters" are obtained as with a private placement). Also, the issuer must reasonably believe that no more than 35 purchasers of the issue are not accredited investors. In addition, any such non-accredited investor purchasers must have sufficient experience to evaluate the investment (in the issuer's reasonable belief) and must have access to Exchange Act reports (or comparable Securities Act registration information) on the issuer.

Since these exemptions are often conditional on limitation of resales of the securities, an issue exemption could be reopened to the extent that subsequent resales are not exempt (or, even where such resale is within an exemption, the particular circumstances negative the necessary conditions for the issue exemption (for instance a resale under the broker/dealer exemption might nevertheless operate to show that the purchaser intended to distribute the securities, and thus reopen a private placement issue exemption)). Exemption on resale following an issue is available for:

(a) A resale of exempt securities as before;
(b) Sales under s. 4(1) by persons other than issuers, underwriters (this term being interpreted on the facts and quite widely to include any person who purchases securities with a view to reselling them, and also any affiliates of the issuer) or dealers;
(c) Sales under s. 4(3) and s. 4(4) by brokers and dealers (including underwriters no longer acting as such) more than 40 days (or 90 days in certain cases) after the first offering of the securities;
(d) Sales under Rule 144 (a safe harbour under s. 4(1) from possible consideration as an underwriter). An SEC safe harbour from consideration of a person as an underwriter within the meaning of s. 4(1) of the Securities Act. Thus, a person within the safe harbour who is not an issuer or dealer can rely on the s. 4(1) resale exemption. The safe harbour allows resales after an initial one year holding period, and requires that resales occur in ordinary market transactions, that notice of resales is filed with the SEC, that periodic Exchange Act reports (or comparable public information) are available on the issuer, and that the volume of resales be within certain limits (these volume limits are dropped after a 2-year holding period for sellers who are not affiliates of the issuer). Prior to April 1997 the initial holding period was 2 years and the volume limit for non-affiliates was 3 years;
(e) Sales under "s. 4(1$\frac{1}{2}$)" (sales that would be a private placement but for the fact that they are not made by the issuer and are therefore outside s. 4(2));
(f) Sale under Rule 904 of Regulation S on a non-US market approved by the SEC as a Designated Offshore Securities Market. In their release of 27 June 1995, the SEC notes that attempts to "wash-off" resale restrictions (e.g. on Rule 144A securities) by selling outside the US under Rule 904 and buying back fungible but unrestricted securities would render the replacement securities subject to the same restrictions.
(g) Sale in the US under Rule 144A (originally intended as a safe harbour codifying the s. 4(1$\frac{1}{2}$) position, but actually differing in scope). Rule 144A (introduced in April 1990) provides a resale exemption from registration under the Securities Act for a securities issue (or part of an issue) that is subjected to the restriction that it may be resold solely to and among QIBs (a qualified institutional buyer – generally speaking, an institution with over US$100m in assets under investment) in the secondary market. Rule 144A is often used immediately following a private placement, which placement is often made to a single investment bank intending immediate resale.

Rule 144A is only available in relation to a class of securities of the issuer (e.g. preferred shares, ordinary shares, debt, ADRs, etc.), which has not already been listed on a US securities exchange or listed on Nasdaq. Rule 144A is not available to an issuer unless current financial statements and statements for the two preceding years, together with basic information on the issuer, is available to each holder of a security, as well as to prospective investors, on request (which requirement is deemed met if the issuer is either subject to the reporting requirements of the Exchange Act, or exempt from such requirements under Rule 12g3-2(b) and therefore required instead to supply home country information).

Further requirements may arise under blue sky laws or regulations.

3.7.2   Taxation provisions – TEFRA

The Tax Equity and Fiscal Responsibility Act 1982 was introduced in the US to counteract tax evasion by US taxpayers on untraceable holdings of bearer securities. Securities with a maturity of 1 year or less (or 183 days or less if US-issued) are exempt from the TEFRA provisions. They require that only registered securities are issued, ownership in which can be traced by the IRS.

Any issue of bearer securities world wide will be subject to adverse US tax consequences for any issuer or purchaser of the securities who becomes subject to US taxation provisions. These adverse consequences are that purchasers of bearer securities in the primary market are required to register them or they will be unable to claim a loss deduction on the securities, while any gain will be taxed as income. Secondary market purchasers are similarly treated, unless the securities are registered or held through specific financial institutions within a recognised clearing system. Issuers are liable to a 1% excise tax on the outstanding principal amount of the securities from year to year, cannot deduct interest payments on the securities against federal income tax and cannot claim the "portfolio interest" exemption for the purposes of US withholding tax.

Issuers will be exempt from punitive tax consequences if:

(a) Arrangements are in place that are reasonably designed to ensure that the securities will only be sold or resold to persons who are not US persons (or to certain financial institutions who are US persons). This requirement is considered met if the issue and resale of the securities falls within one of the TEFRA safe harbours (TEFRA C and TEFRA D) up to the point at which the securities become seasoned securities.

TEFRA C   An issue of bearer securities will fall within TEFRA C if it "is issued only outside the United States and its possessions by an issuer that does not significantly engage in interstate commerce with respect to the issuance of such obligation either directly or through its agent, an underwriter, or a member of the selling group". Although there is no requirement to hold securities in global form as with the more complex TEFRA D requirements, most issuers regard TEFRA C as being too uncertain and vaguely defined to be relied on safely. In particular, it is unclear at what point interstate commerce becomes significant within the meaning of the safe harbour language. Where one of the underwriters is a US entity it is usually considered unsafe to rely on the TEFRA C safe harbour.

TEFRA D   TEFRA D requires that:

(i) Neither the issuer nor any distributor shall "offer or sell the obligation during the restricted period to a person who is within the United States or its possessions or to a United States person". This restriction will be considered to have been met with regard to any distributor if the distributor covenants that "it will not offer or sell the obligation during the restricted period to a person who is within the United States or its possessions or to a United States person" and during the restricted period the distributor has in place "procedures which are reasonably designed to ensure that its employees or agents directly engaged in selling the obligation are aware that the obligation cannot be offered or sold during the restricted period to a person who is within the United States or its possessions or is a United States person".

(ii) Neither the issuer or any distributor delivers the obligation in definitive form within the US or its possessions during the restricted period. To prevent the risk of this occurring, the issue is typically "locked-up" in the form of a global note. If an issue is intended to remain in global form as a permanent global note, it may be considered to be a single definitive, for which reason issues of bearer securities intended to remain in global form are typically made in the form of a temporary global note, which is exchanged for a permanent global note at the end of the restricted period.

(iii) On "the earlier of the date of the first actual payment of interest by the issuer on the obligation or the date delivered by the issuer of the obligation in definitive form" a certificate is provided by each holder of the obligation stating that it is not a US person.

  For the purposes of TEFRA D the restricted period is the period from whichever is the earlier of the closing date or the first date on which the securities are offered, to the date forty days after the closing date. Any subsequent offer or sale by the issuer or a distributor of an original unsold allotment or subscription will also be considered to be made during the restricted period.

(b) Interest on the securities is payable only outside the US and its possessions.

(c) The securities and their coupons bear the TEFRA legend wording, that: "Any United States person (as defined in the United States Internal Revenue Code) who holds this obligation will be subject to limitations under the United States Income Tax Laws, including the limitations provided in Sections 165(j) and 1287(a) of the United States Internal Revenue Code."

3.7.3 Investment Company Act

The Investment Company Act of 1940 defines an investment company as, *inter alia*, any issuer of securities which "is or holds itself out as being engaged primarily ... in the business of investing, reinvesting, or trading in securities" or any issuer that "is engaged or proposes to engage in the business of investing, reinvesting, owning, holding or trading in securities, and owns or proposes to acquire investment securities having a value exceeding 40% of the value of such issuer's total assets ... on an unconsolidated basis". The definition of "securities" is wide and covers "any note ... or evidence of indebtedness".

An affiliated originator is prohibited from transferring financial assets to an investment company under s. 17(a)(2), and any investment company that makes a public offer of securities in the US is required under s. 7(d) of the act to be registered with the SEC. Furthermore, any investment company that makes a placement of securities in the US is also required to be registered pursuant to a no-action letter sent to Touche Remnant in 1987.

An exemption is available under s. 3(c)(1) for "any issuer whose outstanding securities (other than short-term paper) are beneficially owned by not more than 100 [US] persons and which is not making and does not presently propose to make a public offering of its securities". This is an ongoing requirement (and is also therefore relevant to resales), rather than simply a primary issuance requirement.

In addition, Rule 3a-7 (adopted by the SEC in 1992) provides a general exemption for any "issuer who is engaged in the business of purchasing, or otherwise acquiring, and holding eligible assets" (certain financial assets such as receivables that will "convert into cash within a definite time period"), where the securities issued off the back of the assets carry an investment grade credit rating or are sold to QIBs.

An exemption is provided under s. 3(c)(7) (passed into law in 1996 and effective from April 1997) for an issuer whose securities are owned solely by qualified purchasers (either an individual investor with investments which equal or exceed US$5m in value, or a corporate investor who owns and invests on a discretionary basis an investment portfolio which equals or exceeds US$25m in value) and which does not intend to make a public offering of its securities.

3.8   UK SECURITIES LAWS

Securities laws in the UK were revised significantly following the introduction of the Financial Services and Markets Act 2000 (the "FSMA"). The FSMA was first published in draft at the end of July 1998, and received royal assent on 14 June 2000. The FSMA came into effect at midnight on 30 November 2001 (referred to as "N2"), following delays due to consultation and lobbying periods in the City. The Act replaces certain provisions of the Financial Services Act 1986 regime and its wholesale/retail distinction, together with certain provisions of the Banking Act 1987 and the Insurance Companies Act 1982.

Under the FSMA, the supervisory and capital adequacy regulatory functions of several self-regulating organisations (or SROs) were rolled into the Financial Services Authority (the "FSA") from N2, together with the powers of the DTI to regulate insurance companies and of the Building Societies Commission to regulate building societies. In addition, the supervisory and capital adequacy regulatory role of the Bank of England over banks and wholesale markets passed to the FSA with the entry into force of the Bank of England Act 1998 on 1 June 1998, and the FSA (referred to as the UK Listing Authority or UKLA when acting in this capacity) replaced the London Stock Exchange as listing authority from 1 May 2000, when the regulatory portion of the Yellow Book was replaced by the new UKLA Listing Rules.

The intention was to create a single financial services regulator, with powers under the FSMA. The FSA regulates the investment industry generally in accordance with four main principles of: maintaining confidence in the financial system, promoting public understanding of the system, protecting consumers and reducing opportunities for criminal activity.

3.8.1 Financial Services and Markets Act 2000

Under Schedule 11 of the FSMA, an offer of securities to the UK public (or any section of the UK public) which does not fall within one of the exemptions contained in Schedule 11, constitutes an "offer to the public". When such an offer is made for the first time in relation to the securities in question, which offer occurs prior to admission of the securities to a listing, a prospectus must be prepared under s. 85 of the FSMA. The chief exemptions are:

(i)   Offers to professionals, to no more than 50 persons, to members of a club with an interest in the use of the proceeds, to a "restricted circle" of knowledgeable investors, in connection with an underwriting, to public sector entities, in connection with a takeover or merger, which are free offerings of shares or exchange offerings of shares, to the issuing company's employees or their families, resulting from conversion of a convertible, by a charity, or

(ii)   Offers where the securities are: priced less than Euro 40 000 in total, acquired to the extent of at least Euro 40 000 worth by each person, denominated at Euro 40 000 or more each, building society shares, or "Euro-securities" (securities underwritten and distributed by a syndicate at least two members of which are registered in different countries, and which may only be acquired through a credit institution) in relation to which no advertisement (other than an advertisement of a prescribed kind) is issued in the UK.

Exemptions in (ii) may not be combined with each other or with exemptions in (i) in the same offering. Exemptions in (i) may be combined with each other in the same offering.

No offer to the public may be made until the prospectus is published, breach of which requirement is a criminal offence under s. 85 FSMA. Prospectuses are subject to disclosure on specific details as set out in listing rules, as well as to an overriding duty under s. 86 (applying s. 80) FSMA to disclose all information investors would reasonably expect and require to find therein, with liability to compensate investors under s. 86 (applying s. 90) FSMA on responsible persons as specified in s. 86 (applying s. 79(3)) FSMA under regulations to be given by the Treasury (the issuer, its directors and any person who authorised, or is named as accepting responsibility for, the prospectus) for any loss they suffer as a result of untrue or misleading statements in the prospectus or the omission of relevant details. Prospectuses must be registered at Companies House under s. 86 (applying s. 83) FSMA 2000, breach of which requirement is a criminal offence. Prospectuses may also give rise to general criminal liability under s. 86 (applying s. 397) FSMA for misleading or false statements.

The FSMA also establishes:

(a)   Under s. 19, an offence of a person, in or from the UK in the way of business, carrying on a "regulated activity" (to be expanded by the Treasury in secondary legislation, but including the activities set out in Schedule 2 of the FSMA – dealing in investments, arranging deals in investments, deposit taking, safekeeping and administration of assets, managing investments, investment advice, establishing collective investment schemes or using computer-based systems for giving investment instructions) without authorisation or exemption (this is referred to as the "general prohibition");

(b) Under s. 21, an offence of a person, in the course of business, communicating an invitation or inducement to engage in investment activity unless he or she is an authorised person or the content of the communication is approved by an authorised person. If the communication originates outside the United Kingdom, the section only applies if the communication is capable of having an effect in the United Kingdom.

(c) Under s. 118, a civil fine (which can be unlimited) for "market abuse" – behaviour in relation to qualifying investments (UK traded investments) which "is likely to be regarded by a regular user of that market ... as a failure on the part of the person or persons concerned to observe the standard of behaviour reasonably expected of a person in his or her position in relation to the market", and which:

(1) Is based on information not generally available to those using the market but which would be likely to be regarded by a regular user of the market as relevant when deciding the terms on which transactions in investments of the kind in question should be effected;

(2) Is likely to give a regular user of the market a false or misleading impression as to the supply of, or demand for, or as to the price or value of, investments of the kind in question; or

(3) A regular user of the market would, or would be likely to, regard as behaviour that would, or would be likely to, distort the market in investments of the kind in question. There is a defence to market abuse for people who had a reasonable belief that they were not abusing the market, or who took all reasonable precautions to avoid engaging in market abuse. The Act was amended in May 2000 to provide for the FSA to authorise a safe harbour from the market abuse offence if the relevant party has conformed to the City Code (with the FSA the ultimate arbiter on whether market abuse has occurred, but required to keep itself informed of the way in which the Takeover Panel interprets the City Code).

(d) Under ss. 397(1) and (2), an offence of recklessly or knowingly making a misleading, false or deceptive "statement, promise or forecast" to induce (or being reckless as to whether it will induce) a person to enter into a "relevant agreement".

(e) Under s. 397(3), an offence of creating a "false and misleading impression as to the market in or the price or value of any relevant investments" to induce a person to "acquire, dispose of, subscribe for or underwrite those investments or to refrain from doing so or to exercise, or refrain from exercising, any rights conferred by those investments" (dealings in the market for a particular undisclosed purpose (such as a bond buy-back) or disclosure of relevant information to a limited group of investors may fall foul of this provision).

The offences in (a), (b), (d) and (e) are punishable by imprisonment and/or a fine. It is also an offence to breach prohibition orders issued by the FSA (where persons are not fit and proper to carry out a regulated activity), and a civil penalty can be levied for breach of statements of principle (on the conduct of authorised persons). Agreements entered into in contravention of s. 19 or 21 without authorisation or exemption are unenforceable by the contravening party.

Persons exempted from authorisation included recognised clearing houses and recognised investment exchanges (under s. 285) and other bodies prescribed by the Treasury (under s. 38). Authorised persons include persons who have applied for and received permission to carry on regulated activities (under the procedure and threshold conditions set out in ss. 40, 41 and Schedule 6 of the Act) and entities authorised as a credit institution or investment firm in another EU country. The Act establishes a single regulator, the Financial Services Authority, with effect from N2, together with a first instance disciplinary tribunal, the Financial Services and Markets Tribunal (to which contested decisions of the FSA may be referred by the complainant).

Investments include shares, debentures, loan stock, bonds, certificates of deposit and any other instruments creating or acknowledging a present or future indebtedness, government and public securities, warrants or other instruments entitling the holder to subscribe for any investment, depositary receipts (certificates representing securities), units in collective investment schemes, options to acquire or dispose of property, futures, contracts for differences, insurance contracts, participations in Lloyd's syndicates, deposits, mortgage lending (loans secured on land), and any right or interest in anything that is an investment.

Stabilisation provisions apply from N2 on the purchase or sale of new securities in a way designed to stabilise their price on initial distribution into the market. A new subscription should comply with FSMA conduct of business rules on stabilisation set under s. 144 FSMA (allowing use of a safe harbour under s. 397(4) FSMA), or any stabilisation activities subsequently carried out may constitute a criminal offence under s. 397(3) FSMA.

Listing requirements are set out in Part VI of the FSMA. Listing particulars are subject to disclosure on specific details as set out in the listing rules, as well as to an overriding duty under s. 80 FSMA to disclose all information investors would reasonably expect and require to find therein, with liability to compensate investors under s. 90 FSMA on responsible persons as specified in s. 79(3) FSMA (under regulations to be given by the Treasury) for any loss they suffer as a result of untrue or misleading statements in the particulars or the omission of relevant details. Listing particulars must be registered at Companies House under s. 83 FSMA, breach of which requirement is a criminal offence. Listing particulars may also give rise to general criminal liability under s. 397 FSMA for misleading or false statements.

3.9 EU SECURITIES LAWS

The Prospectus Directive replaces and harmonises existing regimes for listing securities across the EU, and regulates two areas:

- Public offer of securities within the EU; and
- Admission to trading on an EU exchange.

The Directive was adopted in July 2003 and is intended to be implemented in member states in 2005, with an 8-year transitional period. The Directive has caused concern for non-EU issuers, as it limits the ability of EU exchanges to waive and vary disclosure requirements, potentially meaning that non-EU issuers that are listed and subject to accounting standards and disclosure requirements outside the EU could, on listing or offering securities to the public in the EU, also be required to comply with EU standards.

3.9.1   Content of the Prospectus Directive

Under Article 3 the Directive requires delivery of a prospectus on an offer to the public or on admission to trading, and works on the basis that the prospectus is vetted by the home authority of EU issuers (defined in Article 2(1) as the authority where the issuer has its registered office or – in respect of debt securities with a denomination of Euro 1000 or more (reduced from Euro 5000 in the March 2003 draft and from Euro 50 000 in drafts prior to November 2002) – either the state where the issuer has its registered office or the state where the securities will be admitted to trading or the state where the securities will be offered to the public, at the option of the issuer).

Categories of offer that are not considered as an offer to the public are contained in Article 3(2) (these exemptions do not apply to admission to trading):

- Offers to qualified investors (defined in Article 2(1) as credit institutions, investment firms, insurance companies, collective investment schemes, pension funds, other financial institutions, corporates whose sole purpose is to invest in securities, supranationals, government agencies, legal entities which are not small or medium-sized enterprises (SMEs), sophisticated individual investors, or SMEs who expressly ask to be treated as qualified investors);
- Offers to less than 100 persons (other than qualified investors) per member state;
- Minimum investment per investor or minimum denomination of Euro 50 000;
- Offers of less than Euro 100 000 in total over 12 months.

Small and medium-sized enterprises are defined in Article 2(1) as entities that have at least two of: less than 250 employees, total balance sheet assets of Euro 43m or less, net turnover of Euro 50m or less.

Other issues which are exempt under Article 4(1) from the obligation to publish a prospectus on an offer to the public include:

- Securities resulting from a merger or takeover, or from conversion of a convertible; and
- Securities offered to employees.

Exemptions under Article 4(2) from the requirement to deliver a prospectus on admission to trading include:

- Small equity tap issues;

- Securities resulting from a merger or takeover, or from conversion of a convertible; and
- Securities offered to employees.

Prospectus filings may be undertaken in a single document, or via separate documents split into:

- Registration Document (a shelf document on the issuer that must be updated annually);
- Securities Note (prepared in relation to a particular issue of securities); and
- Summary Note (giving short details of the most significant items in the first two documents – the summary may have to be translated into the language of countries where offers are to be made).

The information required in a prospectus is set by reference to the type of securities (debt or equity), and also to take into account the size and activities of the company – in particular, in relation to small and medium-sized enterprises.

3.10   TAX TREATMENT

Securitisation transactions involve complex and intricate taxation analysis that will depend on the nature of the receivables and the jurisdiction or jurisdictions involved. In some instances, this can involve cross-border taxation issues. Issues for analysis can arise from:

- **Disposal taxes**   The ability of the originator to dispose of the receivables without generating an accelerated taxation liability (for example, to capital gains tax).
- **Transfer taxes**   Any transfer taxes (such as value added tax, sales tax, stamp duty or registration tax) that may be due on the transfer of the receivables from originator to SPV will need to be considered and limited in an acceptable manner. Traditional methods for stamp duty limitation have included an offer to purchase receivables that is accepted by payment (so that no stampable transfer document is ever created), the execution and holding of documentation outside the jurisdiction of the receivables, or the use of intragroup relief to transfer receivables to bankruptcy remote SPVs within the originator's group.
- **Income and withholding taxation**   Once the receivables are successfully transferred, the SPV will wish to receive income without being liable to income tax on the receivables in the jurisdiction of the originator, and without the originator being obliged to make payments of withholding tax on collections passed over to the SPV (which would result in the SPV receiving income on the receivables net of tax). Any hedging arrangements where currency or interest flows are passed to a swap counterparty or other hedging counterparty, and a return cash flow is paid by the counterparty to the SPV, will need to be examined to ensure that no withholding taxes can be applied to either of these flows.
- **Corporate taxation**   The SPV itself will need to be established in a jurisdiction with no corporation tax, or a jurisdiction where certainty can be achieved as to the amount of tax that will be payable by the SPV (for example, by obtaining a tax ruling from the tax authorities). If the SPV needs to be established in a particular

jurisdiction (for example, to take advantage of a particular double tax treaty in order to obtain collections on the receivables free of withholding tax, or to be able to claim a particular tax relief, such as the (now abolished) MIRAS relief in the UK), then the SPV will need to be structured to ensure that it is tax neutral and can deduct its expenses in full against its income. Any taxation on the SPV will result in money leaking from the transaction that could otherwise be returned to the originator as profit. This may necessitate structural additions to enable crystallisation of losses for tax purposes on the same basis as the losses are taken for accounting purposes. For example, use of a put option for defaulted receivables, to enable them to be transferred to a third party at a nominal value after enforcement has been carried out, and a loss to be taken.

In some jurisdictions, such as the UK, there may be tax issues with establishing an SPV on a limited recourse basis, due to the fact that typical limited recourse language provides for any outstanding debt to be extinguished after the application of all available proceeds within the SPV. This may be interpreted as linking the return on the subordinate classes of securities issued by the SPV to the profitability of the SPV, which may lead to interest payments made on the securities being classified as distributions for tax purposes, rather than deductible interest payments. Consequently, structures may be used where limited recourse language is not inserted into the securities, but the SPV is instead given the right to call the subordinate securities for a nominal amount after having applied all available proceeds within the SPV and if there is any default on the bonds (thus preventing any technical insolvency of the SPV at such point from prejudicing the bankruptcy remoteness of the SPV).

A trust may have fiscal transparency under US tax law (as will a bare trust in the UK), whereas a normal SPV corporate will be subject to taxation and will need to establish full deductibility of its expenses for tax purposes (especially its cost of funds on its debt issuance) in order to ensure that there is no mismatch between its profits for taxation purposes and its profits for accounting purposes.

- **Withholding tax**   It will need to be ensured that the funding instruments of the SPV are not themselves subject to withholding tax on payments of interest made by the SPV to investors. In the UK, payments of interest made on a quoted Eurobond may be made free of withholding tax.
- **Profit extraction**   In any securitisation transaction, credit enhancement will be required which will typically be maintained in the SPV in the form of a cash reserve fund account or other reserve, or as overcollateralisation. In addition, in many cases the interest rate on the receivables will significantly exceed that on the funding instruments, generating a surplus or excess spread in the SPV, even after payment of transaction fees and expenses on a periodic basis. These amounts will need to be returned to the originator in some tax efficient method in order to ensure that the transaction is financially viable for all parties. The methods used will often comprise a combination of subordinated debt or debt instruments, with the originator as the creditor, or a form of deferred purchase price element that is payable to the originator subsequent to the main purchase price on completion of the securitisation if, and only if, the receivables perform beyond the level required to repay the senior investors in full. Alternatively, amounts may be returned to the originator by way of fee payment for provision of servicing functions relating to the

receivables, or under a back-to-back swap between the originator and the counter-party who has entered into the main hedging arrangement with the SPV (through a mismatch of payment flows on either side of the swap). Another favoured alter-native is the use of a receivables trust to split the beneficial ownership of the receivables between the originator and the SPV, so that amounts are only taxed once in either the SPV or the originator. Dividend payments may be used as well, although these are unlikely to be very tax efficient unless tax credits are available to prevent two levels of profits tax, as they will typically be paid on a post-tax basis. Also, ownership of the necessary equity interest to realise the dividend may result in problems achieving off-balance-sheet treatment due to consolidation issues.

3.11   ACCOUNTING TREATMENT

In many cases, one of the objectives of a securitisation will be to ensure that the receivables that are securitised are removed from the accounting balance sheet of the originator. Financial Accounting Standard 140 (FAS 140) and Financial Accounting Standards Board Interpretation No. 46 (FIN 46) in the US, Financial Reporting Standard 5 (FRS 5) in the UK, and International Accounting Standards (in particular, IAS 39, IAS 27 and SIC-12) set guidelines for the requirements of the accounting authorities in order for such a transaction to effectively transfer the receivables off balance sheet. These guidelines are applied in a number of other jurisdictions world wide. Accounting analysis is entirely separate and distinguishable from the legal anal-ysis of whether a transaction is a true sale or a secured loan. Depending on the jurisdiction in question, it may be entirely possible for something to be sold at law while remaining on the accounting balance sheet. Generally, as well as removing the receivables from the originator's balance sheet (or receiving a linked presentation or quasi-subsidiary treatment under FRS 5), it is desirable to ensure that the receivables do not still appear in the consolidated accounts of the originator's group, for example, because the SPV is regarded as a subsidiary of the originator.

In the UK, the key elements of FRS 5 in ensuring that off-balance-sheet accounting treatment can be achieved are that:

- There is limited recourse to the originator for losses on the receivables (a legal transfer as such may not be important). Recourse elements such as deferred purchase price, or rights or obligations to repurchase the assets, will mean that the recourse element, or element in relation to which the repurchase right or obligation exists, will remain on balance sheet.
- No indemnities are given by the originator to the SPV.
- No off-market swaps are written by the originator with the SPV.

In the US, use of a trust has historically enabled receivables to be removed from the consolidated accounts of the originator under the now redundant substantive equity regime, as trust certificates were regarded as equity for US accounting purposes, enabling the trust and its assets to be regarded as off balance sheet for the originator (whereas if funding was arranged via debt instruments, the thin capitalisation of the SPV might have led to the SPV being consolidated with the originator).

The accounting treatment of securitisation transactions is considered in more detail in Chapter 10.

3.11.1 Due diligence and verification

As well as providing advice on the accounting off-balance-sheet treatment of a transaction, accountants are typically employed to undertake due diligence and verification on the data tape, with a data sampling process comparing tape entries against the original loan files to either a 95% or a 99% confidence interval of a particular maximum error rate (generally around 2%). Assuming that the sample does not display more than a particular number of errors (dependent on the pool/sample size, confidence interval and error rate parameters), this should establish a 95% or 99% probability respectively that the error rate across the pool as a whole does not exceed that on the sample (this assumes a log normal distribution and is based on a mean observed deviation from the norm which enables 2 and 3 standard deviations to be plotted).

Accountants are also used to audit the pool as against the eligibility criteria, and to provide verification on the information in the offering circular relating to the pool. In addition, they will typically opine on the SPV capitalisation table in the offering circular, and provide comfort letters as to the financial status of the originator and as to a review of the board minutes of the originator.

3.12 CAPITAL TREATMENT

The adequacy of the amount of capital held by a bank or financial institution to cover losses was originally the subject of the Basel Accord of July 1988. The Basel Committee is currently working on an extensive reworking of the Basel Accord, which is discussed in more detail in Chapter 11.

In securitisations of bank receivables it is typically a requirement of the bank that the receivables be regarded as off balance sheet from the bank's capital adequacy balance sheet for regulatory purposes. Guidelines in this area have been issued by certain central banks and regulators, which establish requirements that must be complied with to ensure that the bank is not still required to put capital against the receivables after the transaction is completed. It is often possible in certain jurisdictions to transfer receivables off the capital adequacy balance sheet without effecting a legal true sale of the receivables (an example being a limited recourse funded sub-participation, where recourse to the originator by the SPV and the investors is limited to amounts received by the originator with regard to the receivables, or a synthetic transaction structured through a credit default swap). These structures are particularly helpful for banks arranging CLO transactions, where preserving customer relationships and confidentiality are often of prime importance.

Key elements of ensuring off-balance-sheet capital treatment are typically to ensure that:

- Recourse against the originator for losses on the pool is limited to any credit enhancement they have provided.
- There is no right or obligation for the originator to repurchase the assets.

- The originator has not entered into any off-market transactions (such as swaps) with the SPV.

Off-balance-sheet rules are under consideration as part of the new Basel Accord.

Capital guidelines are also of relevance for banks acting in providing funding commitments for conduit structures via the provision of liquidity facilities. Undrawn liquidity lines may benefit from a zero capital charge if they have an original maturity of 1 year or less, provided that they are not regarded as providing credit enhancement (in which case they risk being treated as a direct credit substitute). Other loans, such as loans to cover start-up expenses, provided by a bank originator to the SPV may be directly deducted from capital.

Residential mortgage-backed securities may attract a beneficial risk weighting for capital purposes in some jurisdictions, making them an attractive investment instrument to hold for investors who are themselves subject to capital monitoring requirements on their risk-weighted assets.

These areas are also under consideration as part of the new Basel Accord.

3.13 DATA AND CONSUMER REGULATION

3.13.1 Data protection/confidentiality

In order to effect the analysis of data required for the determination of appropriate credit enhancement levels, it is necessary to have pool performance data available. Furthermore, in the event that the appointment of the originator as servicer needs to be terminated due to poor performance of the servicing function or insolvency, it will be necessary to obtain detailed information concerning the debtors, to enable servicing and/or enforcement action to be taken.

In many jurisdictions, bank originators are subject to confidentiality requirements that may render the provision of this information a criminal offence or subject the bank to civil liability. Also, in some jurisdictions information relating to consumers is subject to confidentiality requirements, which may curtail its dissemination. These and any other relevant confidentiality requirements (for example, contractual provisions in the receivables documentation) will need to be considered carefully.

In the EU, data protection legislation has been harmonised under the terms of the Data Protection Directive (discussed in detail in Chapter 13).

3.13.2 Consumer protection

Receivables arising under agreements with consumers may be subject to statutory protections in some jurisdictions, giving consumers the right to cancel agreements within a certain time, the right to set-off amounts owed by them as against any failure of the creditor or a third-party service provider to perform fully, or implying maximum interest rates or other terms into all contracts. Again, any such provisions will need to be considered carefully.

In the UK, for example, issues may arise under the Consumer Credit Act 1974, the Unfair Contract Terms Act 1977 or the Unfair Terms in Consumer Contracts Regulations 1999.

Similarly, the EU has proposed harmonised European consumer credit legislation under the terms of the Consumer Credit Directive (on which more detail is provided in Chapter 13).

3.14   REGULATORY APPROVALS

Regulators for different types of originators (in particular, financial services sector originators) may play a role in the form of approvals required for various types of transaction. Typical regulated areas may include:

- Banking business (in addition to imposing requirements on off-balance-sheet treatment (see section 3.12), many bank regulators may require that securitisation transactions by banks are given their prior approval or consent).
- Investment business (see section 3.6 to section 3.9).
- Mortgage lending.
- Consumer finance.
- Insurance business.
- Money lending.
- Finance companies and other financing entities.

3.14.1   Areas of regulation – the UK

In the UK, the main areas of financial regulation are for deposit-taking, investment business (see section 3.6), mortgage lending and advice, consumer finance (under the Consumer Credit Act 1974 – see under section 3.13.2 above) and insurance business.

Deposit-taking

Deposit-taking is regulated under the general prohibition in s. 19 Financial Securities and Markets Act (replacing ss. 3 and 67 of the Banking Act 1987) and s. 5 of Statutory Instrument 1992/3218 for the EU. Under the Financial Services Act 1986, the issue of bonds, commercial paper, medium-term notes or other securities risked constituting deposit-taking unless it was exempt under the Banking Act 1987 (Exempt Transactions) Regulations 1997. The receipt of proceeds of issue of securities outside the UK (e.g. Jersey) was sometimes used to circumvent deposit-taking provisions.

The new Financial Services and Markets Act 2000 (Regulated Activities) Order 2001 (2001/544), Article 9, provides:

(1) Subject to paragraph (2), a sum is not a deposit for the purposes of article 5 if it is received by a person as consideration for the issue by him of any investment of the kind specified by article 77 or 78.
(2) The exclusion in paragraph (1) does not apply to the receipt by a person of a sum as consideration for the issue by him of commercial paper unless –
  (a) the commercial paper is issued to persons –
    (i) whose ordinary activities involve them in acquiring, holding, managing or disposing of investments (as principal or agent) for the purposes of their businesses; or

(ii) who it is reasonable to expect will acquire, hold, manage or dispose of investments (as principal or agent) for the purposes of their businesses; and

(b) the redemption value of the commercial paper is not less than £100 000 (or an amount of equivalent value denominated wholly or partly in a currency other than sterling), and no part of the commercial paper may be transferred unless the redemption value of that part is not less than £100 000 (or such an equivalent amount).

(3). In paragraph (2), "commercial paper" means an investment of the kind specified by article 77 or 78 which must be redeemed before the first anniversary of the date of issue.

Mortgage lending and advice

In June 2001, the Treasury published a draft *Mortgage Sourcebook*, dealing with the regulation of mortgages under the FSMA. From "N3" on 31 October 2004, regulated activities include lending under a regulated mortgage, advising on a regulated mortgage and administering (servicing or enforcing) a regulated mortgage. Advising on regulated mortgages was not originally intended to be regulated but on 12 December 2001 the Treasury announced that the FSA would also take over regulation for advice on mortgages.

Regulated mortgages are mortgages where:

• The borrower is an individual;
• The mortgage is entered into on or after N3 and the borrower is in the UK at the time;
• The lender has a first charge over property in the UK;
• The property is at least 40% occupied by the borrower or his family.

Mortgage lenders will have to be authorised by the FSA. They will be subject to the rules on advertising and enforcement set out in the *Mortgage Sourcebook*, as well as minimum capital requirements (either 1% of total assets or 20% of total income, with a minimum of £100 000). The *Mortgage Sourcebook* also sets out formalities for mortgage origination and servicing and a cooling-off period for mortgage loans other than for purchase of a property. Regulated mortgages will not fall within the ambit of the Consumer Credit Act 1974. Other consumer credit instruments will remain regulated by the CCA 1974.

Securitisation SPVs are not subject to regulation for administering regulated mortgages, following the wording of Article 62 of the Financial Services and Markets Act 2000 (Regulated Activities) Order 2001 as interpreted in the *Mortgage Sourcebook*. This exempts from authorisation a non-authorised person who arranges for an authorised mortgage administrator to administer mortgages.

3.15   ADMINISTRATION AND SYSTEMS

Securitisations require detailed data analysis, and rely on the ability of the originator (prior to close) and the servicer (post-close) to monitor the receivables and maintain data, such that reports can be extracted and servicing functions can be carried out quickly and efficiently.

Although the servicer is the entity with the primary role of an ongoing nature, other parties will continue to be involved in ensuring that the transaction functions smoothly. Servicing, accounting and cash management systems need to deal with the following issues:

3.15.1 Prior to close

Originator

- Cutting the basic pool data tape
- Producing historic dynamic pool data
- Producing historic static pool data
- Stratification tables
- Final pool cut on the cut-off date prior to close.

3.15.2 On close

Servicer

- Flagging and segregating the securitised receivables from its remaining assets.

Custodian

- Holding items such as post-dated cheques received, notices to be given to debtors, original contracts.

Account Bank

- Bank account transfers.

Paying/calculation/reference agent

- Making cash payments on close.

Accountants/originator

Accounting for the transaction on close (i.e. off-balance-sheet treatment)
  Figure 3.2 illustrates transaction movements on close.

3.15.3 Post-close

Servicer

- Collection and clearing of receipts on the receivables
- Periodic reporting of collections

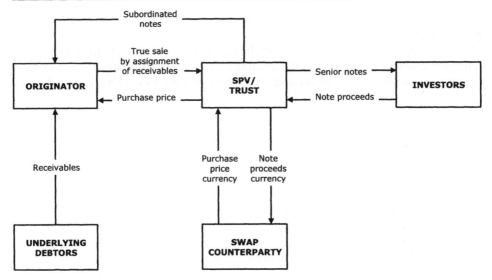

Figure 3.2   Securitisation structure: Day 1

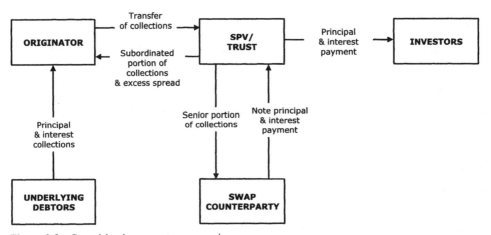

Figure 3.3   Securitisation structure: ongoing

- Liaison with debtors on amendments
- Enforcement.

Account Bank

- Bank account management and reporting.

Cash manager

- Payments to creditors in the priorities
- Reporting of receipts and payments made.

Paying/calculation/reference agent

- Calculation of amounts due on the bonds, and setting periodic coupon on the bonds
- Making payments on the bonds.

Accountants/originator

- Accounting for the ongoing segregation of funds and treatment of any profit strip
- Accounting for VAT and/or tax at the SPV level (including appropriate loss provisioning) and audit at the SPV level.

Figure 3.3 illustrates ongoing transaction movements.

Investor Concerns

4.1 INVESTOR CREDIT ANALYSIS

Assuming that a deal is structured to properly address and mitigate tax and legal risks, the key elements of credit analysis of different asset classes usually come down to two basic fields (which are the same as those used by rating agencies in fixing ratings on ABS tranches), namely the default frequency and the loss severity. In addition, a consideration of the eligibility or substitution criteria for introducing new assets into a deal is essential, as well as a consideration of the structure and credit enhancement (including the cash flow waterfall) for the deal.

For whole business deals, key data fields are different. There is no pool of assets which may individually default, but rather the adequacy or inadequacy of an overall stream of cash flow arising from a business activity. Consequently, the necessary data fields relate to the relevant areas of concern for the generation of revenues in the relevant sector. Some of these will depend on economic and macro factors rather than deal-specific fields.

4.1.1 Default frequency

Default frequency can be clearly recorded for many kinds of assets: for consumer loans, mortgages, leases and the like, it is simply the percentage frequency of assets reaching a certain level of days past due on payments under the assets; similarly for CDOs, the frequency of defaults of underlying corporate debtors can be measured.

For many asset types, significant historic data is available as to the expectation of defaults over time, and forms the basis of rating agency analysis of deals. Default frequency for consumer receivables will be influenced by a large number of factors, including:

- Asset type/product
- Geographic location
- Employment status of borrower (self-employed, employee, etc.)
- Reason for loan (purchase of primary residence, buy-to-let, consolidation of debt, etc.)
- Debt-to-income ratios
- Income multiple
- Prior defaults or arrears.

For small business corporate assets, the default frequency will be tied to the sector in which the corporate operates and the economic outlook for that sector, as well as factors specific to the business in question. For larger corporates, default frequency may be inferred from the credit rating of the corporate.

For synthetic assets, the picture is slightly different as losses to investors will depend on the frequency of credit events under the portfolio default swap for the assets.

Local economic and cultural conditions can greatly affect default frequencies. For example, Fitch has listed its assumed stressed default frequency for residential mortgages in different regions in Italy as follows:

Rating	North	Central	South
AAA	15.8%	27.4%	36.3%
A	9.5%	22.0%	21.8%
BBB	6.3%	11.0%	14.5%

(See Fitch Ratings Pre-sale Report for BPV Mortgages S.r.l. deal of 20 November 2001.)

Thus, geographic data is of significance in assessing a portfolio. Trends towards the occurrence of defaults can in turn be measured by the level of delinquencies or arrears in a portfolio.

4.1.2 Loss severity

The second factor, loss severity (100% minus the recovery rate) can be analysed by reference to initial portfolio criteria and current economic conditions, as well as reported losses to date. For example, the expected loss severity on a 40% LTV mortgage loan is likely to be 0%, as, even in a depressed property market (assume house prices 20% down), with costs of sale (assume 5%) and accumulated loan arrears (assume 5%), the sale will still recover 75 against a capitalised loan balance of 45 – a recovery rate exceeding 100%.

On the other hand, the expected loss severity on subordinated debt issued by a company in insolvency which has few valuable assets may be 100%.

In this respect, clearly receivables with collateral – such as residential property or commercial real estate – are likely to have lower loss severity. Loss severity will therefore be primarily influenced by:

- Level of seniority of claim against debtor (e.g. secured debt, subordinated debt, etc.) – for asset-backed securities, this is most relevant for underlying positions in CDO deals.
- Nature of collateral.
- Geographic location.
- Valuation of collateral and liquidity of local market for collateral.
- LTV.
- Level of enforcement expenses.
- Ranking of security interest (first, second, etc.).

Again, there is likely to be a variant for synthetic structures. These will have different formulations of the loss on a declared credit event, but will often be calculated by reference to the loss following foreclosure of the asset (or, for corporate debt, the price realised on sale of the asset) without including any loss due to accrued unpaid interest or the costs of foreclosure.

4.1.3 Eligibility/substitution criteria

In any deal with a revolving or reinvestment period (see under section 4.3), the addition of new assets to the portfolio is conditional on compliance with eligibility or substitution criteria. These are dealt with in more detail in section 4.2, but typically cover the following areas:

1. Type of asset (mortgage loan, auto loan, etc.)
2. Ranking of asset (first mortgage, senior debt, etc.)
3. Location of debtors
4. Form of interest (fixed/floating, etc.)
5. Arrears
6. Maximum concentration in single debtor
7. Currency
8. Maturity date.

For the substitution of assets in a CDO, additional factors may be of relevance, given the nature of the assets, such as:

1. Industry concentration
2. Diversity score
3. Net loss rate as determined using rating agency model on portfolio
4. Minimum rating level on individual assets
5. WARF (weighted average rating factor) of pool.

4.1.4 Structure and credit enhancement

Analysing default frequency and loss severity will only tell part of the story. The rest is down to the deal structure – in particular the cash flow waterfall for the deal (and any trigger or covenants that modify the application of proceeds in the cash flow waterfall), and the credit enhancement built into the deal structure.

See, in particular, under section 4.3.

These elements can combine to achieve different results for bondholders. For example, the use of excess spread to provide credit enhancement in a deal is often on a "use it or lose it" basis. In other words, if there are no losses during the early stages of a deal, any surplus excess spread may be released to the originator of the deal by way of profit strip, and may not be available to support losses at the end of the deal.

Consequently, if excess spread is valued by totalling the spread over the life of the deal, it will overstate the actual level of credit enhancement available to bondholders. Conversely, if credit is only given to one period of excess spread, this understates the value of the excess spread as credit enhancement, as in the event that small losses happen on a regular basis throughout the deal, the excess spread realised in each period may be enough to cover such losses fully.

Thus, the value given to excess spread by an investor may vary, based on a view over whether losses are likely to occur as larger losses over a few periods, or smaller losses over many periods.

4.2 ELIGIBILITY CRITERIA

The eligibility criteria for a deal are designed to ensure that, on replenishment of new assets into a deal which permits the reinvestment of proceeds from receivables (or on substitution of new assets into a deal generally), the asset quality of the portfolio is not eroded. Consequently, they normally seek to address the main credit drivers of the relevant kind of assets, such as the following areas:

1. **Nature of contract**   The form of each contract should be specified as, for example:

   - A repayment contract, an endowment contract, a deferred interest contract
   - A lease, a hire purchase agreement or a conditional sale agreement, which relates to cars, trucks used for business purposes, equipment
   - A payment for the supply of particular goods or services.

   Each of these forms has different characteristics as to payment of interest and principal. Detail may also be required as to the nature of the property or other assets; for example, as to whether the loan is to finance the purchase of residential or commercial property, where the property is located, whether the property is completed and ready for occupation, the age of the property, whether the vehicles or equipment financed are new or second-hand, due to the diminished resale values on enforcement over older assets.

2. **First lien**   Each contract should (if secured) be secured by a first priority security interest.

3. **Originator and debtors**

   - It is usually a requirement that each contract (or receivable or account) should be originated by the originator contracting as principal to prevent the need to look behind the originator to some other entity when undertaking insolvency unwind analysis, and to ensure that consistency in underwriting and origination criteria has been applied across the pool. The criteria will need to be varied where the originator has purchased and warehoused various contract portfolios and then subsequently arranges a securitisation of them. This also reduces the required legal analysis of the standard form documents used to originate the contracts, as with a single originator contracting on its own account, there are likely to be fewer forms.
   - With regard to the debtor in relation to each contract, it is usual to specify whether debtors are individuals or corporates, as the taxation treatment and consumer protection treatment for individuals and corporates may differ under the relevant law.
   - It is also usual to specify the jurisdiction of the debtor's residence and to require that the debtor is also contracting as principal.
   - Unless the securitisation is a staff receivables transaction (which has additional structural features as this usually bears a subsidised interest rate), it is usually also a requirement that the debtor is not an employee, officer or director of the originator or of an affiliate of the originator.
   - The debtors may also be required to be on an approved list or subject to approval criteria.

4. **Right of debtor to purchase** If any of the contracts contain an option for the debtor to acquire or retain the relevant asset, then they may be reclassified as a hire purchase agreement rather than a finance lease or operating lease, potentially affecting the tax or accounting treatment for the transaction.

5. **Principal amount outstanding** The principal amount outstanding under the contracts as at a particular cut-off date (on which the amount of funding raised is based) should be specified.

6. **Frequency of payments** The periodicity of payments to be made by the debtors should be specified.

7. **Interest** The form of interest (fixed rate, floating rate, etc.) on the contract should be specified. Also:

- The basis interest rate for the calculation of payments due on the contracts will determine any potential basis risk between the rate receivable on the contracts and the rate payable by the SPV on its funding. Consequently, the originator should give details of the rates used to set payments under the contracts, and restrict the basis rates as much as possible, to simplify the hedging of the basis risk.

- For contracts in the pool which bear a fixed interest rate, it may be necessary to specify that each contract should bear an effective interest rate (calculated as the internal rate of return, or APR, of the contract; that is, the rate which, when used to discount each periodic payment to a net present value, results in an aggregate net present value which is equal to the principal amount financed under the contract) of a certain minimum level.

- It will also be necessary to address the interaction of the rate set for the contracts with the rate set for contracts originated by the originator that do not form part of the securitised portfolio. The SPV should not be prejudiced by the fact that, owing to the securitisation, the originator now has different priorities when setting the base rate that applies across its business. To ensure this, a threshold interest margin or threshold rate may be set, with which the originator will covenant to comply, or face losing the ability to set the contract rate with regard to the securitised portfolio.

- For new property leases, a minimum yield may be stated for any new contract within the site, or a certain minimum net present value for the new lease.

- Trade receivables are generally non-interest bearing.

8. **Full amortisation of principal** If the contracts are such that the principal is paid by amortisation using part of the periodic payment, the periodic payments should be sufficient that, after allowing for the interest element of the payments, the contract principal will amortise fully over the term of the contract (or over the "primary period" of any finance lease).

9. **Payment defaults** The contracts should be free of delinquencies or defaults in payment as at the point of sale to the SPV. Contracts where the debtor has been allowed payment extensions or payment waivers to prevent a payment failure should also be excluded. This criterion may be relaxed in certain cases – e.g. for sub-prime contract deals – and may not be relevant in some cases – e.g. for non-performing loan deals.

10. **Collections**   The methods used to collect payments on the contracts, and whether the debtors are to be instructed to pay direct to the SPV (rather than via the originator), should be specified. A multitude of different collection methods will increase the administrative complexity of servicing the contracts, which may give rise to concerns as to the ability of any back-up or substitute servicer to adequately perform servicing if the originator becomes insolvent. Collection methods may include autopay/direct debit payments, post-dated cheques, cash or cheque payments, or payment through paying-in slips.

11. **Law applicable to contracts**   Each contract should be expressed to be governed by the same governing law. This is to prevent arguments that the contract receivables are actually governed by different laws (which might make it necessary to consider the provisions relating to the transfer of receivables that apply in other jurisdictions in order to be sure that a true sale has been achieved from the originator to the SPV). This question is of particular relevance to cross-border export receivables, where an export business which contracts on the standard terms of business of its customers (as may be the case, for example, with emerging markets exporters shipping to OECD countries) may find that its receivables are governed by several different governing laws.

12. **Debtor concentration/size**   There should be no contract which is overly large compared to the other contracts in the pool, and which would therefore represent a concentration of risk in the pool. The size of each contract, the specification of the type of asset which is the subject of the contract, or the number of assets financed by each contract, may also determine which category each contract will fall into in rating agency risk analysis (that is, luxury, investment purposes, etc.). Conformity (within a certain range) of the majority of the pool's contracts will help the rating agencies to assess the likely performance of the pool and should lead to lower credit enhancement requirements than for a pool whose performance is difficult to predict accurately.

13. **Denomination of contracts**   The currency for payments under the contracts should be specified. If more than one currency is to be incorporated in a transaction, additional currency hedging will need to be considered.

14. **Tenor of contracts**   The maximum remaining tenor that is allowed for contracts forming part of the securitised pool should be specified – this will then be used as a backstop date to serve as the legal final maturity of the notes to be issued by the SPV.

15. **Seasoning**   A certain minimum seasoning (that is, a minimum number of payments that have already been made on the contract) is usually required. This is indicative of the debtor's ability to manage his finances and make payment on an ongoing basis.

16. **Loan to value (LTV) ratio**   The existence of an equity cushion in the financed asset through setting a maximum LTV is protective of the SPV's rights on enforcement, when the full "value" of the asset may not be quickly realisable (for example, in a property price recession). This may also be of relevance where residual value risk is part of the transaction. There may also be regulatory restraints on contract lending over certain valuations. The LTV is usually based on the lower of a valuation of the asset from an approved valuer at the time of origination of the contract or the price for which the asset is purchased by the debtor.

17. **Debt-to-income ratio** Contracts should not form part of the pool where they did not, on origination, meet a minimum threshold figure set to determine the coverage of the periodic payments which is provided by the income of the relevant debtor over the same period.

18. **No maintenance obligations** If the contracts provide that the originator will maintain or service the relevant asset, then the SPV may be prejudiced by the originator's failure to do so after sale of the benefit of the contracts to the SPV. In particular, the debtors may seek to withhold payment on the contract, or attempt to set-off the cost of arranging the maintenance against payments due under the contract. Maintenance obligations are of particular relevance for real estate leases, and it should be specified whether lease contracts are triple net (US) or fully repairing and insuring (UK), or whether the landlord is liable for repairs at its own expense.

19. **No exchanges** Vehicle or equipment contracts may provide that the debtor can return the vehicle or equipment and request a replacement. As with maintenance obligations, if the originator does not perform the obligation, the debtor may seek to withhold payment on the contract, or attempt to set-off against payments due under the contract.

4.2.1 Representations and warranties

Representations usually deal with the legal and regulatory, rather than economic, aspects of protection required by the SPV, but also overlap with eligibility criteria in several areas.

1. **Status of debtors** The SPV will be concerned to see that the debtors are not insolvent, or in a compromised position that could bring into question the validity of the relevant contract when executed. This latter usually deals with the death or insanity of the relevant debtor, or, in the case of a guarantor of the debtor, that the guarantor was induced to enter into the guarantee through duress or misrepresentation.

2. **Eligibility criteria** It is required that the originator represent that the contracts meet the eligibility criteria, to establish the mechanism for the remedy of a breach of the eligibility criteria (which is generally the same as that for other breaches of representations relating to the contracts). For mortgages and consumer loans, this is generally that the originator repurchase the offending contracts. For credit cards and trade receivables, the offending accounts or receivables may simply fall out of the calculation of the amounts paid to the originator on eligible funded receivables and into payments back on ineligible unfunded receivables, or the originator may be required to repurchase the offending accounts or receivables.

3. **Standard documents/origination procedures** The contracts should be documented on the basis of one of a limited number of standard forms, or in accordance with standard procedures, allowing for a simplification of the due diligence process.

4. **Ownership of contracts** The originator will be required to represent that it owns the contracts and the accessory rights, and that they are not subject to any third-party encumbrances, such as security interests or prior assignments or transfers.

5. **Consumer protection and licensing**   Representations should be given as to whether the contracts are subject to any consumer protection legislation in the jurisdiction in question, and, if they are, that they comply in full with the terms of such legislation. For example, the Consumer Credit Act 1974 in the UK sets out requirements as to form and substance for agreements regulated under the Act.

6. **Terminations and breaches**   No contract should be in default or have been terminated or cancelled.

7. **Legality and validity**   Each contract should be fully enforceable against the debtor, and, if secured should:

   - Enable sale of the relevant property or asset and/or appointment of a receiver over such property or its income;
   - Have the security registered if required, with any stamp duty paid;
   - Secure all amounts due by the terms of the contract.

   The originator may also be required to represent that it is not aware of any other security interest created in relation to any of the properties where the transaction involves further advances, to gain reassurance that no ruling-off or break in the contract account is required.

8. **Title deeds and records**   The originator will be required to represent that it holds title deeds and complete and up-to-date records in relation to each property and each contract, respectively. For trade receivables, the records should be sufficient to permit the identification of the receivable and the segregation of the receivable from other receivables. This is to assist the transferability of the receivables; without a clear ability to segregate one receivable from another, it is arguable that each individual receivable cannot be sufficiently identified to enable a true sale of that receivable, which may necessitate some kind of undivided interest structure using a trust over the originator's whole portfolio of receivables.

9. **Completed performance/further advances**   All obligations that fall on the originator should have been performed to prevent the accrual of rights in the debtor to set-off or withhold payment if any unfinished obligations are not in fact completed by the originator after the contracts are sold. For mortgages, typically the originator's only obligations will relate to making further advances to the relevant debtor. In such a case, a reserve fund or facility may be required to fund any such further advances.

10. **Credit policies**   The originator should have investigated the debtors in the manner of a reasonably prudent contract lender, thus subjecting the originator's credit policies to an objective standard, and should not have lent to any debtor where anything was discovered that would have caused such a lender not to proceed.

11. **Transferability of the contracts and accessory rights**   The originator will be required to represent that there are no assignability restrictions on its interest in respect of the contracts and the accessory rights. Any such restrictions would usually take the form of a requirement to obtain the prior consent of the relevant debtors. Insurance policies may contain a term which voids the policy on any purported assignment.

12. **Transfer taxes**   The assignment to the SPV may be subject to stamp duty, or to duties on registration of the SPV as the new owner, or to notarial fees. This may arise on the transfer of vehicles or equipment as well as on the transfer of the

contract receivables. The originator will be required to represent that no such amounts apply (if necessary, with the aid of a structural device to ameliorate any such amounts) or, if they are nominal, to describe the amounts due. Depending on the structure used, it may also be necessary to obtain representations relating to no withholding tax applying on collection of the contract receivables (for example, where exemptions from tax may or may not be available depending on the nature of the debtors).

13. **Validity of transfer**   The assignment of the benefit of each contract and the accessory rights to the SPV will be effective. If the transaction is a secured loan transaction, this representation will relate to the validity and perfection of the security interest. If underlying vehicles or equipment are being transferred, then the procedure for transfer of such assets where possession remains in the hands of the debtors will need to be investigated.

14. **Data and disclosure restrictions**   The disclosure of information relating to the contracts and the accessory rights may breach duties of confidentiality owed under general legal principles (for example, by a bank originator to its customers), or specific to certain types of information (for example, in the UK, under the Data Protection Act 1998 with respect to electronically held data).

15. **Set-off**   In a case where the contract receivables are transferred by assignment without notice to the debtors, the debtors' general rights of set-off are preserved until notice is given. If, therefore, they have other relations with the originator (a common example would be where a debtor has a deposit account with the originator), the ability of any debtor to exercise a right of set-off against the originator may prejudice the ability of the SPV to recover the contract receivables in full.

16. **Accurate particulars and valuation**   The originator will be required to represent that the details of the contracts and of the properties or other assets given in the transfer documentation are complete and accurate. With regard to any third-party valuation of real estate or big ticket assets, the owner will be required to represent that the valuation is accurate and that there has been no event affecting the value stated in that valuation since the valuation was performed.

17. **Litigation**   The originator will be required to represent that it does not know of any litigation in relation to any contract, and to provide disclosure of any such litigation that is underway, including any repossession proceedings.

18. **Selection of contracts**   In selecting the contracts to be securitised, the originator, relying on its greater and more detailed knowledge of the contracts than that available to the SPV, may have based its selection on a desire to remove troublesome assets from its portfolio. Unless the transaction is intended to be a securitisation of distressed or non-performing assets, this would unfairly prejudice the SPV and the investors, and the originator will be required to represent that it has not specifically selected contracts that could prejudice the SPV's recovery. Equally, some central bank regulators may have a concern that the originator should not "cherry-pick" by selecting its best assets for securitisation, in order to obtain cheaper funding, leaving the worst assets still on its balance sheet. This may be a matter for representation, if advice is being sought from legal counsel as to compliance with central bank requirements for off-balance-sheet treatment.

19. **Location and use of the assets**   The originator will usually be required to represent that the assets are located in a particular jurisdiction and are being used properly

by the debtors (and, in particular, in accordance with statutory and manufacturer's guidelines). This is designed to minimise any possible lender, manufacturer or supplier liability that could result for the SPV in purchasing an interest in the contracts in the event that the assets are misused by debtors, and personal injury or damage is caused as a result. For real estate, the landlord may be required to represent as to the use to which the property has been put previously, and the use to which it is being put now. This is due to potential environmental concerns that could affect recoveries, or incur lender liability for parties lending against the real estate.

20. **Leasehold property**   The tenor of any leasehold assets should extend for a minimum period beyond the final maturity date of the related contract, to enable the lease remainder to be sold as a valuable asset in the event of default. In addition, it should not be the case that a lease may be forfeited by the landlord on insolvency of the debtor, as this would prejudice enforcement by the SPV.

21. **Insurance**   The originator should represent that each asset has general insurance in the name of the originator (or that there is some other form of access to insurance proceeds, such as a loss payee clause in the insurance requiring payment of insurance proceeds to the originator) for an amount sufficient to pay off the contract, and that the insurance policy allows insurance proceeds to be applied by the SPV in paying off the contract. For high property value CMBS deals, the real estate should be fully insured (for a value at least equal to either the reinstatement value of the property plus loss of rent cover for the expected time taken to reinstate, or the full value of the securitised debt plus accrued interest and other senior items, as appropriate) against all relevant risks, and the originator should represent that it will ensure that the property remains so insured.

22. **Title to the assets**   The debtors (or the owner for CMBS deals) should have good title to the relevant assets (subject only to the terms of the contract) which is not subject to any third-party interest.

23. **Pool policy**   Where a pool policy forms part of the transaction credit enhancement, the originator should represent that each of the contracts is covered by a valid pool policy, the amount of which matches the expected figure.

4.3   CASH FLOW WATERFALL

The cash flow waterfall, or priority of payments, controls the application of cash receipts within the SPV or trust to different parties. Consequently, it is of critical importance in determining the relative creditworthiness of the different tranches of a deal. Generally, there are three waterfalls in a deal – application of revenue pre-enforcement, application of principal pre-enforcement and application of all proceeds post-enforcement (i.e. following the declaration of an event of default by the trustee for the transaction).

4.3.1   Post-enforcement

Generally, events of default in a deal consist of:

1. Failure by the SPV to pay interest or scheduled principal on the senior (Class A) Notes;
2. Failure by the SPV to perform or observe its other obligations under the Notes and the deal documents;
3. Insolvency or insolvency-related events that occur in relation to the SPV.

Although the failure to pay event may use wording that indicates a wider scope than that set out above (for example, "failure to pay interest or principal on any note when due"), it can normally be reduced to this basic formulation, since:

- Failure to pay interest on mezzanine or junior notes (e.g. Class B Notes) may be restricted such that it can only constitute an event of default after the Class A Notes have fully paid off;
- There are normally interest deferral provisions which defer the due date of interest on mezzanine and junior classes in the event that there is insufficient available revenue to make payment of such interest (with the result that the "when due" wording is not triggered);
- Principal which is due on a pass-through basis on the Class A or more junior classes is only due to the extent of cash received, such that failure to make a principal payment when there are no principal receipts will not trigger a default.

The "failure to perform other obligations" event of default may be qualified such that it is only an event of default if it is materially prejudicial to the Class A Noteholders. Insolvency of the SPV is inherently unlikely due to the bankruptcy remote nature of the SPV. Note that the insolvency of the originator is not normally an event of default (although it will constitute an early amortisation event to terminate any revolving period – see below).

The exception to this structure for events of default is synthetic transactions. As these deals do not rely on the sufficiency of cash collections from the underlying portfolio in order to make interest and principal payments, but rather on payments received from the credit swap counterparty and from any collateral (e.g. repo securities or Pfand-briefe) pledged to the notes, the analysis is somewhat different. Notes are written down by reference to losses on the underlying pool, but, in respect of notes that are not yet written down, any failure to pay amounts due on any class of notes implies a failure by the credit swap counterparty to make adequate payment on the credit swap. As such, it is likely to trigger the termination of the swap and the acceleration of all classes of notes. Similarly, the insolvency of the credit swap counterparty will trigger the termination of the swap and the acceleration of the notes. Consequently, events of default in a synthetic deal are more likely to consist of:

1. Failure by the SPV to pay interest or principal on any class of notes when due;
2. Failure by the SPV to perform or observe its other obligations under the notes and the deal documents;
3. Insolvency or insolvency-related events that occur in relation to the SPV;
4. Insolvency or insolvency-related events that occur in relation to the credit swap counterparty.

Waterfall

Post-enforcement, all cash proceeds of the liquidation or continued management of the assets of the SPV will be run down a single waterfall. A typical post-enforcement waterfall would be as follows:

1. Trustees fees and expenses of enforcement;
2. Fees of other parties;
3. Liquidity facility principal and interest;
4. Hedge provider termination amounts (except for subordinated amounts – see 9 below) (NB: termination payments on currency swaps may be required by rating agencies to rank pari passu with the relevant note class);
5. Class A note principal and interest and other amounts;
6. Class B note principal and interest and other amounts;
7. Class C note principal and interest and other amounts;
8. Subordinated liquidity facility amounts (gross-up amounts and increased costs amounts);
9. Subordinated hedge provider termination amounts (gross-up amounts and termination payments where the swap counterparty is in default);
10. Release cash to originator (e.g. deferred purchase price, sub-loan, etc.).

4.3.2   Pre-enforcement

The net effect of the event of default provisions described above is that, other than for synthetic transactions, defaults are generally driven by the failure to pay interest or scheduled principal on the Class A notes, or the failure to comply with other obligations in a way that is significantly prejudicial (i.e. that prejudices the Class A notes).

As significant deterioration could be seen before these events are triggered, the pre-enforcement waterfall is extremely important for all classes of noteholders in a non-synthetic transaction:

- The Class A notes will wish to see that they are adequately protected such that amounts are not paid out to the junior classes early on in the deal leaving the Class A notes to bear losses later on.
- The mezzanine or junior notes will wish to see protections to mitigate the risk that they will be left with notes that are not paying them anything and are simply deferring and capitalising (PIK-ing) interest. This is especially so as in many deals (as outlined above) there is no ability for the mezzanine or junior classes of notes to trigger an event of default for non-payment and thus crystallise some value earlier – potentially leaving these investors with a note which PIKs for the entire life of the deal with no remedy.

Exactly where the waterfall is set between these two opposing views is a matter of negotiation. The particular cash flow waterfall used on a transaction varies on a deal-by-deal basis and is a matter for discussion between the rating agencies, lead manager and originator for the transaction. It is unusual for investors to be directly involved in this process, but the investor's view of the relative strength of the position of different classes of notes in the deal is likely to sway his choice of which class to invest in, or whether to invest in the deal at all.

The pre-enforcement position is often modified by a number of tests or triggers applied to the waterfall which lock-off or increase cash to certain items, usually dependent on the performance of the transaction or the particular point in time. Some of these are credit triggers, and some are structural periods which determine the amortisation profile of the deal.

Revolving period/early amortisation events

The first possible structural period is the revolving period. If this structure is used, principal receipts will be reinvested in new receivables for a initial period, instead of being used to pay-down debt. The revolving period of a deal is typically set as a specific fixed period, which may be terminated early on the occurrence of an early amortisation event. Early amortisation events are generally events such as:

- A deterioration in the quality of the receivables held by the SPV (e.g. an increase in the level of delinquencies or defaults);
- A drop in the level of spread earned from the receivables;
- A failure to generate sufficient new receivables;
- The occurrence of an insolvency-related event with regard to the originator.

Amortisation structure

If a deal does not have a revolving period, it will typically begin to amortise immediately from issue, although there may be specific reasons not to do this. For example, Italian deals may become subject to withholding tax if they are permitted to amortise during the first 18 months of the transaction. Consequently, defeasance or cash-trapping structures may be employed. If a deal does have a revolving period, it will amortise following the end of the revolving period.

Amortisation may be effected by a number of potential different structures:

- **Pass-through structure** All principal receipts are passed directly through to debt, on one of three bases:
  - Sequential pay
  - Pro rata pay
  - Modified pro rata pay.
- **Scheduled amortisation structure** Certain scheduled amounts are used to amortise debt. Again, this can be on a sequential, pro rata or modified pro rata pay basis. Scheduled amortisation is typical in whole business securitisations, where there is no specific limited principal balance of receivables that must be allocated to investors or to reinvestment, but rather a quantum of operating cash flow per period.
- **Accumulation period and bullet pay structure** This retains principal receipts in the deal in order to make payment of principal on a bullet tranche due to mature at the end of the accumulation period. It is often used as part of a master trust.
- **Controlled/turbo amortisation structure** In a master trust, receipts are normally allocated between the seller interest and the investor interest – i.e the portion of the receivables where beneficial ownership is retained by the originator, and the portion owned and funded by the SPV, respectively. The originator and SPV rank pro rata,

and, following the occurrence of an early amortisation event in a controlled amortisation structure, the investor interest will only receive its pro rata share of principal receipts to effect amortisation. In a turbo scenario, the investor interest will receive all principal receipts on the pool, enabling faster amortisation. This latter structure is penalised by capital regulators such as the BIS and the FSA, as it implies that investors are not fully sharing losses with the originator on a pro rata basis during the pay-down.

- **Turbo from spread structure**   In some transactions, often CMBS deals, the junior tranche of the deal may be structured to amortise from excess spread on the deal, which serves to reduce the weighted average life of the tranche, and the tenor of the credit risk taken by investors.

Credit triggers

Aside from early amortisation events, other triggers of relevance to principal amortisation would include the interest cover ratios and overcollateralisation ratios (also known as par value tests) seen in CDOs. In relation to each class of debt the following ratios are calculated:

- Interest cover ratio
- Overcollateralisation ratio (the ratio of the par amount of the transaction collateral to the amount of the debt ranking at or senior to that class).

The results will be compared to set trigger levels. If the ratios are breached in respect of a class, then the cash flow waterfall will be diverted to effect amortisation of that class of debt instead of making payments on more junior classes of debt or on equity, until the ratios are once more in compliance.

Revenue waterfall

Revenue would generally consist of all income receipts, available drawings on any liquidity facility if relevant, and the amount of any reserve fund if relevant. A typical revenue waterfall would be as follows:

1. Fees (generally trustee, paying agent and third party fee amounts)
2. Servicer and standby servicer fees
3. Liquidity facility principal and interest (excluding subordinated amounts such as indemnities)
4. Hedge provider to exchange amounts required for note interest payments
5. Class A1/2 note interest
6. Reduce Class A1/2 note PDL (credit principal waterfall)
7. Class B note interest
8. Reduce Class B note PDL (credit principal waterfall)
9. Class C note interest
10. Reduce Class C note PDL (credit principal waterfall)
11. Top-up reserve fund to required level
12. Subordinated liquidity facility amounts
13. Release cash to originator (e.g. deferred purchase price, sub-loan, etc.).

Principal waterfall

Principal would generally consist of all principal receipts from the redemption or sale of underlying assets, together with receipts credited from the revenue waterfall to make good PDLs. A typical principal waterfall would be as follows:

1. Use to pay unpaid interest on the Class A/B/C notes
2. During revolving period, reinvestment in new receivables
3. After revolving period, Class A1 note principal
4. After revolving period, Class A2 note principal
5. After revolving period, Class B note principal
6. After revolving period, Class C note principal
7. Top-up reserve fund to required level
8. Release cash to originator (e.g. deferred purchase price, sub-loan, etc.).

This is a sequential pay structure for the amortisation of principal. Deals may also use a full or modified pro rata pay structure for the amortisation of principal – in other words the A, B and C notes may be amortised pro rata. Pro rata pay structures are generally subject to financial covenants, triggers or other protections agreed with the rating agencies, in order to protect the more senior notes.

Merged waterfall

Generally mortgage transactions and consumer loan-based transactions will use two separate waterfalls, as principal and interest receipts can be separately allocated and matched to the principal and interest of the issued notes, and the deals may experience prepayment of underlying assets that can be passed down the principal waterfall.

However, income-based transactions such as rental deals and whole business deals tend to use a single merged revenue and principal waterfall both to pay note interest and to amortise the notes. As a result, they tend to follow a scheduled amortisation structure. A typical merged waterfall would be as follows:

1. Fees (generally trustee, paying agent and third party fee amounts)
2. Servicer and standby servicer fees
3. Liquidity facility principal and interest (excluding subordinated amounts such as indemnities)
4. Hedge provider to exchange amounts required for note interest payments
5. Class A1/2 note interest
6. Class A1 note principal
7. Class A2 note principal
8. Class B note interest
9. Class B note principal
10. Class C note interest
11. Class C note principal
12. Top-up reserve fund to required level
13. Release cash to originator (e.g. deferred purchase price, sub-loan, etc.).

Note that this particular sequence of paying interest and principal on each class in sequence (AI, AP, BI, BP, CI, CP), may be partially or fully modified in certain cases, resulting in three combinations:

- Unmodified (AI, AP, BI, BP, CI, CP): used in whole business securitisation;
- Partially modified (AI, BI, AP, BP, CI, CP): may be used where the C Class is rated below investment grade;
- Fully modified (AI, BI, CI, AP, BP, CP): used in non-performing loan transactions, as principal amortisation is usually a pass-through of all remaining cash until the relevant class is paid down to zero.

This is a critical aspect of concern to junior noteholders in a deal, as, unlike in a deal with split revenue and principal waterfalls, the merged waterfall means that interest payments on the B notes are conditional on the payment of principal on the A notes, and that interest payments on the C notes are conditional on the payment of principal on the A and B notes.

Exactly how much principal is required to be paid at these levels is dependent on the amortisation structure as outlined above, but if this amount is significant, or can increase if financial triggers are breached in the deal, there is a much stronger possibility that the B or C noteholders may find that their interest payments are deferred.

Equally, such a deal provides a much stronger protection to the senior noteholders, as all cash receipts in the deal – principal and interest – are available to them prior to making any payments on the more junior classes. For example, if:

```
Cash receipts    = 21
A Interest due   =  5
A Principal due  =  8
B Interest due   =  3
B Principal due  =  6
C Interest due   =  1
C Principal due  =  4
```

Using the unmodified waterfall:

	Waterfall item	Payment made
1.	A interest	5
2.	A principal	8
3.	B interest	3
4.	B principal	5
5.	C interest	
6.	C principal	

- No interest or principal is paid on the C notes
- The interest cover at the B level is $1.31\times$ and the DSCR is $0.95\times$
- The interest cover at the A level is $4.2\times$ and the DSCR is $1.61\times$.

If the partially modified waterfall is used:

Waterfall item	Payment made
1. A interest	5
2 B interest	3
3. A principal	8
4. B principal	5
5. C interest	
6. C principal	

- No interest or principal is paid on the C notes
- The interest cover at the B level is 2.62× and the DSCR is 0.95×
- The interest cover at the A level is 4.2× and the DSCR is 1.31×.

If the fully modified waterfall is used:

Waterfall item	Payment made
1. A interest	5
2. B interest	3
3. C interest	1
4. A principal	8
5. B principal	4
6. C principal	

- The interest cover ratio at the C level is $21/(5+3+1) = 2.33\times$, but no principal is received
- The interest cover at the B level is 2.62×, with a DSCR of 0.91×, as the waterfall will run out of money after paying A, B and C interest and A principal, and 4 out of the B principal due
- The interest cover at the A level is 4.2× and the DSCR is 1.23×.

Other waterfall features

There are many other features that can be included in deal structures and will need to be allowed for in waterfalls. For example:

- Extra classes or sub-classes of debt;
- IO strips used to extract spread at a senior-ranking level;
- Provisions to turbo-pay junior notes prior to trigger events.

4.4 BOND PRICING AND VALUATION

Issuance in the US ABS markets is split between fixed rate and floating rate. Issuance in the European market is, however, primarily floating rate. Pricing of credit spreads for new issuance is primarily off a comparative benchmarking process, with often large variations between sectors for the same credit spread level, as illustrated in Table 4.1. In particular, the wide variation can be seen between different types of CDO issuance, and the much tighter levels achieved on consumer and prime mortgage credits as opposed to commercial and non-conforming mortgage credits.

Table 4.1 Sample European ABS FRN new issue spreads to Libor/Euribor

Class	Deal	Date	WAL	AAA	AA	A	BBB	BB
ABS – Credit cards	Pillar Funding 2003-1	May 2003	5	25		70	170	
ABS – Italian small ticket commercial leases	Ponte Vecchio Finance 2	June 2003	2.1–2.7	33		95		
ABS – Italian small ticket commercial leases	Ponte Vecchio Finance 2	June 2003	4.2–7.5	47		135		
CDO – European leveraged loans	North Westerly CLO I	May 2003	8.9–11.8	65		180	300	700
CDO – Synthetic balance sheet	Daphne Finance 1	April 2003	4.75	90	120	300	500	
CMBS – UK shopping centres	DECO Series 2003-CIT	July 2003	4.8	47	75	105	200	
NPL – Italian mortgages and unsecured loans	Tiepolo Finance 2	April 2003	3.3–4.6		115	185		
RMBS – UK prime	Mound Financing 3	May 2003	5.2	26	55	90	170	
RMBS – German synthetic prime	Provide Green 2003-1	June 2003	7	35	60	85	190	
RMBS – UK non-conforming	RMS 15	June 2003	3.6	45	85	170	350	

4.4.1   Valuation

Valuation is effected by a discounting back to present value of the future cash flows arising under a bond.

Bullet securities

For fixed rate bullet securities, this is relatively straightforward, with the fixed future amounts discounted back over the life of the deal at a particular yield set by reference to a benchmark government security.

For accuracy, this should be performed on a line-by-line basis, to ensure that the correct amount due is calculated for each payment date by reference to the relevant accrual period and the deal day count fraction.

If a deal has equal periodic coupon payments over the course of the year, where the total interest due over the year will be the same as the stated annual coupon – for example, the deal uses a 30/360 day account fraction – then a simplified formula can be used to calculate the bond value by a present value as follows:

$$\text{Bond value} = [(\text{PAO} \cdot \text{Periodic coupon}/r) \cdot (1 - [1/(1+r)^n])] + \text{PAO} \cdot [1/(1+r)^n]$$

where r = discount rate per period
n = number of periods.

This assumes that the bond value is calculated as a clean price (excluding accrued interest) on a coupon payment date.

For floating rate bullet securities, the amount of each coupon will first need to be set – either by assuming they are set at the current quarterly Libor rate, or by setting them off the forward curve. These coupons will then be discounted back at the Libor rate or the forward curve rate respectively.

As floating rate securities are more likely to use an actual/actual or an actual/360 day count fraction, they are unlikely to have equal periodic payments, even if the current Libor rate is used for all coupon resets rather than the forward curve. Consequently the short present value formula will produce a marginally inaccurate result.

More significantly, as the actual/360 day count fraction will produce extra coupon value each year (averaged over a number of years, the total coupon earned will be equal to [face coupon × 365.25/360] (accounting for an average over leap years and non-leap years) the resultant bond value will always be closer to par (a smaller discount or premium) than the present value calculated line-by-line. This latter point can be significantly corrected by "grossing-up" n (the number of periods) by multiplying it by 365.25/360.

Amortising securities

Periodic payments on bonds with scheduled amortisation will need to be present valued payment-by-payment to reach a bond value. If the bond is amortising on an annuity basis with equal periodic payments, comprised of a mixture of principal and interest (rather than on a specific schedule that does not match an annuity profile, or on an annuity profile that is truncated by a call), then a simplified formula can be used to calculate the bond value by a present value as follows:

$$\text{Bond value} = [(\text{Periodic payment}/r) \cdot (1 - [1/(1 + r)^n])]$$

where r = discount rate per period
        n = number of periods.

As for bullet securities above, this assumes that equal periodic payments are made over the course of the year, and that no gain is made on the number of days coupon received over each year, as a result of the day count fraction (in absence of which, the accuracy of the result can be increased by "grossing-up" n as described above). It also assumes that the bond value is calculated as a clean price (excluding accrued interest) on a coupon payment date.

For amortising prepayable ABS securities, the process is more complex. For each valuation date, a set of cash flows for the bond will need to be obtained, which may vary from those determined on origination of the deal. Changes in the CPR, the rate of defaults, and expectations of any likely call date, can all change the expected cash flow profile of a bond.

The cash flows cannot be discounted to a present value in the same way as a bullet-pay security or an annuity amortising security if there is an uneven set of payments, and will need to be present valued payment-by-payment.

Convexity

Certain types of ABS are structured to amortise or prepay with cash received as prepayments on the underlying assets, without any prepayment penalty. These typically include RMBS and consumer loans (where legal restrictions may prevent or limit the charging of prepayment penalties on the underlying assets) but they generally exclude other types of ABS such as CMBS and whole business deals.

Consequently, fixed rate bonds backed by assets that are prepayable without penalty, are generally themselves prepayable without penalty. Fixed rate bonds on other transactions are generally structured with make-whole provisions such as Spens clauses, which require the payment of significant penalties if they are prepaid early by reference to market yields at the time of prepayment. This is to compensate investors, as in the event that the bonds were trading above par when prepaid, the investors will suffer a loss on the mark-to-market value of the bond.

Prepayment is less of an issue for FRNs, as a change in market interest rates without a change in the FRN credit spread will not change the trading price of an FRN. Fixed rate bonds will, however, fluctuate in value with movements in market yields. FRNs will vary in value as credit spreads change over time, but as the related prepayment risk for investors (of receiving par for a bond trading above par) is smaller, FRNs do not generally carry any prepayment penalties (although a small premium on an optional early call of a deal in whole by the issuer may be seen in some cases).

As a result of prepayment risk, the analysis of fixed rate ABS which are prepayable without penalty has to take account of convexity. Convexity is a measure of the curvature, or rate of change, of the relation between yields and bond prices. If the actual bond price exceeds the estimated price extrapolated on a straight-line basis from a small change (i.e. the price/yield relation curves above the straight-line), then

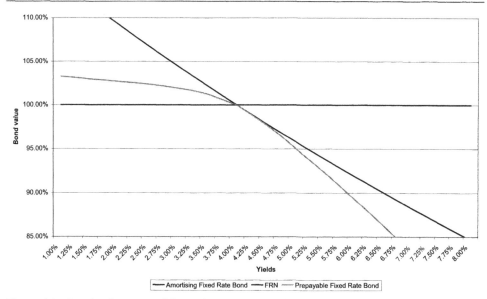

Figure 4.1   Bond values over different interest rate levels

the bond has positive convexity. If the actual bond price is less than the estimated price extrapolated on a straight-line basis from a small change (i.e. the price/yield relation curves below the straight-line), then the bond has negative convexity.

Prepayable ABS are generally negatively convex due to the effect on the bond of underlying (e.g. mortgage) prepayments. As yields fall, the likely increase in prepayment (through refinancing) of the underlying mortgages means that the bond principal reduces, shortening its life and decelerating its increase in value. Conversely, as yields rise, the expected life of the bond is likely to lengthen, as prepayments drop, meaning that the value drops at an accelerating rate.

Similarly, a bond with a call option is likely to have negative convexity, due to the reduced likelihood of the call being exercised in a high-yield environment, and the increased likelihood of the call being exercised in a low-yield environment.

Figure 4.1 displays the variance of bond value over different levels of interest rates for a 4% fixed rate ABS which is prepaying faster as yields fall and slower as yields rise, when compared to an FRN, and to a 4% fixed rate bond which is amortising on a fixed scheduled annuity-amortising basis (e.g. an annuity-style paydown with scheduled amortisation and no prepayments).

Figure 4.2 assumes the same overall change in yields from a combination of interest rates and credit spreads as Figure 4.1, but specifically splits out part of that change as a variation in credit spreads to show the limited fluctuation in value of an FRN.

4.5   PERFORMANCE AND REPORTING

Unlike the market for corporate bonds, the ABS markets have an inbuilt information deficiency. Companies regularly make announcements on matters affecting their

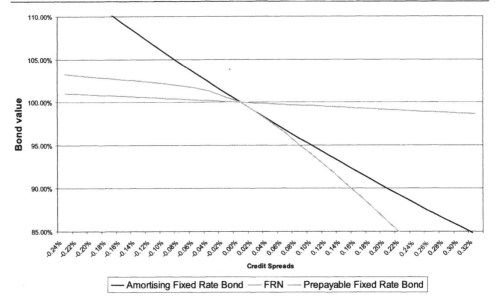

Figure 4.2   Bond values over different levels of credit spreads/interest rates

business, and may be required to do so pursuant to a stock exchange listing where relevant. Profits warnings, strategic announcements, acquisitions and disposals all intersperse quarterly financial reports. The ABS markets, on the other hand, are mainly dependent on quarterly reports for the underlying deals.

The quality, detail and regularity of these reports determine the ability of investors to judge the performance of a deal and to determine fair value pricing for the deal at any point in time. Without more regular performance reports, the value of an ABS bond can be difficult to analyse between report dates.

Reporting has improved over time as the market has grown, and regular issuers can be seen to devote more time and resources to ongoing data production. An example can be seen in the performance reporting provided by Kensington Group, a UK non-conforming mortgage lender, which was established in 1995 and has issued multiple securitisations from December 1996 onwards. Data provided on Kensington's investor website at www.ukmbs.co.uk illustrates key performance variables over the deals issued by Kensington.

Figure 4.3 illustrates the levels of prepayments on Kensington's deals over time, and shows the convergence trend to a rate of 35%. The data shows the value to be garnered for both investor and issuer in accurate data reporting. Both investor and issuer can be reasonably confident, over economic periods (and, in particular, interest rate levels) similar to those experienced during the course of these deals, and absent other major changes (e.g. to origination standards), what the CPR of such a deal will be. This assists the investor in predicting accurately the cash flows that will arise under the bond, and in assessing the level of reinvestment risk they are running as well as the price for the security relative to other securities in the market.

The issuer benefits from understanding the maturity profile of its deals more closely, and from tighter pricing to reflect the level of certainty and familiarity for investors.

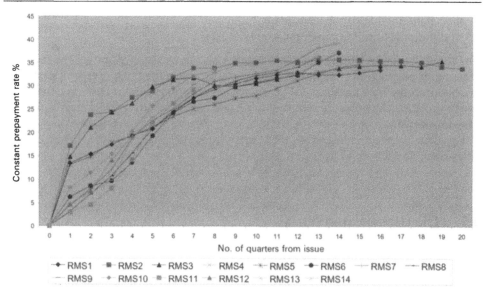

Figure 4.3 Kensington CPR % over time as at June 2003; source www.ukmbs.co.uk (reproduced by permission of the Kensington Group)

4.5.1 Key data

Key data for investors in analysing ABS falls into two categories – credit data and investment data. Credit data tells the investor whether to expect losses on the ABS, or the full payment of principal and interest. Investment data tells the investor the investment performance the investor can expect from the ABS.

Credit data

For initial credit analysis of specific types of transaction, see the relevant asset class in Chapter 5. Ongoing monitoring of transactions will require much the same analysis, but assisted by updated information on the performance of the transaction over time in a number of key areas, to assess whether the deal is performing better or worse than anticipated in the initial credit assessment. In particular, trends over time in the level of defaults or the level of delinquencies or arrears in a portfolio are important, as are trends in the ongoing level of EBITDA and free cash flow in whole business deals.

The level of excess spread over time is also an important item, as it determines the level of ongoing credit enhancement in the deal. Excess spread would normally be expected to drop over time as the pool pays down, due to the fixed costs of the deal and the increase in blended cost of debt (if the deal is sequential pay and the cheaper senior debt is paid off first).

Investment data

Investment data tells the investor what kind of return to expect of the asset absent credit losses. The key field here for most ABS products is the level of prepayments on assets. This is due to the effect that such prepayments have in:

- shortening the life of the asset; and
- entitling the issuer to prepay the bonds at par.

The former concern relates to the reinvestment risk run by the investor – if the investor wishes to invest cash for 5 years, and the assets underlying the bond prepay so fast that the bond average life shortens to 2 years, the investor must find a new investment in which to reinvest the proceeds received, or he will receive a reduced return over the life of his investment.

The latter concern relates to the prepayment risk run by the investor (see "Convexity" in section 4.4.1).

4.5.2 Typical investor report details

Commercial ABS and EETCs

- Data for deals will vary in accordance with the nature of the deal; as many deals will consist of pools of assets leased to different companies, significant items are likely to include the level of defaults and/or lease terminations.
- Also overall DSCR/Interest Cover.

Consumer loans/leases

- Delinquencies
- Defaults
- Cumulative losses.

Credit cards

- Monthly payment rate (% paid each month)
- Yield (annualised %)
- Charge-offs (annualised %)
- Excess spread (after charge-offs and cost of funds, annualised %)
- Delinquencies greater than 30 days (%).

CDOs

- Overcollateralisation ratio (deal collateral versus *pari passu* and senior debt) (%)
- Interest cover ratio
- WARF (weighted average rating factor)
- Diversity
- Defaults to date/credit events to date (for synthetics)
- Cumulative losses (%).

CMBS

- Interest cover ratio

- Occupancy rates
- Arrears
- Defaults.

Future flows

- Asset cover ratio (gross level of receipts generated versus interest cover and total debt service).

Non-performing loans

- Profitability of closed positions versus business plan (%)
- Speed of collections versus business plan (amount versus amount, or %)
- Remaining GBV (Gross Book Value) of unclosed positions
- Purchase price paid for such remaining positions.

RMBS

- Delinquencies greater than 30 days (%)
- Losses (%)
- Prepayment rate (%)
- Excess spread.

An example can be seen from the Kensington website in Figure 4.4, which illustrates cumulative loss rates over time on Kensington's deals to date.

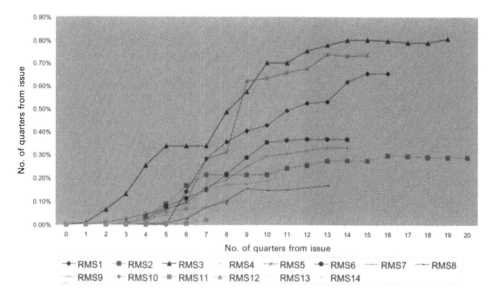

Figure 4.4 Kensington cumulative loss rate as at June 2003; source www.ukmbs.co.uk (reproduced by permission of the Kensington Group)

Trade receivables

- Write-offs
- Delinquencies
- Dilutions.

Whole business

- EBITDA
- Interest cover ratio
- DSCR (EBITDA versus interest and scheduled principal debt service)
- FCF DSCR (EBITDA less Capex versus interest and scheduled principal debt service)
- Rent cover and occupancy rates (Care Homes)
- Barrelage and rent (Pubs)
- RAV (Regulatory Asset Value) (Water).

Synthetics

- Number of credit events
- Cumulative losses
- Incipient credit events (e.g. level of delinquencies greater than 30 days).

5
Asset Classes

Virtually any type of cash flow can be used as a foundation for securitisation technology. It is, however, possible to pinpoint the main classes of asset that have led the development of the international market to its current level. In the US, auto loans, credit cards and residential mortgages have been major staples of the market. Auto loans were a significant area of issuance in the ASEAN countries prior to the Asian crisis. In much of Europe and other countries world wide, residential mortgages are the focus for development of the market and form the backbone of issuance, Australia and Spain being key examples. Trade receivables owed to corporates are a crucial component of the market in bank-arranged CP-funded conduit structures.

Repackagings developed separately from the securitisation market (being naturally more international and cross-border in nature, with no servicing function and often only one or a handful of underlying debtors), but they increasingly overlap the securitisation market, with the establishment of asset-backed MTN programmes designed to allow rapid issuance off a diverse range of underlying bonds or receivables, and the repackaging of securitisation bonds for specific investors.

CDOs bring together the securitisation rationale of combining multiple diversified underlying debtors in order to reduce concentration risk and correlation risk, with a repackaging structure.

The securitisation of non-performing loans has been a more recent development in the international markets, stemming from the high level of non-performing assets to be found in certain world markets due either to local recessions, or to global turmoil such as the Asian crisis. Prime candidates here are real estate loans in the financial system in Japan, and mortgages in the system in Italy, both of which have been the subject of securitisation transactions since 1999, in addition to securitisation of non-performing loans by KAMCO in Korea and by other Asset Management Corporations world wide.

The structural features of a securitisation depend very heavily on the form of the underlying assets, for three main reasons.

- Firstly, the receivable itself may have a number of "credit enhancement" factors already built in. The securitisation should take full advantage of these factors if it is to realise the maximum potential of the assets. For example, a mortgage receivable benefits from a security interest over the mortgagor's property. In the event of default in payment by the mortgagor, the mortgagee can enforce the security by exercising its power of sale or foreclosure, and repaying itself from the proceeds realised. Likewise, a mortgagee will usually insist that the mortgagor take out insurance for the property against fire. If the property burns down, the mortgagee will insist that the insurance monies are used to reinstate the property, or will claim them to discharge the mortgage debt. An auto loan will contain a power for the lender to repossess the vehicle and sell it to effect repayment. If possible, the securitisation structure should allow the SPV, and thus the investors, to benefit from these ancillary rights by ensuring that they are also transferred to the SPV.

- Secondly, the cash flow structure and contract terms of different classes of receivables vary significantly. Trade receivables are, by and large, non-interest bearing. Auto loans made by way of a finance lease carry a single periodic rental payment reflecting the principal cost of the vehicle to the originator together with financing charges. An operating lease may provide for maintenance obligations on the originator. Credit cards do not charge interest on amounts outstanding for the first month, and only bear interest thereafter on debt which remains outstanding after the month end. Mortgages may bear interest at a fixed or floating rate, and may be amortising (a repayment mortgage) or may have a bullet redemption structure (for example, an endowment mortgage where the mortgage principal is paid off from the proceeds of a maturing insurance policy). Non-performing loans will generate cash receipts on an irregular basis off the back of completed enforcement proceedings or settlements. The structure may need funding mechanisms to smooth cash flows over time or multiple classes of notes to match different cash flow structures.
- Thirdly, taxation issues may lead to requirements for particular structural elements. In particular, the tax treatment of leases can be very complex, involving in many countries the payment by the lessee of VAT for leasing services, which must be collected by the lessor and paid to the authorities without prejudicing the bankruptcy remoteness of the SPV (which assumes in part the role of lessor). In addition, tax reliefs such as capital allowances may add complexity to auto, equipment or asset finance structures.

5.1 ABS: COMMERCIAL AND EETCs

The main items falling into this category are securitisations relating to big ticket transportation assets such as ships, aircraft and trains. It also covers securitisations relating to small ticket business items such as equipment leases of computers, plant and so on. Structures typically consist of either:

- Loans secured over assets (e.g. for an airline to raise debt above its corporate credit level, or as a package of loans originated by a lender); or
- Leases of assets.

Structural issues of leases of assets are similar to those that arise for consumer ABS (see 5.2 below), with a distinction between finance leases and operating leases, and an analysis of the VAT and capital allowances position of the originator and the SPV.

For big ticket assets, however, much more analysis is likely to take place of the residual value of the leased assets, as the number of underlying debtors is likely to be much smaller than for a small ticket deal, meaning that a portfolio credit rating approach may be inappropriate. Unless the individual lessees carry high credit ratings themselves, the clearest benchmark for rating value may be the value inherent in the assets, which can be seized if the lessee defaults, and either sold or re-leased. Consequently, the rating analysis may involve examining the liquidity of the sale and re-lease markets for the leased assets, and applying a haircut to market resale values or market re-lease rates to determine a "rated" level of cash flow.

Airlines have typically financed themselves through issuance of asset-based finance (in the form of ETCs or EETCs) against their fleets. They have been largely unable to access more sophisticated asset-backed products, as cash flows are dependent solely on their own routes and business (and the residual value of the aircraft), without the required level of diversification to demonstrate the ongoing robustness of the overall cash flow portfolio. Consequently, the deals are not limited recourse, and are akin to sale and leasebacks in nature.

Consequently, pure asset-backed aircraft deals have centred on the aircraft lessors which run a diversified financing business far more suited to the asset-backed product (such as the ALPS deals for GPA, and the CRAFT deal for Bombardier where CRAFT was established to act as a finance lessor to finance the acquisition of aircraft by airlines from Bombardier, the manufacturer).

Transactions involving narrow body planes are likely to receive better ratings, as they can be used on more routes world wide, and therefore have a wider reuse market than wide body planes used for long-haul flights. Transactions have been structured with both turboprop and jet planes.

Similarly, train deals have centred around train lessors rather than train operators. In the UK, ROSCOs (rolling stock companies) act as lessors to the TOCs (train operating companies), with deals arranged for Angel Trains (dating from the Bullet Finance securitisation arranged in 1996) and for Porterbrook.

There have been few shipping transactions, with the main example being the Latitude Synthetic deal in 2002, which securitised shipping loans made by NIB Capital.

Small ticket commercial ABS has been dominated by Italian lease deals. These have securitised mixed portfolios of longer term real estate leases and shorter term equipment and auto leases.

5.1.1 Credit analysis

For big ticket assets, key considerations will be the nature of the assets and the marketability of the assets – either a direct resale value in the market, or the ability to realise ongoing value through re-lease rates.

This will be heavily influenced by macroeconomic factors and external events. For example, significant disruption was seen in the airline sector post 9/11 as fewer flights were taken, impacting the profitability of airlines and creating surplus capacity in aircraft space. Consequently, the values of aircraft were negatively affected, leading to downgrades in the EETC sector as both primary obligor default probability (the relevant airline) and potential loss severity increased.

Similarly, during a slump in business investment, the resale value of capital goods will drop.

For small ticket assets (i.e. low value assets and small businesses), the analysis will lean more towards that adopted for consumer ABS (see below), although the local business environment of the debtors is also directly relevant.

Key information

- Assets – type, location and quality
- Number/quality of lessees
- Resale/re-lease potential and value
- DSCR/interest cover.

5.2 ABS: CONSUMER AND CREDIT CARDS

Consumer ABS mainly includes:

- Auto loans, leases and hire purchase agreements
- Consumer loans
- Credit cards
- In the US, home equity loans.

Home equity loans are loans secured over private residences which are taken out for reasons other than house purchase – chiefly the consolidation of existing consumer debts, to pay for college or medical bills, or for home improvement. In the past, these have usually been second mortgages, but they are now increasingly consolidated into the first mortgage on the property.

Although this type of loan exists outside the US (for example, significant remortgaging has taken place in the UK over the last few years as people have withdrawn equity from their homes to finance consumer expenditure), such loans are usually grouped with RMBS in most countries (although the innate adverse credit selection of loans which lever home equity tends to lead to deals which contain significant proportions of such loans trading wide of RMBS).

5.2.1 Auto and consumer loans (and leased assets)

As well as covering auto and consumer loan and lease transactions, this section also deals with other leased assets (such as equipment leases), due to the similarities between leasing structures for low value assets.

The US has a simplified filing system for classifying asset-financing transactions under Article 9 of the Uniform Commercial Code (the UCC), which covers title retention, conditional sales, leases and other transactions involving chattels and security interests in chattels.

In the UK and many other jurisdictions, the classifications of the common law survive. The main divisions in the UK are between simple retention of title transactions, conditional sale and hire purchase transactions, and finance leases. In legal terms, all of these devices seek to enable a seller to provide credit to a buyer for purchase of an asset from the seller, while retaining a kind of security interest in the asset being sold to give the seller protection against the insolvency of the buyer. The use of a straightforward loan with security over the asset has been hindered by the onerous legislation on registration of bills of sale, where security is given by an individual, so that these transactions seek, instead, to achieve the same end by a retention of ownership of the asset with the seller.

This similar legal basis does not, however, necessarily equate to the same tax and accounting treatment, especially when other types of agreement, such as operating leases or simple hire contracts (both of which also retain asset ownership in the seller), are also included, making the securitisation of a mixed portfolio potentially complex.

In an operating lease, the substantive economic value of the vehicles (or equipment, for equipment leasing deals) will remain with the lessor at the end of the lease term, leaving the lessor with residual value risk, which differs from a finance lease or hire purchase.

A finance lease is the economic equivalent of purchasing the asset from the lessor on credit terms, in a way that enables the lessor to claim capital allowances on the asset (the benefit of which can be passed on to the lessee as a reduced financing charge). The lessee is not given the right to purchase the asset, but at the end of the "primary period" of the lease (i.e. when the principal amount and financing costs are prepaid), the asset may be sold and part of the proceeds passed to the lessee as a rent rebate, or the lease may be continued for a "secondary period" at a nominal rent. In the UK, it is presumed that a lease is a finance lease if the present value of the minimum lease payments amounts to substantially all (normally 90% or more) of the fair value of the leased asset.

Taxation issues are often of particular complexity for lease receivables, as lease businesses may be reliant on capital allowances derived from leased assets, the treatment of which will have to be unaffected (or at least not adversely affected) by the transaction if the originator is to remain tax neutral with regard to the transaction. This may necessitate the transfer of ownership to the vehicles or equipment together with the leases. If this is so, then in the UK the bills of sale requirements will become relevant again, as they also govern situations where ownership of assets that are not in the possession of the original owner are transferred. Also, in many countries, lease payments are subjected to VAT or other forms of sales or service tax. If the receivables are sold to the SPV, the primary tax liability may also be transferred, such that reserves or structuring at the SPV level may be necessary to cover VAT liability.

Lease payments will usually need to be divided into notional "interest" and "principal" portions for the purpose of matching collections to funding instruments. This is usually carried out by discounting the lease payment to net present value, with the discount rate used being regarded as the implied interest rate charged to the lessee on the lease.

Operating lease or hire contracts may impose maintenance obligations on the originator. If the originator fails to continue to perform these obligations after the contracts have been transferred to the SPV, the receivables debtors may begin to withhold payment, or pay for maintenance separately and withhold the cost from their periodic payments. In either circumstance, the SPV's cash flow is prejudiced. This may not be a concern if the credit rating of the originator is equal to or higher than that being sought on the funding instruments, as the originator's rating can simply be adopted as a dependent rating for the funding instruments. If the originator is not so rated, however, it may be necessary to obtain a commitment from another entity to provide maintenance services if the originator fails to do so. The contracts may also contain further provisions such as set-off rights, upgrade rights, early termination rights, or provisions for downward rental adjustments that will need to be addressed.

Concerns may arise as to which party in a transaction accepts responsibility and liability for defects in vehicles or equipment that give rise to loss, damage or personal injury. In the UK, the Financial Services Authority requires in its guidelines for off-balance-sheet treatment for capital purposes that UK-regulated institutions acting as originators in relation to consumer finance receivables take appropriate steps, such as arranging insurance policies or obtaining an indemnity from the purchaser, to cover against the risk of any such claims after the assets are sold.

Some countries may use an amortisation method known as the "Rule of 78s" in calculating the remaining outstanding balance of auto loans. This method first calculates the amount of each equal instalment on an annuity basis. The amount of the instalment that relates to principal amortisation is then a fraction of the original loan amount equal to the number of the period divided by the total sum of the numerical digits of each period over the life of the deal (so for a 12-period loan, the sum would be $1 + 2 + 3 + 4 + \cdots + 11 + 12 = 78$). For example, in the fourth period of a 12-period loan, the principal amount of the instalment will be equal to 4/78ths of the loan principal. This method of amortisation will normally result in a slower amortisation schedule than that for an annuity loan. Consequently, the interest rate on a rule of 78s loan will be higher than that on a comparable annuity loan at the start of the loan, but falls during the life of the loan, so that it is lower than that on the annuity loan by the end of the loan term. As this method of amortisation allows the originator to collect more cash (absent prepayment penalties) on a loan that is prepaid during its life, it may be utilised as a disincentive to prepayment (or as a compensation measure for the originator).

Comparative amortisation curves for a 12-year annuity-style loan, and a 12-year Rule of 78s loan are shown at Figure 5.1, where both run at an 8% effective interest rate.

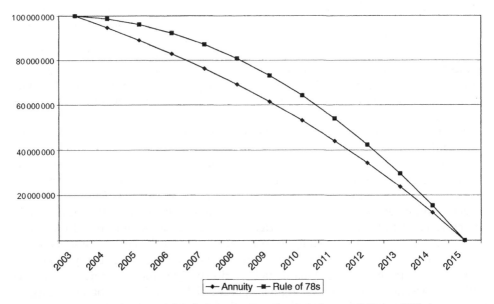

Figure 5.1   Comparative remaining balance on annuity-style loan and Rule of 78s loan

5.2.2   Credit analysis

Due to the granular nature of consumer pools, most analysis is historic benchmarking. Thus, the quality of historic data that can be provided by the originator is crucial. Less importance is attached to the value of the collateral, due to its low value, and its high associated repossession and remarketing costs as a percentage of the collateral value.

Key information

- Volume of origination by originator and historic levels of delinquencies/defaults/ losses
- Seasoning
- Underwriting procedures
- Quality of servicing
- Repossession market and values.

In rating auto loan transactions, Standard & Poor's uses an actuarial approach (see Standard & Poor's *Auto Loan Criteria*, 1999, p. 24) by benchmarking losses on the pool against other pools in the market. Performance can vary widely between different pools, and credit and underwriting standards are therefore considered important. Typical loss multiples against static pool data are 4× to 5× at AAA level, down to 1.75× to 2× at BBB level (if the losses are taken from dynamic pool data, the loss figure will first be factored by the weighted average term).

5.2.3   Credit cards

A retailer from whom goods or services are purchased by a customer on a credit card will seek reimbursement by selling the credit card voucher signed by the customer to a merchant acquirer at a discount to its face value (the discount being referred to as the interchange). The merchant acquirer will then on-sell the voucher to the card clearer (such as VISA or Mastercard) who will in turn on-sell the voucher to the card issuing bank.

The receivable to be securitised can then constitute either:

- the amounts outstanding on the customer's account at the card issuing bank; or
- the amounts outstanding to the merchant acquirer from VISA or Mastercard.

The former are usually referred to as credit card receivables, and are the subject of a credit card receivables deal. The latter are referred to as card voucher receivables, and are usually the subject of a future flows style deal (see section 5.6), as they can enable the merchant acquirer to receive finance against amounts due from credit-worthy entities (VISA and Mastercard) located outside the country of origin of the merchant acquirer, and thus circumvent the sovereign ceiling of that country.

The Day 1 structure of a typical credit card transaction is shown in Figure 5.2.

The payment of amounts outstanding on a customer account is made by customers on a monthly basis in amounts that could equal the whole amount of the outstanding debt. If the initial amounts outstanding on the cards are all that is sold in the securitisation, the weighted average life of the transaction would be extremely short, which would not enable the relatively high front-end structuring costs of the transaction to

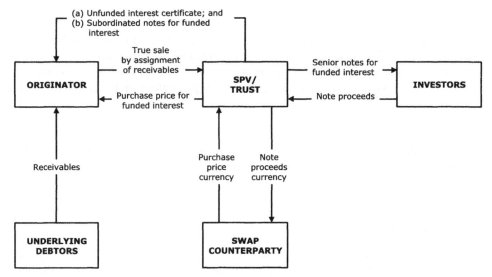

Figure 5.2   Credit card structure: Day 1

be amortised over a sufficient length of time. To enable a longer average life to be set, all receivables under specified credit card accounts will be sold to the SPV. This enables the reinvestment of cash receipts, thus extending the average life.

In turn, however, this generates a new issue; namely that the level of amounts outstanding under a particular account will vary significantly from period to period. If the SPV bought all amounts outstanding, it would need a fluctuating level of funding to match its asset base, which would be complex to structure. The solution that has evolved instead is to give the SPV an "undivided interest" in the receivables under the specified accounts, usually by transferring the whole of the accounts into a trust, with the SPV having an undivided share under the trust (the "funded interest" or "investor interest"). The level of this interest is determined by a fraction known as the "floating allocation percentage" or FLAP, which has as its numerator the principal amount of the SPV's funding (senior and subordinate) and as its denominator the fluctuating outstanding amount from period to period. This enables the SPV's funding to remain fixed. The remaining interest (the "unfunded interest" or "seller interest") is held by the originator.

Amounts outstanding under credit cards do not carry a final maturity date when principal or interest repayment is due. This means that it is not possible to establish a simple final maturity date for the bonds issued under the securitisation, as is possible with mortgages, for example. To establish such a date, the FLAP is converted to a "fixed allocation percentage" after the end of the revolving period so that the SPV's funding is subject to gradual amortisation, until a repayment date for the final portion outstanding is reached. Alternatively, the principal allocation can be accumulated in a principal funding account, and used to defease the debt and make a bullet repayment at the final maturity. This creates a simpler structure for the investor, but has an embedded negative carry on the defeasance account.

Credit card balances are classified as delinquencies after 30 days past the due date.

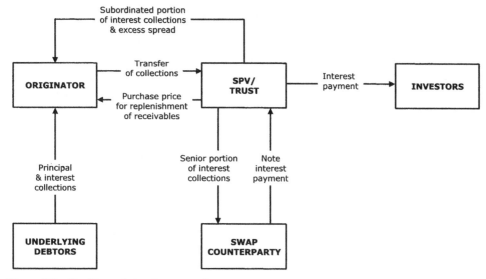

Figure 5.3   Credit card structure: ongoing

After 180 days, amounts due and unpaid on credit cards are classified as charge-offs. In reporting for credit card transactions, the gross yield is monitored, as is the monthly payment rate or MPR (receipts of finance charges and principal collections on card balances). Gross yield less any charge-offs, the cost of funds, and any fees, will give the level of excess spread in a transaction.

The ongoing structure of a typical credit card transaction is shown at Figure 5.3.

5.2.4   Credit analysis

As with other consumer assets, credit cards are assessed primarily off historic data. The key variables are slightly different however, reflecting the fact that a higher level of losses is expected, but that this is compensated by significant excess spread in the portfolio from yield on the card accounts.

Key information

- Monthly payment rate (% paid each month)
- Yield (annualised %)
- Charge-offs (annualised %)
- Excess spread (after charge-offs and cost of funds, annualised %)
- Delinquencies greater than 30 days (%).

In rating credit card transactions, Standard & Poor's stresses charge-offs by a factor of 3× to 5× for an AAA rating (see Standard & Poor's *Credit Card Criteria*, 1999, p. 12).

5.3   COLLATERALISED DEBT OBLIGATIONS

CDOs can be divided into CBOs and CLOs, and also into arbitrage or balance sheet deals. Balance sheet deals are deals that are undertaken to reduce the size of a bank's loan book for regulatory capital relief or to reduce usage of credit lines to particular borrowers. Arbitrage deals generally comprise new assets specifically bought for the transaction, with a view to realising profits from assets under management or from holding tranches of the deal.

Each of these deals can be further subdivided into cash flow transactions, synthetic transactions and market value transactions. Cash flow transactions are akin to other securitisations, in that they rely on the flow of cash from periodic payments on a pool of underlying assets in order to make payments on the issued securities. Synthetic transactions are backed by a credit default swap, and only suffer losses with respect to the occurrence of credit events on the referenced portfolio. These are dealt with in more detail in Chapter 7. Market value transactions rely on a trading analysis of the value that could be realised from liquidating the portfolio at any one point in time.

CDOs may also be static or managed. Static deals are those where it is intended that the underlying assets remain the same throughout the life of the deal. Managed deals on the other hand permit an asset manager to switch into and out of underlying assets, thus changing the credit profile of the deal. Generally, this will permit the removal of "credit improved" or "credit impaired" assets, and also a per annum amount of purely discretionary trading (generally, no more than 20% of the total pool per annum).

CBOs in particular share many characteristics with repackagings, the main differences being the (relative) diversity and granularity of the underlying asset portfolio, and the ability to trade the portfolio. As set out below, trading leads to securities law issues. It also leads to taxation issues akin to those arising in a repackaging programme structure where multiple trades are carried out. In other words, concerns arise as to whether the SPV is tax resident in the jurisdiction of the asset manager who trades the portfolio for profits tax purposes. In the UK, corporation tax is levied on non-resident companies on the profits of a UK branch or agency which is a UK representative of the company, although an investment manager providing services in the ordinary course of business for a market remuneration may be excluded from this risk.

The structure of a typical cash flow CBO transaction is shown at Figure 5.4.

CLOs are potentially more complex, due to the often non-conforming nature of the underlying loan agreements forming the portfolio and the level of due diligence that may therefore be required. This is often exacerbated by restrictions on assignment contained in some loan agreements, which may prohibit assignment of the loans without the consent of the relevant borrower. In practice, restrictions on assignment have meant that many transactions to date have been arranged by way of sub-participation with the originator as a dependent rating, or by using a synthetic structure.

Other key concerns in this market are not to disturb the relationship with the underlying borrowers and not to disclose any more detail of the underlying loans than is strictly necessary. This may be ensured by reliance on investor perception of the originator's own credit scoring system to persuade investors to accept minimal disclosure on the actual identities of the underlying borrowers.

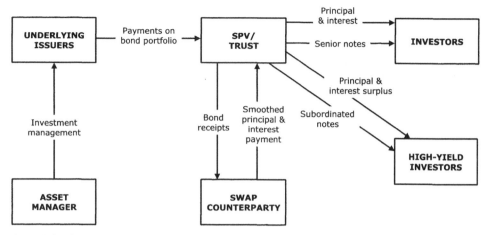

Figure 5.4 CBO structure

As the SPV in a CBO or CLO issue will often engage in trading of its underlying assets, investment company issues are relevant. The US Investment Company Act of 1940 defines an investment company as any issuer of securities that is engaged primarily in the business of investing or trading in securities. Any investment company that makes a public offer or private placement of securities in the US is required to be registered with the SEC. Exemptions are available for an issuer whose outstanding securities are beneficially owned by not more than 100 US persons and which does not intend to make a public offering of its securities, and for an issuer whose securities are owned solely by qualified purchasers (individual investors with investments which equal or exceed US$5 million in value, or corporate investors who own and invest on a discretionary basis an investment portfolio which equals or exceeds US$25 million in value) and which does not intend to make a public offering of its securities.

The ability of an asset manager to trade the assets that form the pool for a CBO may enable the manager to avoid holding defaulted assets, or to realise a profit on assets trading above par. Any such trading ability will be subject to scrutiny by the rating agencies, who will set eligibility or substitution criteria which must be complied with in carrying out trades. These criteria will be aimed at ensuring that the pool does not have a higher probability of default after the trade than it had before, and will address such factors as:

- Maximum concentration in single issuer
- Diversity score
- Net loss rate as determined using rating agency model on portfolio
- Minimum rating level on individual asset
- WARF (weighted average rating factor) of pool.

The diversity score reflects a certain degree of diversity of the assets in the CDO pool across industry sectors and country of origin of the underlying debtors on the assets. The more diverse the portfolio, the lower the perceived default correlation risk in the pool, and the lower the required credit enhancement for the transaction.

In a securitisation, the originator will often retain a certain amount of the credit risk on the securitised assets through subscribing to subordinated notes or some other form of credit enhancement, and in many CDOs a similar first loss piece is often retained by the originator or asset manager.

In some CDOs, however, the arranger may intend to fully sell-down the subordinated tranches to investors. One structure used to assist this is the repackaging of subordinated tranches, either with senior tranches in the same deal (generally issued as combination notes without using a repackaging vehicle), or with highly rated securities such as US Treasuries, in order to achieve a guaranteed return of principal.

5.3.1 Super-senior pieces

The arbitrage achievable on CDO transactions – in terms of either capital relief or funding spread – can depend on the sale of risk related to the most senior level of risk tranching.

For CLO deals, banks seeking capital relief on banking book will wish to reduce the capital treatment on this, the largest section of the portfolio, as much as possible. A sale of bonds issued against the entire super-senior can result in a large transaction size, which may impact pricing. An alternative is to transact a credit default swap for the risk on the super-senior piece (with an OECD bank under the old Basel capital rules) – thus reducing the capital charge against this part of the portfolio to 20% of its normal charge.

As CBO transactions are generally smaller and require funding, more of these deals have sold senior notes into the market against the entire capital structure. However, since economic funding of the super-senior piece may determine the overall economics of the deal, other alternatives have also developed such as:

● Repo funding;
● On-balance-sheet funding;
● Commercial paper funding.

5.3.2 Credit analysis

The credit analysis of CDOs involves an assessment of a number of factors:

● Type of assets in the CDO;
● Flexibility and incentivisation of the deal manager, if the CDO is managed;
● Exact composition of the initial pool (and of the substitution criteria, if the pool is managed).

The role of the deal manager can be analysed by looking at any cash commitment they have to the deal (retaining equity in the deal for example), and considering their structure, resources and alignment of interest with the notes issued under the deal, as well as their relevant expertise to originate and manage the variety of assets in question.

Analysis of the composition of the initial pool involves a corporate credit assessment of each name (or an assessment of each individual ABS name for an ABS pool). This is combined with a view on the homogeneity and granularity of the pool expressed through the average rating, maximum individual concentrations, and the diversity of the pool.

Key information

- Maximum concentration per name
- Diversity
- Main industry sectors
- Interest cover ratio
- Amount of low-rated assets
- WARF (weighted average rating factor).

In rating CDO transactions, Standard & Poor's assigns each underlying asset a default probability (either from an explicit rating scale, or by mapping internal bank rating scores) and the pool is then put through their CDO Evaluator model (a Monte Carlo simulation) to determine the default frequency across the pool at different rating levels on the basis of correlation assumptions on the sector diversity of the underlying pool (see Standard & Poor's *Global Cash Flow and Synthetic CDO Criteria*, 21 March 2002). In the US, the loss severity input ranges from 40% to 50% for senior secured bank debt, 45% to 60% for senior secured bonds, and 72% to 85% for subordinated bonds. In the UK, the loss severity input ranges from 35% to 45% for senior secured bank debt, 40% to 55% for senior secured bonds, and 85% to 90% for subordinated bonds. In continental Europe, the loss severity input ranges from 40% to 55% for senior secured bank debt, 45% to 60% for senior secured bonds, and 75% to 85% for subordinated bonds. CDOs of emerging markets assets are subject to stricter diversification guidelines for concentration levels in different regions, and emerging market debt will be subject to higher loss assumptions (75% loss for sovereign debt, 85% loss for corporate debt).

Moody's calculates a weighted average diversity score for the portfolio based on the weighted average spread of industries in the underlying assets (see *Moody's Rating Cash Flow Transactions Backed by Corporate Debt*, 7 April 1995, pp. 2–3 and Moody's *Emerging Market Collateralized Bond Obligations: An Overview*, 25 October 1996, pp. 2–3). This diversity score is then treated as being equal to the number of homogeneous bonds in the pool for the purpose of a binomial expansion of the pool. A weighted average credit rating for the pool is determined, based on the rating of each underlying asset in the pool, to set the default rates for the binomial expansion. Loss severity is set by reference to loss levels for the particular asset type. Credit enhancement levels are determined as the sum of the loss in each scenario in the binomial expansion of pool. CBOs/CLOs of emerging markets assets are subject to stricter diversification guidelines across regions, and emerging market debt will be subject to higher loss assumptions (75% loss for sovereign debt, 90% loss for corporate debt). A 20% credit enhancement floor may be set for transactions with senior pieces to be rated A or higher.

Fitch assigns each underlying asset a default probability (either from an explicit rating scale, or by mapping internal bank rating scores) and the pool is then put through their VECTOR model (a multi-step Monte Carlo simulation) to determine the default frequency and recovery amounts across the pool at different rating levels on the basis of correlation assumptions on the sector diversity of the underlying pool (see Fitch's *Global Rating Criteria for Collateralised Debt Obligations*, 14 July 2003). Loss severity varies by stress rating level of the CDO debt issued, as well as by investment grade or subinvestment grade status of the corporate, and geographic location of the corporate. Market value CDOs calculate an advance rate for investment grade issuance as against the credit quality and liquidity of the underlying portfolio, and as against the historic market price volatility of the underlying.

5.4   COMMERCIAL MORTGAGE-BACKED SECURITIES

The categorisation of CMBS (commercial mortgage-backed securities) can cover a multitude of different transaction types, including:

- Commercial mortgage transactions (where the originator is a mortgagee lender rather than an owner of real estate);
- Residential real estate (where the originator is an owner of property – typically "multi-family property" – leased to residential tenants);
- Commercial real estate (where the originator is an owner of property leased to commercial tenants);
- Sale and leaseback transactions.

Commercial and residential real estate deals are typically structured to use lease cash flow to service interest payments on the securities issued, with the principal serviced by a balloon or bullet payment made from property disposal or refinancing. In many cases, a secured loan structure is used, so as not to require a transfer (and disposal) of the real estate (which could raise stamp duty and capital gains tax concerns). A transfer could also complicate the preservation of the property equity value in the originator's group, and could potentially require renegotiation of lease terms with tenants. The underlying loan secured over the property is typically designed to mature prior to the securities, due to the length of time taken to enforce the security and sell the property (if necessary due to an inability to refinance).

There are therefore two areas for analysis – the ability of lease income to support payments of interest and principal amortisation, and the ability of the property value to support payment of principal.

The terms of the leases are likely to be relatively standard based on the terms available in the local market, and will need to be analysed to determine the length of the leases until the next break clause.

In the US, commercial leases are typically 5–10 years in length, and may be "triple net" (a lease where the tenant is obliged to pay for taxes and insurance as well as maintenance costs on the property). In the UK, commercial leases have historically been 25-year tenor fully repairing and insuring ("FRI") leases (the tenant is liable for repairs and insurance, and the landlord can recover money spent on these from the tenant through service charges), potentially with break clauses as short as year 15, and 5 year upward only rent reviews.

If it is the owner and landlord of the properties, the originator is subject to various expenses and maintenance obligations (some of which may be reclaimable, e.g. where the lease is an FRI lease) which do not fall on a purely financial originator such as a commercial mortgagee. Consequently, the analysis of real estate transactions is more akin to that applied to whole business transactions, with an analysis of the periodic cash flow and expenses of the originator. Likewise DSCR ratios will be applied (if the leases are long term without break clauses, the DSCR is likely to be tighter to reflect the stronger contracted cash flow stream).

Full insurance will be required for the real estate, and third-party valuations will also be required.

Commercial mortgage and commercial real estate deals will also have to consider the effects that the business characteristics of the tenants have on the real estate (for example, environmental concerns where the tenants are manufacturers, and connected lender liability issues).

5.4.1   Credit analysis

Deals can be categorised by the number of tenants/borrowers, with the main split being:

- Sale and leaseback transactions (single tenant)
- Portfolio transactions (high number of tenants or high number of borrowers such as commercial mortgage borrowers)
- Trophy or high-value property deals (limited tenants).

The key risks in CMBS structures can be broken down into:

- Tenant/borrower default risk
- Lease break/tenant non-renewal
- Sale/re-lease risk
- Balloon refinancing risk.

For sale and leaseback transactions, there is typically a long lease with no lease break during the term of the transaction. The analysis is therefore based on a combination of the corporate credit of the lessor and the potential sale or re-lease recovery value of the real estate on default by the lessor.

For portfolio transactions, the analysis centres on the location and use of the real estate. Sectors are typically divided into:

- Office
- Retail
- Industrial
- Hotel/leisure.

If the pool takes the form of commercial mortgages, it can also be analysed by historic default frequencies. For high value real estate with a limited number of tenants, analysis is similar, but concentration risk (i.e. the focus on a small number of properties) is also relevant.

Key information

- Occupancy rates

- Rent roll, net rental income after expenses, and Capex levels
- Interest cover ratios
- LTVs
- Balloon LTVs
- Lease maturities
- Arrears
- Defaults.

Rating assumptions for real estate deals may vary significantly from country to country.

Under guidelines for rating real estate deals in the US (see Standard & Poor's *CMBS Property Evaluation Criteria*, 1999, pp. 24 and 65–66), Standard & Poor's will determine a figure based on current revenues and expenses (net operating income or NOI) net of cash contributions for capex and retenanting costs (stabilised net cash flow). A stressed capitalisation rate will be applied to the resultant stabilised net cash flow figure to determine an adjusted property value. This gives benchmark LTV and DSCR ratios (against the adjusted property value and the stabilised net cash flow respectively) based on the property type, and the rating level sought (credit levels are generally set higher for deals backed by a single property than for deals backed by multiple property loans – in the latter case credit is given for the increase in diversification). For a US multiple property multi-family deal, indicative levels are 40–50% and 1.65× to 2.05× (AAA), 50–60% and 1.55× to 1.95× (AA), 55-65% and 1.4× to 1.8× (A), 60–70% and 1.3× to 1.7× (BBB), 70–80% and 1.2× to 1.45× (BB) and 75–85% and 1.15× to 1.35× (B).

For UK commercial real estate deals (see Standard & Poor's *UK Commercial Real Estate Criteria*, 1997, pp. 8–14), Standard & Poor's assigns default probabilities to commercial tenants based on their creditworthiness, the length of the lease (a longer term lease means that the tenant is more likely to default), and the rating level sought. A Monte Carlo model is run to see the effect on the DSCR in different scenarios. Lease income is assumed to fall by 30–50% in the UK from the point at which a lease break clause operates, in order to simulate the reduced subsequent rent with a new tenant. Standard & Poor's will instruct a third party valuer to value 75% plus of the pool by value. Due to the typical balloon or bullet principal paydown on these deals, Standard & Poor's will compare default and refinancing scenarios, and take the higher of the two credit enhancement figures (to refinance properties effectively in the UK, the owner will generally need to show that remaining tenants have at least 12–15 years left on their leases). Base market value decline assumptions in the UK are a 35% to 45% drop for a BBB scenario, and a 50% to 65% drop for an AAA scenario (depending on the type of commercial property). As noted, these figures could vary significantly from market to market.

5.5 COVERED BONDS AND PFANDBRIEFE

The word "Pfandbriefe" (singular Pfandbrief, plural Pfandbriefe) is a German term for a variety of secured bond, which is collateralised by a dynamically changing pool of mortgage or public sector assets. Although the term (and product) is uniquely German as its operation is enshrined in German legislation, the term has been used in a generic sense for similar collateralised products that have developed in other European jurisdictions. This is strictly inaccurate, given that these other products differ in their terms, their structures and their risks, and the term "covered bonds" (and "mortgage bonds" for the mortgage-backed variety) is now gaining use, although Pfandbriefe may still be encountered as a convenient label for the product generally in all its national forms (see Table 5.1).

The covered bond market has its roots in the 1700s, with the passing of legislation in Germany in 1769, followed by similar legislation in Denmark in the 1800s, in France in 1852, and in Spain in 1869. Describing the market as a new growth area may therefore seem unusual. In practice, however, until 1995 when "Jumbo Pfandbriefe" were devised, the sector had limited cross-border significance, with the markets for the product being mainly domestic markets in Germany and Denmark. Issuance of French covered bonds was restricted to certain issuers.

In May 1995, the introduction of the issuance criteria for Jumbo Pfandbriefe was designed to significantly increase liquidity in the Pfandbriefe market, and hence investor interest, by standardising terms of issuance, and by setting minimum issuance size for Jumbo Pfandbriefe at Euro 500m. Jumbo Pfandbriefe are required to be listed on a German exchange, and three market-makers are required. This development coincided with increasing restrictions on government issuance across Europe generally as European governments tried to meet the Maastricht economic convergence criteria on public debt levels, thus shrinking the pool of high-quality, liquid AAA-rated assets in Europe. As the single largest and most important market in Europe, the German Pfandbriefe market had a head start, but with the introduction of the Euro, other European issuers had the chance to compete with the German market directly.

Consequently, in November 1997, one year before the Euro was introduced, the Luxembourg authorities introduced covered bond legislation, followed by the French authorities in June 1999 and the Finnish authorities in 2000. The Bank of Spain lowered the risk weighting on Spanish covered bonds in April 2000. Ireland passed covered bond legislation in 2001. Belgium and Italy also proposed legislation in 2001. Many of the Eastern European countries introduced legislation between 1995 and 2000. The market for the product has subsequently grown in importance, and most particularly has moved from being a domestic product to a cross-border product.

Issuance is now substantial in the German and Spanish markets, with rapid growth in the French market and significant growth expected in Ireland following the Euro 4bn first issue in the Irish market in March 2003. Increased issuance in Luxembourg is also expected.

More recently, concern has centred on the potential impact on the covered bonds market of downgrades in the German banking sector and the impending removal of state guarantees for the Landesbank in Germany.

In 2003, HBOS launched a UK covered bond programme permitting the issuance of fixed rate, floating rate or index-linked covered bonds. Although there is no UK legislation on covered bonds, given the flexibility of the UK legal system it is possible to duplicate the form of a covered bond structure. In this case, HBOS transferred a portfolio of mortgages into a new LLP (UK Limited Liability Partnership) by way of equitable assignment. The LLP then guaranteed the issue by HBOS Treasury Services of the covered bond to third-party investors. In the event that HBOS Treasury Services defaults on the bond, the bond is not accelerated but is defeased over time from

Table 5.1 Covered bonds and Pfandbriefe: European regimes

	Name	Capital weighting	Issuance limits	Collateral
Austria	Pfandbriefe	Pfandbriefe have a 10% capital risk weighting and are Tier One ECB eligible.		Pfandbriefe may be backed by a pool of mortgages (*Hypothekenpfandbriefe*) or by a pool of public sector loan assets (Austrian government or public authority loans and EEA/Switzerland government loans) (*öffentlicher Pfandbriefe*)
Denmark	*Realkreditobligationer*	10% capital weighting.		There is no regime for public sector debt
Finland	Mortgage bonds are known as *kiinteistövakuudellinen joukkovelkakirja*, public sector bonds are known as *julkisyhteisövakuudellinen joukkovelkakirja*			Mortgage banks can issue bonds backed by a pool of mortgages (*kiinteistövakuudellinen joukkovelkakirja*) or bonds backed by a pool of public sector loan assets (*julkisyhteisövakuudellinen joukkovelkakirja*). The maximum LTV for loans to be eligible for the pool is 60%
France	Obligations foncières, or OF issued by *sociétés de crédit foncier*, or SCFs	OFs carry a 10% regulatory capital weighting	The law requires that OFs are overcollateralised by eligible assets in the collateral pool, and sets out rules for the level of overcollateral required	The collateral pool for OF issuance can consist of residential or commercial mortgages or other real estate assets meeting certain criteria, public sector loans or securities, asset-backed securities backed to at least 90% of their value by such mortgages or public sector assets, and other liquid instruments. The Law sets out requirements for the quality of the assets to be acquired (LTVs are restricted to 60%, or 80% where additional collateral is provided)
Germany	Pfandbriefe, which can be issued by German Hypothekenbank (or mortgage banks) under the Mortgage Bank Act or by Landesbank under the Public Sector Pfandbrief Act	10% risk weighting for Pfandbriefe. Since January 1999, Pfandbriefe may be used as Tier One repo collateral with the European Central Bank if they are listed and denominated in Euros	Pfandbriefe issued by mortgage banks are subject to an overall cap on the maximum possible issuance of Pfandbriefe equal to 60 times the banks' capital	Pfandbriefe may be backed by an eligible pool of mortgages (*Hypothekenpfandbriefe*) or by an eligible pool of public sector assets (*öffentlicher Pfandbriefe*). The two pools (mortgages and public sector assets) are segregated into separate registers or *Deckungsstock*. Eligible public sector assets can consist of German government, public authority or Landesbank loans and securities and EEA government loans and securities. Public sector or mortgage assets from the EEA are limited to 10% of the pool in respect of countries where the relevant local

			authorities do not recognise the preferential rights of Pfandbriefe holders on insolvency (as at October 1999 only Austria, Luxembourg, Denmark and France accepted these rights). From 1 July 2002, public sector debt from the US, Canada, Japan, Switzerland, the Czech Republic, Hungary, Poland and Slovakia may also be included in pools (up to the 10% limit where preferential rights are not recognised). A trustee is appointed by the BAKred to supervise substitution in the asset pool. Pfandbriefe issued by mortgage banks are subject to stricter criteria than those issued by the Landesbank, including a maximum 60% LTV for mortgage assets backing mortgage Pfandbriefe
Ireland	Covered bonds	Covered bonds are subject to an overall cap on the maximum possible issuance equal to 50 times the banks' capital	Mortgage bonds issued by mortgage credit institutions may be backed by an eligible pool of mortgages, and public sector bonds issued by public credit institutions may be backed by an eligible pool of public sector assets. The pools can be revolving in nature, with substitution of assets in the pool up to 20% of the pool, and each pool can back multiple issues of covered bonds. Public sector and mortgage assets can come from entities within Ireland, the EEA, the G7, or Switzerland. However, no more than 15% of the collateral pool may consist of assets from non-EEA countries. Covered bonds issued by mortgage banks are subject to a maximum 60% LTV or 75% LTV for residential or commercial mortgage assets respectively (with a maximum of an additional 20% LTV or 5% LTV for residential or commercial mortgage assets respectively financed outside the pool), which must be first mortgages over residential or commercial property. Commercial mortgages are restricted to 10% of the pool
Luxembourg	Bonds backed by a pool of mortgages (*lettres de gage hypothecaires*) or by a pool of public sector loan assets (*lettres de gage publiques*)	*Lettres de gage* carry a 10% regulatory capital weighting	The asset pool can consist of assets from throughout the OECD, EU and EEA For mortgage bonds, the portfolio cannot include mortgages with an LTV in excess of 60% (for commercial or residential property)

continued

Table 5.1 *(cont.)*

	Name	Capital weighting	Issuance limits	Collateral
Spain	*cedulas hipotecarias* (CH) for mortgage assets and *cedulas territoriales* (CT) for public sector assets	The Bank of Spain lowered the capital risk weighting attributed to CH from 20% to 10% in April 2000 CT are risk weighted 10% by the Bank of Spain	Requirements restrict issuance to a maximum of 90% of the eligible amount of the eligible portfolio (for CH) or 70% of the amount of the eligible portfolio (for CT)	For CH, only first mortgages are part of the eligible portfolio, and the portfolio cannot include mortgages with an LTV in excess of 70% (for commercial property) or 80% (for residential property) For CT, eligible assets consist of loans to central governments, local administrations or public sector entities within the EEA
Switzerland	Pfandbriefe			Pfandbriefe may be backed by a pool of mortgages over Swiss land. Public sector Pfandbriefe are not permitted
UK	Covered Bonds	20% risk weighted by FSA	No specific legislation – the HBOS covered bond uses a maximum issuance of 93% of the total loan balance. Also, only the portion of each loan up to a 60% loan-to-indexed-value may be issued against	No specific legislation

proceeds from the collateral pool collected under the guarantee. The proceeds are held in a GIC account pending maturity of the bond and overcollateralisation is included to cover the risk of negative carry to the maturity date of the bond.

The strength of the UK security is evident from the delinked AAA rating awarded to the issue by S&P and Fitch, with Moody's treating the issue structure as giving an eight-notch credit uplift over the issuer's long-term unsecured credit rating. The FSA has accorded UK covered bonds a 20% risk weighting – in line with its risk weighting for covered bonds issued in other European countries. However, as most other European countries accord covered bonds from their own country a 10% risk weighting, and use the weighting in the country of the home regulator for covered bonds issued in other countries, UK covered bonds are less likely to be purchased by investors in continental Europe than other covered bonds.

The bulk (some 80%) of Pfandbriefe issuance is backed by public sector debt rather than mortgage bonds, and the vast majority (around 99%) of Jumbo Pfandbriefe issuance is backed by public sector debt. The Jumbo Pfandbriefe market alone had over Euro 400bn outstanding at the end of 2002.

5.5.1 Differences between covered bonds and ABS

Traditional ABS are off-balance-sheet instruments backed by a pool of assets segregated in an SPV. Covered bonds are not off balance sheet in the same way, and are backed by a changing pool of collateral that remains part of the balance sheet of the issuing institution. They typically have a bullet maturity. In rating covered bonds, the rating agencies are concerned to address two key areas:

- The degree to which any insolvency of the issuer could either attach to the collateral pool, or lead to delays in use of the collateral pool to repay the covered bonds (in other words, the extent to which the collateral pool is bankruptcy remote from the issuer); and
- The credit quality of the collateral pool (and the manner in which it can dynamically change), and level of funding issued against the pool.

5.5.2 Bankruptcy remoteness

In order to address the first concern, covered bonds are subject to a particular legal regime under the legislation that introduced them. This legislation will provide for one of a variety of different solutions which seek to ring-fence the collateral pool from the insolvency of the issuer.

The level of protection varies from jurisdiction to jurisdiction, with France and Ireland being seen as countries with stronger ring-fencing protection for covered bonds, and Spain weaker.

In Germany the collateral pool is divided into two separate pools of public sector assets and mortgage assets, with each of the pools being separated from any insolvency proceedings of the issuer, which is seen as reasonably strong, although Moody's in particular still considers there to be a level of credit-linkage to the issuer credit rating (see "Rating" below).

5.5.3 Collateral pool

The covered bond legislation in each country sets out eligibility requirements for the permitted composition of the collateral pool used to back covered bond issuance. The key requirement for mortgage collateral is usually the maximum LTV on the mortgage loan for it to be eligible for inclusion in the pool. This varies from 60% LTV in Germany and Finland to 80% for residential property in Spain. For public sector collateral, the restriction is typically geographic, with limits to OECD or EEA public sector assets, and in many cases the proportion of these assets which originate outside the country of the issuer is also restricted (e.g. to 10% of the pool in Germany).

In Luxembourg, the pool can consist entirely of non-Luxembourg OECD assets (which has raised the possibility of arbitrage issuance against lower credit rated OECD public sector assets under the covered bond umbrella).

In some cases, the level of issuance against the collateral pool is restricted to provide overcollateral for the issuance. For example, in Spain, issuance volume cannot exceed 90% of the amount of the collateral pool (for mortgages) or 70% of the collateral pool (for public sector assets).

In the HBOS covered bond issue in the UK, the maximum issuance is 93% of the total loan balance at any point in time. In addition, although loans of any LTV may be included in the pool, only the portion of the loan up to a 60% loan-to-indexed-value may be issued against. Thus overcollateralisation would be the greater of 7% and the amount required to reduce all loans to a 60% loan-to-indexed-value. Additional over-collateralisation will be included to cover potential set-off risk and negative carry.

5.5.4 Capital weighting

As full recourse on-balance-sheet instruments, covered bond issues do not serve to reduce the amount of capital which the issuer is obliged to hold against its risk-weighted assets.

Due to their low risk profile, however, covered bonds benefit from a low-risk weighting as assets held by investors in some countries. Covered bonds are 10% weighted in Austria, Denmark, France, Germany, Luxembourg and Spain, and 20% weighted in the UK.

German mortgage banks in particular have lobbied the Basel Committee to retain the 10% risk weighting for covered bonds under the new Basel capital proposals, rather than the 20% weighting for highly credit rated bank or ABS issues (although in any event they will lose a degree of comparative advantage against other issues if the Basel proposals come in and give highly rated issues a 20% weighting).

5.5.5 Spreads

Covered bonds are typically issued as fixed rated bonds.

Spreads on covered bonds are consistently tighter than asset-backed deals with the same ratings, reflecting their greater liquidity, their long history (in Germany), their lack of prepayment risk (as they are typically structured on a bullet basis) and their lower capital risk weighting.

This has enabled covered bonds to act as an effective funding mechanism for low yielding assets such as public sector loans (which might generate a negative return if they were securitised). The volume of issuance in this area (particularly for Jumbo Pfandbriefe) and the cheap funding rates on issuance has also led to increasing arbitrage issuance, taking the form of a directional interest rate play. Thus, if German public sector Schuldscheine are trading inside the Jumbo Pfandbriefe curve, issuers may originate public sector debt in volume and warehouse it pending a downward shift in the yield curve (enabling issuance at a positive spread). Alternately, they may pre-fund and put the proceeds on deposit as collateral backing the issuance, then buy in Schuldscheine subsequently when rates have gone up.

Covered bonds will generally trade near to swaps, at a small (2-5 bps) discount (for shorter maturities) or premium (for longer dated maturities), although spreads on German Pfandbriefe in particular have widened out recently with the credit deterioration of German banks.

5.5.6 Rating

Rating of covered bonds depends on a composite view of the strength of the rating of the issuer and the rating of the collateral pool; neither can be used solely – the issuer may be less relevant in jurisdictions with stronger insolvency ring-fencing, and more relevant in other jurisdictions. The credit of the collateral pool may change with the ability to dynamically substitute the pool.

Moody's takes a more linked approach to issuer credit rating in looking at covered bonds than Standard & Poor's or Fitch. From 2003, Moody's links Pfandbrief ratings to the issuer rating, but with a floor of Aa2 (public sector Pfandbrief) or Aa3 (mortgage Pfandbrief) for investment grade issuers.

The three agencies have a strong view of covered bonds from France and Ireland, and a weaker view of the protections offered by the Spanish legislation. For Spanish covered bonds, they will typically only permit the issue to be rated up to two rating notches above the credit rating of the issuer as they are not regarded as being truly ring-fenced. This is due to the potential for delays to be suffered in realising payment on the covered bonds if insolvency occurs, as the covered bonds simply have priority claims in insolvency over the assets of the bank.

UK covered bonds have been awarded a delinked rating by Standard & Poor's and Fitch, with Moody's treating the issue structure as giving an eight-notch credit uplift over the issuer's long-term unsecured credit rating.

5.6 FUTURE FLOWS

Future flows deals bear a superficial similarity to whole business deals, as they are reliant on amounts not yet contracted to repay the funding raised. In future flows, however, only a specific asset pool is sold (albeit some of this pool is to be generated in the future) rather than the general cash flow of the business. Security is not required, as a true sale of the current and future receivables is usually used (in some jurisdictions, this may necessitate that periodic legal documentation is executed effecting transfer of future receivables as and when they arise).

These are not true asset-backed structures, as the investors are dependent on the continued generation by the originator of new receivables on a periodic basis in order to repay the funding. In other words, the transaction is not entirely self-liquidating from the receivables which are in existence on Day 1.

Insolvency of the originator will generally prevent the originator from continuing to generate the receivables, and a failure to generate sufficient receivables in its business to cover interest and principal payments on the funding will leave investors exposed to an unsecured credit risk on the originator. There is thus the risk that the backing for the deal could disappear and, consequently, the deals are linked in some way to the credit rating of the originator.

The main benefit of future flows deals is to circumvent sovereign ceilings (see Chapter 2, section 2.1.18) by trapping cash flow outside the country, and hence achieve an arbitrage between the rating of the originator and the rating of the sovereign. They are therefore useful in countries like Turkey, with strong corporates but a weak sovereign rating. Trapping cash flow is achieved by directing the correspondent banks (in a workers remittance deal), the credit card clearers (VISA or Mastercard) (in a card voucher deal – see section 5.2.3 above) or the customers (in an export receivables deal) to make payment direct to an offshore account in the name of the SPV where the cash can be trapped in hard currency.

Deals are structured with the annual debt service covered 4× or 5× by the annual future flows stream, in order to ensure that the deal can be wound down fairly rapidly if problems are encountered, by fast amortisation of the bonds from all cash flows coming in.

5.6.1 Credit analysis

The stability of the perceived future level of business generation is crucial in analysing future flows deals.

A detailed analysis of the originator is also essential. In the event that the future flows deal involves the pledge of significant income streams by the originator, this may prejudice the ability of the originator to service other (e.g. unsecured) debt, or general operating expenses, leading to a default by the originator.

Key information

● Asset cover ratio (gross level of receipts generated versus interest cover and total debt service).

In rating future flows transactions, Standard & Poor's will generally limit the rating to the local currency rating of the originator. Moody's will analyse the fundamental importance of the originator's field of business to the economy of the country to determine the likelihood of performance continuing regardless of originator insolvency (although the originator's local currency rating is still important). Fitch considers that the originator local currency rating may act as a ceiling, but it may be possible to rate a deal above this level.

5.7 NON-PERFORMING LOANS

Structures for the securitisation of non-performing loans vary significantly with the specific asset type of the loan. Common asset classes which have been securitised in this way are non-performing mortgages (e.g. in Italy) and non-performing loans backed by real estate (e.g. in Japan). Both these types of loan benefit from the security backing them, with the consequence that much of the structure and rating analysis for these deals focuses on procedures and timing for the enforcement of the loan or mortgage security, and consequent sale of the secured residential or commercial real estate.

At the most basic level then, the structure needs to ensure, as with a performing mortgage or real estate transaction, that the SPV can take all the necessary steps to enforce the security and realise value from the property. This may entail registration of the SPV as mortgagee and the payment of transfer or registration taxes. In most cases, however, given that problem loans typically become systemic in a bad recession or asset price collapse, in areas where there are significant regulatory or tax hurdles it is relatively common to find that the government will set up a short- or medium-term regime designed to deal with some of these transaction costs and hurdles.

For example, Law 130 on securitisation in Italy (which provides for a simplified transfer regime without requiring registration of the SPV transferee as mortgagee) has been subject to amendments which specifically address the risk that the SPV might not have full beneficial enforcement rights to the mortgage security, and set out a beneficial loss-accounting regime for Italian institutions which engaged in securitisation within 2 years after the law came into force. In Japan and Thailand, specific legislation on funds was passed to enable overseas investors to invest in real estate, and revive the local moribund real estate markets, by offering them tax incentives. In Korea, KAMCO has been active in securitisation of non-performing assets, and has made use of the Korean ABS and MBS laws.

Valuations and rating analysis of property-backed loan portfolios requires a significant degree of due diligence – as the borrower has already defaulted, the property is the only way that realisation of value can be guaranteed.

For the same reason, an analysis of the level of liquidity and demand in the local property market may be required.

For unsecured non-performing transactions, such as the INPS deal for the Italian government in November 1999, realisation of value to a rated standard can prove much harder. In that transaction, comfort is derived from the state backing behind the collection authority (itself a state entity) and the significant level of overcollateralisation contained in the deal – of the entire collateral pool of Euro 42.3bn, rated notes were only issued against the top 11% (although that achieved an AAA rating from four rating agencies).

Ensuring that the servicer is properly motivated to perform its role efficiently and to consider all options for resolution is essential. Pools which have been bought off the originator by a third party at a discount are likely to be serviced thoroughly and rapidly. If the purchaser is servicing the pool themselves, they will seek to prove out their purchase price and realise equity as quickly as possible, while if they have employed a third party special servicer (a servicer that specialises in the collection of non-performing assets) they will incentivise them with fee payments and contractual terms which reward overachievement. Consequently, investors are likely to have more confidence in the performance of any bond structured against such a pool.

By way of contrast, where an originator structures a deal off its own book, the customer base in the pool is likely to reflect the residual customer base of the originator, and strong enforcement tactics used in these areas may damage other areas of the originator's ongoing business or customer relations. Consequently, investors may feel that the originator as servicer is not motivated to act in investors' interests, and have less confidence in the eventual outcome of the collection process. Furthermore, transactions put together by an originator off its own book will not have been subjected to market bidding to fix a price for the pool. To the extent that the originator has not fully written down its position in the loan pool to a market benchmark value, the originator will be motivated to ensure that recoveries are maximised in order to prevent any further write-downs impacting its balance sheet. This can also reduce the volume of transactions going through the real estate market where the problem is systemic – for example, banks may continue to hold loans at levels based on out-of-date valuations, and be reluctant to sell property backing one loan at current prices as they may then have to provision other loans based on the new price benchmark set.

Servicing strategies are likely to include:

- Court proceedings – enforcement against, and sale of, secured assets;
- Real estate owned (REO) strategies involving bidding for foreclosed real estate at auction in order to acquire a free title and realise greater value, as court auctions may be badly publicised or attended and yield levels below market;
- Negotiated settlements or discounted pay-offs (DPOs), which provide the borrower with a discount for timely payment;
- Property swaps to take the secured property from the borrower by agreement, in return for debt forgiveness;
- Onward sale of parts of the portfolio which are unlikely to realise significant value, or which are outside the scope of the main skills of the servicer to collect.

Cash flows from a non-performing transaction are likely to be lumpy in nature, as the process of negotiating settlements and court enforcement will not permit exact timing predictions. Consequently, liquidity lines may be required, both for payment of senior level interest to investors on securities issued, and for payment of the expenses of collection, which necessarily pre-date enforcement receipts. Liquidity lines for non-performing deals are often structured in the form of a servicer advance facility, whereby the servicer will advance cash for collection expenses, and subsequently recover it from the proceeds of collection (together with interest on their initial advance).

Cash flows are also likely to need interest rate hedging. The cash flows coming from a non-performing portfolio are clearly subject to a potentially wide degree of variance. Interest rate fluctuations may indirectly affect quantum of realisations (for example, where they affect activity and pricing in the secondary market for real estate), but there is unlikely to be any provable correlation. The financing for the pool is likely to be floating rate, due to the possibility of break costs on fixed rate financing resulting from the uncertainty of timing of receipts, and financing costs are therefore likely to rise as interest rates increase (which would also make the quantum of realisation correlation inverse, as an increase in interest rates would cause the property market and realisations to fall, as financing costs rise).

Generally interest rate caps are likely to be the most appropriate hedge. Due again to the uncertainty of timing of receipts, the amortisation schedule for the securities will be uncertain, and a swap set at the expected amortisation level could leave the portfolio underhedged or overhedged as amortisation fluctuates – with the resultant two-way payments under the swap reintroducing interest rate risk into the transaction on the hedge mismatch. A cap can be fixed at the most conservative recovery scenario, leaving the portfolio either correctly hedged (if collections are slow) or overhedged (but given that the payments are one-way, without interest rate implications for the transaction).

5.7.1 Credit analysis

The likely recoveries from a portfolio of non-performing loans are determined by an assessment of:

- How much will be recovered on each loan;
- When the recovery will be received.

The recovery amount can be quantified by reference to the collateral value and fore-closure process for secured loans, and to historic recoveries levels on similar positions for unsecured loans.

Time to recovery can similarly be quantified for secured loans by the likely length of foreclosure proceedings, with unsecured loans tracked off historic time to recovery.

Key information

- Gross book value (GBV) of portfolio
- Net book value (NBV) of portfolio after provisions to date by the originator
- Sale price of portfolio, if acquired by a third party from the originator
- Collateral
- Valuations
- Historic recovery experience (timing, level of recoveries, and degree of expertise)
- Local legal process on foreclosures.

In rating non-performing loan transactions, the rating agencies are likely to apply similar approaches to determination of loss severity as those used for the relevant class of performing assets, although the approach will be more developed and detailed, as it forms a greater part of the final rating levels. By way of contrast, little analysis is done of default rates, as in most cases the default level will be assumed to be 100% given the non-performing nature of the assets.

In rating non-performing loans backed by real estate, Fitch are likely to require a lock-out on payments to junior equity classes until the senior classes have paid down (see Fitch *Securitizing Distressed Real Estate*, 9 April 1999, pp. 5–6). They may cap the amount of investment grade debt that can be achieved against non-performing loans relative to the appraised asset value of the loans, and/or against the price at which the loans trade in the market.

5.8 REAL ESTATE INVESTMENT TRUSTS

REITs, or Real Estate Investment Trusts, are a US invention. They are a form of closed-end fund which invests in real estate and real estate related assets (e.g. RMBS and CMBS), and enjoys certain tax benefits. In their original form in the US, they are exempt from corporation tax provided that they meet requirements set out in the US Tax Code (including requirements as to the distribution of net income to investors).

They have subsequently been copied in other jurisdictions, notably Japan and Singapore. To date there has been relatively little focus on the product in Europe, although Europe has instead seen extensive use of the covered bond product (see section 5.5 and Table 5.1).

European REITs exist in Belgium (in the form of FBIs), France (in the form of *societés d'investissements immobiliers cotées* (SIIC)) and the Netherlands (in the form of *societes d'investissement à capital fixé en immobilier* (SICAFI)).

5.8.1 Japanese REIT

The Japanese REIT, or J-REIT, was brought into being by amendments to the Investment Trust Law (The Law Relating to Investment Trusts and Investment Corporations) in effect from November 2000. The amendments permit an investment trust or investment company to invest directly in real estate (prior to the amendment they were restricted to investing primarily in securities), and to act as an ongoing investor in real estate.

The J-REIT will carry tax benefits and will be restricted in the activities it can carry out. The J-REIT must outsource all its activities, and must appoint an investment manager to manage its assets. The investment manager will be required to avoid entering into transactions that could give rise to a conflict of interest. The potential for conflicts of interest (and lack of historical track record for most managers) is a key area of concern for rating agencies.

The Tokyo Stock Exchange published listing rules for J-REIT corporations in early 2001, requiring that:

- Property must constitute at least 75% of the portfolio of a J-REIT and that the remaining 25% must constitute cash or equivalent.
- The majority of the investment portfolio must consist of long-term investments in cash-generating properties.
- An independent real estate valuer must appraise asset values on acquisition and sale.
- Major transactions must be disclosed when booked.

Property registration and acquisition taxes are reduced under the J-REIT provisions. J-REITs will also be permitted to deduct dividends against income for corporation tax purposes provided that they distribute more than 90% of earnings to shareholders as dividends (which may give rise to requirements for liquidity facilities for the J-REIT). J-REITs will not be free of tax on contributions of assets to the J-REIT in the manner of the UPREIT in the US (to which assets can be contributed at book value without triggering a tax charge), which may generate capital gains tax charges for originators.

5.8.2 Singapore REIT

The Singapore REIT, or S-REIT, was updated with guidelines published by the MAS on 28 March 2003, which enable them to borrow up to 35% of their assets, and to borrow in excess of 35% if all their debt is rated at least single A. S-REITs may invest in property outside Singapore.

5.8.3 Other developments

In Hong Kong on 30 July 2003, the Securities and Future Commission published a code which proposes the establishment of REITs, shares in which could be sold to retail investors. The REIT must be listed on the Hong Kong Stock Exchange, and may only invest in Hong Kong real estate. They may hold real estate through SPV holding companies. At least 90% of the net income of such a REIT must be distributed. They may borrow up to 35% of their gross assets.

In Taiwan, the draft Real Estate Securitisation Act provides for the establishment of REIT-style trusts, which would be exempt from certain land taxes.

5.9 REPACKAGINGS

Unlike securitisation transactions, where generally only a single transaction is carried out through an SPV, SPVs used for repackagings are often established to carry out several transactions as a method of reducing the individual transaction costs and the length of time required to carry out a transaction. Furthermore, repackagings are generally required to be completed far more rapidly than securitisations, in order to meet individual investor requirements. These factors mean that far more of the administrative and other functions to be carried out by the SPV are in fact carried out by the bank that has established the SPV and acts as arranger or underwriter of the instruments issued by the SPV. This raises concerns as to whether the SPV is tax resident in the jurisdiction of the arranging bank for profits tax purposes. For example, in the UK corporation tax is levied on non-resident companies on the profits of a UK branch or agency which is a UK representative of the company. Although investment managers providing services in the ordinary course of business for a market remuneration are excluded from being UK representatives, this exemption may not be available where the bank is also managing the SPV's liabilities (that is, its funding), a function not usually carried out by an investment manager.

The services carried out for the SPV could also raise the possibility that the SPV would be consolidated on the accounting or capital adequacy balance sheet of the arranging bank, as some jurisdictions may require consolidation for accounting or capital purposes of entities that are directly or indirectly controlled by another entity.

If an SPV is being used for multiple transactions, some method will need to be found to ensure that the costs and expenses of the SPV can be met on an ongoing basis. Any such method will need to be tax efficient and should not be classified as support of the SPV in a way that could consolidate the SPV with the party covering the expenses (for example, indemnities to the SPV or the directors of the SPV may cause accounting issues under FRS 5 in the UK, and recurrent expense payments may cause off-balance-sheet issues under regulatory capital guidelines). Methods typically used include the up-front provision of an expense fund (sized to cover programme expenses over the life of the programme) by way of a subordinated loan, the provision of expenses on a trade-by-trade basis through adjustment of the price of a swap or other derivative used for the trade, or the use of excess spread.

If an SPV is making multiple issues of securities where one or more of the issues carry a credit rating and not all issues have the same credit rating, requirements of the rating agencies with regard to the ring-fencing of one series from another series will need to be met, in order not to taint the rating of the higher-rated issues with that of the lower-rated or unrated issues. These requirements mean that effective limited recourse language must be incorporated in the documentation for each trade to limit the recourse of investors to the underlying assets for that trade, and that security over the relevant underlying assets should be granted to a trustee for the investors so that the assets cannot be attached by investors under other trades.

The structure of a typical ring-fenced repackaging programme is shown in Figure 5.5.

A related concern may arise as to whether or not the SPV is bankruptcy remote, given the possibility of a shortfall in provision for expenses. This may lead the directors of the SPV to ask for an indemnity against the risk of a technical insolvency, unless they can be reassured that there are sufficient provision for expenses. Provision of such an indemnity may again give rise to accounting or capital consolidation issues for the repackaging institution.

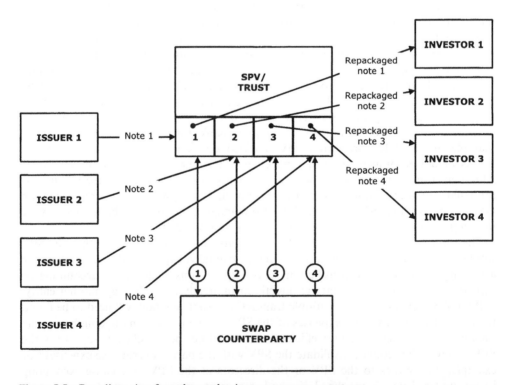

Figure 5.5   Paradigm ring-fenced repackaging programme structure

The successful creation of a security interest in the assets underlying a repackaging trade will depend on the nature of the assets. For bond repackaging, one of the main concerns will be as to whether the bonds are held in a clearing system or whether they are held directly in material form by a custodian.

The legal analysis of the rights of different parties in intermediate securities (securities where some kind of certificate has been issued but the certificate is held by an intermediary such as a custodian) and dematerialised securities (securities where there are no certificates) is complex and not fully resolved. Attempts have however been made to address the issues in the US through the introduction of the revised Article 8 of the UCC, and in the EU through the Settlement Finality Directive of 1998 and the Financial Collateral Directive of 2002 (see Chapter 11, section 11.4.9).

In the UK, the UKLA Listing Rules set out minimum disclosure requirements for the listing of issues on the London Stock Exchange where the underlying assets relate to obligations of 10 or fewer obligors, or where an obligor accounts for 10% or more of the assets. These may cause difficulty for black box issues where it is intended that limited disclosure be given of the underlying assets.

Due to the fact that swaps in repackaging structures are often arranged by the bank that establishes the structure, the bank will often be more concerned with the protection of the rights of the swap provider than in a standard securitisation. This will generally lead to the swap provider ranking equally with, or ahead of, the investors in the event that it becomes necessary to enforce against the underlying bonds. If the notes issued to investors are credit rated, the rating agencies will generally only permit the swap provider to rank ahead of investors if the enforcement is due to a default on the underlying bonds (see Chapter 2, section 2.3.5), although for credit-independent events (such as a change of tax law) the swap provider may rank equally with investors.

5.10 RESIDENTIAL MORTGAGE-BACKED SECURITIES

Mortgage transactions generally divide into:

- Prime issuance
- Sub-prime or non-conforming issuance
- Master trust issuance
- Reverse mortgages.

The sub-prime market comprises credits where there are some negative credit characteristics such as arrears, while the non-conforming market comprises credits with unusual characteristics such as self-certification of income (e.g. self-employed individuals). In practice, the two pieces of terminology are often used interchangeably. The US, the UK and (more recently) Australia are the only significant sub-prime mortgage markets to develop to date, although a form of negative equity mortgage (effectively, an unsecured consumer loan to the extent it exceeds 100% LTV) has been seen in Hong Kong.

The master trust structure provides for the transfer of a large pool of collateral into a trust to back multiple series of issuance, allowing the issuance of tranched soft bullet MBS, including MBS with legal final maturities shorter than the maturity of the mortgages within the pool, by diverting principal receipts from the entire pool to each bullet class in the accumulation period running up to its maturity. Investors are effectively backed by a revolving pool of assets due to the relatively higher levels of substitution in such a portfolio. In the UK, master trust structures for mortgages have been used since the Mound Financing series from the Bank of Scotland was first issued in April 2000.

Reverse mortgages (also known as equity release mortgages) are products designed for older or retired borrowers as a means of extracting value from their houses. A roll-up mortgage loan is advanced at a low LTV (25–30%), which accretes in value against the property until the death of the borrower (or earlier prepayment on sale of the property). As zero coupon assets, deals backed by these mortgages rely on large liquidity lines to service interest for the first few years of the deal.

Fundamental to any mortgage securitisation is the need to transfer the mortgage security interest effectively to the SPV, in order to enable the SPV to enforce the interest against individual debtors in the event of non-payment. This may give rise to a require-ment to register mortgage transfers at the relevant land registry, which may lead to administrative complexities and fee costs. In order to be protected against the loss of property value that would result from any event that damages or destroys the property, the transfer of general property insurances over the properties is also important. In addition, in some markets the use of pool policies or MIG policies by originators to cover losses on a pool is prevalent as a form of credit protection for a pool of mortgages prior to any securitisation. Where the insurer carries a high credit rating, this may in turn form a valuable component of the transaction credit enhancement if the rights to claim against the pool insurer can be properly transferred. Pool insurance was a feature of many UK mortgage securitisations prior to the recession and property price falls of the early 1990s, and is still used in Australian transactions.

There may also be government concerns with consumer issues relating to the proper management of the mass transfer of mortgages (typically the largest and most signifi-cant financial commitment of many people during their life) to offshore SPVs, which can manifest themselves in different ways.

The range of mortgage products, with differing interest and principal payment struc-tures, may necessitate complex interest rate hedging requirements, depending on the nature of the market for ABS issuance, and may mean that an issue needs to be split up into different tranches relating to different products. In the US, many mortgages are fixed rate, but the market for fixed rate pass-through mortgage bonds has developed, thus reducing requirements for hedging as fixed rate bonds may be issued to finance the mortgages.

In most other markets, floating rate bonds are prevalent. In Hong Kong, a limited range of mortgage products is on offer (which are, almost without exception, floating or variable rate based on HIBOR or Hong Kong Prime). In the UK, more complex structures have developed to cover fixed rate and floating rate mortgages, as well as deferred rate products, stabilised rate products, repayment and endowment mortgage structures and more recent products such as flexible mortgages. Consequently:

- Fixed rate products will generally be hedged with caps.
- Floating (or variable) rate mortgages will rely on the calculation of a minimum floor or "threshold interest margin" for the rate the originator charges on its variable rate mortgage portfolio (this rate will continue to affect the securitised

mortgages unless and until the right of the originator to set the rate for the securitised pool is specifically terminated).
- Deferred or stabilised rate products may rely on a reserve fund created at the start of a transaction, which is used to fund any roll-up in the amount of deferred or stabilised rate mortgages due to the operation of the initial low rate (for deferred rate mortgages) or the stabilisation calculation (for stabilised rate mortgages).
- Flexible mortgages may use a revolving credit line to cover redrawing.

The mortgage documentation in simpler products may contain other additions, such as the provision for further advances to be made by the originator to the mortgagor in certain circumstances (in some cases, these may be mandatory further advances which the originator is required to advance). The transfer of the mortgages must be effected in such a way that the originator can continue to make such advances without them being unsecured (due to the fact that the mortgage security interest has been transferred to the SPV). Protection for investors may also be needed in the form of a committed facility to cover the making of any mandatory further advances, as in the event that these are not made by the originator, the individual debtor could otherwise attempt to withhold payments on the mortgage due to the breach of the requirement on the originator to make the advance. Concerns as to the ability to "tack" the further advance under the same security interest at a senior level may also be relevant if further advances are to be bought by the SPV.

Mortgages may carry tax reliefs for individuals, often used by the local government to stimulate the local property market or to incentivise home ownership. In the UK for example, prior to its abolition on 6 April 2000, MIRAS (or mortgage interest relief at source) allowed UK individuals tax relief on mortgage interest payments by a deduction at source mechanism. Thus, any transfer of the mortgages had to be effected in such a way that claims for the tax relief were not impaired. In the UK this historically necessitated the use of a UK SPV as purchaser of the mortgage loans who was established as a "qualifying lender" for the purpose of the MIRAS legislation, and led to the Inland Revenue requirement that the beneficial interest in mortgage loans where MIRAS was being claimed were not divided among two or more people (making it difficult to use a receivables trust as a profit strip mechanism for residential mortgage deals).

Prepayment risk has a significant effect on mortgages. In many countries, individuals have a relatively unfettered right to make prepayments on a property mortgage at any time. In particular, in most jurisdictions, a mortgage loan is prepaid in full each time that an individual moves house. The resultant prepayment risk and reinvestment risk may require a careful analysis of the weighted average life and constant prepayment rate (see below), and the use of GICs to protect against reinvestment risk within the transaction during an interest period (see Chapter 2, sections 2.3.3 and 2.3.4).

Levels of prepayment are generally modelled from a constant prepayment rate, or CPR, which is an assumed percentage rate of prepayment each year, as a percentage of the principal balance of receivables outstanding at the start of the year, less scheduled principal payments over the year. The US uses standardised prepayment speeds based on 100% PSA, which is a prepayment rate of 0.2% CPR, increasing by 0.2% CPR every month until it reaches 6% CPR after 30 months, and then remaining flat at 6% CPR. The other standardised speeds are multiples of 100% PSA (e.g. 200% PSA

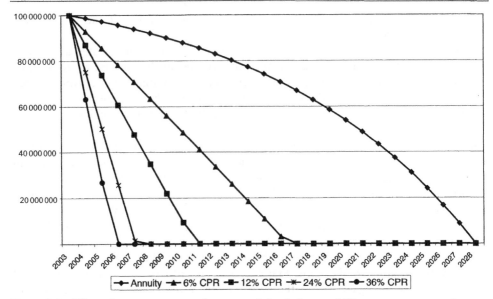

Figure 5.6 Effect of prepayment speeds on remaining balance of 25-year mortgage pool

assumes a prepayment rate of 0.4% CPR, increasing by 0.4% CPR every month until it reaches 12% CPR after 30 months, and then remaining flat at 12% CPR).

The effect of these different prepayment speeds can be seen in Figure 5.6, which compares an annuity-style paydown (i.e. no prepayments) with different levels of constant prepayment speed.

5.10.1   Credit analysis

Mortgage deals are analysed by reference to the characteristics of the borrower pool, and the value achievable from the collateral for the loans.

Key information

- Conforming/non-conforming borrowers
- Reason for loans (purchase, buy-to-let, second home, etc.)
- Income multiple
- Prior arrears
- Seasoning
- LTV
- Location/geographic diversity of properties.

In rating mortgage transactions, Standard & Poor's compares the mortgage pool to a benchmark pool exhibiting certain common characteristics as to LTV, underwriting, geographic concentration and seasoning. For the UK (see Standard & Poor's *Credit-Week*, 29 March 1993, pp. 73–77 and Standard & Poor's *Revised Criteria*, 5 July 2001), the benchmark is a minimum of 300 loans which are geographically diverse, with not more than 80% LTV ratios and a maximum loan size of 2.5× the borrower's income. The benchmark is set differently for each market – for example the benchmark LTV ratio for Hong Kong is 70% (see Standard & Poor's *Structured Finance Asia 1997*, pp. 32–33).

For this benchmark, a certain default frequency (ranging from 15% for an AAA rating down to 6% for a BBB rating in the UK (12% down to 4% under the *Revised Criteria* of July 2001) or 15% down to 8% in Hong Kong and a certain loss severity (ranging from 47.8% for an AAA rating down to 31.5% for a BBB rating in the UK (not expressly stated in the new criteria) or 71% down to 54% in Hong Kong) are assumed.

Loss severity levels are predicated on property market value declines of 37% for an AAA rating down to 24% for a BBB rating in the UK (47% down to 30% (the south of the UK) or 25% to 16% (the north of the UK) under the new criteria) (or 60% down to 48% in Hong Kong).

These initial figures are then analysed by reference to characteristics in the pool, which vary from the benchmark (with adjustments up or down depending on the weighted average value of certain key attributes of the pool), and to other characteristics of the transaction, in order to come up with default frequency (weighted average foreclosure frequency, or WAFF) and loss severity (weighted average loss severity, or WALS) figures for the transaction, the product of which forms the basic floor level of credit enhancement for the transaction (which therefore varies from 7.2% for an AAA rating to 1.9% for a BBB rating under the old criteria in the UK, or 10.6% for an AAA rating down to 4.3% for a BBB rating in Hong Kong).

Defaults are assumed to occur at Month 1, Month 13 and Month 25 for cash flow modelling, with recoveries assumed to be received 18 months later. The model is stressed at different interest rate and prepayment rate levels.

Moody's compares the mortgage pool to a benchmark pool exhibiting certain common characteristics – for the UK, a minimum of 300 loans which are geographically diverse, with a maximum of 2× to 3× the borrower's income (see Moody's *Approach to Rating UK Residential Mortgage-Backed Securities*, April 1998, p. 4). For this benchmark, the pool is subdivided into buckets of different LTV ratios which are indicative of the level of home-owner equity in the property, and the benchmark credit enhancement for the pool is determined by the average benchmark credit enhancement level for each such LTV ratio (ranging from 17.32% for 100% LTV, through 8.48% for 80% LTV to 2.5% for 55% LTV at an AAA rating level), weighted by reference to the principal amount of the pool in each bucket. A loan-by-loan analysis is also carried out on the product of the expected default frequency on a loan and the anticipated loss severity to give credit enhancement figures. Initial figures are then analysed by reference to other characteristics in the pool that vary from the benchmark, and to other characteristics of the transaction.

Fitch determines indicative credit enhancement levels by a loan-by-loan analysis (see Fitch *UK Mortgage Default Model*, 15 April 1996, pp. 4 and 10) of the product of the expected default frequency on a loan (the level of which is set by reference to the value of the home-owner's equity in the property and the amount of the mortgage loan as a multiple of annual income, giving an 11% to 18% range at different loan multiples at an 80% LTV for an AAA rating in the UK) and the anticipated loss severity on the loan (determined on the basis of the LTV ratio, enforcement costs and assumed property market value declines of around 40% for an AAA level down to around 25% for a BBB level in the UK), to give figures for the base credit enhancement on a loan, which are then aggregated on a weighted average basis across the pool.

5.11 TRADE RECEIVABLES

Trade receivables relate to payments by businesses for goods or services on trade credit. Contractual documentation is therefore less formal than for other mortgages or leases, and typically consists of standard terms of business which are incorporated by reference in each shipment or supply. Where the receivables relate to export supplies, it is likely that some of the receivables will be backed by letters of credit issued by the exporter's or importer's bank (known as a buyer credit where payment is made by the issuing bank to the buyer for onward transmission to the seller, and as a seller credit where payment is made by the issuing bank to the seller direct). The letters of credit are a form of credit protection for the seller, as the creditworthiness of the issuing bank is likely to be better than that of the importer. The letters of credit may therefore form part of the credit analysis of the receivables, in which case it will be important to try to trap the cash flows arising from them. Chapter 13 contains analysis of:

- Letters of credit (including documentary credits and standby credits)
- Bills of exchange
- General trade financing terminology such as CIF, FOB and INCOTERMS.

Trade receivables are short-term in nature and non-interest bearing. The ideal form of matched funding for these receivables is therefore commercial paper issued at a discount, where the amount of funding required can be adjusted rapidly and easily. As the receivables are short-term, trade receivables deals are revolving in nature, with regular replenishment of receivables. Generally, trade receivables structures set a specified end date for the last purchases under the transaction, but otherwise allow continual purchases unless and until an early amortisation event occurs (see Chapter 4, section 4.3.2). Continual purchases mean that the systems of the originator have to be up to regular calculations and reporting requirements. It may also necessitate a mechanism for dealing with receivables that are sold to the SPV but turn out not to meet the eligibility criteria for receivables, as there may not be sufficient time to establish if all sold receivables meet the criteria prior to transfer. Generally this is dealt with by a downward adjustment of the purchase price to remove the ineligible receivables from the calculation, rather than by the repurchase requirements that exist for mortgages and other receivables, due to the short-term nature of the receivables, with collections on the unfunded ineligible receivables being passed direct to the originator.

Figure 5.7 shows the Day 1 structure of a typical trade receivables conduit structure.

This use of commercial paper funding gives rise to liquidity risk in the structure in the event that periodic rollover of the commercial paper is unsuccessful. Often the rating agencies for a conduit structure will expect 100% coverage of the maturing face value of the commercial paper by a liquidity facility. In turn, this may lead to discussions on the appropriate definition for the "borrowing base" for the facility, so that the liquidity banks can be sure that they will not be subject to an adverse capital adequacy treatment on their participation in the facility (which would be the case if the facility was con-

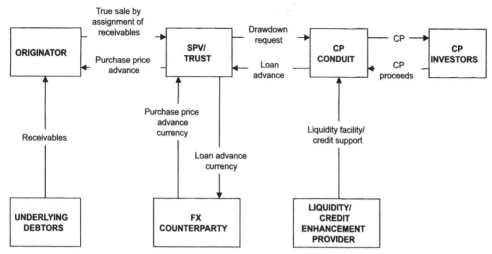

Figure 5.7 Trade receivables/CP conduit structure: Day 1

sidered to provide credit enhancement). The borrowing base is the maximum amount that may be drawn under the facility from time to time. It is a dynamic figure, and is designed to ensure that drawings only assist liquidity problems and do not provide credit enhancement by being set by reference to receivables which are not in default. On some occasions, however, it may be set wider than this and provide a full or partial wrap to CP investors – for example, the "look-back" style of borrowing base, which ensures full CP coverage by basing drawings against defaulted receivables as shown in the previous periodic report on the basis of which CP was issued.

Conduit structures which incorporate an option to switch issuance from US commercial paper to Eurocommercial paper may also include a swingline facility that is used to bridge the two-day settlement gap between same day availability of funds against issuance in the US-CP market and spot availability of funds against issuance in the Euro-CP market.

The rollover of a typical trade receivables conduit structure is illustrated at Figure 5.8.

As the underlying receivables contract in an export transaction is between parties in two different jurisdictions, in the absence of an express choice of governing law in the contract and in the absence of the exporter insisting on the same governing law across all its contracts, different receivables may be governed by different governing laws. This may necessitate investigation under the laws relating to transfers of receivables in a wide range of jurisdictions in order to ensure that the receivables pool has been properly transferred under all relevant legal systems.

5.11.1 Credit analysis

The risk of a trade receivables deal can be analysed by reference to historic levels of:

- Write-offs
- Delinquencies
- Dilutions (i.e. reductions in invoices due to rebates, etc.).

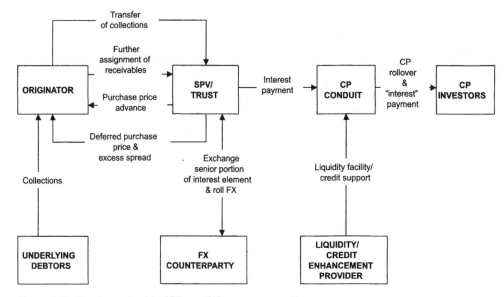

Figure 5.8   Trade receivables/CP conduit structure: rollover

In rating trade receivables transactions, Standard & Poor's applies stress factor multiples to the quantum of losses embedded in the pool (as demonstrated by the highest rolling 3-month average historic loss and dilution levels over the last year) to determine the initial indicative level of credit enhancement (see Standard & Poor's *Trade Receivable Criteria*, 1999, p. 23). Stress factor multiples typically vary from 2.5× (for an AAA rating) to 1.5× (for **BBB** rating). A floor level of enhancement may also be set, calculated on the assumption of a certain number of debtor defaults, based on the creditworthiness of the underlying debtors.

Moody's examine historic data, but base their credit enhancement levels off a detailed examination of the originator, its business position and other factors relevant to the pool (see Moody's *Trade Receivables Update: Concentrating on Dilution – Focus on Capital Goods and Consumer Products Receivables*, 17 January 1996, p. 1).

5.12   WHOLE BUSINESS SECURITISATION

Whole business securitisations, or WBS, are a hybrid form of securitisation falling somewhere between secured corporate debt and future flows style transactions. Many have centred around assets in the form of real estate, such as pubs or hospitals, meaning that they also resemble CMBS.

Probably the most significant difference to other forms of ABS concerns the level of operating risk taken by investors in the deal. Future flows have a level of protection from operating risk, in the specific pledge of future cash flows and the fact that debt is amortised from these cash flows in priority to payment of operating expenses of the issuer. Corporate bonds have full exposure to the operating risk of the company.

Whole business deals need to allow the payment of operating expenses prior to debt service as, by definition, there is no other cash source available to make these payments unlike a future flows deal, where only a portion of the receivables of the issuer are pledged in the transaction. The most significant difference to secured corporate debt is the predictable nature of the business and cash flows in companies considered suitable for whole business securitisation, and thus the relatively low level of operating risk compared to other corporate debt.

The vast majority of transactions to date are UK deals in a limited number of sectors, such as:

- Motorway service stations (Welcome Break, RoadChef)
- Pubs (Punch Taverns, Unique, Punch Funding, Spirit, Pubmaster)
- Media and entertainment (Tussauds, Formula One)
- Transport and Infrastructure (Wightlink, City Aviation, THPA Finance, Steam Packet Finance)
- Water (Dwr Cymru, Anglian, Southern)
- Healthcare (GHG, UK Hospitals (BUPA), Craegmoor Funding, Priory Finance)
- Funeral services (Dignity).

Of these, pub deals have generally performed well, with a combination of strong, steady cash flow, and real estate value. Water deals have also performed satisfactorily.

Some other sectors have had a more chequered performance. The motorway service station deals have had a particularly bad performance track record, stemming in large part from their high leverage and uneven debt service structure. These deals are examined in detail in Chapter 8.

The transport and infrastructure deals have been affected by events such as 9/11, and by the financial difficulties of corporates that contribute to the cash flows for the deal (such as Corus, which is a significant contributor to the earnings of THPA Finance).

The RHM Finance deal, a whole business structure for Rank Hovis McDougall, has frequently been distinguished from other whole business transactions owing to the competitive industry sector of the company and the low leverage of the deal relative to other whole business deals – reflective of the higher level of operating risk.

Outside the UK, there has only been a handful of deals – the closest to the UK model being the Tornator Finance deal in Finland and the Romulus Finance deal in Italy. The Tenovis Finance deal in Germany is also important.

Whole business securitisations are examined in detail in Chapter 8.

5.12.1 Credit analysis

The nature of credit analysis on whole business transactions varies significantly, based on the relevant industry sector. The view is akin to that of analysing a corporate credit, but with a greater view to certain common features of these structures, such as:

- Strength of competitive position
- Industry sector – resilience to new technology/reduced demand
- Stability of earnings (EBITDA)
- Level of required maintenance Capex.

Transaction specific elements include:

- Rent cover and occupancy rates (Care Homes)
- Barrelage and rent (Pubs)
- RAV (Regulatory Asset Value) (Water).

6

Opportunities and Challenges

6.1 INTRODUCTION

The asset-backed markets have been subject to many challenges over their short life, but have generally proved themselves to be extremely resilient. Indeed, on occasion (such as following 9/11 in 2001), ABS securities have been regarded as a safe haven for bond investors, away from the more volatile and reactive corporate bond markets. As a market founded on innovation, the ABS markets have often had to adapt to changing regulatory or tax environments, and this flexibility has stood them in good stead for the current level of uncertainty facing the market.

This Chapter and Chapters 7 to 11 deal with some developing areas of opportunity for the market, as well as issues that may cause difficulties for the ABS markets going forward.

- **Synthetics** The development of synthetic technology for CDOs and for ABS deals has increased the scope and flexibility of securitisation technique considerably. Synthetics have seen great use in Europe in particular, as they permit the securitisation of assets from several different jurisdictions simultaneously without having to comply with local rules on ring-fencing and true sale in all the relevant jurisdictions. Synthetic technology also allows the securitisation of particular risk slices of a capital structure – a technique that is likely to have significant applications when the new Basel Accord is implemented, as it will enable the sale of only those tranches where the capital required to be held by the originator is too high. See Chapter 7.
- **Whole business** The development of whole business securitisation in the UK (and, increasingly, in Europe and elsewhere) permits funding through the ABS markets to be raised by an ever-wider section of the corporate market, and has attracted great interest from private equity sponsors and leveraged loan market participants. See Chapter 8.
- **European Union** The EU is attempting to create a single European market for capital and investment, and, if successful, could create a domestic capital market to rival that of the US. There is still much work to do to approach this goal, although the introduction of the euro has done more in moving towards this than any other measure to date. The ABS markets present particular complexity in trying to achieve harmonisation, due to the complex nature of asset-backed deals which rely on local market mechanics of consumer and commercial finance markets, cultural attitudes to home-ownership and debtor responsibility, and the operation of legal and regulatory provisions on the transfer of assets and issuance of securities. See Chapter 9.
- **Accounting** Challenges to the off-balance-sheet nature of securitisation deals have been launched in the wake of the Enron and WorldCom accounting scandals, with reform of accounting treatment under:

- FASB Interpretation No. 46 (FIN 46) and draft amendments to FAS 140
- IAS 39 amended draft.

See Chapter 10.

- **Capital** Key challenges to the fundamentals of the ABS market are being launched from a regulatory capital perspective, with ongoing discussions on potential reforms to capital off-balance-sheet treatment under drafts of the new Basel Accord. See Chapter 11.

6.2 SIGNIFICANCE OF ACCOUNTING AND CAPITAL OFF-BALANCE-SHEET REFORM

Obtaining off-balance-sheet treatment for accounting or capital purposes has often been a reason to securitise. The nature of these challenges to existing off-balance-sheet treatments are considered in more detail in Chapters 10 and 11, but it is worth first considering what actual impact these changes may have.

6.2.1 What is the practical impact of transactions remaining on-balance-sheet?

Securitisation and structured transactions are undertaken for many reasons – funding, risk transfer and capital release being among the most important.

Accounting standards on off-balance-sheet treatment for securitisations have generally set requirements on either giving up control and decision-making, or on giving up the risk of losses and the ability to receive profits from the assets (and sometimes both, due to the ability to make securitisation transactions "auto-pilot" in nature, which can remove direct decision-making without limiting the risk of loss or share of profits taken by the originator). Historically, whether or not a securitisation SPV would fall back into the originator's consolidated accounting group has depended on whether the originator has control or voting rights in relation to the SPV.

Groups for capital purposes have generally followed the basis determined by accounting treatment.

The more recent accounting reforms have shifted accounting treatment, particularly in relation to the consolidation treatment of the SPV, under:

- SIC-12 interpretation under IAS 27 (increasingly relevant as International Accounting Standards are used by more companies)
- FIN 46 interpretation of January 2003 (and subsequent draft amendments to FAS 140 of June 2003).

These new requirements (Table 6.1) reduce the possibility of removing SPVs from consolidated accounts where the right to benefits is retained, rendering an analysis of the transfer from the originator to the SPV less relevant.

Corporates

The main impact of the new measures on corporate originators will be to change their ability to manage financial covenants in bank debt and other debt. At present, the securitisation of receivables or other assets results in cash in place of the assets. This

Table 6.1   Requirements for accounting off-balance-sheet treatment and non-consolidation

	US	UK	IAS
Initial	FAS 140: cede control (transfer to QSPE) or 3% external equity	FRS 5: cede all risks/ rewards (OR cap risks/ rewards for linked presentation)	IAS 39/IAS 27/SIC-12: cede control and decision-making, and substantially all risks/ rewards
Evolving	FAS 140: cede control (transfer to QSPE) and do not provide liquidity or credit lines, or FIN 46 FIN 46: 10% external equity, or cede majority risks/rewards (variable interest)	FRED 30: work towards joint standard to replace FRS 5 and IAS 39	Revised IAS 39: no continuing involvement (right to call assets or provision of uncapped guarantee) at originator or SPV level enables "look-through" treatment. Any capped guarantee amount remains on-balance-sheet

can enable the originator to either pay down existing debt (thus shrinking the balance sheet of the company), or to reinvest the proceeds in new assets (thus increasing profitability). In either situation, the company can improve its ratios – in the former, by reducing its gearing, and in the latter, by increasing its net cash flow (thus improving its debt service and interest cover).

If the securitised assets remain on balance sheet following consolidation, then the company's balance sheet will increase in size to reflect the new assets (cash) and the new liabilities (limited recourse debt). In effect, the balance sheet will be "grossed-up" by the securitisation.

- The gearing of the company will likely be increased by the size of the debt in the deal against assets in the deal (relative to the ratio in the remainder of the company's balance sheet).
- Although the reinvestment in new assets will benefit total income, total debt service will also increase, due to the inclusion of the debt service cost of the securitised debt.

Clearly, whether or not the securitisation is consolidated in accounting terms does not affect the actual net cash flow generated in the company or the net assets available to repay liabilities. The change in covenant ratios illustrates an issue that has been identified by the rating agencies in relation to companies that use securitisation extensively. Namely, that residual cash flows (excess spread, etc.) and residual assets (net equity in securitised assets) are of lower credit quality than cash flows or assets which are not levered, and should not be attributed the same value in financial covenants.

This issue is taken into account by rating agencies in assigning corporate ratings (with the rating agencies in some cases regarding securitised assets as consolidated in calculating ratios). The agencies have noted the effect of heavy usage of securitisation on existing unsecured debt.

In effect, the potential to manage financial covenants through securitisation can be used as a mechanism for arbitraging the banking sector, and it is in the ability of corporates to access the banking sector that any effect of bringing assets back on balance sheet is most likely to be felt.

Financial institutions

The single biggest impact for financial institutions of tougher consolidation standards will be on regulatory capital. Banks are not as dependent on financial covenants in borrowings, but are tied in to regulatory capital requirements which closely affect the perceived risk of dealing with the institution, and its cost of doing business.

Under capital standards, financial institutions are monitored on a solo and consolidated basis, with institutions generally required to consolidate owned financial entities, and to deduct from capital equity holdings in commercial entities. Entities relevant for consolidation are generally defined by reference to majority ownership and/or control.

It has long been the case that the risk of loss on assets may be transferred in such a way as to reduce capital held against those assets, without the assets themselves being transferred off the accounting balance sheet. Key examples of this are sub-participation (historically) and credit derivatives (more recently). For securitisation vehicles which are not consolidated, a financial institution would deduct from capital any equity piece retained in the securitisation. If, instead, the vehicle is consolidated, then the entire amount of assets of the vehicle would need to be taken into account in the consolidated capital calculation, unless a "look-through" treatment (as proposed under the draft amendment to IAS 39) can be adopted.

CP conduits have been seen as the main victim. If these are consolidated, the capital treatment for the institution would then be the same as if the conduit assets had been originated by it on balance sheet.

To date, it appears that European conduits may be able to avoid accounting consolidation under SIC-12 where the primary assets in a conduit are third-party assets, as the ownership benefits achieved for the sponsor by the conduit are limited compared to those available to the third parties.

US conduits have also sought to avoid accounting consolidation, but this is now more difficult. Concerns with the scope of FIN 46 in the US led to bank activity focused on trying to ensure that CP conduits fell within the QSPE provisions of FAS 140, but this was stalled by an Exposure Draft of June 2003 (replaced in late 2003), which limits the ability of sponsors to enter into liquidity lines with QSPEs. Following this, attention shifted to trying to structure expected loss notes for CP conduits that could be sold to third-party investors, thus ensuring that more than 50% of the losses on the conduit would be absorbed away from the conduit sponsor, and maintaining accounting non-consolidation under FIN 46. Consideration has also been given in CDOs to giving voting rights to investors.

6.2.2   How much effect will consolidation have?

The institution would still benefit from risk transfer – with its credit risk capped by the level of its conduit support – and potentially from a lower cost of funds. Consolidation is unlikely to have an effect on the credit rating of an institution, as the ratings agencies will have already considered the economic risks being taken by the institution in connection with the conduit.

Even if not consolidated, banks sponsoring CP conduits will still be subject to higher capital charges on liquidity lines following implementation of the new Basel Accord. However, this will be offset by the lower capital charges for higher-rated assets, such as those held in conduits, under the new Basel Accord. Also, given the effect of the new Basel Accord, with lower capital requirements for higher-rated assets, the use of CP conduits to reduce capital requirements may simply be of less relevance going forward.

Balance sheet CDOs may encounter difficulties

Given the volume of some of these deals, and the capital relief rationale behind them in the first place, the potential for capital concerns on consolidation is more significant here. As a result, these deals may be structured differently; perhaps by means of a credit default swap with a market counterparty, and without use of an SPV.

6.2.3 Look-through treatment

The IAS 39 draft of June 2002 provides an escape route for accounting consolidation, with their look-through treatment for limited recourse debt. To the extent that this treatment is developed, it may significantly counteract the increasing risk of consolidation for European companies and institutions.

The statement on 29 October 2002, that the FASB in the US and the IASB would work to achieve convergence between US standards and IAS by 1 January 2005 using the principles-based approach of the IASB rather than the rules-based approach of the FASB, may alleviate some of the effect of the FASB Interpretation for US companies and institutions.

6.3 NEW BASEL ACCORD

The drafts of the new Basel Accord are considered in more detail in Chapter 11, but it is worth considering the big picture view of the overall effect of the Accord.

Currently, capital is held on the same basis across many different asset types. The new Accord will adjust this so that the level of capital held will more directly reflect the credit risk of the relevant asset. This credit risk may be measured in different ways, from the use of external ratings through to the use of internal models and data to demonstrate historic losses. The overall relevance of this is that regulatory capital will begin to more correctly reflect the level of prudential economic capital held by an institution against the relevant credit risk. How closely will depend on the quality of the systems and reporting of the institution in question.

6.3.1 What are the consequent trends to be expected from this?

Institutions with the best and most advanced systems, or who are most specialist in particular areas of the market and can thus form detailed views of the credit risk of certain asset types, will find that their economic and regulatory capital become more closely aligned.

On the other hand, institutions with poor quality systems, or who are dabbling in particular areas without more detailed historic knowledge, will find that the Accord is dictating regulatory capital charges to them. These may be an improvement on current levels (e.g. for AAA assets), or a worsening (e.g. for sub-investment grade assets).

The consequence of this is that those banks that have already built the systems appropriate to their businesses should enjoy a competitive advantage, as their competitors are either forced to spend to develop these systems, or to adjust their capital/ asset mix.

6.3.2   What is the consequence for the asset-backed markets?

1. More sophisticated institutions are likely to use securitisation more sparingly. Why use relatively expensive securitisation debt to securitise high-grade assets, where the capital released is minimal? Instead, deals could be structured synthetically which are entirely composed of mezzanine and subordinate risk on asset pools.
2. Less sophisticated institutions may use securitisation to rebalance their capital base away from certain areas, or to continue to support new origination in areas with higher capital charges.
3. Securitisation may become more important as a funding tool for financial institutions, than as a capital release tool. This would be a significant trend, given the level of issuance to date in sectors such as the balance sheet CDO market, where many trades are for capital release. The trend towards funded deals and away from synthetics in Germany is elsewhere remarked upon, as funding costs for the German financial sector rise due to deteriorating credit quality of its institutions.

6.3.3   Is this negative for the asset-backed markets?

As remarked before, the asset-backed markets are extremely flexible, and have repeatedly shown maximum growth as a consequence of points of stress in the wider financial markets – witness the growth in Italian NPL issuance following house price falls in Italy, the growth in Italian state issuance following Maastricht, or the growth in the Japanese balance sheet CDO market following rising NPLs at banks in Japan.

The flexible nature of the market means that most "issues" become new opportunities. There is no reason to believe that entities which currently use the ABS markets as a funding tool will change their issuance patterns. Spreads may evolve to reflect the capital charge of regulated institutions for holding them, but given the preponderance of institutions which are not regulated for capital as investors (hedge funds, SIVs, CP conduits, pension funds), this is unlikely to disrupt the market. Also, additional entities will likely begin to use the ABS markets for funding – such as German banks.

Entities which seek capital release may change their issuance patterns, but the new weightings are likely to create opportunities as well as destroy them. The mega-RMBS master trusts may begin to look increasingly unwieldy (with new plans for cheaper funding via covered bonds taking over), but the issuance of rated ABS debt by low-rated corporates (whose bank funding costs will rise in line with increased capital charges) will surely increase.

Indeed the drop in the funding cost of highly rated corporates (though fewer and further between now than a few years ago) and financial institutions will itself lead to further opportunities for acquisition-based activities, and the potential for refinancings or whole business style leveraged transactions.

7
Synthetics and Credit Derivatives

Credit derivative products first made their way onto the scene in the 1990s, and have since grown and diversified significantly into both an individual financial product line of their own, and a financial tool that can be used to manage and transfer credit risk in an increasing liquid and standardised form.

The investment demand for credit risk has always existed directly in the corporate and government bond markets, and synthetically via asset swaps, but has been dependent on the supply and demand of the bond markets. As with other derivative areas, the credit derivatives market is an attempt to create a large and liquid trading market on a synthetic basis, whether or not the underlying product itself is widely available or liquid.

In early credit derivative products, however, the pioneers of the market focused almost exclusively on sovereign credit risk. The availability of a liquid government bond market to lay off risk as a hedge was an encouraging factor, as was the wider level of market knowledge and information on governments than on individual corporates. Since then, the market has grown and diversified:

- Significant market players have invested in developing the research and pricing infrastructure necessary to move the market into a stand-alone pricing structure, rather than a pure cost-to-hedge intermediary role (such as JP Morgan with their CreditMetrics product).
- ISDA has undertaken the production of standardised documentation formats for credit default swaps, and standardised terminology for credit derivatives generally (leading to the publication in July 1999 of the *1999 Credit Derivatives Definitions* booklet and short-form credit default swap confirmation, updated in February 2003).

The market for credit default products in particular has developed more in Europe than in the US due to the smaller and less-developed corporate bond market. Increasingly, synthetic CDO transactions have been constructed using a portfolio of credit derivative positions. Credit derivatives are also featuring with ever greater regularity as risk transfer mechanisms in securitisation transactions – an area where their use has the potential to revolutionise multi-jurisdictional securitisation.

The credit derivatives market saw a significant boost in early 2003 with the publication by ISDA of its new *2003 Credit Derivatives Definitions* on 11 February 2003 to replace the *1999 Credit Derivatives Definitions*. The *2003 Definitions* are in use from 20 June 2003 and incorporate the Restructuring, Convertibles and Successors supplements published during 2001. They also provide clarification on the issue of what constitutes a "Not Contingent" obligation for deliverability purposes (the new definition is centred around obligations that preserve principal and would include bonds with Spens repayment formulae), and make modifications to physical settlement and buy-in procedures, as well as to credit events. The *2003 Definitions* also provide for different bases for using guarantees – parties can choose whether they want all guarantees given by a reference entity in respect of third parties to be able to trigger a credit event and to be deliverable (the position favoured in Europe), or just guarantees given in respect of "Qualifying Affiliates" (the position favoured in the US).

7.1 SYNTHETIC SECURITISATION: CREDIT DERIVATIVES

Synthetic securitisations have grown in usage in Europe in three main fields: CDOs, CMBS and RMBS. They are conducted by execution of a credit default swap between the originator and the SPV, which references a basket of credits (a pool of bonds for a synthetic CDO, a pool of mortgages for a synthetic RMBS deal, and so on). The SPV agrees to reimburse the originator for losses on the reference pool, in return for receipt of a periodic premium.

The SPV issues notes to investors, and invests the proceeds, typically in collateral in the form of:

- Government bonds
- Pfandbriefe or covered bonds
- Repo
- GIC
- Notes issued by the originator.

The collateral is pledged to both the originator and the note investors in respect of their respective claims on the credit default swap and on the notes.

A typical synthetic securitisation structure is shown in Figure 7.1. The combination

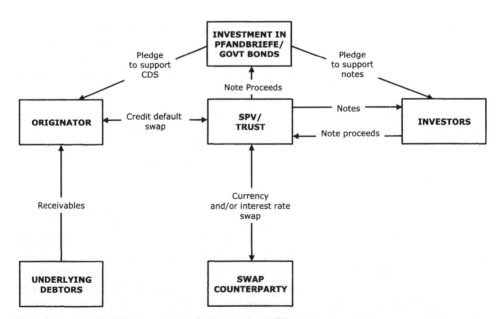

Figure 7.1 Credit default swap synthetic structure: Day 1

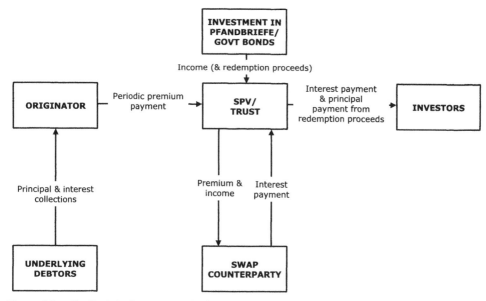

Figure 7.2   Credit default swap synthetic structure: ongoing – no default

of the investment return on the collateral, and the premium on the credit default swap, are used to make payment to investors. The ongoing structure of a typical synthetic securitisation is shown in Figure 7.2.

In the event that a loss is suffered on the referenced assets, part of the collateral is liquidated, and the proceeds are paid to the originator. On maturity of the deal, the remaining notes (i.e. net of any amounts written-down in respect of losses suffered) will be redeemed with the remaining collateral. The structure of a typical synthetic secur-itisation on occurrence of an underlying default is shown in Figure 7.3.

The form of the collateral for the deal is important, as the investors have bivariate risk in a synthetic deal – they are exposed to a loss on the referenced assets, but they are also at risk on the value of the collateral, which is the only source the SPV has in order to repay the notes. Transactions in which the collateral takes the form of notes issued by the originator (or a deposit with the originator) are exposed to unsecured credit risk on the originator, and are thus not delinked from the credit rating of the originator.

The originator may have the right to substitute assets into and out of the reference pool from time to time – generally subject to meeting certain substitution criteria (see Chapter 4, section 4.1.3).

The primary benefits that the use of credit derivatives bring to a securitisation structure are:

- **Simplicity**   Credit derivatives effect a synthetic transfer of risk, by creating a new asset (the derivative), rather than transferring the existing asset. Consequently many of the issues raised by a transfer which give rise to detailed and complex structural issues (assignment notification requirements, insolvency unwind, capital gains tax, stamp duty, true sale, etc.) do not arise (although the derivative itself may of course give rise to some of these issues on its own). This has been a particular

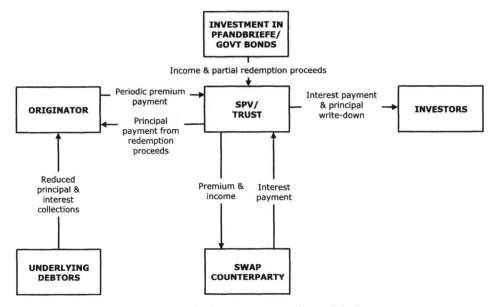

Figure 7.3   Credit default swap synthetic structure: ongoing – default

reason (together with "Funding cost" below) for the development of the synthetic market in Germany, due to the potential trade tax costs which could arise on an SPV in a German true sale deal.

- **Administrative ease**   Synthetic transfers of risk may serve to circumvent some of the administrative complexity and separation of accounts and payment records required for a full transfer.
- **Flexibility**   As the underlying assets are not transferred, substitution or replenishment of assets can also be done without the requirement for further transfers (which could themselves necessitate extra opinions, tax issues, and documentation on the occasion of each transfer). Instead, specific substitution criteria as to the eligibility of reference obligations in relation to which risk is transferred can be set.
- **Ability to transact**   In countries with onerous bank secrecy and disclosure requirements, or restrictions on the transfer of receivables (or where the receivables in question contain transfer prohibitions), a synthetic risk transfer may offer an alternative transfer route which is the only way to actually undertake a transaction.
- **Multi-jurisdictional transactions**   Although the single European currency is now in place, the desire of the European Union to create a single market in financial services is, of course, still subject to differences in the tax and legal regimes extant in each jurisdiction. Harmonisation of these regimes is at best peripheral. In Asia, the market is even more fragmented, with multiple currencies and regulatory regimes. Synthetic transfers of risk bypass regimes relating to receivables which in some cases date back hundreds of years, in favour of regimes relating to credit derivatives, which as a new and growing area are only now being developed. Due partly to the desire of most countries to ensure that their local institutions are not disadvantaged in competing for business in this area, and partly to the acknowledged complexity of the products and the desire of regulators to

match regimes that have been tried and tested elsewhere, there is a remarkable degree of homogeneity in criteria for credit derivatives across different jurisdictions. This enables a product to be created which is otherwise too complex for many trades – a multi-jurisdictional (and even multi-continent) securitisation.

- **Regulatory capital arbitrage**   The credit risk transfer criteria developed for credit derivatives by most central banks are generally less onerous than those they have developed for securitisation, allowing benefits which might be difficult to achieve on a real asset basis to be realised on a synthetic basis.

- **Funding cost**   A synthetic transfer can be used to leave the originator's current funding mechanisms in place intact. This can offer a significant funding benefit where the originator is currently funding in the retail deposit market. Weighing up the options between a full capital transfer and synthetic hybrids will depend on the economic position of the originator and its cost of capital as against its on-balance-sheet funding costs. Full capital relief will be more cash expensive (in terms of reducing the residual return realised on the assets), due to sale of the most junior risk tranches.

7.2   SUPER-SENIOR PIECES

Consider the relatively common structure illustrated in Figure 7.4 for a synthetic CDO transaction. In this structure, the risk on a corporate loan portfolio is divided into a first loss piece (which is sufficiently large as against the portfolio that at least part of it would qualify for an AAA credit rating) and a remainder. The remainder of the risk is, by definition, greater than AAA and can be sold to an OECD bank on an unfunded basis relatively cheaply under a super-senior credit default swap. This will entitle the protection buyer to reduce its capital held against this remainder from a 100% risk weighting to a 20% risk weighting.

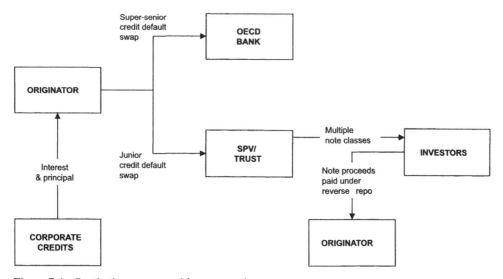

Figure 7.4   Synthetic structure with super-senior

The exact attachment point of the super-senior default swap will vary deal-by-deal, both with the quality of the underlying pool of assets (which will determine the exact amount of the capital structure that is below AAA) and with the risk profile of the super-senior buyer. For example, during the period of significant spread widening seen in the corporate bond market in 2002, attachment points on super-seniors moved higher.

The OECD bank may, in turn, back out the risk on the super-senior default swap to another party, such as a monoline insurer.

This form of structure is increasingly used in the market, particularly for large transactions, due to the size of some transactions and the commensurate cost of selling large AAA-rated classes of funded notes into the market. It has been seen mostly for CDO transactions, but has also been used for CMBS and RMBS deals by German banks.

The credit risk of the first loss piece is sold to an SPV under a junior credit default swap. The SPV issues note classes against the risk to investors, ranging from an AAA rating down to an equity piece – generally 2% or 3% of the total pool. The proceeds of the issue are passed by the SPV to the originator under a reverse repo in return for government securities or (often) Pfandbriefe. As the portfolio has been created synthetically, the originator can substitute loans within the portfolio on a simple basis within certain criteria.

Since the SPV will pledge the government or Pfandbriefe collateral both to investors (to repay the notes issued in the event that the underlying note portfolio performs) and to the originator (to make payment on the CDS in the event that the underlying loan portfolio does not perform):

- The notes can be delinked from the credit rating of the originator (for the benefit of investors).
- The originator can benefit from a 0% or 10% capital weighting on the first loss portion according to the form of the collateral, and a 20% risk weighting on the super-senior.

Assuming an 80% super-senior, this structure can therefore reduce the 8% capital haircut on corporate debt to:

$$(80\% \times 20\% \times 8\%)[\text{super-senior}] + (18\% \times 10\% \times 8\%)$$
$$[\text{junior swap with Pfandbriefe}]$$
$$+ 2\% [\text{assumed first loss held}]$$
$$= 3.424\% \text{ (or } 1.424\% \text{ if the first loss can be sold)}$$

Assuming a 95% super-senior (achieved on some German RMBS deals), this structure can reduce the 4% capital haircut on mortgage debt to:

$$(95\% \times 20\% \times 8\%)[\text{super-senior}] + (4.5\% \times 10\% \times 8\%)$$
$$[\text{junior swap with Pfandbriefe}]$$
$$+ 0.5\% [\text{assumed first loss held}]$$
$$= 2.056\% \text{ (or } 1.556\% \text{ if the first loss can be sold)}$$

In both cases, the capital reduction can be even more significant if the first loss piece is sold.

7.3   PROs AND CONs OF SYNTHETIC SECURITISATIONS FOR INVESTORS

Pros:

- **Defined risks**   The only risk taken by investors on the referenced assets is default risk resulting in a loss. The investor is not at risk on a movement in FX rates, a drop in the average margin on the assets, or other non-performance which does not result from a credit event (such as trading losses in a managed CDO deal).
- **Limited loss**   Generally, the loss is designed to cover loss of principal only and not costs of foreclosure, or loss of accrued interest.
- **Manager flexibility**   If the deal is managed (e.g. a managed CDO structure), then the synthetic basis provides the manager with more flexibility to substitute assets. As synthetic structures are unlikely to contain any kind of spread test or par value test, the manager can make clear credit decisions. The mechanics of substitution are also simpler than a cash-based structure.

Cons

- **No excess spread**   The investor will not have the benefit of excess spread that could be used to repair losses over time (e.g. compared to a mortgage deal where excess loss is used to cover losses on foreclosure in previous periods). Once a loss has occurred, an investor's notes will be written down permanently.
- **Credit linkage**   If the ABS proceeds are invested in collateral that loses value, the investors will suffer loss regardless of the performance of the reference assets. This is a particular risk if the collateral takes the form of notes issued by the originator (or by another entity susceptible to downgrade), as the investors suffer from outright credit linkage to such credit, and the notes will be downgraded in line with such credit.
- **Manager quality**   In a managed CDO structure, the increased flexibility of the manager to substitute assets (see above) can give investors a greater risk of loss with a synthetic structure than a cash structure, if the manager in question is of poor quality.

7.4   TERMINOLOGY AND TYPES OF CREDIT DERIVATIVE

The market has its own terminology, centred around three basic definitions of the participants and the subject-matter:

- **Protection seller**   The party that is selling protection and assuming risk under a credit derivative (also known as the credit risk buyer)

- **Protection buyer**   The party that is buying protection and shedding risk under a credit derivative (also known as the credit risk seller)
- **Reference obligation**   The asset whose default or performance determines the pay-out on the credit derivative.

The function of any credit derivative is to transfer credit risk in relation to the defined reference obligation from the protection buyer to the protection seller. There are four main types of credit derivative:

- **Credit default swap**   The most common type. The protection buyer pays a periodic premium to the protection seller. If certain trigger default events occur in relation to the reference obligation (or certain other obligations of the reference entity as detailed in the credit events), the protection seller pays to the protection buyer an amount equal to the fall in the value of the reference obligation.
- **Total return swap**   The basis of the asset swaps market. The protection buyer passes through periodic amounts based on the cash receipts on a notional principal amount of a particular security (the reference obligation) to the protection seller (the pass-through is equal to receipts – if less is received, less is paid over). The protection seller pays periodic amounts based on LIBOR or another market interest rate charged on the same notional principal amount to the protection buyer. The swap may also reflect the appreciation or depreciation in value of the reference obligation (e.g. where the swap relates to equities).
- **Credit-linked note**   The synthetic version of limited recourse notes issued from a securitisation or a repackaging. Investors subscribe cash up-front for a note that pays principal and interest. If certain trigger default events occur in relation to the reference obligation (or certain other obligations of the reference entity as detailed in the credit events), the amount due to be repaid to the investor is reduced by an amount equal to the fall in the value of the reference obligation.
- **Credit spread products**   A more complex product, where the protection buyer receives a pay-out if the spread between the yield on a particular security (the reference obligation) and the yield on a benchmark (such as a government bond) widens beyond a certain point (indicating that the credit of the issuer has deteriorated relative to that of the relevant government).

7.5   USE AND PRICING FOR CREDIT DERIVATIVES

Credit default swaps

These have a similar rationale to securitisation products. They can be used to:

- Free up capacity on credit lines to a particular client;
- Effectively repackage an asset held by the bank, by passing on credit risk in a different currency or interest rate basis;
- Sub-participate risk without prejudicing direct relations with the client;
- Release bank capital held against credit risk;
- Leverage a position by assuming first loss risk.

As credit default swaps are off balance sheet, they can also be used as an alternative to taking on an on-balance-sheet exposure. This can be particularly useful where the protection seller has a high cost of funds, as they can use a credit default swap to take on exposure in an unfunded form, meaning that their return is not diluted by having to fund at a higher level than the market average.

Credit default swaps were historically traded off sovereigns, but are now used across a range of corporates, banks and synthetic exposures (including baskets of different credits). The hedge for a credit default swap is to create a synthetic short or long position in the relevant corporate or government risk by borrowing the relevant security and short selling it to invest in government bonds, or by borrowing cash and buying the relevant security, respectively.

Consequently, arbitrage opportunities will cause the CDS premium to revert to the spread of the relevant security over the risk-free benchmark.

Credit-linked notes

As a funded version of the credit default swap, these instruments are virtually identical to a repackaged note or securitisation issue in terms of their uses and pricing.

Total return swap

As another way of shifting credit risk on an off-balance-sheet basis, total return swaps may be used in a similar way to credit default swaps. They are often used to warehouse assets off balance sheet on a temporary basis. Pricing is similar to credit default swaps, as effectively the market funding cost is added to both legs, giving a LIBOR base on the risk-free leg and a LIBOR plus credit spread on the risk leg.

Credit spread option

These can be used to take a trading view that is "market neutral", by creating a synthetic spread between two credits, or between short-term and long-term credits, which will be unaffected by a rise or fall in the overall market.

7.6 STRUCTURE AND CONCERNS

Unlike other derivative products, where many of the relevant legal, regulatory and structural issues have been debated at length and (broadly) resolved over several years, the debate for credit derivatives is more recent.

7.6.1 Gaming and insurance issues

Credit derivatives raise the same gaming issues that are raised by other derivative products, but they also raise a further issue of key importance to market participants – namely, the possibility that credit derivative contracts could be construed as insurance contracts for regulatory and legal purposes.

Gaming or wagering agreements are void and unenforceable under English law but are upheld if they fall within s. 412 of the Financial Services and Markets Act 2000 (i.e. if they are regulated investments under the Act such as contracts for differences).

The risk of categorisation of credit derivatives as insurance contracts arises due to the manner in which a credit derivative is protective of the protection buyer. Treatment of a credit derivative as an insurance contract could lead to providers of credit derivatives being subjected to regulation by insurance regulatory bodies, or to credit derivative contracts being void where they are provided by unregulated entities. On the other hand, buyers of credit derivatives could become subject to the duty of *uberrimae fides* (or utmost good faith) under insurance law, requiring them to disclose all information connected to a transaction that could affect the decision of the credit derivative provider to enter into the derivative, or the price at which they enter into the derivative.

Credit derivatives have, however, been differentiated from insurance contracts in the UK, on the grounds that they do not make payment by way of compensation for a loss suffered by the buyer, but rather that payment is obliged to be made whether or not the buyer has suffered a loss.

7.6.2   Confidentiality and insider dealing

The use of credit derivatives in portfolio balance sheet trades by banks has led to concerns about confidential client information on referenced names that may be available to the bank through bank-lending relationships. This has two aspects:

- Whether such information can be produced to evidence the occurrence of credit events, given typical bank restrictions on client confidentiality.
- Whether or not the bank is using such information as insider information in entering into credit derivative trades.

The former is a question for the bank confidentiality laws of the jurisdiction in question. The latter is a wider question that has been raised by the dealer community generally, amid concerns that banks may unfairly exploit the market. Even assuming that banks do not use such information inappropriately, they will still in any event need to ensure some segregation of relationship staff with inside information from staff engaged in credit derivatives activity, in order to avoid the risk of falling within insider dealing prohibitions.

7.6.3   Documentation

In order to ensure netting of trades where appropriate, trades are increasingly documented on a confirm under an ISDA Master Agreement, which serves as a framework netting agreement. ISDA has published a format for a credit default swap trade, together with standardised definitions for the product, which centre around the following key concepts:

- **Reference obligation**   The obligation that is the subject of the derivative. Either a specific reference obligation (for cash settlement trades, where it is used to calculate the payment on the derivative on occurrence of a credit event) or categories of deliverable obligations (for physical settlement trades, such as "Not contingent", "Transferable", "Maximum maturity") may be specified.

- **Reference entity**   The entity that has issued or created the reference obligation.
- **Obligation**   Those obligations of the reference entity in relation to which a credit event can occur (generally specified by way of categories such as "Reference obligations only", "Bond or loan" or "Borrowed money").
- **Credit event**   Those events that serve as a trigger to payment by the protection seller to the protection buyer under the derivative.

7.6.4   Hedging and basis risk

The key to ensuring an effective protection contract from the point of view of the protection buyer is successfully correlating the risks and exposures that the buyer is taking on its underlying position, with the payment triggers and amount on the credit derivative.

For example, a credit derivative may be structured off a reference entity, which is a key supplier of the underlying entity to which the protection buyer is exposed, on the basis that insolvency of the reference entity will force the underlying entity into insolvency. This is in practice an imperfect hedge, as the underlying entity may become insolvent for some other reason wholly unrelated to the reference entity, but leaving the protection buyer with no ability to seek payment on the credit derivative.

Likewise, using a bond issued by the reference entity as the reference obligation, where the underlying exposure is to a loan or a derivative, may result in a mismatch as to the timing and amount of any payment triggered on the derivative as against the loss on the underlying exposure.

The credit derivative should therefore be structured to be as close a hedge as is available in the market, unless there is some other reason for using the product.

7.6.5   Credit events

Standard credit events under the *1999 Credit Derivatives Definitions* were:

- Bankruptcy
- Failure to pay
- Obligation default
- Obligation acceleration
- Repudiation/moratorium
- Restructuring.

Obligation default was subsequently dropped in most trades, and on 5 April 2002, ISDA also agreed to drop obligation acceleration and repudiation/moratorium as credit events in standard corporate credit default swaps. This has left bankruptcy, failure to pay and restructuring as the commonly used credit events.

The restructuring credit event has been widely debated since 2001 following the restructuring of the insurer Conseco. The ISDA standard definition of "restructuring" as a credit event triggered payout on credit swaps linked to Conseco, following the restructuring of bank loans owed by Conseco, without there being an economic default. This resulted in a gain for dealers who had bought protection on Conseco, which was widely considered to be unfair.

Consequently, a new ISDA standard definition of the "restructuring" event – now known the market over as "modified restructuring" – was published on 11 May 2001, which excludes from the restructuring trigger any obligation that is narrowly held (among less than four unaffiliated holders).

At the same time, an amendment was made allowing for the parties to specify a maximum final maturity of assets eligible for delivery under "physical settlement" on occurrence of a restructuring (being 30 months after the date of the restructuring). This was designed to counter cases where very long-term or perpetual securities (which lose more value than other securities where the issuer is in financial difficulties and are hence "cheapest to deliver") were delivered to create arbitrage profits for the protection buyer. A requirement for deliverable obligations to be "fully transferable" was also inserted.

As well as the issues arising out of the Conseco case, the rating agencies' views on default assessment for transactions using the restructuring event are having an impact on the development of the market. Due to the rating agencies assessing lower default frequencies for the new modified restructuring language in CDO and repack trades, dealers which hedge market credit default swap positions with CDO deals are keen to use modified restructuring in traded market positions to ensure a matching risk on both sides.

While standard traded swaps in the US market largely switched to the new modified restructuring definition, swaps in Europe continued to trade off the old definition. Credit derivative end-users were concerned by the limitations contained in the modified restructuring provision that only "fully transferable" assets (defined as assets freely transferable to a relatively wide range of transferees as set out in the modified restructuring definition) may be delivered into the derivative, due to the wide range of limitations on loan transfer contained in many European loan documents. This would make the modified language an imperfect hedge as it would prevent physical settlement in relation to some hedged loan obligations.

The lines were therefore drawn between dealers keen to prevent the Conseco scenario arising again and to hedge their books, and end-users keen to ensure that their protection was as watertight as possible. The discussions took another turn with the publication of the *2003 Definitions*. These added a further option, and now allow for four possible outcomes on the restructuring credit event:

- **Restructuring**   The original form, favoured in Japan.
- **Restructuring with modified restructuring maturity limitation and conditionally transferable obligation**   The new so called "modified modified restructuring" language introduced in the *2003 Definitions* and favoured in Europe, which permits non-bond deliverables that are only transferable with the consent of the reference entity or the guarantor or any agent, and limits the maturity of the deliverable to at most 5 years after the scheduled termination date of the trade.
- **Restructuring with restructuring maturity limitation and fully transferable obligation**   The so-called "modified restructuring" form put forward in 2001 and adopted in the US, which limits deliverables to assets transferable without the

consent of any person and which limits the maturity of the deliverable to at most $2\frac{1}{2}$ years after the scheduled termination date of the trade.
- **No restructuring**.

7.6.6 Calculation of Payout

Most standard market credit default swaps settle on a physical settlement basis. However, most synthetic securitisation structures (including CDOs) settle on a cash settlement basis, due to the difficulties involved in transferring physical assets to the SPV to work out on behalf of investors.

Cash settlement

Cash settlement involves payment by the SPV to the originator of an amount equal to the loss on the relevant underlying assets, generally calculated by reference to:

- Market quotes (for corporate bonds or other traded assets)
- Loss after applying recoveries on foreclosure (for mortgages, receivables, etc.).

The loss on foreclosure is usually calculated as the gross sale proceeds less the principal amount of the loan, thus not covering the protection buyer for any costs of foreclosure, or for any loss of accrued interest on the loan between falling due and eventual recovery. In some cases, however, it may also include one or other of these amounts.

It is apposite here to comment on the role of the calculation agent, which, in a trade that is settled for a cash payment, will act as agent to determine the amount of the loss on the credit derivative. In a trade between financial and non-financial counterparties, this would typically be the financial counterparty.

Although the ISDA form envisages independent third-party quotes as to the residual value of the reference obligation in order to determine the loss, using such an objective process may not be possible where the subject-matter of the credit derivative is an illiquid obligation. In such a case, the calculation of any loss amount may be a relatively subjective matter, and this is a prime area in which disputes can arise.

Physical settlement

Physical settlement involves delivery of the underlying asset against a cash payment equal to the full par value of the asset. The administration of Railtrack on 7 October 2001 led to discussion on the possibility of delivering a convertible bond issued by Railtrack under the credit derivative. The discussion centred on the meaning of the ISDA definition of "Not contingent", which was specified as applying to deliverable obligations in many trades.

Advice from Robin Potts QC on 18 October 2001 confirmed the view that convertibles should not be regarded as contingent and are therefore deliverable even where "Not contingent" is specified. Convertibles carrying a "widows and orphans" clause under which the trustee is the party who decides to convert could be construed as creating a contingency on repayment. However, they would be unlikely to be regarded by the courts as contingent within the intention of the ISDA definitions, where there is no real possibility of the trustee exercising the option (as would be the case in credit-impaired scenarios where the conversion option would be heavily out-the-money).

On 13 February 2003 the UK High Court ruled on the dispute between Nomura and CSFB over CSFB's refusal to accept Railtrack convertibles as deliverables under a credit default swap following the Railtrack administration proceedings in October 2001. CSFB had argued that the convertibles were "Contingent" due to the conversion option, but the High Court ruled that this was not the case, distinguishing between bonds convertible at the option of the bondholder (which are not contingent) and bonds convertible at the option of the issuer (which are contingent).

7.6.7 Additional terminology

Further features of credit derivatives that have assumed less importance as the market has developed are:

- Materiality
- Publicly available information.

Materiality thresholds have been used in some credit derivatives to require deterioration of the reference obligation below a certain point before a claim can be made (in order to prevent claims for small amounts of money being made on the derivative). Due to the dislike of regulators for materiality thresholds, who may deduct these thresholds from capital or require that such thresholds are approved in advance when considering the protection offered by a credit derivative, they are now less commonly used.

The requirement that there must be publicly available information verifying the occurrence of a credit event prior to a claim being made has been hard to use in practice, especially where the reference obligation is not publicly traded, and it is now an optional requirement in ISDA forms.

7.7 REGULATORY CAPITAL ADVANTAGES OF SYNTHETICS

The requirements for a proper credit risk transfer under a credit derivative in each country are set out in guidelines promulgated by financial regulators, as are the guidelines for a "true sale" risk transfer under a securitisation. In most cases however, the credit derivatives rules are shorter and less comprehensive, with the primary focus being on establishing a proper risk hedging match between the protected asset and the credit derivative.

For example, in the UK the securitisation guidelines permit transfer of assets by novation or assignment (legal or equitable) or by the use of a declaration of trust or a funded sub-participation. The use of other methods requires the prior approval of the FSA and a supporting legal opinion. Transferors are also expressly required to comply with a long list of detailed requirements (see under United Kingdom in Chapter 12 for more detail) including:

- The transferor has no right or obligation to repurchase the assets – except pursuant to: (a) a call option of the originator when the portfolio of securitised assets is less than 10% of their maximum value and the assets are still fully performing; (b) a call and step-up (this is limited to mortgage deals and will be considered on a case by case basis); (c) a breach of a warranty given at the time of sale on a matter within the control of the transferor (warranties on the future credit of the underlying borrowers are not permitted).

- Evidence from the transferor's legal advisers that the transferor will not be liable to investors for losses.
- Auditors should be satisfied that the deal complies with FRS 5.
- The originator will be required to confirm in writing that they have evidence that their lawyers and auditors are satisfied that the FSA's requirements have been met.

For credit derivatives, however, the UK requirements are significantly less strict, including requirements that:

- For funded credit derivatives, there must be no obligation on the protection buyer to repay any funding received under a credit derivative (except at termination of the credit derivative, or as a result of a "credit event" trigger, or for breach of warranty in relation to the reference obligations).
- The derivative is only permitted to be cancelled pursuant to an option of the protection buyer when the reference obligation is still fully performing (or in a basket structure, where the remaining uncollected value of the basket of reference obligations is less than 10% of their maximum value and the assets are still fully performing).

It can be seen from this that the credit derivative requirements are less detailed (e.g. the provision of legal and audit confirmations) and less restrictive as to form (e.g. as to the use of particular transfer methods).

7.8 INTERNATIONAL CAPITAL TREATMENT FOR CREDIT DERIVATIVES

The capital treatment of credit derivatives in the banking book is largely developed from the capital treatment that applies to guarantees, reflecting the most common use of credit derivatives in the form of an unfunded credit default swap. Funded products are generally treated either as funded sub-participations, or as cash collateralised exposures. In the trading book, credit derivatives are typically treated as short or long positions in the reference obligation.

Regulatory releases on the capital treatment applicable to credit derivatives were prominent in 1998 and 1999 following releases by the Federal Reserve in 1996 and 1997, the draft view of the Bank of England which was first published in November 1996, and the guidelines released by the Canadian authorities in October 1997. The French regulators released guidelines in April 1998, followed shortly by the UK authorities. The German regulators released draft guidelines in July 1998 and September 1998 and a final version in June 1999. They were followed by the Japanese authorities in December 1998 and March 1999. Hong Kong released guidelines in December 1999, Singapore in December 1999 and September 2000, Australia in April 2000 and Finland in December 2000.

This speed of progress by regulators is a response to the increasing globalisation of financial products and the need to establish a level playing field for local market players operating on a global level. Consequently, the guidelines are all very similar in nature, varying only in a few limited areas, which can be summarised as follows:

- Whether or not credit derivatives may be admitted to the trading book for capital purposes.
- Whether the reference obligation must be exactly the same as the protected asset in order for protection to be recognised (or whether it must simply be issued by the same issuer and rank at the same priority level or a more junior priority level than the protected asset).
- Whether capital benefits can be gained from derivatives with a shorter maturity than that of the underlying exposure.
- The treatment of basket trades.
- The level of "add-on" for potential future exposure to credit risk on the mark-to-market value of credit derivatives in the trading book.

Most regulators have deferred judgement on credit spread products until they have seen more instances of their use in the market and are better able to decide the appropriate treatment.

7.8.1   Australia

Guidelines on the capital treatment of credit derivatives were released in April 2000 by APRA. The guidelines cover both banking book and trading book treatment.

- **Maturity Mismatch**   A sliding scale is applied.

7.8.2   Canada

Credit derivative guidelines were published in October 1997.

7.8.3   Finland

Guidelines on credit derivatives were published on 5 December 2000.

7.8.4   France

In April 1998, the Commission Bancaire published a paper on the capital treatment of credit derivatives. Credit derivatives are regarded as trading book instruments if the derivative is marked-to-market daily with quotes from market-makers and held with intent to sell, and if the institution has expertise in the credit derivatives market and accurate valuation models.

Banking book treatment

- **Reference obligation**   Same issuer required.
- **Minimum tenor**   If the reference obligation has less than one year to maturity, then no protection value is recognised.

- **Maturity mismatch** If the credit derivative has a shorter term than the protected asset, then no protection value is recognised if the credit derivative has less than one year to expiry. If the credit derivative has one year or more to expiry, then a charge is made on the protection buyer for the residual exposure as an undrawn commitment exceeding one year (or, if the residual exposure is an undrawn commitment, at half the usual weight for an undrawn commitment) (thus the weighting on a 5-year drawn position protected by a 3-year credit default swap with an OECD bank would be 70% of the principal amount, i.e. 20% for the protected period plus 50% for the residual).
- **Basket trades** A "first to default" basket structure gives the buyer protection against the default of the asset with the lowest risk weighting in the basket. Sale of a "first to default" credit derivative basket structure generates a capital charge for the protection seller equal to the addition of the respective capital charge for each asset in the basket.

Trading book treatment

- **Reference obligation** Exact match required.
- **Maturity mismatch** The credit derivative must have the same maturity as the protected asset. (If the credit derivative has a shorter term than the protected asset, then both the specific risk of the protected asset and the specific risk of the credit derivative will be recorded.)
- **Basket trades** A "first to default" basket structure allows the buyer to record a short position for the worst risk weighted asset in the basket. Sale of a "first to default" credit derivative basket structure creates a long position for the protection seller in each asset in the basket.
- **Add-ons** In addition to market risk assessments, unfunded credit derivatives such as total return swaps and credit default products (but not funded credit derivatives such as credit-linked notes) are subjected to a counterparty risk haircut by calculating the mark-to-market value of the derivative plus an "add-on" percentage, which is the interest rate add-on (investment grade) or the equity add-on (non-investment grade) for the protection seller, and the equity add-on (investment grade) or the commodity add-on (non-investment grade) for the protection buyer. The relevant add-on percentage is applied to the notional principal, with the aggregate figure then being multiplied by counterparty risk weight and weighted by a factor of 8%.

7.8.5 Germany

On 16 June 1999, BAKred published Circular 10/99 on the Treatment of Credit Derivatives. TRORS and CDS are regarded as trading book instruments if the underlying asset is a security, or banking book instruments if the underlying asset is a loan (unless it is marked-to-market daily and held with intent to sell, in which case it may be held in the trading book). The guidelines are silent on basket structures.

Banking book treatment

- **Reference obligation** Same issuer required.

- **Maturity mismatch** The credit derivative must have the same maturity as the protected asset. (If it is shorter, no protection value is recognised but no additional exposure is incurred by the credit derivative.)

Trading book treatment

- **Reference obligation** Same issuer required.
- **Maturity mismatch** The credit derivative must have the same maturity as the protected asset. (If it is shorter, then both the specific risk of the reference obligation and the specific risk of the credit derivative will be recorded.)
- **Add-ons** In addition to market risk assessments, unfunded credit derivatives such as total return swaps and credit default products (but not funded credit derivatives such as credit-linked notes) are subjected to a counterparty risk haircut by calculating the mark-to-market value of the derivative plus an "add-on" percentage which is the interest rate add-on (for investment grade) or the equity add-on (for non-investment grade), for both the protection seller and the protection buyer. The relevant add-on percentage is applied to the notional principal, with the aggregate figure then being multiplied by counterparty risk weight and weighted by a factor of 8%.

In February 2000, German banks requested the BAKred to relent on its treatment of derivatives on loan assets solely in the banking book, and to refine its approach to maturity mismatches.

7.8.6 Hong Kong

The HKMA published guidelines on the capital treatment for credit derivatives in the banking book in December 1999. The guidelines require the institution to consult with the HKMA on the treatment of credit derivatives in the trading book.

- **Reference obligation** Same issuer required.
- **Maturity mismatch** Consultation with the HKMA is required.
- **Basket trades** Consultation with the HKMA is required.

7.8.7 Japan

The MOF released short credit derivative guidelines in December 1998, followed by more detailed rules released by the Bankers Association of Japan in March 1999, which duplicate the rules released by the FSA in the UK.

7.8.8 Singapore

The MAS published guidelines on the capital treatment for credit derivatives in the banking book and the trading book in December 1999 and September 2000.

   Credit derivatives are regarded as trading book instruments if the derivative is traded and is marked-to-market daily.

Banking Book Treatment

- **Reference obligation**   Same issuer required.
- **Maturity mismatch**   If the credit derivative has a shorter term than the protected asset, then no protection value is recognised if the credit derivative has less than one year to expiry. If the credit derivative has between one year and five years to expiry, then protection is recognised on a sliding scale. If the credit derivative has more than five years to expiry, full protection value is recognised.
- **Basket trades**   A "first to default" basket structure gives the buyer protection against the default of one asset in the basket. Sale of a "first to default" credit derivative basket structure generates a capital charge for the protection seller equal to the addition of the respective capital charge for each asset in the basket (capped at the amount of the maximum payout). A proportionate basket structure will give protection or generate charges on a proportion of the assets in the baskets.

Trading Book Treatment

- **Reference obligation**   Same issuer required.
- **Maturity mismatch**   If the credit derivative has a shorter term than the protected asset, a forward position (i.e. an obligation to acquire the bond or other protected asset in the future) in the specific risk of the reference obligation is recorded by the protection buyer for the residual exposure.
- **Basket trades**   A "first to default" basket structure allows the buyer to record a short position for any one of the assets in the basket. Sale of a "first to default" credit derivative basket structure creates a long position for the protection seller in each asset in the basket, capped at a direct deduction from capital. A proportionate basket structure only creates a long or short position by reference to the proportionate weighting of each asset in the basket.
- **Add-ons**   In addition to market risk assessments, credit derivatives are subjected to a counterparty risk haircut by calculating the mark-to-market value of the derivative plus an "add-on" percentage which is the interest rate add-on (qualifying assess) or the equity add-on (non-qualifying assets), and multiplying by the counterparty risk weight and the BIS factor.

7.8.9   UK

The FSA first published credit derivative guidelines in 1998, and has since revised them periodically. The latest revision, effective from 1 September 2003, provides for the treatment of second to default baskets, and offers a revised treatment for first to default baskets. The FSA permits credit derivatives to be admitted to the trading book.

Banking book treatment

- **Reference obligation**   Same issuer required.
- **Maturity mismatch**   If the credit derivative has a shorter term than the protected asset, then no protection value is recognised if the credit derivative has less than one year to expiry. If the credit derivative has one year or more to expiry, then a charge

is made on the protection buyer for the residual exposure as an undrawn commitment exceeding one year (or, if the residual exposure is an undrawn commitment, at half the usual weight for an undrawn commitment) (thus the weighting on a 5-year drawn position protected by a 3-year credit default swap with an OECD bank would be 70% of the principal amount, i.e. 20% for the protected period plus 50% for the residual).

- **Basket trades**   A "first to default" basket structure gives the buyer protection against the default of any one of the assets in the basket. Sale of a "first to default" credit derivative basket structure generates a capital charge for the protection seller equal to the addition of the respective capital charge for each asset in the basket, capped at a direct deduction from capital (although the FSA will consider disapplying this treatment if they are satisfied that the assets in the basket display a very strong degree of correlation). Under the 1 September revision, sale of a "second to default" credit derivative basket structure generates the same capital charge for the protection seller, but ignoring the single worst asset in the pool. The revision effective from 1 September 2003 provides that if the first to default or second to default basket takes the form of a credit-linked note which is rated as a qualifying debt item (i.e. investment grade), the protection sellers may instead include the basket at the weighting of the single worst asset in the pool. A proportionate basket structure only relieves or generates a capital charge by reference to the proportionate weighting of each asset in the basket.

Trading book treatment

- **Reference obligation**   Same issuer required.
- **Maturity mismatch**   If the credit derivative has a shorter term than the protected asset, a forward position (i.e. an obligation to acquire the bond or other protected asset in the future) in the specific risk of the reference obligation is recorded by the protection buyer for the residual exposure.
- **Basket trades**   A "first to default" basket structure allows the buyer to record a short position for any one of the assets in the basket. Sale of a "first to default" credit derivative basket structure creates a long position for the protection seller in each asset in the basket, capped at a direct deduction from capital (although the FSA will consider disapplying this treatment if they are satisfied that the assets in the basket display a very strong degree of correlation). Under the 1 September revision, sale of a "second to default" credit derivative basket structure generates the same long position for the protection seller, but ignoring the single worst asset in the pool. A protection seller who is acquiring a multiple-name credit-linked note which is rated as a qualifying debt item (i.e. investment grade) only records a long position in the credit-linked note itself at the specific risk weight for the note issuer. A proportionate basket structure only creates a long or short position by reference to the proportionate weighting of each asset in the basket.
- **Add-ons**   In addition to market risk assessments, unfunded credit derivatives such as total return swaps and credit default products (but not funded credit derivatives such as credit-linked notes) are subjected to a counterparty risk haircut by calculating the mark-to-market value of the derivative plus an "add-on" figure of between 0% and 15% (set by reference to the residual term of the contract and the contract

type (0% to 1.5% for qualifying debt items), 6% to 10% for non-qualifying debt items – e.g. non-investment grade debt) of the notional principal (in total, the "credit equivalent amount"), with the aggregate figure then being multiplied by counterparty risk weight. Prior to the introduction of the proposals contained in the 1999 Basel paper, the counterparty risk weights are between 0% and 50%. The 50% cap is removed under the new paper. The resultant figure is then weighted by a factor of 8%.

7.8.10 US

On 12 August 1996 and 13 June 1997, the US Federal Reserve published guidance on the capital treatment of credit derivatives.

Banking book treatment

- **Reference obligation** Must cross-default to protected asset.
- **Basket trades** A "first to default" basket structure gives the buyer protection against the default of the smallest and least risky risk weighted exposure in the basket. Sale of a "first to default" credit derivative basket structure generates a capital charge for the protection seller equal to the most risky risk weighted asset in the basket.

Trading book treatment

- **Reference obligation** Exact match or correlation is demonstrated.
- **Basket trades** A "first to default" basket structure allows the buyer to record a short position for the smallest and least risky risk weighted asset in the basket. Sale of a "first to default" credit derivative basket structure creates a long position for the protection seller in the most risky risk weighted asset in the basket.
- **Add-ons** In addition to market risk assessments, unfunded credit derivatives such as total return swaps and credit default products (but not funded credit derivatives such as credit-linked notes) are subjected to a counterparty risk haircut by calculating the mark-to-market value of the derivative plus an "add-on" percentage (which is based on either equity add-ons or commodity add-ons) of the notional principal, with the aggregate figure then being multiplied by counterparty risk weight and weighted by a factor of 8%.

8
Whole Business Securitisation

As discussed in section 5.12, whole business transactions are securitisations of the cash flow arising from a certain line or area of business of the originator over the long term. The transaction does not attach to certain contractual payments over time (as is the case with a mortgage or auto loan transaction), and does not operate within a particular contractual framework (such as the customer card agreement for a credit card transaction). It also cannot be defined by means of eligibility criteria (as is the case with future flows receivables), but rather attaches to general cash flow arising from a business.

Given this definition, whole business deals at first resemble plain corporate bonds rather than asset-backed securities. In fact they lie somewhere in between. As well as an overlap with corporate securities in some respects, there are also a number of differences, which are key to the benefits of whole business securitisations:

- A whole business deal is secured over the business generating assets (most corporate bonds are unsecured with negative pledge provisions against security for other debt to protect bond investors).
- Whole business deals are reserved for companies in particular sectors and competitive positions which have strong and stable cash flow positions.

8.1 BENEFITS AND REQUIREMENTS OF WHOLE BUSINESS DEALS

- **Leverage** This is the single biggest benefit from whole business transactions, and the ultimate rationale behind the preponderance of deals so far. Bank deals rarely exceed 100% gearing and thus only lever 50% of the enterprise value of the business. High-yield issues may be able to achieve up to 200% gearing, accessing two-thirds of the enterprise value of the business. Whole business transactions, however, are typically able to achieve a much greater degree of leverage, with deals so far raising from 60% all the way up to 90% of the appraised enterprise value of the business.
- **Quantum** The quantum of debt that can be raised against cash flow is larger than for a bank or high-yield deal, due to the long-term amortisation profile of the debt. Typically, debt can be raised to an EBITDA multiple of 6 to 10×, compared with 3.5 to 4× for senior LBO bank debt and 4.5 to 5× for mezzanine debt or a high-yield bond.
- **Tenor** Due to the ability of the bond market to absorb much longer debt maturities at an investment grade level than the bank market, maturities on whole business deals already issued (in this relatively young market sector) have

stretched to 30 years. This compares to 7 to 10 years for the bank and high-yield markets.

- **Cost** Whole business deals have cost benefits for two reasons:

  (a) As noted above, since the maturity of a whole business deal is significantly longer than other alternatives the absolute debt service cost in any one period is likely to be lower due to a longer debt amortisation period; and

  (b) Due to the reduced stress on current cash flow from the lower level of debt service, interest cover and debt service cover ratios are higher, leading to an investment grade credit rating and a more robust transaction which is more resistant to short-term market difficulties. Consequently, the coupon on the securities is likely to be lower.

- **Covenants** Covenants generally allow the management a degree of flexibility in running the day-to-day business of the company which exceeds that available to them in a bank deal or a high-yield deal.

Given such benefits, it is unsurprising that the nascent sector has aroused a high level of interest among the securitisation industry and the wider corporate sector. The key reason that the sector has not taken off in a bigger way is inherent in the basic analysis approach taken. As the deal attaches to operating cash flow, it is important for rating purposes that such cash flow can be predicted with reasonable certainty over the long term. Consequently, whole business deals are reserved for companies with:

- Stable and predictable cash flow
- A protected industry position – in other words, companies with little competition or high barriers to entry, where the competitive position is not likely to change significantly over time
- No dependence on particular managers or management elements to continue successful operations
- A solid regulatory position, where interference or action that could prejudice cash flow is unlikely
- No significant capital expenditure required.

As a result, deals to date have focused on particular sectors or companies with relatively protected competitive positions, such as the following:

- Motorway service stations
- Pubs, where the stability of cash flows and more granular nature of the business is combined with real estate value
- Dominant long-term entertainment groups (Tussauds)
- Globally dominant broadcasting groups (Formula One)
- Transport and infrastructure assets
- Water companies
- Healthcare concerns.

Related deals which have borrowed some of the "whole business" analysis approach have been in:

- Media (transactions such as the Bowie bond and the Cecchi Gori deal)

- Stock deals, which raise finance against the cash flow derived from trading stock (such as the Marne & Champagne deal)
- Real estate (transactions such as Broadgate which amortise rather than using a bullet or balloon debt repayment structure, and hence operate more on a cash flow basis).

8.2 STRUCTURES

Due to the nature of the cash flow that is being transferred, there is no true sale transfer analysis of a portfolio of receivables as would usually be found in other types of securitisation. It is still necessary, however, to ensure that the operating cash flow from the business can be properly ring-fenced from other liabilities in the business, and from the risk of insolvency of the business generally. This is especially the case given that the transaction will operate to significantly increase the leverage of the company and to reduce its available equity cushion for creditors. As a consequence, a very similar form of analysis will be done to ensure that the chosen ring-fencing mechanism is sufficient to ensure that other creditors cannot access the cash flow ring-fenced in favour of the securitisation.

8.2.1 UK transactions

The most common form of structure so far is that of a secured loan. This has been used extensively in UK transactions due to the creditor-friendly regime in the UK which permits an administrative receiver to block moratorium proceedings that could otherwise prejudice the timely payment of cash flows under the structure (although see section 8.6.2).

This structure is illustrated in Figure 8.1.

As well as a direct security interest over the assets of the operating companies, share pledges may be taken over the shares in the companies in order to give an extra degree of control. Share pledges may also be used to take a level of control in cash-generating companies that are peripheral to the main transaction, and where creating security interests over their assets would be difficult.

The apparent simplicity of a structure using secured notes issued by an asset-holding operating company is complicated by several factors:

- Financial assistance laws
- Securities laws
- Tax
- Corporate structure.

As most whole business deals are the refinancing of a leveraged acquisition, financial assistance rules are relevant. These require that a target is not permitted to provide assistance to enable the acquisition of its shares. These rules can be overcome by several methods, one of the most common of which is a "whitewash" procedure in which the director of the target provides a statutory declaration that the company will be able to pay their debts for at least 12 months after the provision of the assistance. However, such a declaration may only be given by a private company, and not by a public

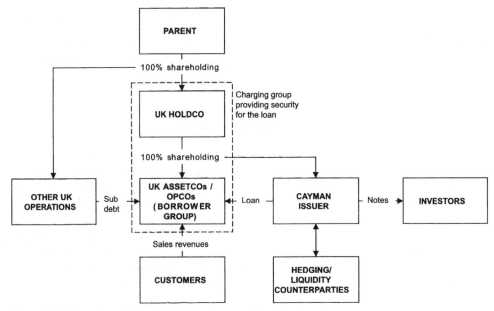

Figure 8.1 Paradigm UK whole business securitisation structure

company. Conversely, only a public company may issue securities that are to be listed for sale to investors.

Consequently, most structures to date have used a Cayman Islands special-purpose company to issue securities to investors, as this does not fall within the UK public company prohibition on using the whitewash procedure, and Cayman Islands securities laws are straightforward. The Cayman issuer then passes the proceeds on to the UK private companies which constitute the main asset-holding or operating companies in the group by way of loan secured over the assets of these group companies, with a floating charge over all assets of these companies to enable appointment of an administrative receiver (and block appointment of an administrator) where necessary to ensure that creditor control over the business is retained in any insolvency-related proceedings.

In order to ensure that the inter-company loan from the issuer to the borrowing group is not subject to withholding tax on interest payments, the Cayman issuer has usually been owned by the holding company of the borrowing group, so that the group income election for intra-group payments could be claimed. This is now of less importance, however, following the introduction of the inter-company exemption from withholding tax in s. 85 of the Finance Act 2001.

The particular corporate structure of a group may add complexity to the challenge of creating security over the necessary assets under the loan and ring-fencing the correct parts of the business.

8.2.2 Water deals

An active area of securitisation finance in the UK has been for the water sector. Although the structure differs from the whole business template in one key area –

lack of security over the water assets (the pipes, etc.) – the deals are otherwise sufficiently similar to be grouped as whole business deals. In particular, they are highly levered financings that are dependent on the results of the business and take operating risk on the business. The first deal, the Dwr Cymru transaction for Welsh Water (Glas Cymru), was launched in May 2001. Aside from being the first deal in the water sector, the Dwr Cymru transaction also employed a unique not-for-profit structure, where a company limited by guarantee was established to acquire the business. Consequently, all profits have to remain in the business or be used for reinvestment or rebates to customers. Although the Welsh Water structure has been duplicated by several companies in the water sector (most prominently Anglian Water and Southern Water) this has not included the not-for-profit shareholding structure.

The rationale for the financing of UK water companies is linked to the regulatory framework that governs water companies since the privatisation of the UK water sector in 1989, and is tied into the RAV (or RAB) – regulatory asset value (or base) – of the companies. RAV is a figure that was determined at privatisation for each water company. It is not intended to reflect a full asset value, and would only cover a small percentage of the replacement cost of the pipe network and infrastructure. Instead, RAV operates as a capital base for the company, on which it is permitted to earn a return under the regulatory framework.

Ofwat, the UK water regulator, fixes price limits every 5 years at a level that will enable water companies to cover their operating costs and maintenance Capex, and to cover a reasonable cost of capital on RAV. This is on the basis of an increase of RPI plus or minus "K" (an element designed to reward efficiency improvements or penalise underperformance). Water companies have the ability to request an "interim determination of K" (IDOK) during this 5-year period as a result of events such as increased capital obligations and substantial adverse effects (the latter is known as the "shipwreck" clause).

The RAV itself is increased by enhancement Capex (not maintenance Capex), and is decreased by current cost depreciation. RAV is also increased by RPI.

As a result of the regulatory framework, water companies have been able to raise finance as a percentage of RAV with a high level of certainty that their free cash flow post expenses and Capex will be able to service the debt. For example, the total debt issued in the Dwr Cymru transaction of £2.06bn (including a VFN) represented 93.6% of RAV – of which £1.96bn, or 89.1% of RAV, was investment grade. The senior class (rated A–/A3, part of which was wrapped) was £1.56bn, or 77.7% of RAV. Furthermore, as the regulatory formula allows RAV to increase by enhancement Capex, water companies have raised this finance by way of debt programmes that will allow them to issue further debt to fund enhancement Capex.

Despite the high level of stability of water companies, there are some residual concerns in these structures. The water licence granted to water companies in the UK can be revoked, although 10 years' notice of revocation must be given, terminating on or after 2014 (i.e. notice from 2004). In a transfer of licence, the structure would need to "take members and creditors into account" in determining the transfer value.

No security can be created over the water licence, or over protected assets needed to maintain the water supply, in such a way as would interfere with the appointment of a special administrator under the special administration regime applicable to water companies. This regime enables Ofwat to appoint an administrator whose appointment cannot be blocked by a security package (as appointment of an administrator for a normal corporate can be blocked by the holder of a floating charge over substantially all the assets of the company). Given the inability to take security over the water network itself, the water deals are structured with an 18-month standstill on occurrence of an event of default. This is designed to prevent the water regulator putting the company into special administration, and to enable a solution to the issue that has caused the event of the default to be worked out. Failing this, enforcement may be effected by the sale of the shares in the water company.

8.2.3   Non-UK transactions

In some countries, there may be no ability to prevent moratorium proceedings with a security interest, and consequently a variety of other mechanisms have evolved (see section 8.5).

Always at the core of this analysis is the level of control that the bond trustee (directly or via a receiver) has over the relevant cash-generating assets, and its ability to intervene in the business and either dispose of assets or run the business itself (or via delegates) if things go wrong.

This imposition of market discipline on the company through the use of the bond trustee makes it more likely that the bond will be called in and enforced promptly if operating cash flow is beginning to fall, assisting in the rating analysis. This puts pressure on the business managers to take the interests of bondholders more seriously, although it is adverse to the interests of the equity holders, who have given up a certain level of control that they would otherwise have.

8.2.4   Other structural features

Note classes for whole business deals are typically structured with short-dated floating rate classes (which are redeemable without penalty) and long-dated fixed rate classes (with Spens prepayment penalties). The short classes are designed to allow flexibility for redemption (both to bring funding costs down, and to have the ability to de-lever in the event that an IPO is to be considered as an exit option for the equity in the business). The long classes are designed to access the long-dated investor base, and to increase the maturity of the debt (and reduce the quantum of periodic amortisation payments) sufficiently to allow for the increased leverage.

The wide range of business types that could be considered for whole business securitisation means that a variety of other issues will also be relevant in any structure.

This is well highlighted by the Formula One transaction, where the consideration of the structure of the Formula One industry (and consequently the broadcasting and advertising revenues forming the securitisation pool) by the European Commission on competition grounds was seen as a major risk factor in the deal on launch (and subsequent to launch, with the formation of a company to establish the Grand Prix World Championship (GPWC) as a rival championship by some of the teams).

Media and intellectual property deals generally are likely to encounter issues with the exact valuation of the intellectual property rights that constitute the deal, due to their uncertain future value. In addition, they are likely to need careful structuring to ensure that the contractual and proprietary basis of the rights is sound, and can be adequately secured or transferred without breaching their terms (both with regard to head rights between the originator and the relevant copyright or patent holders, and with regard to sub-rights granted to exploit the rights, which are the cash generative portion of the business).

8.2.5 Taxation

Structures may be used to minimise tax, the most common being the use of subordinated debt or zero coupon debt provided by an entity outside the securitisation borrowing group to introduce a further source of tax deductions within the securitisation borrowing group.

If this debt can be supported (and does not lead to thin capitalisation issues or reclassification of coupons as equity dividends or distributions), then the payment (or non-payment but accrual) of interest on it will act as a deduction to offset tax on surplus income, enabling tax efficient profit extraction.

Tax structures can be particularly helpful when considering rating agency recession stress scenarios, where the accrual of (unpaid) interest on junior debt can reduce the overall tax burden and enable full repayment of debt over time without default.

8.2.6 Acquisition finance

Most countries have financial assistance prohibitions which introduce additional structural complexities for the use of whole business securitisation to refinance acquisition finance. In the UK, this will often mean using a private company whitewash structure to approve the debt security package, or any upstreaming of cash from the target to repay acquisition debt. As discussed in section 8.2.1, this may involve the use of a particular company structure, or the requirement to comply with other regulatory provisions.

8.3 CORPORATE VALUATION

Whole business deals introduce a new methodology for company valuation. Traditional corporate valuation methods are typically a combination of the following:

- **Book value**   The value of the company on this measure is equivalent to its net asset value. That is, the balance sheet value of its assets, net of the balance sheet value of its liabilities (and minority interests held in companies consolidated into its balance sheet). This reflects the value of the equity capital and reserves of the company, but does not give credit for the use to which those assets have been put in generating goodwill and ongoing earnings.
- **Comparison value**   This method values the company by comparing features of the company to the same features in other companies, where the price or value of the other companies is more readily calculated (for example, because the other companies are listed). The most common example is by calculating a benchmark price/earnings ratio for the company to be valued, by reference to listed companies in the same sector as the company to be valued. This can then be compared with the

earnings of the company to be valued, in order to determine its comparative price per share.

- **Discounted value**   This method seeks to value the company on the basis of discounted cash flow, by looking at the likely dividend flow over the first 5 years or so and a prospective future sale price at the end of Year 5.
- **Liquidation value**   This is the value that would be achieved by a liquidation of the company and sale of its assets. This is also known as its break-up value, and, like the book value, does not reflect the nature or value of the business as a going concern. It does, however, reflect the current value that could be realised by the assets on a realistic market sale basis, rather than their historic book values.
- **Replacement value**   This is the cost of replacing the assets of a company, and hence the cost of entry of competitors to the market. This is seen by some economists as a cap on the value of the company, as, if a company or sector was persistently valued in excess of its replacement value, there would be a clear inducement for competitors to enter the market to compete, thus driving values down again.

To these, new "internet economy" methods of valuation surfaced in 1998 and 1999. They attempted to recognise the fact that the initial business growth period for an internet company was greatly time-compressed, and consequently sought to value the business off the basis of the position it would be in when its initial growth surge had reached a plateau and its business was more stable, with developed revenue streams. Two main methods were:

- **Discounted value**   This method seeks to value the business off a discount back on a comparative valuation of the company in 5 years' time. The method assumes that in 5 years the high-growth period will stabilise, and applies a 5-year compound annual growth rate (CAGR) (benchmarked against levels seen in the internet market, which for start-ups are typically in excess of 50% and can be in excess of 100%) to current gross revenue levels to determine revenues in 5 years' time. Having calculated gross revenues at the end of the high-growth period, these revenues are then discounted back to present at a plain equity market level discount rate. Without having specific regard to current expense levels (which are assumed to outweigh revenues in the first few years anyway, as the cost base of the business leads the revenues base in terms of brand creation and advertising), a net margin for the business is set on an old economy comparative basis for the relevant line of business. The resultant earnings figure can then be applied through a comparative P/E approach to determine the value of the company.
- **Value per user**   This method is premised on the importance of the customer base of the company, and the assumption that, in the future, ways will be found to realise revenue from that customer base. Consequently, a comparative valuation is performed by looking at the value of other traded internet companies by the customers they have, and placing the company to be valued among them.

In whole business securitisation valuation, rating agency whole business modelling approaches can be used to increase the level of investment grade rated debt that can be raised in the market against the value of the business. Raising this debt serves to leverage the residual equity position of the owner of the business, thus increasing the return on equity. As this increase is likely to take the return on equity above previous levels in the market, it is likely to increase the prices that acquirers are prepared to pay to acquire companies in that sector generally, thus feeding through into an increase in the valuation of businesses in that sector.

Consequently, it is likely to become imperative for companies in sectors suitable for whole business analysis to consider securitisation and an efficient leverage structure, or they are likely to become targets for leveraged buy-outs, which will be re-financed through securitisation. Many companies in the UK carry debt levels around $1.5\times$ EBITDA with 50% gearing – levels which can easily be leveraged significantly with whole business securitisation. A significant proportion of whole business transactions to date have been carried out either to refinance an acquisition of the company, or (as with Formula One) to enable the existing owner to cash out maximum value against equity as an alternative to IPO.

8.4   RATING ANALYSIS

As with any other transaction, the credit analysis will be designed to ensure that there is sufficient coverage of scheduled debt service (interest and amortisation) by cash flow in the company, and that this is likely to remain so over the course of the transaction. Rating analysis for whole business deals is therefore typically based around the EBITDA of the company (or around operating profit with non-cash items such as depreciation added back in) less capital expenditure required for the core business. Once this is adjusted to remove one-off or uncertain earnings streams, this derives a base-case-stabilised free-operating cash flow figure.

Reflecting the rating agency stressed analysis, it is likely that the level of annual cash flow that will be assumed by the rating agencies to exist within the company to an investment grade level will be lower than that assumed within a high-yield structure to a lower-rated level. Consequently, the level of annual payments that can be supported by a whole business deal to an investment grade level is likely to be lower than the level that could be supported by a high-yield deal.

The advantage to be gained from a whole business deal is the long-term view of the business that can be taken by the rating agencies, as a result of the factors mentioned above (i.e. the security that is taken over the key assets, and the strong competitive position and stable cash flows of the company). Given the longer term of a whole business deal, the quantum of debt that can be raised is larger than that that can be raised as bank debt or high-yield debt, while still amortising the debt at a lower rate per annum. The short-term risk on the debt is actually lower than that on the high-yield debt, due to the greater debt service coverage (actual base case DSCR for interest and amortisation on a whole business deal on close could be up to $2\times$, compared to $1.5\times$ for a high-yield deal, $2.5\times$ for bank debt and $4\times$ to $5\times$ for future flows deals where the annual cash flow stream is more volatile). The risk is maintained over a longer time horizon however, and is dependent on an investor base prepared to accept this view.

The rating analysis will also examine the level of residual equity in the business, as this will incentivise the business owners and managers to continue to run the business and service the debt.

As general requirements for the deal going forward, the rating agencies will expect to see that the transaction structure provides sufficient protection against the insolvency of the originator (see section 8.2), and will require covenants that:

- A certain DSCR will be preserved at a certain level. There are generally two triggers – breach of the higher one means that no dividends can be paid, and breach of the lower one means that the deal will default. The dividend trigger has typically been set around the $1.5\times$ level, and the default trigger around the 1.25 level (both on a rolling 4-quarter basis), although these would be higher for deals with more variable cash flows or a higher level of embedded operating risk.
- The originator and its group must act to a prudent industry standard in operating its business (for example, in deciding future capital expenditure plans).
- The originator must not borrow, or dispose of or charge its assets in a way that could prejudice the ability of the business to repay the debt (but freedom to dispose is allowed within these limitations).

Analysis may also be required of the need for a back-up servicer to be able to run all or part of the business as delegate of a receiver if the business experiences difficulties.

8.5   FEASIBILITY IN DIFFERENT COUNTRIES

The feasibility of whole business securitisations for different companies is largely dependent on two factors:

- The nature of the business and market in which the company operates.
- The country in which the company's main assets and operations are based.

Companies in a monopolistic or competition-protected position with strong, stable cash flow have a sound foundation for these transactions. In order for the cash flow from the company's operations to be ring-fenced for the benefit of securitisation investors, however, the insolvency regime in the country where the company's main assets are based will need to be analysed to ensure that, in an insolvency of the company, a receiver acting for investors can continue to realise cash flow from operations without interruption.

It is generally not enough for the receiver to have valid security over hard assets such as real estate, as, by definition, the value in the business for bond investors lies in the continued operation and cash flow of the business over time. Exceptions to this are CMBS and inventory stock transactions.

The UK has formed the basis of development of whole business structures due to a creditor-friendly insolvency regime. This regime has been threatened to a certain extent by the Enterprise Act (see section 8.6.2), but the UK remains far ahead of other jurisdictions in developing whole business technologies.

Development of whole business structures in other countries has been more limited and complex, with a number of potential structures being utilised to circumvent difficulties with national insolvency regimes, such as:

- Franchise arrangements (used in the Arby's structure)
- Grant of a lease/synthetic lease to a bankruptcy remote entity

- Usufruct
- Inventory/stock security (used in the Marne et Champagne and the Rosy Blue Carat transactions)
- Ring-fencing of intellectual property rights
- Owner/operator split into two companies, with servicing outsourced by the owner to the operator
- Licence
- Hive-down of the main business generating assets into a bankruptcy remote subsidiary (holding assets through single-purpose subsidiaries is also commonly found in the property sector world wide)
- Grant of a security interest, reinforced by a share pledge over the shares in the company.

A country by country analysis is presented in Table 8.1.

8.5.1 Finland

Finland has seen the first true whole business deal in continental Europe, with the Tornator Finance transaction of November 2002 for Tornator Timberland – a whole business deal that took the form of a spin-off of Stora-Enso's forestry assets. This deal securitised forestry receipts from 594 000 hectares of forest in Finland.

The transaction creates security over the forestry assets, combined with a share pledge over the parent. Also, Finland has moratorium-type proceedings, which cannot be blocked by a creditor with a security interest. Consequently, the deal is structured to limit the number of potential creditors who could seek to exploit this mechanism.

8.5.2 France

Although not a whole business deal, the Marne & Champagne Finance transaction is an example of the export of secured loan technology to continental Europe. Notes are secured over a loan from Jersey SPV to an A-rated bank in France. The bank in turn lends to three champagne companies, secured by a possessory pledge over their champagne stocks (and security over the stock insurance policies). Possession is with a third-party holder.

In the event that there are disruptions in payments, a liquidity facility (sized to cover two years of debt service) can be drawn. If an administrator is appointed and it looks as though a delay in payments will arise, the note trustee will be able to sell the SPV loan rights to another champagne house to undertake enforcement (thus circumventing the usual risk of being unable to enforce rights in a moratorium).

In this case, the secured loan is dependent on the particularly strong nature of the security interest that can be granted over champagne stocks in France. Consequently, the deal technology is relatively difficult to transfer to other assets except for real estate (which has been securitised under secured loan-style CMBS deals).

Table 8.1 Country-by-country analysis

	Ability to seize and control assets		Interruptions to cash flow		Other		Deals
	Full security interest	Creditor regime on insolvency	Chapter 11, etc.	Priority creditors	Hive-down and legal merger	Financial assistance	
Finland			Reorganisation proceedings cannot be blocked by secured creditor				Tornator Finance deal in November 2002
France	No floating charge	• Creditors lose control of security enforcement if a creditor files for insolvency • Insolvency proceedings are controlled by court • Primary aim of insolvency proceedings is to protect employees • Marne relies on 1. Sale of once-removed loan rights (i.e. distressed value) 2. 2 years bank liquidity 3. 3 years between note maturity/loan maturity	Stay during: • Debtor commenced reglement amiable (3 months) • Creditor commenced 1. Redressement judiciaire or 2. Liquidation judiciaire (20 months)	Behind: • Employees • Proceedings costs • Taxes and social security • Post-insolvency creditors		• Can only use reduction of capital by disposal of surplus assets • May dispose of non-surplus to parent to reduce capital further • Also share pledge	None outside CMBS
Germany	No floating charge – security over real estate enforced by court auction	• Creditors lose control of security enforcement if a creditor files for insolvency • Court-appointed insolvency administrator (creditors can replace with their choice) must produce an insolvency plan • View to rehabilitation • Take account of all classes of creditors in considering whether to liquidate/restructure/transfer, etc.	Stay from filing for insolvency until insolvency plan produced and approved • Time taken to approve plan likely to be around 3 months • Can cover with liquidity facility (e.g. 18 months line in Tenovis) • Insolvency plan to present business continuance as best for all creditors	Behind: • Proceedings costs	• May be able to use sale and leaseback of entire business with economic benefit retained by seller (so no tax event) to "hive-down" or ring-fence	• GmbH can upstream from reserves • AG cannot upstream	Tenovis Finance in November 2001

Country				Behind	Legal merger		Deals
Ireland			Stay for examinership; can only be blocked if receiver in office for more than 3 days prior to application for examinership			Have whitewash procedures	
Italy	Limited Article 46 floating charge to bank lenders		Stay under amministrazione controllata for up to 2 years; cannot block with Article 46 floating charge		• Legal merger possible	• Cannot upstream value • Can merge Target into Newco if have two-thirds majority of target • May be challenged if merge Newco into Target	FILMS plc deal for Cecchi Gori in 1998; Romulus Finance deal for AdR in February 2003
Japan					• Legal merger possible		
Malaysia						Have whitewash procedures	1st Silicon deal in June 2001
Netherlands	No floating charge		Limited moratorium for maximum of 2 months				
Spain					• Legal merger possible	• Cannot upstream value • Can merge Target into Newco	
UK	Floating charge	• Creditors can control process	Stay can be blocked by creditor with floating charge	Behind: • Proceedings costs (and preferential creditors if only have a floating charge)	• Legal merger not possible • On hive-down, employees travel with business • Tax on disposal	• Private company can whitewash use of distributable reserves (need reduction of capital for anything more) • Public company can only use "larger purpose"	Multiple deals from 1997
US		• Arby's relies on transfer of franchise receivables/rights and logo to SPV	Automatic stay applicable under Chapter 11	Behind: • Post-insolvency creditors • Proceedings costs • Wages, taxes	• Legal merger possible	• Cannot transfer assets without reasonable return if become insolvent or retain unreasonably small capital	Arby's deal in November 2000

8.5.3 Germany

One of the most promising continental European jurisdictions for development of whole business structures is Germany, as the German insolvency code gives strong creditor protection and adequate security packages for most assets. The most difficult point of argument to date in Germany has been the ability to control the insolvency process. The crux of the process lies in understanding the reaction of an insolvency administrator on initiation of insolvency proceedings. The administrator can be replaced by the creditors committee, and must decide on the insolvency plan for the business.

The main choice here is in deciding whether to try to sell the business assets for a lump sum to pay off creditors, or in continuing to run the business for ongoing cash flow. Once made, the decision reached by the insolvency administrator is irrevocable.

In reaching a decision, the insolvency administrator must take into account:

- The value achieved for all classes of creditors.
- The job security of the employees of the business.

Almost by definition, given that the structure is designed to protect a whole business cash flow securitisation, running the business for cash flow will achieve greater value for creditors than disposing of the assets. Clearly, continuing to run the business should also act as a greater protection for employees than an asset disposal.

Against this must be weighed the management burden and time involved to run the business. This is particularly the case where the business has just entered insolvency and its suppliers and customers may be thinking of terminating business arrangements rather than continuing them. In addition, the provisions of the new Insolvency Code (which was passed in 1999) are not yet tested.

Tenovis Finance

The first deal close to a whole business transaction in Germany closed in 2001, with the Tenovis Finance transaction for Tenovis GmbH. A whole business style secured loan technology was used, although the collateral pool and structure was much closer to a standard securitisation, with a pool of Euro 1.15bn present value of leasing contracts for PABX systems (with maintenance obligations) supporting only Euro 350m of debt (Euro 300m of notes and Euro 50mn of revolving facility). Clearly, most UK-based whole business structures have less contractually based revenues streams (e.g. pub income).

Despite the significant overcollateralisation, the maintenance obligations in the contracts and the risk of termination by an insolvency administrator combined to limit the deal to the A rating level. The rating agencies accorded value to the appointment of EDS Holding (guaranteed by A-rated EDS Corporation) as back-up servicer. EDS committed to take over the servicing obligations of the company on insolvency (with an 8-year commitment matching the expected maturity of the notes), in terms of:

- Taking over from the administrator the burden of dealing with the running of the business;
- Ensuring that the staff in the business will enjoy job security going forward; and

- Enabling a rapid transition to a new (and well-known) entity, which serves to protect supplier and customer relationships. This is particularly relevant in light of the rights of customers to terminate for failure to service in this transaction.

This would provide comfort to the insolvency administrator that a reputable firm would be available to run the business and would encourage the administrator to opt to renew business contracts rather than terminate them.

The potential for termination by the customers is protected by penal termination provisions which generate termination payments of up to 95% of the net present value of the contract (provided that maintenance continues to be provided). This would be a less significant issue in a monopolistic-type business with limited competition, or where customers are locked into the business in some other way.

The rating agencies also questioned several German insolvency practitioners, and obtained comfort from them that they would be likely to continue the operations of the business on insolvency. As further protection, the servicing operations were split off into a separate company, and the back-up servicer was given a call option over the shares of the servicing company to enable the back-up servicer to obtain the necessary staff and expertise in the event that they were called upon to act as servicer. The trustee was given the ability to control the shares in the servicing company and to direct the sale of the company if necessary. In Germany, the state will provide for payment of the salaries of employees of an insolvent business for up to 3 months after insolvency, giving the trustee up to 3 months at the most in which to act to find a substitute servicer, before employees leave to find other work (and clearly, the longer the delay the greater the likelihood that they will look for other work anyway).

The potential liquidity gap arising from the time delay while insolvency proceedings are dealt with was covered by 18 months of liquidity (the expected time period for the insolvency procedure to be worked through was 3 months).

8.5.4   Italy

The Romulus deal of February 2003 marks the first sizeable whole business-style deal in Italy (since the FILMS plc deal for Cecchi Gori in 1998). Although the Romulus deal is based on an operating concession (which allows for a less complex security ring-fencing structure than other types of whole business deal), this is a positive development and shows the continued development that has marked the Italian market out as the largest and most sophisticated cash securitisation market in continental Europe.

8.5.5   Malaysia

Malaysia saw the first Asian whole business deal, with the US$ 250m 1st Silicon deal for 1st Silicon Malaysia in June 2001. Although ultimately guaranteed by the Sarawak Economic Development Corporation, the structure nonetheless followed whole business techniques, compatible with Malaysian laws through Malaysia's English law colonial heritage.

8.6 THREATS TO WHOLE BUSINESS TECHNOLOGY

8.6.1 Ratings volatility

As with the CDO sector, the whole business sector has seen ratings volatility in excess of that seen in the mainstream ABS, RMBS and CMBS markets. Much of this is accounted for by a few deals, with the Welcome Break and RoadChef transactions in particular being downgraded several times.

Some of this volatility is due to particular structural features surrounding these deals, as outlined below. However a higher level of volatility remains more likely to be seen in this sector going forward, as by their nature whole business deals carry more operating risk (and thus exposure to consumer and business sentiment), and are less granular and diverse, than most other ABS.

Welcome Break

The Welcome Break transaction was the first ever whole business securitisation. It was a securitisation of 21 motorway service stations (two of which – Gretna Green and Ross Spur – were owned on a JV basis and originally excluded from the deal) in August 1997 that was undertaken to refinance their acquisition by Investcorp for £476m in March 1997. The acquisition was financed through £320m of senior and mezzanine debt that was replaced by £321m of securitisation debt in Classes A1, A2, A3 and B.

The structure of the deal is illustrated in Figure 8.2.

On acquisition, EBITDA was running at £35.6m, giving a Debt/EBITDA multiple of

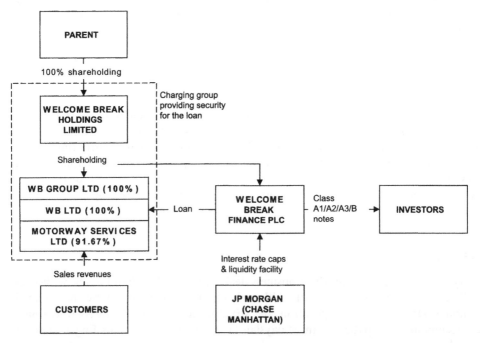

Figure 8.2 Welcome Break Finance plc

9.02×. This Debt/EBITDA multiple increases to 10.28× if an undrawn but senior-ranking revolving facility of £45m is added back in. The deal was tapped in October 1998 for a further £55m of Class A1 and A2 notes, at which point EBITDA had increased to £47m, giving a new Debt/EBITDA multiple of 8.00× (10.56× measured against original EBITDA). This Debt/EBITDA multiple increases to 8.96× if the revolving facility of £45m is added back in (11.83 × measured against original EBITDA).

Two further service stations were subsequently added: Hopwood Park in August 1999, and Wheatley in late 1999.

The business was considered to be a suitable candidate for long-term financing, as it operated under service station concessions granted by the government, which are limited in number. Consequently, the ability of other participants to enter the market was limited. Revenues were seen as linked to traffic growth on the road network.

The notes began trading downwards in value following December 1998 and March 1999 quarterly figures that showed EBITDA trending below the levels seen in the same quarters in previous years (the business is seasonal in nature, with peak revenues in the summer quarter (July, August and September). The decline was exacerbated by poor figures for summer 1999.

Although EBITDA subsequently recovered over 2000 and 2001, it declined again in 2002, raising doubts as to the ability of the company to meet debt service payments going forward. This was a particular concern for this deal as, despite the drop in debt service due to the fall in market Libor rates on the Class A1 and A2 notes, the debt service profile of the deal increased significantly from June 2004 onwards as the Class A1 notes were to begin to amortise.

Between February and May 2002, the notes suffered several downgrades from the rating agencies, the net effect of which was to reduce:

- The Class A notes (rated A on issue) to BBB (S&P)/BBB (Fitch)
- The Class B notes (rated BBB on issue) to BB (S&P)/BB- (Fitch).

Further downgrades followed in mid-2003, on the back of restructuring proposals which involved potential note write-downs:

- The Class A notes to BB (S&P)/BB (Fitch)
- The Class B notes to B (S&P)/CC (Fitch).

The deal was the first in the whole business sector, and has some valuable lessons about the nature of the field. Foremost among these is the structure of the debt service schedule. The deal was structured with a rising level of debt service, with an assumption that growth in the early years of the transaction would enable the business to cope with such increased debt service.

As can be seen from Figure 8.3, assuming EBITDA at £41.6m (the average of the June 2002 and September 2002 annualised figures), the transaction would not support debt service on the Class A or B notes across 2005. EBITDA is required to grow at 5.09% per annum to support a 1 × DSCR.

Thus, not only would the deal breach its financial covenant to maintain EBITDA at 1.25× Debt Service, but it would be at risk of having to defer interest payments on the Class B notes and potentially even trigger a payment event of default through failure to make interest payments on the Class A notes.

In fact, EBITDA has subsequently dropped further, falling below £40m.

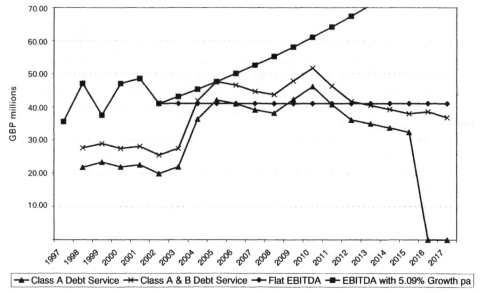

Figure 8.3   Welcome Break Finance plc; source offering circular, investor reports

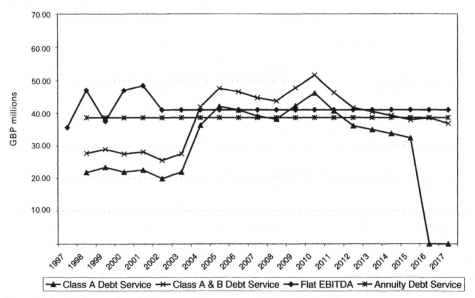

Figure 8.4   Welcome Break Finance plc; source offering circular, investor reports

The significance of this debt service structure can be seen by comparing it to a typical annuity debt service structure as set out in Figure 8.4 (which is commonly used on new whole business deal structures). This generates a stable level of debt service for interest and principal payments combined, which, although higher in the early years, is ultimately more stable.

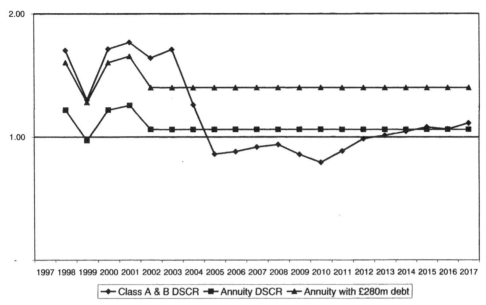

Figure 8.5 Welcome Break Finance plc debt service cover; source offering circular, investor reports

In practice, given the stress shown on an annuity style basis in Figure 8.4 in the early years of the deal, the annuity-style structure would have been combined with a lower total level of debt.

Figure 8.5 shows the DSCR on the current Welcome Break structure assuming flat EBITDA of £41.6m, compared with the DSCR on an annuity-style payment structure, and the DSCR on an annuity-style payment structure combined with a lower total debt of £280m (eight times start EBITDA of £35.6m).

The rule-of-thumb measure of 8–9× EBITDA to an investment grade level has developed from a number of whole business deals since Welcome Break closed, with many pub transactions and transport/infrastructure deals closing around this level. Some deals have exceeded this – for example, Romulus Finance, which benefited from a long operating concession, achieved 9.5× EBITDA. However, multiples on new deals with more significant operating risk or Capex requirements are increasingly less levered than this (e.g. healthcare deals which have mostly reached around 6× EBITDA to an investment grade level).

The high level of leverage seen in Welcome Break including the senior revolving facility, and the significant increase in debt service over the life of the deal, are unlikely to be seen in the same form again. Furthermore, the tap issue in October 1998, only one year into the deal, followed an early upward trend in the EBITDA of the group and exacerbated the underperformance of the deal following the downturn in EBITDA.

The key to structuring transactions that will survive 25 or 30 years of debt repayment is to ensure that the volatile swings of corporate business patterns are minimised. This is partly accomplished in the selection of businesses from stable sectors, but the deal structure also needs to avoid introducing unwarranted stresses.

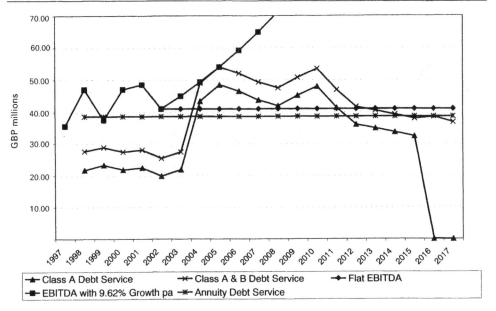

Figure 8.6   Welcome Break Finance plc; source offering circular, investor reports

A further potential stress can be seen in the method of hedging the floating rate liabilities in the form of the A1 and A2 notes. In Welcome Break this takes the form of interest rate caps set at 7.5% for an initial period. If the scenarios illustrated in Figures 8.3 and 8.4 are re-run with Libor on the floating rate notes reset at 7.5% going forward, the result is as set out in Figure 8.6. As can be seen, there is no change to the annuity debt service profile, as this is modelled on a fixed rate based on the blended cost of debt as at the time the Welcome Break deal was launched (i.e. assuming that any floating rate was swapped to a fixed rate cost for the issuer at the point of issue).

However, the Class A and B debt service requirement increases on an increase in floating rates to 7.5%, as the A1 and A2 note coupon rises. In a rising interest rate environment this would introduce additional volatility into the business profile, and further impact the transaction. The required growth in EBITDA to reach 1× debt service would then be 9.62% per annum.

On 5 June 2003, Welcome Break announced a potential restructuring proposal, which serves to illustrate the manner in which the deal could be rebalanced. The proposal was to effect a sale and leaseback of nine of its motorway service stations, with the proceeds to be used to tender for the majority of the Class A notes and all of the existing Class B notes below par. The effect would be to reduce consolidated debt (and thus debt service), and to convert debt service to a more even basis (with debt service payments on the sale and leaseback made by way of rentals), thus reducing the volatility of the structure, as well as cutting the absolute leverage of the deal.

RoadChef

A valid comparison can here be made with the RoadChef Finance transaction of November 1998, which has also encountered difficulties since launch. As with

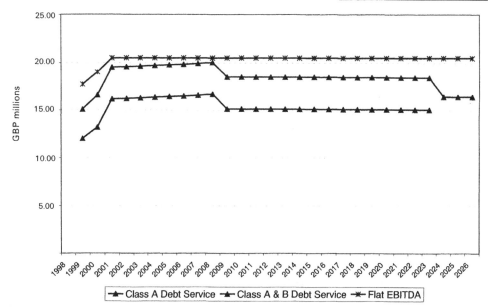

Figure 8.7 RoadChef Finance Limited; source offering circular, investor reports

Welcome Break, RoadChef was a whole business securitisation of motorway service stations (17 in this case) and was heavily levered, with debt of £210m on EBITDA of £17.69m – a Debt/EBITDA multiple of 11.87×.

As with Welcome Break, EBITDA of the RoadChef group has not increased as expected since the launch of the deal. However, the RoadChef deal had a less stepped debt service structure, as shown in Figure 8.7.

As with Welcome Break, between February and May 2002, the notes suffered several downgrades from the rating agencies, the net effect of which was to reduce:

- The Class A notes (rated A on issue) to BBB (S&P)/BBB+ (Fitch)
- The Class B notes (rated BBB on issue) to BB.

Despite these pressures, the more stable nature of the RoadChef deal is clearly displayed. Even though the DSCR would, in the absence of EBITDA growth, fall over time, it would not breach a 1× DSCR. Although there would be the potential to breach the deal's 1.25× DSCR financial covenant, the transaction permits the sponsor to deposit equity in the securitisation group, which can be added to EBITDA to enable it to meet its ratios. In practice, EBITDA has subsequently risen, reaching £21.8m in June 2003.

8.6.2 Enterprise Act

The insolvency ring-fencing structure of whole business deals in the UK is dependent on the ability of the holder of a floating charge to appoint an administrative receiver (in order to block the appointment of an administrator and moratorium proceedings) and the ability of that receiver to run the business. This enables control to be exerted over the business in insolvency proceedings, maximising value and timing of collections for creditors.

The Enterprise Act limits the use of administrative receivership, and promotes the use of administration proceedings, in order to encourage business start-ups and entrepreneurship. It also reforms the system of preferential debts which rank ahead of floating charge creditors. The Act received Royal Assent on 7 November 2002, and the relevant provisions came into force in September 2003.

Exclusions from the provisions of the Enterprise Act were prepared for securitisation, but concerns remain over their effect on warehousing and acquisition finance structures which are not immediately financed or refinanced through the issuance of bonds or commercial paper.

Administrative receivership

The Act provides at s. 250 for new sections 72A through G to be inserted in the Insolvency Act 1986. New s. 72A provides that the holder of a qualifying floating charge may not appoint an administrative receiver of the company. A qualifying floating charge is defined in paragraph 14 of Schedule 16 (which is inserted as Schedule B1 of the Insolvency Act 1986) as a floating charge which expressly states that paragraph 14 applies to it, or which purports to empower the holder of the floating charge to appoint an administrator or an administrative receiver of the company, and which – either by itself, or together with other charges or security interests – is secured over "the whole or substantially the whole of the company's property".

Under s. 72A(4), the new provision restricting the appointment of an administrative receiver would apply to a floating charge created on or after a date appointed by the Secretary of State by order made by statutory instrument (effectively retaining the old rules for existing charges).

There are a series of exceptions to the new provision, which permit the appointment of an administrative receiver, including:

- Under s. 72B and Schedule 18 (which is inserted as Schedule 2A of the Insolvency Act 1986), where there is security to a trustee/nominee/agent for holders of an instrument (or there is a third-party guarantee or security interest, or there is an arrangement involving options, futures or contracts for differences) under which a party incurs (or is expected to incur) debt of at least £50m (or currency equivalent as at the time when the arrangement is entered into) at any time during the life of the arrangement, where the arrangement involves the issue of:

  – A debt instrument which is rated by an internationally recognised rating agency, admitted to the official list in the UK, or admitted to trading on a market established under the rules of a recognised investment exchange or on a foreign market (or is designed to be so rated, listed or traded). Or:
  – A bond (construed in accordance with Article 77 of the FSMA 2000 (Regulated Activities) Order 2001) or commercial paper (which must be redeemed before its first anniversary) issued to investment professionals, high net worth individuals or sophisticated investors.

- Under ss. 72C, D and E and Schedule 18, in respect of a project company (a company which holds property for the project, or has sole or principal contractual responsibility for carrying out all or part of the project (either directly or through agents), or is one of a number of companies which together carry out the project, or has the purpose of supplying finance to enable the project to be carried out, or is a holding company of any of these, unless in any of such cases it also performs another function which is neither related to any of these nor related to the project) for a public–private partnership project, a utility project or a project under which a party incurs (or is expected to incur) debt of at least £50m (or currency equivalent as at the time when the project begins) at any time during the life of the arrangement, where in each case a person who provides finance for the project has contractual step-in rights to assume sole or principal contractual responsibility for carrying out all or part of the project.

Administration

An administrator may not be appointed while an administrative receiver is in office, unless the floating charge holder who appointed the administrative receiver consents, or the floating charge is in some way prejudiced (as set out in paragraph 39 of Schedule 16). The appointment of an administrator takes effect for an initial period of 1 year (under paragraph 76 of Schedule 16), subject to extension by the court or by consent.

Preferential debts

Under s. 251, those categories of preferential debt due to the Crown (the Inland Revenue, Customs & Excise and social security – set out in paragraphs 1 through 7 of Schedule 6 to the Insolvency Act 1986) – primarily PAYE and NI Contributions due in the last 12 months and VAT due in the last 6 months – are abolished. Other preferential debts (mainly wages due in the last 4 months and occupational pension contributions) remain as preferential debts. Under s. 252, an amount prescribed by order by the Secretary of State will be ring-fenced in favour of unsecured creditors (and will not be available to holders of a floating charge to the extent that there are any such unsecured creditors).

9
The European Union

The laws and regulations of the European Union do not yet serve to cover the majority of areas relevant to securitisation, but the recent increase in the issuance of Directives in the field of financial services have served to render a more detailed overview of European provisions relating to securitisation relevant.

The European Union was formed pursuant to the Treaty of Rome, and brings constituent member states in Europe into a single harmonised marketplace, designed to promote free movement of goods, services, labour and capital. Since 1995, the 15 member states of the European Union have consisted of Austria, Belgium, Denmark, Finland, France, Germany, Greece, Ireland, Italy, Luxembourg, the Netherlands, Portugal, Spain, Sweden and the United Kingdom. The next wave of enlargement of 10 new member states from 1 May 2004 consists of Cyprus, the Czech Republic, Estonia, Hungary, Latvia, Lithuania, Malta, Poland, Slovakia and Slovenia. Bulgaria and Romania are in the next wave, and Turkey is expected to follow behind them.

The key EU institutions consist of the Council (of Heads of State), the Commission (the European civil service), the Parliament (of elected members) and the European Court of Justice. The balancing of the Council as legislature, the Commission as executive and the European Court of Justice as judiciary leaves the Parliament with relatively little power.

The publication of a Draft EU Constitution on 20 June 2003 was designed to acknowledge the extensive enlargement planned for the EU, and to rework the governmental framework of the EU. More areas are shifted towards qualified majority voting, and the constitution provides for a President of the Council, and for an EU Foreign Minister, as well as providing for the ability of an EU state to leave the EU.

European Union law consists of (a) the Treaty of Rome and amendments thereto (including the Single European Act, which extensively rewrites the Treaty) which are directly applicable and enforceable by or against member states or private individuals or companies if capable of being so construed; and (b) legislative instruments consisting of Regulations, Directives and Decisions. These instruments are proposed by the Commission and are submitted in draft to the European Parliament, Economic and Social Committee (ECOSOC) and Council for comment. They are updated and referred to the Committee of Personal Representatives (COREPER) and then to the European Parliament once more, before being finalised and sent to the Council, who vote to accept or reject them. Recommendations or Opinions given by the Council or Commission are not legally binding.

A resolution was put forward in the EU Parliament in December 2002 to rename Regulations as "Laws" and to rename Directives as "Framework Laws".

9.1   RING-FENCING AND TRUE SALE

There is no common European position on the transfer or ring-fencing of assets, or on the establishment of securitisation SPVs. These areas are however dealt with by legislation in several European jurisdictions, mainly in one of two different forms:

● The fund structure adopted in France and Spain
● The company structure adopted in Italy.

Some jurisdictions have adopted legislation providing for either of these at alternatives, such as Belgium and Portugal.

9.1.1   Moratorium/automatic stay

Although the EU has not put in place its own harmonisation of insolvency laws, it has put in place, under the Insolvency Proceedings Regulation No. 1346/2000 of 29 May 2000, provisions for which jurisdiction's insolvency proceedings are relevant to an entity. This has a potentially significant effect in that neither the country of formation of the entity nor the legal form of the entity would now act as a block to the application of the insolvency or moratorium proceedings of any other European jurisdiction where the entity has the centre of its main interests (CMI).

The Regulation came into force on 31 May 2002 with direct effect in all member states except Denmark (where separate rules are expected to be enacted), and overrides domestic legislation to the extent that the two are incompatible. The CMI is presumed to be the jurisdiction of the company's registered office unless proved otherwise, but this has successfully been proved in the UK case of *Brac Rent-a-Car International Inc (2003) Ch* where the company was a Delaware company, but the court held that its CMI was in the UK. The Regulation applies if the CMI is within the EU. The main proceedings in respect of a company's insolvency are to be undertaken in the CMI in respect of that company, and encompass all assets of the company save those subject to secondary proceedings. Secondary proceedings can be undertaken in any jurisdiction in which the company has an establishment, but only in respect of assets situate in that jurisdiction. Insolvency proceedings will be carried out in accordance with the *lex fori* of the jurisdiction of proceedings. The Regulation does not apply to insurance undertakings, credit institutions, investment undertakings or collective investment undertakings.

9.1.2   Covered bonds

This is an area where significant legislative activity has been seen across Europe over the last few years. In particular, France, Ireland, Luxembourg and Spain have all introduced new legislation, or revived old laws, in order to aid the development of a market in covered bonds to rival the German Pfandbrief market. Covered bonds have also been issued in the UK without specific enabling legislation.

9.2 SECURITIES LAWS

The EU has developed many different proposals which affect the issuance and sale of securities within the EU, including the Listing Particulars Directive and the Prospectus Directive.

The Listing Particulars Directive requires that companies should be able to use a single prospectus to raise capital across the EU. The prospectus is checked by the listing authority in the home state of the issuer, and needs to be updated annually via a shelf registration. The directive also applies to the smaller companies markets across Europe (such as AIM).

Discussions on the Prospectus Directive began in May 2001, when the EU Commission set out its proposal for a directive to harmonise prospectuses across Europe. The Directive was adopted in July 2003 and is intended to be implemented in member states in 2005, with an 8-year transitional period. The Directive replaces and harmonises existing regimes for listing securities across the EU, and regulates public offer of securities within the EU and admission to trading on an EU exchange.

The Directive requires, under Article 3, delivery of a prospectus on an offer to the public or on admission to trading, and works on the basis that the prospectus is vetted by the home authority of EU issuers (defined in Article 2(1) as the authority where the issuer has its registered office or – in respect of debt securities with a denomination of Euro 1000 or more (reduced from Euro 5000 in the March 2003 draft and from Euro 50 000 in drafts prior to November 2002) – either the state where the issuer has its registered office or the state where the securities will be admitted to trading or the state where the securities will be offered to the public, at the option of the issuer).

Categories of offer that are not considered as an offer to the public are contained in Article 3(2) (these exemptions do not apply to admission to trading) and include offers to qualified investors (defined in Article 2(1) as credit institutions, investment firms, insurance companies, collective investment schemes, pension funds, other financial institutions, corporates whose sole purpose is to invest in securities, supranationals, government agencies, legal entities which are not small or medium-sized enterprises (SMEs), sophisticated individual investors or SMEs who expressly ask to be treated as qualified investors), offers to less than 100 persons (other than qualified investors) per member state, offers with a minimum investment per investor or minimum denomination of Euro 50 000, and offers of less than Euro 100 000 in total over 12 months. Small and medium-sized enterprises are defined in Article 2(1) as entities that have at least two of: less than 250 employees; total balance sheet assets of Euro 43m or less; net turnover of Euro 50m or less.

The information required in a prospectus is set by reference to the type of securities (debt or equity) and also to take into account the size and activities of the company – in particular, in relation to small and medium-sized enterprises.

The Market Abuse Directive (Directive 2003/6 of 28 January 2003) entered into force on 12 April 2003 and must be implemented in member states by 12 October 2004. The Directive covers all financial instruments admitted to trading on a regulated market within the EU and requires that each member state specify a regulator to prevent incidences of market abuse (insider dealing and market manipulation).

9.3 TAX TREATMENT

9.3.1 Withholding tax

The Savings Tax Directive (Directive 2003/48) was eventually signed in June 2003 after 5 years of discussion. The Directive is to be implemented in member states by 1 January 2004, and applied from 1 January 2005. The UK and the Netherlands have agreed to ensure the adoption of the same measures in their dependent territories (the Channel Islands, Isle of Man and Caribbean dependencies).

The Directive provides for all EU states except Austria, Belgium and Luxembourg to exchange information on non-resident savings from 1 January 2005, to enable the domestic state to tax the individual properly. Paying agents or collecting agents established in the EU will be required to provide information on payments of interest made on bonds and bank deposits to individuals (not corporates) who are EU residents in another state (regardless of the location of the bond issuer or deposit bank itself). Austria, Belgium and Luxembourg would instead impose a withholding tax of 15% from 2005 to 2007, 20% from 2008 to 2010 and 35% from 2011 (as will Switzerland), and would only move to information exchange if the EU is unanimously satisfied that Switzerland and the US (in particular) are meeting EU information exchange requirements.

Bonds issued prior to 1 March 2001 would be exempt from the provisions, and (under a further decision of the ECOFIN Council on 2 March 2001), any issues prior to 1 March 2002 which are fungible with bonds issued prior to 1 March 2001 would also be exempt. Bonds issued by governments or state-related entities on or after 1 March 2002, which are intended to be fungible with bonds issued prior to 1 March 2001, will result in both the original issue and the new issue being subject to the new regime. Bonds issued by corporate entities on or after 1 March 2002 will be subject to the new regime, and will not be fungible with issues prior to 1 March 2001.

9.4 ACCOUNTING TREATMENT

On 7 June 2002 the European Parliament and Council adopted a Regulation on International Accounting Standards. The Regulation requires EU companies that are listed on an EU market to use International Accounting Standards and International Financial Reporting Standards in their consolidated accounts from each financial year starting on or after 1 January 2005. Member states may opt to also apply the Regulation to non-listed companies, and may delay the application of the Regulation to financial years starting on or after 1 January 2007 for companies that only have debt securities listed.

The relevant IAS standards for off-balance-sheet treatment are IAS 27 on consolidation (as well as SIC-12, an interpretation of IAS 27 issued by the Standing Interpretations Committee) and IAS 39 on derecognition.

IAS 27 requires the consolidation of all subsidiaries and of all entities controlled by a company (and the preparation of consolidated financial statements to include such subsidiaries and entities). An entity may be regarded as being controlled by a company even where the company owns little or no equity in the entity. SIC-12 is an interpretation applicable to IAS 27, and contains guidance as to when an entity is controlled and is consequently required to be consolidated. Control requires being able to direct or dominate the decision-making of the SPV (or establishing an "auto-pilot" mechanism so that the entity acts in a predetermined manner), and having the objective of obtaining benefits from the activities of the SPV.

IAS 39 requires that in order for an asset to be considered off balance sheet of a company for accounting purposes in a securitisation transaction control over the assets must be lost or surrendered by the company. This can be achieved where the transferee acquires the right to pledge or exchange the assets, and the transferor does not retain effective control over the assets (via a right and obligation to take back the assets at a certain point, or a right to take back the assets other than at fair market value at the time of repurchase). If this is the case, the assets are granted "derecognition" and removed from the originator's balance sheet into the SPV, to be replaced with the resulting components of the sale at fair value, and any fair value adjustment on the sale price against the carry value of the assets. Derecognition is not available if the transferor retains substantially all the risks and benefits of the assets. On 20 June 2002 the IASB published an exposure draft for a revised version of IAS 39, which emphasises the concept of "continuing involvement" in the asset or a portion of the assets that have been transferred.

For more details see Chapter 10.

On 3 July 2002 Eurostat (the EU statistics agency) published guidelines on account-ing for securitisations undertaken by EU states, to tie-in with compliance with the Maastricht criteria on public sector borrowing. The guidelines set out principles that future flows deals and deals with state guarantees will be regarded as government borrowing, as will deals with deferred purchase price or further payments from the SPV to the state, where the initial payment proceeds are more than 15% less than the market price of the assets transferred.

9.5   CAPITAL TREATMENT

The Commission released a First Consultative Document on the new Basel Accord proposals on regulatory capital in November 1999, and a Second Consultative Docu-ment on 5 February 2001. A Working Document was published on 18 November 2002, and a Third Consultative Document was published on 1 July 2003 following the publication by the Basel Committee of CP3 in April 2003. The Documents provide for the Standardised Approach and the IRB Approach.

The Documents set out the draft provisions detailed below.

9.5.1   Method of transfer

In order for an originator to exclude securitised assets from its capital calculation, the following requirements should be complied with:

- Significant credit risk should have been transferred to third parties.
- The transferor does not maintain effective or indirect control (e.g. via a right or obligation to take back the assets at a certain point).

- The assets should be transferred beyond the reach of the transferor and its creditors or liquidator in bankruptcy.
- The securities issued are not obligations of the transferor.
- The transferee is an SPE and the holders of beneficial interests in the SPE have the right to pledge or exchange those interests without restriction.
- Any clean-up call should be at the bank's discretion, should not exceed 10% of the overall issuance, and must not be used to provide credit support.
- The deal should not require the originator to improve the quality of the pool, or provide for the credit enhancement to increase post-close, or provide for enhanced yield to investors on a drop in credit quality.

To the extent that the originator provides implicit support for a transaction, it will be required under the Documents to hold capital against all exposures in the transaction, and must publicly declare that it has provided support, and the capital impact of so doing.

9.5.2 Synthetic securitisations

The Documents specifically assess the risk on super-senior pieces under a "look-through" approach for the Standardised Approach, and off inferred ratings for the IRB Approach. The Documents also set out requirements for an originator to exclude securitised assets from its capital calculation under a synthetic securitisation as follows:

- There should be no provisions that materially limit the transfer of credit risk (e.g. significant materiality thresholds, etc.).
- The deal should not require the originator to improve the quality of the pool, or provide for the credit enhancement or retained first loss position to increase post-close, or provide for either an increase in the cost of credit protection, or an enhanced yield to investors, on a drop in credit quality.
- Legal opinions on enforceability in relevant jurisdictions.
- Any clean-up call should be at the bank's discretion, should not exceed 10% of the overall issuance, and must not be used to provide credit support.
- Time calls may be included, provided that they are set outside the weighted average life of the credit pool.

The level of reduction in capital achieved by the transfer of risk in synthetic form will depend on the collateral, if any, backing the credit protection (in accordance with the new system for collateral provided in the Documents) and the counterparty risk weighting of the credit protection seller.

If there is a maturity mismatch between the underlying credit exposures and the term of protection bought under the synthetic securitisation, the originator will be required to hold capital to reflect the maturity mismatch. If a mismatch exists, then no protection value is recognised if the synthetic securitisation has less than one year to expiry. If the synthetic securitisation has one year or more to expiry, then the benefit of tranches sold will be reduced by multiplying the tranche amounts by the synthetic securitisation residual term over the underlying exposure residual term (in risk weight terms, equivalent to averaging an unprotected amount and a protected amount by tenor).

9.5.3   Credit enhancement and liquidity facilities

On-balance-sheet items will be risk weighted as for other assets. For off-balance-sheet items such as commitments under liquidity facilities, an assessment is undertaken as to whether a facility is "eligible". To be eligible:

- The facility must identify clearly in what circumstances it may be drawn, and may not be used for credit enhancement, or to cover losses, or to provide permanent funding
- Drawings on the facility should not be subordinated to investors and the fees for the facility should not be subordinated
- The facility cannot be drawn after credit enhancement for the deal has been exhausted
- The facility should contain a provision for preventing the facility being drawn against past due or defaulted assets
- The facility should contain a provision resulting in a reduction of the amount that can be drawn if the average pool quality falls below investment grade

In the Standardised Approach, eligible facilities may be treated as normal business commitments (a 20% credit conversion factor (CCF) for one year or less, or a 50% CCF for more than one year). If the facility is only available in the event of general market disruption (rather than in relation to liquidity shortfall on underlying assets), then a 0% CCF is proposed. A 0% CCF is also available for eligible servicer cash advances which rank senior to other claims, subject to national discretion. Other off-balance-sheet items are given a 100% CCF.

In the IRB Approach, eligible facilities that may only be drawn in the event of general market disruption are treated as on-balance-sheet items in respect of their full notional amount, but the bank is then only required to recognise 20% of the resulting capital charge. Other off-balance-sheet exposures are treated as on-balance-sheet items in respect of their full notional amount.

9.5.4   General capital treatment

Most of the EU materials track the new Basel proposals closely (see details in sections 11.6 to 11.8). The key differences relate to the treatment of commercial mortgages and covered bonds.

Unlike the 1988 Basel Accord, the current EU rules weight commercial mortgages at 50% for Denmark, Germany and Greece (where there is a maximum 60% LTV, and the mortgages are over completed residential property or offices or multi-purpose commercial premises located within the relevant country).

The new Basel proposals recognise the potential 50% weighting for commercial mortgages going forward. They do not recognise a different weighting for covered bonds. The current EU rules weight covered bonds at 10% for Austria, Denmark, France, Germany, Luxembourg and Spain.

The new regime proposed under the Consultative Documents would have the effect of changing the covered bond weightings to the following in the Standardised Approach:

- 10% risk weighting: covered bonds issued by 20% risk weighted entities, and (at national discretion) claims on institutions specialising in the inter-bank and public debt markets and which are fully secured over assets which are 0% or 20% risk weighted

- 20% risk weighting: covered bonds issued by 50% risk weighted entities
- 50% risk weighting: covered bonds issued by 100% risk weighted entities
- 100% risk weighting: covered bonds issued by 150% risk weighted entities.

In the Foundation IRB Approach, the Loss Given Default would be 20% for covered bonds (in the Advanced IRB Approach, the bank is required to calculate the LGD).

9.6   DATA PROTECTION/CONFIDENTIALITY

The Data Protection Directive 1995/46 on the processing of personal data set out certain requirements for dealing with "personal data", including the requirement that personal data should not be transferred outside the European Economic Area unless the recipient territory has adequate personal data protection provisions. A compromise on a "safe harbour" has been agreed with the US, under which US companies that sign up to oversight by regulatory authorities in the US can receive such information. The EU has also approved standard contractual clauses for the transmission of personal data to a data processor outside the EU who acts on behalf of the data controller who has sent the information.

9.7   CONSUMER PROTECTION

On 11 September 2002, the EU Commission published a proposal for a directive on consumer credit (the Consumer Credit Directive) to replace Directive 87/102. The new draft Directive is designed to harmonise consumer credit across the EU by preventing member states from adding to the new rules (except in certain specific areas) under Article 30. The new draft governs the regulation of "credit agreements" where credit is granted to a "consumer" (an individual acting outside his trade) by a "creditor" (an individual or legal entity granting credit in the course of business), and "surety agreements" (ancillary agreements guaranteeing the fulfilment of credit, granted by a guarantor who is a consumer).

There is no minimum or maximum amount of credit under regulation. Certain agreements are exempt from the provisions of the Directive under Article 3; namely loans for the purchase or transformation of immovable property (as opposed to equity release mortgages where the proceeds are used for other purposes), hire agreements where there is no option to purchase, credit agreements where debts must be discharged by a single payment within a period not exceeding 3 months (e.g. debit cards), credit agreements granted by creditors outside their normal business activity at lower than market rates which are not offered to the public generally and certain credit agreements with investment firms (which are subject to regulation on information and advice under the investment services Directive).

Under Article 28, creditors and "credit intermediaries" (an individual or legal entity who acts as an intermediary in concluding credit agreements for a fee) must be registered and subject to inspection or monitoring.

Credit agreements and surety agreements should be entered into on business premises under Article 5. Under Article 11, consumers are given a 14-day right of withdrawal from an agreement, which runs from the date on which a copy of the agreement is transmitted to the consumer. The agreement must meet certain requirements as to form, including a statement of the "total lending rate" charged by the lender under the agreement and the "annual percentage rate of charge" or APR (which reflects the total cost of credit to the consumer).

9.8   OTHER ISSUES

The EU Financial Collateral Directive (Directive 2002/47 of 6 June 2002) applies to collateral arrangements over securities or cash between two entities, where at least one of them is a financial institution, and the other is not a natural person. In relation to book-entry securities, the Directive sets out conflict of laws provisions which provide that perfection of any security interest and completion of any other steps required to make the security interest effective on third parties should be carried out in accordance with the requirements of the jurisdiction where the account is held, as should any steps for enforcement of the security interest. The Directive extends the scope of the Settlement Finality Directive.

10
Accounting for Securitisation

The primary issues raised in accounting for securitisation relate to:

- The claim for derecognition, or off-balance-sheet treatment, of the securitised assets and finance by the originator; and
- The treatment of the securitisation SPV as a subsidiary of the originator, or as an independent non-consolidated entity.

Within the securitisation industry, accounting rules centred around the US accounting standards first embodied in FAS 77. The US led the rest of the globe in addressing accounting issues relating to securitisation due to the predominance of securitisation activity in the US. Standards were developed in the UK in 1994 with FRS 5, and many other countries around the world have relied on the US or UK standards in developing their own treatments. The latest US standard (FAS 140) applies from 1 April 2001. The IAS standard (IAS 39) was published in December 1998 and applies from 1 January 2001.

The UK standards focus on the transfer of risks and rewards in the assets to the SPV. To the extent that risks are retained but are capped, an element of the assets may be transferred off balance sheet (resulting in a "linked presentation" showing gross and net figures in a caption on the accounts). By contrast, the US standards have focused on the transfer of control over the assets (although the new FIN 46 interpretation shifts this focus), with any elements of risk retained being recorded as separate residual risks.

IAS 39 follows the trend of US standards, with the predominant focus being on control. However the interaction of IAS 39 with IAS 27 and SIC-12 (effective from 1 July 1999) on consolidation means that it goes much further in preventing off-balance-sheet treatment on a consolidated basis. SIC-12 widens the group definition to include entities that are directed or operate on autopilot, where the company realises benefits from them. This is likely to include most SPVs – with the possible exception of SPVs in synthetic deals where excess spread is not paid out from the SPV.

Accounting standards have undergone significant change and development from 2001 to date, following accounting scandals such as Enron and WorldCom, and EU attempts to apply standardised accounting rules across the European Union. The impact of the collapse of Enron in December 2001 led to pressure for full and clear disclosure of off-balance-sheet arrangements in company accounts, and the more rigorous enforcement of the rules on minimum levels of equity for off-balance-sheet transactions in the US. This has been followed by an increased level of scrutiny on companies that use securitisation (in terms of the risks they shed and the risks they retain in the transaction structure), as well as on corporates with complex accounting structures.

10.1   US ACCOUNTING STANDARDS

10.1.1   FAS 140

FAS 140 was published in September 2000 to replace FAS 125, and applies to transfers and servicing of financial assets that take place after 31 March 2001 (excluding some transfers committed to prior to such date – for example, further tranches of revolving transactions). The Standard applies to securitisations and to resecuritisation of existing deals.

FAS 140 accords a transfer one of four treatments:

- Sale (if the requirements set out in FAS 140 are met);
- Financing (if the requirements are not met);
- Swap (for example, where loans are exchanged for notes); or
- Partial sale (if the requirements of FAS 140 are met, but the originator retains servicing or one or more classes of securities issued). In this latter case, the sold assets are accorded sale treatment, and the retained assets (i.e. servicing rights to the extent that a more than adequate compensation is received for servicing, or securities) will appear on the balance sheet.

To qualify as a sale, the transferor must:

- Surrender control over the assets, such that they are isolated beyond the reach of the transferor, affiliates, liquidator or creditors;
- Transfer the assets to an SPV where:

  - For a QSPE (see below), noteholders have the right to pledge or exchange their notes or certificates; or
  - For other entities, the SPV itself has the right to pledge or exchange the underlying assets;

- Not retain effective control over the assets via a right and obligation to take back the assets at a certain point, or a right to take back specific assets (other than under a clean-up call where the transferor retains or subcontracts servicing, but not where the transferor sells servicing); and
- Receive cash proceeds from the sale (as opposed to a note or interest in the assets). This requirement has led to the introduction of a second onward transfer step to an issuing trust in some bank securitisations in the US, where previously a "one-step" transfer to a subsidiary in return for a note would have sufficed under FAS 125.

A Qualifying Special Purpose Entity or "QSPE" is never consolidated in the financial statements of the seller. An SPV which is not a QSPE may be consolidated with the seller (see below). To qualify as a QSPE, an SPV must:

- Be "demonstratively distinct" from the seller (i.e. where it cannot be unilaterally dissolved by the transferor or its affiliates or agents, and where at least 10% of the fair value of its beneficial interests are held by entities other than the transferor or its affiliates or agents);
- Have permitted activities that are significantly limited and specified up-front;
- Only hold passive financial assets (i.e. where no decisions other than servicing are

made by the QSPE – the QSPE cannot, for example, hold controlling equity stakes), cash and investments; and

- Have limited powers to choose when to dispose of assets, such that it may only dispose of assets if required to do so as a result of an event of default outside its control, or where funds are required on exercise of a put or call or predetermined maturity or liquidation date.

If the SPV is not a QSPE then it will be consolidated on the accounts of its majority owner unless it falls within FIN 46 (see below).

If sale treatment is accorded to a transaction, this amounts to derecognition, and the seller is required to use "gain on sale" accounting. Some sellers have structured securitisations as financings rather than sales, specifically in order to avoid gain on sale treatment. This is due to the fact that gain on sale is disliked by the equity market as it generates current accounting profit from future excess spread revenue (leading to earnings volatility if default and prepayment assumptions in the gain on sale calculation prove to be incorrect).

On 19 July 2001, the FASB issued guidance extending the ability of QSPEs to dispose of assets, by allowing servicers acting on behalf of QSPEs to buy loans out of a securitised pool at fair value without prejudicing QSPE treatment. This followed industry concerns over the ability to dispose of non-performing loans in CMBS transactions.

10.1.2   FIN 46

On 2 December 2001 Enron filed for Chapter 11. Increasing pressure began to be exerted by the SEC in terms of full and clear disclosure of off-balance-sheet arrangements in company accounts. At this point, non-QSPE entities could be divided into:

- Entities that met the SEC 3% equity rule (that entities must have a minimum equity equal to at least 3% of their total capital structure in order to permit off-balance-sheet transactions);
- Thinly capitalised entities that did not meet this rule.

Entities that were non-QSPEs would be consolidated on the accounts of their majority owner unless they were thinly capitalised (in which case they would be consolidated with the seller).

The concern in the Enron situation was with the use of entities that apparently met the 3% requirement, and could therefore avoid consolidation by ensuring external voting control, but were nonetheless thinly capitalised and the losses on which were effectively borne by the seller. Consequently, the 3% equity rule for off-balance-sheet treatment of non-QSPEs was more rigorously enforced. On 25 June 2002 WorldCom announced a $3.8bn misstatement of expenses as capital expenditure. Its ratings were downgraded to Ca/CCC–/CC on 26 June following the announcement.

Following these developments, the FASB announced on 27 February 2002 that they were considering increasing the minimum equity requirement for deconsolidation from the transferor of assets of SPVs that were not QSPEs within FAS 140 from 3% to 10%. This was the start of a developmental process (with extensive discussions throughout the latter part of 2002), with the publication of a draft interpretation on consolidation on 28 June 2002 for comments by 30 August 2002. This process was concluded on

17 January 2003 with the publication of FASB Interpretation No. 46 (FIN 46) on Consolidation of Variable Interest Entities, to be applied from 1 February 2003 in respect of entities created after 31 January 2003, and from the first fiscal period beginning after 15 December 2003 (originally 15 June 2003) in respect of entities created before 1 February 2003.

The Interpretation does not apply to QSPEs. It does apply if an entity is a "Variable Interest Entity" (VIE), that is:

- Its equity is insufficient to permit the entity to finance its activities without subordinated financial support (for this purpose equity of less than 10% of total assets is considered insufficient unless the entity can demonstrate its ability to finance its activities, or it has at least as much equity as comparable entities which operate without subordinated financial support, or it can demonstrate that its equity exceeds its expected losses); or
- Its equity investors do not have votes, the obligation to absorb losses or the right to receive residual returns.

If an entity is a VIE it will be consolidated by the entity (the "Primary Beneficiary") that will absorb the majority of the expected losses of the VIE, and/or that is entitled to a majority of the VIE's expected residual return, as a result of holding "Variable Interests" in the entity. If different entities absorb the losses and receive the return, the entity that absorbs the losses will consolidate. If a VIE has no primary beneficiary it will not be consolidated.

"Variable interests" are defined as "contractual, ownership, or other pecuniary interests in an entity that change with changes in the entity's net asset value". Variable interests can include equity and debt instruments, guarantees, put options, derivatives, servicing contracts, leases and other items. For this purpose, an entity will consider variable interests held by itself and by its related parties (which include certain de facto agents).

In addition to consolidation considerations, holders of variable interests are required to meet disclosure requirements. The primary beneficiary (as well as consolidating) must disclose the nature, purpose, size and activities of the VIE, the carrying amount and classification of VIE collateral, and any lack of recourse by creditors of the VIE to the primary beneficiary. Holders of significant variable interests must disclose the nature of involvement with the VIE and when such involvement began, the nature, purpose, size and activities of the VIE, and the maximum exposure to loss as a result of the involvement with the VIE.

10.1.3   Amendment to FAS 140

Following the Enron and WorldCom accounting scandals and the publication of FIN 46, further discussions were held throughout 2003 on the scope of the permitted activities of QSPEs, amid concerns that the exemption of QSPEs from FIN 46 might lead to the exploitation of QSPE status as a way of circumventing FIN 46 (in particular, in order to ensure that CP conduits remain off balance sheet). This resulted in the issuance on 10 June 2003 of an Exposure Draft to amend FAS 140. This was replaced by a new Exposure Draft in late 2003.

The Exposure Draft provides that the permitted activities of QSPEs should not include entering into liquidity or credit enhancement agreements with the seller. In addition, the permitted activities of any QSPE which "reissues beneficial interests" (e.g. revolving commercial paper) should not include entering into liquidity or credit enhancement agreements with any party (together with its affiliates) that provides more than half of the relevant commitment or makes decisions about the reissuance of beneficial interests.

10.2   UK ACCOUNTING STANDARDS

10.2.1   FRS 5

In the UK, Financial Reporting Standard 5 of the Accounting Standards Board on reporting the substance of transactions, came into effect on 22 September 1994. FRS 5 requires that in order for an asset to be considered off balance sheet for accounting purposes in a securitisation transaction, all significant risks and benefits attached to that asset must be transferred to another entity.

If this is the case, "derecognition" will result in the assets being removed entirely from the balance sheet of the originator. If this is not the case, but:

- The maximum risk of the originator on the assets has been capped; and
- The SPV and investors have "no recourse whatsoever, either explicit or implicit, to the other assets of the [originator] for losses",

then a hybrid treatment known as "linked presentation" will be used. This groups the gross asset value with the risk portion that has been transferred to leave the remaining net exposure, all in a separate caption in the originator's accounts.

A linked presentation is only available to the extent that:

- The originator has no right or obligation to repurchase the assets. Any repurchase right (e.g. the 10% clean-up call permitted by Financial Services Authority guidelines) or obligation means that the portion of the assets over which the right or obligation extends will not be deducted from the gross asset value in the accounts. The clean-up call, tax call and call and step-up embedded in most deals may be structured at the SPV level rather than the originator level in order to avoid the risk of losing FRS 5 linked presentation treatment;
- Any swap or cap provided by the originator: (i) is on market terms; (ii) is not based on rates under the control of the originator; and (iii) merely replaces existing hedges that the originator had for the asset portfolio prior to its sale.

Indemnities given by the originator which allow access to all assets of the originator may prevent linked presentation treatment. There are different interpretations on the extent of this restriction, for example as to whether it includes an indemnity to directors of an SPV for legal liability (which is not direct support of losses on a deal, but rather other legal liabilities that could arise). Typically, this would cover any liability that the directors could incur for trading while insolvent, and if a deal has been correctly structured to be bankruptcy remote, a claim should never arise in practice (save possibly in a programme structure where the directors could be concerned over the incidence of ongoing expenses in the SPV).

If the transferee entity is directly or indirectly controlled by the originator, and the transferee represents a source of benefits for the originator, this may lead to the transferee itself being included in the originator's consolidated accounts in a linked presentation as a "quasi-subsidiary". If the transferee is also an actual subsidiary, then full consolidated accounts including the transferee will be required instead.

10.2.2 Amendment to FRS 5

On 10 September 1998, the Accounting Standards Board published an amendment to FRS 5 with immediate effect to deal with the balance sheet treatment of properties (such as hospital, schools, prisons, etc.) that form part of PFI transactions or of other similar transactions. The amendment requires that:

- Elements of the overall transaction which are capable of being separately attributed to the provision of services, rather than to the use of the property, are split out (for example, where the service element runs for a different period from the property element, has different terms and conditions or termination provisions, or can be renegotiated separately);
- If non-separable service elements remain linked to the property payments, then the amendment to FRS 5 is applied;
- If there are no remaining non-separable service elements, then SSAP 21 is applied, which treats the payments for the property as lease payments, and uses the test of who bears "substantially all the risks and rewards of ownership" to establish whether the payments create a finance lease or an operating lease. If the lease is a finance lease, then the lease payments are discounted to NPV to create a capital figure to be entered into the accounts of the payor.

With regard to any remaining use of property payments that contain non-separable service elements (and are thus subject to the amendment to FRS 5), the amendment sets out a number of risk factors to be considered. Each of these factors should be considered where the relevant risk is significant (i.e. there is a high degree of uncertainty involved), and there is a genuine commercial possibility of the risk or scenario materialising. The factors are indicative as to whether the property appears as an asset on the balance sheet of the user (in PFI transactions, the government) or of the operator, depending on who bears the risks. The main risk factors are:

- Who bears the risk of demand for the property (a fixed payment by the user regardless of reduced or increased use of the property indicates that the user has demand risk);
- Whether the operator has access to third-party revenues to cover the property (or, for example, relies on a guaranteed minimum level of payment from the user);
- Who determines the nature of the property (or whether, for example, the operator is free to use another property to fulfill its obligations);
- Whether underperformance is penalised (in which case the property is likely to be an asset of the operator);
- Whether the operator can pass on its specific increases in costs to the purchaser (or is restricted to increasing costs in line with general indices such as the RPI);

- Who bears the risk of obsolescence; and
- Who bears residual value risk.

Other subsidies or contributions made by the user may result in on-balance-sheet items for the user related to such payments. Also, if the user has agreed to buy the property at the end of the contract term for a price other than the residual market value at that future time, the difference between the price and the expected residual value should be accrued in the accounts over the length of the contract.

10.2.3 FRED 30

Financial Reporting Exposure Draft 30 (FRED 30) was issued by the Accounting Standards Board in June 2002 in relation to the intended adoption of IAS 32 and 39 in the UK as part of convergence to IAS generally by 2005. FRED 30 recommends that the derecognition portions of IAS 39 not be applied in the UK at present, with a view to working on a joint standard to replace both FRS 5 and IAS 39 on derecognition prior to 2005.

10.2.4 IAS

On 17 July 2003, the DTI announced that all UK companies would be entitled at their option to use International Accounting Standards instead of UK standards from January 2005 in both their individual accounts and their consolidated accounts. This option is over and above the requirement of the EU Regulation on International Accounting Standards (see below), that publicly traded companies be required to use IAS in their consolidated accounts from January 2005.

10.3 INTERNATIONAL ACCOUNTING STANDARDS

Accounting standards around the world enjoy a greater degree of harmonisation than legal or tax regulations due to the work of the International Accounting Standards Committee (IASC), the standards of which have been adopted by many countries and by many multinational corporations. The IASC was formed in the UK in 1973 to prepare International Accounting Standards (IAS) that could be adopted on an international basis, and published its first standard in 1975.

The IASC was restructured in 1999, resulting in the formation of the International Accounting Standards Board (IASB), which took over from the IASC on 1 April 2001. From 1 April 2001, new reporting standards issued by the IASB are designated as International Financial Reporting Standards (IFRS). The IASB has no mandatory authority. However, much like the Basel Committee, its pronouncements are likely to become ever more important as more countries around the world harmonise their standards to international standards. In particular:

- Many countries allow the financial statements of listed companies to be prepared in accordance with IAS (e.g. China (for B shares), France, Germany, Italy, the Netherlands, Switzerland, Thailand and the UK), while more countries permit foreign-listed companies to use IAS (e.g. Australia, Hong Kong, Singapore, Turkey and the US (if reconciled to US GAAP)).

- Some countries are applying IAS standards uniformly across local companies or harmonising their standards to accord with IAS (e.g. Hong Kong, where the Hong Kong Society of Accountants has been gradually harmonising standards with IAS (rather than UK GAAP) since 1993).

- On 7 June 2002 the European Parliament and Council adopted a Regulation on International Accounting Standards. The Regulation requires at Article 4 that all EU companies which are admitted to trading on a regulated market in the EU must use IAS and IFRS in their consolidated accounts from each financial year starting on or after 1 January 2005. Member states may opt to also apply the Regulation to non-consolidated accounts and to accounts of non-listed companies, and may delay the application of the Regulation to financial years starting on or after 1 January 2007 for companies that only have debt securities listed.

- On 29 October 2002, the FASB in the US and the IASB announced that they would work to achieve convergence between US standards and IAS by 1 January 2005, using the principles-based approach of the IASB, rather than the rules-based approach of the FASB.

The attractions of a uniform global set of accounting standards are clear. They would enable:

- Multinationals to ease reporting requirements across many jurisdictions;
- Companies to list on different global exchanges more rapidly and easily (encouraging competition and the global flow of capital);
- Investors to compare financial statements of companies around the world directly.

The IASC published IAS 27 on consolidation in April 1989 (effective for financial years beginning on or after 1 January 1990) and IAS 39 on derecognition in December 1998 (effective for financial years beginning on or after 1 January 2001). The IASC issued SIC-12 (an interpretation of IAS 27 issued by the Standing Interpretations Committee) in June 1998 (effective for financial years beginning on or after 1 July 1999) (the terms of IAS 1 require that financial statements under IAS meet the requirements of both the Standards and the SIC interpretations).

On 19 June 2003, the IASB published IFRS 1, giving details of the transition requirements to using IAS and IFRS. These originally included a requirement that the submitted set of accounts should include a set of accounts for the previous year for comparison purposes, which would have required EU companies migrating to IAS and IFRS to begin to calculate their accounts using IAS and IFRS from the first accounting period starting on or after 1 January 2004 in order to provide such a comparison, but this requirement was removed on 23 July 2003.

10.3.1 IAS 39

IAS 39 requires that in order for an asset to be considered off balance sheet of a company for accounting purposes in a securitisation transaction, control over the assets must be lost or surrendered by the company. This can be achieved where the transferee acquires the right to pledge or exchange the assets, and the transferor does not retain effective control over the assets (via a right and obligation to take back the assets at a certain point, or a right to take back the assets other than at fair market value at the time of repurchase).

If this is the case, the assets are granted "derecognition" and removed from the originator's balance sheet into the SPV, to be replaced with the resulting components of the sale at fair value, and any fair value adjustment on the sale price against the carry value of the assets. Derecognition is not available if the transferor retains substantially all the risks and benefits of the assets. There may be a requirement to consolidate the SPV with the originator, under the provisions of IAS 27 and SIC-12. If control has not been surrendered, the transaction will be accounted for as secured borrowing.

IAS 39 also deals with accounting for derivatives and hedging.

10.3.2   IAS 27

IAS 27 requires the consolidation of all subsidiaries and of all entities controlled by a company (and the preparation of consolidated financial statements to include such subsidiaries and entities). An entity may be regarded as being controlled by a company even where the company owns little or no equity in the entity (see examples given at IAS 27.12).

10.3.3   SIC-12

SIC-12 is an interpretation applicable to IAS 27, and contains guidance as to when an entity is controlled and is consequently required to be consolidated. Control requires:

(a) Being able to direct or dominate the decision-making of the SPV (or establishing an "autopilot" mechanism so that the entity acts in a predetermined manner); and
(b) Having the objective of obtaining benefits from the activities of the SPV.

SIC-12 gives scenarios that can be considered as the control of an SPV by an originator:

- The activities of the SPV are conducted on behalf of the originator such that the originator obtains benefits for the operation of the SPV.
- The originator has the decision-making powers to obtain the majority of the benefits from the SPV, or uses an "autopilot" mechanism to obtain them.
- The originator has the right to the majority of the benefits of the SPV and may thus be exposed to the risks of the SPV.
- In substance, the originator retains the majority of the ownership risks of the SPV in order to obtain benefits from the activities of the SPV.

10.3.4   Revised IAS 39

SIC-12 may mean that where funding is required, deals are more likely to be on balance sheet. Where capital is required, synthetics may be used rather than cash deals to avoid a benefit arising in the SPV, or the transaction may be undertaken with a market counterparty instead. This may also lead to the increasing use of specific group structures with entities established specifically for the origination and securitisation of assets.

The European Securitisation Forum expressed concern to the IASB in October 2001 on the effect of SIC-12 and the IAS 27 and IAS 39 standards on the securitisation industry. Since then, efforts have focused on the possibilities suggested by the limited recourse nature of the debt issued in a securitisation – such as removing the debt from the balance sheet of either the originator or of any SPV issuer, regardless of whether the issuer itself is off balance sheet. In effect, the debt issued would be regarded in accounting terms as giving an interest in the securitised assets to the bond investors. This has led to the publication of a draft amendment to IAS 39 in June 2002.

On 20 June 2002, the IASB published an Exposure Draft for a revised version of IAS 39 for comments by 14 October 2002, modifying its provisions dealing with derecognition. The IASB held public roundtable discussions on the draft in 2003, for a new paper in December 2003.

The new exposure draft emphasises the concept of "continuing involvement" in the asset or a portion of the assets that have been transferred. Where continuing involvement is present, derecognition will not be permitted. Examples of continuing involvement are where the transferor:

- Has the ability or obligation to reacquire control of the transferred asset, to the extent of such ability or obligation; or
- Provides compensation based on the performance of the transferred assets – e.g. by way of guarantee – to the extent of such potential compensation.

The new exposure draft removes the requirement for the transferor to transfer substantially all the risk and benefits of the assets in order for derecognition for any part of the assets to be considered, and for the transferee to obtain the right to pledge or exchange the assets. The new amendment also sets out the basis for "pass-through arrangements" based on the limited recourse nature of securitisation deals. If an entity transfers its contractual rights to a financial asset and continues to collect cash flows from the transferred asset, the transfer qualifies for derecognition provided that the transferor does not otherwise have a continuing involvement and that:

- The transaction is limited recourse based on amounts collected;
- The transferor is not permitted to sell or pledge the transferred asset or otherwise use that asset for its benefit; and
- The transferor must remit collections without material delay and is not entitled to reinvest such amounts for its own benefit.

In effect, the debt issued would be regarded in accounting terms as giving an interest in the securitised assets to the bond investors, thus removing the assets from the balance sheet of the securitisation SPV, and rendering consideration of whether or not the securitisation SPV is consolidated with the originator far less important.

The structure would, however, potentially require both the originator and the SPV to meet the requirements for pass-through treatment, in absence of which the assets may remain on balance sheet at either one level or the other, if the SPV is consolidated under IAS 27 and SIC-12.

10.4   THE INFLUENCE OF THE EUROPEAN UNION

As discussed, the EU is already influencing accounting standards by the imposition of IAS from 2005. However, it has also made its presence felt more directly by its oversight of sovereign accounting to comply with the Maastricht criteria on public sector borrowing.

On 3 July 2002 Eurostat (the EU statistics agency) published guidelines on accounting for securitisations undertaken by EU states. The guidelines set out these principles:

1. Future flows deals will be regarded as government borrowing.
2. Deals with state guarantees will be regarded as government borrowing.
3. Where the deal provides for further deferred purchase price or payments from the SPV to the state, and the initial payment proceeds are more than 15% less than the market price of the assets transferred, the transaction will be regarded as a borrowing as it is an insufficient risk transfer.
4. Where the deal is within the 15% range, the initial proceeds are treated as the sale price, with any deferred purchase price considered only when it arises.

The guidelines apply to all government deals, including deals previously closed. Greece had launched four deals through 2000 and 2001 – Hellenic (2000), Ariadne (2000), Atlas (2001) and Aeolas (2001) – all of which are future flows deals relying on elements of state guarantee. Likewise, the Blue Danube deal for the State of Lower Austria in 2001 carried a state guarantee. Italy had securitised lottery receivables (the SCCPP deal in 2001) on a future flows basis, and real estate (the SCIP deal in 2001) for Euro 2.3bn – significantly less than its value of Euro 5.1bn. The INPS and INAIL deals realised significantly less than book value of the assets transferred (although arguably closer to the assets' market value).

Greece announced a hold on state securitisation following the initial announcement by Eurostat in April that they were examining the issue of accounting for state securitisation, leading market players to believe that future volumes in the public ABS sector in Europe were likely to be reduced.

Italy, however, has continued its securitisation programme, but has modified it to ensure that the Eurostat criteria are met, with tranched deals that are more closely structured to market standards for accounting off-balance-sheet treatment in the corporate and bank sectors.

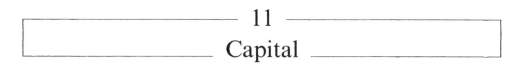

11

Capital

Regulatory capital for financial institutions around the world is set by local central banks. Since the Basel Accord of July 1988, this has been based on the guidelines produced by the Basel Committee in most countries. These guidelines attempt to set a level playing field for banks to hold certain minimum levels of capital against the risk of losses arising on their assets. This arises from the concern that banks are fundamentally heavily leveraged institutions, and that the collapse of one bank may lead to the collapse of other banks due to the interlinked nature of the financial markets. Capital levels and periodic provisions are designed to cover expected and unexpected losses on the bank's loan assets, so that only the capital providers (i.e. equity investors) suffer if the bank's loans default, rather than depositors or other creditors losing money.

11.1 BANKING BOOK

The Basel Accord set capital at an arbitrary minimum of 8% of the amount of the bank's loan assets, with each loan asset being "risk-weighted" to reflect the relative risk of the relevant borrower. To do this the amount of the loan is multiplied by a factor between 0 and 1 – set by figures between 0% and 100% (0% for an OECD government borrower or a cash collateralised exposure, 20% for an exposure guaranteed by an OECD bank or a regulated investment firm, 100% for a corporate borrower, and so on) – such that no capital is required to be held for a loan risk-weighted at 0%, and the full 8% of capital is required to be held for a loan risk-weighted at 100%. The OECD (the Organisation for Economic Cooperation and Development) includes most European countries and other developed countries world wide.

11.2 TRADING BOOK

Since then, further standards have been introduced, which reflect the market risk that arises in the trading book of banks and other investment institutions (i.e. the risk that the bank's trading assets – shares, bonds etc. – fall in value, generating losses). Consequently, the rules are now divided between the "banking book" of a bank (where capital is held against assessed credit risk) and the "trading book" of a bank (where capital is held against assessed market risk). Other institutions such as securities houses are assessed in ways similar to the trading book assessment of banks. The trading book generally relates to items held "with trading intent", which are marked-to-market daily. Generally, the trading book regime charges each position in a bond, share, etc. to a certain amount of capital (there is no "8% of risk-weighted assets" approach) via a "general" risk amount (reflecting the risk of a loss due to general market movements such as a change in interest rates) and an additional "specific" risk amount (reflecting the risk of loss from that particular position, e.g. due to a downturn in the fortunes of the relevant issuer). For example, for debt securities, the charge is to:

- A "general" risk amount (which can be offset by hedging the risk with a matching position in a security with a similar interest rate and duration); plus
- A "specific" risk amount of 0% of the exposure to an OECD government, between 0.25% and 1.6% of the exposure to a "qualifying debt item" such as a security issued by an OECD bank or regulated investment firm or a security that carries an investment grade credit rating, and 8% of the exposure to other securities (which exposures can only be offset by hedging the risk with the sale of a comparable instrument issued by the same issuer).

Complex items in the trading book (such as derivatives) are generally broken down into constituent parts of long and short positions to reflect the trading book approach of a collection of "long" positions (i.e. assets bought and held by the bank) and "short" positions (i.e. assets sold short by the bank, generating a "negative" holding). As trading book capital requirements are based on the potential loss that could be suffered as a result of market movements, both assets bought and assets sold short can generate a loss and require capital to be held against them.

The general policies of any particular bank as to which items will be entered on that bank's trading book must be agreed with regulators, due to the generally favourable capital treatment for items entered on the trading book.

11.3   NEW BASEL ACCORD

With the advent of more advanced bank systems, and with more sophisticated banks pushing for the ability to use their own advanced models to assess the correct level of capital to hold against their exposure, the Basel capital guidelines are currently under review. On 3 June 1999, the Basel Committee published a consultative paper on amendments to the 1988 regime, and further papers followed over the subsequent years. The papers proposed a new system centred on the internal credit rating systems of banks, known as the Internal Ratings Based approach, with a fallback to external credit ratings.

Given the complexity of the subject, however, implementation of the proposals has been delayed several times and ABS industry professionals in particular have objected to the proposed higher risk weighting given to asset-backed securities compared to corporate securities. The proposals are now intended to be brought into effect by the end of 2006.

See sections 11.6 to 11.8 below for more details.

11.4   BASEL CAPITAL ARBITRAGE

11.4.1   Return on capital

Return on capital is a significant motivation for institutions to engage in securitisation.

- Financial institution originators ensure that they obtain proper relief from regulatory requirements to hold capital against their risk-weighted assets, by transferring the assets off their regulatory capital balance sheet.

- Financial institution investors price the spread on asset-backed securities to reflect the capital required to be held against it on the basis of the relevant regulatory capital treatment applying to the securities in question.
- Non-financial institution originators comply with accounting off-balance-sheet rules (under FRS 5 in the UK) enabling the institution to remove the assets from its accounting balance sheet (and thus potentially from the scope of financial covenants on gearing which limit its ability to leverage its equity any further).

11.4.2 Examples

A few examples can help to illustrate the capital relief available through securitisation. Each of these examples assumes that:

1. The all-in cost of the securitisation matches the all-in cost of the originator funding the assets on its own balance sheet (in practice, the all-in cost of a securitisation for a credit-worthy bank may be somewhat higher than its on-balance-sheet cost of funds)
2. Return on capital was previously 15% (and that a productive use can be found for capital released by the securitisation)
3. The junior class of securities is retained by the originator.

Example 1: Bank securitising residential mortgage pool

Before
Pool = US $800m
Capital = Pool × 50% (residential mortgage risk weight) × 8% (BIS ratio) = **US$ 32m Capital**

After
Size of Senior ABS Classes = US$ 800m × 98.1% (S&P benchmark 1.9% credit enhancement below BBB) = US$ 785m
Size of Junior ABS Class held by bank = US$ 800m − US$ 785m = US$ 15m
Capital = Direct deduction of Junior Class = **US$ 15m Capital**

The release of US$ 17m of capital (US$ 32m − US$ 15m) will increase return on capital to 32% (15% × 32/15).

Example 2: Bank securitising corporate loan pool

Before
Pool = US$ 5000m
Capital = Pool × 100% (risk weight − assumes all loans to corporates) × 8% (BIS ratio) = **US$ 400m Capital**

After
Size of Senior ABS Classes = US$ 5000m × 98% (assumed investment grade levels) = US$ 4900m

Size of Junior ABS Classes = US\$ 5000m − US\$ 4900m = US\$ 100m
Capital = Direct deduction of Junior Class = **US\$ 100m Capital**

The release of US\$ 300m of capital (US\$ 400m − US\$ 100m) will increase return on capital to 60% (15% × 400/100).

Example 3: Corporate securitising trade debtors pool

Before
Total Assets = US\$ 1000m (of which US\$ 350m for securitisation)
Net Worth = US\$ 400m
Gearing = [(1000 − 400)/400] × 100% = **150% Gearing**
Earnings = US\$ 60m
Return on Capital = 15% (60/400 × 100%)

After
Size of Senior ABS Classes = US\$ 300m (assumed levels)
Size of Junior ABS Class = US\$ 50m
Total Assets = US\$ 700m (of which US\$ 50m is Junior Class)
Net Worth = US\$ 400m
Gearing = [(700 − 400)/400] × 100% = **75% Gearing**
Earnings = US\$ 60m
Return on Capital = 15% (60/400 × 100%).

In this last example, the return on capital remains the same, as the capital benefit is not redeployed elsewhere in the company, but is used to reduce gearing. This could subsequently be used to gear up again to the 150% gearing level by taking on another US\$ 300m of debt.

11.4.3   Banking book arbitrage

The 1988 Basel guidelines set a simple calculated method of determining the minimum level of capital that banks are required to hold in their banking book. This is set at 8% of their risk-weighted assets, with haircut capital charges and risk weights as follows:

General on-balance-sheet assets

The haircut capital charges under the regime prior to the new Basel Accord coming into force are as follows:

- **0% (0% risk weighting)**   Cash or claims on an OECD central government/central bank
- **0%/0.8%/1.6%/4% (0%/10%/20%/50% risk weighting)**   Claims on an OECD public sector entity
- **1.6% (20% risk weighting)**   Claims on an OECD bank or an OECD securities firm regulated by a similar regime
- **4% (50% risk weighting)**   Residential mortgages (either owner-occupied or rented)
- **8% (100% risk weighting)**   Other

- **100% (1250% risk weighting; 1-for-1 deduction)**   First loss enhancement provided by an originator or sponsor and second loss enhancement provided by an originator.

A key additional point to note is that Pfandbriefe/covered bonds enjoy a 10% risk weighting in Austria, Denmark, France, Germany, Luxembourg and Spain, and a 20% risk weighting in most other countries.

General off-balance-sheet assets (other than derivatives)

Off-balance-sheet items other than derivatives (including guarantees, undrawn commitments, and liquidity facilities) are reported by multiplying the notional principal amount of the item by a "credit conversion factor" between 0% and 100% before multiplying by the counterparty risk weight and the 8% factor (sub-participations are reported as an exposure at the higher of the risk weighting of the underlying borrower and that of the participating bank), as follows:

- **1-for-1 deduction**   Liquidity facilities which do not meet qualification requirements (for example, as to a use of a borrowing base calculation) and are therefore treated as credit enhancement in a case where there is no other first loss enhancement (assets will simply remain on balance sheet where a liquidity facility is provided by the originator and it does meet the requirements). Also, any off-balance-sheet first loss enhancement provided by an originator, sponsor or repackager and off-balance-sheet second loss enhancement provided by an originator.
- **100%**   Off-balance-sheet items that are a "direct credit substitute" (guarantees given should be reported as an exposure for the full principal amount on the party guaranteed, or on the reference entity for a credit derivative).
- **50%**   An undrawn commitment with an original maturity exceeding 1 year.
- **20%**   Self-liquidating trade finance items.
- **0%**   An undrawn commitment with an original maturity of 1 year or less. The deemed beginning of the commitment for lines with a maturity of 1 year or less is 30 days after the firm offer to enter the commitment (or 60 days after the firm offer for syndicated lines). Any firm offer to extend such a line may only be made in the last 30 days (or 60 days for a syndicated line) prior to expiry of the line, or the new line and the old line will be treated as a single line with the aggregate tenor of the two lines.

This simplistic approach enables a relatively easy calculation of bank capital requirements, but it also leads to some significant arbitrage opportunities. For example, in January 1998 after the start of the Asian crisis, the Republic of Korea had been downgraded to a Ba1 level with Moody's and a B+ level with Standard & Poor's, and spreads on Korean issuance had widened significantly. As an OECD sovereign, however, Korea ranked as a 0% risk-weighted entity for loan claims. By comparison, top multinational corporate credits with AAA ratings would be 100% risk weighted.

Clearly in such a case, the regulatory capital requirement does not match the true default risk being taken on by the creditor. While the institution will provide adequately against the exposure if it is prudently managed in any event, this nonetheless creates competitive distortions in the market. With the advent of the New Basel Accord, banking book risk weightings are set to change to reflect external (or internal) credit ratings in assessing capital to hold against different risks (see section 11.7). These benefit higher-rated obligations at the expense of lower-rated obligations.

11.4.4 Conduits and Repackaging Programmes

Off-balance-sheet commercial paper conduits and repackaging programmes have long been viewed as useful market arbitrage mechanisms. For CP conduits, the arbitrage comes from two sources. One is a yield curve arbitrage which arises by virtue of the issuance of short-term commercial paper to fund the acquisition of long-term financial assets. The other is capital arbitrage due to the unregulated nature of conduits – the conduit itself is not obliged to hold capital under bank capital rules, and will not be consolidated onto the regulatory capital balance sheet of the bank that established the conduit, provided that it meets criteria for separation set by the domestic financial regulator. For repackaging vehicles (which generally match-fund their assets), only the capital arbitrage from separation is typically relevant.

Conduits will still require credit support and liquidity support for transactions they take on; however, these costs are generally sufficiently low that an arbitrage can still be realised, provided that the support can be properly treated for capital purposes. In the UK, FSA guidelines set out requirements for both credit support and liquidity support.

Credit enhancement is classified into either "first loss" enhancement that will be directly deducted from capital, or "second loss" enhancement (enhancement that benefits from the protection of a "substantial" first loss layer that covers some multiple of historic losses and can only be drawn after the first loss credit enhancement is exhausted) which will be normally weighted where the extent of involvement of the bank is fully explained to investors. Programme-wide enhancement is likely to constitute second loss enhancement, as it will be drawn after any first loss enhancement on the individual deals put through the conduit.

Liquidity lines that contain a borrowing base provision for reducing the facility if the asset quality in the SPV deteriorates will be normally weighted if provided by a sponsor where the extent of involvement of the sponsor is fully explained to investors.

Example

Suppose that an A1/P1 rated conduit acquires an asset-backed security that is rated AA and carries a coupon of Dollar Libor + 75 basis points. The conduit itself can issue short-term commercial paper at sub-Libor levels, and when dealer and programme costs are added in funds at Libor flat.

Programme-wide credit enhancement may be needed – assuming that this is at 5% of the asset amount, and is normally weighted, it will require capital of [100% × 5% × 8%] or 40 basis points of the asset amount. To generate a 15% return on that capital, 6 basis points should be set aside for PWE costs. Credit enhancement should not be needed for the trade itself, as an AA long-term credit rating should be capable of supporting an A1/P1 short-term rating.

Consequently, the conduit should be able to earn 69 basis points on the asset amount, from which it needs to pay liquidity costs. If the liquidity line was charged to 4% capital [100% × 50% credit conversion factor on an undrawn line exceeding 1 year × 8%], then paying the entire 69 basis points over to the liquidity bank would achieve a return on capital of 17.25% for the liquidity bank, and leave the conduit making zero profit/zero loss.

However, using a 364-day liquidity line reduces the capital required to be held to 0%, meaning that any return at all to the liquidity bank effectively generates an infinite return on capital. As a consequence, the conduit should be able to sign-up liquidity banks for less than 69 basis points, keeping an arbitrage profit for itself. This profit, while real enough in cash terms, is not a zero risk profit. The following risks are embedded in this structure:

- Volatility in market CP rates (at the time of the 1998 Russian debt default, CP rates spiked up by more than 30 basis points).
- Insufficient return on capital (although the regulatory capital for a 364-day liquidity line is zero, the line is not zero risk. If risks are not reflected in the return on capital equation, the risk/reward picture within the institution is skewed).

New Basel Accord

Clearly in this case, the Basel system of zero capital can lead to an incentive to mis-price risk. Concerns over this area have clearly been perceived by the Basel Committee, which in its proposals has announced its intent to require banks to hold capital against 364-day liquidity lines on the basis of a one-fifth credit conversion factor unless they can be cancelled unconditionally. This would result in a 1.6% capital haircut [$100\% \times 20\%$ credit conversion factor $\times 8\%$] for an underlying 100% risk-weighted asset.

In the example given above, paying the entire 69 basis points over to the liquidity bank would now generate a return on capital for the bank of just over 43% (at 100% risk weighting on the underlying asset) or 215% (at 20% risk weighting on the underlying assets using the new proposed Basel rules for AA asset-backed securities).

Assuming a requirement for a 25% return, the liquidity bank will require a commitment fee of 40 basis points (at 100% weighted) or 8 basis points (at 20% weighted), leaving the residual spread with the conduit.

11.4.5 Trading book

The trading book regime was introduced in the 1990s, and is intended to reflect the different nature of risks taken by financial institutions (both securities houses and banks that engage in proprietary trading) that trade their portfolios continuously (as opposed to the banking book "buy and hold" mentality).

Due to the fact that the trading portfolio is assumed to be liquid and that institutions are assumed to operate stop-loss policies and limits on trading capacity, the guidelines are designed to reflect the holding of margin against the potential for significant price fluctuations over a short period of time, rather than long-term credit risk. Consequently the general risk requirements (relating to the embedded market risk that the whole market moves due to interest rate or economic growth perceptions) and the specific risk requirements (relating to the risk of market movements due to credit risk or operating risk for the individual issuer in which an exposure is held) for capital on the trading book are generally less onerous than the equivalent levels for the same instrument held on the banking book.

Arbitrage here centres around illustrating that an instrument is sufficiently liquid to be held on a trading book, and that the regulatory capital to be held should therefore reflect trading book levels rather than banking book levels. For example, under UK rules a 5-year loan of 100 to an AA-rated corporate paying 3-month Libor plus a spread that is held on banking book would generate a capital charge of:

$$100 \times 8\% = 8$$

The same loan held in the form of a bond on trading book would attract charges under the UK interest rate regime rules for fixed income instruments, where unmatched positions are assessed for general (or position-related) market risk at a fraction of 0% to 12.5% of the principal amount to reflect the residual maturity of the security (floating rate securities are weighted by reference to the time to the next interest determination rather than the residual maturity – the 3-month band incurs a charge of 0.2%) weighted by a factor of 100%, and are also assessed for specific (or counterparty-related) risk on a haircut in a range of:

- 0% (issues of or collateralised by OECD central government/central bank securities);
- 0.25% for "qualifying debt items" (such as securities issued or guaranteed by an OECD bank, securities carrying a 50% risk weighting and investment grade rated securities) with 6 months or less residual maturity;
- 1% for "qualifying debt items" with 6+ to 24 months residual maturity;
- 1.25% for "qualifying debt items" with more than 24 months residual maturity; and
- 8% (for other securities)

of the gross position. This would give a capital charge of:

General risk: $100 \times 100\% \times 0.2\% = 0.2$
Specific risk: $100 \times 1.6\% = 1.6$

Total charge $= 1.8$

Again the new Basel Accord would change the position here. It would bring in a new credit-related capital regime for the banking book, under which an AA corporate risk would be charged at a 20% risk weighting on the external ratings basis, generating a capital charge of:

$$100 \times 20\% \times 8\% = 1.6$$

(in other words less than the equivalent trading book charge).

Classification of an item as trading book or banking book depends on the local regime. Under the 1988 Basel Accord the trading book of a bank consists of its proprietary holdings of, or principal broking positions in, financial instruments that are held for short-term resale and holdings in financial instruments taken in order to hedge such exposures.

The New Basel Accord revises this definition such that the trading book consists of its positions in financial instruments and commodities that are held either with trading intent or in order to hedge other elements of the trading book. Positions are considered to be held with trading intent if they are held intentionally for short-term resale and/or with the intent of benefiting from actual or expected short-term price movements or to lock in arbitrage profits. Trading intent can be evidenced by documented trading strategies and policies such as regular mark-to-market and trading desk management. A bank will be subject to close supervision as to the allocation of items between the banking book and the trading book, with particularly close scrutiny given to the classification of assets with limited liquidity as trading book assets.

11.4.6 Arbitrage under the New Basel Accord

The New Basel Accord would have the effect of changing the current haircuts and weightings, and also removing limitations on the range of collateral to reduce risk weightings. See detail in section 11.6. The arbitrage that the New Accord presents is the fact that the capital required to be held against AAA and AA corporate bonds and AAA and AA asset-backed bonds will drop. As this will have a direct impact on the return on capital that can be earned from these securities by a financial institution investor, it is anticipated that spreads on these securities will tighten. In contrast to this, the amount of capital required to be held against B corporate bonds and BB and B asset-backed bonds will increase, which is expected to lead to a widening of spreads on these securities.

11.4.7 Principal protected structures

This is a development from the retail markets, where a mixture of high-risk and low-risk investments are structured to offer a potentially significant upside with a limited downside.

Proceeds are invested partly in government or other low-risk securities, and partly in high-risk assets such as warrants, derivatives, or high-risk loan assets. The issued securities can benefit both in credit terms (from the government collateral) and in capital terms (from the protection of the high-risk first loss piece which would otherwise constitute a direct deduction from capital).

Example

For example, a benchmark residential mortgage pool of 100 has a 7.2% piece below AAA, and an average life of 4.5 years:

- Bonds are issued for a principal amount of 125
- 100 of the proceeds is used to acquire the mortgages
- The other 25 is used to acquire 5-year zero coupon UK gilts yielding 5.8% compounded annually.

Principal redemption on the mortgages to an AAA certainty will be 92.8. At 5.8%, the redemption proceeds of the gilts at year 5 will be 32.22, giving 125.02 of principal proceeds to an AAA-rated level. In capital terms, the bonds can be issued in two tranches:

- A senior tranche of 92.8, which will attract a capital charge of $92.8 \times 50\%$ risk weight $\times 8\% = 3.71$, and
- A junior tranche of 32.2, which should be charged at $32.2 \times 10\%$ risk weight $\times 8\% = 0.26$ (subject to ensuring that the lack of support from the gilts for interest on the junior tranche does not prejudice the capital treatment)

for a total capital charge of 3.97.

If, instead, a first loss piece of 7.2 had been issued (on the assumption that there was no tranching below the AAA tranche), the capital would have been:

- 3.71 on the senior tranche, and
- 4 on the junior tranche (a direct deduction capped at the amount of capital on the pool – 7.2, capped at $100 \times 50\%$ risk weight $\times 8\% = 4$)

for a total capital charge of 7.71.

This structure does have an economic cost, due to the negative carry on the gilts against the bond coupon (and is effectively akin to paying a premium to guarantee the junior piece), but may still be able to improve return on capital.

11.4.8 Use of guarantees

Guaranteed exposures typically carry the risk weighting of the guarantor. This foundation has been used for:

- Straightforward bank guarantees, which will serve to reduce a 100% risk-weighted capital charge against a corporate exposure to the risk weighting of the bank (20% if it is an OECD bank);
- The packaging of MBS through government-sponsored agencies such as Ginnie Mae and Fannie Mae in the US and the HKMC in Hong Kong to reduce risk weighting to 20% (or 0% in the case of Ginnie Mae);
- Put options written by an OECD bank (which will also serve to reduce a 100% risk-weighted capital charge against a corporate exposure to the risk weighting of the bank). Put options were also used as part of a round trip trade in Japan in the mid- to late-1990s. In these trades, a put option between a Japanese bank and a foreign bank was used, where the foreign bank agreed that the Japanese bank could put certain loan assets to it at par. This enabled the Japanese bank to report the assets at a 20% risk weight to reflect the OECD bank commitment they had obtained (and by itself this would have fallen within the scope of the put concept as used elsewhere in the world). In these cases however, the deal was backed out into a round trip by the foreign bank agreeing an onward put to an SPV company, secured over a committed facility to the SPV from the Japanese bank (on an undrawn 364-day zero-weighted basis). This resulted in a 20% capital risk weight for the Japanese bank and a 20% capital risk weight for the foreign bank (but with the Japanese bank taking primary risk on the loan assets, and the foreign bank having primary risk on the Japanese bank and only being at risk on the loan assets on a secondary basis if the Japanese bank becomes insolvent).

- The capital treatment of credit derivatives, reflecting the most common use of credit derivatives in the form of an unfunded credit default swap, which is akin to a guarantee.

11.4.9   Use of collateral/repo

Use of collateral in the form of government securities, or Pfandbriefe/covered bond securities (for example by German banks who recognise Pfandbriefe as having a 10% risk weighting), is a common method of supporting an exposure to ensure that the credit risk on the exposure can be reduced, and that a capital benefit can also be obtained.

- **Banking book**   Collateral held against exposures in the banking book can be used to reduce the risk weighting of the exposure to that of the collateral. Reduction of risk weighting is only permitted in respect of that part of the exposure covered by the collateral. The added credit benefit of "first loss" collateral is not recognised in capital terms over and above the amount of the exposure covered.
- **Trading book**   Collateral can be held against counterparty risk in the trading book to reduce the counterparty risk weighting in the same way as for banking book assets. For trading book purposes, a collateral risk weighting is only permitted in respect of that part of the exposure covered by the collateral. The added credit benefit of "first loss" collateral is not recognised in capital terms over and above the amount of the exposure covered. Collateral is required to be marked-to-market daily and a cushion subtracted to take account of future market movements.

Repo agreements are a particular example of capital efficient financing. The cash lender/securities borrower can report them as a collateralised loan and give them the risk weighting appropriate to the collateral.

Restrictions on the use of collateral are chiefly:

- Ensuring that the type of collateral used is a form of collateral that can be recognised for capital purposes; and
- Ensuring that the collateral is taken in a form that is valid and recognised in the relevant jurisdictions to ensure that it will not be forfeit in an insolvency of the collateral provider.

Distinguishing collateral and structural look-through

Collateral that will enable a reduction in capital risk weighting (and the relevant capital haircuts and risk weightings) under the old Basel rules are as follows:

- **0% (0% risk weighting)**   Cash collateralised assets or assets collateralised by OECD central government/central bank securities or assets guaranteed by an OECD central government/central bank;
- **1.6% (20% risk weighting)**   Assets guaranteed by an OECD bank or an OECD securities firm regulated by a similar regime.

As can be seen, the use of mortgage-backed securities or other low-risk weight assets as collateral will not enable a reduction in risk weighting. It should be noted, however, that the structure of some asset-backed securities (with mortgage-backed securities themselves being the most obvious example) permits them to carry a risk weighting below 100%, on the basis of an acceptance that the SPV issuer is bankruptcy remote (and that the exposure to the SPV should therefore be disregarded and looked-through), and that the correct weighting of the ABS should match that of the worst risk on the components of the underlying structure (for example, that of the underlying assets or that of the swap counterparty).

New Basel Accord

The New Basel Accord envisages widening the types of collateral that can be used, such that investment grade corporate or bank paper would reduce the weighting of the collateralised exposure to that of the collateral (which would itself carry a lower risk weighting under the new rules).

Validity of collateral interest over securities held in a clearing system or with a custodian

In the UK, the FSA requires that banks have legal opinions as to the validity of a security interest over securities. This is a particular issue for security interests taken over securities held in clearing systems, where:

- Firstly, it is not entirely clear what interest an owner holding a security through a clearing system has that they can give security over;
- Secondly, perfection of that interest may be complex and expensive; and
- Thirdly, insolvency of the clearing system or one of the other intervening parties may prejudice the rights of the owner and consequently of the secured party to which the owner grants collateral.

Clearing systems typically operate on a fungible pooled account basis, with title to any physical global securities held with a depositary on behalf of the clearing system, and all securities of one nature commingled in a single pool. The interest of clearing system participants in part of the pool is recorded in electronic account entries. The sub-interest of the ultimate owner of the securities which holds its interest in the securities via the clearing system participant (the participant will act as a custodian of the interest of the ultimate owner where the ultimate owner is not itself a participant in the clearing system) may be recorded at the clearing system level by the transfer of the relevant securities into a segregated account. This, in practice however, is rarely done, as it adds to the cost and administrative burden of the custodian, resulting in further account charges. Consequently, the interest of the ultimate owner is typically not recorded at the clearing system level, but only at the custodian level, and clearing system terms and conditions often specifically state that they will only recognise the rights of clearing system participants unless a participant opens a segregated account clearly held in favour of a certain party.

As the ultimate owner does not have any legal title in the securities (which resides with the clearing system depositary as nominee for the clearing system), and has no interest at the clearing system level, the ultimate owner has either:

- A pure contractual right against the custodian to arrange re-delivery of the securities that the custodian has received on instructions from the ultimate owner; or
- A proprietary interest in the fungible pooled account of securities (at either the custodian level or the clearing system level) as a pro rata share under a tenancy-in-common; or
- A direct proprietary interest in specific securities within the pool.

The first option is an unsatisfactory solution, as the potential then exists for the ultimate owner's rights to be prejudiced by insolvency of the custodian if it cannot prove some kind of proprietary interest in the securities themselves. The last option had been considered unlikely, given the fungible nature of the account, but see the case of *CA Pacific Securities Ltd* below.

The second option, of a proprietary ownership interest in a pool of fungible collateral, has however long been a complex issue under English law. The issues that arise are the same as those that arise on consideration of an undivided interest structure in a securitisation – namely, that share of the ultimate owner in the fungible pooled account is not allocated by reference to a particular divided part of the receivables, and in the absence of a declaration of trust by the custodian in favour of the ultimate owner the owner may not obtain any proprietary interest in the securities.

In the case of *Re London Wine Company (Shippers) Ltd (1975)*, it was held that sales of unascertained goods from a pool of goods did not operate to transfer any interest in the goods to the purchaser, either by way of equitable assignment or by constitution of a trust, due to lack of appropriation or identification of the goods in which a proprietary interest was to pass (cf. Certainties). By way of contrast, it was further held that the seller "could by appropriate words, declare himself to be a trustee of a specified proportion of [the whole pool of goods] and thus create an equitable tenancy in common between himself and the named beneficiary, so that a proprietary interest would arise in the beneficiary in an undivided share of the [pool of goods]". This distinguishes between the sale of a number of unallocated items from a pool (on the one hand) and a sale of an unallocated and undivided percentage of a pool with an express declaration of trust (on the other hand). Most English law securitisation structures attempting to fund through an undivided interest mechanism protect against the risk that no proprietary interest is transferred by a true sale of the entire interest in the receivables, with the receivables sold into a trust (constituted by an express declaration of trust over the whole of the pool), whereby the originator and investors are entitled to trust interests matching their respective shares. For example, in credit card securitisations, it is common to divide the trust assets into originator and investor shares ranking equally with each other and determined by use of a floating allocation percentage.

More recently, in the case of *Re Goldcorp Exchange Ltd [1994] 2 All ER 806*, the Privy Council confirmed *London Wine*, when it held that it "would not be right to impose a remedial constructive trust or a restitutionary proprietary interest" in favour of purchasers of unallocated shares of a stock of bullion. In the case of *Hunter v. Moss [1994] 3 All ER 215 CA*, however, the Court of Appeal held that a person can "declare himself trustee of [a specified number of] shares in [a specific company] ... and that is effective to give a beneficial proprietary interest to the beneficiary under the trust". *London Wine* was distinguished as it dealt with passing of property in chattels rather than a declaration of trust.

Academics have disputed the correctness of *Hunter v. Moss*, but the judgement in *Re Harvard Securities Ltd [1997] 2 BCLC 369* followed it in determining that an equitable assignment of an unappropriated interest in shares was effective to pass a proprietary interest to the purchaser. *London Wine* was distinguished, as it related to chattels rather than shares.

Form of security interest

In order to cover all possibilities, most attempts to create security interests over securities held in fungible accounts in clearing systems state that the collateral provider grants security over any rights they have against the custodian (in order to attach to any re-delivery rights), and under the custody agreement (in order to attach to any equitable interest in the securities evidenced by the custody agreement) and in and to the securities themselves (in the event that the collateral provider can be seen to have an interest directly against the securities at some level).

Provided that some local law considerations are observed (for example, Belgium, where Euroclear is located, does not recognise security interests created in the form of a floating charge – a pledge form should be used), this is relatively simple to provide for. It does not, however, address the further issue of how best to perfect the security interest so that, on insolvency of the collateral provider, the interest of the secured party will be recognised by the relevant court considering the circumstances of the winding-up. The matter could come before a court in the jurisdiction of the collateral provider, the custodian, the clearing system, the depositary or the issuer of the underlying security, and in practice the issue is typically dealt with by perfecting the interest in the jurisdictions where enforcement is considered most likely or vital. This generally comes down to the jurisdictions of the security document itself, of the governing law of the custody agreement, and of the jurisdiction of the relevant clearing system.

Finally, consideration should be given to the risk that one of the parties in the chain becomes insolvent, and the rights to the securities are prejudiced in the insolvency. The major clearing systems such as Euroclear and Clearstream have contractual provisions and legislation that protect against the possibility of the securities being caught up in their insolvency, or insolvency of their depositaries. Separation of the securities from the insolvency of the custodian will depend on an analysis of the custody agreement for terms implying that the securities are held on trust for the ultimate owner (or are otherwise segregated in its favour), and reliance on the rationale of cases such as *Hunter v. Moss*.

Recent developments

In the US, provision has been made under Article 8 of the Uniform Commercial Code for a simplification of the classification and perfection of ownership and security interests in securities held through a clearing system or custodian, where the owner's entitlement is reflected by a book entry. The ownership interest of the owner is classified under Article 8 as a bundle of rights (known as a "securities entitlement") which includes rights against the custodian and (under s. 8-503(b)) a pro rata proprietary interest in the pool held by the custodian of which his account is part. Under s. 8-503(a) the securities do not form part of the custodian's insolvency estate. The custodian is obliged to take due care to obtain payment from the underlying issuer of the securities under s. 8-505(a). Under s. 9-103(d) of Article 9, the relevant law to determine the steps required for perfection of a security interest over an owner's securities entitlement is that of the law of the custodian's jurisdiction.

In the Hong Kong SAR, the doctrine in *Hunter v. Moss* has been further developed by the first instance decision in the case of *CA Pacific Securities Ltd* in December 1998. The court determined that client securities held by broker CA Pacific in a fungible CCASS account pooled with its own securities were acquired by CA Pacific as agent for its clients as principals, and that consequently the clients did have proprietary interests in the securities despite the fungible nature of the CCASS account. This was decided on the basis of a construction of the terms of the client agreement. Furthermore, the clients had specific interests in certain of the securities in the account (rather than interests in an undivided portion of the account as tenants in common), as the client agreement clearly envisaged separate client interests rather than an interest in a changing pool with other clients. Appropriation of particular securities to a particular client was held to be unnecessary due to the nature of the securities themselves where, unlike tangible goods, the securities are fungible and segregation therefore serves no purpose. Exactly how to trace a particular interest through the pool was left undetermined.

In the EU, the Settlement Finality Directive (Directive 98/26) provided that where registered securities are provided as collateral for "securing rights and obligations potentially arising in connection with a system" (a settlement system such as Euroclear or Clearstream), the law governing provision of the securities as collateral will be the jurisdiction where the register is held.

This was extended by the Financial Collateral Directive (Directive 2002/47 of 6 June 2002), which member states are required to enact through national legislation by 27 December 2003. The Directive applies to collateral arrangements over securities or cash between two entities, where at least one of them is a financial institution, and the other is not a natural person. In relation to book entry securities, the Directive sets out conflict of laws provisions which provide that perfection of any security interest and completion of any other steps required to make the security interest effective on third parties should be carried out in accordance with the requirements of the jurisdiction where the account is held, as should any steps for enforcement of the security interest.

A further recent development of global significance is the "Place of the Relevant Intermediary Approach" (PRIMA) used in The Hague Convention on Indirectly Held Securities 2002 to determine the law applicable to transactions involving securities held via an intermediary. The law is at the choice of the account holder and its intermediary, subject to the proviso that the intermediary must have an office in the relevant jurisdiction. The Convention was agreed in December 2002 and presented to be ratified by the 62 members of the Hague conference.

11.5   OFF-BALANCE-SHEET TREATMENT UNDER BASEL

The Basel Committee published guidelines titled Asset Transfers and Securitisation in September 1992. The guidelines set out when an originator bank may regard assets as transferred off balance sheet for capital purposes.

The originator should be seen to have transferred the assets to an unrelated entity such that there is no obligation on the originator to repurchase the assets and such that there is no recourse to, or apparent moral obligation on, the originator for non-performance of the assets (as would be the case if, for example, the originator has ownership or management control over the SPV, the SPV uses the name of the originator, or the originator consolidates the SPV).

For revolving pools, there needs to be an adequate method of ensuring control of the amortisation process, and ensuring appropriate distribution of risks.

A one-off provision of credit enhancement to an SPV may be permitted, although it will be directly deducted from capital. Other credit enhancement may prevent an off-balance-sheet transfer. Credit enhancement may be weighted as a direct credit substitute for the full pool size if provided by an unconnected third-party bank, or directly deducted from capital.

Liquidity facilities may not be drawn for the purpose of credit enhancement.

11.5.1   Revisions to the policy – New Basel Accord papers

The policy is revised under a Supporting Document to the First Basel Consultative Paper of 1999 (CP1), the Second Consultative Paper in January 2001 (CP2) and a working paper on securitisation in October 2001, as well as under Quantitative Impact Study 3 (QIS3) on 1 October 2002 and a Second Working Paper on Securitisation on 28 October 2002.

The October 2001 paper raised new areas for consideration in relation to development of the IRB approach for securitisation structures – in particular, scaling factors for ABS and the appropriate treatment for revolving securitisations and liquidity facilities. The scaling factors were replaced in QIS3 and the Second Working Paper in October 2002. Subsequently a Third Basel Consultative Paper (CP3) was published on 29 April 2003.

The papers provide for the Standardised Approach and the IRB Approach (see section 11.7), and set out the following draft provisions:

Method of Transfer

In order for an originator to exclude securitised assets from its capital calculation the following requirements should be complied with:

- Significant credit risk should have been transferred to third parties.
- The transferor does not maintain effective or indirect control (e.g. via a right or obligation to take back the assets at a certain point).
- The assets should be transferred beyond the reach of the transferor and its creditors or liquidator in bankruptcy (this appears to still allow for the inclusion of sub-participation as a method of transfer, as this is specifically cited as an example).
- The securities issued are not obligations of the transferor.
- The transferee is an SPE and the holders of beneficial interests in the SPE have the right to pledge or exchange those interests without restriction.
- Any clean-up call should be at the bank's discretion, should not exceed 10% of the overall issuance, and must not be used to provide credit support.

- The deal should not require the originator to improve the quality of the pool, or provide for the credit enhancement to increase post-close, or provide for enhanced yield to investors on a drop in credit quality.

To the extent that the originator provides implicit support for a transaction, it will be required under CP3 to hold capital against all exposures in the transaction, and must publicly declare that it has provided support, and the capital impact of so doing.

Synthetic securitisations

In CP2, the Committee stated that it might require super-senior pieces to be transferred, unless they were of high quality, the mezzanine piece had been transferred, and the originator was not able to buy back or retain any piece except the super-senior piece. Alternatively, that it might require a minimum level of transfer of risk to the market, or that protection is acquired against a retained super-senior.

The Second Working Paper, and subsequently CP3, specifically assess the risk on super-senior pieces under a "look-through" approach for the Standardised Approach (see section 11.7), and off inferred ratings for the IRB Approach. The Second Working Paper and CP3 also set out requirements for an originator to exclude securitised assets from its capital calculation under a synthetic securitisation (in addition to the general requirements for credit derivatives – see section 11.7.7) as follows:

- No provisions that materially limit the transfer of credit risk (e.g. significant materiality thresholds, etc.).
- The deal should not require the originator to improve the quality of the pool, or provide for the credit enhancement or retained first loss position to increase post-close, or provide for either an increase in the cost of credit protection, or an enhanced yield to investors, on a drop in credit quality.
- See legal opinions on enforceability in relevant jurisdictions.
- Any clean-up call should be at the bank's discretion, should not exceed 10% of the overall issuance, and must not be used to provide credit support.

The level of reduction in capital achieved by the transfer of risk in synthetic form will depend on the collateral, if any, backing the credit protection (in accordance with the new system for collateral provided in CP3) and the counterparty risk weighting of the credit protection seller.

If there is a maturity mismatch between the underlying credit exposures and the term of protection bought under the synthetic securitisation, the originator will be required to hold capital to reflect the maturity mismatch. If a mismatch exists, then no protection value is recognised if the synthetic securitisation has less than 1 year to expiry. If the synthetic securitisation has 1 year or more to expiry, then the benefit of tranches sold will be reduced by multiplying the tranche amounts by the synthetic securitisation residual term over the underlying exposure residual term (in risk weight terms, equivalent to averaging an unprotected amount and a protected amount by tenor).

Disclosure

Public disclosure of quantitative data on the securitised portfolio, the roles undertaken by the originator, and any credit or liquidity facilities provided in connection with the portfolio is also required in order to gain off-balance-sheet treatment.

Future margin income

FMI that is capitalised as an asset must be deducted from Tier 1 Capital.

Credit Enhancement and liquidity facilities

On-balance-sheet items will be risk weighted as set out in section 11.7. For off-balance-sheet items such as commitments under liquidity facilities, an assessment is undertaken as to whether a facility is "eligible". To be eligible:

- The facility must identify clearly in what circumstances it may be drawn, and may not be used for credit enhancement, or to cover losses, or to provide permanent funding.
- Drawings on the facility should not be subordinated to investors and the fees for the facility should not be subordinated.
- The facility cannot be drawn after credit enhancement for the deal has been exhausted.
- The facility should contain a provision for preventing the facility being drawn against past due or defaulted assets.
- The facility should contain a provision resulting in a reduction of the amount that can be drawn if the average pool quality falls below investment grade.

In the Standardised Approach, eligible facilities may be treated as normal business commitments (a 20% credit conversion factor (CCF) for 1 year or less, or a 50% CCF for more than 1 year). If the facility is only available in the event of general market disruption (rather than in relation to liquidity shortfall on underlying assets), then a 0% CCF is proposed. A 0% CCF is also available for eligible servicer cash advances which rank senior to other claims, subject to national discretion. Other off-balance-sheet items are given a 100% CCF.

In the IRB Approach, eligible facilities that may only be drawn in the event of general market disruption have a 20% CCF. Other off-balance-sheet securitisation exposures have a 100% CCF.

11.6   BASEL CAPITAL TREATMENT AND NEW BASEL PROPOSALS

The Basel Accord of July 1988 agreed by the Basel Committee on Banking Supervision (established by the G-10 countries in 1974) established that the ratio of an institution's own capital to its risk-weighted assets should have an absolute minimum value of 8% (higher levels may be set by individual regulators or for individual institutions). Given the reduction of asset principal value by these weightings, bank capital as a percentage of actual principal value of assets tends to be less than 8%. The Basel Accord has no legal force, but is regarded as best practice, and has been implemented by almost all countries with international banks.

Subsequent to the Basel Accord, the Basel Committee reached agreement on amendments and additions to the Accord; principally, to include an assessment of market risk from January 1998, and to permit the use of approved bank internal VAR type models to set market risk capital charges.

Also on 27 October 1998, the Basel Committee approved the issuance of perpetual preferred securities to qualify as Tier 1 capital (subject to a limit of 15% of total Tier 1 capital), interest on which is tax deductible. The debt can only be callable a minimum of 5 years after issue (and only with the regulator's prior approval), and must be subordinated to depositors and creditors. Coupon step-ups are permitted.

On 3 June 1999, the Basel Committee published a Consultative Paper ("**CP1**") on amendments to the 1988 regime, which heralded the start of a lengthy development process:

- 18 January 2000: The Committee published a further consultative paper on the internal credit rating systems of banks.
- 16 January 2001: The Committee issued a new Consultative Paper of their proposals ("**CP2**") for comments by 31 May 2001, which included the foundation of the Internal Ratings Based approach. The proposals were intended to be finalised by the end of 2001, for implementation in 2004.
- June 2001: Following extensive comments on the proposals, the Committee decided to issue a further proposal in early 2002, to finalise by the end of 2002 for implementation in 2005. Particular concern was voiced on the capital costs of funding SMEs (small/medium-sized enterprises) and on the operational risk charge (20% of current capital having been discussed as the appropriate level for this charge).
- September 2001: Following comments from ISDA and other parties, the Basel Committee announced that they would consider moving the "W" factor charge on collateral, guarantees and credit derivatives from the first "pillar" on minimum capital to a consideration of appropriate measures under the second "pillar" on supervisory review.
- Late 2001: Papers on individual topics were issued (including a paper on operational risk in September 2001 and a working paper on securitisation in October 2001).
- 5 November 2001: Press release set out potential revisions of some risk weighting details set out in CP2 in January 2001.
- December 2001: The Committee further announced the delay of issuance of further proposals into 2002.
- 10 July 2002: A new press release gave a revised timetable for implementation, with a new quantitative survey to be launched and details of new treatment for SME loans.
- 1 October 2002: Quantitative Impact Study 3 ("**QIS3**") released, giving more detail on corporate and retail capital calculations, use of collateral to reduce capital charges, and also on weightings for securitisations.
- 28 October 2002: Basel Committee published Second Working Paper on Securitisation.

- 29 April 2003: A new Consultative Paper ("**CP3**") was published for comment by 31 July 2003.
- 11 October 2003: Basel Committee published press release delaying publication of the final Accord from November 2003 to June 2004 and announcing further items for comment by year-end 2003, including taking into account provisions made for expected credit losses and replacement of the Supervisory Formula approach outlined below.

Implementation is intended for the end of 2006.

The proposals contain three "Pillars" for capital regulation:

- Minimum capital requirements
- Supervisory review
- Market discipline (e.g. disclosure requirements).

Banks are required to hold banking book capital equal to 8% of the risk-weighted assets in their banking book, and to hold trading book capital equal to the sum of each capital charge in their trading book (in relation to some of which the 8% ratio may be used to compute counterparty risks).

Under CP3, for the first 2 years after implementation of the new accord at the end of 2006, banks using the IRB approach (see below) will be subject to a minimum capital floor based on the capital they would have to hold if calculated under the old accord, set at 90% of such level in 2007 and 80% in 2008.

Capital is required to be held by banking entities on a solo and consolidated basis, with the normal expectation that subsidiaries will be consolidated. CP3 tightens this basis to include holding companies which are parents of banking groups, and requires financial subsidiaries (including securities firms and unregulated entities) to be consolidated where they form part of the same group as a bank.

11.6.1 Banking book versus trading book

The trading book of a bank consists of its proprietary holdings of, or principal broking positions in, financial instruments that are held for short-term resale and holdings in financial instruments taken in order to hedge such exposures. A bank will be subject to close supervision as to the allocation of items between the banking book and the trading book.

CP3 revises this definition such that the trading book consists of its positions in financial instruments and commodities that are held either with trading intent or in order to hedge other elements of the trading book. Positions are considered to be held with trading intent if they are held intentionally for short-term resale and/or with the intent of benefiting from actual or expected short-term price movements or to lock in arbitrage profits. Trading intent can be evidenced by documented trading strategies and policies such as regular mark-to-market and trading desk management. There is no requirement to comply with trading book capital treatments for a book below a certain size. A bank will be subject to close supervision as to the allocation of items between the banking book and the trading book, with particularly close scrutiny given to the classification of assets with limited liquidity as trading book assets.

11.6.2   Netting

Netting is permitted in respect of off-balance-sheet items for OTC derivatives and forwards where they are subject to a netting agreement, in relation to which legal opinions have been obtained, and which do not contain a "walkaway" clause (a provision limiting the liability of a non-defaulting party to make any termination payment due to a defaulting party on termination of the derivative).

CP3 permits on-balance-sheet netting in respect of loans and deposits.

If the netting positions do not match in maturity, then no netting value is recognised if the positions are less than 1 year to expiry. If the positions are 1 year or more to expiry, then the netted amount will be reduced by multiplying it by the shorter exposure over the longer exposure (in risk weight terms, equivalent to averaging a netted amount and an unnetted amount by tenor).

11.6.3   Collateral or guarantees in the banking book

Collateral held against exposures in the banking book can be used to reduce the risk weighting of the exposure to that of the collateral. Reduction is only permitted in respect of that part of the exposure covered by the collateral. Permitted collateral and relevant haircut/risk weightings are:

- **0% (0% risk weighting)**   Cash collateralised assets or assets collateralised by OECD central government/central bank securities or assets guaranteed by an OECD central government/central bank.
- **1.6% (20% risk weighting)**   Assets guaranteed by an OECD bank or an OECD securities firm regulated by a similar regime.

CP3 revises the treatment of collateral significantly, and sets out two approaches (the simple approach and the comprehensive approach) for use of collateral. In relation to both collateral and guarantees, CP2 provided for a "W" factor of 15% of the covered exposure, which is weighted as though it were not collateralised or guaranteed (in addition to any uncovered exposure). The Basel Committee announced in September 2001 that they would consider moving the charge relating to the "W" factor from the first "pillar" on minimum capital to a consideration of appropriate measures under the second "pillar" on supervisory review. QIS3 made further significant amendments to this framework (including removing the "W" factor).

Under CP3, in the:

- *Banking book (Standardised Approach)*, either the simple approach or the comprehensive approach may be used;
- *Banking book (IRB Approach)*, only the comprehensive approach may be used;
- *Trading book*, only the comprehensive approach may be used.

Legal opinions must be taken confirming the validity of a security interest over the relevant collateral, or of a guarantee, as appropriate.

1. **Simple approach**   The collateral must be marked-to-market at least every 6 months. Exposure that is collateralised by the mark-to-market value of the collateral will be given the risk weight of the collateral (subject to a floor risk weighting

of 20% unless the collateral is cash or is subject to daily mark-to-market and other requirements). Uncollateralised exposure is given the risk weighting of the counterparty. CP3 permits collateral in the form of cash, gold, debt securities (which are sovereign and public sector securities rated BB− and above, corporate, bank or securities firm securities rated BBB− and above, securities rated at least A3/P3 or certain listed bank senior debt with an implied investment grade rating), main index equities and certain mutual fund units.

2. **Comprehensive approach**   The exposure is haircut (i.e. increased) for volatility in the exposure amount, and the collateral is haircut (i.e. decreased) for volatility in value and FX rate volatility (if there is a currency mismatch). The difference between the two haircut figures is treated as the uncollateralised amount, and is risk weighted against the counterparty (the collateralised portion attracts no charge). CP3 permits collateral in the same form as for the simple approach, with the addition of listed equities not on the main index. Haircuts may be either standard Basel volatility haircuts, or as determined by the bank. Standardised Basel volatility haircuts vary from 0% (cash) to 25% (equities not part of a main index) assuming daily mark-to-market and margin calls and a 10-day holding period. A haircut of zero may be applied for collateral in respect of repo of government securities by a core market participant that is marked-to-market daily.

Permitted financial asset collateral can be taken into account in order to reduce the LGD in the Foundation IRB Approach. After application of haircuts to the value of the collateral (for volatility of the underlying exposure, volatility of the collateral, and exchange rate volatility), the LGD on the covered portion can be reduced to a floor of 0% for financial collateral.

Receivables collateral can also be used to reduce the LGD down as far as 35% (where the value of the collateral exceeds 125% of the exposure). Real estate (commercial or residential) collateral will reduce the LGD down as far as 35% (where the value of the collateral exceeds 140% of the exposure). Other collateral will reduce the LGD down as far as 40% (where the value of the collateral exceeds 140% of the exposure).

Guaranteed exposures are given the risk weighting of the guarantor in the Standardised Approach, or are used to reduce the PD or LGD in the IRB Approach. Eligible guarantors are sovereigns, public sector entities, banks and securities firms, as well as corporates rated A− or higher in the Standardised Approach, and also lower rated corporates in the IRB Approach.

Materiality thresholds should be directly deducted from capital in the Standardised Approach.

Where the reference obligation is denominated in a different currency, the level of protection recognised will be reduced by a haircut (to reflect the currency risk) in the Standardised Approach.

In both the Standardised Approach and the IRB Approach if the credit protection has a shorter term than the protected asset, then no protection value is recognised if the protection has less than 1 year to expiry. If the protection has 1 year or more to expiry, then the protected amount will be reduced by multiplying it by the protection residual term over the exposure residual term (in risk weight terms, equivalent to averaging an unprotected amount and a protected amount by tenor).

11.6.4 Collateral or guarantees in the trading book

Collateral can be held against counterparty risk in the trading book to reduce risk charges using the comprehensive approach as set out above.

11.6.5 Derivatives and credit derivatives

In addition to any trading book market risk assessments, OTC derivatives are subjected to a counterparty risk haircut by calculating the mark-to-market value of the derivative plus an "add-on" figure of between 0% and 15% (set by reference to the residual term of the contract and the contract type (0% to 1.5% for interest rates, 1% to 7.5% for FX, 6% to 10% for equities, 7% to 8% for precious metals or 10% to 15% for commodities)) of the notional principal (in total, the "credit equivalent amount"), with the aggregate figure then being multiplied by counterparty risk weight.

The counterparty risk weights are between 0% and 50%. The resultant figure is then weighted by a factor of 8%. This gives rise to counterparty risk haircut charges for OTC derivatives (which arise in addition to any trading book market risk assessment) of 0% to 4% of mark-to-market and add-on.

CP3 removes the 50% counterparty risk weight cap, giving counterparty risk haircut charges of 0% to 8% of mark-to-market and add-on.

CP3 provides for "add-on" charges for credit derivatives of 5% to 10%.

11.6.6 FX

Banks are required to hold 8% of capital against their net foreign exchange position and their net gold position (banks with minimal FX activity whose net open position does not exceed 2% of capital may be exempted from this charge by local regulators).

11.6.7 Commodities

Banks are required to hold 15% of capital against their net commodity position, together with 3% against their gross commodity position.

11.6.8 Models

Approved VAR type models are permitted in assessing capital requirements in respect of the FX and/or commodity position risk of a bank, as well as the interest rate, equities and derivatives risk of the bank on its trading book (as well as in assessing specific risk if further requirements are met).

11.7 CAPITAL FOR BANKING BOOK EXPOSURES

Capital for the purpose of banking book exposures consists of Tier 1 (equity and disclosed reserves less goodwill and investments in non-consolidated entities engaged in financial services activities and less capital issued by other banks (if the local regulator so determines (e.g. in the UK) under the original rules, and in any event under

CP3)) and Tier 2 (undisclosed reserves, revaluation reserves, general (i.e. non-specific) loss reserves and subordinated debt with a minimum five-year term). Tier 2 may only be included up to the level of the Tier 1 capital, and Tier 2 subordinated debt only up to the level of 50% of the Tier 1 capital. Assets on the banking book are risk-weighted as follows:

11.7.1 General on-balance-sheet assets

The haircut capital charges under the regime prior to the New Basel Accord coming into force are as follows:

- **0% (0% risk weighting)** Cash or claims on an OECD central government/central bank.
- **0%/0.8%/1.6%/4% (0%/10%/20%/50% risk weighting)** Claims on an OECD public sector entity.
- **1.6% (20% risk weighting)** Claims on an OECD bank or an OECD securities firm regulated by a similar regime.
- **4% (50% risk weighting)** Residential mortgages (either owner-occupied or rented).
- **8% (100% risk weighting)** Other.
- **100% (1250% risk weighting; 1-for-1 deduction)** First loss enhancement provided by an originator or sponsor and second loss enhancement provided by an originator.

The new regime under CP3 would have the effect of changing these haircuts and weightings to one of two options, to be chosen by the bank, as set out in section 11.7.2 and section 11.7.3.

11.7.2 Standardised (external ratings based) approach

The haircut capital charges using the external ratings option would be as follows:

- **0% (0% risk weighting)** Cash or netted or cash collateralised assets or claims on or guaranteed or collateralised by an AAA to AA− sovereign.
- **1.6% (20% risk weighting)** Claims on or guaranteed or collateralised by an AAA to AA− bank (or securities firm regulated by a similar regime) or corporate or public sector entity or asset backed issue, or on an A+ to A− sovereign.
- **2.8% (35% risk weighting)** Residential mortgages.
- **4% (50% risk weighting)** Claims on or guaranteed or collateralised by an A+ to A− bank (or securities firm regulated by a similar regime) or public sector entity or corporate or asset backed issue, or on a BBB+ to BBB− sovereign, and (subject to national discretion) well-developed and long-established mortgage lending secured on commercial premises which is not past due to the extent of the lower of a Loan-to-Market-Value of 50% or a Loan-to-Mortgage-Value of 60% which carries losses in any one year to the extent of such lower LTV of 0.3% or less and overall losses to any LTV of 0.5% or lower. Also, at national discretion, residential mortgage loans which are past due for more than 90 days with at least 50% provisions.
- **6% (75% risk weighting)** Claims of a retail nature other than residential

mortgages, including SME loan portfolios managed as a retail portfolio and which are highly granular (no loans in excess of Euro 1m).

- **8% (100% risk weighting)**   Claims on or guaranteed or collateralised by a BBB+ to B– bank (or securities firm regulated by a similar regime) or public sector entity, a BBB+ to BB– corporate, a BBB+ to BBB– asset-backed issue, a BB+ to B– sovereign, or a bank (or securities firm regulated by a similar regime) or corporate or sovereign which does not carry a credit rating, or by commercial mortgages (save as noted under 50% above). Also loans that are past due for more than 90 days with at least 20% provisions, and residential mortgage loans that are past due for more than 90 days with less than 50% provisions.
- **12% (150% risk weighting)**   Claims on or guaranteed or collateralised by a less than B– bank (or securities firm regulated by a similar regime) or public sector entity or sovereign, or by a less than BB– corporate, and unsecured claims that are more than 90 days past due (net of specific provisions). Also loans that are past due for more than 90 days with less than 20% provisions.
- **28% (350% risk weighting)**   Claims on or guaranteed or collateralised by a BB+ to BB– asset-backed issue (for an originator of the deal in question this would be a 1250% weighting).
- **100% (1250% risk weighting; 1-for-1 deduction)**   Claims on or guaranteed or collateralised by a B+ or less asset-backed issue (in addition to other credit enhancement items as with the old rules).

Short-term bank claims (for 3 months or less) would move up one category. There is also an option, at national discretion, for a regulator to risk weight banks incorporated in its country at one category worse than the risk weight of the sovereign.

In relation to unrated exposures, which are the most senior securitisation exposure, second loss positions of investment grade quality associated with ABCP programmes, and eligible liquidity facilities, a "look-through" treatment is proposed:

- For the most senior securitisation exposure, the exposure is risk weighted at the average risk weight of the underlying credit exposures.
- For second loss or better positions of investment grade quality associated with ABCP programmes, a 100% risk weight is applied.
- For eligible liquidity facilities (see below), the facility is risk weighted at the highest risk weight of the underlying credit exposures.

CP3 provides that short-term ratings may be used on an issue-specific basis for short-term rated facilities as follows:

- **1.6% (20% risk weighting)**   Claims on an A1+ to A1 bank or corporate or asset-backed issue.
- **4% (50% risk weighting)**   Claims on an A2 bank or corporate or asset-backed issue.
- **8% (100% risk weighting)**   Caims on an A3 bank or corporate or asset-backed issue.
- **12% (150% risk weighting)**   Claims on banks or corporates rated below A3.
- **1250% (1250% risk weighting; 1-for-1 deduction)**   Claims on an asset-backed issue rated below A3 or unrated.

In order to use external ratings for a particular market segment, the paper envisages that a methodology for such rating in the relevant market segment should have been established for at least 1 year (and preferably at least 3 years).

CP3 also contains an opt-out which allows regulators national discretion to permit banks to apply a 100% risk weight to all corporates regardless of external rating.

11.7.3   Internal Ratings Based (IRB) approach

In this approach, the bank is required under CP3 to classify its exposures into five categories: corporate, sovereign, bank, retail and equity (excluding equities on trading book).

The bank can initially adopt the IRB approach for a single one of these classes, but will then be expected to adopt it for all other classes as well, although CP3 recognises that there may be a lag in implementation, or a phased roll-out over time.

The more simplistic "foundation approach" applies initially to corporate, sovereign and bank exposures and requires banks to estimate the Probability of Default (PD) for an exposure. Under the "advanced approach", banks must also estimate Maturity (M) and may also estimate Loss Given Default (LGD) and Exposure At Default (EAD). There is no difference between foundation and advanced approach for retail exposures.

Corporate, sovereign and bank categories

Aside from mainstream corporate lending, there are five sub-categories of specialised lending in the corporate category (which encompass forms of lending to an entity which relies on specific assets to make repayment, and has little or no other material assets), as follows:

● Project finance
● Object finance (i.e. asset finance)
● Commodities finance (e.g. inventory, receivables)
● Income-producing real estate (e.g. offices, multifamily, hotels, etc.)
● High-volatility real estate (e.g. construction or other scenarios where the finance is repaid by sale proceeds or the expected cash flow to be generated by the real estate is uncertain).

The bank first calculates a 1-year Probability of Default (PD) for each of its internal ratings grades.

For specialised lending, where the bank does not meet requirements for estimation of PD, the bank will be required to map the exposure to one of five regulatory categories (with classifications and risk weights for maturity of less than 2.5 years/equal to or more than 2.5 years of: strong 50%/75%, good 75%/100%, satisfactory 150%/150%, weak 350%/350%, default 625%/625%). These categories broadly correspond to BBB– or higher, BB+/BB, BB–/B+, B/C–, default. If the bank does meet the requirements, it may use the foundation or advanced approach.

For high-volatility real estate exposures, banks must use one of five regulatory categories (with classifications and risk weights for maturity of less than 2.5 years/ equal to or more than 2.5 years of: strong 75%/100%, good 100%/125%, satisfactory 175%/175%, weak 350%/350%, default 625%/625%). If they meet requirements for estimation of PD, they may use the foundation or advanced approach subject to national discretion, with a separate risk weight function specifically for high-volatility real estate.

The Maturity (*M*) of all exposures is assumed under QIS to be 2.5 years under the foundation approach. The bank is required to calculate the effective maturity under the advanced approach.

In the foundation approach under CP3, LGD (the Loss Given Default) is a standardised percentage (expressed as a number equal to the percentage) of:

- 45% (for senior claims on a corporate, bank or sovereign); or
- 75% (for subordinate claims on a corporate, bank or sovereign).

In the advanced approach, the bank is required to calculate the LGD.

For SME loans (loans where the borrower has less than Euro 50m of annual sales), CP3 provides for a lower risk weight which reduces the capital charge on a sliding scale (from businesses with turnover of Euro 50m, down to businesses with a turnover of Euro 5m or less). If the SME portfolio is managed as a retail portfolio and is highly granular (no loans in excess of Euro 1m), the retail risk weight curve may be used instead.

Capital requirements (*K*) are calculated from these component inputs, and the risk weight attributable to an asset is equal to 12.5 times the capital requirement calculated.

$$K = LGD \times N[(1 - R)^{-0.5} \times G(PD) + (R/(1 - R))^{0.5} \times G(0.999)]$$

$$\times (1 - 1.5 \times b(PD))^{-1} \times (1 + (M - 2.5) \times b(PD))$$

where

$$b = (0.08451 - 0.05898 \times \log(PD))^2$$

$$R = 0.12 \times (1 - \exp(-50 \times PD))/(1 - \exp(-50)) + 0.24$$

$$\times [1 - (1 - \exp(-50 \times PD))/(1 - \exp(-50))]$$

Retail category

Retail is divided into residential property, qualifying revolving (revolving, unsecured and uncommitted exposures to individuals of Euro 100 000 or less with a high ratio of spread – or Future Margin Income – to losses) and other retail. To be classified as retail, exposures must either be to individuals or be residential mortgages to owner-occupiers (also buy-to-lets where buildings only contain a few units) or SME loans with no exposure larger than Euro 1m which are managed as retail exposures. The exposures should also form a large pool and be managed on a pooled basis. The retail category is split into segments by product type and by other features that are designed to consist of homogeneous assets with no undue concentration. Each segment should be large enough to allow for statistical measures of default and loss to be applied across the segment as a whole.

To calculate capital, the bank calculates a PD and LGD off internal estimates (rather than internal ratings grades) for each segment as a whole, assuming 90 days past due (and/or the occurrence of bankruptcy or other credit events) as a reference level for default.

Capital requirements (K) are calculated from these component inputs, and the risk weight attributable to an asset is equal to 12.5 times the capital requirement calculated.

- Residential:

$$K = \text{LGD} \times N[(1 - R)^{-0.5} \times G(\text{PD}) + (R/(1 - R))^{0.5} \times G(0.999)]$$

where $R = 0.15$.

- Qualifying revolving:

$$K = \text{LGD} \times N[(1 - R)^{-0.5} \times G(\text{PD}) + (R/(1 - R))^{0.5}$$
$$\times G(0.999)] - 0.75\text{PD} \times \text{LGD}$$

where

$$R = 0.02 \times (1 - \exp(-50 \times \text{PD}))/(1 - \exp(-50)) + 0.11$$
$$\times [1 - (1 - \exp(-50 \times \text{PD}))/(1 - \exp(-50))]$$

- Other retail:

$$K = \text{LGD} \times N[(1 - R)^{-0.5} \times G(\text{PD}) + (R/(1 - R))^{0.5} \times G(0.999)]$$

where

$$R = 0.02 \times (1 - \exp(-35 \times \text{PD}))/(1 - \exp(-35)) + 0.17$$
$$\times [1 - (1 - \exp(-35 \times \text{PD}))/(1 - \exp(-35))]$$

Equity category

Equities are risk weighted on either a market-based approach (either at a simple risk weight of 300% for publicly traded equities and 400% for other equities, or using a VaR methodology), or on a PD/LGD basis (using an LGD of 90%).

Securitisation

To calculate capital for a securitisation, the IRB approach is subdivided into the Ratings Based Approach (RBA) and the Supervisory Formula approach (SF) (proposed to be replaced under the Press Release of 11 October 2003). The proposed capital treatment varies between originators (entities that directly or indirectly originate credit exposures included in a securitisation, and sponsors of CP conduits or similar programmes), servicers and investors (any other entities that assume economic risk in a securitisation). The SF is primarily for use by originators, and the RBA by investors.

Banks that apply the IRB approach for a class of underlying assets must also use the IRB approach for any securitisation of such class of assets.

An originator using the IRB Approach is required to calculate K_{IRB} – the capital charge for the securitised assets were they to be held on balance sheet – which is expressed in decimal form (e.g. 15% would be expressed as 0.15). Also the credit enhancement level (L), tranche thickness (T), number of loans in the pool (N) and weighted average loss-given-default (LGD).

The K_{IRB} is used as a cap on the maximum capital charge to originators under the

IRB Approach (see below). It is also used to determine the level of capital charged on more senior positions under the SF:

- The total capital charge across all issued tranches under the SF is set at $(1 + \text{Beta}) \times K_{IRB}$, where Beta is a premium (originally discussed at the 20% level, but which is risk-sensitive under the new proposals and would be higher for a non-granular pool than for a granular pool).
- For positions in excess of the K_{IRB} level (for which there is a direct deduction from capital), this calculates capital on a curvilinear function dropping off from a full deduction level.
- The result is a total capital charge across all tranches equal to the K_{IRB} plus Beta as a percentage of the K_{IRB}.

The capital charge on a tranche is calculated as

$$S[L + T] - S[L]$$

where L = credit enhancement level

       T = thickness of tranche.

If L is less than or equal to K_{IRB}, the charge is equal to L.
   If K_{IRB} is greater than L, then:

$$S[L] = K_{IRB} + K[L] - K[K_{IRB}] + (d \cdot K_{IRB}/w)[1 - e^{w(K_{IRB}-L)/K_{IRB}}]$$

As a "safe harbour" to limit the burden of assessing granularity, if the single largest exposure in the pool is 3%, then an LGD of 50% may be assumed in the K_{IRB} capital calculation.

Originators

Under the IRB Approach, an originator is required to calculate K_{IRB} for a securitisation.

- Positions between zero and K_{IRB} which are retained by the originator will be directly deducted from capital.
- Positions in excess of K_{IRB} should use RBA based on external or inferred ratings where available (see under "Investors" below), and the SF calculation of capital on a curvilinear function where external or inferred ratings are not available.
- Positions straddling K_{IRB} should be divided into two portions and treated appropriately.

Funded cash reserve funds can be taken into account as credit enhancement below a risk piece. The maximum total capital requirement for the originator bank will be the K_{IRB} level of capital.

Investors

The capital required to be held by investors under the IRB approach as proposed in the paper of October 2001 evaluated the issued securities using the RW under the corporate assets IRB approach at 50% LGD. This was then multiplied by a scaling factor which operated to increase the capital charge. The scaling factor approach was replaced in QIS3 with a new set of risk weights, under the Ratings-Based Approach (RBA).

Investors will be required to use the RBA to calculate the capital charge on external or inferred ratings. If external or inferred ratings are not available, the exposure should be deducted from capital unless supervisory approval is given to use the SF.

The RBA categorises positions into:

- Senior positions (seniority greater than or equal to $0.1 + 25$/(no. of assets in pool)) backed by highly granular pools (100 or more exposures);
- Base; and
- Non-granular pools.

This gives risk weights as follows (haircut capital charges are stated first):

- **0.6/1.0/1.6% (7/12/20% RW)** for Aaa level (senior and granular/base/non-granular, respectively)
- **0.8/1.2/2.0% (10/15/25% RW)** for Aa level (senior and granular/base/non-granular, respectively)
- **1.6/1.6/2.8% (20/20/35% RW)** for A level (senior and granular/base/non-granular, respectively)
- **4% (50% RW)** for Baa1 level
- **6% (75% RW)** for Baa2 level
- **8% (100% RW)** for Baa3 level
- **20% (250% RW)** for Ba1 level
- **34% (425% RW)** for Ba2 level
- **52% (650% RW)** for Ba3 level
- **100% (1250% RW)** for below Ba3 level and unrated.

Short-term:

- **0.6/1.0/1.6% (7/12/20% RW)** for A1 level (senior and granular/base/non-granular, respectively)
- **1.6/1.6/2.8% (20/20/35% RW)** for A2 level (senior and granular/base/non-granular, respectively)
- **6% (75% RW)** for A3 level
- **100% (1250% RW)** for below A3 level and unrated.

11.7.4 Resultant on balance sheet capital haircuts

The result of the new Basel Accord external ratings based (ERB) and internal ratings based (IRB) capital calculations can be seen in Table 11.1, which uses the sample IRB calculations in CP3. As can be seen, the new Basel Accord is extremely penal for ABS tranches compared to other assets, even such as specialised lending exposures on project finance, in both the ERB and the IRB approach. These capital haircuts are also illustrated graphically in Figure 11.1.

11.7.5 General off-balance-sheet assets (other than derivatives)

Off-balance-sheet items other than derivatives (including guarantees, undrawn commitments, and liquidity facilities) are reported by multiplying the notional principal amount of the item by a "credit conversion factor" between 0% and 100% before

Table 11.1 Sample capital under the new Basel Accord; source Basel Committee April 2003 Consultative Document

	ERB ABS	ERB Corporate	IRB ABS Base	IRB Corporate/ Bank/Sovereign	IRB Corporate SME (not retail)	IRB Corporate Specialised (2.5 yrs+)	IRB Retail Mortgages 25% LGD	IRB Retail Other 85% LGD	IRB Retail Revolver 45% LGD
AAA	1.6%	1.6%	1.0%	1.2%	0.9%	6.0%	0.2%	0.8%	0.2%
AA	1.6%	1.6%	1.2%	1.2%	0.9%	6.0%	0.2%	0.8%	0.2%
A	4.0%	4.0%	1.6%	1.6%	1.3%	6.0%	0.3%	1.1%	0.3%
BBB+	8.0%	8.0%	4.0%	2.4%	1.9%	6.0%	0.5%	1.9%	0.6%
BBB	8.0%	8.0%	6.0%	4.1%	3.2%	6.0%	1.0%	3.6%	1.1%
BBB−	8.0%	8.0%	8.0%	5.2%	4.1%	6.0%	1.4%	4.9%	1.5%
BB+	28.0%	8.0%	20.0%	6.9%	5.5%	8.0%	2.3%	7.0%	2.1%
BB	28.0%	8.0%	34.0%	8.6%	6.9%	8.0%	3.3%	9.0%	2.7%
BB−	28.0%	8.0%	52.0%	10.1%	8.0%	12.0%	4.4%	10.5%	3.1%
B+	100.0%	12.0%	100.0%	11.6%	9.2%	12.0%	5.7%	11.7%	3.4%
B	100.0%	12.0%	100.0%	14.3%	11.3%	28.0%	7.8%	13.4%	3.9%
B−	100.0%	12.0%	100.0%	20.0%	16.4%	28.0%	11.6%	17.8%	5.6%
CCC+	100.0%	12.0%	100.0%	24.6%	20.7%	28.0%	14.2%	23.4%	7.2%
CCC	100.0%	12.0%	100.0%	28.2%	24.3%	28.0%	16.2%	29.1%	8.6%

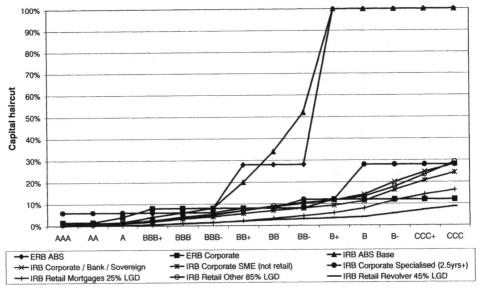

Figure 11.1 Sample capital under the New Basel Accord; source Basel Committee April 2003 Consultative Document

multiplying by the counterparty risk weight and the 8% factor (sub-participations are reported as an exposure at the higher of the risk weighting of the underlying borrower and that of the participating bank), as follows:

- **1-for-1 deduction** Liquidity facilities that do not meet qualification requirements (for example, as to a use of a borrowing base calculation) and are therefore treated as credit enhancement in a case where there is no other first loss enhancement (assets will simply remain on balance sheet where a liquidity facility is provided by the originator and it does meet the requirements). Also, any off-balance-sheet first loss enhancement provided by an originator, sponsor or repackager and off-balance-sheet second loss enhancement provided by an originator.
- **100%** Off-balance-sheet items that are a "direct credit substitute" (guarantees given should be reported as an exposure for the full principal amount on the party guaranteed).
- **50%** An undrawn commitment with an original maturity exceeding 1 year.
- **20%** Self-liquidating trade finance items.
- **0%** An undrawn commitment with an original maturity of 1 year or less.

The new regime under CP3 changes this as follows for the Standardised Approach:

- **100%** Off-balance-sheet items that are a "direct credit substitute" (guarantees given should be reported as an exposure for the full principal amount on the party guaranteed) and liquidity facilities that are not eligible, as well as other off-balance-sheet items relating to a securitisation.
- **50%** An undrawn commitment or eligible liquidity facility with an original maturity exceeding 1 year.

- **20%** An undrawn commitment or eligible liquidity facility with an original maturity of 1 year or less and self-liquidating trade finance items.
- **0%** An undrawn commitment with an original maturity of 1 year or less which is unconditionally cancellable and an eligible liquidity facility which may only be drawn in the event of general market disruption.

In the IRB Approach, off-balance-sheet items will carry the same credit conversion factors as under the standardised approach, except that committed undrawn facilities which are not unconditionally cancellable at any time would be given a 75% credit conversion factor regardless of maturity (under the foundation approach) or converted at the expected Exposure At Default (EAD) level (under the advanced approach). In relation to off-balance-sheet securitisation exposures, eligible facilities that may only be drawn in the event of general market disruption have a 20% CCF. Other off-balance-sheet securitisation exposures have a 100% CCF.

For securitisation of revolving pools, the Committee first proposed an additional charge in CP2 (in the form of a "credit conversion factor" of 10% on the notional amount) to reflect the risk of early amortisation bringing the issue back on balance sheet.

CP3 develops this with a sliding scale of credit conversion factor (CCF) for off-balance-sheet exposures where there are early amortisation features, based on the level of excess spread in the deal. For controlled early amortisation of uncommitted retail credit lines, the CCF starts at 0% for excess spread levels of 450 bps or more, down to 40% for spread of less than 112.5 bps. Non-retail credit lines and committed lines have a 90% CCF. For uncontrolled early amortisation of uncommitted retail credit lines, the CCF starts at 0% for excess spread levels of 450 bps or more, down to 100% for spread of less than 112.5 bps. Non-retail credit lines and committed lines have a 100% CCF.

11.7.6   Repo/stock loans

Reverse repos and stock borrowings are reported by the cash lender/securities borrower as a collateralised loan and given the risk weighting appropriate to the collateral (the collateral weighting may be reduced to 0% for certain repos, such as repo of government securities with daily mark-to-market – see section 11.6.3).

11.7.7   Credit derivatives

Credit default swaps and total return swaps are treated as guarantees in respect of the amount of exposure to which they relate (see section 11.6.3). Credit spread products do not give any capital benefit to the buyer.

As with guarantees, CP2 required a "W" factor of 15% of the covered exposure be weighted as though not protected (in addition to any uncovered exposure). Similarly, the Basel Committee announced in September 2001 that they would consider moving the charge relating to the "W" factor from the first "pillar" on minimum capital to a consideration of appropriate measures under the second "pillar" on supervisory review. QIS3 removed the "W" factor.

CP3 set out as general requirements for credit derivatives:

- The credit derivative must be a direct claim which is explicitly referenced to specific exposures, and must be irrevocable save in the case of non-payment by the protection buyer.
- There must be no provision permitting the unilateral cancellation of the credit cover by the protection seller or increasing the cost of the credit cover as a result of a deterioration in the credit quality of the protected assets.
- The credit derivative must at the very least include "credit event" triggers relating to failure to pay, bankruptcy, and restructuring involving forgiveness or postponement of payment (CP3 acknowledges that the restructuring event may not be necessary if the bank has control over whether there is a restructuring or not – e.g. by withholding its consent – although its discussions on this are ongoing).
- The reference obligation must be the same as the protected asset, or must be issued by the same issuer and rank junior to or *pari passu* with the protected asset and cross-default must apply.

Eligible credit protection providers are sovereigns, public sector entities, banks and securities firms, as well as corporates rated A– or higher in the Standardised Approach (and also lower rated corporates in the IRB Approach).

Materiality thresholds should be directly deducted from capital in the Standardised Approach.

Where the reference obligation is denominated in a different currency, the level of protection recognised will be reduced by a haircut (to reflect the currency risk) in the Standardised Approach.

If the credit derivative has a shorter term than the protected asset, then no protection value is recognised if the credit derivative has less than 1 year to expiry. If the credit derivative has 1 year or more to expiry, then the credit protected amount will be reduced by multiplying it by the protection residual term over the exposure residual term (both capped at 5 years) (in risk weight terms, equivalent to averaging an unprotected amount and a protected amount by tenor).

CP3 provides, in relation to basket trades, that:

- A "first to default" basket structure gives the buyer protection against the default of any one of the assets in the basket.
- On sale of a "first to default" credit derivative basket, if the structure is externally rated it is charged as a securitisation tranche with such rating; if not rated, the structure generates a capital charge for the protection seller equal to the addition of the respective capital charge for each asset in the basket (capped at a direct deduction from capital of the exposure).
- In a "second to default" basket structure, the buyer may only count protection as capital relief where first-to-default protection has also been obtained, or one of the assets has already defaulted.
- On sale of a "second to default" credit derivative basket, if the structure is externally rated it is charged as a securitisation tranche with such rating; if not rated, the structure generates a capital charge for the protection seller equal to the addition of the respective capital charge for each asset in the basket, excluding the single worst asset in the basket.

11.7.8   Operational risk

CP2 proposed that additional banking book capital charges be set for operational risk, depending on the nature of the business of the bank. CP2 proposed 20% of minimum regulatory capital, the September 2001 paper on operational risk proposed reducing this to 12%.

CP3 sets out three methods for calculating operational risk charges – the Basic Indicator Approach, the Standardised Approach and the Advanced Measurement Approach. In the Basic Indicator Approach the formula is 15% of the average annual gross income over the last 3 years.

The Committee has backed away from their original position that there should be an additional capital charge for interest rate risk for "outliers" with extensive interest rate risk, but stress that supervisors should be attentive to banks where value would drop by more than 20% of Tier 1 and Tier 2 capital following a 200 basis point interest rate shock.

11.8   CAPITAL FOR TRADING BOOK EXPOSURES

Capital for trading book exposures consists of Tier 1 and Tier 2 capital as with the banking book, but in addition banks may use Tier 3 capital (subordinated debt with a minimum 2-year maturity) against certain trading book exposures (Tier 2 and Tier 3 capital set against trading book cannot exceed 250% of Tier 1 capital set against trading book) of an institution. Certain elements are required to be directly deducted from capital (giving an equivalent risk weighting of 1250%). In particular in relation to the provision of credit enhancement to an SPV in a securitisation structure where the bank is the originator of the transaction. Capital haircuts for assets on the trading book are as follows.

11.8.1   Debt

Fixed income instruments are assessed for general (or position-related) market risk on matched long and short positions in the same maturity band at a fraction of 0% to 12.5% of the offsetting amount without double counting (to reflect the residual maturity of the security – floating rate securities are weighted by reference to the time to the next interest determination rather than the residual maturity and will thus often fall into the 1 month or less band of 0%, the 1+ to 3 month band of 0.2% or the 3+ to 6 month band of 0.4%), which is then subject to two levels of offset – firstly, within each of three zones (short term, medium term and long term) and, secondly, between these zones. Unmatched positions are assessed at a fraction of 0% to 12.5% of the principal amount, weighted by a factor of 100%. This gives rise to a general haircut of gross exposure ranging from 0% to 12.5% (unmatched), and less for matched positions.

The debt securities specific (or counterparty-related) haircut as a percentage of the gross position is:

- 0% (the same issues of the same issuer where the long and short positions offset (see also section 11.8.3) or which are issues of or collateralised by central government/central bank securities);

- 0.25% for 6 months or less residual maturity "qualifying debt items";
- 1% for 6+ to 24 months residual maturity "qualifying debt items";
- 1.6% for more than 24 months residual maturity "qualifying debt items"; or
- 8% for other securities.

Qualifying debt items broadly consist of public sector securities and investment grade rated securities, and also, at the discretion of the local regulator, securities issued by a bank or by a securities firm subject to a similar regime to the Basel Accord.

11.8.2 Equity

The general haircut for equities is 8% of net position. Equities are specific risk weighted at 8% of the gross position, or 4% for equities that are liquid and part of a diversified portfolio of equities.

11.8.3 Credit derivatives

CP3 provides that complete specific risk offset may be gained by use of a total return swap. Only partial offset to the extent of 80% is gained from a credit default swap or a credit linked note. To benefit from these offsets, the reference asset must exactly match the underlying asset, and it must also match maturity and currency.

If the reference asset is issued by the same issuer as the underlying exposure, and ranks junior to or *pari passu* with the protected asset, or there is a currency or maturity mismatch, then the higher of the two specific risks (the credit derivative and the underlying) will be taken. Materiality thresholds or fixed payout amounts will limit the protection value.

11.8.4 Derivatives

Exchange-traded and OTC derivatives are generally broken down into their individual risk components (interest rate, equity risk, etc.) that are included in the relevant assessment of market risk requirements, as set out above. Long positions in options and warrants are generally assessed to a haircut equal to the lesser of the charge for a position in the underlying, or the amount of the market value of the instrument. Short positions in options and warrants are generally assessed to a haircut equal to a position in the underlying, but the assessment reduces by any amount that the option is out of the money. Assessments are reduced fully or partially for positions taken to hedge an underlying asset.

Global Securitisation Markets

12.1 ARGENTINA

Most transactions to date in Argentina have been domestic deals. The first securitisation of distressed assets (a mixture of secured and unsecured corporate loans) in Argentina was completed in May 2001 using the CNV trust structure. Following the forced conversion of US Dollar-denominated assets and liabilities into Argentine Peso and the devaluation of the Peso in January 2002 (see "Other issues" below), a number of transactions were downgraded by Standard & Poor's in January 2002 over concerns about the transferability of funds.

Ring-fencing and true sale

The implementation of the Housing and Construction Financing Law (otherwise known as the Trust Law) – Law No. 24,441 of 9 January 1995 – permitted assets to be transferred to a trust and managed by a trustee, and provided that the transfer would not be unwound save in cases of fraud.

Onshore SPV

A trustee of a trust established under the Trust Law can issue bonds or trust certificates against the assets of the trust, and acts on behalf of the holders of these securities as beneficiaries of the trust.

Securities laws

An offer of securities to the public is subject to the prior approval of the *Comision Nacional de Valores* or CNV (the Argentine SEC).

Tax treatment

Withholding tax   Interest payments on bonds issued by a trustee under the Trust Law will be free of withholding tax if offered to the public with CNV approval, and will otherwise be subject to withholding tax. Trust certificates are likely to be free of withholding tax.

Profits tax   A trust can claim a tax deduction for interest payments on bonds (with the possible exception of bonds with equity-type characteristics), but not for distributions on trust certificates.

VAT   The Trust Law exempts transfers under the terms of the law from liability to VAT on transfer.

Other issues

On 6 January 2002, Emergency Law 25,561 was brought into force. Together with Decree 214 of 3 February 2002, this provided for the mandatory conversion of assets and liabilities denominated in US Dollars which are governed by Argentine law into Argentine Peso. Prior to this, the Peso had been fixed to the Dollar at 1 : 1. The Emergency Law repealed the fixed rate and converted bank deposits to Peso at Peso 1.4 per US$ 1, while loans and other obligations (including ABS) were converted at Peso 1 per US$ 1. The Peso devalued sharply over 2002.

12.2 AUSTRALIA

Australia has proved a fertile ground for securitisation, with mortgage-backed transactions and asset-backed commercial paper conduits in particular showing significant volume. From 1999 onwards, Australian issuers have accessed the Euromarket and US market, in addition to their traditional Australian investor base. More recently, synthetic securitisations have come to the fore. Almost 90% of term issuance in 2001 comprised RMBS, although this dropped to 84% in 2002. Many mortgages in Australia are covered by pool insurance from AAA- or AA-rated entities such as Housing Loan Insurance or CGU, resulting in highly rated junior tranches on many deals.

Australia is a common law jurisdiction, historically based on English law. The country operates a federal system, with six states and two territories.

Ring-fencing and true sale

Transfer can be carried out by equitable assignment without the need to give notice.

Set-off

The debtor can obtain good discharge by making payments to the originator until notice of the assignment is given to the debtor, at which point the debtor is obliged to pay to the SPV direct. The SPV will take subject to any defects in the title of the originator and, until notice is given to the debtor, the SPV is subject to any further equities (such as set-off) arising in favour of the debtor through relations between the originator and the debtor subsequent to the assignment.

Onshore SPV

Australian SPVs are often used to avoid withholding on receivables collections.

Foreign ownership

No foreign person is permitted to acquire more than 15% ownership of an Australian company without notifying the Commonwealth Government (the treasurer has the power to dismantle an ownership in excess of this level). Foreign ownership of Australian banks may not exceed 15% of voting rights. Acquisitions of more than 5% in a listed company and each subsequent 1% must be notified to the stock exchange.

Securities laws

The Financial Services Reform Act 2001, which streamlines Australian securities laws, came into effect on 11 March 2002.

Tax treatment

Stamp/registration/etc. The stamp duty regime in Australia was put under review in 1996. Significant stamp duty may be levied on assignments, leading many deals to use the "acceptance by payment" basis to avoid creating a stampable document. Specific exemptions exist in New South Wales, Victoria, Queensland and Tasmania for assignments relating to a mortgage-backed programme.

The stamp duty regime in some states is unclear in relation to the amount of stamp duty that could become payable if the originator entered insolvency and a transfer needed to be perfected. This has led rating agencies to require a stamp duty reserve on some mortgage deals, where the originator is not investment grade rated.

Withholding tax Receivables interest paid to an offshore entity is subject to withholding tax at a rate of 10%. Collection agents (such as the originator) would be obliged to pay this on to the tax authorities. This tax is not reduced by any double tax treaty entered into by Australia.

Under s. 128F of the Income Tax Assessment Act 1936, an exemption from withholding is available for interest paid by an Australian resident SPV company (or a trust, provided that the trust is not a charitable trust and the beneficiaries of the trust are acting for themselves and not as trustee for other parties) on bonds that are issued pursuant to a "public offer". There are a number of ways in which the public offer test can be satisfied, but, in general, this includes bonds that are issued to professional investors, are listed on a stock exchange, or are in global form. The exemption will not be available if the SPV knew, or had reasonable grounds to suspect, that the bonds were being, or would later be, acquired by an "associate" of the SPV. The "public offer" test replaces the earlier "wide distribution" test.

Prior to the passing of legislation on 29 June 1999, the bonds also had to be issued to investors outside Australia to qualify for the exemption, with interest to be paid outside Australia. The new legislation removed this requirement for new issues after such date (but not for existing issues prior to such date).

Profits tax Australia applies an "income source" methodology in taxing entities, such that income sourced in Australia (which includes under s. 25(2) of the Tax Act interest in respect of money secured over Australian property) may result in an offshore SPV becoming liable to Australian profits tax. If the SPV is located in a tax treaty jurisdiction, the Australian source income will need to be attributable to a permanent establishment in Australia before it will be taxable. Purchase of Australian assets will not create an Australian permanent establishment, however, administration of those assets may, unless performed by an independent agent.

In order to prevent withholding tax arising on payments on the receivables (see above), it may be desirable to ensure that the SPV is located in Australia, and it would therefore be necessary to confirm tax neutrality by ensuring that all expenses can be fully deducted against receipts.

SPVs located in Australia may be subject to thin capitalisation rules – historically these recharacterised debt in excess of a 6:1 ratio as equity, where the bonds were bought, or guaranteed, by the originator. The Ralph Report of September 1999 on business tax in Australia proposed reforms to the thin capitalisation rules, leading to an exposure draft of new rules on 21 February 2001. These new rules were introduced on 1 October 2001, and apply to debt issued on or after 1 July 2001 (the date when the rules were originally scheduled to come into effect). Issues prior to 1 July 2001 remain subject to the old rules until 1 July 2004. The new rules restrict interest deductibility for corporates with debt in excess of a 3:1 ratio (measuring debt in Australia against assets in Australia), or for banks with equity of less than 4% of risk-weighted assets. There is also a specific exemption for securitisation vehicles raising debt on an arm's-length basis.

VAT   Australia introduced a goods and services tax (GST) from 1 July 2000 at a rate of 10%.

Accounting treatment

The Australian Accounting Standards Board Urgent Issues Group released an abstract relating to Accounting Standard 1024 on consolidated accounts in July 1999 (Abstract 28 on Consolidation of Special Purpose Entities), which potentially requires the consolidation of SPVs onto the balance sheet of the originator where the majority of economic benefits in the SPV are distributed to the originator, or the SPV acts on an automatic basis (i.e. without independent consideration). In addition, Australia generally follows IAS standards, and the approach set out in IAS 39 is increasingly being used.

Capital treatment

The Australian Prudential Regulatory Authority (APRA) was established to take over regulatory authority for banking institutions from the Reserve Bank of Australia (RBA) from 1 July 1998, and enforced the RBA's Prudential Statement C2 (PSC2) of October 1995 on "Funds Management and Securitisation", which set out guidelines for the transfer of assets off balance sheet by banking institutions, and the involvement of bank entities in securitisations as liquidity providers, credit enhancers, et al.

A new APRA Prudential Standard (APS 120) became effective on 1 October 2000. APS 120 replaces PSC2, and applies to authorised deposit-taking institutions as well as banks. APS 120 requires that there be a clear separation between the originator and the SPV. The originator may not hold an ownership interest in the SPV, and may only have a limited number of directors on the board of the SPV. A clear statement must be made to investors in any offering materials that the originator will not support the SPV in excess of any specific facilities provided by the originator to the SPV. If the originator fails to comply, it must hold capital against all the securities issued in the transaction. The risks and rewards of the assets must be fully transferred to the SPV (although rights to excess spread may be retained if further conditions are met). First-loss credit enhancement will be directly deducted from capital (up to a cap equal to holding capital against all the securities issued in the transaction); second-loss enhancement will simply be treated as a normal direct credit substitute.

Guidelines on the capital treatment of credit derivatives were released in April 2000 by APRA. The guidelines cover both banking book and trading book treatment, and apply a sliding scale to deal with maturity mismatches.

In June 2001, APRA welcomed the new Basel proposals, with reservations on the suitability of internally calculated capital charges for some institutions.

Data protection/confidentiality

Financial service providers are required to keep customer information confidential.

Consumer protection

The Consumer Credit Code of November 1996 regulates consumer contracts.

12.3 AUSTRIA

Austria has legislation which allows for the issue of Pfandbriefe. The Austrian market opened up in late 2001 with its first publicly rated transactions – the FACT-2001 auto loan transaction for Porsche Bank and the Euro 2.5bn Blue Danube Loan Funding deal (a securitisation of subsidized housing loans) for the State of Lower Austria.

Ring-fencing and true sale

Covered Bonds   Legislation allows for the issue of Pfandbriefe. Pfandbriefe may be backed by a pool of mortgages (*Hypothekenpfandbriefe*) or by a pool of public sector loan assets (Austrian government or public authority loans and EEA/Switzerland government loans) (*öffentlicher Pfandbriefe*). The maximum LTV for mortgage loans to be eligible in the pool is 60%. Pfandbriefe have a 10% capital risk weighting and are Tier 1 ECB eligible.

Tax treatment

Stamp/registration/etc.   A transfer of receivables is subject to 0.8% stamp duty. The re-registration of mortgages on transfer is subject to registration duties of 1.2%.

12.4 BELGIUM

The securitisation market in Belgium opened up with its first transactions in 1996, and has rapidly established itself with predominantly mortgage issuance, in particular from repeat issuer BACOB Bank (now Artesia Banking Corporation). Mortgage deals slowed in 1999, due to extremely high prepayment rates arising from borrowers seeking to refinance at lower interest rates.

Belgium operates a civil law system.

Ring-fencing and true sale

Receivables may be assigned in a manner that is binding on third parties without a requirement to give notice to the debtor (since amendments to Article 1690 of the Civil Code in July 1994), but any mortgage transfer must be registered unless the transferee is an SIC or FPC (see below). Consumer loans may only be transferred to a regulated entity or an SIC/FPC.

Notice to the debtor is still required for the transfer to be enforceable against the debtor.

Future receivables   Future receivables cannot be transferred effectively.

Recharacterisation   Deferred purchase price elements are considered to be compatible with a sale characterisation.

Moratorium/automatic stay   Moratorium proceedings can prevent the enforcement of security.

Set-off

The debtor can obtain good discharge by making payments to the originator until notice of the assignment is given to the debtor, at which point the debtor is obliged to pay to the SPV direct. The SPV will take subject to any defects in the title of the originator, and until notice is given to the debtor, the SPV is subject to any further equities (such as set-off) arising in favour of the debtor through relations between the originator and the debtor subsequent to the assignment.

Onshore SPV

Vehicles may be established in the form of a company (an SIC or *société d'investissement en créances*) (also known as a VBS or *vennootschap voor belegging in schuldvorderingen*) or a fund (an FPC or *fonds de placement en créances*) (also known as an FBS or *fonds voor belegging in schuldvorderingen*) under a law in November 1993 (modified with effect from July 1997).

An FPC requires a management company (distinct from the originator) with share capital of at least Euro 125 000. Both SICs and FPCs require a credit institution to act as custodian and an independent supervisory company (unless they are solely engaged in private offerings, following the amendment of July 1997). SICs must have a minimum capital of circa Euro 30 000. SICs/FPCs may be used as programme vehicles for more than one deal, and may engage in deal-related hedging and borrowing activities.

Belgium has a type of REIT in the form of FBIs.

Foreign ownership

Any foreign person acquiring more than 10% ownership of a Belgian company must notify the company. Acquisitions of more than 5% in a listed company and each subsequent 5% must be notified to the stock exchange.

Tax treatment

Stamp/registration/etc.   There is a registration cost of 1% of the value of the assets on mortgage transfers. This may be avoided if an SIC or FPC is used (see above).

Withholding tax   Belgium charges withholding tax at a rate of 15%. Both SICs and FPCs are exempt from withholding tax on interest received. An exemption from withholding tax is available on interest paid to offshore investors (but generally not domestic investors), where the bonds are held in registered form in the National Bank of Belgium clearing system; this exemption is generally not available to FPCs. The double tax treaty with the Netherlands reduces offshore withholding to zero.

From 5 June 2003 a new decree came into force, which allows listed Belgium holding companies, and companies which act as treasury providers to their group, to pay interest to offshore banks free of withholding tax.

Profits tax   An offshore SPV will need to be structured carefully to avoid being viewed as a permanent establishment. SICs are largely exempt from corporate tax except on profits from off-market transactions (abnormal or gratuitous advantages). FPCs are not subject to corporate tax.

VAT   Transfers of receivables are not charged subject to VAT. Servicing fees are likely to be liable to VAT, although there are a number of exemptions from VAT for SICs/FPCs on services rendered to them. SICs/FPCs cannot recover input tax incurred.

Capital treatment

The *Commission Bancaire et Financière* (CBF) requires that transfers should not put the originator under any moral obligation to support the transaction if they are to achieve off-balance-sheet treatment. Where the assets of an SIC/FPC are pledged to note-holders and certain other requirements are met, the notes may carry the same capital risk weighting as the underlying assets.

Regulatory approvals

Publicly offered transactions are subject to prior approval by the CBF of the deal and of the prospectus for the offering, and must be rated (prior to the amendments which came into force in July 1997, these limitations also applied to private offerings).

Issues by offshore SPVs are subject to CBF approval if the securities are offered in Belgium.

Other issues

The effectiveness under Belgian law of an interest in collateral taken by means of an outright transfer of ownership (rather than a security interest) was called into doubt by the Belgian Supreme Court in the Sart-Tilman case of October 1996. As of 9 September 1998, however, a law reform bill promulgated by the Belgian government entered into force. This provides that collateral taken by outright transfer from a financial institution which is in the form of book entry securities or cash, and where there are provisions for redelivery of the collateral, will be effective.

12.5 BOLIVIA

A secondary mortgage company was established to operate from Autumn 1999.

Ring-fencing and true sale

Securities Law 1834 of 31 March 1998 provides for issuance via securitisation companies.

Regulatory approvals

Regulations relating to mortgage deals were put forward to be passed by the CNV in mid-1999.

12.6 BRAZIL

Brazil has the largest securitisation market in Latin America, with export receivables and other future flows transactions, as well as political risk insurance (PRI) transactions (which wrap convertibility and transferability risks attached to a corporate credit).

Ring-fencing and true sale

Notice is required to be given for an assignment of receivables to be effective under the Civil Code. A general agreement by the debtor to assignment in the terms of the contract is considered to be effective to permit assignment.

Future receivables   Future receivables may be assigned under the Civil Code.

Substantive consolidation   Separate management and control of the SPV should be instituted to prevent any risk of substantive consolidation.

Moratorium/automatic stay   Moratorium proceedings (*concordata*) are similar to US Chapter 11.

Onshore SPV

Resolution 2097 of 2001 provided for the establishment of *fundos de investimentos em direitos creditorios* (FIDCs – open-ended or closed-ended investment funds), which can be used to purchase and securitise receivables.

Tax treatment

Stamp/registration/etc.   Transfers are subject to registration fees.

Profits tax   FIDCs are exempt from many taxes.

Data protection/confidentiality

Banks are subject to strict bank secrecy laws.

Regulatory approvals

Resolution 2696 of January 2000 of the national monetary board (the *Conselho Monetario Nacional* or CMN) provides regulatory approval for securitisation, and replaced the previous resolution 2493 of May 1998 (which in turn replaced resolution 2026 of 1993).

Resolution 2696 provides for the transfer of assets to an SPV which bears the title *companhia securitizadora de creditos financeiros* and which is registered with the securities regulator (the *Comissao de Valores Mobiliarios* or CVM).

Other issues

Trusts are not generally recognised, and fiduciary structures are used instead.

12.7   CANADA

Canada has a large and developed domestic securitisation market, which has historically focused on ABCP issuance rather than term issuance. Offshore development has been hindered by withholding tax on payments overseas, although it is anticipated that this will improve following renegotiation of the Canada–US double tax treaty to remove withholding tax, opening up the US investor base for Canadian deals.

Issuance in 2002 was up 2% on 2001.

Canada is a common law jurisdiction, historically based on English law (save for Quebec, which is a civil law system).

Ring-fencing and true sale

Most of the provinces of Canada operate a registration and filing system similar to the UCC filing system in the US. Quebec operates a central registry system under the provisions of its Civil Code.

Recharacterisation   In deciding whether a transaction is a true sale or a secured loan, the court will construe the deal documents to determine the intention of the parties. Other factors such as whether the originator has the right to repurchase the receivables, or is obliged to compensate the SPV for any loss on the receivables, will also be considered.

Onshore SPV

Due to the application of capital tax (see "Other tax issues" below), trusts are typically used as issuers rather than corporations.

Securities laws

Canada has undertaken reform to enable issuers to seek a single securities approval from Ottawa for public issues, rather than having to seek approval from each of the 10 provincial regulators (a factor that has held up public issuance in the Canadian market in the past).

Tax treatment

Withholding tax   Canada charges withholding tax on interest on receivables paid to an offshore entity. Withholding is also charged on securities issued to offshore investors, at a rate of 25% (which is generally only reduced to 10% by double tax treaties). There is no withholding tax on discount elements.

An exemption from withholding tax is available for issues by a corporation (but not issues by a trust) if at least 75% of the principal of the securities cannot be repaid (in whole or part) within 5 years from issue. There are also specific exemptions for certain asset classes such as certain pass-through MBS issues.

Discussions in 2002 may lead to the removal of withholding tax on interest paid between US and Canada during 2003 (charged at 10%).

VAT   Canada charges a goods and services tax (GST).

Other tax issues   Canada introduced an annual capital tax on the balance sheet capital (equity plus long-term debt) of corporations (the tax is not charged on capital of a trust) at both the federal and the provincial level in 1989. In 2003, it was proposed to remove the federal level charge over a 5-year period (the provincial level charge will remain).

Accounting treatment

Canadian accounting standards EIC 9 and EIC 54 on off-balance-sheet treatment historically limited recourse to the originator to a measurable and "reasonable" level of around 10% in order to obtain off-balance-sheet treatment.

Revisions to these accounting guidelines were discussed by the Accounting Standards Board of the Canadian Institute of Chartered Accountants (the CICA) in 1999 and 2000 in order to bring Canadian standards in line with the revised FAS 125 published in late 1998. Following publication of FAS 140 in September 2000 to replace FAS 125 in the US, the CICA adopted Accounting Guideline 12 applying to the transfer of receivables in 2001, which largely follows FAS 140. New guidelines which follow FIN 46 of January 2003 are expected.

Capital treatment

The Office of the Superintendent of Financial Institutions (OSFI) published guidelines in 1994 which move towards a standard of allowing off-balance-sheet capital treatment where the significant risks and rewards of ownership are transferred. Credit derivative guidelines were published in October 1997.

Canadian liquidity facilities are not structured as full or partial credit enhancement, and can be cancelled and not drawn against defaulted assets. The argument has therefore been advanced that they would not be subject to the capital requirement levied on liquidity lines via the new proposed 20% credit conversion factor for 364-day lines that cannot be cancelled unconditionally in the latest Basel capital proposals.

12.8   CHILE

Ring-fencing and true sale

Notice of an assignment must be given to the debtor in order for the assignment to be effective to transfer the receivables out of the insolvency estate of the originator.

Onshore SPV

Law No. 18,045 of 1994 (amended by Law No. 19,301) provides for mortgage SPVs. Law No. 19,623 was passed in August 1999, which extends the regime to other kinds of asset.

Tax treatment

Withholding tax   Chile charges withholding tax at a rate of 35%.

Regulatory approvals

Securities issued under a transaction must be registered with the Securities Regulator (the SVS).

12.9   CHINA

As a result of the legal, tax and regulatory uncertainty which pervades the People's Republic of China (the PRC), securitisations in the PRC to date have been limited to future flows deals securitising offshore receivables (which to a certain extent reduce PRC regulatory issues) – such as the COSCO deals of 1997 and 1999 – or deals financed through CP conduits, where bank liquidity lines ease the rating agency analysis of the credit risk on the CP. Strong support exists amongst officials within the PRC to develop a more securitisation-friendly structure.

Cinda Asset Management Corp, the Chinese state asset management corporation, is owned by the Ministry of Finance and has Renminbi 10bn of capital. It auctioned its first pool of assets (of around Renminbi 60m par) in late 1999, achieving a sale price of some 12% of par. Cinda has taken equity in some enterprises via debt-equity swaps, and aims to use securitisation for some of its assets.

In 1999, Asset Management Companies were established by the big four Chinese banks – Bank of China, the Industrial and Commercial Bank of China, the Construction Bank of China and the Agricultural Bank of China. Renminbi 1400bn (US$ 169bn) of non-performing loans was transferred to the four AMCs by the Big Four banks in 2000. Roadshows for the auction of the first package of these loans to external investors (from Huarong AMC) commenced in 2001, with Renminbi 16bn (US$ 1.9bn) of loans on offer. In June 2001, the IFC stated that it would finance successful bidders for the assets. The state announced rules to ease the auction of non-performing loans in November 2001 by permitting foreign ownership of equity stakes in AMCs. Parcels of NPLs were bought by Morgan Stanley in November 2001 and Goldman Sachs in December 2001. The process of cleaning up NPLs was accelerated in July 2003, when Morgan Stanley was given permission to approach banks direct to buy NPLs, rather than having to purchase NPLs from the AMCs by auction.

In April 2000, the People's Bank of China approved a plan by the China Construction Bank to issue MBS backed by residential loans and construction loans. In May 2000, the US and China announced a cooperation agreement for the US to lend China its expertise on establishing an MBS market.

In May 2003, a US$ 1.5bn CDO called Great Wall One was launched for the Agricultural Bank of China. The deal comprises investment grade CDS on mostly US and European names.

In the Cultural Revolution of the sixties and seventies, the legal system of the PRC was largely disassembled. It has only been reinstated in piecemeal fashion since the late seventies by means of laws which cover specific areas, and through the Civil Code adopted in 1986, and custom and practice continue to be of importance in interpreting these provisions. Administrative decisions and rulings also play a large part in the legal framework and have a major impact on transactions. Laws may be passed at a local level or at a national level. The ultimate legislative body is the National People's Congress.

Ring-fencing and true sale

A new Contracts Law was passed on 22 March 1999, and came into force on 1 October 1999. Prior to the passing of the new Contract Law, the sale of receivables was only considered to be effective if the consent of the debtors was obtained. The new Contract Law provides however that no such consent is necessary. Instead, a transfer will be effective provided that notice of the transfer is given to the debtor. Any such transfer will also operate to transfer ancillary rights.

Terms in the receivables documentation which prohibit assignment or transfer by the originator of its rights under the contract, or which require that the originator must obtain the consent of the relevant debtor in order to assign or transfer its rights under the contract, will prevent any assignment or transfer being effective unless the consent of the debtor to the transfer is in fact obtained.

Insolvency unwind   Transactions undertaken within 6 months prior to the insolvency of the originator may be unwound on the basis of fraud, undervalue, or granting security with no fresh consideration.

Set-off

The SPV is subject to set-off rights in favour of the debtor through relations between the originator and the debtor.

Securities laws

Approval of the China Securities Regulatory Commission ("CSRC") is required for an offer of securities to the public in the PRC. The issue of H shares, N shares or S shares (shares in PRC businesses, which shares are listed on the Hong Kong, New York or Singapore stock exchanges respectively) is subject to approval of the CSRC. Listing on domestic PRC exchanges is subject to detailed listing requirements under the Securities Law.

A new Securities Law was passed on 29 December 1998, and came into force on 1 July 1999. The Securities Law regulates corporate bonds and shares and other securities designated from time to time and sets out the regulatory requirements to be met by securities houses, and procedures for the listing and offering of securities in the PRC, as well as false market and insider dealing provisions.

Foreign ownership

Foreigners may only invest in "B" shares. "A" shares are for residents only. From February 2001, residents may also acquire "B" shares. Acquisition of more than 5% of the shares in a listed company requires reporting to the CSRC and the relevant stock exchange.

Tax treatment

Stamp/registration/etc.   Stamp duty may be charged on a transfer of receivables at *ad valorem* rates.

Withholding tax   Interest payable offshore is subject to withholding tax at a rate of 10%.

VAT   There is no VAT on the transfer of receivables.

Capital treatment

The People's Bank of China ("PBOC") is the central bank and regulator for bank entities.

Regulatory approvals

The completion of a securitisation transaction in the PRC may require consents or approvals from a wide range of governmental agencies responsible for different aspects of financing transactions, such as the State Administration of Foreign Exchange ("SAFE") among others.

Other issues

Trusts are generally not recognised in the PRC, but a draft trusts law is under consideration.

Exchange restrictions exist on the Renminbi capital account. In the wake of the Asian crisis, SAFE tightened its monitoring of transactions on the Renminbi current account.

The new Contracts Law permits contracts involving a foreign party to be governed by foreign law (although contracts involving real estate in the PRC must be governed by PRC law). It is unclear whether the new Contract Law applies to contracts with state entities. Contracts solely between Chinese entities may be declared void if they breach government policy.

12.10   COLOMBIA

Ring-fencing and true sale

Resolution 400 of 1995 provides for the securitisation of real estate, securities and other receivables through a trust structure or a fund structure. Law 546 of 1999 provides for the securitisation of residential mortgages. The Financial Reform Law No. 510 of 1999 provides for transfers to an SPV under a securitisation to be bankruptcy remote.

12.11   CZECH REPUBLIC

Development work has been undertaken for securitisation issuance in the Czech Republic. Czech law is a codified civil law system. Since the overthrow of the Communist regime in 1990, the Czech Republic has undertaken a substantial privatisation programme, and has introduced various market reform measures.

Ring-fencing and true sale

Collateral for a receivable travels with the receivable on transfer. Terms in the receivables documentation which require that the originator must obtain the consent of the relevant debtor in order to assign or transfer its rights under the contract, will, depending on their wording, prevent any assignment or transfer being effective unless the consent of the debtor to the transfer is obtained.

Insolvency unwind   Transactions carried out within 3 years prior to insolvency by the insolvent entity with an intention to prejudice creditors, where the party dealing with the insolvent entity had actual or constructive knowledge that the insolvent entity intended to prejudice creditors, may be unwound under s. 16 of the Bankruptcy Act. Transactions entered into within 6 months prior to insolvency which are an undervalue or which are onerous to the insolvent entity may be unwound under s. 15 of the Bankruptcy Act.

Set-off

The debtor can obtain good discharge by making payments to the originator until notice of the assignment is given to the debtor, at which point the debtor is obliged to pay to the SPV direct. The SPV will take subject to any set-off rights against the originator (and, until notice is given to the debtor, the SPV is subject to any further set-off rights with regard to amounts which accrue due from the originator to the debtor prior to receipt by the debtor of the notice).

Securities laws

The consent of the Securities Commission is required for an issue of securities by a Czech company.

Tax treatment

Stamp/registration/etc.   There is generally no stamp duty on assignments.

Withholding tax   The Czech Republic charges withholding tax on the payment of interest to an offshore entity. The Czech Republic has double tax treaties with Ireland and the Netherlands which reduce withholding to zero.

VAT   Sales of receivables are generally not subject to VAT. VAT may apply to servicing fees at a rate of 22%.

Capital treatment

The Czech National Bank monitors capital adequacy, applying marginally different standards than those used under the BIS rules.

Data protection/confidentiality

Banks are required to keep customer identity and any borrowing relationships confidential (whether the customer is an individual or not) unless the customer consents to disclosure. The Data Protection Act requires customer consent to be obtained for the transfer of information relating to individuals.

Regulatory approvals

An offshore SPV should not be required to be licensed in the Czech Republic.

Other issues

Powers of attorney given by Czech companies are revocable on insolvency. Trusts are not recognised in the Czech Republic, and subordination provisions may not be recognised in the Czech Republic.

In a bankruptcy, secured creditors are only entitled to priority ranking in respect of part of their claim (the remainder may be subordinated to certain preferred creditors such as costs of the bankruptcy, taxes and social security payments), and must cede control over the enforcement process to the bankruptcy trustee.

12.12   DENMARK

Covered bonds can be issued in Denmark under provisions dating back to the 1800s.

Ring-fencing and true sale

Transfers of receivables must be notified to the debtors.

Insolvency unwind   Transactions may be unwound on insolvency (without time limit) in the event that a party dealing with the insolvent entity knew or ought to have known that the insolvent entity was insolvent at the time the transaction was entered into, or that it became insolvent as a result of the transaction, and that the transaction was improper. Transactions at an undervalue entered into within 12 months prior to in-solvency may be unwound.

Recharacterisation   A transfer may be considered as a secured loan instead of a true sale if the transferor retains significant risk in relation to the assets, or the transferee does not acquire the right to pledge or exchange the assets, or the transfer is otherwise conditional.

Covered bonds   The issuance of *realkreditobligationer* (a form of Pfandbriefe) began in the 1800s, and the Mortgage Bank Act was passed in 1850. There is no regime for public sector debt.

Foreign ownership

Acquisitions of more than 5% in a listed or unlisted company and each subsequent 5% must be notified to the stock exchange (if the company is listed) and the company.

Tax treatment

Stamp/registration/etc.   There is no stamp duty on the transfer of receivables. There is a 0.6% registration fee on the transfer of real estate. Mortgage registration fees stand at 1.5%.

VAT   VAT is due on servicing fees. An SPV is unlikely to be able to recover input tax.

Accounting treatment

IAS standards are likely to be followed.

Regulatory approvals

An offshore SPV which is incorporated in the EU or EEA should not be required to be licensed as a credit institution. A Danish SPV, or an SPV incorporated outside the EU or EEA, may be required to be licensed in respect of the issuance of securities.

Other issues

Under Danish law, there is no concept of a floating charge. A security trust may not be recognised in Denmark.

12.13   EGYPT

The first asset-backed deal from Egypt was closed in September 2002, with a US$ 250m credit card deal for Banque Misr. Egypt has a civil law system derived from French law.

Tax treatment

Stamp/registration/etc.   Assignments are subject to stamp duty at a rate of 0.6%, although it may be possible to avoid this by ensuring that documentation is executed outside Egypt.

Withholding tax   Egypt charges withholding tax on Egyptian source income at 32%.

12.14   FINLAND

Issuance in Finland to date has been dominated by the Fennica series of issues from the Finnish Housing Fund, the first of which closed in 1995. The Mortgage Bank Act came into force on 1 January 2000 and the first tranche of mortgage bonds was issued by Suomen Asuntoluottopankki (part of the Leonia group) in April 2000. The Act was amended from 1 January 2001.

In November 2002, the Tornator Finance Deal was launched for Tornator Timberland – a spin-off of Stora-Enso's forestry assets in Finland. This was an important and innovative deal, as it relied on whole business techniques to securitise cash flows arising from the management of the forests over a 30-year period, and is one of the first mainstream whole business deals outside of the UK.

Ring-fencing and true sale

Under Finnish law, notice of a transfer of receivables is required to be given to debtors in order for the transfer to be effective on insolvency of the originator. The notice should, however, be able to be given informally on an account statement provided that it is readily apparent to the debtor. Receipt of the notice must be established, but again, it should be possible to establish receipt by the conduct of the debtor in paying to a new account specified in the notice of transfer.

Certain receivables are founded on the issue of a bearer promissory note, and are transferable by simple delivery of the promissory note to the transferee. Possession of the note must be transferred in order to move the receivable out of the insolvency estate of the originator.

Future receivables   The ability to transfer future receivables is unclear.

Insolvency unwind   A transfer of receivables may be unwound if it favours one creditor over another. Transfers within 5 years prior to a petition for insolvency may be unwound if they prejudice creditors.

Recharacterisation   True sale analysis is based on the transfer of risks and rewards relating to the assets, and on the originator not retaining repurchase rights or obligations.

Moratorium/automatic stay   Finland has reorganisation proceedings, which cannot be blocked by a secured creditor.

Covered bonds   The Mortgage Bank Act was adopted on 23 December 1999 and came into effect on 1 January 2000. The Act provides for the establishment of mortgage banks or *kiinnitysluottopankki*, which are restricted activity institutions supervised by the Finnish Financial Supervision Authority (the FSA) that can issue bonds backed by a pool of mortgages (*kiinteistövakuudellinen joukkovelkakirja*) or bonds backed by a pool of public sector loan assets (*julkisyhteisövakudellinen joukkovelkakirja*) on a ring-fenced basis by entering the assets onto a register. The bonds have a preferential claim on the pool on insolvency of the issuing institution. The maximum LTV for loans to be eligible for the pool is 60%. The Act was amended from 1 January 2001 to provide better protection for investors, and to allow for the use of derivatives.

Set-off

Once a debtor has received notice of an assignment to an SPV, the debtor is obliged to pay to the SPV direct. The SPV will take subject to any claims the debtor may have against the originator (although, for a receivable evidenced by a promissory note, such claims will be limited to claims arising under express terms on the face of the note itself).

Foreign ownership

Acquisition of more than one-third of the equity of large companies in sensitive areas such as defence or public health requires consent of the Ministry of Trade and Industry. Acquisition of more than 10%, 20%, 33%, 50% or 66% of the shares in a listed company must be notified to the Finance Control Authority. Acquisitions or disposals to more or less than 5%, 10%, 15%, 20%, 25%, 33.3%, 50% or 66.6% of the shares in a Finnish company listed in the European Economic Area must be notified to the company and the FSA.

Securities laws

The offering of securities to the public in Finland is subject to prospectus requirements.

Tax treatment

Stamp/registration/etc.   There is no stamp duty on transfers of receivables.

Withholding tax   Interest on receivables may be paid to an offshore entity free of withholding in reliance on a ruling from the Finnish Central Tax Board in 1993.

Profits tax   An offshore SPV will be liable to corporate tax in Finland in relation to any income of a permanent establishment in Finland.

Accounting treatment

There are no specific Finnish standards on off-balance-sheet treatment, and IAS will generally be followed.

Capital treatment

The FSA issued guidelines on securitisation on 16 January 1996 requiring that:

- The SPV should be independent;
- Transfers should be notified to the debtors;
- The originator should not be obliged to repurchase the assets;
- Securitisation by a credit institution should be notified to the FSA; and
- Subordinated debt and reserves provided by a bank originator should be directly deducted from the bank's capital.

The FSA published guidelines on the capital treatment for credit derivatives on 5 December 2000.

Data protection/confidentiality

Banks are subject to customer confidentiality requirements under s. 58 Deposit Bank Act unless the customer's consent to disclosure is obtained or disclosure is required by law. However, the 1996 FSA guidelines permit the disclosure of information on underlying debtors (including names and addresses) for securitisation purposes.

Regulatory approvals

Offshore SPVs purchasing Finnish assets should not become subject to regulatory requirements on credit institutions in Finland, unless they offer securities to the public in Finland.

Other issues

There is no trust concept under Finnish law.

12.15 FRANCE

Following the first transactions in the early 1990s, the French market quickly developed into one of the largest European markets, capturing 27% of the European market in 1997 and 17% in 1998. Paribas closed the MasterNoria deal for Cetelem's consumer loans in 1998, which was the first revolving-style deal in France using an FCC. Since 1999 however, there has been less growth in the public term markets and more growth in the commercial paper and private markets. In addition, following the introduction of

Law 99-532 of 25 June 1999, which provides for the establishment of *sociétés de credit foncier*, or SCFs, to issue *obligations fonciéres* (a variety of Pfandbriefe), the volume of covered bonds issued has been significant. The first issue under the new law was brought by Credit Foncier de France in October 1999. As a result the public French market was only 5% of the European market in 2002.

The Law on Financial Security (Law 2003-706 of 1 August 2003) amends the FCC legislation in order to:

1. Permit the FCC to directly own assets other than receivables on enforcement
2. Permit FCCs to issue bonds as well as units
3. Permit FCCs to enter into credit derivatives
4. Protect cash collected by the seller/servicer and held pending transfer to the FCC from the seller/servicer's own insolvency
5. Ring-fence different transactions undertaken by an FCC from each other.

These new changes will assist in establishing bankruptcy remoteness for FCC transactions, and in enabling FCCs to undertake synthetic securitisations.

France operates a civil law system.

Legislative history

Prior to 1988, the sale of receivables under French law carried onerous requirements of the French Civil Code. The only alternatives to such a sale were the simplified procedure under the *Loi Dailly* (which could only be used where the receivables were due from commercial debtors and the purchaser was a credit institution), or the subrogation of the purchaser to the rights of the originator (where the full par value of the receivables was paid over by way of purchase price). To relieve the difficulties of using these structures, and create a securitisation market in France, a series of laws were passed:

- **Law 88-1201 of 23 December 1988** (implemented by **Decree 89-158 of 9 March 1989**, and subsequently codified at Articles L.214-5 and L.214-43 to 49 of the Financial Code) permitted the establishment of a French onshore SPV known as an FCC (see detail below). The law contained various restrictions. An FCC was not permitted to purchase receivables from corporates (leading to a two-step transfer technique, with a transfer to a credit institution under the *Loi Dailly* followed by a transfer to an FCC), and was prevented from purchasing more than one pool of assets, or assets with a tenor of less than 2 years. Debtors had to be notified of a transfer to an FCC by letter (the effect of not giving such notification was unclear under the law). Establishment of an FCC required prior approval by the *Commission des Opérations de Bourse* (the COB) and any issue required a credit rating. FCC issues were required to bear credit enhancement in one of three specified forms – subordinated debt (acquired by the originator, an affiliate, or a credit institution), overcollateralisation, or a guarantee (by the originator, an affiliate, or a credit institution). Servicing had to be carried out by the originator, and could not be transferred to another entity. Units issued by the FCC had to have a minimum denomination of French Francs 10 000.
- **Law 93-6 of 4 January 1993** (implemented by **Decree 93-587 of 27 March 1993**) removed the requirements for credit enhancement in a specified form or for a

minimum 2-year asset tenor, and permitted FCCs to purchase extra assets after issuing funding (which helped in setting up pre-funding structures and substitutions, but did not permit tap issues). The 1993 Law also reduced the minimum denomination on issued units to French Francs 5000, and allowed servicing to be transferred to a credit institution or to the *Caisse des Depots et Consignations*. Requirements for COB approval, and to obtain a credit rating on issued units, were limited to public issuance undertaken by an FCC.

- **Law 96-597 of 2 July 1996** (implemented by **Decree 97-919 of 6 October 1997**) permitted FCCs to purchase non-performing receivables and lease receivables, and to issue securities and/or purchase assets denominated in currencies other than French Francs. The Decree also permitted FCCs to issue additional funding; and purchase assets of a different class from those previously purchased.
- **Law 98-546 of 2 July 1998** permitted FCCs to buy future receivables, receivables from corporate originators, and removed the requirement for debtors to be informed of a transfer by letter.
- **Decree 98-1015 of 6 November 1998** permitted FCCs to borrow for the purpose of liquidity, and to borrow from the originator or a credit institution for the purpose of credit enhancement. FCCs may enter into FX, swaps or other derivatives with credit institutions or members of the originator's group (provided that the transaction is entered into to hedge the position of the FCC). The minimum issuance denomination was reduced from French Francs 5000 to French Francs 1000 (after introduction of the Euro, this became Euro 150). A 10% clean-up call was permitted.
- **Law of 25 June 1999** permitted FCCs to dispose of loans which are past due (e.g. to crystallise a loss and claim tax relief for corporation tax and VAT purposes). Also provided for the ring-fencing of multiple portfolios within a single FCC.

Ring-fencing and true sale

The sale of receivables under French law presents particular difficulties due to the onerous requirements of the French Civil Code. Under general principles, notice is required to be given to debtors of the transfer in order for the transfer to be effective to pass a proprietary interest in the receivables. However, it is not merely sufficient that notice should be given; the notice must be given by the medium of a court official or *huissier*. This route is therefore not only unattractive from the commercial perspective of the originator, but can involve considerable expense and administrative difficulties where the pool of receivables relates to a large number of debtors.

An alternative transfer method available to originators seeking to securitise receivables due from commercial (that is, non-consumer) debtors is the *Loi Dailly*, a law that provides for a simplified method of transfer involving the delivery of a *bordereau* (that is, a detailed list) of the receivables being transferred, with no requirement to give notice to debtors. It is, however, essential that a purchaser under the *Loi Dailly* is a credit institution.

Alternatives for other kinds of receivables were, until 1988, limited to the use of subrogation, whereby the SPV makes payment to the originator which allows the SPV to step into the shoes of the originator as regards the originator's rights against the debtors. This route has structuring flaws, namely that it only allows the SPV to assume rights to the extent of the payment by the SPV, and only existing rights can be assumed (not future rights). To obtain full rights against the debtors, the SPV therefore has to pay the full face value of the receivables to the originator, making use of a deferred purchase price structure difficult. Structures permitting the transfer of some funds back from the originator to the purchaser are required, such as a transfer of collateral or of a fee.

In 1988, a law was passed which permits the establishment of a French onshore SPV known as a *Fonds Commun de Créances* or FCC (see "Legislative history" above). An FCC is permitted to purchase receivables from credit institutions, insurance companies, the *Caisse des Dépots et Consignations* or corporates. The law allows FCCs to buy more than one pool of assets, to buy mortgages without registration of a mortgage transfer, to engage in tap issues, to purchase assets of different classes, to purchase non-performing receivables, lease receivables and future receivables, and to issue securities and/or purchase assets denominated in currencies other than French Francs. FCCs may borrow for the purpose of liquidity, and can borrow from the originator or a credit institution for the purpose of credit enhancement. FCCs may enter into FX, swaps or other derivatives with credit institutions or members of the originator's group (provided that the transaction is entered into to hedge the position of the FCC). From 25 June 1999, FCCs may dispose of loans which are past due, and the ring-fencing of multiple portfolios within a single FCC is possible.

The new Law on Financial Security of August 2003 amends the FCC legislation in order to permit FCCs to directly own assets other than receivables on enforcement, to issue bonds as well as units, and to enter into credit derivatives (which will assist in enabling FCCs to undertake synthetic securitisations). The new changes also strengthen provisions on insolvency remoteness for FCCs (see below).

Assets are transferred to an FCC by the delivery to the management company of a *bordereau* of the receivables being transferred (as with the *Loi Dailly* above). FCCs may not hold physical assets (such as real estate), or synthetic claims.

Terms in the receivables documentation that prohibit assignment or transfer by the originator of its rights under the contract, or require that the originator must obtain the consent of the relevant debtor in order to assign or transfer its rights under the contract, may not be binding on the transferee unless the transferee has accepted the prohibition (following a decision of the *Cour de Cassation*).

Article 442-6IIc of the Commercial Code provides, from 14 May 2001, that prohibitions on assignment in commercial contracts (excluding those in favour of consumers or banks), or provisions which require that consent to assignment be obtained, are ineffective to prevent assignment or transfer of rights (both as against the transferee or other third parties, and as between the contract parties).

Future receivables   The transfer of future receivables to an FCC is permitted since 1998. Future receivables can also be transferred under the *Loi Dailly*. However, a decision of the *Cour de Cassation* on 26 April 2000 held that future receivables falling due after the beginning of insolvency proceedings relating to the originator that were transferred under the *Loi Dailly* may still belong to the insolvency estate of the originator, thus potentially prejudicing the value of future receivables structures under either the *Loi Dailly* or the FCC provisions.

However, a further decision by the *Cour de Cassation* on 22 November 2002 appeared to rule against this.

The new Law on Financial Security had been expected to safeguard the transfer of future receivables, but provisions on this issue were removed in parliamentary debate.

Insolvency unwind   Law 85-98 of 25 January 1985 sets out insolvency unwind provisions at Article 107 (for transactions at an undervalue entered into within 18 months prior to the commencement of insolvency proceedings) and Article 108 (for transactions, where the buyer knew that the seller was insolvent, that were entered into within 18 months prior to the commencement of insolvency proceedings).

The new Law on Financial Security amends the FCC legislation in order to protect cash collected by the seller/servicer and held pending transfer to the FCC from the seller/servicer's own insolvency, and to ring-fence different transactions undertaken by an FCC from each other.

Moratorium/automatic stay   A stay may be imposed by the court during the *règlement amiable* proceeding which may be commenced by a debtor (the stay is designed to assist the debtor and creditors in reaching a voluntary solution). If a creditor or debtor requests the commencement of insolvency proceedings (the *redressement judiciaire* or *liquidation judiciaire*), an "observation period" lasting up to 20 months commences automatically, during which time a stay operates. Enforcement of security following insolvency is dealt with by the courts rather than by the creditor.

Covered bonds   *Obligations foncières*, or OF (a French variety of covered bond based on the German Pfandbriefe), may be issued under the terms of Law 99-532 of 25 June 1999 (updating and replacing the previous act of 1852), which provides for the establishment of *sociétés de crédit foncier*, or SCFs, with the sole purpose of acquiring certain eligible mortgage assets or public sector assets and issuing OFs. Insolvency of an SCF will not automatically accelerate OFs. OFs benefit from statutory protection under Article 98 of the law which ring-fences eligible assets backing the OF for the benefit of the OF holders (and any counterparty to swaps or other hedging transactions linked to the OF), in priority to any other creditors (including normally preferred creditors such as tax authorities and employees). OFs are backed by all assets of the SCF, such that assets backing other OF issued by the SCF will also be available to the OF holders in priority to other creditors (in practice it is considered unlikely that a single SCF would mingle mortgage assets and public sector assets, but rather that two separate SCFs would be set up). SCFs are not SPVs in the strict sense. They require operational systems and employees in order to function, and are regulated as credit institutions by the Commission Bancaire and required to meet regulatory capital requirements. Consequently, they are not bankruptcy remote. Their assets must be managed by themselves or by a credit institution. Article 105 of the law provides that the transfer of eligible assets to an SCF is subject to the same beneficial transfer treatment as that which applies to FCCs (i.e., the transfer is made through delivery of a *bordereau*, which operates to transfer title to the loan and any related security without the risk of recharacterisation of the sale as a loan), although the transfer of other eligible assets (such as securities) must be made in the normal fashion. Article 101 of the law operates to disapply some of the French insolvency unwind provisions on transfers to an SCF. The collateral pool for OF issuance can consist of residential or commercial mortgages or other real estate assets meeting certain criteria, public sector loans or securities, asset-backed securities backed to at least 90% of their value by such mortgages or public sector assets, and other liquid instruments. The law sets out requirements for the quality of the assets to be acquired (LTVs are restricted to 60%, or 80% where additional collateral is provided). The law requires that OFs are overcollateralised by eligible assets in the collateral pool, and sets out rules for the level of overcollateral required. OFs carry a 10% regulatory capital weighting.

Set-off

Where there is a transfer by way of assignment or subrogation or under the *Loi Dailly* or to an FCC, the debtor can obtain good discharge by making payments to the originator until notice of the assignment is given to the debtor, at which point the debtor is obliged to pay to the SPV direct. Where there is a transfer by way of assignment or subrogation, the debtor may maintain rights of set-off that accrued up to the point at which he is notified of a transfer.

Onshore SPV

FCCs have no legal personality but constitute a "co-ownership". They are established jointly by a *dépositaire* (depository) of the receivables (the depository must be established in France as a credit institution, and is typically the originator) and a *société de gestion* (management company) (which can sue on behalf of the FCC, and which monitors and manages the FCC and represents investors). They are not subject to insolvency proceedings and are exempt from corporation tax and VAT. They can issue units to investors in minimum denominations of Euro 150.

Servicing must be carried out by the originator, a credit institution or the *Caisse des Depots et Consignations*.

Where an FCC is established to undertake public issuance, prior approval by the *Commission des Opérations de Bourse* (the COB) is required, and any issue must carry a credit rating.

France has a type of REIT in the form of *sociétés d'investissements immobiliers cotées* (SIIC).

Foreign ownership

Acquisition of a controlling interest (more than 20% for a listed company) in companies in sensitive areas, such as defence or public health, requires consent of the Ministry of Finance. Acquisitions of more than 5%, 10%, 20%, 33%, 50% or 66% of the shares in a listed company must be notified to the company and to the stock exchange regulator.

Securities laws

Prospectus requirements arise for offerings listed on the French Stock Exchange, or which are otherwise offered to the public in France. There is a safe haven from public offer requirements for sale to qualified investors (credit institutions, insurance companies and corporates with a net worth in excess of French Francs 1bn) or to a limited circle of 100 investors or less. Under Article 10 of Decree No. 89-938 of 29 December 1989, authorisation of the French Treasury is required for the offering or placing of securities issued by a non-OECD issuer into France.

The *Loi Toubon* (Law 94-665 of 4 August 1994) requires that certain documents be prepared in the French language. On 20 December 2000, the *Conseil d'Etat* determined that this law applied to prospectuses to be approved by the COB, which therefore had to be prepared in French. This rescinded previous regulations of the COB, which permitted issuers to use a common language in prospectuses for all their issuance, and only prepare a summary in French. On 20 November 2001, a law was passed by the French government which provides that the French language should normally be used in prospectuses, but that the COB may make exceptions to this rule, provided that a summary of the prospectus is prepared in French. On 6 April 2002, the COB published Regulation 2002-03 which allows issuers to draft prospectuses in a common language for financial prospectuses from 8 April 2002, with a summary in French.

Tax treatment

Stamp/registration/etc.   Nominal stamp duty is charged on a transfer of receivables. Transfer tax is charged at 4.8% on the transfer of shares, and at 4.89% on the transfer of real estate. Registration tax is charged on registration of a mortgage (at 0.615%), and on release of a mortgage (at 0.1%).

Withholding tax   France levies withholding tax on interest or payments recharacterised as interest at a rate of 15%. Double taxation treaties with certain European countries reduce the rate of withholding to zero. Amounts paid on FCC units are free of withholding when paid to French corporates, or when paid to offshore investors (subject to certification of non-residence).

Profits tax   The originator may be regarded as a permanent establishment of the SPV if it is permitted to enter into contracts in the SPV's name. FCCs are exempt from corporation tax.

Tax consolidation may be used to assist in debt service following a leveraged buy-out where the acquirer holds at least 95% of the shares of the target. The tax saving of grouping the acquirer's debt service against the target's income may be booked at the acquirer level as a (non-taxable) profit.

VAT   Fees paid by an FCC to a receivables servicer are exempt from VAT.

Other tax issues   Tax is charged in an up-front lump sum on the grant of a lease longer than 12 years, in an amount of 0.615% of the lifetime rent (i.e. the annual rent times the number of years in the lease) up to 20 years.

Real estate tax (*taxe foncière*) is charged on ownership of real estate based on the taxable value of the relevant property as fixed by the local authority each year.

Accounting treatment

The accounting treatment for French banks is determined by the *Comité de la Reglementation Comptable* (the "CRC"), which took over the role from the *Comité de la Reglementation Bancaire et Financière* (the "CRBF") under the law of 6 April 1998 (implemented in December 1998). CRBF Regulation 93-6 of 21 December 1993 permits off-balance-sheet treatment for assets sold to an FCC but requires the transaction to be described in a note to the accounts.

Capital treatment

Credit enhancement provided by the originator is subject to a direct deduction from capital, up to a cap of the amount of capital that would be required if the securitised assets were still on balance sheet.

In April 1998, the *Commission Bancaire* published a paper on the capital treatment of credit derivatives. Credit derivatives are regarded as trading book instruments if the derivative is marked-to-market daily with quotes from market-makers and held with intent to sell, and if the institution has expertise in the credit derivatives market and accurate valuation models. Credit spread products are not covered by the Circular. There is no specific differentiation between funded and unfunded products.

Banking book   Credit derivatives are treated as guarantees in the banking book in respect of the amount of exposure to which they relate, with credit for cash collateral where they are funded. As general requirements for credit derivatives:

- The reference obligation must be the same as the protected asset, or at least issued by the same issuer (if it is only issued by the same issuer levels of credit protection recognised will be reduced by 10% where there is an FX match or 20% where there is an FX mismatch).
- The reference obligation must rank junior to or *pari passu* with the protected asset.
- If the reference obligation has less than 1 year to maturity, then no protection value is recognised.
- If the credit derivative has a shorter term than the protected asset, then no protection value is recognised if the credit derivative has less than 1 year to expiry. If the credit derivative has 1 year or more to expiry, then a charge is made on the protection buyer for the residual exposure as an undrawn commitment exceeding 1 year (or, if the residual exposure is an undrawn commitment, at half the usual weight for an undrawn commitment) (thus the weighting on a 5-year drawn position protected by a 3-year credit default swap with an OECD bank would be 70% of the principal amount – 20% for the protected period plus 50% for the residual).
- A "first to default" basket structure gives the buyer protection against the default of the asset with the lowest risk weighting in the basket.
- Sale of a "first to default" credit derivative basket structure generates a capital charge for the protection seller equal to the addition of the respective capital charge for each asset in the basket.
- The protection buyer should be seen to have transferred the credit risk such that the protection seller has no recourse to the protection buyer for losses.

Trading book   The exposure to the reference entity is treated as a long/short specific risk position. As general requirements for credit derivatives:

- The reference obligation must be the same as the protected asset.
- The credit derivative must have the same maturity as the protected asset (if the credit derivative has a shorter term than the protected asset, then both the specific risk of the protected asset and the specific risk of the credit derivative will be recorded).
- A "first to default" basket structure allows the buyer to record a short position for the worst risk weighted asset in the basket.
- Sale of a "first to default" credit derivative basket structure creates a long position for the protection seller in each asset in the basket.
- The protection buyer should be seen to have transferred the credit risk such that the protection seller has no recourse to the protection buyer for losses.

In addition to market risk assessments, unfunded credit derivatives such as total return swaps and credit default products (but not funded credit derivatives such as credit-linked notes) are subjected to a counterparty risk haircut by calculating the mark-to-market value of the derivative plus an "add-on" percentage which is the interest rate add-on (investment grade) or the equity add-on (non-investment grade) for the protection seller, and the equity add-on (investment grade) or the commodity add-on (non-investment grade) for the protection buyer. The relevant add-on percentage is applied to the notional principal, with the aggregate figure then being multiplied by counterparty risk weight and weighted by a factor of 8%.

On 26 April 2002, the *Commission Bancaire* announced new asset-backed risk weightings applicable to French banks investing in ABS. Senior tranches will continue to be weighted as per the underlying assets (50% for mortgages and 100% otherwise), but tranches rated below BBB+ or Baa1 will be treated as a direct deduction from capital. It has since become unclear as to whether senior MBS are still entitled to 50% risk weighting or now fall into the 100% bucket, and also as to whether BBB securities will be a direct deduction from capital, or just securities rated BB or below.

Consumer protection

Law 78-92 of 10 January 1978 contains protective provisions for consumers in consumer credit transactions below a certain value threshold.

Regulatory approvals

If a non-FCC SPV (or other purchaser) acquires receivables which are not yet due from a non-credit institution, it may be required under Law 84-46 of 24 January 1984 to be licensed as a credit institution if it has an establishment in France, unless it is in the same corporate group as the originator. Furthermore, French banks can only sell receivables to banks or FCCs. Sales to other purchasers require the prior consent of the *Commission Bancaire*, save for sales to offshore securitisation SPVs where the receivables are not past due and certain other requirements are met.

Due to these restrictions, and the limitations of the assignment or subrogation routes for transferring receivables, deals which do not use a simple FCC structure will typically use a two-step structure. This will entail a first transfer to an offshore group entity by way of subrogation (only where the originator is not a bank) or to an FCC or a bank (whether the originator is a bank or not), and a second transfer to the ultimate SPV, thus removing consent requirements whilst maintaining transfer advantages.

Other issues

There is no concept of floating charge in France.

Article 313 of the Consumer Code on usury makes it a criminal offence to charge interest on a conventional loan at a rate in excess of one-third above the official Central Bank base rate from time to time. It has been unclear whether this provision applies to subordinated debt or to capital market instruments such as high-yield bonds, but in January 2003 the Minister of Economy published a statement that the usury laws do not apply to the issue of bonds by French companies. The economic initiative law published on 5 August 2003 reinforced this, providing that the usury provisions in the Consumer Code are not applicable to loans "granted to a legal entity engaged in industrial commercial, artisanal, agrigultural or commercial activity."

Secured creditors in France rank behind employees, costs of enforcement proceedings, taxes and social security payments and creditors who advanced money after the entry of the company into insolvency.

The granting of a guarantee or other security by a target company to support the acquisition of the shares in the target is not permitted under financial assistance provisions. Cash proceeds of loans against the target's assets cannot be upstreamed, nor can upstream security or guarantees be granted.

A reduction of capital may be effected from the sale or disposal of assets by a target post-acquisition and return of cash to shareholders. A certain amount of cash may also be upstreamed by the use of tax consolidation (see "Profits tax" above) where relevant.

12.16   GERMANY

Development of the securitisation market in Germany has been slowed by the established market in Pfandbriefe (which can be issued by Hypothekenbank – mortgage banks – or by Landesbank), and by regulatory resistance to the product up until 1997, when regulations were relaxed.

In December 1999, the German government announced that tax on capital gains arising on the sale of stakes in German companies would be exempted from the tax otherwise due (which could be up to 50%) from 1 January 2001. This date was subsequently postponed to 1 January 2002, when the proposal was introduced.

In December 2000 Kreditanstalt für Wiederaufbau (KfW), the German development bank, launched its "PROMISE" programme for the packaging and securitisation of SME loans, followed in October 2001 by its "PROVIDE" programme for the packaging and securitisation of housing loans. Both of these use synthetic structures, and have proved successful and been utilised by a number of institutions in the German market.

On 17 July 2001, the German government agreed with the EU Commission to abolish government guarantees for new obligations of the Landesbanks by July 2005 (the EU had argued that the guarantees distorted competition in the financial sector due to the low borrowing costs enjoyed by the Landesbanks as a result of the state backing).

Existing obligations will be covered until December 2015. On 6 November 2001, Deutsche Bank, Dresdner Bank and Commerzbank announced a merger of their mortgage lending subsidiaries – Eurohypo, Deutsche Hyp and Rheinyp respectively – to form Eurohypo AG.

On 1 January 2002 a new takeover law came into effect in Germany, which permits "poison pill" defences to hostile takeovers to be put in place by German companies, if supported by 75% of shareholders.

On 23 April 2003, a group of leading German banks announced an initiative to speed the development of true sale securitisation in Germany, following the announcement of trade tax reforms on 29 January 2003. The historic tendency of German banks to use synthetic structures has resulted from the low cost of funds enjoyed by German banks on Pfandbriefe issuance (possible against residential mortgages up to a 60% LTV) and on other debt, compared to funded ABS issuance. In addition, synthetics have been used to split mortgages into a first lien position up to a 60% LTV (which carries a 50% weighting for regulatory capital and can be financed through Pfandbriefe) and second lien positions above a 60% LTV (carrying a 100% weighting) – with the second lien position being securitised to give greater capital release. Synthetic trades have been closed in Germany for CLOs, CMBS and RMBS. This has also been influenced by the beneficial capital treatment obtained from the use of the synthetic PROMISE and PROVIDE structures developed by the KfW (under which the bank buys credit protection on a portfolio of mortgages or loans from KfW – a 0% risk weighted entity – which then participates the risk out to the market). The potential for trade tax costs on true sale structures has further inhibited true sale issuance. As the balance sheets and credit ratings of German banks have come under pressure, funding costs have risen and funded ABS issuance has become a more attractive option. The new initiative was backed by six institutions – Deutsche, Dresdner, Commerzbank, Hypovereinsbank, DZ Bank and KfW – and was joined on 9 July 2003 by another seven institutions – Citibank Germany, Bayerische Landesbank, DekaBank, Eurohypo, HSH Nordbank, Landesbank Hessen-Thuringen and WestLB – each of whom will contribute Euro 10m in capital to the establishment of a joint venture vehicle for the securitisation of corporate loans.

On 1 May 2002, the *Bundesaufsichtsamt für das Kreditwesen* (BAKred, the German Banking Supervisory Authority), the *Bundesaufsichtsamt für das Versicherungswesen* (BAV, the German insurance regulator) and the *Bundesaufsichtsamt für den Wertpapierhandel* (BAWe, the German securities market regulator) were merged into the Financial Services Supervisor (the *Bundesanstalt für Finanzdienstleistungsaufsicht* or BAFin).

Ring-fencing and true sale

Receivables may be transferred by assignment without the need to give notice to debtors of the transfer. Terms in the receivables documentation that prohibit assignment or transfer by the originator of its rights under the contract, or require that the originator must obtain the consent of the relevant debtor in order to assign or transfer its rights under the contract, may prevent any assignment or transfer being effective unless the consent of the debtor to the transfer is in fact obtained, or unless the assignment falls within the terms of section 354a of the Civil Code. This provides that receivables arising under business transactions governed by German law that are due from corporates or public sector entities are assignable despite a prohibition on assignment, where the prohibition was contracted after 30 July 1994.

Future receivables   Future receivables can be sold, but if they are general receivables which are not clearly defined they may not survive insolvency of the originator.

Insolvency unwind   Under Article 131 of the new Insolvency Code, which was brought into force from 1 January 1999 to consolidate and replace prior legislation, a transaction occurring within 1 month prior to insolvency which was not at arm's-length can be unwound. A transaction intended to prejudice other creditors can be unwound within 10 years prior to insolvency.

Recharacterisation   A transfer is likely to be considered as a true sale if the transferee has no recourse against the originator in relation to default on the transferred assets, the originator retains no credit risk on the transferred assets and the originator is not obliged to return the purchase price for the assets. Otherwise, it may be considered to be a secured loan. If a purported true sale is recharacterised as a secured loan, the originator may be liable to account for trade tax (see "Other tax issues" below).

Moratorium/automatic stay   Following application by a creditor or debtor to the court, a stay will be imposed if the court resolves to commence insolvency proceedings. An insolvency administrator will be appointed by the court; another administrator can subsequently be elected by the creditors at the first creditors' meeting, which is called within 3 months of the decision to commence insolvency proceedings. The administrator can be required by the creditors' meeting to put forward within a reasonable time an insolvency plan to determine whether the most appropriate course of action is to realise the assets of the debtor, or to continue to run the business. The insolvency plan must be approved by a majority of each class of creditor (both by number and by value), including unsecured creditors.

Covered Bonds   Pfandbriefe (a variety of collateralised bond – singular Pfandbrief, plural Pfandbriefe) may be issued by German Hypothekenbank (or mortgage banks) under the Mortgage Bank Act or by Landesbank under the Public Sector Pfandbriefe Act. Pfandbriefe may be backed by an eligible pool of mortgages (*Hypothekenpfandbriefe*) or by an eligible pool of public sector assets (*öffentlicher Pfandbriefe*). The two pools (mortgages and public sector assets) are segregated into separate registers or *Deckungsstock*, each of which are subject to separate insolvency proceedings from insolvency proceedings connected with the issuing institution (although the pools remain on the balance sheet of the issuing institution). Consequently, holders of Pfandbriefe have preferential rights to the relevant pool of assets supporting the Pfandbriefe, which are liquidated separately for the benefit of the Pfandbriefe holders on insolvency of the issuer, as well as a residual right as an unsecured creditor against the other assets of the issuer in the event that the asset pool is insufficient. The pools can be revolving in nature, with substitution of assets in the pool, and each pool can back multiple issues of Pfandbriefe. Pfandbriefe are typically issued in bearer form with bullet redemption, although they can be issued in registered form and with structured paydown unless they are issued as Jumbo Pfandbriefe (see below). Most Pfandbriefe are fixed rate, although they can be issued as floating rate or zero coupon instruments. Eligible public sector assets can consist of German government, public authority or Landesbank loans and securities and EEA government loans and securities. Public sector or mortgage assets from the EEA are limited to 10% of the pool in respect of countries where the relevant local authorities do not recognise the preferential rights of Pfandbriefe holders on insolvency (as at October 1999 only Austria, Luxembourg, Denmark and France accepted these rights). From 1 July 2002, public sector debt from the US, Canada, Japan, Switzerland, the Czech Republic, Hungary, Poland and Slovakia may also be included in pools (up to the 10% limit where preferential rights are not recognised). A trustee is appointed by the BAKred to supervise substitution in the asset pool. Pfandbriefe issued by mortgage banks are subject to stricter criteria than those issued by the Landesbank, including a maximum 60% LTV for mortgage assets backing mortgage Pfandbriefe. Pfandbriefe issued by mortgage banks are subject to an overall cap on the maximum possible issuance of Pfandbriefe equal to 60 times the banks' capital. German mortgage banks have lobbied Basel to retain the 10% risk weighting for Pfandbriefe, rather than the 20% weighting for senior ABS under the new 1999 Basel proposals. Since January 1999, Pfandbriefe may be used as Tier 1 repo collateral with the European Central Bank if they are listed and denominated in Euro (in addition to the government agency securities which could be used previously).

Jumbo Pfandbriefe, which were first issued in May 1995, are designed to offer greater trading liquidity due to their size, and increased transparency due to standardisation. They are required to be listed on a German exchange, and are issued as bullet securities in bearer form (or registered form for any portion of the issue which is sold into the US). They have a minimum issue size of Euro 500m, and three market-makers are required.

From 10 April 2001, the BAKred requires German mortgage banks to calculate the impact of interest rate changes on their mortgage pools by calculating the change in net present value of their exposure resulting from a 100 bp positive or negative shift in interest rates. If the change exceeds 10% of capital, the regulator may take action, and is very likely to do so if the change exceeds 20% of capital.

Set-off

The debtor can obtain good discharge by making payments to the originator until notice of the assignment is given to the debtor, at which point the debtor is obliged to pay to the SPV direct. The SPV will take subject to any defects in the title of the originator, and until notice is given to the debtor, the SPV is subject to any further equities (such as set-off) arising in favour of the debtor through relations between the originator and the debtor subsequent to the assignment.

Onshore SPV

German entities are liable to pay trade tax, which has made German SPVs unattractive to date. See however "Other tax issues" below in relation to new trade tax rules.

Foreign ownership

Acquisition of more than 5%, 10%, 25%, 50% or 75% of the shares in a listed company must be notified to the Federal Securities Trading Supervisory Authority Office.

Tax treatment

Stamp/registration/etc.   Stamp duty is not charged on a transfer of receivables.

Withholding tax   There is no withholding tax on interest payments except on interest paid by banks. Withholding may arise on rental payments. Tax may be assessed on loans secured on real estate situated in Germany.

Profits tax   An offshore SPV may become liable to corporate tax in Germany if it has a fixed place of business in Germany, or a dependent agent in Germany. This could potentially be an issue where the SPV employs a servicer in Germany to service German assets. If the servicer has substantial other assets and operations, the servicer may not be viewed as being a "dependent" agent. However, if the servicer has no other significant operations, it may be viewed as being "dependent" and render the SPV liable to German tax (although deductions against income should still be available to the SPV).

A residence held by an individual for more than 2 years may be sold free of capital gains tax.

Tax reforms in 2000 tightened thin capitalisation rules, such that debt provided by an offshore shareholder or related entities to a company in excess of 1.5 times its equity will be disallowed for interest deductibility purposes (previously, the ratio was in excess of 3 times). The rules also apply where an offshore bank lender lends to a company in reliance on support from the company's parent (which render the loan similar to a loan made by the parent to the company). The fact that the regime only applied to offshore shareholders (who cannot claim a tax credit) was challenged in front of the European Court of Justice in 2003, which ruled that the offshore-only nature of the regime was discriminatory.

VAT   VAT is likely to be due on servicing fees if the SPV is based in the EU, but not if the SPV is based outside the EU. The SPV will not be able to recover input tax.

Other tax issues   Trade tax (*Gewerbesteur*) is due from all German businesses, and from non-German businesses with a fixed place of business in Germany, or a dependent agent in Germany (except for entities which carry out no activities other than the lease of real estate, which are exempt from trade tax). The tax is due on income less expenses, but only 50% of interest charges on long-term debt (defined as debt which is financing fixed assets which is longer than 1 year in tenor – not debt which is financing current assets, although this is difficult to monitor, as the debt would need to be paid down from realisations on current assets) can be deducted against income for trade tax purposes – although credit institutions can deduct 100% of such interest charges. Consequently, taxable income for trade tax purposes should equal normal net taxable income plus 50% of long-term interest charges. Trade tax is charged at between 12% and 18% (depending on the German region from which the income originates).

Trade tax can be relevant for securitisation either at the originator level (if a true sale transfer is recharacterised as a secured loan on the originator's balance sheet – a low degree of recourse to the originator will be needed in order to persuade the German tax authorities that the transfer is a true sale, not a secured loan) or at the SPV level (if the SPV is established in Germany or has a fixed place of business in Germany or a dependent agent in Germany).

For non-German SPVs, the dependent agent category could potentially be an issue where the SPV employs a servicer in Germany to service German assets. If the servicer has substantial other assets and operations, the servicer may not be viewed as being a "dependent" agent. However, if the servicer has no other significant operations, it may be viewed as being "dependent" and render the SPV liable to trade tax (which could result in trade tax on the SPV at 6% to 9% of total interest charges – the 12% to 18% rate over 50% of the debt service charge – on long-term debt, assuming the SPV has zero normal net taxable income).

S&P released a warning on 31 January 2001 that they had become aware of rumours that some German states were looking to clamp down on the use of offshore SPVs, and that a Generally Applicable Letter might be issued by German tax authorities in March (seeking to make offshore SPVs used to securitise German assets with a German servicer liable to German corporate and trade tax). In synthetic deals, there are no potential dependent agents of the offshore SPV, as there are no assets which the SPV owns which are to be serviced. Hence, no trade tax issues are likely to arise.

On 29 January 2003, the German Ministry of Finance announced new rules which were passed on 11 July 2003, under which SPVs purchasing bank receivables would benefit from the same trade tax regime as banks – allowing the deduction of 100% of interest charges in calculating trade tax. The change does not however apply to SPVs used in transactions by corporate originators. The change should encourage banks to use true sale securitisation in order to realise funding benefits from cash securitisations, as well as the capital relief benefits gained to date from synthetic deals.

Accounting treatment

The Accountants' Institute published guidelines on the treatment of securitisations on 1 October 2002. In order for a transaction to be off balance sheet, the SPV must obtain the right to pledge or exchange the assets, the originator should have no right or obligation to re-acquire the assets (except for any clean-up call) and the originator may not retain any credit risk on the assets (although a group entity may provide a subordinated loan to the SPV, and a fair market level of discounted purchase price is permissible).

Capital treatment

Guidelines published by the BAKred on 20 May 1997 provide that:

- Banks may sell assets subject to prior notification to the BAKred and the Bundesbank.

- An auditor's statement should be given as to potential deterioration in the originator's remaining portfolio ("cherry-picking" of assets is not permitted).
- There should be no recourse to the originator.
- There should be no obligation on the originator to repurchase any of the receivables other than for breach of warranty when sold.
- No substitution is permitted.
- A 10% clean-up call is permitted, provided that the assets are repurchased at their then market value.
- Any subordinated loan made by the originator should be disclosed and will be directly deducted from capital.
- Overcollateralisation, purchase price discounts, subordinated note issuance and reserve accounts are acceptable forms of credit enhancement.
- The originator should not be an underwriter or purchaser of the notes in the primary market, or no off-balance-sheet treatment will be accorded until all the notes are sold down.
- The originator and the SPV should not be connected and the names of the originator and the SPV should not be identical or similar.
- The prospectus should state that the originator is not liable on the notes.
- Data may be transferred on a portfolio basis or encrypted and held by a custodian bank without breaching confidentiality requirements.

The guidelines were expanded by the BAKred with the publication of requirements for the securitisation of revolving assets in September 1998.

On 16 June 1999, BAKred published Circular 10/99 on the Treatment of Credit Derivatives. TRORS and CDS are regarded as trading book instruments if the underlying asset is a security, or banking book instruments if the underlying asset is a loan (unless it is marked-to-market daily and held with intent to sell, in which case it may be held in the trading book). Credit spread products are not covered by the Circular. There is no specific differentiation between funded and unfunded products. The guidelines are silent on basket structures.

Banking book Credit derivatives are treated as guarantees in the banking book in respect of the amount of exposure to which they relate – protection buyers also obtain the benefit of cash collateral treatment where the credit derivative is funded. As general requirements for credit derivatives:

- The reference obligation must be the same as the protected asset, or at least issued by the same issuer.
- The reference obligation must rank junior to or *pari passu* with the protected asset.
- The credit derivative must have the same maturity as the protected asset (if it is shorter, no protection value is recognised but no additional exposure is incurred by the credit derivative).
- The protection buyer should be seen to have transferred the credit risk (without such transfer constituting a breach of the term of the reference obligation) such that the protection seller has no recourse to the protection buyer for losses.
- The credit derivative must detail "credit event" triggers relating to the reference obligation.

Trading book Total return swaps are treated as a long/short position in the reference obligation (carrying specific and general risks) and a short/long position in a benchmark security (carrying general risk) paying the same rate. Credit default swaps are treated as a long/short position in the reference obligation (carrying specific risk only). Premium payments may be treated as a notional position in a benchmark security for general risk. Credit linked notes are treated as a long/short position in the note (carrying specific risk of the issuer and general risk) and also as a long/short position in the reference obligation (carrying specific risk only). As general requirements for credit derivatives:

- The reference obligation must be issued by the same issuer as the protected asset.
- The reference obligation must carry the same ranking in liquidation as the protection asset.
- The credit derivative must have the same maturity as the protected asset (if it is shorter, then both the specific risk of the reference obligation and the specific risk of the credit derivative will be recorded).
- The protection buyer should be seen to have transferred the credit risk (without such transfer constituting a breach of the term of the protected asset) such that the protection seller has no recourse to the protection buyer for losses.
- The credit derivative must detail "credit event" triggers relating to the reference obligation.

In addition to market risk assessments, unfunded credit derivatives such as total return swaps and credit default products (but not funded credit derivatives such as credit-linked notes) are subjected to a counterparty risk haircut by calculating the mark-to-market value of the derivative plus an "add-on" percentage which is the interest rate add-on (for investment grade) or the equity add-on (for non-investment grade), for both the protection seller and the protection buyer. The relevant add-on percentage is applied to the notional principal, with the aggregate figure then being multiplied by counterparty risk weight and weighted by a factor of 8%.

In February 2000, German banks requested the BAKred to relent on its treatment of derivatives on loan assets solely in the banking book, and to refine its approach to maturity mismatches. In March 2001, BAKred confirmed that German investors can attribute a 10% risk weighting to *cedulas hipotecarias* issued by Spanish mortgage banks.

On 28 January 2002, the BAKred gave indications that it might not permit off-balance-sheet treatment for transactions where interest sub-participations are used to support junior pieces. This indication was expanded on 19 April 2002, when the BAKred published a checklist requiring prior approval of the BAKred in order to gain regulatory relief on synthetic securitisations. The checklist also requires that:

- Interest sub-participations should only relate to the risk premium on the relevant reference pool. They should not relate to the return that covers funding costs, or to the risk premium or the return that covers funding costs on assets other than the reference pool.
- Restructuring losses should be for the account of the protection seller.
- Assets can only be substituted to the extent that they were in breach of eligibility/replenishment criteria at the time of inclusion, and on an arm's-length basis.

- Termination of protection should only occur in limited circumstances; these should not include a call on occurrence of a step-up, or a put at the right of the protection seller.

Data protection/confidentiality

See "Capital treatment" above.

Other issues

Companies in Germany can issue shares in either bearer or registered form. Historically, many companies have issued shares in bearer form, although the use of registered shares is increasing due to the ease of communicating with investors.

No more than 20% of the mortgage book of a Hypothekenbank may be invested in second mortgages. There is no concept of floating charge in Germany.

The new Insolvency Code provides at s. 166(2) for the enforcement of security (including an assignment by way of security) by a liquidator, who can oust secured creditors (other than a first ranking creditor secured over property) from enforcing. The liquidator is entitled to keep up to 9% of the value of the collateral by way of enforcement costs. Enforcement of security over real estate is carried out by asking the court to appoint an administrator to manage the property and look for new lessees, or by asking for a sale by court auction.

The new Insolvency Code also abolished Article 419 of the Civil Code (which provided that a secured creditor assuming all or substantially all the assets of a borrower under a security interest could be liable for the debts of the borrower).

Secured creditors in Germany rank behind costs of enforcement proceedings. Employees and taxes are not preferred creditors and do not rank above unsecured creditors.

Section 613 of the Civil Code requires that employee contracts be assumed by the transferee on any transfer of the business as a going concern.

Usufruct rights can be granted which entitle the beneficiary to the income on an asset (but not to the capital value of the asset). Usufruct rights are not transferable.

The granting of security or guarantees by an AG (a stock corporation) to support the obligations of its parent is prohibited. The granting of security or guarantees by a GmbH (a limited liability company) to support the obligations of its parent is permitted, provided that it does not exceed the reserves (total assets less registered share capital and liabilities) of the GmbH, as s. 30 of the GmbH Act prohibits financial assistance from registered share capital.

On 3 May 2002, the insurance regulator published guidelines formally allowing insurers to invest up to 7.5% of their restricted assets in certain investment grade products (RMBS, CMBS, CDO, synthetics and certain ABS – although not leases or future flows). Free assets of insurers can be invested in equity tranches as before. Although German insurers were already active investors in the asset-backed market, the regulator was previously silent on the suitability of asset-backed securities as investments.

12.17   GREECE

Securitisation in Greece saw significant public sector activity in 2000, with the government securitisation of dividend receipts from CDLF (the state-owned mortgage bank) in the Hellenic Securitisation deal, and of lottery ticket receipts from state lotteries in the Ariadne deal. A new law on public sector securitisation was passed in 2000 (and subsequently amended) in order to facilitate these deals. A law governing non-public sector securitisation was passed in June 2003 to ease development of the securitisation market for non-government originators.

Ring-fencing and true sale

Assignments under the Civil Code must be notified. Law 2801/2000 (as amended by Law 2843/2000) allows the Greek government to assign current and future receivables such that they are insolvency remote from the government, the transferee, and any other third party (except for the secured creditors of the transferee).

Article 10 of Law 3156/2003 of June 2003 permits the transfer of a variety of receivables and assets (including future receivables and real estate assets) by banks, insurers and listed companies to a securitisation SPV. The transfer must be registered, but need not be notified to obligors. A Greek or non-Greek SPV may be used (although a Greek SPV must be used for real estate assets).

Future receivables   The 2003 law permits the transfer of future receivables.

Insolvency unwind   Transactions that are preferences may be unwound. However, transactions under the 2003 law will not be unwound under these provisions.

Tax treatment

Stamp/registration/etc.   Stamp duty at 2.4% may be payable on assignments, unless effected between credit institutions operating in Greece. A sale of receivables under the 2000 law or the 2003 law is exempt from stamp duty.

Withholding tax   Withholding tax is charged on payments on receivables made to offshore entities.

Profits tax   Greek SPVs under the 2003 law are exempt from corporation tax in Greece.

Data protection/confidentiality

The 2003 law provides for exemptions from bank confidentiality and data protection laws requirements in respect of the transfer of receivables (which requirements could normally include the consent of the Data Protection Agency and of the debtors). The exemptions also permit the transfer of information in respect of performance or enforcement of receivables to the SPV, the servicer and the noteholders in a securitisation.

Other issues

There is no concept of a trust under Greek law.

12.18   HONG KONG SAR

The Hong Kong market developed apace during 1996 and 1997 (following a lull in 1995) off the back of mortgage and single property financing transactions. The Asian currency crisis slowed down the Asian markets, but Hong Kong continued to demonstrate significant issuance through 1998 and 1999 – mostly CMBS deals.

On 28 July 1998, the HKMA relaxed its 1994 guideline that banks hold not more than 40% of their loan book in property exposure. In August 1998, the government intervened to prop up the stock market by buying stocks with foreign exchange reserves and at the end of September, the government launched Exchange Fund Investments Limited as a separate entity to manage the stocks acquired. Part of these stocks were packaged in the form of a unit trust tracking the Hang Seng index, called TraHK, which was launched in November 1999 and was widely subscribed.

Issuance slowed down significantly in 2000, and has remained subdued to date, for a combination of reasons – economic slowdown has been hard-felt in Hong Kong due to the effect of the Hong Kong Dollar peg to the US Dollar, preventing devaluation in line with other Asian economies following the Asian crisis, but giving rise to a deflationary environment. Consumer borrowing and spending has slowed down in line with a depressed stock market and a collapse in housing prices, removing the rationale for banks to release capital for reinvestment and bringing down the margins on new loan origination.

Property developers have found the bank market simpler and more flexible than the ABS markets, and banks looking to securitise mortgage portfolios have taken advantage of the ability of the Hong Kong Mortgage Corporation to guarantee MBS to a 20% risk weighting by selling their mortgages to the HKMC from 1998-1999 onwards, rather than securitising them directly.

In March 2003, the Hong Kong government announced plans to dispose of or securitise up to HK$ 112bn (US$ 14.3bn) of assets by 2008.

The Stock Exchange of Hong Kong, the Hong Kong Futures Exchange and the Hong Kong Clearing Company merged into the Hong Kong Exchanges and Clearing on 6 March 2000 following a government proposal in March 1999 and approval of the merger in September 1999.

The government sold Exchange Fund Notes (EFNs) (the Exchange Fund manages Hong Kong's currency reserves) to retail investors for the first time in August 1999, in order to develop a retail investor bond market for other issuers.

Mandatory Provident Fund contributions were required to be made by employers and employees from 1 December 2000. A percentage of each MPF scheme is required to be invested in Hong Kong Dollar-denominated investments, increasing the demand for capital markets instruments in Hong Kong.

The Hong Kong Special Administrative Region operates a common law system, historically based on English law.

The Joint Declaration of 19 December 1984 between the UK and the PRC provided for the PRC to legislate for the preservation of Hong Kong's capitalist system after the 1 July 1997 handover under the "one country, two systems" principle. Under Article 8 of the Basic Law enacted by the PRC legislature on 4 April 1990, the laws in force in Hong Kong as at 30 June 1997 remain so after the handover save for any laws that contravene the Basic Law. The Basic Law sets out general principles on areas such as the political structure, the judiciary, the economy (including the right of private property, the right to tax and the continued existence and free convertibility of the Hong Kong Dollar), education, religion, labour and external affairs. The Basic Law also provides that the capitalist system shall be preserved in Hong Kong for at least 50 years.

The Hong Kong Reunification Ordinance (No. 110 of 1997) preserves the laws of Hong Kong with a provision similar to that of Article 8. The Basic Law can only be amended by the National People's Congress of the PRC.

Guidelines on the capital treatment of credit derivatives were released in December 1999.

Mandatory Provident Fund contributions are required to be made by employers (5% of each employee's salary, to a maximum of HK$ 20 000 per month) and employees earning more than HK$ 4000 per month (a matching amount) from 1 December 2000.

In February 2001, the HKMA published a draft of guidelines on syndicated lending as part of a new banking supervisory policy manual, in order to encourage management of interest rate risk and credit risk associated with syndicated lending.

An increase in corporate taxes (from 16% to 17.5%) and personal taxes (from 15% to 16%) was announced in the March 2003 budget, following a widening budget deficit.

The Securities and Futures Ordinance came into force on 1 April 2003.

The Hong Kong Mortgage Corporation

The Hong Kong Mortgage Corporation (the HKMC), which is a government-owned corporation mandated to purchase residential mortgages and issue mortgage backed securities, was established in March 1997 with capital of HK$ 1bn and a minimum capital/assets ratio of 5%. The HKMC experienced a strong pick-up in purchases in the first quarter of 2000 from previous levels, as they relaxed the previous guideline requiring them to buy only loans originated at or above Prime (due to excess liquidity and strong mortgage price competition throughout 1998 and 1999, most mortgages were being originated at Prime, and a significant percentage below Prime). The new guidelines call for the rate to be agreed between HKMC and the lender.

The HKMC has also attempted to create appetite among banks to originate a fixed rate mortgage product, in order to reduce the impact of interest rate increases (necessary to defend the HK Dollar peg to the US Dollar) on the wider economy. To this end, it launched a pilot scheme in March 1998 with Dao Heng Bank and Chase Manhattan, committing to acquire HK$ 250m of fixed rate mortgages meeting certain purchase criteria. The scheme was expanded to include six more banks in September 1998.

The HKMC has also established a mortgage insurance scheme that enables originators approved by the HKMC to lend up to a 90% LTV (i.e. in excess of the normal 70% limit on lending by authorised institutions). The HKMC provides a guarantee of the 20% portion between 70% and 90% LTV, in return for a guarantee fee.

The HKMC established a HK$ 10bn revolving credit line from the Hong Kong Monetary Authority (the HKMA), and launched a HK$ 20bn Note Issuance Programme in January 1998 (which was listed on the Hong Kong Stock Exchange in October 1999) and a HK$ 20bn Debt Issuance Programme in June 1998, and has purchased mortgage pools from local banks to build up a mortgage portfolio.

The HKMC also undertakes securitisation of mortgage pools, with its first securitisation of a pool from Dao Heng Bank in October 1999. The HKMC acquires mortgages from originators, which it on-sells to an orphan SPV. The SPV issues pass-through notes back to the originating bank, which notes are guaranteed by the HKMC. The HKMC charges a guarantee fee for this service, which is taken from collections on the mortgages. The notes are 20% risk-weighted, reducing the originator's capital requirements from the usual 50% residential mortgage risk weighting, and are treated as liquid assets for the purpose of the 25% liquidity ratio required to be maintained by authorised institutions (see "Regulatory approvals" below). The originating bank continues its role as servicer of the mortgages.

The second stage in the HKMC mortgage securitisation programme was launched in January 2002, with the establishment of Bauhinia MBS Limited, a multi-issuance Cayman SPV that can issue off segregated ring-fenced pools of mortgages in multiple currencies. The first issuance off this programme was launched in March 2002.

In February 2001, the HKMC acquired a portfolio of HK$ 17bn subsidised loans from the Hong Kong Housing Authority at par, backed by an interest make-whole to market levels.

The HKMC purchase criteria for variable rate mortgages are:

- Maximum original loan size of HK$ 5m
- Original loan-to-value ratio of no more than 70%
- Original debt-service-to-income ratio (DTI) of no more than 50% (60% for certain high-income borrowers)
- Six-month seasoning requirement on acquisition of floating rate mortgages was dropped in October 1999
- Maximum 30-year original term
- Minimum 3-year remaining term to maturity
- Sum of the original term and the age of the property cannot exceed 40 years.

The HKMC purchase criteria for fixed rate mortgages are:

- Maximum loan size of HK$ 4m
- Original loan-to-value ratio of no more than 70%
- Original debt-service-to-income ratio (DTI) of no more than 50% (60% for certain high-income borrowers)
- Maximum 25-year original term
- Minimum 10-year remaining term to maturity
- Sum of the original term and the age of the property cannot exceed 40 years.

The HKMC mortgage insurance scheme criteria are:

- Maximum original loan size of HK$ 5m (HK$ 4m for fixed rate loans)
- Original loan-to-value ratio of no more than 90%
- Original debt-service-to-income ratio (DTI) of no more than 50%
- Maximum 30 year original term up to 85% LTV (25 years up to 90% LTV)
- Minimum 10 year remaining term to maturity
- Sum of the original term and the age of the property cannot exceed 40 years.

Ring-fencing and true sale

Under conflicts of laws principles, the assignability or non-assignability of an intangible, such as the benefit of receivables under a contract, is determined by the governing law of the underlying contract giving rise to the receivables. The parties' choice of governing law for the underlying contract will be upheld, with the law of the country with which the contract is most closely connected being applied in default of such a choice.

Receivables may be transferred by equitable assignment without the need to give notice to debtors of the transfer under s. 9 Law Amendment and Reform (Consolidation) Ordinance (which is very similar to s. 136 of the Law of Property Act 1925 in the UK). There is no requirement for equitable assignments of equitable interests to be in writing unless they relate to land (s. 5(1) of the Conveyancing and Property Ordinance). An assignment of future receivables can be executed and will be effective to transfer the future receivables to the assignee automatically as and when they come into existence. The assignment would not be prejudiced by the originator entering into insolvency prior to the receivables coming into existence.

If a transfer of mortgages is registered at the relevant Land Registry, the transferee will be able to take up the priority of the original registration. Registration of a mortgage transfer is no longer strictly required by the rating agencies, as the risk resulting from non-registration is primarily fraud by the originator. See also "Stamp/registration/etc." below.

The tacking of a further advance under an existing mortgage, to take priority to a subsequent mortgagee, is possible under s. 45 of the Conveyancing and Property Ordinance: (a) if the subsequent mortgagee so consents; (b) where the further advance does not exceed the stated maximum secured by the first mortgage; or (c) where the first mortgage is an all moneys mortgage in favour of an authorised banking institution.

Terms in the receivables documentation which prohibit assignment or transfer by the originator of its rights under the contract, or which require that the originator must obtain the consent of the relevant debtor in order to assign or transfer its rights under the contract, will, depending on their wording, prevent any assignment or transfer being effective unless the consent of the debtor to the transfer is in fact obtained, and may also prevent the declaration of a trust over the contractual rights in favour of the SPV. The 1998 Don King case, which was decided in the UK after the handover of Hong Kong to the PRC, is not a precedent in Hong Kong. The principles of Don King (which recognised a declaration of trust as being effective to circumvent a prohibition on the assignment of receivables on the basis that a clause prohibiting assignments is prima facie restricted to assignments of the benefit of the obligation and does not extend to declarations of trust of the benefit unless it is the intention of the parties that it should cover a trust as well) may however apply in Hong Kong on the basis that the case simply interpreted the law existing prior to that point.

Undivided interest   An attempt by an originator to achieve a true sale of an undivided interest in receivables is at risk of being regarded as a mere contractual right against the originator, due to lack of appropriation or identification of the goods in which a proprietary interest was to pass. It is possible to protect against the risk that no proprietary interest is transferred by a true sale of the entire interest in the receivables, with the receivables sold into a trust (constituted by an express declaration of trust over the whole of the pool), whereby the originator and investors are entitled to trust interests matching their respective shares. More recently however, in the first instance decision in the case of *CA Pacific Securities Ltd* in December 1998, the court determined that client securities held by broker CA Pacific in a fungible CCASS account pooled with its own securities were acquired by CA Pacific as agent for its clients as principals, and that consequently the clients did have proprietary interests in the securities despite the fungible nature of the CCASS account. This was decided on the basis of a construction of the terms of the client agreement. Furthermore, the clients had specific interests in certain of the securities in the account (rather than interests in an undivided portion of the account as tenants in common), as the client agreement clearly envisaged separate client interests rather than an interest in a changing pool with other clients. Appropriation of particular securities to a particular client was held to be unnecessary due to the nature of the securities themselves where, unlike tangible goods, the securities are fungible and segregation therefore serves no purpose. Exactly how to trace a particular interest through the pool was left undetermined.

Insolvency unwind   There are no transaction at an undervalue provisions – s. 59 of the Conveyancing and Property Ordinance specifically states that no "purchase, made bona fide and without fraud, of any interest in property of any kind within Hong Kong shall be opened or set aside merely on the ground of undervalue", although s. 60 allows unwind of transactions made with intent to defraud creditors where there is no valuable consideration. The Companies Ordinance deals with extortionate credit transactions at s. 264B, unfair preferences at s. 266B and disclaimer of onerous property by a liquidator at s. 268.

Substantive consolidation   There is no doctrine of substantive consolidation in Hong Kong save for the limited circumstances in which the Hong Kong courts may ignore the corporate veil of a company and seek to make members liable for the company's liabilities. This is very rare and typically arises where there is evidence that the company is used to perpetrate a fraud, or where the company is used for an illegal or improper purpose. Specific cases in which the corporate veil may be ignored arise:

- Where a company has a single member for more than 6 months. In this case the member will become liable for the debts of the company; and
- Under the Transfer of Businesses (Protection of Creditors) Ordinance. Under these provisions, transferees of the business of a company (or of part of the business where not acting bona fide and for value) will become liable for the debts of the company. There are exemptions for transfers pursuant to a charge registered for a year or more (this leaves a residual risk for a transferee from a receiver under a floating charge less than 1 year old).

Moratorium/automatic stay   In Hong Kong, provisions akin to an automatic stay or moratorium are limited in nature. Proposals for moratorium style proceedings were put forward by the Law Reform Commission (the LRC) in a report on Corporate Rescues in October 1996. These were developed in the report of the LRC in July 1999, and led to the Companies (Corporate Rescue) Bill, which was put before the Legislative Council in May 2001 but which has not yet been enacted. The intention is to implement a procedure called "provisional supervision", which is supported by a 30-day moratorium for the company to formulate a plan with creditors. If the plan is approved the moratorium could be extended by up to 6 months, and from the date on which a petition for winding-up of a debtor is presented the court would have a discretion to stay any pending court proceedings undertaken against the debtor.

Set-off

The debtor can obtain good discharge by making payments to the originator until notice of the assignment is given to the debtor, at which point the debtor is obliged to pay to the SPV direct. The SPV will take subject to any defects in the title of the originator, and until notice is given to the debtor, the SPV is subject to any further equities (such as set-off) arising in favour of the debtor through relations between the originator and the debtor subsequent to the assignment.

Foreign ownership

There are limitations on foreign ownership in certain sectors – e.g. banking, insurance and broadcasting. Under the Securities and Futures Ordinance s. 406, the acquisition (including a stake held as a stock borrowing under a stock loan arrangement, and other equity derivatives arrangements) of more than 5% of the shares in a listed company and each subsequent change that crosses a percentage point level (upwards or downwards, but once the holding drops below 5%, no further disclosure is required) must be notified to the stock exchange and the company. This replaces the old Securities (Disclosure of Interests) Ordinance s. 315 acquisition notification threshold of 10%.

Securities laws

There are requirements under the Companies Ordinance to produce a prospectus for any offer of securities to the public in Hong Kong, which must be registered with the Registrar of Companies, unless the securities are offered to professionals or are privately placed.

The Securities and Futures Ordinance was passed on 13 March 2002, and came into force on 1 April 2003. The Ordinance was originally put forward in a consultation paper on 7 April 2000, but underwent a lengthy discussion process due to its complexity and scope.

The Securities and Futures Ordinance consolidates the multitude of regulatory ordinances in Hong Kong and provides for the regulation of offers of securities to the public, and regulates:

- Dealing in securities
- Dealing in futures contracts
- Leveraged foreign exchange trading
- Advising on securities
- Advising on futures contracts
- Advising on corporate finance
- Providing automated trading services
- Securities margin financing
- Asset management.

On 30 July 2003, the Securities and Futures Commission published a code which proposes the establishment of REITs, shares in which could be sold to retail investors.

The REIT must be listed on the Hong Kong Stock Exchange, and may only invest in Hong Kong real estate. They may hold real estate through SPV holding companies. At least 90% of the net income of such a REIT must be distributed. They may borrow up to 35% of their gross assets.

Tax treatment

Stamp/registration/etc. Registrations of transfers of mortgages are subject to a nominal registration fee. In addition, stamp duty is chargeable at sliding rates on the transfer of interests in land (including a transfer of mortgages), depending on the price paid for the property (HK$ 100 up to HK$ 1m, 0.75% for HK$ 1–2m, 1.5% for HK$ 2–3m, 2.25% for HK$ 3–4m, 3% for HK$ 4–6m and 3.75% for more than HK$ 6m). The Collector of Stamp is willing to give adjudications that a mortgage transfer is not subject to stamp. Otherwise, stamp is only chargeable on a transfer of stock that is repayable in Hong Kong dollars and is not loan capital, or on the issue of a bearer instrument that is repayable in Hong Kong Dollars. The rate is 0.2% for transfer of stock, and 3% on the issue of Hong Kong Dollar bearer instruments. For transfers of stock, the rate is paid half by the seller and half by the buyer on the bought and sold contract notes for the transfer. There is an exemption from stamp duty for qualifying stock loan transactions under s. 19 Inland Revenue Ordinance. Indemnities for stamp duty are valid.

Withholding tax   There is no withholding tax on interest payments in Hong Kong.

Profits tax   Hong Kong taxes "every person carrying on a trade, profession or business in Hong Kong" in respect of profits "arising in or derived from Hong Kong ... from such trade, profession or business" (s. 14(1) Inland Revenue Ordinance), which may render an offshore SPV liable to Hong Kong tax. Under s. 20A of the Inland Revenue Ordinance, an offshore entity may be chargeable to tax "either directly or in the name of his agent ... whether such agent has the receipt of the profits or not". An entity will not be treated as an agent where it is an investment adviser or dealer registered under the Securities Ordinance, which is an independent entity charging a market fee for transactions in the ordinary course of business.

If the debtors in question are business debtors, the originator will be concerned to ensure that the debtors can maintain a profits tax deduction for interest paid on the receivables after the securitisation has closed, so that the securitisation does not adversely affect them (this will also be relevant to the originator, where the transaction is a secured loan transaction, with regard to interest on the secured loan). The main provisions on interest deductions in the Inland Revenue Ordinance allow for a deduction where (i) the loan is made by or to a financial institution (s. 16(2)(a) and (d)); (ii) the loan is made by a non-financial institution and the interest is chargeable to Hong Kong tax in the hands of the lender (s. 16(2)(c)); or (iii) the interest is payable on an instrument issued "bona fide and in the course of carrying on business and which is marketable in Hong Kong or in a major financial centre outside Hong Kong approved by the Commissioner" (s. 16(2)(f)).

The easiest way for a Hong Kong debtor/originator to claim a tax deduction for interest payments to an offshore SPV is under s. 16(2)(c) of the Inland Revenue Ordinance, for which it will be necessary to establish that the SPV is indeed chargeable to Hong Kong tax on the interest. To reinforce the argument that the SPV is indeed carrying on business in Hong Kong for tax purposes, the SPV may be registered under the Companies Ordinance as having established a place of business in Hong Kong.

To ensure tax neutrality for the SPV, the liability to Hong Kong tax has previously been dealt with by ensuring that the SPV's interest expenses (the major constituent of the SPV's expenses) are tax deductible under s. 16(2)(f) of the Inland Revenue Ordinance, by having the SPV issue listed securities.

Tax avoidance transactions may be disregarded in assessing tax under s. 61 (an artificial or fictitious transaction which reduces taxes) and s. 61A (a transaction with the sole or dominant purpose of enabling the person to claim a tax benefit).

Hong Kong does not tax capital gains.

VAT   There is no VAT in Hong Kong.

Other tax issues   A tax relief which allows a deduction from taxable income of up to HK$ 100 000 of mortgage interest paid by an individual on property owned and occupied by the individual (where the relevant mortgage was used for the purchase of the property and where the lender is a financial institution, a credit union, a money lender, the Hong Kong Housing Society, the individual's employer, or an organisation or association approved by the Commissioner of Inland Revenue) was introduced with effect from 1 April 1998.

Accounting treatment

The Hong Kong Society of Accountants (the HKSA) issued an Exposure Draft of an accounting standard for "Consolidated financial statements and accounting for investments in subsidiaries" on 15 August 2000. It was issued as Statement of Standard Accounting Practice (SSAP) 32 on 9 February 2001, and is effective for accounting periods beginning on or after 1 January 2001. The standard is intended to bring Hong Kong standards in line with International Accounting Standard (IAS) 27, and may require some SPVs that are currently off balance sheet to be consolidated back into the consolidated financial statements of the reporting enterprise.

The standard requires an enterprise to use a definition of subsidiary based on whether an enterprise is in substance controlled by another enterprise (e.g. where the reporting enterprise has decision-making powers over the SPV and rights to the majority of benefits of the SPV) rather than the definition in s. 2(4) of the Companies Ordinance. However, Hong Kong incorporated companies must still use the Companies Ordinance definition when it conflicts with the new standard (which may result in the financial statements of Hong Kong and non-Hong Kong incorporated companies not being directly comparable).

Capital treatment

The HKMA published guidelines in March 1995 (revised in August 1997) that follow the pre-1998 Bank of England guidelines very closely. The guidelines do not specify particular permitted methods of transfer, and provide that:

- There should be a clear statement in offering documents that the originator will not support losses suffered by investors and evidence from the transferor's legal advisers that the transferor will not be liable to investors for losses.

- The originator should not own any shares in the transferee or have control of the board of directors of the transferee (although they may have one director) and the name of the transferee must not imply a connection to the originator.
- Any mortgage transfer documentation should be sent to the Collector of Stamp Duty for adjudication.
- The transfer should not contravene the terms of the underlying assets.
- The transferor has no right or obligation to repurchase the assets (except: (a) for breach of a warranty given at the time of sale on a matter within the control of the transferor (warranties on the future performance of the assets are not permitted); (b) pursuant to a call option of the originator when the portfolio of securitised assets is less than 10% of their maximum value and the assets are still fully performing; or (c) where the assets are fully performing and they are repurchased for the purpose of making further advances).
- A one-off provision of expenses or subordinated debt to an SPV is permitted, although this will be directly deducted from capital for capital adequacy purposes, being treated as a "direct credit substitute" of a capital nature. Such a deduction would, however, be capped at the level of capital the institution would be required to hold if it was providing a direct credit substitute for the full value of the securities issued by the issuer. Third parties providing credit enhancement to a transaction will also be required to deduct the enhancement from capital, subject to the same cap (subordinated notes will be simply risk weighted at 100% if the HKMA does not consider that they are a form of credit enhancement facility to the SPV).
- The originator should not underwrite the issue without the consent of the HKMA or act as market-maker for the securities and should hold no more than 5% of them. Any subordinated notes held by the originator will be directly deducted from capital.
- The originator cannot bear recurring expenses of the SPV or fund the SPV.
- Swaps may only be entered into at market rates.

The intent behind the guidelines is to ensure that the originator bank should be seen to have transferred the assets such that there is no recourse to the originator for non-performance of the assets.

Senior MBS tranches are eligible for a 50% risk weighting if they meet the following conditions:

- The mortgage borrowers are individuals
- The LTV on the mortgages is not more than 90%
- The mortgages are secured by a first legal charge over residential property that is occupied by the borrower or a tenant of the borrower
- The mortgages are performing when they are transferred to the SPV
- The SPV must be independent of the seller and its activities must be restricted to the deal
- The SPV must not hold assets with a risk weighting in excess of 50%
- The SPV should obtain legal advice that the deal allows investors or the trustee to initiate legal proceedings directly against the SPV, secures all the assets of the SPV in favour of the investors or the trustee, and contains provisions that would enable

investors or the trustee to acquire legal title to the mortgage security and to realise that security following an event of default

- The investors should not be absorbing more than a pro rata share of losses on the mortgage loans.

Subordinated tranches bought at market prices will be risk weighted at 100%. If the purchase is regarded by the HKMA as credit enhancement, it will be deducted from capital.

The HKMA published guidelines on the capital treatment for credit derivatives in the banking book in December 1999. An institution should have appropriate risk control systems, and should consult legal advisers as to the use of credit derivatives. Credit derivatives are treated as either cash-collateralised or non-cash-collateralised guarantees in the banking book in respect of the amount of exposure to which they relate depending on whether they are funded or unfunded. The guidelines do not deal with credit spread products. Credit derivatives with binary payouts are treated as guarantees to the extent of the binary payout. As general requirements for credit derivatives:

- The reference obligation must be the same as the protected asset, or at least issued by the same issuer.
- The reference obligation must rank junior to or *pari passu* with the protected asset.
- The protection buyer should be seen to have transferred the credit risk (without such transfer constituting a breach of the term of the reference obligation) such that the protection seller has no recourse to the protection buyer for losses.
- The credit derivative must at the very least include "credit event" triggers relating to the reference obligation.

The guidelines require the institution to consult with the HKMA on the treatment of credit derivatives in the trading book, on credit derivatives that have a maturity mismatch or currency mismatch to the protected asset, or on basket trades.

Data protection/confidentiality

There is a duty on banks to keep customer information confidential. Customer information may only be disclosed in limited circumstances, such as disclosure with the consent of the customer. There is also a duty on anyone collecting or using personal information relating to an individual, from which it is reasonably practicable to identify the individual, to treat the information in accordance with the Personal Data (Privacy) Ordinance. The Ordinance requires that the information should only be used for the purposes for which it was collected, and provides that the information may not be transferred outside Hong Kong (unless the individual so consents), save to a location that also operates data privacy requirements.

In June 2003, the HKMA published guidelines on standards for the sharing of consumer credit information through credit reference agencies, in order to protect the confidentiality of the information.

Consumer protection

The Control of Exemption Clauses Ordinance imposes a reasonableness test on contractual exemption clauses in standard form contracts.

Regulatory approvals

Any authorised institution (i.e. an institution authorised by the HKMA) should approach the HKMA prior to undertaking a securitisation. The HKMA authorises three classes of deposit-taking entity under the provisions of the Banking Ordinance – Deposit-Taking Companies (DTCs) (requiring minimum paid-up capital of HK$ 25m) which may only take deposits of a minimum of HK$ 100 000 for a minimum 3-month term, Restricted Licence Banks (RLBs) (requiring minimum paid-up capital of HK$ 100m) which may only take deposits of a minimum of HK$ 500 000 and licensed banks (requiring minimum paid-up capital of HK$ 300m – increased from HK$ 150m in 2002 following a review in December 2001). The capital ratio may be increased from the minimum of 8% to a maximum of 16% (for DTCs and RLBs) or 12% (for licensed banks). Authorised institutions are also subject to a minimum 25% liquidity ratio. Authorised institutions are not permitted to lend by way of residential mortgage in excess of a 70% LTV ratio.

Other regulatory ordinances include the Money Lenders Ordinance (regulating parties whose business includes the making of loans) and the Companies Ordinance (dealing with disclosure requirements for Hong Kong companies issuing a prospectus, and overseas companies issuing a prospectus in Hong Kong).

The Securities and Futures Ordinance at s. 406 consolidates and replaces many of the other regulatory ordinances in Hong Kong, such as the Leveraged Foreign Exchange Trading Ordinance (which covered the licensing of parties carrying on a business of FX trading), the Commodities Trading Ordinance (which dealt with the registration of commodities dealers and commodities trading advisers), the Securities Ordinance (which set out requirements for the registration of securities dealers (parties carrying on a business of dealing in securities) and of investment advisers (parties advising other persons concerning securities)) and the Protection of Investors Ordinance (which prohibited invitations or advertisements to the public to enter into agreements relating to acquisition or disposal of securities). The Securities and Futures Ordinance provides for these various licensing mechanisms to be replaced by a single license.

On 5 July 2002, the HKMA released guidelines on the main points of the new Securities and Futures Ordinance as they relate to banks that carry out securities activities. In particular, setting out the interaction of the HKMA and the Securities and Futures Commission (the SFC) in regulating such institutions, and requiring banks with securities businesses (which were previously classed as exempt dealers) to meet SFC criteria for regulation.

Other issues

There are no wrongful trading provisions in Hong Kong, although fraudulent trading provisions exist under s. 275 Companies Ordinance. Inability to pay debts may be founded on a failure to pay a debt of at least HK$ 5000 within 3 weeks of service of formal demand on the company by the creditor at the company's registered office. Insolvency set-off is mandatory under s. 35 Bankruptcy Ordinance and s. 264 Companies Ordinance (similar to Rule 4.90 in the UK).

Preferred creditors include the state for all taxes due within the 12-month period prior to winding-up (the 1999 report of the LRC proposed removing the government's preferential status). There are no statutory powers of sale or appointment of receivers except in relation to security over land (legal security over land is effected as a charge by deed expressed to be a legal charge) taken as a legal charge or equitable mortgage made by deed.

The Conveyancing and Property Ordinance implies covenants as to title into a legal charge or assignment over land where given "as beneficial owner".

Security over shares held in the Central Clearing and Settlement System (CCASS) can be taken by way of charge or mortgage, perfected by transfer of the securities into the name of the chargee (notice should be given to CCASS as a protective measure).

The Charge Card decision in the UK on taking security over cash accounts was disapplied by statute in Hong Kong under s. 15A Law Amendment and Reform (Consolidation) Ordinance.

Hong Kong authorised institutions are not permitted to charge more than 5% of their total assets.

Any person holding themselves out as being prepared to deal in Hong Kong listed securities on the basis that completion will occur later than the trading day after the trade date commits a criminal offence under s. 76 Securities Ordinance, unless the transaction is a qualifying stock loan.

Deeds are required to be sealed by companies and individuals (for individuals, s. 19 Conveyancing and Property Ordinance allows that a document that describes itself as a deed or states that it has been sealed shall be presumed to have been sealed). Requirements in the relevant company's articles should also be complied with. The Conveyancing and Property Ordinance provides at s. 20 that a deed executed by a company is considered duly executed if the seal was affixed in the presence of a director and secretary or of two directors.

Land is held under leasehold title, on a Crown Lease from the SAR government. Multi-storey buildings do not have a separate Crown Lease for each unit, but a Deed of Mutual Covenant between the tenants, which notionally divides the building into shares, with a number of undivided shares allocated to each unit. The tenants are then tenants-in-common of the undivided shares in the building.

12.19   HUNGARY

There has been limited activity in securitisation in Hungary to date.

Ring-fencing and true sale

Receivables can be effectively transferred without notice to the debtors.

Insolvency unwind   Transactions at an undervalue or which defraud creditors may be unwound if entered into within 1 year prior to insolvency.

Set-off

The debtor can obtain good discharge by making payments to the originator until notice of the assignment is given to the debtor, at which point the debtor is obliged to pay to the SPV direct. The SPV will take subject to any defects in the title of the originator, and until notice is given to the debtor, the SPV is subject to any set-off rights arising in favour of the debtor through relations between the originator and the debtor.

Securities laws

Prior to 2002, companies other than financial institutions could only issue securities up to the amount of their capital. Following the entry into force of the new Capital Markets Act on 1 January 2002, companies can issue debt securities in excess of their capital, provided that they have been operating for at least 1 tax year and that the securities carry a rating from a recognised rating agency. Companies which have not been operating for at least 1 tax year may still issue debt securities in excess of their capital, provided that the securities are secured over specific assets and that the securities carry a rating from a recognised rating agency.

Tax treatment

Profits tax   Hungarian SPVs are subject to corporation tax. Investment funds are not subject to corporation tax.

VAT   Sales of receivables are not subject to VAT.

Data protection/confidentiality

There is a duty on banks to keep customer information confidential.

Regulatory approvals

A Hungarian SPV set up to buy receivables on a revolving basis must be licensed as a factoring company by the Financial Supervisory Authority.

Other issues

Floating charges are recognised in Hungary.

12.20   INDIA

The first securitisation in India was a securitisation by Citibank of auto loans in 1991. Deals since then have been small securitisations of auto and truck loans, or future flows transactions, and have been conducted on a domestic basis.

The National Housing Bank has been attempting to promote the issuance of MBS, with their first deal issued in late 2000.

The Reserve Bank of India (RBI) set up a Working Group on securitisation in June

1999, which published a report in December 1999 carrying recommendations in various areas, including:

- Providing for the transfer of assets under securitisation
- Rationalising stamp duty at 0.1% for securitisation in all states
- Reduction of registration charges
- Including ABS under the scope of regulation by the Securities Contract Regulation Act
- Permitting mutual funds to invest in MBS
- Ensuring tax neutrality of SPVs
- Establishing risk weightings for ABS and MBS paper
- Establishing listing requirements for ABS and MBS
- Accounting rules to enable off-balance-sheet treatment for securitised assets
- Disclosure requirements for offering documents
- Prudential guidelines for banks and finance companies for true sale (see "Capital treatment" below).

The RBI has asked the government to amend the Reserve Bank of India Act 1934 and the Banking Regulation Act 1949.

In April 2000, the Ministry of Finance attempted to impose 30% capital gains tax on investments in India by foreign institutions based in Mauritius (which were claiming exemption from the tax under the India–Mauritius double taxation treaty), but was forced to drop the measure due to protests. Institutions which are certified by the Mauritian tax authorities as resident in Mauritius can continue to claim the exemption.

Ring-fencing and true sale

The sale of unsecured receivables is governed by the Transfer of Property Act 1882, which requires that a transfer be made in writing. Notice to the debtor is not required.

Transfers of mortgages are required to be registered.

Future Receivables   Only receivables that are in existence can be transferred.

Onshore SPV

The Securitisation and Reconstruction of Financial Assets and Enforcement of Security Interest Act 2002 was passed in November 2002. Its intention was to strengthen secured creditors' enforcement rights (see "Other issues" below) and stem the growing tide of NPLs in India. The Securitisation Act provides for the establishment of Securitisation and Asset Reconstruction Companies (SARCs). SARCs may acquire financial assets from financial institutions and fund themselves through the issue of notes or debentures. They are required to be registered with the Reserve Bank of India and are subject to capital adequacy requirements.

Foreign ownership

Foreign ownership of a company is restricted to 24%, with holdings by a single entity limited to 10%.

Tax treatment

Stamp/registration/etc.   Stamp duty is chargeable on the assignment of receivables at an *ad valorem* rate, and may also be due on securities or trust certificates issued in a deal. Interpretation of the correct classification of a transaction and of the securities issued under a transaction for the purposes of the stamp legislation is complex, which may enable structuring to avoid some of the charges. Rates vary from state to state across the 26 states of India and are significant, although they were reduced to 0.1% in Maharashtra (1994), Karnataka and Tamil Nadu (1997), Gujarat (1998) and West Bengal (1999).

Withholding tax   Withholding tax is charged at 20% on interest income, but should not apply to approved external commercial borrowings.

Other tax issues   Mortgage borrowers who obtain loans from "eligible mortgage lenders" are entitled to tax relief. The potential status of an SPV as an eligible mortgage lender remains to be clarified.

Accounting treatment

There are no specific accounting standards for securitisation, but the Working Group paper proposes that FRS 5 be followed, allowing for derecognition or linked presentation.

Capital treatment

The RBI Working Group report of December 1999 carries recommendations on prudential guidelines for banks and finance companies for true sale. If the following criteria are met, the transaction will be considered to have achieved a clean sale, and can be excluded from the balance sheet of the originator for capital purposes (if the requirements are not met, the transaction is regarded as a financing and remains on balance sheet):

- Transaction price between the transferor and the transferee must be arm's-length.
- The assets must be put beyond the reach of the creditors or receiver of the originator in insolvency.
- The transferor must not maintain effective control over the assets.
- All risks and rewards on the assets have been transferred (save as provided below).
- The transferor must have written opinions from its legal advisors and auditors that it is not liable to investors for the assets.
- The transferee must have no formal recourse to the transferor (save as provided below).
- The transferor must not give warranties except as to existing facts (not future performance of the assets).
- The transfer should not contravene the terms of the underlying assets.
- The transferor must not be under any obligation to repurchase assets except in relation to breach of a warranty given at the point of transfer.
- The transferor must not make a market in the issued securities.

- The transferor may purchase senior securities issued by the transferee up to 5% of the issued amount.
- The transferor may only enter into swaps with the transferee at market rates.
- The transferee would be subject to the terms of any renegotiation of the assets.
- The transferor must not be obliged to pay over collections on the assets unless and until they are received.
- The transferor may not own a substantial interest in the transferee.
- The transferor may only have one director on the board.
- The name of the transferee must not have any resemblance to that of the transferor.

Credit enhancement facilities must meet the following conditions:

- Must be documented in writing
- There should not be any further recourse beyond the terms of the enhancement facility itself
- Must be on arm's-length terms
- Must be clearly limited in amount and duration.

If these requirements are not met, capital must be held against the value of all securities issued. If these requirements are met, the credit enhancement is directly deducted from capital for capital adequacy purposes.

Liquidity facilities must meet the following criteria:

- Must not bear recurring expenses
- May not be drawn for the purpose of credit enhancement
- Must be documented in writing
- There should not be any further recourse beyond the terms of the facility itself
- Must be on market terms
- Must be clearly limited in amount and duration
- Must provide for reduction in funding if asset quality deteriorates below specified levels
- Funding must be provided to the transferee, not to investors
- Repayment of the facility cannot be subordinated to investors.

If these requirements are not met the facility will be treated as credit enhancement.

Servicing provided by the transferor must meet the following conditions:

- Must be documented in writing
- There should not be any further recourse beyond the terms of the agreement
- Must be provided on arm's-length market terms.

The guidelines also deal with revolving structured and financing of equipment and consumer goods. Risk weights for ABS paper are based on rating level, to match the new Basel proposals.

Regulatory approvals

An Indian SPV may be subject to regulation by the RBI.

Other issues

Regulations restrict the potential uses for proceeds of a securities issue that are regarded as deposits taken from non-corporate depositors.

Mortgage enforcement proceedings are lengthy.

The Securitisation Act entitles a secured creditor to seize and manage secured assets without a court administered process, and includes the ability to take over management of a company where relevant.

12.21   INDONESIA

Following on from the first Indonesian securitisation, of auto loans, in August 1996, other auto and credit card issues followed rapidly in 1997. The development of the market (and in particular of potential mortgage deals) was halted by the Asian currency crisis.

On 21 May 1998, the long-standing president of Indonesia, President Suharto, resigned. On 4 June 1998, a debt-restructuring package was announced, which established the Indonesian Debt Restructuring Agency (INDRA) to protect trade financing and to provide FX rate protection for Indonesian non-bank corporates. The government announced the closure and liquidation of 38 banks with low levels of regulatory capital in March 1999. A debt-restructuring package was agreed through the Paris Club in April 2000 (resulting in a downgrading of the sovereign foreign currency rating to "selective default" by Standard & Poor's while the restructuring terms were put in place).

The Indonesian Bank Restructuring Agency (or "IBRA" – known in Indonesia as *Badan Penyehatan Perbankan Nasional* or "BPPN") was established in 1998 to manage the restructuring of Indonesian financial institutions. Following government decrees of 26 and 28 January 1998, which introduced a government guarantee of certain obligations of Indonesian banks to depositors and creditors, Bank Indonesia and IBRA issued joint guidelines on 6 March 1998 as to the implementation of the guarantee. Indonesian banks were required to register with the IBRA within 60 days (which subjects them to restrictions on their lending policies and tighter regulatory supervision) in order to benefit from the guarantee. Once registered, the guarantee covered most debts maturing on or before 31 January 2000, excluding obligations which were off-market or which did not meet prudent lending practices, loan capital obligations and subordinated loans. Significant additional powers for IBRA to enforce claims against non-performing debtors were granted by regulation in June 1999, which enabled IBRA to sue debtors of institutions it was restructuring directly and gave IBRA the rights of a preferential creditor in some cases.

IBRA has been active in asset disposals in 2002.

In early 2001, the government put out to tender a US$ 1bn future flows deal to be backed by natural gas exports from Indonesia to Singapore. However, opposition to the deal was subsequently voiced by the IMF and the World Bank on the grounds that it could result in the pledge of assets required to service debt to the IMF or World Bank.

Indonesia operates a civil law system, historically based on Dutch law.

New ABS regulations were passed in December 1997 (see "Securities laws" below) and a new Bankruptcy Act was passed on 22 April 1998 and came into effect on 20 August 1998.

Ring-fencing and true sale

Receivables may be transferred by assignment without the need to give notice to debtors, although the originator's insolvency may adversely affect the ability to subsequently perfect an assignment by giving notice. Consequently, it may be considered necessary to incorporate originator financial covenants in the documentation, breach of which enables the SPV to give notice to debtors on deterioration in the originator's financial condition. Also, it may be necessary to obtain the consent of debtors to a transfer of vehicles or equipment in the possession of the debtors.

The transfer of receivables to an entity outside Indonesia is permitted.

Transfers of mortgages must be registered.

Any notice that is given to debtors must be served by court bailiff to be effective, or written acknowledgement of the notice must be obtained from the debtor; general forms of notice on account statements will not be effective.

Terms in the receivables documentation that prohibit assignment or transfer by the originator of its rights under the contract, or require that the originator must obtain the consent of the relevant debtor in order to assign or transfer its rights under the contract, will prevent any assignment or transfer being effective unless the consent of the debtor to the transfer is in fact obtained.

Future receivables   Transfers of future receivables (other than future payments under a current contract) or of an undivided interest in receivables are unlikely to be effective.

Insolvency unwind   The preference unwind provisions in Indonesia are open-ended; a transaction that the company knew would prejudice creditors may later be unwound without time limit. If the transaction took place within 40 days prior to the company's insolvency and involves an undervalue or lack of consideration, then it is presumed that the company knew that the transaction would prejudice creditors. This may lead to issues for structures such as deferred purchase price mechanisms where the price paid by the SPV is below market value.

Moratorium/automatic stay   Moratorium proceedings exist in Indonesia.

Set-off

A debtor will retain a right of set-off unless and until notice of transfer is served on him by court bailiff, or notice of transfer has been duly acknowledged by him.

Onshore SPV

Bapepam published regulations on 26 December 1997 for the issuance of asset-backed participations in a pool of receivables pursuant to a collective investment contract (a *kontrak investasi kolektif* or KIK) signed by an investment manager (who must have a minimum capital of Rp 25bn and who will be responsible for representing noteholders and for the accuracy of the offering prospectus) and by a custodian (who acts as the depositary holding the legal title to the receivables and is instructed by the investment manager). The investment contract must be notarised. Different classes of participations (that is, senior and subordinated) may be issued. The regulations do not seek to address the potential taxation of the participations or the asset pool in Indonesia (beyond stating that the pool does not constitute a mutual fund), and do not clarify the exact legal nature of the interest of the holders of participations *vis-à-vis* the custodian.

Foreign ownership

Foreign ownership of Indonesian companies in certain sectors is restricted in accordance with the "negative list". In June 1999, legislation was passed to permit foreigners to acquire up to 99% of a listed Indonesian bank, provided that they are of good reputation. Listed company shares owned by foreigners are traded on a separate board from shares in the same company held by Indonesians. Acquisitions of more than 5% in a listed company and each subsequent change must be notified to the stock exchange and the company.

Securities laws

Where an Indonesian issuer is used, Bapepam regulations must be complied with, requiring that a company be established for a minimum of 3 years with a minimum of 2 years of profitability before it can issue securities.

Where an investment pool is used (pursuant to the Bapepam regulations of 26 December 1997 – see "Onshore SPV" above), a prospectus must be issued which should contain all material facts relating to the offering.

Tax treatment

Stamp/registration/etc.   There is a 1% notarisation fee on mortgage transfers.

Withholding tax   Indonesia imposes domestic withholding tax (at a rate of 15%) on payments of interest, discount or premium made by companies in Indonesia to other residents (unless the payee is a financial institution). In addition, offshore withholding tax (at a rate of 20%) is imposed on payments made by any resident of Indonesia to an offshore payee. Consequently, both offshore deals and onshore deals (in the latter case, where the debtors are companies, the originator is a bank and the SPV is not a bank) may require structuring for withholding tax. The popular European structuring route of using double taxation treaties is only of limited use, as Indonesia has no treaties that reduce the rate to zero. There are treaties with the Netherlands and Singapore that reduce the rate to 10%.

Withholding tax structuring in previous transactions has utilised an interest purchase mechanism. In such a structure, the rights to interest which the offshore SPV purchases are periodically sold to an offshore branch of an Indonesian bank, which pays a periodic purchase price in return, relating to each group of collections. Collections on the receivables are then paid to the Indonesian bank. The offshore branch is treated as an Indonesian entity for tax purposes, and the possibility of domestic withholding if the debtors are corporates is avoided as the entity is a bank. The passing on of the collections in the form of a purchase price for the interest receivables takes the amounts outside the scope of the offshore withholding tax charge, as they no longer constitute "interest" but are now purchase price for a capital asset.

Another mooted structure is the use of a transfer to an onshore SPV, which funds itself through a yen loan, ensuring that the interest payment which is passed offshore, and which is subjected to withholding, is minimised. It appears that in circumstances where a yen funding is combined with currency swaps, such that the Indonesian borrower receives a different currency, and the entity providing the funding is actually the same as the swap counterparty, withholding tax may be charged on the coupon which the borrower is paying under the swap.

Profits tax   An offshore SPV may be liable to Indonesian tax if it has a permanent establishment in Indonesia.

VAT   VAT was introduced on "factoring services" by decree no. 292 of 1996. It does not, however, appear to cover a sale of receivables. VAT is charged on services at a rate of 10%. Services provided wholly outside Indonesia should not be subject to VAT.

Accounting treatment

US accounting standards are followed. Off-balance-sheet treatment will be dependent on the level of credit enhancement provided by, and the degree of recourse to, the originator.

Data protection/confidentiality

Under the Banking Law Amendment (Law No. 10/1998), the previous strict duty on banks to keep all customer information confidential was replaced by a lesser duty to keep information relating to depositors confidential (prior to the new law, customer information could only be disclosed in limited circumstances, such as disclosure with the consent of the customer, and the effectiveness of a general advance customer consent to disclosure was questionable).

Consumer protection

A Consumer Protection Law (Law No. 8/1999) was passed in March 1999, and came into effect on 20 April 2000. The law introduces minimum requirements on the provision of goods and services to consumers, and regulates the use of exemption clauses in consumer contracts.

Regulatory approvals

Indonesia imposes restrictions on offshore borrowings undertaken by Indonesian companies, through operation of the governmental "PKLN Team". Companies which are state owned or which are undertaking government projects, are required to seek consent of the PKLN Team prior to entering into any offshore borrowing. Other companies are required to report offshore borrowings to the PKLN Team, but no consent is required. PKLN requirements will not need to be met if the originator achieves accounting off-balance-sheet treatment for a securitisation, but may for relevant transactions such as secured loans.

It appears unlikely that an offshore SPV would be required to be licensed as a finance company provided that it does not engage in origination in Indonesia. Indonesian SPVs may be subject to regulation.

The Companies Law requires that approval of 75% of the shareholders of the originator must be obtained for a disposal of all or a substantial part of the originator's assets (in practice more than 50% of its assets). Consent of shareholders is also required by Bapepam for "material" transactions by listed companies; material is probably circa 5%.

Other issues

Normally powers of attorney terminate on insolvency and can be revoked at any time. If a power of attorney is given by way of security, it is possible that it may be irrevocable but this is still uncertain. Express provision for sub-delegation should be inserted in the power of attorney.

In order to take security over post-dated cheques used to make payments, each individual cheque must be endorsed over. Due to the difficulty of carrying this out, an assignment may be taken instead of the right to the proceeds of the cheques on presentation.

Foreign judgements are not enforced by Indonesian courts.

Indonesian bank branches within Indonesia cannot make loans to offshore entities.

Indonesia does not recognise the concept of a trust save in limited circumstances, such as the *obligasi* concept (a form of note issued by the originator and limited in recourse to an underlying pool of receivables, which may utilise a form of security trust over the receivables in favour of a changing pool of investors).

A security interest cannot be granted to a party that is not a creditor of the secured debt. Hence, in a structure with a security trustee who is not also the note trustee, or where there is no note trustee (and where it is therefore not a creditor under the bond covenant to pay), a "parallel debt" structure may be necessary, whereby the full debt is covenanted to the security trustee as well as to bondholders, with a discharge of one covenant operating as a *pro tanto* discharge of the other covenant. The security interest is then simply granted to the security trustee; the bondholders are technically unse-cured, but can sue the trustee under the terms of the security trust deed. The Fiducia Law (law No. 42/1999) passed in September 1999 recognises the *"fiducia"* as a form of security interest over movable assets that does not require delivery of possession of the assets.

12.22   IRELAND

In addition to direct securitisation of assets, Ireland has become a focus for the estab-lishment of SPVs for use in transactions involving assets originated in other jurisdic-tions. This is due to the favourable tax regime applying to Irish securitisation SPVs (in particular companies which operate in the International Financial Services Centre (or IFSC) (which is located in the Dublin Docklands)), the fact that Ireland is within the EU and benefits from EU regulatory approval under passport directives, and a network of double tax treaties unlike many tax haven jurisdictions (in particular, the treaty with Korea providing for a reduction in cross-border withholding tax on interest payments to zero). Beneficial tax status for companies which operate in the IFSC, and which appoint a manager in the IFSC, was introduced as an incentive to aid development and regeneration of the Dublin Docklands area.

A new tax regime was introduced for Irish securitisation SPVs outside the IFSC in the Finance Act 1999. This regime gives non-IFSC companies some advantages over IFSC companies for securitisation purposes, as such non-IFSC companies are not required to obtain certification from the Ministry of Finance. Direct securitisation issuance in Ireland has grown on the back of increasing MBS issuance (in particular the Celtic MBS series from First Active) and the extension of beneficial tax treatment under the Finance Act 1999.

Following the introduction of Covered Bond legislation by Ireland in December 2001, the first Irish Covered Bond issue was finally launched in March 2003, with a Euro 4bn issue by Depfa Deutsche Pfandbriefbank.

Companies set up with IFSC certification from the Ministry of Finance have enjoyed a number of benefits, including the ability to make payment of interest overseas exempt from withholding tax, trading company status for tax deduction purposes, and liability to profits tax at a reduced rate as against non-IFSC companies. Certification from the Minister of Finance, and appointment of a manager in the IFSC, was needed to enable a company to claim IFSC tax benefits.

As a response to EU criticism on tax distortions resulting from the favourable IFSC tax regime, a new corporate taxation system was brought in for non-trading income, and was phased in for trading income by a reduction in the corporate tax rate each year. This was intended to harmonise the 10% IFSC tax rate and the 32% non-IFSC tax rate. The new system taxed non-trading income at 25% from 1 January 2000, and eventually taxed trading income at 12.5% by the beginning of 2003. IFSC companies set up before 31 December 1999 were still liable to profits tax at the reduced rate of 10% until the beginning of 2003, but since then are subject to the new tax rate of 12.5%. IFSC companies set up after 31 December 1999 were subject to 12.5% tax immediately.

Following the harmonisation of tax rates and the introduction of a range of tax deductions for non-IFSC companies, the IFSC regime is now rarely used, and most new Irish SPVs are set up as non-IFSC companies.

New ABS listing rules were issued by the Irish Stock Exchange in 2000.

Ring-fencing and true sale

Under conflicts of laws principles, the assignability or non-assignability of an intangible such as the benefit of receivables under a contract is determined by the governing law of the underlying contract giving rise to the receivables. The parties' choice of governing law for the underlying contract will be upheld, with the law of the country with which the contract is most closely connected being applied in default of such a choice.

Receivables may be transferred by equitable assignment without the need to give notice to debtors of the transfer. Terms in the receivables documentation that prohibit assignment or transfer by the originator of its rights under the contract, or require that the originator must obtain the consent of the relevant debtor in order to assign or transfer its rights under the contract, will prevent any assignment or transfer being effective unless the consent of the debtor to the transfer is in fact obtained.

Moratorium/automatic stay   Ireland has moratorium proceedings in the form of examinership, which can prevent the enforcement of security. Appointment of an examiner can only be blocked if a receiver has been in office for at least 3 days prior to an application for examinership. The proceedings were amended under the Companies Amendment (No. 2) Act 1999 which limited the risk that "related companies" (e.g. SPVs) could be caught up in an examinership of the originator.

Covered bonds   New legislation for covered bonds was introduced in Ireland with the publication of the Regulation of Mortgage and Public Credit Institutions and Securities Act in 2001. The Act was passed into law on 18 December 2001. The legislation is modelled on the German Pfandbriefe market, with mortgage bonds issued by mortgage credit institutions backed by an eligible pool of mortgages, and public sector bonds issued by public credit institutions backed by an eligible pool of public sector assets. The pools can be revolving in nature, with substitution of assets in the pool up to 20% of the pool, and each pool can back multiple issues of covered bonds. Public sector and mortgage assets can come from entities within Ireland, the EEA, the G7, or Switzerland. However, no more than 15% of the collateral pool may consist of assets from non-EEA countries. Covered bonds issued by mortgage banks are subject to a maximum 60% LTV or 75% LTV for residential or commercial mortgage assets respectively (with a maximum of an additional 20% LTV or 5% LTV respectively financed outside the pool), which must be first mortgages over residential or commercial property. Commercial mortgages are restricted to 10% of the pool. Covered bonds are subject to an overall cap on the maximum possible issuance equal to 50 times the banks' capital.

Tax treatment

Stamp/registration/etc.   Stamp duty is charged at 1% on a transfer of receivables, although a transfer of mortgages is exempt. Documents may be executed and held outside Ireland to delay triggering the stamp tax charge on the transfer of receivables until the documents are brought into Ireland for enforcement against the relevant debtor (if necessary). Alternately, the sale may be carried out on an "acceptance by payment" basis, where the only written documentation for the transfer is an offer, which is then accepted by payment from the SPV to the originator, without any actual stampable transfer documentation being produced.

Withholding tax   A quoted Eurobond exemption allows the issuance of securities by an Irish SPV free of withholding. In addition, SPVs that are licensed in the IFSC are exempt from withholding tax on interest paid overseas. The Finance Act 1999 also exempts from withholding payments of interest in the ordinary course of business to a company that is resident in another EU country outside Ireland.

Profits tax   The terms of s. 110 of the Taxes Consolidation Act 1997 (TCA) (from s. 31

of the Finance Act of 1991 and subsequent Finance Acts) provide for a favourable tax deduction regime for both IFSC and non-IFSC companies.

IFSC companies are regarded as carrying on a trade. Non-IFSC companies which meet the following criteria are treated as non-trading companies (and are taxed at 25%), but are given the benefit of calculating tax deductions on the favourable trading company basis (including deductions for certain bad debts). The criteria were widened by reforms to s. 110 TCA contained in s. 45 of the Finance Act 2003 (effective from 4 April 2003):

- The company is resident in Ireland.
- It carries on a business of the management of qualifying assets (financial assets).
- It acquires or holds assets, or enters into a contract which is itself a qualifying asset (prior to the Finance Act 2003, it had to acquire such assets from the original lender or originator).
- It does not carry on any other business apart from ancillary activities.
- It holds initial up-front qualifying assets of at least Euro 10m (prior to the Finance Act 2003, it had to hold qualifying assets of at least Euro 12.69m (IR£ 10m prior to adoption of the Euro) for at least 3 months after first acquisition).
- Provided that subordinated debt does not account for more than 25% of the asset portfolio, profit strip payments are deductible (prior to the Finance Act 2000, profit strip payments on subordinated debt that extracted all remaining cash flow from the SPV could potentially be reclassified as equity distributions, leading to the use of swaps or fee payments instead).

The Irish tax authorities may require that an SPV established in Ireland make taxable profits of at least 1 basis point of the value of its assets.

Accounting treatment

UK accounting standard FRS 5 is followed by the Institute of Chartered Accountants in Ireland.

Capital treatment

The Central Bank of Ireland published guidelines in 1992 similar to the Bank of England guidelines, intended to ensure that the originator does not assume a moral obligation to support the SPV.

Data protection/confidentiality

The Data Protection (Amendment) Act 2003 (in force from 1 July 2003) implements the EU Data Protection Directive.

Regulatory approvals

Confirmation may be needed that an onshore SPV is not carrying on a business as an investment intermediary. Security interests granted by an Irish company (or an offshore company with an established place of business in Ireland) may need to be registered with the Companies Office.

12.23   ISRAEL

The first securitisation from Israel (a US$ 150m trade receivables programme) was closed in August 2001 for Makhteshim Agan Industries.

Tax treatment

Stamp/registration/etc.   The transfer of mortgages was exempted from stamp duty in June 1999.

VAT   The transfer of mortgages was exempted from VAT in early 1999.

12.24   ITALY

A new Securitisation Law came into force on 29 May 1999 which eased transfer tax and notification requirements, debt issuance restrictions and minimum share capital requirements that had hindered issuance previously, as well as providing for a beneficial tax treatment for losses on non-performing assets that were securitised within 2 years of the new law coming into force. Since then, securitisation issuance has grown significantly, with initial emphasis on deals backed by non-performing mortgage loan assets (a problem for many Italian banks following the property price crash of the early 1990s) to take advantage of the tax break, and subsequent growth into performing mortgages, consumer loans and other classes.

The potential concerns in August 2000 arising out of the collections on the INPS social security payments transaction were satisfactorily explained as an under-reporting issue rather than a cash shortfall, enabling S&P to confirm their rating on the deal in October 2000.

In 2001, Italian issuance increased massively and Italy became the second largest market in Europe for cash (as opposed to synthetic) deals, accounting for 21% of the European market with over Euro 7bn of public sector issuance alone.

A decree of September 2001 was passed into law in November 2001 which permits the securitisation of future receivables for certain deals and also gives tax benefits. The Italian Bankers Association drafted a proposal for legislation to establish a covered bond market in 2001. This was taken up by the legislature in 2003 after requests from the Bank of Italy and the banking sector.

Italy operates a civil law system.

Ring-fencing and true sale

As with several other civil law jurisdictions, the development of securitisation in Italy has suffered from the requirement under the Civil Code for debtors to be notified of a transfer of receivables owed by them, in order for a transfer under Article 2160 of the

Civil Code to be effective to remove the receivables from the insolvency estate of the originator. The use of a *pubblico proclamo* (public notice) of the transfer in a national newspaper has been used as an alternative to notice.

Law 52 of 21 February 1991 (known commonly as Law 52) provides for an alternative method of transfer. Law 52 allows for transfer to a company which meets the requirements of Law 52 (known as a Law 52 company, and generally including banks and factoring companies; see details below) to be made without notice to debtors being required, provided that the date of the transfer is fixed with certainty (a *data certa*) (for example, by having the transfer notarised). As with a notified assignment, it is important that the assignment be a *pro soluto* assignment (an assignment without recourse to the seller for losses suffered by the purchaser if the receivables debtors default) rather than a *pro solvendo* assignment (an assignment with recourse) in order for the transfer to avoid recharacterisation as a secured loan rather than a true sale.

Article 58 of Law 385 of 1 September 1993 (known as the Banking Law) provides an additional alternative method of transfer for receivables where the receivables have common characteristics that enable them to be regarded as a portfolio, and the assignee is an Italian or EU bank, or an Italian branch of another bank. A transfer under Article 58 will be binding on third parties and on the receivables debtors if details of the receivables transferred are published in the *Gazzetta Ufficiale della Repubblica Italiana*. Publication also serves as notice of the transfer to the debtors.

The new Securitisation Law (Law 130 of 30 April 1999 which came into force on 29 May 1999) extends the Article 58 transfer method to a transfer of a homogeneous pool of receivables to an SPV set up in accordance with the new law. Law 130 specifically provides for the segregation of the assets of a Law 130 company in favour of the noteholders and creditors for debts due in relation to the note issuance in question, to the exclusion of other creditors of the company. The new law also relates to transfers of assets to mutual funds, and loan or sub-participation structures (although it is unclear exactly which provisions of the new law apply in these cases). To ensure the homogeneous nature, criteria for the selection of the portfolio are required to be set out in the transfer agreement, which should exclusively identify those assets transferred, and not also identify any assets remaining with the originator. Transfers of assets on a revolving basis (under a trade receivables deal for example) may cause problems for identification under these criteria, which may necessitate a new publication in the *Gazzetta Ufficiale* each time that assets are transferred.

On 24 October 2003, the Italian Supreme Court published a court ruling of 9 April 2003 where a liquidator of a small insolvent leasing company that was not regulated by the Bank of Italy was permitted to cancel *traslativo* lease contracts and sell the leased asset, even though the lessee was not in default. This raised significant concerns for investors in Italian lease securitisations, and on 5 November 2003 the Italian Treasury announced plans to amend the 2004 budget law to remove the ability of liquidators to cancel *traslativo* leases.

The new Companies Law (see "Other issues" below) will, from 1 January 2004, permit the segregation of a group of assets from the rest of a corporate entity with the ability to issue notes against this pool of assets. This ring-fencing provision may provide a foundation for whole business structures in Italy, which are otherwise difficult to create due to the existence of *amministrazione controllata* proceedings (see "Moratorium/automatic stay" below) and limitations on the ability to create floating charges (see "Other issues" below). The ring-fencing takes two possible forms – the *patrimonio destinato* (which can ring-fence up to 10% of a company's net assets which are used for a specific business activity, together with the cash flow generated from such assets) and the *finanziamento dedicato* (which gives a priority right to lenders under loans or Law 130 bonds in respect of cash flows derived from a specific business activity, but not in respect of specific assets). The *finanziamento dedicato* structure does not give control over insolvency or enforcement proceedings – just a priority in insolvency – so control would need to be obtained through separate security interests.

Registration with the Land Registrar may be required for an effective transfer of mortgages, but it may be possible to postpone registration by having the mortgages transferred by a separate transfer from the mortgage debt, and notarised outside Italy. The transfer would then only be registered with the Land Registry if enforcement is necessary. No registration of transfer is required for a transfer under Article 58 (or under the new Securitisation Law).

Terms in the receivables documentation that prohibit assignment or transfer by the originator of its rights under the contract, or require that the originator must obtain the consent of the relevant debtor in order to assign or transfer its rights under the contract, will prevent any assignment or transfer being effective unless the consent of the debtor to the transfer is obtained.

Future receivables   The Civil Code only permits the transfer of future receivables where they can be sufficiently identified, and where they arise under an existing framework contract. Even then, a liquidator can void a claim to future receivables (including a security interest) which have not yet come into existence when the originator becomes insolvent.

Law 52 widens this to allow the transfer of future receivables arising within the next 2 years even where there is no contractual framework yet, provided that the debtors can be readily identified, and the transfer is made to a Law 52 company.

The new Securitisation Law expressly covers future receivables, although it is unclear whether this would cover non-contracted cash flows. It is possible that future receivables originated pursuant to a contractual framework could be transferred without the need to effect a new registration each time that new receivables arise.

Decree no. 350 of 25 September 2001 (which was passed in November 2001 specifically for the benefit of the Lotto deal and the subsequent SCIP real estate deal, both in December 2001) permits the transfer of future receivables in deals specified by the Ministry of Finance, and envisages transfers by public sector entities. The Decree also provides for exemption from the requirement for the SPV to use a registered bank or financial institution as servicer and provides for certain tax benefits (see under "Withholding tax" below).

Insolvency unwind   Transactions may be unwound on insolvency in the event that a party dealing with the insolvent entity had actual or constructive knowledge that the insolvent entity was insolvent at the time the transaction was entered into, in relation to transactions carried out within 1 year prior to insolvency (or 2 years where the party was not at arm's-length from the insolvent entity, or was not bona fide). In the event that the party dealing with the insolvent entity is an SPV under the new Securitisation Law, these periods are reduced to 3 months and 6 months respectively.

Transactions at an undervalue entered into within 2 years prior to insolvency may be unwound, unless the party dealing with the insolvent entity can establish that they did not have actual or constructive knowledge that the insolvent entity was insolvent at the time the transaction was entered into.

Recharacterisation   Transactions are likely to be regarded as a true sale, and are unlikely to be recharacterised, provided that there is no recourse back to the originator other than for breach of warranty.

Substantive consolidation   There is no general substantive consolidation regime in Italy, unless a company has a single shareholder, in which case the sole shareholder is liable for the debts of the company.

Moratorium/automatic stay   A company may be put into *amministrazione controllata*, which creates a moratorium on enforcement, following application to the courts by the company where there is a substantial likelihood of recovery of the company. The moratorium lasts 1 year and can be renewed once, for a maximum period of 2 years.

Set-off

A proper transfer under Article 58 or to a Law 130 company should prevent further set-off rights accruing, although previously accrued set-off rights will continue to exist unless consent to waive such rights is obtained from the debtor.

Onshore SPV

For a company to be effectively established under Law 52, it must be set up with an issued share capital of at least Italian Lire 1bn (Euro 516 457) and registered in Italy with the *Ufficio Italiano Cambi* to carry on a factoring business.

The new Securitisation Law provides for the establishment of an Italian SPV which can undertake either a single or multiple securitisation transactions, and which must be established with a minimum share capital of Lire 200m (Euro 103 292) paid up as to at least Lire 60m (Euro 30 988) (which must be fully paid-up prior to the shares being transferred) as a *societa per azioni* – an S.p.A. or joint stock company. The SPV could also be set up with Lire 20m (Euro 10 330) of share capital as a *societa a responsibilita limitata* – an S.r.l. or ordinary limited liability company, although it is not entirely clear to what extent the Securitisation Law overrides the general provision of Italian law that only certain entities such as S.p.A. companies can issue debt securities. The SPV must be registered as a financial institution with the *Ufficio Italiano Cambi* which can take up to 60 days. The SPV must use a registered bank or financial institution as servicer (see "Regulatory approvals" below).

Law No. 340 of 24 November 2000 simplified the procedure for establishing companies in Italy by removing the requirement for the articles of the company to be subject to *omologazione* (a court review that took up to 40 days).

Foreign ownership

Acquisitions of more than 2% in a listed company and each subsequent change must be notified to the financial regulatory authority and the company. Acquisitions of more than 10% in an unlisted company and each subsequent 5% must be notified to the financial regulatory authority and the company.

Securities laws

Prior to the entry into force of the new Companies Law on 1 January 2004 (see "Other issues" below), a normal Italian S.p.A. company can only issue securities up to an amount equal to its fully paid-up capital under Article 2410 of the Civil Code, and normal S.r.l.s cannot issue securities. From 1 January 2004, an S.p.A. will be able to issue bonds up to twice its fully paid-up share capital plus its legal reserves (or potentially in excess of this for issues subscribed by professional investors or which are listed), and an S.r.l. will be able to issue bonds that are subscribed solely by professional investors.

An SPV under the new Securitisation Law is not subject to these limits, although it must obtain an investment grade credit rating from a qualifying rating agency for its securities if it sells them to private investors. CONSOB has prepared regulations on the qualification requirements for rating agencies on deals under the new law.

The new Securitisation Law sets out specific requirements for the contents of the offering circular if the securities are to be sold to professionals. If the securities are to be sold to private investors, then the public offer requirements of CONSOB (the *commissione nazionale per le societa e la borsa* – the Italian Stock Exchange regulator) apply instead.

Tax treatment

Stamp/registration/etc.   Stamp duty is charged at a nominal rate on most contracts. Stamp duty can be avoided by executing a contract as an exchange of letters. Registration tax is also chargeable on most contracts but at differing rates depending on the nature of the contract. If a contract is executed by way of exchange of letters, then registration tax would not be incurred unless and until there is a need to bring the letters before a court in Italy to enforce their provisions. Documents may be executed outside Italy to delay triggering stamp and registration tax charges until the documents are used in court in Italy for enforcement against the relevant debtor (if necessary).

Some of the main registration tax charges are as follows:

- Transfers and security interests are charged to registration tax at an *ad valorem* rate of up to 0.5% of the par value of assets which are transferred, or over which security is created, in order to enable the transfer documents to be used in Italian court proceedings, and up to 3% on amounts awarded by way of judgement in Italian court proceedings.
- A transfer of mortgages is subject to a 0.5% registration tax and a 2% mortgage tax (see also "Ring-fencing and true sale" above), although these charges can be avoided if the transfer of mortgages is made to a relevant bank under the terms of Article 58 of the Banking Law (see above).
- Medium- or long-term bank loans from an Italian bank of over 18 months in tenor are subject to *imposta sostitutiva* tax on creation, as are certain other receivables. The tax is charged at 0.25% of the amount of the loan or receivable, but payment of the tax effectively "franks" the loan from the payment of registration taxes on any security interest related to the bank (enabling the bank to create and register security in relation to such receivables without incurring further registration tax

costs). EU banks operating in Italy which are not Italian banks are not obliged to pay the tax, but can elect to do so in order to gain the "franking" benefits of exemption from registration tax.

- Under the new Securitisation Law, a transfer of receivables that fall outside the *imposta sostitutiva* regime may be regarded as a VAT-exempt transaction, leading to a reduction of registration tax to Lire 250 000 (Euro 130) (but potentially giving rise to VAT reclaim issues for an originator).
- The transfer of receivables subject to the *imposta sostitutiva* tax on creation is exempt from registration tax under the new Securitisation Law.

Withholding tax   Withholding tax may be charged on interest-bearing receivables unless they are bought by an Italian bank or a non-Italian bank acting through an Italian branch. No withholding tax is charged on discount elements. Italy has a complex withholding tax regime on bond issues. A broad outline is that withholding tax is levied on payments made by an Italian issuer on bonds:

- At 12.5% (in the form of a final substitutive tax or *imposta sostitutiva* – a term used here in a general sense and not to be confused with the specific *imposta sostitutiva* regime for certain loans and other receivables set out in the section on "Stamp/registration/etc." above) where the investor is an Italian resident individual;
- At 0%, where the investor is an Italian resident company;
- At 0% under Decree No. 239 of 1 April 1996 (effective 1 January 1997) where the investor is resident for tax purposes in a double tax treaty country (and not in Italy or a tax haven) that has a double tax treaty with Italy that provides for the exchange of information. The notes must be held through an Italian custodian, and the noteholder must provide an annual residence declaration (on form *modulario* 116) on or before 31 January of each year. Most OECD countries have tax treaties with Italy that meet these requirements, including the US and the UK, but not including Switzerland;
- At 12.5% (in the form of an *imposta sostitutiva* tax – used in a general sense) where the investor is not an Italian resident, but the Decree requirements cannot be met.

These provisions are subject to higher rates regardless of the location of the investor and regardless of treaty relief (the 27%/20% withholding applied to short-term bonds is not reduced by treaty relief, as the bonds are not considered to be "bonds" within the treaty meaning) as follows:

- At 27% if the bonds are issued by an unlisted Italian company and pay a coupon which exceeds Prime by a certain amount;
- At 27% if the bonds are shorter than 18 months in tenor;
- At 20% if the bonds are longer than 18 months in tenor but are called/put/redeemed/amortised/novated in whole or in part prior to 18 months after issue.

Decree No. 350 (see under "Future receivables" above) provides for an exemption for bonds issued by an SPV under the Decree from tax otherwise arising on redemption within 18 months of issue, or on sale to investors in jurisdictions where the Decree No. 239 information exchange requirements cannot be met.

Bonds issued by an Italian SPV under the new Securitisation Law are given the same tax treatment as bonds issued by a listed Italian company, and may therefore be subjected to 20% withholding if they are short-term, or amortise in the short term.

Withholding tax avoidance methods have included the payment of interest via a bank or other institution established in a jurisdiction such as Luxembourg or the Netherlands, which do not charge withholding tax, where the bank can reclaim any withholding suffered on payments received by it. Until 1996, the "conduit" method (that is, the making of loans to an Italian borrower by an offshore branch of an Italian bank, funded by sub-participation to foreign banks) was used to avoid withholding. Conduit interest was, however, expressly subjected to 15% withholding by Decree No. 323 of 20 June 1996. It may still be possible to avoid withholding through the use of back-to-back loans through a conduit-type structure, where one of the loans is a limited recourse loan giving the lender (e.g. an Italian bank) sole recourse and enforcement rights against the ultimate borrower, and the other is a full recourse loan made by an offshore bank to the Italian bank, such that there is no look-through to the underlying loan.

Profits tax   Italy charges IRPEG corporate tax on profits, and also IRAP on profits with certain items (staff costs and financing costs) added back in (financial companies may avoid the add-back of financing costs). An SPV under the new Securitisation Law is subject to corporate tax as a financial company, which should enable it to avoid adding back financing costs when calculating IRAP.

The announcement from the Bank of Italy on 29 March 2000 was expected to clarify the tax status of SPVs under the new law by ruling that assets acquired and bonds issued by the SPV should not appear on the accounting balance sheet of the SPV (effectively meaning that the SPV would not be subject to profits tax, and that multiple transactions could be undertaken by a single SPV without the risk that tax liabilities could breach the ring-fencing of one portfolio of assets from another portfolio of assets within the same SPV). In the event however, the announcement simply provided that the assets and bonds should be dealt with below the line in the accounts.

On 24 October 2002, the local revenue in the Lombardy region released an interpretation that Law 130 SPVs should be taxed annually over the life of a deal. This was superseded on 6 February 2003, when the Italian Revenue published Circular No. 6 providing an interpretation that Law 130 SPVs should only be taxed on their taxable income at the end of the relevant securitisation programme, to the extent of amounts left after the repayment of noteholders, in relation to its taxable income net of deductible expenses over the life of the deal.

Interest accrued or paid on financing is deductible, as are business expenses. Loan provisions are deductible in the year taken up to 0.5% of the loan amount per annum, with amounts in excess of this deductible over 7 years. Provisions are only deductible up to an overall cap of 5% of the loan amount. Actual losses on bad debts are only deductible for tax purposes in calculating profits when they are definitively crystallised (which may lead to an accounting/tax profit mismatch unless the loss can be crystallised at the right point).

An offshore SPV may be liable to Italian tax if it has a permanent establishment in Italy. Also, if a two-tiered structure is used (with an onshore Law 52 SPV and an offshore funding SPV), there is a risk that the offshore SPV would become liable to Italian tax as a controlling entity of the Law 52 SPV. This may be avoided if it can be demonstrated that the Law 52 SPV is making a profit, by retaining a spread within the Law 52 SPV.

Recognition of losses on the sale of assets for securitisation under the new Securitisation Law within 2 years of the effective date of the law (i.e. until 29 May 2001) were allowed to be spread over 5 years in the profit and loss account for accounting purposes but were debited immediately in full against reserves in the balance sheet. The tax treatment followed the accounting treatment, so that one-fifth of the loss was written through the profit and loss account (and taxable profit) in the first year, and the other four-fifths were written as a reduction of financial reserves in the balance sheet. In each subsequent year, a further one-fifth of the original loss was entered through the profit and loss account (and taxable profit) and reversed through the balance sheet. Losses can generally be carried forward for tax purposes for 5 years, but cannot be carried back.

VAT   There is no VAT on the transfer of receivables or on the provision of financial services. Servicing fees for enforcement services are subject to VAT.

Other tax issues   Italy has mortgage interest relief in the form of a tax deduction for interest on mortgage loans. The servicer of the loan is required to make a statement to the borrower annually on 30 April to ensure that the borrower can continue to claim this. An SPV under the new law should be able to make the statement in its role as a mortgage lender (it should not be necessary for the SPV to be licensed as a bank).

Accounting treatment

The transfer must be made *pro soluto* in order to achieve off-balance-sheet treatment.

Capital treatment

A sale under Article 58 of the banking law or Law 130 can achieve off-balance-sheet capital treatment. The Bank of Italy issued guidelines on the capital treatment of mezzanine and junior notes issued under a Law 130 securitisation in March 2000. Junior notes are directly deducted from capital (subject to a cap equal to the amount of capital held against the pool prior to securitisation, or to a pro rata share of such cap relative to the share of junior notes held). Mezzanine notes are normally weighted unless the amount of the junior notes is less than the original capital held against the pool, in which case the mezzanine notes are subject to the higher of a direct deduction from capital (subject to a cap equal to the excess of the amount of capital held against the pool prior to securitisation over the amount of the junior notes, or to a pro rata share of such cap relative to the share of mezzanine notes held), or a normal weighting.

If the securitisation is not carried out under Law 130, holdings of junior and mezzanine notes are directly deducted from capital.

The Bank of Italy issued guidelines on the capital treatment of synthetic securitisations on 31 December 2001 that have the same effect as the Law 130 guidelines. As with Law 130 deals, junior default swaps are directly deducted from capital (subject to the cap) and mezzanine default swaps are subject to the higher of a direct deduction from capital (subject to the cap), or a normal weighting. Senior default swaps are normally weighted.

Consumer protection

Consumers are entitled to cancel credit transactions (other than mortgage loans) on the basis of fraud, non-disclosure or misrepresentation.

Regulatory approvals

The Bank of Italy imposes reporting requirements on bank originators. Italian issuers, and issuers issuing securities in Italy, are required to notify the Bank of Italy under Article 129 a minimum of 20 days and a maximum of 30 days prior to the issue, where the securities are issued in an amount in excess of Euro 150m or are unusual in nature. The Bank of Italy can prevent the issue, but only in limited circumstances.

An SPV under the new Securitisation Law should not be subject to capital requirements, but will be required to make quarterly reports to the Bank of Italy. An SPV under the new securitisation law must use a bank or financial institution registered under Article 107 of the Banking Law as servicer of its receivables (which may necessitate appointing a third-party servicer where the originator is not so registered).

A servicer under Article 107 will be subject to requirements set out in Bank of Italy guidelines published on 23 August 2000. The servicer will not be subject to full capital requirements, but must have minimum capital of Euro 0.5m (if they service deals with an aggregate value up to Euro 100m in value), Euro 1m (for value of Euro 100m to 500m) or Euro 1.5m (for value upwards of Euro 500m), and will be subject to large exposure limitations that prevent it assuming exposures to any single company or company group that exceed 25% of its capital base. The servicer will be required to carry out electronic reporting to the Bank of Italy on a quarterly basis.

Prior approval of the Bank of Italy may be required for certain transactions by Italian banks and Italian branches of non-EU banks.

Other issues

Floating charges over variable assets can be created under Article 46, but solely in favour of an EU bank lender, and they are not recognised otherwise (to the extent that the security interest relates to assets that have not yet come into existence at the point at which the borrower becomes insolvent, the security interest is voidable by a liquidator). Such charges will not prevent a company entering *amministrazione controllata*.

Italy's main insolvency procedures are *fallimento* (insolvent liquidation), *concordato preventivo* (voluntary arrangement with creditors) and *amministrazione controllata* (administration). There is also an administration procedure for large enterprises (*amministrazione straordinaria per le grandi imprese in crisi*) and a special liquidation procedure for financial institutions and other enterprises of public interest (*liquidazione coatta amministrativa*).

Trusts are not recognised, such that security interests granted in favour of a security trustee, or over a fluctuating pool of assets, may not be valid. However, Articles 2410 to 2420 of the Civil Code provide for the role of a representative of noteholders on a bond issue (who has certain roles in relation to notifications on a security package and amendments of the bonds, but who does not actually hold the security package), and for a real estate security package that can be registered in the name of the noteholders as a class (even where bearer). Law 130 disapplies these provisions, but it is unclear whether this is intended to simply remove some of the more restrictive provisions on the role contained in the Civil Code, or to disapply it (and the commensurate security benefits) entirely in relation to deals using the new Securitisation Law. Other representatives (such as a *mandatario* or an English law trustee) may be used instead.

The Italian Usury Law (Law 108 of 7 March 1996) set maximum interest rates (usury rates) chargeable on different kinds of loan. The Usury Law defines the usury rate as any interest rate which is more than 50% higher than current average loan rates. The average loan rate is reset quarterly by the Treasury, which publishes the relevant average loan rate for each quarter. The Usury Law was thought to apply only to loans advanced after the Usury Law came into force on 24 March 1996, with the effect that if the interest rate on any such loan during an interest period exceeded the usury rate applicable during that period, the interest amount otherwise due during that period would be void and could be reclaimed by the debtor if paid. Charging interest in excess of the usury rate is also a criminal offence.

On 17 November 2000, Italy's highest court (the Cassazione) ruled that the Usury Law would also be applied to loans advanced prior to 24 March 1996, and that payments made on these loans by debtors where the loan interest rate breached the then relevant usury rate for any historic period could be reclaimed. The statute of limitations (which limits claims after 10 years) would prevent claims prior to 1991.

This decision caused great concern among banks in Italy, due to the high level of interest rates prevalent in Italy prior to entry into the Euro in 1999, with the result that many fixed rate mortgages entered into prior to 1996 bore rates in excess of the usury rate. Estimates of the potential cost to the Italian banking sector of reimbursing these payments were as high as Euro 25bn.

As a result, the Italian parliament passed Law No. 24 of 28 February 2001 preventing any claim by a debtor for reimbursement for rates charged on fixed rate loans prior to 1 January 2001. They also set the new usury rate for mortgages at 9.96% (or 8% for first-time buyers buying a house with a value of less than Euro 75 000), and provided that loans becoming usurious in the future would automatically be reduced by operation of law to the usury threshold (resulting in a loss to the lender of only the surplus interest portion, not the entire interest amount).

Consequently, the loss to lenders in respect of loans advanced prior to 24 March 1996 is now limited to reimbursement of amounts paid after 1 January 2001 in excess of the usury threshold, and the ongoing limitation of interest on such loans to the level of the usury threshold.

Article 1283 of the Civil Code only permits capitalisation of accrued interest from 6 months after its due date (or from the date of legal proceedings for its recovery if earlier), or in accordance with recognised customary practices. Banks traditionally capitalised accrued interest every 3 months in reliance on this being a customary practice. However, judgements in 1999 from the Cassazione held that such practices are not recognised customary practices and are unlawful. Decree 342 of 4 August 1999 was introduced to validate the practice historically (Article 25(3)), and to permit capitalisation in the future in accordance with resolutions of the CICR ministerial committee (Article 25(1)). The CICR accordingly passed a resolution on 9 February 2000 (which came into force on 22 April 2000) allowing compounding in accordance with the terms of the relevant agreement. On 17 July 2000, the Constitutional Court struck down Article 25(3) as *ultra vires*, although Article 25(1) is still applicable.

Penalty interest can be charged at the lower of the basic contract interest rate and the legal rate (which is an announced rate that is revised periodically) for the calendar year of foreclosure (not of default) and the 2 previous calendar years. For other years prior to or after this period, the maximum rate chargeable is 2.5%, and any amount charged in excess of this is unsecured.

Enforcement of security rights over land is by court auction; there is no foreclosure remedy. Enforcement and court auction proceedings can take between 3 and 8 years. Enforcement costs will include court fees, lawyers fees, auction fees and notaries fees. Enforcement procedures were revised by Law 302 of 3 August 1998 (effective from 8 September 1998), which provides for procedures for the preparation of court auctions to be carried out by notaries instead of by the court. As the courts were becoming increasingly overstretched, this could speed up the enforcement process by as much as 2 years.

Article 58 was amended at the end of 1999, such that where a portfolio of mortgages has *fondiario* status (which applies to loans originated by a bank, which are first ranking mortgages, have a tenor in excess of 18 months, and have an LTV of less than 80%), a transfer under Article 58 to a Law 130 SPV will enable the Law 130 SPV to continue to claim the benefit of *fondiario* status (which enables enforcement to be carried out more rapidly).

Mortgages typically pay interest semi-annually rather than monthly, and are generally only for a fixed amount (as stated in the mortgage), rather than being "all monies".

There are no bankruptcy procedures for private individuals. Company legislation introduced in July 1998 reformed some features of corporate governance to assist transparency and protect shareholders.

Financial assistance (including upstream security) given by a company for the acquisition of its shares is not permitted under Article 2358 of the Civil Code, breach of which is a criminal offence (in addition, the relevant contracts will be invalid). There is no "whitewash" procedure for either public or private companies. To date, most leveraged buy-out transactions in Italy have utilised provisions that enable targets and acquisition vehicles to be merged by an extraordinary resolution of shareholders, which requires a majority vote by two-thirds of the shareholders in attendance at the shareholders meeting. It has been argued that this does not constitute an indirect breach of the financial assistance prohibition, where the acquisition vehicle is the company that remains post-merger, and is hence the only company ever liable for the acquisition debt. This has been disputed (in particular where a reverse merger is effected and it is the target that remains post-merger).

Law 366 of 3 October 2001 (known as the Mirone Law) gave the Italian government the authority to draft a reform of Italian company law. As a result, Decree 61 of 11 April 2002 and Decree 6 of 17 January 2003 were published, forming the basis of a new Companies Law. These provisions cover a range of different areas (see "Ring-fencing and true sale" and "Securities laws" above). In relation to financial assistance, Decree 61 removed the potential criminal liability for breach of Article 2358 of the Civil Code, and provides instead, under modified Article 2629, that it is a criminal offence to arrange a merger transaction that causes damage to creditors. Decree 6 (in force from 1 January 2004) legitimises post-acquisition mergers, provided that a merger plan is produced that sets out the funding to be used for fulfilment of the merged entities' obligations post-merger. This must be accompanied by a report from the board of directors (setting out the reasons for the transaction), an expert's report, and an auditors' report. The form of the Decree has raised concerns that it would not cover asset-stripping or leverage plays by financial buyers that do not have other independent valid business reasons for a merger.

To date, post-acquisition balance sheet management has relied on a "double Newco" structure – gearing up the target and merging it into a Newco (Newco 2) funded entirely through equity, of which the vast majority is distributable. The combined entity then dividends the cash proceeds of the gearing to its parent (Newco 1) and to other third-party shareholders, significantly reducing the net worth of the entity, prior to merging it into Newco 1, which is mainly debt funded. This achieves a merger without significantly diluting the majority shareholder.

The exchange ratio is based on preserving the absolute value of the net worth that the minority shareholders had rights to, by setting their ratio of the merged entity at the value of the minority net worth as a percentage of the net worth of the merged entity (the valuation methods used to assess the value of both merging entities will be verified by an expert appointed by the court, and could be based on net worth, cash flow valuation, or market value of shares if traded). For example, Newco 2 will be equity financed to the level of 100% of the value of the Target's shares. If 70% of the shares are acquired, Newco 2 will have assets of 70 (Target shares) and 30 (cash) backed by 100 of equity. The "worth" of the Target will be 100 (assuming that the "worth" equals the market value of the shares), with minority shareholders holding 30 of this through their 30% stake. The value of the merged entity would be 100 (value of Target) plus 30 (amount of cash over and above the share value), rather than 200 (as counting the shares in the Target held by Newco would be "double-counting" net worth). Consequently, the minority shareholders would receive 30 (value of minority stake) divided by 130 (value of merged entity), expressed as a percentage, i.e. 23% of the merged entity.

12.25 JAPAN

Lease receivables and consumer loans were the historic mainstay of the Japanese market, under the securitisation-friendly provisions of the MITI Law (see below), from 1994 onwards. However, the announcement in November 1996 of the Big Bang deregulation of the Japanese financial markets and the publication on 31 March 1997 of resultant liberalisation proposals (affecting securitisation, and also the fund management and FX industries) led to significant growth in the CDO section of the securitisation market.

Over the course of 1997, bank balance sheet CDO issuance for Japanese financial institutions began to gather pace ahead of the financial year end on 31 March 1998. Securitisation of loans from US branches was particularly popular in order to ease transfer perfection requirements, as was contingent perfection (the use of which reduced with time due to scepticism from rating agencies) and subsequently, the declaration of trust technique used in the Aurora deal for Sumitomo in April 1998.

Heavy CDO issuance continued through 1998 and 1999, but the market for CDO issuance slowed down significantly in 2000, as government funds were injected to recapitalise the banking sector. Two failed banks were auctioned off, with the US group Ripplewood buying LTCB in 1999 and the Japanese consortium of Softbank, Orix Leasing and Tokio Marine buying Nippon Credit Bank in 2000. Following the recapitalisation, banks halted their asset disposal programmes, and put the extra capital to use with new corporate lending programmes focused on asset quality and better quality corporate credits, rather than shrinking their balance sheets with securitisation and focusing on return on equity.

As the CDO market slowed down, however, so the mortgage market opened up in 2000, with the Government Housing Loan Corporation (GHLC) (which accounts for 38% of the Japanese residential mortgage market), announcing in January 2000 its intent to securitise Yen 50bn of its residential mortgage portfolio (finally closed in March 2001), and several other significant MBS deals in 2000, including:

- The Yen 33bn issue from Mitsubishi Trust and Banking Corp deal, structured as a fixed-rate pass-through; and
- The Yen 211bn deal from Dai-Ichi Mutual Life Insurance.

In addition, activity in the CMBS market opened up significantly in 2000, with a multitude of domestic transactions.

From 2001 onwards, most sections of the market have seen growth, with issuance reaching US$ 26.8bn in 2001 (a 23% increase on issuance in 2000). Japan has seen the additional development of securitisation of unusual asset types not found elsewhere in the world, such as revolving consumer loans (similar in form to credit card receivables), other shopping loans (such as loans for the purchase of silk kimono) and non-performing loans. There has been little credit card activity, as cards are mostly paid off in full in Japan and do not generate significant finance charges. A planned J-REIT listing by Goldman Sachs of an US$ 800m property portfolio in November 2001 was pulled shortly before listing on the back of deteriorating real estate conditions.

In February 2001, the government announced new tougher measures whereby it could require banks to write-off outstanding non-performing loans by March 2001. Subsequent to this, several bank mergers were announced:

- MTFG – Mitsubishi Tokyo Financial Group (Bank of Tokyo Mitsubishi, Mitsubishi Trust & Banking) in April 2001
- SMFG – Sumitomo Mitsui Financial Group (Sakura Bank, Sumitomo Bank) in April 2001
- UFJ – United Financial of Japan (Sanwa Bank, Tokai Bank, Toyo Trust) in January 2002
- Mizuho (Dai-Ichi Kangyo Bank, Fuji Bank, Industrial Bank of Japan) in April 2002
- Resona (Asahi Bank, Daiwa Bank) in March 2003.

A challenge to the market was also launched in 2001, when a CMBS sale and leaseback transaction by Mycal was questioned in the bankruptcy of Mycal in November 2001. The bankruptcy trustee unsuccessfully challenged the true sale of the property on the basis that the leaseback rent was off-market. Despite this, in 2002 there was significant growth in MBS and also in CDOs once again, with issuance reaching US$ 40bn (up 49% on 2001). December 2001 saw the launch of Shinsei Bank's master trust funding CLO programme for its corporate loan book (which was entrusted with Yen 1.44

trillion, and an initial issuance of Yen 115bn) and September 2002 saw the massive Yen 1.27 trillion (over US$ 10bn) CuBic One deal for Mizuho, which comprised US$ 2bn in issued form below a super-senior default swap.

On 14 May 2003, Mizuho announced a plan to recover Yen 4.6 trillion (US$ 39.4bn) of its problem loans, forming a joint venture advisory vehicle with UBS, Morgan Stanley, Merrill Lynch, Deutsche Bank and Cerberus (each taking 6%) and the Development Bank of Japan (taking 10%). Mizuho will take the remaining 60%. The plan seems to be focused on helping to restructure loans to help improve cash flow from troubled borrowers, rather than on securitisation or disposals, although given the size of the book, it is likely that several solutions will be proposed.

On 17 May 2003 the government announced a rescue plan for Resona, recapitalising the bank to the extent of Yen 2 trillion (US$ 17bn), following its announcement that its capital adequacy ratio had fallen to 2%. The recapitalisation increases Resona's capital ratio to 10%.

Legislative history

Prior to 1992, the key legislation and notices relating to securitisation in Japan were largely restrictive of the securities markets and preventative of the development of securitisation. These included:

- Article 467 of the Civil Code of 1896 ("Article 467")
- The Law Regulating the Acceptance of Deposits and Interest (Law No.195 of 1945) (the "Shusshi-ho Law")
- The Securities and Exchange Law (Law No. 25 of 1948) (the "Securities and Exchange Law")
- The Lawyers Law (Law No. 205 of 1949) (the "Lawyers Law")
- Foreign Exchange and Foreign Trade Control Law (Law No. 228 of 1949) (the "FX Law")
- The Interest Rate Restriction Law (Law No. 100 of 1954) (the "IRRL")
- The Law Relating to Money Lending Business (Law No. 32 of 1983) (the "Money Lending Law")
- MOF Notice of 30 April 1992 on transfer of Bank Loans (the "1992 MOF Notice").

Since 1992, the climate has turned from regulatory measures to liberalisation measures that have assisted in the development of securitisation, such as:

- The Law Concerning Amendment of Laws for Reform of Securities Trading (Law No. 87 of 1992), which came into force on 1 April 1993 (the "1993 Additions")
- The Law Relating to the Regulation of the Business of Specified Claims (Law No. 77 of 1992), which came into force on 1 June 1993 (the "MITI Law")
- MOF Notice on Treatment of Asset-Backed Bonds Issued Outside Japan of 16 September 1994 (the "1994 Additions")
- Amendment allowing issuance of Bonds and CP backed by Specified Claims into the Japanese capital markets, which came into force on 1 April 1996.

The Japanese market in securitisation began to open up in 1993 and 1994 on the back of these liberalisations, and in particular due to the easier method for the transfer of receivables brought about by the MITI Law, which was sponsored by the Ministry of International Trade and Industry (MITI) (which regulates leasing and finance companies). The relaxation of securities regulations by the Ministry of Finance (MOF) (which regulates banks) cleared other obstacles:

Securities laws

Prior to the 1993 Additions, only a limited class of instruments qualified as "securities" (making them more easily marketable) under the Securities and Exchange Law. The 1993 Additions added commercial paper, housing loan trust interests and trust interests in a loan pool issued by a non-Japanese legal entity to this list. Under the 1994 Additions, the MOF agreed to the designation of bonds issued by offshore SPVs that are backed by Divided Claims under the MITI Law as foreign corporation corporate bonds under the Securities and Exchange Law and as qualifying as "securities". Such bonds may only be sold or resold outside Japan, or to institutional investors regulated by the MOF inside Japan. The J-Cars transaction of October 1994 marked the first transaction after the lifting of the ban and was structured as a repackaging of Divided Claims. This was expanded by the 1 April 1996 amendment allowing issuance of bonds and CP backed by Specified Claims into the Japanese capital markets.

Issuance has been helped by an ever-increasing raft of supportive legislation such as:

- The relaxation of the 1992 MOF Notice on 1 June 1997
- The Foreign Exchange and Foreign Trade Law, which came into force on 1 April 1998 (the "Trade Law")
- The Law on Securitisation of Specific Assets by an SPC, which came into force on 1 September 1998 (the "SPV Law")
- The Law Prescribing Exceptions to the Civil Code Requirements on Assignment of Claims (Law No. 104 of 1998), which came into force on 1 October 1998 (the "Perfection Law")
- The Law for Special Measures Relating to Debt Collection Business (Law No. 126 of 1998), which came into force in April 1999 (the "Servicing Law")
- The Law Relating to the Issue of Bonds by Finance Companies for Money Lending Business (Law No. 32 of 1999), which came into force in April 1999 (the "Bond Law")
- The Law to amend the Law Relating to Money Lending Business and others (Law No. 155 of 1999), which came into force on 1 June 2000 (the "1999 Amendment")
- The Chukan-houjin Law of 1 April 2002.

These legislative developments have cleared certain obstacles that previously limited deals:

Transfer of bank loans   Under the 1992 MOF Notice, transfers of bank loans in the domestic market required the consent of the debtor and could only be made to financial institutions and sophisticated institutional investors and not to an SPV, under MOF guidelines. These guidelines were relaxed, however, as part of the 31 March 1997 reforms, with the 1 June 1997 MOF amendment to their previous guidelines to the effect that SPVs are now permitted to purchase bank loans.

Transfers to a non-Japanese resident   Prior to 1 April 1998, transfers of receivables to a non-Japanese resident were required to be approved by the MOF under the FX Law, leading to the use of a Japanese branch of an offshore SPV (which was considered a Japanese resident for the purposes of the Law) as the receivables purchaser. As a loan by a Japanese resident to a non-Japanese resident also required prior notification to the MOF unless the loan was made in Yen, the Japanese branch typically funded itself by a Yen-denominated intra-company loan from its offshore head office. The requirement for MOF approval was replaced by a simple requirement to report the transfer under the Trade Law from 1 April 1998, and the requirement to notify the MOF unless the intra-company loan is in Yen was also dropped (although the Japanese branch structure is still typically used for withholding tax purposes (see below)).

Further amendments have also been brought in more recently, such as:

- The amendment of the SPV Law; and
- The creation of J-REITs by amendment to the Law Relating to Investment Trusts and Investment Corporations (the "Investment Trust Law")

both of which came into force in November 2000.

SPVs The SPV Law allowed for the establishment of a corporate entity with a minimum share capital of Yen 3m to undertake securitisation of receivables or real estate, or of trust interests relating to receivables or real estate, and to issue ABS, ABCP and preferred equity. The law was criticised, however, as it required the SPV to prepare a detailed outline of the transaction to be incorporated in the SPV's constitutive documents, and to register the plan with the Financial Rehabilitation Commission (FRC), which could take up to 2 months. The SPV could not dispose of assets or borrow outside the transaction outline, and the outline was difficult to amend, thus not allowing sufficient flexibility for changes in transactions. Furthermore, the law did not permit preferred equity to be established without voting rights, which prejudiced the bankruptcy remoteness of the structure. The amendment to the SPV Law reduced the minimum capital requirement further to Yen 100 000 and the requirement for FRC registration was reduced to a requirement for FRC notification of a plan (furthermore, the plan is no longer required to be included in the articles of the company, making amendments to the transaction outline easier to carry out). The SPV is now permitted to borrow, and preferred equity can be issued without voting rights attached.

Ring-fencing and true sale

Assignment of a receivable must be carried out in compliance with the law of the country of residence of the obligor. Notice of a transfer of receivables must be given to the underlying debtors in order for the transfer to be effective against third parties under Article 467; alternatively, the consent of the debtors to the transfer must be obtained. This notice should have a confirmed date stamp (*kakutei hizuke*) fixed by a notary, and should be sent by certified registered mail.

Alternatively, under the Perfection Law (The Law Prescribing Exceptions to the Civil Code Requirements on Assignment of Claims (Law No. 104 of 1998), which came into force on 1 October 1998), corporations may transfer certain types of receivables in a manner that is effective against third parties by registration of the transfer at the Legal Affairs Bureau, without a requirement to give notice (although notice must be given for the transfer to be effective against the debtors, and to prevent them exercising set-off rights). Detailed information is required about the receivables in the registration, including the identity of the obligors.

The MITI Law (The Law Relating to the Regulation of the Business of Specified Claims (Law No. 77 of 1992), which came into force on 1 June 1993) also provides an alternative route for the transfer by credit card and leasing finance companies of credit card and lease receivables and hire purchase/deferred purchase obligations (e.g. auto loans and shopping loans for specific purchases – but not general revolving consumer loans or credit card receivables) (Specified Claims or *tokutei saiken*). Transfer only requires publication of a general notice in a national daily newspaper, detailing the date of the transfer, the transferee and giving a general description of the Specified Claims. Transactions under the MITI Law may take the following forms: (i) the Assignment Method: a sale of Specified Claims to an SPV licensed as a Specified Claims Purchaser under the MITI Law, with the originator obtaining a "Basic Claim" (*kihon saiken*) to the price for the Specified Claims, which the originator then divides into "Divided Claims" (*koguchi saiken*) and sells to investors in its capacity as a licensed Divided Claims Distributor; (ii) the Trust Method: a transfer of Specified Claims to a trust, with the trustee (a trust bank licensed by the MOF) then marketing the resultant Divided Claims to investors on behalf of the originator (who receives the proceeds of sale); or (iii) the Partnership Method: a pooling of contributions by investors acting in the form of either: (a) a *tokumei kumiai* limited partnership governed by the Commercial Code; or (b) a *nini kumiai* unlimited partnership governed by the Civil Code, with the general (i.e. unlimited) partner/managing partner then purchasing the Specified Claims from the originator. Most public transactions to date have used the Trust Method, while most conduit structures have used the Assignment Method.

Transfers under the MITI Law and under the Perfection Law each carry certain advantages. The MITI Law can operate to perfect the transfer against the debtor and prevent future set-off rights accruing but requires approval over 60 days from the Structured Finance Institute of Japan. The Perfection Law means that expensive newspaper advertisements are not required each time that a further transfer into the deal is made (for example on revolving issuance) and no plan is required to be approved allowing transactions to be closed faster; however greater disclosure of information is required. Consequently, deals with MITI Law eligible assets and originators may seek to use a combination of the two regimes (a combination may also be appropriate where the assets being transferred are a mix of assets falling within the MITI Law scope, and those outside it).

There are three historic forms of mortgage product in Japan. The first type, the Mortgage Certificate (*teito shoken*), was created under the Mortgage Certificates Law (Law No. 15 of 1931) as a negotiable instrument issued by the Land Registration Office on behalf of the originator over a pool of residential or commercial mortgages. They are transferable by endorsement and delivery, but do not constitute securities under the Securities and Exchange Law (Law No. 25 of 1948). Furthermore, they are not limited recourse, and have full recourse back to the originator for defaults. A MOF Notice of 1974 introduced the second type, the Residential Mortgage Certificate (*jutaku teito shosho*). These instruments are issued by the originator against a homogeneous pool of mortgages, but are also not limited recourse, and have full recourse back to the originator for defaults. The third type, the Residential Mortgage Trust (*jutaku loan saiken shintaku*) was originally used in 1973, and is more akin to full securitisation. The originator places mortgages on trust with a trust bank, which then issues trust certificates to investors that can be structured as limited recourse.

Transfers of mortgages must be made to a bank or financial institution.

Terms in the receivables documentation that prohibit assignment or transfer by the originator of its rights under the contract, or require that the originator must obtain the consent of the relevant debtor in order to assign or transfer its rights under the contract, will prevent any assignment or transfer being effective unless the consent of the debtor to the transfer is in fact obtained.

Prohibitions on assignment are relatively common in Japanese contracts.

Future receivables   Future receivables were considered only to be assignable up to 12 months in advance, but a recent Supreme Court case has confirmed that they are generally assignable, provided that they are sufficiently identifiable.

Insolvency unwind   Transfers within a suspect period prior to the bankruptcy of the originator may be unwound if the originator knew that the sale would prejudice other creditors. Also, transfers within 1 month prior to the bankruptcy may be unwound unless the transferee can prove it did not know that the sale would prejudice other creditors of the originator.

Recharacterisation   A true sale characterisation under Japanese law is likely to depend on the intention of the parties, a transfer of material risks on the assets to the SPV, whether there is any obligation on the originator to repurchase the receivables, a fair value sale price viewed against historic norms, the degree to which the transfer has been perfected and the accounting treatment accorded to the transaction by the originator.

Substantive consolidation   Substantive consolidation may be applied where a company has no independent substance or where it is used for illegitimate purposes.

Moratorium/automatic stay   Moratorium-style proceedings exist in Japan.

Set-off

The debtor may accrue rights of set-off until he is notified of a transfer, even if the transfer is effected under the Perfection Law. Public notice under the MITI Law will, however, prevent any further set-off rights from accruing, as the notice perfects the transfer against the obligor as well as third parties. If the debtor has acknowledged the transfer without qualification, he is then precluded from asserting any set-off, even of accrued rights.

Onshore SPV

The SPV Law (the Law on Securitisation of Specific Assets by an SPC, which came into force on 1 September 1998) (as amended with effect from November 2000 – also known as the Asset Securitisation Law) allows for the establishment of a *tokutei mokuteki kaisha* corporate entity (or TMK) with a minimum share capital of Yen 100 000 (rather than the Yen 10m usually required for a *kabushiki kaisha* joint stock company) and a sole director, to undertake securitisation of a range of assets, including receivables or real estate, or of trust interests relating to receivables or real estate. The

SPV can issue ABS, ABCP and preferred equity. The SPV bears certain tax benefits and is primarily focused on the securitisation of real estate. The SPV cannot be listed. The SPV Law requires the SPV to prepare an outline of the transaction and to file it with the FRC. The SPV is permitted to borrow.

Amendments to the Investment Trust Law (the Law Relating to Investment Trusts and Investment Corporations) in effect from November 2000 introduce the concept of a J-REIT by permitting an investment trust or investment company to invest directly in real estate (prior to the amendment they were restricted to investing primarily in securities), and to act as an ongoing investor in real estate. The J-REIT will carry tax benefits and will be restricted in the activities it can carry out. The J-REIT must outsource all its activities, and must appoint an investment manager to manage its assets. The investment manager will be required to avoid entering into transactions that could give rise to a conflict of interest. The potential for conflicts of interest (and lack of historical track record for most managers) is a key area of concern for rating agencies.

The Chukan-houjin Law of April 2002 created the *chukan-houjin*, a non-profit-making entity that may be used in transactions as a holding entity in order to orphan an SPV for a transaction.

Foreign ownership

Prior notification to the MOF is required for a non-resident to acquire shares in a Japanese company in certain sectors such as utilities, weapons and broadcasting (for other sectors, only subsequent notification is required). Under the Securities and Exchange Law, acquisition of more than 5% of the shares in a listed company, and each subsequent change of 1% or more, must be reported to the MOF within 5 days.

Securities laws

The Securities and Exchange Law sets out a list of items that constitute "securities" and are subject to regulation by the MOF (items that are not listed are subject to selling restrictions on direct resale to other investors, which restrict their marketability), such as shares and bonds issued by Japanese corporations, commercial paper, housing loan trust interests, trust interests in a loan pool issued by a non-Japanese legal entity, bonds issued by offshore SPVs that are backed by Divided Claims (such offshore bonds may only be sold or resold outside Japan, or to institutional investors regulated by the MOF inside Japan). Instruments issued by an SPV created under the SPV Law are also classed as securities.

The transfer of subordinated Divided Claims retained by the originator may be restricted under the terms of the deal, in order to ensure that the originator continues to have an interest in keeping a deal performing.

Investment in the Divided Claims created under a MITI law structure requires approval. If the investors are "specified investors" (investors with a minimum of Yen 500m share capital, or are financial institutions), then approval can be sought under Article 6 of MITI Law (which may take 1 month). For an investment by investors with less than Yen 500m capital, MITI and Structured Finance Institute of Japan (SFIJ) approval must be sought under Article 3, which may take 2 months, and requires that the transaction credit enhancement is at least the greater of 10% or 5 times historical default levels. Consequently, many deals set up a further SPV with Yen 500m share capital (typically injected by way of redeemable preference shares) to act as Divided Claims investor, which then issues offshore bonds backed by the Divided Claims. The capital is then used to fund a reserve account, or transaction expenses, and is paid back on a subordinated basis at the end of the deal. Although such an SPV is typically set up in the Cayman Islands, use of the SPV for multiple deals may still be subject to rating scrutiny in relation to limited recourse and ring-fencing provisions, in the event that attempts are made to wind the SPV up in Japan. Japanese companies must have a minimum share capital of Yen 1bn in order to issue bonds.

The Tokyo Stock Exchange published listing rules for J-REIT corporations in early 2001, requiring that:

- Property must constitute at least 75% of the portfolio of a J-REIT and that the remaining 25% must constitute cash or equivalent.
- The majority of the investment portfolio must consist of long-term investments in cash-generating properties.
- An independent real estate valuer must appraise asset values on acquisition and sale.
- Major transactions must be disclosed when booked.

Tax treatment

Stamp/registration/etc.   Nominal stamp duty is charged on an assignment. There are no other transfer taxes on the assignment of receivables. Significant property registration and acquisition taxes exist on the acquisition of real estate. These are reduced under the new SPV Law. They are also reduced under the J-REIT provisions.

Withholding tax   The interest element of collections on Japanese receivables is subject to withholding tax if paid to an offshore company, but can be paid free of withholding to a Japanese company or a branch or permanent establishment of an offshore company (provided that the company obtains a tax exemption certificate from the district tax office, and delivers it to the originator). In many transactions the transfer is made to the Japanese branch of an offshore SPV which funds itself intra-company from its offshore head office (intra-company arrangements are not generally subject to withholding). For these purposes, a trust is likely to be regarded as a pass-through, such that a trust certificate holder is regarded as a part-owner of the trust assets.

Withholding tax is charged on interest payments on loans or bonds to offshore investors (but not on discount or redemption premium). Bond withholding is only charged where the SPV is a Japanese corporation (which entails having a head office in Japan), whereas loans will be subject to the withholding if the loan relates to the business of the SPV in Japan (hence, issuance of bonds by a Cayman SPV is less likely to become subject to Japanese withholding than borrowing under a loan). Bonds are at risk of being recharacterised as loans if they are not transferable, or are not widely distributed.

Double tax treaties between Japan and countries where investors are located have two effects on this basic position:

- Issuance on a discount basis benefits from discount not being subject to withholding tax under Japanese law, but it may lose this beneficial treatment under the

OECD model double tax treaty (the benefit is maintained under the Japan/US double tax treaty, and hence still works for conduit CP issuance through a US conduit); and

- Where a bond is issued in connection with a permanent establishment of the issuer in Japan, the source of income on bond interest payments is regarded as being Japan, with the result that withholding tax will apply to the payments at the rate relevant between Japan and the country of the investor.

Consequently, structures may consist of:

- The SPV, which acquires the Specified Claims (if the Assignment Method under the MITI Law is used) or receivables;
- The second SPV, which acquires the Divided Claims through a Japanese branch and funds itself intra-company through its offshore branch (and may have Yen 500m of share capital to overcome securities laws approval requirements on the purchase of Divided Claims as set out above) and issues bonds; and
- The third SPV, which acts as investor in the bonds (and is set up in a jurisdiction that does not have a double tax treaty with Japan, so that the Japan source rules do not apply) and issues notes into the market.

This final link enables the adverse look-through withholding tax treatment contained in double tax treaties between Japan and the jurisdictions of the ultimate investors to be displaced (the final link would be unnecessary for an issue at a discount to a US investor such as a Delaware conduit).

Article 6 of the Special Taxation Measures Law adopted on 5 December 1997 (which applied to securities issued on or after 1 April 1998 and before 31 March 2000) allowed issuers and paying agents to pay interest free of withholding on securities issued outside Japan by Japanese corporations, certain Japanese government agencies and (for securities not denominated in Yen) the Japanese government, where the noteholder: (i) was a beneficial owner who is not an individual resident of Japan or a Japanese corporation for Japanese tax purposes; (ii) fell within a class of designated Japanese financial institutions (broadly, Japanese banks, securities houses and insurance companies) holding for its own account; or (iii) was an individual resident of Japan or a Japanese corporation for Japanese tax purposes who receives interest through a payment handling agent in Japan.

Profits tax   The originator will be liable to tax on any capital gain on sale of receivables. An originator may not be permitted to deduct losses incurred on non-performing loans for tax purposes where they still hold the equity piece in the deal.

A Japanese SPV will be liable to corporation tax in Japan. Japanese SPVs under the new SPV Law which distribute more than 90% of earnings to shareholders as dividends, and which meet certain other conditions, are permitted to deduct such distributions as a loss against income for corporation tax purposes.

J-REITs will also be permitted to deduct dividends against income for corporation tax purposes provided that they distribute more than 90% of earnings to shareholders as dividends (which may give rise to requirements for liquidity facilities for the J-REIT). J-REITs will not be free of tax on contributions of assets to the J-REIT in the manner of the UPREIT in the US (to which assets can be contributed at book value without triggering a tax charge), which may generate capital gains tax charges for originators.

A Japanese branch of an offshore SPV will be liable to tax on Japanese source income (including income from Japanese receivables), with permitted deductions for reasonable expenses relating to the business carried on in Japan, including fees paid to the originator. Interest expenses to investors on head office finance can be deducted (the use of proceeds of the issue should be clearly stated to be for intra-company finance to the Japanese branch). Losses arising from defaults can only be deducted provided that enforcement of the debts is properly pursued.

Controlled foreign corporation legislation may attribute any profits made by an offshore SPV to Japanese shareholders, whether or not distributed. In addition, thin capitalisation rules may disallow a deduction for interest expenses of the SPV to off-shore investors, where debt incurred by the SPV exceeds three times equity and the debtholders of the SPV are also shareholders in the SPV (this can be applied on a look-through basis, so that setting up a dual-SPV structure with the same shareholders (e.g. the same charitable trustee) for both SPVs may lead to thin capitalisation issues).

Accounting treatment

Guidelines on the derecognition of transferred assets, which apply from April 2000, require a perfected transfer and the lack of a right or obligation for the originator to repurchase the assets.

The Institute of Certified Public Accountants published principles for accounting for transfers of real estate to SPVs completed after 30 September 2000. The principles require that the originator seeking to obtain off-balance-sheet treatment for a transfer of assets retain not more than 5% of the risks and rewards associated with the assets, which was seen as likely to lead to development of a market in real estate mezzanine pieces in order to reduce the equity to 5% or less. Consequently, different accounting rules apply for real estate and non-real estate transactions.

Capital treatment

Assets may be transferred off the capital balance sheet by means of an assignment or a funded sub-participation, but an unfunded risk participation will not be considered a transfer. An MOF notice of June 1995 sets out three requirements for off-balance-sheet treatment for a sub-participation. The sub-participation must: (a) identify the loans clearly and make the sub-participants subject to the same terms as the loans; (b) release the originator from all risk and all benefit under the loans; and (c) not give the originator any obligation or right to repurchase the sub-participated loans.

Prior to March 1997, transfers of bank loans in the domestic market required the consent of the debtor and could only be made to financial institutions and sophisticated institutional investors and not to an SPV, under MOF guidelines. These guidelines were relaxed, however, as part of the 31 March 1997 reforms, and on 1 June 1997 the MOF issued an amendment to their previous guidelines to the effect that SPVs are now permitted to purchase bank loans.

The MOF released short credit derivative guidelines in December 1998, followed by more detailed rules released by the Bankers Association of Japan in March 1999, which duplicate the rules released by the FSA in the UK.

Data protection/confidentiality

Banks are subject to a general duty of confidentiality. The Law on the use of Personal Information was enacted on 23 May 2003, which provides for personal information held by a business to be kept secure and not disclosed to third parties without the consent of the person to whom the information relates.

Consumer protection

Consumer finance companies regulated under the Money Lending Law (the Law Relating to Money Lending Business (Law No. 32 of 1983)) are required to notify borrowers on each occasion that their receivables are transferred (which, on a revolving receivable, would include the date of each new drawdown). Due to the onerous nature of this requirement, originators considering securitisation of consumer assets have taken steps to change their standard form contracts to provide for consent by the customer to transfer of receivables, in order to obviate the need for such notification.

Regulatory approvals

An SPV buying Specified Claims under the MITI Law is required to be licensed with the MITI under the MITI Law, and will be subject to monitoring. The originator in such a structure is required to obtain a license as a Divided Claims Distributor. A plan setting out receivables collection and investor repayment details is required to be produced jointly by the originator and the SPV and submitted to the Structured Finance Institute of Japan and to MITI, which have 60 days to review it and require changes. Any transfer of receivables to a non-Japanese resident is required to be reported to the MOF.

Non-bank finance companies (including leasing and credit card finance companies) were until recently prohibited from raising funding for their lending activities via an issue of bonds or commercial paper to a large number of investors under Article 2 of the Shusshi-ho Law (the Law Regulating the Acceptance of Deposits and Interest (Law No. 195 of 1945)). It has been argued on a number of transactions that this provision should not affect securitisations, where the SPV (rather than the originator) is the issuing vehicle, but in any event the proceeds of the issue that are on-lent to the originator may still not be available to make fresh loans, limiting the potential uses for a securitisation issue to capital investment. The prohibition was relaxed in April 1999 under the Bond Law (the Law Relating to the Issue of Bonds by Finance Companies for Money Lending Business (Law No. 32 of 1999), which came into force in April 1999), such that a finance company may use the proceeds of a deal to make fresh loans, where it registers as a "specified financial institution" with the FRC and complies with detailed disclosure requirements set out in the Bond Law.

Other issues

Floating charges are not recognised under Japanese law, but a pledge over a fluctuating pool is possible if the pledged assets can be specified. Fixed charges over a bank account are difficult to obtain. A security interest can only be granted to a creditor; thus a charge to a trustee is not possible, except under the provisions of the Secured Bond Trust Law (Law No. 52 of 1905) on secured bonds.

Japan imposes a usury restriction on interest rates chargeable on loans of 15% (loans for Yen 1m or more), 18% (loans for Yen 100 000 to Yen 1m) or 20% (loans for less than Yen 100 000) (or 30% to 40% for default interest – reducing to 21.9% to 29.2% from 1 June 2000 under the 1999 Amendment), depending on the nature of the loan in question. Any amounts charged in excess of the limit are not enforceable, except by consumer finance companies regulated under the Money Lending Law where the company meets certain notice and procedural requirements set out in the Money Lending Law (both on execution of the loan, and each time a repayment is made) and the borrower makes payment of the excess over the threshold voluntarily. There are questions over the ability of lenders to fully comply with these requirements, and rating agencies may not give credit for amounts charged in excess of the limit in a default scenario. It is a criminal offence under the Shusshi-ho Law for any consumer finance company regulated under the Money Lending Law to set an interest rate on a loan in excess of a higher limit of 40.004% (29.2% from 1 June 2000 under the 1999 Amendment) set out in the Shusshi-ho Law.

The originator is required to act as servicer of any transaction under the MITI Law to protect individual debtors, and can only be terminated for justifiable cause. In addition the Lawyers Law (Law No. 205 of 1949) requires generally that only the creditor itself or a lawyer can be appointed to collect and enforce debts where payment of the debt is in default (which can lead to issues with appointing the originator as servicer after it has sold receivables and is no longer the creditor, or with the appointment of a back-up servicer, or of a special servicer for non-performing loan transactions). The Servicing Law (the Law for Special Measures Relating to Debt Collection Business (Law No. 126 of 1998), which came into force in April 1999) allows entities with at least Yen 500m share capital and a lawyer on their board to apply for licences to act as servicers of third-party receivables other than consumer receivables.

A sale of a significant portion of the assets of a Japanese originator will require its board approval.

Real estate in Japan is subject to numerous taxes and regulations, and the involvement of banks in the real estate market has historically been limited.

Residential mortgages in Japan are often granted in favour of a guarantee company, which then issues a guarantee to the mortgage lender of the borrower's obligations under the mortgage loan. The consequence of this is that the mortgage loan is in fact guaranteed but unsecured. Analysis may be required to show that if the mortgage lender calls the guarantee in relation to a defaulted borrower and the guarantor is bankrupt at such time, the mortgage lender is able to enforce the mortgage granted to the guarantor company. For example, the MBS deal from Dai-Ichi Mutual Life Insurance in 2000 contributed the security rights of the guarantor in favour of the trust holding the mortgage loans.

Japanese tenants have the ability to request from their landlord a decrease in rent on their leases under the Land Lease Law, in the event of economic conditions worsening or property/rental values falling. If the landlord does not agree a decrease, the tenant is entitled to seek court action. Since March 2000, the tenant may waive these rights.

12.26 KOREA

The Korean market was poised to open up in late 1997, but multiple transactions were postponed following the downgrade to speculative grade of the sovereign's foreign currency rating in the aftermath of the Asian crisis. The Korea Asset Management Corporation (KAMCO) (a government entity established to manage distressed assets of Korean financial institutions) acquired a significant volume of non-performing assets from the financial sector for sale or securitisation. It achieved a sale price of around 13% of par for its first auction of some of these assets towards the end of 1998, and subsequently achieved significantly greater values of up to 50% of par on further sales. KAMCO issued multiple securitisations of non-performing loans in 1999 and 2000. Typically, KAMCO acquires assets on a recourse basis with a put back to the seller institution.

The Korean Mortgage Corporation (KOMOCO) was established in October 1999 under the MBS Law by the Korean government, a group of Korean financial institutions and the International Finance Corporation with capital of Won 100bn to develop the MBS market in Korea by buying mortgages and packaging them for sale as MBS. It closed the first mortgage securitisation in Korea in March 2000.

The government-owned Korea Land Corporation (KoLand) was also active in securitising land sales receipts on a domestic basis throughout 1999.

Korea First Bank was bought by Newbridge Capital (the US private equity house) at the end of 1999, with the planned acquisition of Seoulbank by HSBC falling through.

Although cross-border issuance has grown, the market has been led by significant domestic issuance in 1999 (US$ 5.9bn), 2000 (US$ 43bn) and 2001 (US$ 39bn) following passing of the ABS Law in September 1998, making the Korean market the largest market in Asia excluding Japan.

In 2001, multiple domestic deals were issued that developed the market, in particular from Samsung (credit card and auto loan deals), Kookmin (credit cards) and LG (credit cards), as well as the first non-supported NPL deal (packaging via the Resurgence Korea vehicle loans acquired by Morgan Stanley). Cross-border issues also appeared. Many issues have been consumer credit oriented, following the rapid growth in the Korean credit card market from 1999 onwards. Consumer credit marketing was targeted on a wider basis than previously, giving rise to higher delinquency rates going forward.

In April 2002, the Financial Supervisory Commission stopped Samsung Card and LG Card opening new accounts for a 2-month period, following a sharp upward spike in reported charge-offs on credit cards in excess of 13% in the second quarter of 2002.

The market has since seen fall-out in 2003 from spread widening following accounting issues at SK Global under which it had overstated its earnings. On 3 April 2003, the Korean government announced plans to recapitalise credit card companies. A report by Moody's in February 2003 illustrates, however, that delinquencies and charge-offs have been lower on rated credit card deals than in the market generally, due to seasoning and performance data requirements for collateral in rated deals.

The first cross-border Korean RMBS deal priced in early December 2002 from Samsung Life – a US$ 299.6m deal through the Bichumi Global I SPV. Due to the significant market share held by the two main mortgage lenders – Kookmin Bank and the National Housing Fund – further development here may depend on their view of the product.

Lehman announced a significant investment in Korea in May 2002, with a US$ 250m equity purchase in Woori Financial (the distressed banks group set up by the government after the Asian crisis), and a US$ 750 investment in a joint venture to sell Woori's NPLs ahead of Woori's listing.

The Republic of Korea has a civil law system derived from French and German law principles. Legislation to simplify the issuance of asset-backed securities was passed by the National Assembly in the form of a new ABS Law in September 1998. An MBS Law was also passed in April 1999, which provides for the establishment of mortgage companies.

Ring-fencing and true sale

Under the Korean Civil Code, for a transfer of receivables to be effective against third parties in Korea the transfer must be notified to debtors and be notarised with a fixed date. It may be possible for notice to be given in the form of a general notice on an account statement, and it may be possible to avoid notice requirements where the receivable is evidenced by a promissory note issued by the debtor to the originator, as promissory notes are freely transferable without notice.

The ABS Law introduces a simplified procedure where the originator is:

- A Korean financial institution; or
- One of certain government-related entities (including KAMCO, KDB and KoLand); or
- A Korean or overseas institution that is approved by the Financial Supervisory Commission (the FSC) (these were originally restricted to investment grade companies, but may be extended to include BB-rated companies).

The law provides that if a transfer of receivables is registered with the FSC, it will be enforceable against third parties from the date of registration.

Notice to the debtor is still required for the transfer to be enforceable against the debtor under Article 7 of the ABS Law, but the law allows for notice to be given by way of advertisement in two newspapers in the event that formal notification has been tried and has failed at least twice.

Article 8 of the ABS Law provides that mortgages will be transferred automatically if the underlying receivables are transferred, upon registration of the transfer with the FSC, and that real estate will be automatically transferred for securitisations of non-performing loans by KAMCO or KoLand.

Mortgages in Korea are often in the form of a kun-mortgage (an all-monies mortgage that can cover a revolving debt). These mortgages were hard to transfer, due to a ruling by the Supreme Court in Korea that only mortgages for a stated amount could be transferred, until the amendment of the ABS Law in January 2000. The amendment provided that kun-mortgages could be transferred provided that the debtor had been notified that no further advances would be made to him under the loan and had been given 10 days to object to the transfer to the SPV.

Future receivables   Future receivables that can be identified with reasonable certainty may be transferred.

Insolvency unwind   A transfer may be unwound under s. 406 of the Civil Code if the assignee is aware that the transfer would prejudice the creditors of the assignor (for example, as an undervalue).

Recharacterisation   Under general Korean law, the potential for recharacterisation of a transfer as a secured loan is unclear, and could occur where the originator retains a right to profit on the assets under a subordinated loan or a right or obligation to repurchase the assets, or if the transfer otherwise resembles a secured loan. The issue of subordinated notes to the originator, or the use of deferred purchase price, are viewed more favourably, and are the most commonly used methods of structuring deals.

The ABS Law clarified true sale characterisation for transactions under the law by providing that, in order for a true sale to occur: (a) the transfer must be made by a written sale contract; (b) the buyer must have the right to profits on the assets, and the right to sell the assets; (c) the seller must not have the right to require repurchase of the assets; and (d) the buyer must assume all risk on the assets except for a limited period or in respect of warranties on sale. However, the definition of "risk" here remains unclear when considering credit enhancement to be provided by the originator. The ability to use subordinated loans remains uncertain, although the purchase of subordinated notes is regarded as less of an issue.

Moratorium/automatic stay   Moratorium-style proceedings exist in Korea.

Set-off

The underlying debtors may continue to assert pre-notification set-off rights unless they have given their consent to the assignment.

Onshore SPV

The ABS Law provides for the establishment of a Korean SPV that can undertake activities limited to those connected to a securitisation transaction (including the issuance of debt securities). The SPV is required to outsource all its activities to third parties.

The MBS Law passed in April 1999 provides for the establishment of FSC-approved mortgage companies with share capital of Won 25m, and provides that these companies will be subject to the same benefits as companies established under the ABS Law.

Due to the restrictive nature of the security interests that can be created under the Secured Bond Trust Act 1962 in respect of note issues, and other limiting regulatory requirements, in most deals to date a two-tier structure has been used, where the first (Korean) SPV purchases the assets with an onward sale to the second (Cayman) SPV. More recent deals have also used trust structures – e.g. for credit card deals and transactions where further issuance is intended – with transfer into a Korean trust which then issues trust interests to a Korean SPV and the originator (with the Korean SPV then funding itself through a Cayman SPV).

Foreign ownership

Following the Asian currency crisis of late 1997, the limit on foreign ownership of a Korean company was increased to 55% (with a maximum holding of 50% by a single foreign investor) in December 1997, and increased to 100% for many company sectors (excluding politically sensitive sectors) on 25 May 1998. Acquisitions of more than 5% in a listed company and each subsequent change must be notified to the FSC and the stock exchange.

Securities laws

The Commercial Code prohibits Korean companies from issuing debt in excess of a 4 : 1 debt to equity ratio. Korean SPVs under the ABS Law are exempt from this provision. The approval of the MOF is required for the issuance of short-term (less than 1 year) securities.

Tax treatment

Stamp/registration/etc.   Assignments are usually not subject to stamp duty, and any duty that does arise may be avoided by ensuring that documentation is not executed within Korea. Assignment notarisation costs are nominal. Registration tax is charged on the acquisition of real estate, but there is an exemption for acquisitions under the ABS Law prior to 31 December 2003 under provisions of the Tax Exemption and Limitation Law.

Withholding tax   Korea charges withholding tax on Korean source income unless the payee is a Korean SPV established under the ABS Law. Withholding tax is also charged on interest paid offshore at 25%, unless reduced by tax treaty provisions. Ireland has a double taxation treaty with Korea under which this withholding is reduced to 0%. Interest paid by a Korean SPV under the ABS Law to offshore investors is not subject to withholding tax.

Profits tax   An offshore SPV should not become liable to Korean profits tax unless it has a permanent establishment in Korea, which may include an agent in Korea, but should not include the appointment of the originator as servicer for the collection of receivables. A Korean SPV under the ABS Law is liable to profits tax in Korea, but can claim a deduction for dividends if it pays out 90% or more of its distributable profits. There was a reduction of the capital gains tax charge for gains on real estate acquired by an SPV under the ABS Law prior to 31 December 2000.

VAT   SPVs under the ABS Law are exempt from VAT.

Capital treatment

Companies established under the MBS Law are subject to minimum capital requirements. In 2002, risk weightings for mortgages were increased from 50% to 60% if:

1. They are 30 days past due; or
2. The total number of days past due in a year exceeds 30; or
3. The debt-to-annual income ratio of the borrower exceeds 250%.

If the loan falls into 3 as well as either 1 or 2, the risk weighting is increased to 70%.

Data protection/confidentiality

There is a duty on banks to keep customer information confidential, unless the customer has consented to the disclosure. The ABS Law permits disclosure of performance data by the originator and the SPV to relevant parties.

Regulatory approvals

The approval of the MOF is required for any transfer of receivables to an offshore entity. Loans from non-resident lenders may give rise to reporting requirements with the MOF under the Foreign Exchange Transaction Acts. Approval is required from the MOF for any loan from a non-resident lender to be redeemed in whole or part within 1 year of being granted.

The ABS Law requires a plan to be registered with and approved by the FSC, giving details of the receivables and of the securities to be issued, as well as the main documents for the deal.

Other issues

The Secured Bond Trust Act only permits bonds to be secured over certain asset types (many domestic deals are issued on an unsecured basis as a result). It is uncertain whether non-petition provisions would be enforceable in Korea. Securitisations carried out under the ABS Law are required under Article 10 of the Law to use a servicer which is one of the same institutions as the potential originators under the law – in other words, a Korean financial institution, one of certain government-related entities, or a Korean or overseas institution which is approved by the Financial Supervisory Commission (the FSC).

12.27   LUXEMBOURG

Luxembourg introduced provisions for the establishment of mortgage banks in a 1997 law.

Ring-fencing and true sale

Covered bonds   A new law of 21 November 1997 provides for the establishment of *banques d'emission de lettres de gage* (mortgage bond issuing banks), which must be domiciled in Luxembourg. They are restricted activity institutions which can issue bonds backed by a pool of mortgages (*lettres de gage hypothecaires*) or by a pool of public sector loan assets (*lettres de gage publiques*) on a ring-fenced basis comparable to Pfandbriefe. The first issue under the law was completed in January 2000.

The asset pool can consist of assets from throughout the OECD, EU or EEA. For mortgage bonds, the portfolio cannot include mortgages with an LTV in excess of 60% (for commercial or residential property). *Lettres de gage* carry a 10% regulatory capital weighting.

Tax treatment

Withholding tax   Luxembourg does not charge withholding tax on interest payments.

Other issues

The effectiveness under Luxembourg law of an interest in collateral taken by means of an outright transfer of ownership was confirmed under a law of 1 August 2001, provided that at least one party to the transfer is a finance industry professional and that there is some Luxembourg nexus for the transaction (such as a Luxembourg account for the collateral).

12.28   MALAYSIA

There has long been the potential for Malaysia to be a significant securitisation market, but it was not until October 1999 that the first Ringgit-denominated deal was completed on a quasi-securitisation basis.

Cagamas Berhad is the Malaysian mortgage corporation and funds itself through capital markets issuance. Its issuance is not directly linked to assets (mortgages and housing loans) it acquires. Since January 2003, Cagamas has also acquired other non-housing receivables. Establishment of Danaharta Nasional Berhad as a wholly-owned government entity to purchase non-performing assets from the financial sector was announced in May 1998. Danaharta Nasional Berhad was established with an initial seed capital of M$ 50m and intended working capital of M$ 25bn, and had circa M$ 5.5bn of rehabilitated loans by early 2001. Danamodal Nasional Berhad was established in 1998 to finance bank recapitalisation; the first issue from Danamodal Nasional Berhad was placed in October 1998.

A plan to strengthen the Malaysian financial system in advance of liberalisation and increasing globalisation was commenced with an announcement of the merger of the 58 banking institutions in the Malaysian financial sector into six "anchor" banks, which was put forward by the Malaysian government. The plan was dropped in October 1999 to give the institutions a chance to merge voluntarily into groups. In April 2000, the Securities Commission announced a similar consolidation for the securities sector, requiring the existing 63 brokers to merge into 15 groups by the end of 2000 and to meet capital adequacy requirements.

There was an increase in issuance in 2001, with the first Asian whole business-style deal completed for 1st Silicon in June 2001, and the M$ 255m Prisma Asset CBO for

Arab-Malaysian Merchant Bank in July 2001. In 2002, the market saw an Islamic financing for the Republic of Malaysia in July for the Federal Lands Commissioner under a sale and leaseback structure via Malaysia Global Sukuk, and Affin Bank issued an unusual CLO deal in November through the Aegis One vehicle – a M$ 1bn primary market CLO under which the SPV lends money directly to end borrowers.

The first auto loan deal was seen in February 2003, with the Auto ABS One deal for Bumiputra Commerce Finance.

Malaysia operates a common law system, historically based on English law.

Malaysia introduced extensive currency controls on 1 September 1998 in an attempt to limit the effect of speculative activities on the Malaysian currency and economy, by pegging the Ringgit at M$ 3.80 to US$ 1 and requiring Ringgit held outside Malaysia to be repatriated within a month (in default of which it would be declared void and no longer legal tender). A requirement for central bank approval was introduced for many FX-related activities. Proceeds from the sale of Malaysian stocks were not permitted to be repatriated overseas until 1 September 1999. On 4 February 1999, the regime was relaxed by permitting the repatriation of proceeds of equity sales subject to payment of an exit tax. The exit tax was abolished in May 2001.

In 1999, Bank Negara Malaysia (BNM), the central bank, released guidelines on securitisation.

On 11 April 2001 securitisation guidelines were published by the Securities Commission which require a high level of detail to be provided prior to transactions being approved. New guidelines were published on 1 April 2003.

Ring-fencing and true sale

Receivables may be transferred by equitable assignment without the need to give notice to debtors of the transfer. Terms in the receivables documentation which prohibit assignment or transfer by the originator of its rights under the contract, or which require that the originator must obtain the consent of the relevant debtor in order to assign or transfer its rights under the contract, will prevent any assignment or transfer being effective unless the consent of the debtor to the transfer is obtained.

Future receivables   A transfer of future receivables may be void in bankruptcy in respect of receivables which have not yet arisen.

Insolvency unwind   The Bankruptcy Act 1967 provides at s. 53 that payments made within 6 months prior to bankruptcy are deemed to be preferential and may be void.

Set-off

The debtor can obtain good discharge by making payments to the originator until notice of the assignment is given to the debtor, at which point the debtor is obliged to pay to the SPV direct. The SPV will take subject to any defects in the title of the originator, and until notice is given to the debtor, the SPV is subject to any further equities (such as set-off) arising in favour of the debtor through relations between the originator and the debtor subsequent to the assignment.

Foreign ownership

Foreign ownership of more than 30% of the voting rights, or more than 15% by a single entity, requires the prior approval of the Foreign Investment Committee. Acquisitions of more than 2% in a listed company and each subsequent change must be notified to the stock exchange and to the company.

Securities laws

The Securities Commission of Malaysia published guidelines on securitisation on 11 April 2001 (and revised guidelines on 1 April 2003), which apply to any person issuing ABS. The guidelines require the issuer to submit an application to the Securities Commission for approval of the securitisation issue declaring their compliance with the requirements set out in the guidelines, together with a preliminary rating report, a legal opinion on true sale and a valuation report (if the securitised assets are real estate). The Commission will give its approval within 28 days of receipt of all the documentation.

The guidelines contain a lengthy set of requirements as to the structure and integrity of the transaction, including requirements as to:

- True sale
- Bankruptcy remoteness of the SPV
- Disclosure and the contents of the information memorandum
- Servicing.

There is also a requirement that the SPV must be tax resident in Malaysia.

Tax treatment

Stamp/registration/etc.   Stamp duty is charged on transfers at up to 4% of the amount transferred. Stamp duty is charged on a sale of shares at 0.3% on the sale price. Documents may be executed and held outside Malaysia to delay triggering the stamp tax charge on the transfer of receivables until the documents are brought into Malaysia for enforcement against the relevant debtor (if necessary). Alternately, the sale may be carried out on an "acceptance by payment" basis, where the only written documentation for the transfer is an offer, which is then accepted by payment from the SPV to the originator, without any actual stampable transfer documentation being produced.

The transfer of assets under a securitisation was proposed to be exempted from stamp duty for the year 2000 to encourage issuance.

Withholding tax   Interest paid offshore is subject to 15% withholding tax.

Accounting treatment

It is likely that UK or US accounting standards would be followed.

Capital Treatment

In 1999 BNM issued detailed guidelines on securitisation in Malaysia. These are similar to the guidelines of the FSA in the UK. They provide that the assets must be sold in a true sale which isolates them from the originator's credit risk and/or control in order to exclude them from the capital balance sheet of the originator, which would prevent off-balance-sheet transfers via sub-participation.

The SPV must be independent and bankruptcy remote. The originator is permitted to retain a repurchase option for fully performing assets, either to fund further advances or as a clean-up call. Replenishment of assets is permitted, provided it does not have a material effect on the credit quality of either the securitised pool or the originator's remaining assets. The guidelines envisage the originator providing "first loss" or "second loss" credit enhancement (against a direct capital deduction) and/or liquidity facilities.

Data protection/confidentiality

Banks are subject to a general duty of confidentiality with regard to information relating to their customers. Consent to disclosure may be granted by BNM. The 1999 BNM guidelines (see above) also require observance of these secrecy provisions.

Regulatory approvals

Approval must be sought from the BNM for securitisations by financial institutions in Malaysia. All ABS issued in Malaysia must be approved by the Securities Commission.

Other issues

Malaysian financial assets may be structured as non-interest bearing Islamic loans.

12.29   MEXICO

The first Mexican MBS deal was issued by Hipotecaria Su Casita in August 2001.

Securities laws

The Securities Market Law of June 2001 regulates the issuance of securities in Mexico.

Accounting treatment

US accounting standards are followed.

12.30   THE NETHERLANDS

Securitisation issuance in the Netherlands has been consistently high relative to the size of the economy, making it one of the leading European markets, which includes large mortgage deals (such as the Euro 2.5bn European Mortgage Securities III issue launched by ABN Amro in September 1999) and repeat issuers. The Netherlands also continues to be an important jurisdiction for the establishment of SPVs for non-

Dutch transactions, due to the lack of withholding tax in the Netherlands and wide range of double tax treaties which the Netherlands has with other countries (particularly within the EU).

The Netherlands operates a civil law system.

Ring-fencing and true sale

Prior to 1992, the transfer of receivables governed by Dutch law was not required to be notified to debtors to be effective against third parties. In the new Dutch Civil Code of 1992, however, a requirement to notify debtors of a transfer in order for it to be effective was added. Transfers of receivables with international elements may be made under the law of a country which does not require notice to be given, following a court ruling in May 1997 enabling such transfers to choose the law governing them.

In May 2003 a bill was submitted to the Dutch parliament for implementation in early 2004, which would reverse the 1992 Civil Code amendments, and would provide for transfers to be made by a registered deed of assignment. The deed would not need to be notified to the debtor in order to be effective (although the debtor may continue to pay to the assignor until notified).

Methods of circumventing the 1992 restriction have included the use of a two-tiered structure. The first transfer would be to an SPV which is bankruptcy remote save for the fact that it is a subsidiary of the originator, with the transfer notified to debtors as an inter-group transfer to minimise the commercial impact of notice. There would then be an onward transfer to an orphan SPV without notice to debtors.

As another method, many Dutch transactions have used a conditional sale (i.e. an assignment which has not been notified) to transfer receivables; in order to protect the SPV and the bondholders from the risk of losing claim to the receivables on the insolvency of the originator, financial and/or credit rating triggers are set which are designed to enable notification to be carried out prior to insolvency if the originator begins to experience financial difficulties. As further protection, the sale agreement may include a penalty payable by the originator in the event that the transfer is not effective. The penalty is in an amount equal to the amount of the receivables and accrued interest, and is supported by a pledge granted by the originator over the receivables. Although the pledge is not notified, it is capable of being notified after insolvency and still being valid.

Under a July 2002 regulation, Dutch non-bank corporate borrowers must ensure that their debt is owned by professional market parties at all times. From 12 February 2003, any company which has a credit rating, or has issued rated securities, is considered to be a professional market party for this purpose (thus including most SPVs). The 2002 regulation also covers notes issued by a Dutch SPV (unless held in a clearing system).

Terms in the receivables documentation which prohibit assignment or transfer by the originator of its rights under the contract, or which require that the originator must obtain the consent of the relevant debtor in order to assign or transfer its rights under the contract, will prevent any assignment or transfer being effective unless the consent of the debtor to the transfer is in fact obtained.

Substantive consolidation   Substantive consolidation is only likely to be permitted where the operations of two or more bankrupt entities are so entwined that creditors could not be expected to view them as separate.

Moratorium/automatic stay   Dutch moratorium proceedings exist, which will prevent the enforcement of unsecured claims, but not the enforcement of security interests. These proceedings are limited to 2 months in duration.

Onshore SPV

An SPV may be established in the Netherlands in a bankruptcy remote fashion by a *stichting*, which is a form of Dutch foundation similar to an English law charitable trust. A Dutch trust company can establish the *stichting* and use it to incorporate an SPV.

Dutch companies can take the form of a *Besloten Vennootschap met beperkte aansprakelijkheid* (or BV, a private limited company with a minimum paid-up share capital of Euro 18 000), or a *Naamloze Vennootschap* (or NV, which has a more public character and a minimum paid-up share capital of Euro 45 000).

The Netherlands has a type of REIT in the form of *sociétés d'investissement à capital fixe en immobilier* (SICAFI).

Foreign ownership

Acquisitions of more than 5%, 10%, 25%, 50% or 66% in a listed company and each subsequent change must be notified to the Minister of Finance and to the company.

Securities laws

Prospectus requirements are relevant where an offering is made in the Netherlands.

Tax treatment

Stamp/registration/etc.   The Netherlands does not charge transfers of receivables to stamp duty.

Withholding tax   There is no withholding tax on interest in the Netherlands. Dividends are subject to a 25% withholding tax.

Profits tax   An offshore SPV will be liable to tax in the Netherlands if it is deemed to have a permanent establishment in the Netherlands.

Advance rulings from the Dutch tax authorities can be obtained as to the amount of taxable profit that will be attributed to an onshore SPV. Historically, the authorities have required that an onshore SPV make annual taxable profits of at least 12.5 bps, and potentially up to 25 bps, of its asset value (which are then taxed at 35%, giving an actual cost of around 4.5 bps to 9 bps). On 30 March 2001, new Decrees were passed which set a requirement that the SPV have "sufficient substance" in the Netherlands, namely that:

- At least half of its directors are resident in the Netherlands;
- Management decisions are taken in the Netherlands;
- Bank accounts and books are held in the Netherlands; and
- The SPV must have the level of equity required to carry on its business (this can be

nominal for an SPV where its liabilities are non-recourse to general corporate assets).

Under the new Decrees, the SPV is required to make an arm's-length return.

On 23 October 2000, anti-avoidance proposals on equity disguised as debt were put forward in the Tax Reform 2001 bill, which stated that a loan will be considered as equity instead of debt, and no deduction will be permitted for interest payments, if the loan has at least two of the following characteristics:

1. Payments are dependent on profits.
2. The loan has a tenor of more than 30 years, or is perpetual.
3. The loan is subordinated.

Such a loan would also be subject to dividend withholding tax.

The proposals were intended to be retrospective to 12 January 2000, and the law was scheduled to be passed in early January 2001. The proposals could have applied to all mezzanine and junior pieces on securitisation deals, potentially prejudicing the bankruptcy remote nature of the SPV issuer and leading to a cash shortfall to investors not able to reclaim the withholding tax. They were dropped on 9 November 2000 following significant financial industry pressure, in favour of more detailed examination by the Ministry of Finance of alternative options.

New proposals were passed into law on 1 January 2002. These stated that a loan will be considered as a "hybrid loan", and no deduction will be permitted for interest payments, if either:

1. Payments are wholly or partly dependent on profits and the loan has a maturity of more than 10 years; or
2. The loan is subordinated, and either has a tenor of more than 50 years or is perpetual.

There are exemptions for loans where unpaid interest is capitalised.

VAT   The transfer of receivables is not subject to VAT in the Netherlands. VAT is, however, charged on the supply of goods or services.

Accounting treatment

There are no published accounting standards, but if the transaction transfers the risks and benefits attached to the assets, and there is no obligation on the originator to repurchase the assets, sale treatment should be available.

Capital treatment

The Dutch Central Bank issued guidelines on securitisation on 25 September 1997. If the transfer is a true sale, the risks of the transaction are clearly set out and the recourse to the originator is limited to an acceptable level, the transaction will qualify for off-balance-sheet treatment.

Guidelines on the use of credit derivatives that were published on 31 January 1997 were replaced with new guidelines effective from 1 January 2002. The securitisation guidelines continue to apply to the transfer of credit risk through portfolio default swaps. Credit derivatives are regarded as trading book instruments if the derivative is held with the intention of making a short-term gain. Credit derivatives are treated as guarantees in the banking book in respect of the amount of exposure to which they relate. As general requirements for credit derivatives:

- The credit derivative must include credit events for failure to pay, bankruptcy and restructuring.
- The credit derivative should not have a substantial materiality threshold (any threshold should be less than one coupon payment on the underlying obligation and less than 3% of the notional).

Data protection/confidentiality

Data protection regulations exist, which may hinder the disclosure of information.

Consumer protection

Consumers are given various protections under the Dutch Civil Code and the Dutch Consumer Credit Act 1992.

Regulatory approvals

Prior to 1 July 2002, a Dutch SPV was required to be licensed as a credit institution unless the securities it issued were offered solely to professional investors and had a minimum tenor of 2 years (save for prepayments made at the option of the SPV within the first 2 years). The 2-year restriction was relaxed by the Ministry of Finance on 18 July 1997 for some rated issues.

Following the terrorist attacks of 11 September 2001, a decree was issued by the Ministry of Finance on 18 December 2001. This Decree provided that, with effect from 29 January 2002, SPV issuers that issued bearer securities that were not listed on an EU or US exchange were required to be licensed as a credit institution. The Decree also required SPV issuers to provide the Central Bank with detailed information on the parties to a transaction and the use of the proceeds of the transaction at least 4 weeks prior to close.

The provisions of the December 2001 Decree were cancelled with effect from 1 July 2002, and the previous exemptions from licensing were replaced by an exemption for issues to a circle of professionals.

Other issues

Floating charges are not recognised in the Netherlands.

The Netherlands do not recognise the concept of a trust.

Under Dutch law, a security interest cannot be granted to a party that is not a creditor of the secured debt. Hence, where a security trustee is to be used, a "parallel debt" structure may be necessary, whereby the full debt is covenanted to the security trustee as well as to bondholders, with a discharge of one covenant operating as a *pro tanto* discharge of the other covenant. The security interest is then simply granted to the security trustee; the bondholders are technically unsecured, but can sue the trustee under the terms of the security trust deed.

The Netherlands has strict financial assistance provisions preventing a company from providing assistance in relation to the acquisition of its shares.

12.31   NEW ZEALAND

There has been significantly less issuance in New Zealand than in Australia to date, with slower market development.

New Zealand operates a common law system, historically based on English law.

Ring-fencing and true sale

Receivables may be transferred by equitable assignment without the need to give notice to debtors of the transfer, although transfers creating instruments under the Chattels Transfer Act are not effective unless exempt or registered. Offer and acceptance may be used to avoid creating such instruments. Terms in the receivables documentation that prohibit assignment or transfer by the originator of its rights under the contract, or require that the originator must obtain the consent of the relevant debtor in order to assign or transfer its rights under the contract, will prevent any assignment or transfer being effective unless the consent of the debtor to the transfer is in fact obtained.

Recharacterisation   Prior to 2002, transfers were structured to take the form of a true sale. The Personal Property Securities Act 1999, which came into effect in 2002, provides for transfers to be governed by substance rather than form, and specifically provides that transfers of book debts will take the form of security interests. Consequently, transfers are now followed by precautionary filings in order to ensure that they are perfected as security interests, by registration of a financing statement. The PPSA does not apply to the transfer of land or interests in land.

Set-off

The debtor can obtain good discharge by making payments to the originator until notice of the assignment is given to the debtor, at which point the debtor is obliged to pay to the SPV direct. The SPV will take subject to any defects in the title of the originator, and until notice is given to the debtor, the SPV is subject to any further equities (such as set-off) arising in favour of the debtor through relations between the originator and the debtor subsequent to the assignment.

Foreign ownership

Foreign ownership of more than 25% of the shares in companies where the transaction value exceeds NZ$ 10m or certain land sites are involved requires the prior approval of the Overseas Investment Commission. Acquisitions of more than 5% in a listed company must be notified to the stock exchange and to the company.

Tax treatment

Stamp/registration/etc.   There is no stamp duty except on transfers of commercial property.

Accounting treatment

FRS 37 of 31 December 2002 requires the consolidation of an SPV with an entity which has the power to determine its operating policies and which enjoys significant benefits from the SPV. This is similar to the operation of IAS 27 and SIC-12, as no such power is required for an SPV on an "auto-pilot" mechanism, such that an entity which derives significant benefit from the SPV will be required to consolidate it.

Consumer protection

Consumers are given certain protections for consumer contracts.

Regulatory approvals

The Reserve Bank of New Zealand published statement BS 2 in 1996, setting out guidelines for the transfer of assets off balance sheet by banking institutions, and the involvement of bank entities in securitisations as liquidity providers or credit enhancers.

12.32   NORWAY

There has been little securitisation activity in Norway, with the exception of the Viking Consumer Receivables deal for Thorn Nordic in 2000.

Ring-fencing and true sale

A transfer of trade receivables need not be notified to debtors, but the transfer of most other forms of receivables will need to be notified.

Insolvency unwind   Transactions at an undervalue and preferences may be unwound where they take place within 3 months of insolvency. In addition, any transaction defrauding creditors may be unwound if it takes place within 10 years of insolvency.

Foreign ownership

Acquisition of more than 10%, 25%, 50% or 75% of the shares in a listed company must be notified to the stock exchange.

Tax treatment

Stamp/registration/etc.   There is no stamp duty on transfers of receivables. Stamp duty of 2.5% is charged on the transfer of real estate.

VAT   VAT is due on servicing fees. An SPV is unlikely to be able to recover input tax.

Accounting treatment

IAS standards are likely to be followed.

Capital treatment

The Bank of Norway supports the majority of the Basel Committee's recommendations.

Data protection/confidentiality

Data protection is enshrined in the Data Protection Act (which closely follows the provisions of the EU Data Protection Directive).

Regulatory approvals

An offshore SPV that buys Norwegian receivables should not be required to be licensed as a credit institution, although a credit institution is not permitted to sell loan portfolios to such an SPV. A Norwegian SPV may be required to be licensed.

A new regulation of 13 December 2002, expected to come into force in late 2003, permits the transfer of loan portfolios from credit institutions to Norwegian SPVs with prior notice to the regulator, provided that the SPV is set up as independent (without ownership or board representation of the originator), and that the originator holds no more than 5% of the securities issued by the SPV. In this case, the Norwegian SPV will not be required to be licensed.

12.33 PAKISTAN

Securitisation was launched in Pakistan with the US$ 250m telecoms receivables deal for Pakistan Telecoms in 1997. Rules on securitisation were finalised by the SEC on 13 November 1999, but do not remove many of the local difficulties seen in the development of securitised product.

12.34 PANAMA

Ring-fencing and true sale

The Civil Code provides for the transfer of receivables under an *escritura publica* (a written and notarised sale agreement) under Articles 1232 to 1234.

Future receivables   Future receivables which are determinable at the point of sale may be transferred.

12.35   PARAGUAY

Ring-fencing and true sale

Law No. 1036 of 1997 provides for the establishment of securitisation companies to acquire financial assets.

12.36   PERU

Ring-fencing and true sale

Decree No. 861 of 1996 provides for the transfer of assets.

Accounting treatment

US accounting standards are followed.

12.37   THE PHILIPPINES

Use of securitisation in the Philippines has been limited to date. The Philippines announced the creation of an asset management company in November 1998, with initial capital of Peso 1bn, operational from early 1999. A Circular containing guidelines on securitisation was released by the *Bangko Sentral ng Pilipinas* (the Philippine Central Bank) in December 1998.

Legislation on the establishment of SPVs to act as asset management companies (AMCs) and acquire NPLs was passed on 10 January 2003.

Ring-fencing and true sale

Receivables may be transferred by equitable assignment without the need to give notice to debtors of the transfer. The assignment should, however, be evidenced by a public notarised instrument for it to be valid against third parties. There are no regulations preventing transfer of receivables to a non-Philippine transferee.

Recharacterisation   A sale may be recharacterised as a secured loan if the originator retains a right to repurchase the receivables, or the court considers that it was the true intention of the parties that the sale should be a secured loan.

Moratorium/automatic stay   Moratorium style proceedings exist in the Philippines.

Set-off

The debtor can obtain good discharge by making payments to the originator until notice of the assignment is given to the debtor, at which point the debtor is obliged to pay to the SPV direct. The SPV will take subject to any defects in the title of the originator, and until notice is given to the debtor, the SPV is subject to any further equities (such as set-off) arising in favour of the debtor through relations between the originator and the debtor subsequent to the assignment. General forms of notice (such as on an account statement) are sufficient if reasonably conspicuous.

Foreign ownership

Foreign ownership is restricted in sectors such as mass media, the retail trade, advertising and national resource development. Acquisition of more than 5% of the shares in a listed company and each subsequent change in such level must be disclosed.

Securities laws

The SEC published regulations on asset-backed securities in March 1991, which require that any asset-backed securities offered for sale to the public in the Philippines must be registered with the SEC or exempt from registration. The registration rules require that the SPV must be a trust, and that it may only hold one asset pool at any one time. A prospectus should be prepared in accordance with SEC requirements, and a registration fee of 1% of the principal amount is payable to the SEC. Subsequent to issuance, there are periodic reporting requirements to the SEC.

Tax treatment

Stamp/registration/etc.   An instrument of transfer is subject to nominal stamp duty, as well as the notary's fees (which are negotiable). Registration/exemption fees of the SEC may also be payable.

Withholding tax   Withholding tax is charged at 20% on payment offshore of Philippine source income. If a Philippine SPV is used, withholding would apply to payments of interest made to foreign investors.

Profits tax   An offshore SPV should not be liable to Philippine profits tax unless it engages in business in the Philippines.

VAT   There should be no VAT on an assignment of receivables.

Accounting treatment

In order for an asset to be considered off-balance-sheet of a company for accounting purposes: (a) control over the assets or effective control (for example, through repurchase obligations, or repurchase rights when assets default) must be surrendered by the company; (b) the transferee must acquire the right to pledge or exchange the assets; and (c) the assets must be transferred beyond the reach of any liquidator or creditor of the company.

Capital treatment

The *Bangko Sentral ng Pilipinas* Circular No. 185 of 8 December 1998 provides for true sale requirements for banks that are established in the Philippines. The originator may not retain any interest in the securitised assets except for a residual note, and must not be under any obligation to repurchase the assets (although substitution or replenishment is permitted), save for breach of a representation or warranty given at the time of the transfer. The originator may retain a clean-up call for 10% or less of the assets, provided that it is exercised at market value. The assets must also be transferred off balance sheet for accounting purposes. Up-front expenses may be borne (as a deduction from capital), but not recurrent expenses.

Data protection/confidentiality

There is a general constitutional right to privacy that prevents the disclosure of private information. In addition, banks are prohibited from revealing customer information without customer consent.

Consumer protection

No consumer protection regulations exist.

Regulatory approvals

A securitisation may require central bank approval.

Other issues

The Philippines does not recognise floating charges. The Philippines would probably recognise a trust constituted under a law other than the law of the Philippines, but a trustee may experience difficulties in enforcing directly in the Philippines. Foreign judgements should be recognised in the Philippines.

12.38   POLAND

The first domestic transactions were completed in Poland in 1999.

Data protection/confidentiality

Poland has bank secrecy laws which prohibit disclosure of customer information without the consent of the customer.

Other issues

Poland passed a law in July 2000 which requires all contracts with Polish entities from 8 May 2000 to be made in Polish in order to be admissible in evidence.

12.39   PORTUGAL

No securitisations were closed in Portugal until the summer of 1998, due to restrictive regulatory and tax impediments. The market opened up significantly in 1999 with auto loan and consumer finance deals structured around these restrictions, but using complex structures to circumvent withholding tax and stamp duty.

Combined with mortgage registration duties, these limitations prevented the development of a mortgage market until a decree of August 2001. This led to the first Portuguese mortgage deal – Magellan Mortgages No. 1 – in December 2001.

Issuance in excess of Euro 3bn was seen in 2002.

A new ABS Law of 5 November 1999 (Decree 453/99) eased notification restrictions. A Decree of the Ministerial Council of 4 August 2001 (Decree 219/01) eased concerns on restrictive withholding taxes and mortgage stamp duty and registration fees. A new decree was passed on 21 February 2002 (Decree 82/2002) which amends various provisions of the ABS Law.

Ring-fencing and true sale

Receivables are generally transferable under Article 577 of the Portuguese Civil Code without the need to notify the debtors. Under Article 6 of the new ABS Law, a transfer of receivables arising under a legal relationship to an SPV under the new law is effective when notified to the debtors; however, a transfer by a credit institution is effective against third parties immediately when made without any requirement to notify the debtor.

Prior to the new ABS Law, a transfer of mortgages had to be carried out by way of public deed, which was subject to notarisation and registration. For a transfer of mortgages to an SPV under the new ABS Law, Article 7 of the law simply requires that the transfer be in writing and it is not required to be notarised.

Insolvency unwind Preferential transactions where the obligations of the originator exceed those of the SPV and the transaction was entered into within 2 years prior to insolvency of the originator may be unwound. Transactions which reduce the assets of the originator may also be set aside.

Set-off

A transfer by a credit institution to an SPV under the new ABS Law is effective to stop any further set-off rights immediately.

Onshore SPV

The new ABS Law provides for the establishment of securitisation SPVs in the form of:

- *sociedades de titularizacao de creditos* or "STCs" (companies). Companies must be established with minimum share capital of Euro 250 000 (Euro 2.5m prior to Decree 82/2002). STCs are limited to activities related to the securitisation transaction and cannot list their shares. No Portuguese credit institution may hold more than 25% of the voting share capital of an STC for more than 3 years.
- *fundos de titularizacao de creditos* or "FTCs" (closed-end or open-ended funds). Funds must be managed by an independent Fund Manager company and must appoint a custodian bank. Fund Managers must be established with minimum share capital of Euro 250 000 (Euro 750 000 prior to Decree 82/2002).

Fund Managers (for FTCs) and STCs are subject to minimum own fund requirements as a percentage of net assets under management (0.5% of assets up to Euro 75m – reduced from 1% prior to Decree 82/2002 – and 0.1% of assets over Euro 75m), and must be based in Portugal.

The FTC fund vehicle has been used to date due to its lower cost.

Tax treatment

Stamp/registration/etc.   Stamp duty is chargeable at an *ad valorem* rate of 0.5% on the interest component of any assets that are transferred to an offshore entity. Transactions to date have been structured with a sale of the interest element of receivables to an onshore branch of an institution, which grants offshore security over the interest element in favour of an offshore SPV, which operates to defer payment of stamp duty until the security is enforced.

The new 2001 Decree exempts the transfer of mortgages from stamp duty and registration fees.

Withholding tax   Prior to 2001, distributions from a new securitisation fund either onshore or offshore were subject to 20% withholding and interest payments to offshore investors were subject to 20% withholding tax, with the exception of payments from an onshore credit institution to an offshore credit institution. Transactions prior to 2001 were structured to rely on this exemption, with a sale of the interest element of the receivables to an onshore credit institution (separately from the sale of the principal element of the receivables), which accepts a limited recourse deposit from an offshore credit institution (typically in the same group), which was in turn funded by a limited recourse deposit paid by the SPV from the transaction issuance proceeds. The risk of insolvency of the credit institution was covered by call provisions of the SPV for the interest element in the event of insolvency, and by reserves to cover subsequent withholding tax costs.

The 2001 Decree permits domestic obligors to make payment to a Portuguese SPV free of withholding tax, and for a Portuguese SPV to pay interest on bonds held by foreign investors free of withholding tax.

Accounting treatment

US accounting standards are likely to be followed.

Capital treatment

The Bank of Portugal guidelines contained in Regulation 10/2001 require junior tranches held by the originator to be directly deducted from capital.

Regulatory approvals

A Portuguese entity which acquires receivables may be required to be licensed as a credit institution. Approval from the *Comissao de Mercado de Valores Mobiliarios* (the CMVM, or National Securities Market Commission) is required for the establishment of a Fund Manager or an STC under the new ABS Law. In addition, the establishment of a Fund Manager requires the approval of the Bank of Portugal.

Other issues

Trusts are not recognised in Portugal.

12.40 RUSSIA

Russia imposed a moratorium on payment of foreign debts – including payments on asset-backed securities – in August 1998, but has since seen a resurgence in its economy. A new Insolvency Law was passed in October 2002.

Tax treatment

Withholding tax   Russia imposes withholding tax on interest paid from residents to non-residents at a rate of 20% (increased in January 2002 from 15%). This rate is reduced to zero under double taxation treaties with the UK, the US, the Netherlands and Germany.

12.41 SCOTLAND

Assets in Scotland are typically combined with assets in the rest of the United Kingdom in most transactions.

Ring-fencing and true sale

For an effective transfer of receivables by "assignation" (that is, assignment) under Scots law, "intimation" (that is, notice) of the assignment must be given to the debtor. In addition, acknowledgement of receipt of notice, either in writing or by conduct (such as paying to an account stipulated in the notice), may be necessary.

As an alternative, the originator may effect an unnotified assignment, which is then supported by a declaration of trust by the originator over the receivables in favour of the SPV. This form of Scots law trust only confers on the SPV a contractual claim against the trustee, rather than a proprietary claim in the assets. The claim of the SPV is, however, protected against the creditors of the originator for most purposes, and can be reinforced by the grant of a security power of attorney by the originator to allow serving of notices on debtors by the SPV on a self-help basis.

Terms in the receivables documentation which prohibit assignment or transfer by the originator of its rights under the contract, or which require that the originator must obtain the consent of the relevant debtor in order to assign or transfer its rights under the contract, will prevent any assignment or transfer being effective unless the consent of the debtor to the transfer is in fact obtained.

12.42 SINGAPORE

Since the first transactions in Singapore in mid-1998, issuance of commercial property securitisations has taken off rapidly. Many of these are quasi-securitisations however, with varying levels of recourse back to the originator. DBS Land has been one of the key issuers in the market, and, due to local investor demand, has been able to sell to both institutional and retail investors in Singapore without producing a high level of detail in offering documentation (although typically it has retained the junior piece). Structures have used a transfer of the shares in the property holding company from the originator to a new orphan company for cash equal to the property value. An ongoing revenue profit strip is taken by way of a property management fee paid to an originator group company. The orphan company gives a share pledge and real estate mortgage to support the bonds it issues.

Singapore announced a "Big Bang" package of reforms in May 1999 liberalising restrictions on the foreign ownership of Singaporean banks, and offering six licenses as "qualifying full banks" (QFBs) to foreign banks. Measures to further liberalise the international use of the Singapore dollar were announced by the MAS on 26 November 1999.

The first internationally rated transaction was the Peridot Investments CMBS deal arranged for CapitaLand in June 2001 and rated by Fitch. This was an interesting deal, securitising periodic future payments to be made for apartments bought off-plan pending completion of the developments. Also in June 2001, Raffles Holdings announced their intention to securitise the Raffles City shopping mall. The first REIT from Singapore (the SingMall Property Trust from CapitaLand) was due to be launched in November 2001, but was delayed due to lack of demand and was launched again in June 2002 as the CapitaMall Trust.

In 2002 and 2003 Singapore has shown further issuance, in particular CDO transactions for local asset management firms. Many of these have combined US and European assets as well as Asian assets, in order to gain scale and diversity. The most recent of these is also the largest – the United Global Investment Grade CDO III deal managed by United Overseas Bank in Singapore. The US$ 1.7bn deal packages CDS exposures to US, European and Asian names.

From 1 January 2003, the state-owned Housing Development Board will no longer provide mortgage finance to individuals buying public housing (the bulk of the mortgage market in Singapore), freeing the way for private sector development.

Singapore operates a common law system, historically based on English law. Real estate in Singapore is typically on a long leasehold of 99 years from the Singapore government.

In September 2000, the Monetary Authority of Singapore (the MAS) issued guidelines for securitisation by regulated entities, and for the capital treatment of credit derivatives (first published in draft in January 1999 and December 1999, respectively).

Singapore operates a Central Provident Fund (CPF) as a savings fund to provide for pensions, healthcare and housing of Singapore residents. Payments are made by mandatory deduction from employee salaries. Residents can use CPF funds to purchase residential property, with the CPF then receiving a mortgage over the property purchased. Properties are usually purchased with a combination of funds from the CPF and funds borrowed from the banking sector. Until July 2002, the CPF enjoyed a first mortgage over residential properties relative to bank lenders, who took a second mortgage over the property.

In July 2002, however, the CPF first charge was switched to a second charge position. The new rules apply to mortgages and re-mortgages entered into on or after 1 September 2002. A maximum of 10% of the property purchase price may be taken from CPF assets, with a maximum of 80% provided by bank lenders. The new measures are designed to promote prudence in individuals by allowing banks to have a first charge on the property.

Ring-fencing and true sale

Equitable assignments without notice are effective to transfer receivables. Prohibitions on transfer will prevent a transfer taking effect unless the debtor consents.

Insolvency unwind Transactions at an undervalue and preferences may be unwound on insolvency.

Recharacterisation The characterisation of a transaction as a transfer or a secured loan is based on the true intention of the parties, as evidenced by the circumstances surrounding the transaction (and in particular, the transfer of risks and rewards under the transaction).

Set-off

The debtor can obtain good discharge by making payments to the originator until notice of the assignment is given to the debtor, at which point the debtor is obliged to pay to the SPV direct. The SPV will take subject to any defects in the title of the originator, and until notice is given to the debtor, the SPV is subject to any further equities (such as set-off) arising in favour of the debtor through relations between the originator and the debtor subsequent to the assignment.

Onshore SPV

New S-REIT guidelines were published by the MAS on 28 March 2003. S-REITs may now borrow up to 35% of their assets (up from 25% previously), and may borrow in excess of 35% if all their debt is rated at least single A. In addition, fuller disclosure in the fund documents is required of the inherent illiquidity and gearing of property funds. S-REITs may invest in property outside Singapore.

Foreign ownership

Foreign ownership is only restricted in strategic industries such as newspapers, banks, insurers, finance companies, airlines and defence companies, generally to between 15% and 49% of the shares in a company. Acquisitions of more than 5% of the shares in a listed company and each subsequent change must be notified to the company, which must in turn notify the stock exchange. Big Bang reforms were announced in May 1999, under which the MAS lifted the 40% restriction on foreign ownership of Singaporean banks.

Securities laws

Issues through a trust structure may be required to comply with the prospectus requirements of Part 5 of the Companies Act.

Tax treatment

Stamp/registration/etc.   Disposals of real estate are liable to stamp duty.

Withholding tax   Singapore charges withholding tax on payments of interest on receivables or securities made to offshore entities. An amendment under the 1999 Budget provided that interest paid offshore on "qualifying debt securities" arranged by Singapore financial institutions prior to March 2003 was free of withholding tax. A Singapore financial institution could apply to the MAS for Approved Bond Intermediary (ABI) status, which would mean that any bond issue lead managed by the institution would then automatically be treated as a qualifying debt security.

Capital treatment

In September 2000, the MAS issued guidelines for securitisation by banks in Singapore, which also apply to the Singaporean branches of foreign banks (in relation to their requirements, but not the actual capital treatment). They do not allow an off-balance-sheet capital treatment for sub-participations, and do not deal with revolving pools, replenishment or substitution, or additional requirements on the transfer of instalment purchase receivables for equipment or goods.

If the following criteria are met, the transaction will be considered to have achieved a clean sale, and can be excluded from the balance sheet of the originator for capital purposes (if the requirements are not met, the transaction is regarded as a financing and remains on the balance sheet):

- Transactions between the transferor and the transferee must be arm's-length.
- There must be clear disclosure to investors of the risks of the investment, and the originator will not support losses suffered by investors.
- The transferor may not own any shares in the transferee (an amendment of 4 December 2000 permits certain preference shares to be held).
- The name of the transferee must not imply any connection with the transferor.
- The transferee must have independent directors (although the transferor may have a minority of directors where there are at least three directors).
- The transferor must not directly or indirectly control the transferee.
- The transferor must not support losses or expenses of the transferee or investors (except under a permitted credit enhancement facility), and the transferor may only enter into swaps with the transferee at market rates.
- The beneficial interest in the assets has been transferred.
- All risks and benefits on the assets have been transferred (save as permitted below).
- The transfer should not contravene the terms of the underlying assets.

- The transferor receives a fixed consideration for the assets at the time of transfer.
- The transferor must not have any obligation to repurchase the assets except pursuant to a breach of a warranty given at the time of sale and as to existing facts (not future performance of the assets).
- The transferee would be subject to the terms of any re-negotiation of the assets.
- The transferor must not be obliged to make a market in the issued securities.

The transferor must confirm that it has written opinions from its legal advisers and auditors that the transaction meets these requirements. The transferor may purchase senior securities issued by the transferee up to 10% of the issued amount.

Servicing may only be provided by the transferor where:

- It is documented in writing;
- There is no further recourse beyond the terms of the agreement;
- It is clearly limited in duration;
- The servicer has written opinions that it is protected from liability to investors (save for normal contractual liability);
- The servicer is not obliged to pay over collections on the assets unless and until they are received;
- The servicing fee is on market terms.

If these requirements are not met, the assets remain on balance sheet.

Credit enhancement facilities must meet the following conditions:

- They must be documented in writing.
- There should not be any further recourse beyond the terms of the enhancement facility itself.
- They must be clearly limited in amount and duration.

If these requirements are not met, the assets remain on balance sheet. If these requirements are met, the credit enhancement is directly deducted from capital for capital adequacy purposes (capped at the normal risk weight of the underlying assets) for a "first loss" facility, or normally weighted for a "second loss" facility (which benefits from a substantial first loss facility and cannot be drawn until the first loss facility is exhausted).

Liquidity facilities must meet the following criteria:

- They must be documented in writing.
- There should not be any further recourse beyond the terms of the facility itself.
- They must be clearly limited in amount and duration.
- The facilities must be documented separately from any other facilities.
- Funding must be provided to the transferee, not to investors.
- The facilities may not be drawn for the purpose of credit enhancement, to support losses or to provide permanent revolving funding.
- Repayment of the facilities cannot be subordinated to investors.
- There must be substantial credit enhancement in place (or the assets must be of very high quality and the liquidity facilities must expressly provide for reduction in funding if asset quality deteriorates below specified levels).

If these requirements are not met the facility will be treated as credit enhancement.

Exposure of a bond investor to obligors in an underlying pool should be taken into account with any other exposure of the bond investor to such obligors.

Investment grade MBS tranches are eligible for a 50% risk weighting if they meet the following conditions:

- The mortgages are secured on residential property.
- The mortgages are performing in accordance with MAS notices when they are transferred to the SPV.
- The SPV must not hold assets with a risk weighting in excess of 50%.
- The investors should not be absorbing more than a pro rata share of losses on the mortgage loans.

Non-investment grade tranches will be normally weighted. If the purchase is regarded by the MAS as credit enhancement, it will be deducted from capital.

The MAS published guidelines on the capital treatment for credit derivatives in the banking book and the trading book in December 1999 and September 2000. Credit derivatives are regarded as trading book instruments if the derivative is traded and is marked-to-market daily. Credit spread products are not covered by the guidelines.

Banking book   Credit derivatives are treated as guarantees in the banking book in respect of the amount of exposure to which they relate, with credit for cash collateral where they are funded. Credit-linked notes bought by a protection seller are weighted at the higher of the risk weight of the underlying or the buyer as long as both risk weights are investment grade (this relaxation was introduced in an amendment of 30 November 2000), or at the sum of both risk weights if one of the risk weights is below investment grade. As general requirements for credit derivatives:

- The reference obligation must be the same as the protected asset, or at least issued by the same issuer.
- If it is only issued by the same issuer, the reference obligation must rank junior to or *pari passu* with the protected asset, the reference obligation and the protected asset must cross-default, and the protected amount will be reduced to the spot FX value of the protection if denominated in a different currency.
- If the credit derivative has a shorter term than the protected asset, then no protection value is recognised if the credit derivative has less than 1 year to expiry. If the credit derivative has between 1 year and 5 years to expiry, then protection is recognised on a sliding scale. If the credit derivative has more than 5 years to expiry, full protection value is recognised.
- A "first to default" basket structure gives the buyer protection against the default of one asset in the basket.
- Sale of a "first to default" credit derivative basket structure generates a capital charge for the protection seller equal to the addition of the respective capital charge for each asset in the basket (capped at the amount of the maximum payout).
- Proportionate basket structures will give protection or generate charges on a proportion of the assets in the basket.

Trading book   Credit derivatives are broken down into legs.

- Total return swaps are treated as a long/short position in the reference obligation (carrying specific and general risks) and a short/long position in a Singapore government security (carrying general risk) paying the same rate.

- Credit default swaps are treated as a long/short position in the reference obligation (carrying specific risk only). Premium payments may be treated as a notional position in a Singapore government security.
- Credit-linked notes are treated as a long/short position in the note (carrying specific risk of the issuer and general risk) and also as a long/short position in the reference obligation (carrying specific risk only).
- A "first to default" basket structure allows the buyer to record a short position for any one of the assets in the basket.
- Sale of a "first to default" credit derivative basket structure creates a long position for the protection seller in each asset in the basket, capped at a direct deduction from capital.
- A proportionate basket structure only creates a long or short position by reference to the proportionate weighting of each asset in the basket.
- The reference obligation must have the same issuer and coupon as the protected asset (credit derivatives in a different currency than the reporting currency of the institution are subject to an FX charge).
- If the credit derivative has a shorter term than the protected asset, a forward position (i.e. an obligation to acquire the bond or other protected asset in the future) in the specific risk of the reference obligation is recorded by the protection buyer for the residual exposure.

In addition to market risk assessments, credit derivatives are subjected to a counter-party risk haircut by calculating the mark-to-market value of the derivative plus an "add-on" percentage which is the interest rate add-on (qualifying assets) or the equity add-on (non-qualifying assets), and multiplying by the counterparty risk weight and the BIS factor.

Data protection/confidentiality

Banks are required to keep customer details confidential.

Regulatory approvals

Any bank acting as seller or manager in a securitisation in Singapore requires the prior approval of the MAS. The MAS reserves the right to impose limits on the volume or type of issuance by an originator, and will need to be satisfied that the originator has appropriate risk management systems to cope with securitisation management.

Prior to 2000, the MAS regulated the use of the Singapore dollar in the bond, equity and derivatives markets. The market was deregulated gradually over 2000 and 2001 (starting with the use of the Singapore dollar to transact derivatives with offshore counterparties announced by the MAS on 26 November 1999), with a final deregulation of activities from 20 March 2002, save that:

- Loans for more than S$ 5m may not be made to non-resident financial institutions where there is reason to believe they will be used for speculation against the Singapore dollar; and

- Loans in Singapore dollars used by non-residents to fund offshore activities must be swapped out of Singapore dollars.

Other issues

Foreign residents are restricted from acquiring residential property in Singapore under the Residential Property Act (which limits ownership to Singapore citizens, Singapore companies and certain other companies).

12.43   SOUTH AFRICA

The first public securitisation out of South Africa was the FirstRand Bank future flows credit card voucher deal closed in June 2000 through a receivables trust structure. The first South African MBS deal, a Rand 1.25bn called Thekwini 1 from South Africa Home Loans (a non-bank mortgage lender), closed in November 2001, with a second issue – Thekwini 2 – closed in November 2002. There was significant further development in the South African market at the end of 2002, with an equipment lease deal from Fintech (Rand 680m) and a Rand 1bn mortgage deal from Investec in December 2002. Regulations on securitisation were published by the South African Reserve Bank in December 2001.

Tax treatment

Stamp/registration/etc.   Stamp duty is charged on the transfer of mortgages. The Thekwini transaction uses origination directly in the securitisation vehicle in order to minimise stamp duty.

Accounting treatment

It is likely that FRS 5 or FAS 125 would be followed.

Capital treatment

The South African Reserve Bank published guidelines on securitisation in December 2001, which follow the form of the old UK guidelines and the new Basel proposals. The guidelines use a classification of the role of the institution into primary roles of:

- Originator (a transferor of an asset or package of assets to an SPV (where less than 10% of the assets come from a company, the company will be classified as a repackager or sponsor instead));
- Remote originator (a lender via an SPV);
- Sponsor (a repackager of assets originated by a third party); and
- Repackager (a seller of government securities or listed loan stock).

The guidelines also define secondary roles of servicer, credit enhancer, liquidity provider, underwriter, investor and counterparty.

The guidelines permit transfer of assets by assignment. Transfers are required to comply with the following guidelines:

- The transfer should not contravene the terms of the underlying assets.
- The transferee should not have recourse against the transferor (except for breach of warranty).
- The transferee would be subject to the terms of any renegotiation of the assets.
- The transferor is only obliged to pay over collections on the assets as and when received.
- The transferor cannot own more than 50% of the shares in the transferee.
- The transferor should not have control of the board of directors of the transferee.
- The transferor cannot be under an obligation to repurchase assets from the transferee, but can repurchase assets at fair market value up to 10% of an asset pool.

A credit conversion factor of 10% is applied to revolving pools.

First loss credit enhancement will be directly deducted from capital (if the bank is acting in a primary role). Second loss enhancement will be normally weighted (investment grade ABS are regarded as second loss).

Liquidity facilities can be provided by sponsors or repackagers if they contain a provision for reducing the facility if the asset quality in the SPV deteriorates (e.g. if the remaining undrawn credit enhancement falls below the outstanding liquidity commitment), and if repayment of the liquidity facility is not subordinated to investors. If these requirements are not met the facility will be treated as first loss credit enhancement.

An originator can underwrite the issue of bonds, but no off-balance-sheet treatment will be recognised until at least 80% of the bonds have been sold. Investment in ABS will be risk weighted in accordance with the standardised approach under the new Basel proposals (i.e. 20% (AAA to AA−), 50% (A+ to A−), 100% (BBB+ to BBB−), 150% (BB+ to BB−), direct deduction (below BB−)).

12.44 SPAIN

Spanish deals up until 1998 largely consisted of mortgage transactions and the 1998 government securitisation of nuclear moratorium credits (brought under the scope of specific legislation). Legislation in 1998 relating to funds for a wider range of receivables operated to expand the range of transactions that could be structured.

Mortgage deals have flourished since mid-1998 on the back of the June 1998 announcement from the Bank of Spain that mortgage-backed securities and asset-backed securities would be eligible for repo with the European Central Bank. This led to an increase in the use of securitisation as a means of increasing the liquidity of assets on the balance sheet of financial institutions. Deals were structured at below market spreads, with the intention that the securities would be subscribed in main or in whole by the originator, and only subsequently sold if spreads tightened significantly. In the interim, the bonds were used as repo collateral. Mortgage securitisation funds, which have been established by several institutions to undertake pooled issuance against their assets, are now operating.

Argentaria issued the first international issue of Pfandbriefe-style *cedulas hipotecarias* in 1999, and was quickly followed by other Spanish banks. The first Spanish CLO to be funded publicly (rather than via a conduit) was launched by BBVA at the end of February 2000.

Issuance (excluding *cedulas hipotecarias*) has increased from Euro 8.8bn in 2001 to Euro 15.4bn in 2002, primarily as a result of a significant increase in consumer ABS deals. The Spanish market has now widened into mortgage transactions, CLO issuance (primarily SME loans under the government guarantee scheme), *cedulas hipotecarias* and consumer ABS transactions, although mortgage deals continue to dominate the market.

In May 1999, a government decree was introduced, under which the government would guarantee up to Euro 1.8bn per annum of investment grade ABS tranches issued under securitisations of loans to small and medium-sized enterprises (SMEs) in each year, through the FTPYME programme. The guarantee covered 80% of value for tranches rated AA or above, 50% for tranches rated A, and 15% for tranches rated BBB. The guarantee was revised in 2001 to limit it to tranches rated A or higher, and again in 2002 to limit it to assets rated AA or higher.

Ring-fencing and true sale

Spanish law allows for the transfer of receivables from the originator to an SPV without a requirement to give notice to the debtors. There is, however, a requirement for transfers to be notarised as a public document (*escritura publica*), which serves to publicly fix the date of the transfer. In the absence of such a notarisation, the transfer will still be enforceable against the debtors, but may not be effective against third parties such as a liquidator, who may attempt to argue that the transfer took place after the point at which the originator became insolvent.

For a transfer of mortgages, the Spanish Mortgage Law originally required notice to debtors and notarisation and registration of the transfer at the Land Registry. Failure to register would result in the transfer being ineffective against third parties. Law 2/1981 of 25 March 1981 provides for an alternative method of financing mortgage portfolios, through the issuance of *participaciones hipotecarias* or PH (a form of limited recourse negotiable debt instrument issued by the mortgage originator). Law 19/1992 of 7 July 1992 created a fund framework for PHs (see "Onshore SPV" below), and amended the 1981 regime to allow PH to be off balance sheet.

Decree 926/1998 of 14 May 1998 permitted a wider range of receivables to use a similar fund structure, although in the case of future receivables other than toll road receipts, there are still restrictions leading to a requirement for prior approval by the CNMV (the *Comision Nacional del Mercado de Valores*, or National Securities Market Commission) (see "Regulatory approvals" below). The new law may be used by an originator who has at least 3 years of audited accounts. A written assignment should be signed and notified to the CNMV. The originator is not permitted to guarantee the assets, although overcollateralisation is allowable.

On 9 June 2003, the Spanish government passed the Law on Public Contracts, which provides for the securitisation of public concession revenues and their ring-fencing in favour of bondholders, in order to facilitate private financing of infrastructure projects.

Terms in the receivables documentation that prohibit assignment or transfer by the originator of its rights under the contract, or require that the originator must obtain the consent of the relevant debtor in order to assign or transfer its rights under the contract, will prevent any assignment or transfer being effective unless the consent of the debtor to the transfer is in fact obtained.

Covered bonds   Law 2/1981 of 25 March 1981 updated the legislation of 1869 relating to the issuance of *cedulas hipotecarias* (CH) by banks on a portfolio-backed basis (in addition to the regime for the issuance of *participaciones hipotecarias* or PH, which are backed by a specific pool of mortgages). CH are backed by the entire eligible mortgage portfolio of the bank. The CH holders have preferential rights to claim against the portfolio on insolvency of the originator (as well as recourse to the issuing bank), but payments may be interrupted as the mortgages are not kept in a separate register as with German Pfandbriefe. Consequently, CH are not regarded as truly bankruptcy remote by the rating agencies, and may only be able to exceed the originator's unsecured credit rating by a couple of notches. CH are on-balance-sheet instruments. Only first mortgages are part of the eligible portfolio, and the portfolio cannot include mortgages with an LTV in excess of 70% (for commercial property) or 80% (for residential property). Overcollateralisation requirements restrict issuance to a maximum of 90% of the amount of the eligible portfolio. The Bank of Spain lowered the capital risk weighting attributed to CH from 20% to 10% in April 2000.

The new Financial Law (the *Ley de Medidas de Reforma del Sistema Financiero*, Law 44/2002) was passed on 22 October 2002, and became effective on 25 November 2002, after a 2 year passage through parliament. The Law introduced a public sector covered bond regime for the issue of *cedulas territoriales* (or CT), which may be backed by an eligible pool of public sector assets. The CT holders have preferential rights to claim against the portfolio on insolvency of the originator and are only subordinated to government claims for taxes and employees salaries. CT are not regarded as truly bankruptcy remote by the rating agencies. Eligible assets consist of loans to central governments, local administrations or public sector entities within the EEA. Overcollateralisation requirements restrict issuance to a maximum of 70% of the amount of the eligible portfolio. CT are risk weighted 10% by the Bank of Spain.

Set-off

The debtor can obtain good discharge by making payments to the originator until notice of the assignment is given to the debtor, at which point the debtor is obliged to pay to the SPV direct. The SPV will take subject to any defects in the title of the originator, and until notice is given to the debtor, the SPV is subject to any further equities (such as set-off) arising in favour of the debtor through relations between the originator and the debtor subsequent to the assignment.

Onshore SPV

Law 19/1992 of 7 July 1992 created a framework for the grouping of PHs together in mortgage securitisation funds (*fondos de titulizacion hipotecaria*) which finance themselves through the issuance of debt securities, and can collect income on the PHs free of withholding. They are closed-end in nature.

Decree 926/1998 of 14 May 1998 provided for a similar fund structure for a wider range of receivables (*fondos de titulizacion de activos*) (as originally put forward in Law 3/1994 of March 1994). They have no separate legal personality, and can be closed-ended or open-ended in nature (in the latter case, allowing the modification of fund assets or liabilities and revolving issuance). They must prepare reports on their assets for the CNMV.

Both varieties of fund are established by notarial deed, registered with the CNMV and managed by a licensed management company (a *sociedad gestora*, which is required to have a fully paid-up share capital of Peseta 150m and which acts as legal representative of the fund). The originator of the assets continues as servicer unless otherwise specified.

Foreign ownership

Approval is required for a more than 50% holding in a company where one or more of the foreign shareholders is resident in a tax haven, and approvals may be required for holdings in defence companies or the media. Acquisitions of more than 5% of the shares in a listed company and each subsequent 5% must be notified to the company, the stock exchange and the CNMV.

Tax treatment

Stamp/registration/etc.   Stamp duty is not charged on a transfer of receivables. Fees for notarising the transfer amount to circa 0.03% of the receivables, although lower fees may be negotiated with a stockbroker rather than a public notary. Notaries fees for transaction under the 1998 Decree are halved.

Withholding tax   Spain charges domestic withholding tax on interest payments by corporates or banks (which may include the payment by the originator to the SPV of receivables collections) to entities within Spain, unless made to a bank or a securitisation fund (see "Onshore SPV" above). Bonds have been exempted from this withholding since January 1999.

Offshore withholding tax is charged on interest payments made offshore and on the discount element on sales of assets at a rate of 18%, unless the SPV is resident in an EU member state and does not have a permanent establishment in Spain (this exemption has made establishment of an SPV in Ireland or the Netherlands a popular structure). Spanish law funds are also subject to withholding on payments made offshore, limiting their uses for deals to be distributed internationally. The rate may be reduced if a claim can be made under a double tax treaty.

Profits tax   An offshore SPV will only be liable to tax in Spain if it has a branch or agency in Spain which is effectively connected with the relevant income, or the SPV's principal place of management is in Spain. A *fondos de titulizacion hipotecaria* is liable to corporate tax.

Accounting treatment

There are no established principles, other than for banks where the requirements of Circular 4/91 (see below) must be met, but it is likely that off-balance-sheet treatment can be obtained if the SPV has no recourse against the originator other than in respect of the receivables.

Capital treatment

The Bank of Spain Circular 4/91 of 14 June 1991 (effective from 1 January 1992) requires that transfers must be a full transfer of all risks, rights and obligations attached to the assets. Thus, the originator is not generally allowed to support the assets or to agree to repurchase assets (not even for breach of warranty).

An issue of PHs can be treated as a transfer of assets out of the balance sheet of the originator for capital purposes.

Regulatory approvals

A Spanish SPV may be regarded as a credit institution in certain circumstances. A transaction under the new law which relates to future receivables other than toll road receipts is required to obtain the prior approval of the CNMV. The prospectus for the transaction is also required to be approved by the CNMV. Each time that further assets are sold into a *fondos de titulizacion de activos*, a report containing details of such further assets is required to be signed by the originator and submitted to the CNMV (this requirement can be difficult to comply with for transactions with short-term revolving structures such as trade receivables deals).

Other issues

Spain does not use trusts, but a trust under English law or another legal system should be recognised where there is a valid reason for the parties to select the law in question.

Financial assistance (including upstream security) given by a company for the acquisition of its shares is not permitted. There is no "whitewash" procedure for either public or private companies. Acquisition targets and acquirers can be legally merged.

The new Financial Law of November 2002 introduced a number of significant reforms of the Spanish legal system relating to derivatives and other financial transactions, as well as a new covered bond regime for public sector debt (see "Covered bonds" above). In particular, the law recognised close-out netting and the use of an outright transfer of title as a means of giving collateral. The law also simplified the perfection of security interests and recognition of security interests created under foreign law. The law is expected to encourage the growth of onshore synthetic structures.

12.45   SWEDEN

Sweden gave rise to one of the original secured loan structures through the St Erik deal. A bill to establish a covered bonds market was put forward in June 2003. Changes were passed in June 2001, which permit the establishment of limited purpose Swedish SPVs without the requirement for such SPVs to meet minimum capital requirements.

Ring-fencing and true sale

Under Swedish law, notice of a transfer of receivables is required to be given to debtors in order for the transfer to be effective on insolvency of the originator. The notice should, however, be able to be given informally on an account statement, provided that it is readily apparent to the debtor. Receipt of the notice must be established, but again, it should be possible to establish receipt by the conduct of the debtor in paying to a new account specified in the notice of transfer.

For a transfer of lease receivables, it may also be necessary to transfer the leased equipment, or there is a risk that a liquidator of the originator could try to sell the leased assets free and clear of the lease. To effect a transfer of leased equipment, notice to the lessee must be given.

Insolvency unwind Transactions entered into within 5 years of insolvency may be unwound in the event that the party dealing with the insolvent entity knew or ought to have known that the insolvent entity was insolvent at the time the transaction was entered into, or that it became insolvent as a result of the transaction, and that the transaction was improper. Transactions at an undervalue entered into within 6 months prior to insolvency may be unwound.

Recharacterisation To ensure that a transaction is regarded as a true sale, the documentation should express the parties' intent in a way that is consistent with a true sale. Other factors that are relevant include whether the originator has the right to repurchase the receivables, whether the originator is obliged to compensate the SPV for a loss on sale of the receivables, and whether or not the SPV has the right to dispose of the receivables.

Tax treatment

Stamp/registration/etc. There is no stamp duty on transfers of receivables. Stamp duty of 3% is charged on the transfer of real estate.

Withholding tax Interest on receivables may be paid to an onshore or offshore SPV free of withholding tax.

Accounting treatment

IAS standards are likely to be followed.

Capital treatment

The Swedish Financial Services Authority published guidelines in 2001 as to when bank assets will be considered to have been transferred off balance sheet for capital adequacy purposes following a securitisation or loan transfer by the bank. The guidelines permit transfer of assets to an unrelated SPV entity where there is no right of repurchase except in certain limited cases (including a 10% clean-up call). Credit enhancement must be directly deducted from capital.

Data protection/confidentiality

There are licensing requirements for entities holding personal data. The consent of the Data Inspectorate may be required for the transfer of information outside Sweden.

Regulatory approvals

Prior to 1 June 2001, a Swedish SPV may have been regarded as a credit institution and become subject to regulatory requirements of the Financial Supervisory Authority (the *Finansinspektionen*) (including minimum capital requirements of Euro 5m). Changes to these rules came into effect on 1 June 2001, which permit a Swedish SPV to operate without being subject to such regulation provided that they do not purchase receivables regularly, and that they do not issue debt to the public frequently.

An offshore SPV should not be so regarded as a credit institution provided that it is not regarded as conducting financing activities in Sweden.

Other issues

Trusts are not recognised in Sweden.

12.46   SWITZERLAND

The first mortgage securitisation (Tell Mortgage Backed Trust 1998-1) was closed for Swiss Bank Corp in March 1998 under Federal Banking Commission approval, but no further mortgage deals followed until the Swissact 2001-1 Sub-Trust deal for Zurcher Kantonalbank in November 2001.

A number of transactions for receivables such as trade receivables deals and leases have been closed each year since the market opened. The first Swiss CMBS deal, Eiger Trust, was closed in May 2003.

Ring-fencing and true sale

Receivables may be transferred without the need to give notice to debtors of the transfer (although see "Data protection/confidentiality" below).

Future receivables   The validity of a transfer of future receivables which come into existence after the insolvency of the originator is unclear.

Covered bonds   Legislation permits the issuance of Pfandbriefe. Pfandbriefe may be backed by a pool of mortgages over Swiss land. Public sector Pfandbriefe are not permitted.

Set-off

The debtor can obtain good discharge by making payments to the originator until notice of the assignment is given to the debtor, at which point the debtor is obliged to pay to the SPV direct. The SPV will take subject to any defects in the title of the originator and, until notice is given to the debtor, the SPV is subject to any further equities (such as set-off) arising in favour of the debtor through relations between the originator and the debtor subsequent to the assignment.

Onshore SPV

A Swiss SPV may be subject to certain thin capitalisation issues with deductibility of interest expenses, and to capital taxes on incorporation. Both areas have, however, recently been relaxed or removed in some cantons.

Foreign ownership

Acquisitions of more than 5%, 10%, 20%, 33%, 50% or 66% of the shares in a listed company must be notified to the company and the stock exchange.

Securities laws

The Swiss Stock Exchange published rules for the listing of ABS issues in Switzerland in September 1997. These rules relax requirements as to a minimum trading history of 3 years and minimum capital, where the issuer is an ABS issuer. The issue must have at least one credit rating.

Tax treatment

Withholding tax   Switzerland applies withholding tax at a rate of 35% on interest payable on a security which is regarded as an issue from Switzerland. This may be the case even where an offshore SPV issuer is used and the proceeds of the issue are paid to a Swiss originator, unless the SPV can be shown to be independent of the originator and to have purchased the receivables in a true sale. Withholding tax is also charged on interest on mortgage loans paid to offshore entities.

Profits tax   An offshore SPV should not be liable to Swiss tax unless it has a permanent establishment in Switzerland.

Other tax issues   Securities issued by a Swiss entity are liable to annual stamp duty at 0.12% per annum of the amount issued. Switzerland allows a limited tax deduction for interest on residential mortgages.

Capital treatment

On 26 March 1998, the Federal Banking Commission (FBC) determined that securitised assets may be removed from the capital balance sheet (even in cases where the originator provides liquidity or credit support to the transaction) provided that the SPV is independent of the originator and that the originator is not obliged to support the SPV beyond the amount of any defined credit support. Credit support will be deducted directly from capital.

Data protection/confidentiality

Switzerland has strict bank secrecy laws, which require debtor consent to be obtained for a transfer of receivables. Banks in Switzerland have begun using standard waiver provisions in customer documentation to circumvent these provisions.

Regulatory approvals

Any securitisation by a bank entity should be submitted to the Federal Banking Commission for approval. The FBC has confirmed that Swiss SPVs will not be required to be authorised as banking entities.

Other issues

Switzerland does not always recognise trusts, and it is advisable to structure trusts with foreign trustees and constitute them under a governing law other than Swiss law.

On 1 October 1997 a law (the Lex Koller) was passed that enables non-Swiss investors to hold Swiss commercial real estate. Foreign investment in residential real estate (including taking the benefit of security interests over a substantial part of the value of a property) remains regulated. As a result of this restriction, a security interest cannot be granted over Swiss residential real estate to an offshore entity to support debt that exceeds 80% of the value of the real estate. This restriction dictated the structure of the Swissact 2001-1 deal, which transferred residential mortgage loans to a Swiss SPV with no onward security given to the offshore SPV issuer.

12.47   TAIWAN

The Financial Institution Merger Act 2001 was passed in 2001, allowing the establishment of Asset Management Companies (AMCs). In January 2001, Goldman Sachs and Chinatrust Commercial Bank of Taiwan announced the establishment of an Asset Management Corporation to buy non-performing loans from the banking sector. At the same time, another group of 20 Taiwanese banks, together with Deutsche Bank, Lehman Brothers and Orix announced the establishment of a similar AMC to buy non-performing loans. An AMC planned by China Development Industrial Bank and Morgan Stanley foundered in June 2001.

On 14 September 2001, Taiwan forced 35 local financial institutions burdened by non-performing loans to merge with 10 commercial banks. In April 2002, First Commercial Bank announced the sale of T$ 13bn of NPLs to Cerberus at 40% of book, and its intention to sell a further T$ 50bn, with the losses to be amortised over 5 years under new rules designed to encourage disposal of NPLs.

The Real Estate Securitisation Act on the securitisation of real estate, which was expected to be passed by the end of 2002, was passed in 2003.

The first Taiwanese securitisation was launched in February 2003, with the NT$ 3.6bn balance sheet CLO for the Industrial Bank of Taiwan.

In March 2001, proposals were put forward to allow foreigners to own land in Taiwan.

Securitisation legislation for the securitisation of financial assets (the Financial Assets Securitisation Act – the "FAS") was drafted by the Ministry of Finance in August 2001, and passed into force on 22 June 2002.

Ring-fencing and true sale

The FAS allows for the securitisation of credit cards, leases, auto loans, mortgages, corporate bonds and other consumer assets. Originally under the FAS, the originator had to be a financial institution, or another institution approved by the Ministry of Finance. In July 2003, the Ministry of Finance announced an interpretation that institutions other than financial institutions would be permitted to use the FAS. Transfer only requires publication of a general notice in a national daily newspaper.

Notice to the debtor is still required for the transfer to be enforceable against the debtor.

Terms in the receivables documentation that prohibit assignment or transfer by the originator of its rights under the contract, or require that the originator must obtain the consent of the relevant debtor in order to assign or transfer its rights under the contract, will prevent any assignment or transfer being effective unless the consent of the debtor to the transfer is in fact obtained.

Onshore SPV

The FAS permits securitisation via an SPV or a special purpose trust (an SPT). An SPV originally required minimum capital of NT$ 1m under Taiwanese company law, but this has been reduced to NT$ 100 000 for securitisation SPVs from October 2002. The Real Estate Securitisation Act of July 2003 provides for the establishment of REIT-style trusts, which would be exempt from certain land taxes.

Foreign ownership

Foreign ownership of a listed company is restricted to 50%. Acquisitions of more than 10% in a listed company, and each subsequent change, must be notified to the Securities and Exchange Commission.

Securities laws

Public offerings will be required to be approved by the Securities and Futures Commission.

Tax treatment

Stamp/registration/etc.   Transfer of shares is subject to a securities transaction tax at 0.3%. Transfers under the FAS are exempt from stamp duty and from registration fees.

Withholding tax   Taiwan has 20% withholding tax. This has been reduced to 6% for withholding on interest paid to offshore entities holding securities issued by a deal under the FAS.

Profits tax   SPTs under the FAS have fiscal transparency.

Regulatory approvals

The FAS requires a plan to be approved by the Ministry of Finance.

12.48   THAILAND

After the first Thai securitisation in August 1996 two subsequent transactions followed, prior to the Thai baht devaluation in July 1997 and the subsequent Asian currency crisis. All three transactions were auto loan transactions, as were many of the deals in the pipeline, which were postponed following the currency crisis. The Thai government brought in various measures through 1997, including legislation on onshore SPVs and reform of the financial sector, which were designed to ease obstacles for securitisation of mortgages and other receivables and to stabilise the financial system.

The Financial Sector Restructuring Authority (FRA) was established in 1997 and was mandated to assess restructuring plans in the finance company sector. The FRA initially suspended 58 of the 91 company finance company sector (16 on 24 June 1997 and a further 42 on 5 August 1997), but by an announcement on 8 December 1997, two of the companies were allowed to continue in business. The FRA appointed new management to the remaining 56 companies from the Ministry of Finance (MOF) and auctioned their assets off over 1998 and 1999. The sale of assets from the finance companies by the FRA was largely completed in August 1999, with the sale of a pool of commercial loans. Overall realisations were c. 19% of book value, and less than half of the expected realisation amount.

The Asset Management Corporation (AMC) was established on 22 October 1998 as a government entity wholly owned by the MOF, and was mandated as a bidder (together with private investors) in these auctions, with capital of THB 15bn (increased in August 1998), and a 10% capital/assets ratio. It subsequently paid in excess of THB 30bn for assets at an average price of around 15% of par.

The Union Bank of Bangkok was merged with 12 failed finance companies to create BankThai, a new government-owned institution, with the bad loans on its books separately guaranteed by the government. Thailand also established a mortgage corporation, the Secondary Mortgage Corporation (SMC), to purchase and securitise the mortgage portfolios of Thai banks.

In January 2000, the Government Land Department reduced property valuations (which are used to determine the level of provisions made by banks against property loans, and the amount of property tax paid by developers) by 25%, which was anticipated to increase activity in the domestic property market as owners would be forced to recognise the extent to which prices had fallen since the property bubble burst in the 1990s.

Deals after the Asian crisis were mostly domestically issued and distributed, due to the high costs of obtaining currency swaps and of credit enhancing transactions sufficiently to achieve ratings over the Thai sovereign ceiling. Surplus domestic liquidity (due to the flight to quality of deposits to some of the stronger banks, and the reluctance of these banks to risk lending to any but the strongest corporates while the economy was still heavily burdened with non-performing debt and debt restructuring) created a natural investor base for these domestic issues.

In July 2002, Lehman refinanced its purchase of non-performing mortgage loans from the FRA in 1998, and from DBS Thai Danu Bank in 2000, with THB 7.17bn of notes and loans via GT Stars II.

In November 2002, the first Thai-based CP conduit, Osprey Series I Co. Ltd, was established. The conduit acquired THB 607.9m (c. US$ 15m) of bonds from an SPV backed by residential housing hire purchase contracts originated by the National Housing Authority.

Thailand operates a civil law system.

Several steps were taken to remove legal and tax obstacles to the FRA auctions in 1998:

- An Emergency Decree of 22 May 1998 was introduced which provided for the true sale of the auction assets through newspaper advertisement of the auction, without notice being given to the debtors, and prevented debtors undertaking set-off against any amounts due from the finance companies.
- The Emergency Decree also provided that a purchaser under an FRA auction may charge interest at the rate set out in the underlying contract even where it is in excess of 15%, provided that the rate under the original contract was permitted under usury laws (see "Other issues" below).
- In May and June 1998 the MOF and the Land Department acted to enable a non-credit foncier purchaser of mortgage assets in the FRA auctions to be registered as mortgagee.
- On 26 May 1998 the Securities and Exchange Commission (SEC) acted to approve the establishment of Thai funds to acquire financial assets.
- The reduction of mortgage transfer fees from 1% to 0.01% and waiver of certain specific business tax and value-added tax costs was decided on 11 August 1998.

The Bankruptcy Act was amended in 1998 and 1999.

Ring-fencing and true sale

Until 1997, any transfer of receivables under Thai law required that notice be given to the debtors under s. 306 of the Commercial Code in order for the transfer to be effective to transfer the receivables out of the insolvency estate of the originator. Notice is not required to be served in any particular formal manner, although a general form of notice on an account statement is unlikely to be effective. In Thailand it is generally advisable to register a transfer of mortgages to protect against fraud risk. This could take the form of a second fraudulent transfer by the seller of the same mortgages, or the use of the sale proceeds when a customer moves (proceeds will usually be paid to the party registered in the mortgage register). Registration of the purchaser as mortgagee will also allow the purchaser to give the owner a valid release of the mortgage if the property is sold. Registration of a mortgage transfer is subject to a 1% mortgage transfer fee (subject to a maximum of THB 200 000 per mortgage) (but see above). It is possible that a purchaser of mortgages which is not set up under the new ABS law may find that the registrar will not be permitted to register the purchase, as the purchaser is not a credit foncier company (but see above in relation to purchasers of mortgage loan assets under the FRA auction process).

To promote the use of securitisation, a new ABS Law (Decree of B.E. 2540 on Special

Juristic Persons for Securitisation) was passed on 27 June 1997, s. 15 of which allows for an effective transfer of receivables to be made without giving notice to debtors, where the purchaser is an onshore Thai SPV (see details below) established and supervised under the provisions of the new law. The provisions of the new law also require, however, that the requirement for notice is only removed if the originator remains as servicer of the receivables after they are transferred. If the servicer is required to be removed (for example, due to its bankruptcy or due to its default in carrying out its services), then the requirement to serve notice on debtors revives at such point in time. This could be problematic, as bankruptcy of the originator/servicer is the primary situation in which the SPV wants to be assured that the transfer to it of the receivables is not likely to be challenged for any reason. The new law can be used by originators who are commercial banks, finance companies, securities companies, credit foncier and corporates.

Insolvency unwind   The main insolvency unwind provisions in the Commercial Code in Thailand relate to:

(a) the cancellation of fraudulent transactions (s. 113);
(b) the unwind of transfers made within 3 years prior to bankruptcy unless they are made in good faith and for consideration (s. 114); and
(c) the cancellation of transfers to a creditor within 3 months prior to bankruptcy (or 1 year where the creditor is a relative or business associate of the bankrupt) which were intended to give undue preference to the creditor (s. 115).

Under s. 116, the rights of third parties dealing with the bankrupt in good faith and for consideration will not be affected by any unwind or cancellation under ss. 114–115. An undue preference which is a fraudulent act and which is done for low (or no) consideration may be cancelled if it is carried out within 1 year prior to bankruptcy.

Recharacterisation   A transfer under the new ABS Law will be regarded as a true sale, and will not be liable to be unwound, provided that it was made for fair market value, that the SPV takes on the risks and benefits of the assets and that the SPV holds title to the assets.

Moratorium/automatic stay   The Bankruptcy Act amendments of April 1998 and April 1999 introduced provisions for a moratorium following application to the courts by creditors owed THB 10m or more. Once the application is accepted, the moratorium will prevent court proceedings against the debtor and enforcement of security by secured creditors without court consent. Subsequently, a moratorium plan must be formulated and accepted by a creditors' vote, and then approved by the court.

Set-off

Until debtors are notified of a transfer, they may continue to accrue new rights of set-off.

Onshore SPV

The new ABS Law allows companies to undertake securitisations through the use of an SPV (which can take the form of a limited company, a public limited company or a mutual fund) which is approved and regulated by the SEC. The SPV enjoys certain advantages in the transfer of receivables (see above) and mortgage transfer registration costs (see below), as well as clarification on its regulatory position (see below). The SPV cannot issue convertible securities, and in most cases cannot incur debt (other than the securities it issues). The SEC did not permit the establishment of a fund under the new ABS law, but in some cases, use of a fund outside the ambit of the new law may be feasible.

On 26 May 1998, an SEC press release provided for the establishment of Thai mutual funds in the form of real estate funds (holding not less than 75% of their assets in real estate), real estate receivables funds (holding not less than 75% of their assets in real estate or loans secured over real estate) or funds holding other assets. The funds are established by a fund manager, a registrar, a custodian/trustee (who holds the asset documentation) and an investment committee. Funds require SEC approval. Certain activities of a fund may require approval of the unitholders or SEC approval, but, in other respects, the fund manager carries out the stated policy of the fund with the investment committee deciding discretionary areas. The three fund types are broadly similar, with a minimum permissible initial size of THB 500m (there is no minimum ongoing size), and a minimum of 10 institutional investors (such as banks, finance companies and non-residents who have licensed investment advisers) holding a maximum of 10% of the fund units each. The funds are mostly required to be closed-ended with no redemptions, but regular capital reductions may be made.

Foreign ownership

The Alien Business Law prohibited the involvement of foreigners as majority owners of many types of business, but did not restrict foreign management. The Foreign Business Act of 1999, which replaced the Alien Business Law, relaxes these limitations and maintains the beneficial treatment available to US investors (which permits them to establish wholly-owned Thai subsidiaries).

Listed company shares owned by foreigners are traded on a separate board from shares in the same company held by Thais. Acquisitions of more than 5% (and each multiple of 5%) in a listed company must be notified to the stock exchange and the Securities and Exchange Commission.

Tax treatment

Stamp/registration/etc.   Mortgage transfer registration fees are charged by the Land Registry on the registration of a transfer of mortgages at an *ad valorem* rate of 1% (subject to a maximum of THB 200 000 per mortgage). A transfer under the ABS Law is exempt. Stamp duty is charged at an *ad valorem* or fixed rate on different instruments, but is nominal in most cases.

The waiver of stamp duty on securitisation transactions under the new ABS Law was announced on 22 July 1998, and promulgated as a Royal Decree in November 1998 to exempt transactions between an originator and an SPV.

Withholding tax   Thailand charges withholding tax at a rate of 15% on interest payments made by an onshore SPV to Thai individual investors (there is no withholding on interest payments from an onshore SPV to Thai corporate investors). Withholding is charged at 15% on interest and rental payments made to an offshore entity, and at 10% on dividend payments. The popular European structuring route of using double taxation treaties is only of limited use, as Thailand has no treaties that reduce the rate to zero. Withholding tax on interest payments made to a Bangkok International Banking Facility is charged at a reduced rate of 10%.

If interest-bearing receivables are sold offshore, withholding may, for some kinds of receivables, be applied to the receivables interest. The most prevalent method of structuring to reduce withholding tax has utilised a transfer to an onshore SPV, which funds itself through a yen loan, ensuring that the interest payment that is passed offshore, and is subjected to withholding, is minimised. On 20 March 1996, the Bank of Thailand gave a ruling to cover circumstances where a yen funding is combined with currency swaps, such that the Thai borrower receives a different currency. The ruling states that if the entity providing the funding is actually the same as the swap counterparty, withholding tax should be accounted for on the coupon that the borrower is paying under the swap.

Fees may also be subject to withholding at a 3% rate.

Withholding tax costs are not waived under the new ABS law.

There is an exemption from withholding tax or Thai corporate tax on dividends and capital gains paid from a Thai fund to offshore institutional investors who are not engaged in a business in Thailand. Thai tax resident institutional investors in the fund will be subject to corporate tax on capital gains, and may be subject to corporate tax on dividends (although if Thai investors hold the fund units for a minimum of 3 months prior and 3 months after each dividend date, they will be entitled to a tax reduction on their normal corporate tax bill on dividends – reducing the normal corporate tax rate (30%) to 0% for listed investors and to 15% for unlisted investors).

Profits tax   Corporate profits tax is charged at a rate of 30%. Expenses that are incurred by a company solely in furtherance of the business of the company are tax deductible in calculating profits. Mutual funds are exempt from tax on income or capital gains.

VAT/SBT etc.   A disposal of receivables (as opposed to a secured loan structure) is chargeable either to VAT at a rate of 7% on the principal amount of the receivables or to Specific Business Tax (SBT) at a rate of 3.3% on the profit or discount on the sale. Whether a disposal would be liable to VAT or SBT would depend on the nature of the business of the seller. SBT is chargeable in relation to certain businesses only, such as finance, securities or banking businesses. VAT charged is not likely to be recoverable by an offshore SPV and will only be recoverable over time, if at all, by an onshore SPV. VAT is also charged on servicing fees.

In addition, as SBT is generally chargeable on all interest, fees or profits derived by a Thai entity from a finance, securities or banking business, loans forming part of a secured loan structure will also be liable to SBT at a rate of 3.3% on the interest amounts if the loan is made by a Thai entity considered to be carrying on a finance, securities or banking business. An exemption from SBT is available for payments of interest made to an entity that has been owned to at least 25% by the payor entity for at least 6 months prior to the date of payment.

Certain financial activities are liable to Specific Business Tax (SBT) (at 3.3%). The tax will be charged at 3.3% on the interest income arising on the mortgages, and can be charged on a cash or an accruals basis, as selected by the payor (although once a basis is selected, the basis cannot be changed without the agreement of the Revenue). SBT will also be charged at 3.3% (reduced to 0.11% for the period from 28 June 2000 until December 2001) on the total sale proceeds arising from enforcement of a mortgage by auction of the relevant property.

The waiver of VAT and SBT on securitisation transactions under the new securitisation law was announced on 22 July 1998, and promulgated as Royal Decrees in November 1998 to exempt transactions between an originator and an SPV from VAT and SBT.

Other tax issues   Thailand allows a deduction from taxable income for up to THB 50 000 per annum (THB 10 000 per annum prior to 28 June 2000) of interest paid to a Thai bank or financial institution on a loan made for the purpose of purchasing or building a residence for the borrower, which is secured over the relevant land.

Consumer protection

Unfair Contract Terms legislation was brought into force on 15 May 1998, and applies to standard form contracts and consumer contracts with unfair provisions.

Regulatory approvals

Commercial banks (deposit-taking entities which make loans), finance businesses (businesses which procure funds from the public to make certain varieties of loan) and credit foncier businesses (entities lending money on security over land) are regulated by the Bank of Thailand and the Ministry of Finance and carry licensing, minimum share capital and capital adequacy requirements. Leasing business is not generally regulated. If the SPV is considered to be carrying on a regulated activity, it may be required to be licensed. There is an exemption in the new ABS Law from the requirement for such a new SPV to obtain approvals, even where the business it is undertaking prima facie falls within one of the regulated categories. Thai SEC approval for such a new SPV is, however, required.

Prior approval of the Bank of Thailand or the MOF is required for securitisations by regulated entities. The Bank of Thailand currently requires that securitisations by regulated entities utilise the new ABS Law.

Other issues

Only credit foncier companies, finance companies and banks may charge loan interest in excess of a rate of 15%, pursuant to the provisions of s. 654 of the Commercial Code. SPVs under the new ABS law may charge loan interest in excess of a rate of 15% where the interest rate was validly charged on the relevant loan prior to the sale of the loan to the SPV. The new mutual fund provisions are silent on this area. If a higher rate is charged there is a risk that the entire interest obligation will be void. The limit does not apply to the effective interest rate comprised in rental payments under a lease.

Thai companies must have at least seven shareholders.

In most cases, trusts will not be recognised in Thailand. Where a security trust is intended, it may therefore be necessary to appoint the security trustee as a security agent instead. In such a case, all the secured creditors should be party to the security document, and they should appoint the security agent as agent on their behalf for the purposes of enforcement. Concerns with commingling of collections in an account of the originator may have to be addressed with a pledge over the account or regular sweeps of the account.

There are strict time limits and procedural requirements (the serving of demand notices, etc.) on the presentation of bills of exchange in Thailand. If they are not complied with, claims of creditors under the bills of exchange may be invalidated.

Foreign judgements are not enforced by the Thai courts.

Mortgages generally only secure a fixed amount (as stated in the mortgage), and are not usually "all monies".

Non-Thais are prohibited from owning land in Thailand.

Thai law provides for two methods of enforcing mortgage security over land. There is no provision for a private sale of the property, or for a seized property to be rented out by the lender to receive income pending sale (the property must remain vacant).

The first method is a court enforcement order that will allow the mortgagee to seize and auction the property by court auction over a 1–3 year procedure (longer if the procedure is contested). Enforcement costs will include court fees (2.5% of the principal amount of the mortgage), lawyers fees, auction fees (5% of the amount of the sale price), property transfer tax (2%, but reduced to 0.01% where a Thai fund is the purchaser from the court auction), stamp tax (0.5% of the sale price) and specific business tax (at 3.3% – or 0.11% as described in VAT/SBT etc. above – of the total sale price).

The second is foreclosure, where the mortgagee assumes ownership of the land, thus extinguishing any rights of the mortgagor in the land. Foreclosure may be exercised after the mortgagor has failed to pay any amounts on the mortgage for a period of at least 5 years, and where the value of the property is less than or equal to the value of the mortgage debt (but may only be exercised by Thai entities as non-Thais are prohibited from owning land in Thailand – a Thai mutual fund will be considered to be a Thai entity for this purpose, but is restricted to holding land received from foreclosure for a maximum of 2 years prior to selling it). The foreclosure law was revised in certain minor respects in April 1999.

12.49 TURKEY

Transactions in Turkey have largely focused on future flows offshore transactions, due to the low sovereign ceiling as against the creditworthiness of some of its corporates and banks, and the level of hard currency receipts from tourism and remittances from Turkish workers overseas (especially from Germany).

Most transactions to date have been at the low investment grade level, with occasional AAA wrapped transactions.

Transactions increased from 1999 to 2001, until the Turkish crisis.

Ring-fencing and true sale

Receivables can be transferred without the requirement to notify debtors. Terms in the receivables documentation that prohibit assignment or transfer by the originator of its rights under the contract, or require that the originator must obtain the consent of the relevant debtor in order to assign or transfer its rights under the contract, will prevent any assignment or transfer being effective unless the consent of the debtor to the transfer is in fact obtained.

Insolvency unwind   Transactions at an undervalue or gratuitous transactions may be cancelled if entered into within 2 years prior to insolvency. Transactions granting further security for an existing debt may be cancelled if entered into within 1 year prior to insolvency.

12.50   UNITED KINGDOM

The UK is the leading European securitisation market, as well as being the oldest and the most innovative to date. This is due to a combination of factors, including the flexibility and workable nature of the legal and tax systems, the location in the UK of the leading European financial centre (the City of London), and the early transplantation to the UK of US methods of asset origination.

The establishment of the Mortgage Corporation in the UK in 1986 by Salomon Brothers led to the opening up of the UK mortgage securitisation market in 1987, and issuance of between Euro 2bn and Euro 8bn equivalent per annum followed until 1992.

The 1992 property price recession and slump in mortgage lending reduced activity in the mortgage securitisation sector significantly, but issuance in other asset classes picked up significantly, widening the scope of the market dramatically and making it the most diverse and developed market outside the US.

Issuance levels have increased from Euro 25bn in 1999, to Euro 41.7bn in 2000, Euro 51.3bn in 2001 and Euro 54bn in 2002. Much of this is still down to RMBS issuance, although the old centralised lenders have been replaced by multi-billion pound issues under the mortgage master trust programmes of Abbey National, HBOS and Northern Rock (the largest of which have securitised some £5bn (Euro 7bn) of mortgages under a single issue). Credit card master trusts set up by Barclaycard, Capital One and MBNA have been another prime contributor to issuance levels.

The UK has also seen significant CMBS issuance, in particular under bank conduit programmes, and developments in principal finance and whole business securitisation techniques from 1997 onwards have made securitisation more widely used in corporate and acquisition finance – leading the US markets in this field.

In the Budget of 9 April 2003 Professor David Miles, professor of finance at Imperial College in London, was commissioned to research the nature and cause of the lack of development of long-dated fixed rate mortgage products and demand for such products. The underlying concern here was the volatility of UK house prices relative to those in continental Europe due to the preponderance of floating rate mortgages in the UK, and the consequent sensitivity of house prices to the level of interest rates in the economy. Attempts to reduce this volatility by developing a long-dated fixed rate mortgage market in the UK would be beneficial to considerations on the UK joining the Euro, and giving control on interest rate setting over to the European Central Bank.

One of the more significant recent developments in the UK is the introduction of the insolvency provisions of the Enterprise Act from September 2003. The Act provides for reform to insolvency law to encourage the use of administration and voluntary procedures. The Act contains a prohibition on the ability of a creditor to appoint an administrative receiver except in certain cases relating to capital markets issuance (there are exemptions for most securitisation transactions), and develops more detailed provisions for the use of administration.

The law of England and Wales is a common law system based on statute and case law.

Ring-fencing and true sale

Under English law conflicts of laws principles (pursuant to Schedule 1, Article 12 of the Contracts (Applicable Law) Act 1990), the assignability or non-assignability of an intangible such as the benefit of a contract is determined by the governing law of the underlying contract giving rise to the intangible.

To determine the governing law of contracts entered into after 31 March 1991, the UK courts will apply the terms of the Rome Convention on the Law Applicable to Contractual Obligations as enacted in the Contracts (Applicable Law) Act 1990, which, at Schedule 1, Articles 3 and 4, upholds the parties' choice of law, applying the law of the country with which the contract is most closely connected in default of such a choice.

For contracts governed by English law, transfer is normally effected by assignment, which can be legal or equitable. Legal assignments are rarely used, as they must, under s. 136, Law of Property Act 1925:

- Be in writing and signed by the assignor;
- Be absolute (i.e. be unconditional or by way of mortgage and not merely by way of charge);
- Cover the whole of the debt or chose in action;
- Be notified in writing to the borrower or other obligor.

In particular, the requirement to notify the borrower of the transfer has led to a reluctance to use legal assignments. As the alternative – an equitable assignment – has long been considered sufficient to effect a true sale, this is generally used instead. An equitable assignment is an assignment that does not meet all the s. 136 criteria. No specific requirement needs to be met (e.g. the assignment need not be in writing), although an equitable assignment of an equitable chose in action must comply with the requirements of s. 53(1)(c) Law of Property Act 1925; that is, it must be in writing and signed by the assignor. An equitable assignment is effective against the assignor and third parties, but is only effective against the debtor where there is privity of contract between the debtor and the assignee. Thus, in most cases, the assignee must sue the debtor in the assignor's name by joining him in proceedings (although this does not prejudice the assignee's proprietary interest in the debt). An equitable assignment is only effective to transfer the full extent of the title held by the assignor. Any defences that the debtor could have raised against the assignor will be effective against the assignee and the debtor can obtain good discharge by making payments to the assignor. When notice of the assignment is given from the assignee to the debtor, the debtor is obliged to pay to the assignee direct. Until such notice is given, the assignee is subject to any further equities (such as set-off rights with regard to amounts which accrue due from the assignor to the debtor prior to receipt by the debtor of the notice) arising in favour of the debtor through relations between the assignor and the debtor.

The transfer of a mortgage will automatically operate to transfer with it the debt secured by the mortgage under s. 114, Law of Property Act 1925.

The burden of a contract cannot be transferred without novation, which is rarely used as it requires the signed agreement of the underlying borrower.

There are no restrictions preventing a sale of receivables to an SPV located outside the originator's jurisdiction.

Under s. 94, Law of Property Act 1925, tacking of further advances is permitted where: (a) an agreement to that effect is reached with the intervening creditor; (b) the original lender had no notice of the intervening security when the further advance was made; or (c) the original lender is under an obligation to make the further advance by the terms of the original security (whether or not notice of the intervening security has been given). By s. 30 of the Land Registration Act 1925, a different regime applies to registered land; here, priority may only be maintained until the original lender receives (or ought to have received) notice from the registrar of the intervening security, unless there is an obligation on the original lender to make the further advance and the obligation is actually noted on the register.

Terms in the receivables documentation that prohibit assignment or transfer by the originator of its rights under the contract, or require that the originator must obtain the consent of the relevant debtor in order to assign or transfer its rights under the contract, will, depending on their wording, prevent any assignment or transfer being effective unless the consent of the debtor to the transfer is obtained. A declaration of a trust over the contractual rights in favour of the SPV may however be used instead under the terms of the 1998 Don King case, which recognised a declaration of trust as being effective to circumvent a prohibition on the assignment of receivables on the basis that a clause prohibiting assignments is prima facie restricted to assignments of the benefit of the obligation and does not extend to declarations of trust of the benefit unless it is the intention of the parties that it should cover a trust as well.

See under "Assignment" and "Declaration of trust" in Chapter 13 for more detail.

Contracts that are personal in nature (e.g. contracts dependent on the personal skill of the individual in question) are not assignable, although amounts accrued due under a personal contract remain assignable.

Future receivables   A future receivable can be transferred provided that it is properly and clearly identified, such that "on its coming into existence, it shall answer the description in the assignment, or, in other words, that it shall be capable of being identified as the thing, or as one of the very things assigned" (per Lord Watson in *Tailby v. Official Receiver (1888) (HL)*). The transfer will take effect as an agreement to assign, which will give rise to an equitable assignment of the receivables the moment that they come into existence, without any further act being required to be done.

Undivided interest   An attempt by an originator to achieve a true sale of an undivided interest in receivables is at risk of being regarded as a mere contractual right against the originator, due to lack of appropriation or identification of the goods in which a proprietary interest was to pass. It is possible to protect against the risk that no proprietary interest is transferred by a true sale of the entire interest in the receivables, with the receivables sold into a trust (constituted by an express declaration of trust over the whole of the pool), whereby the originator and investors are entitled to trust interests matching their respective shares. More recently, however, *Re Harvard Securities Ltd [1997] 2 BCLC 369* decided that an equitable assignment of an unappropriated interest in shares is effective to pass a proprietary interest to the purchaser (and distinguished previous cases as relating to chattels rather than shares).

Insolvency unwind   The main insolvency unwind provisions in the UK relate to transactions at an undervalue and preferences. A transaction at an undervalue occurs where, within 2 years of the commencement of a winding-up the company enters into any transaction with a person "for a consideration the value of which, in money or money's worth, is significantly less than the value, in money or money's worth, of the consideration provided by the company" or for no consideration (except where entered into in good faith and for the purpose of carrying on the company's business and reasonable grounds existed to believe that the transaction would be beneficial to the company). A preference arises where, within 6 months of commencement of a winding-up (2 years if with a person connected to the company), any person is a creditor of or a guarantor for a company, and the company "does anything or suffers anything to be done which ... has the effect of putting that person into a position which, in the event of the company going into insolvent liquidation, will be better than the position he would have been in if that thing had not been done". In addition, any transaction undertaken in order to place assets beyond the reach of a creditor may be unwound as a transaction defrauding creditors by court order at the request of a liquidator or the prejudiced creditor.

Recharacterisation   In determining whether the transaction is a true sale or a secured loan (with the resultant possibility that the so-called security may be void for lack of registration or failure to comply with other requirements for security interests), a UK court will look at whether the documentation for the transaction is a sham to conceal the parties' true intention. If they consider it is not a sham, they will construe the documentation to determine the parties' intent and hence the true characterisation of the transaction. A right of the originator to repurchase the receivables, or an obligation to compensate the SPV for a loss on sale of the receivables, may prejudice a true sale characterisation; however, no single feature is determinative and the court will look at the nature of the relationship between the parties as a whole. See "Recharacterisation" in Chapter 13 for more detail.

Substantive consolidation   There is no doctrine of substantive consolidation in the UK save for the limited circumstances in which the UK courts may ignore the corporate veil of a company and seek to make members liable for the company's liabilities. This is very rare and typically arises where there is evidence that the company is used to perpetrate a fraud, or where the company is used for an illegal or improper purpose.

Moratorium/automatic stay   In the UK, provisions akin to an automatic stay or moratorium are limited to administration proceedings. Secured creditors are prevented from taking action to enforce security from the date of commencement of an administration until the administration is over. Administration can be blocked by the appointment of an administrative receiver, although the use of administrative receivership is limited by the insolvency provisions of the Enterprise Act which came into force in September 2003. The Enterprise Act contains a prohibition on the ability of a creditor to appoint an administrative receiver under a floating charge, but there are a series of exceptions to the new provision, which permit the appointment of an administrative receiver.

The key provision is s. 250, which provides an exception where there is security to a trustee/nominee/agent for holders of an instrument (or there is a third-party guarantee or security interest, or there is an arrangement involving options, futures or contracts for differences) under which a party incurs (or is expected to incur) debt of at least £50m (or currency equivalent as at the time when the arrangement is entered into) at any time during the life of the arrangement, where the arrangement involves the issue of:

- A debt instrument that is rated by an internationally recognised rating agency, admitted to the official list in the UK, or admitted to trading on a market established under the rules of a recognised investment exchange or on a foreign market (or is designed to be so rated, listed or traded); or
- A bond or commercial paper (which must be redeemed before its first anniversary) issued to investment professionals, high net worth individuals or sophisticated investors.

There is also an exception in s. 250 in respect of a project company (a company that holds property for the project, or has sole or principal contractual responsibility for carrying out all or part of the project (either directly or through agents), or is one of a number of companies which, together, carry out the project, or has the purpose of supplying finance to enable the project to be carried out, or is a holding company of any of these, unless in any of such cases it also performs another function which is neither related to any of these nor related to the project) for a public–private partnership project, a utility project or a project under which a party incurs (or is expected to incur) debt of at least £50m (or currency equivalent as at the time when the project begins) at any time during the life of the arrangement, where in each case a person who provides finance for the project has contractual step-in rights to assume sole or principal contractual responsibility for carrying out all or part of the project.

Special administration regimes in relation to water and sewage undertakers, protected railway companies, air traffic services, public–private partnerships and building societies are preserved by s. 249 of the Act.

Set-off

The debtor can obtain good discharge by making payments to the originator until notice of the assignment is given to the debtor, at which point the debtor is obliged to pay to the SPV direct. The SPV will take subject to any defects in the title of the originator and, until notice is given to the debtor, the SPV is subject to any further equities (such as set-off rights with regard to amounts that accrue due from the originator to the debtor prior to receipt by the debtor of the notice) arising in favour of the debtor through relations between the originator and the debtor.

Onshore SPV

Only a public company may make an offer of securities to the UK public or apply for a listing for a securities issue. Public companies are required to have a minimum issued share capital of at least £50 000, of which at least £12 500 must be paid-up.

Foreign ownership

Acquisition of more than 3% of the shares in a listed company and certain other public companies, and each subsequent 1% increase or decrease in shareholding, must be notified to the company under ss. 198–200 of the Companies Act 1985. Acquisitions of stakes of 10% or more in a listed company from more than one person during a 7-day period which takes the total stake to 15% or more are not permitted. Any person acquiring 30% of more of a company is required to make a mandatory offer for a simple majority (more than 50%) of the shares in the company.

Securities laws

There are requirements to produce a prospectus for any offer of securities to the UK public (or any section of the UK public) that is not exempt or a listed issue (if listed, it will be subject to the Financial Services Authority listing rules on prospectuses instead). Chief exemptions include offers to professionals, offers to a "restricted circle" of knowledgeable investors, offers with a denomination of Euro 40 000 or more each, or offers of "Euro-securities" in relation to which no advertisement (other than an advertisement of a prescribed kind) is issued in the UK. Securities offered pursuant to an exemption will subsequently become subject to prospectus requirements if later offered in a way that is an offer to the public and is not exempt, unless the securities have been listed prior to the making of the offer. See "Prospectus" and "Offer to the public" in Chapter 13 for more detail.

Tax treatment

Stamp/registration/etc. UK stamp duty was largely abolished in the Finance Act 2003. The Finance Act 2003 provides for a new form of tax called stamp duty land tax to be chargeable under s. 42 on land transactions relating to UK land and provides at s. 125 for the abolition of stamp duty except in relation to stamp duty on stock or marketable securities from 1 December 2003. In particular, the new regime will remove stamp duty on the transfer of debts.

Stamp duty was prior to this charged at either a fixed or an *ad valorem* rate on instruments (largely, any document) which fall within one of the heads of charge, the most important being:

(a) A conveyance or transfer on sale of any property for more than £60 000, or for any amount with regard to securities (including an assignment or a declaration of trust);
(b) A limited category of agreements for such a sale – agreements for the sale of land, goods and securities are excluded (in respect of each of (a) and (b), charged at 1% – or 0.5% for securities – on the price paid; increasing to 3% for prices between £250 000 and £500 000, and to 4% for prices of more than £500 000); and

(c) A lease or agreement for a lease (charged on any premium at 1%, and on the rent at a rate of up to 2% for a lease up to 35 years in length and from there to up to 24% for a lease of more than 100 years in length).

Stamp duty on the creation and transfer of mortgages was abolished by s. 64 of the Finance Act 1971. In securitisation transactions, methods that have been used to avoid payment of stamp duty include:

- Documents may be executed and held outside the UK to delay triggering the stamp tax charge on the transfer of receivables until the documents are brought into the UK for enforcement against the relevant debtor (if necessary).
- The sale may be carried out on an "acceptance by payment" basis, where the only written documentation for the transfer is an offer, which is then accepted by payment from the SPV to the originator, without any actual stampable transfer documentation being produced (this method may be difficult to achieve for a declaration of trust route).
- Drawn or undrawn stamp duty reserve facilities.
- Intra-group transfers (these are exempted from stamp under the provisions of s. 42 of the Finance Act 1930), with a transfer by the originator to an intra-group but otherwise bankruptcy remote SPV.

Stamp duty land tax is, under s. 42, Finance Act 2003, charged on land transactions relating to UK land which are chargeable transactions, whether or not there is any instrument for the transaction (and whether or not executed in the UK). Land transactions are acquisitions of a "chargeable interest", defined in s. 48 as any estate, interest or right in or over land in the UK (thus including freehold transfers and the grant or surrender of lease), and include under s. 44 contracts or agreements for such transactions which are "substantially performed" without having been completed (i.e. where the purchaser takes possession of – including receiving or being entitled to rents or profits – the whole or substantially the whole of the land, or the vendor receives a substantial amount of consideration for the land). Security interests are exempt. Land transactions are "chargeable transactions" if they are not exempt transactions (transactions with no chargeable consideration – any consideration in money or money's worth – and other transactions such as testamentary or divorce settlements) (s. 49 and Schedule 3).

Stamp duty land tax is chargeable at the same rate on the whole consideration for residential transactions at 0% for consideration up to £60 000, 1% for consideration more than £60 000 up to £250 000, 3% for consideration more than £250 000 up to £500 000 and 4% for consideration more than £500 000. Tax is chargeable at the same rate on the whole consideration for commercial transactions at 0% for consideration up to £150 000, 1% for consideration more than £150 000 up to £250 000, 3% for consideration more than £250 000 up to £500 000 and 4% for consideration more than £500 000. Sales of properties in "disadvantaged areas" will have a nil value threshold set at £150 000 for residential properties, while sales of all commercial properties in disadvantaged areas will be exempt from stamp. Identification of disadvantaged areas is based on the average income of residents in local council wards. Tax will be calculated at 1% on the NPV of future lease payments if the NPV is over £60 000 (residential) or £150 000 (commercial) (the old system taxed the grant at 2% on the first year's rent).

Withholding tax   Withholding tax is a deduction of tax at source by a payor prior to making payment to a payee, collected by assessing the payor for the tax. Grouped here are the main heads of UK withholding tax liabilities (and UK income tax liabilities which may nevertheless operate in a similar way to withholding tax) relevant to securitisations. Tax is principally due:

- Under s. 349(2)(a) and (b) ICTA, on UK source income which is yearly interest of money paid by a company or partnership (unless paid:

  - on a loan from a bank (or originally made by a bank and assigned) where the person beneficially entitled to the interest is within the UK corporation tax charge;
  - on a loan from a building society (but not on loans originally made by a building society and assigned);
  - by a bank in the ordinary course of its business;
  - on a quoted Eurobond;
  - in the ordinary course of his business by a person who is authorised for the purposes of the FSMA and whose business consists wholly or mainly of dealing in financial instruments as principal; or
  - where the payor reasonably believes that the person beneficially entitled to the payment is a UK resident company, a partnership all of whose partners are UK resident companies, a non-UK resident company which is within the UK corporation tax charge on the payment in question, or a local authority or health services body or charity or one of a number of other bodies that are exempt from UK tax.

  A bank for this purpose means a bank authorised under the FSMA or a European bank authorised as a credit institution in its home state in accordance with the reciprocal recognition provisions of Statutory Instrument 1992/3218).
- Under s. 349(2)(c) ICTA, on UK source income which is yearly interest of money paid overseas (unless paid by a bank in the ordinary course of its business, paid on a quoted Eurobond, or paid in the ordinary course of his business by a person who is authorised for the purposes of the FSMA and whose business consists wholly or mainly of dealing in financial instruments as principal. A bank for this purpose means a bank authorised under the FSMA or a European bank authorised as a credit institution in its home state in accordance with the reciprocal recognition provisions of Statutory Instrument 1992/3218).
- Under s. 349(3A) ICTA, on any dividend or interest paid on a security issued by a building society (unless paid on a qualifying certificate of deposit, on a security that is listed on a recognised stock exchange (such as the LSE), or on a quoted Eurobond, or where the payor reasonably believes that the person beneficially entitled to the payment is a UK resident company, a partnership all of whose partners are UK resident companies, a non-UK resident company which is within the UK corporation tax charge on the payment in question, or a local authority or health services body or charity or one of a number of other bodies that are exempt from UK tax).
- Under s. 21 and s. 59 ICTA, on UK source or non-UK source income within Schedule A (s. 21) or Schedule D (s. 59) which a person (e.g. a trustee) receives

or is entitled to and which has not yet been brought into the charge to income tax (e.g. charged under s. 151 Finance Act 1989 for an interest in possession trust, or s. 151 Finance Act 1989 and s. 686 ICTA for a discretionary trust), such as the income of a bare trust (unless (i) the persons owning the income are within the UK corporation tax charge, in which case they are not liable to UK income tax (s. 6(2), ICTA) and the trustee can resist any assessment to tax, (ii) the income is non-UK source income and the persons owning the income are non-UK residents, in which case no UK income tax liability arises, or (iii) the trustee authorises the payment of the income to be made direct from the payor to the beneficiary and notifies the Revenue accordingly, in which case the trustee is not liable under s. 76, Taxes Management Act 1970).

See "Withholding tax" in Chapter 13 for more detail.

Profits tax An offshore SPV will only become liable to UK corporation tax on the profits of a UK branch or agency that is a UK representative of the SPV. Brokers and investment managers providing services in the ordinary course of business for a market remuneration are excluded from being UK representatives (see "Investment manager" in Chapter 13 for more detail). Where the SPV is located in a country with a double tax treaty with the UK, the SPV may only be liable in respect of profits of a UK "permanent establishment" instead.

VAT VAT is chargeable on taxable supplies of goods or services in the UK (or on importation into the UK) made by a person registered for VAT in the course or furtherance of a business, as a percentage of the price of the supply. A taxable person may recover a proportion of the VAT paid by them on supplies received (input tax) equal to the proportion of supplies made by them which are taxable supplies (excluding exempt supplies). Sales of receivables are exempt from VAT. VAT is levied on servicing fees.

Accounting treatment

Financial Reporting Standard 5 of the Accounting Standards Board on reporting the substance of transactions, came into effect on 22 September 1994 and requires that in order for an asset to be considered off balance sheet for accounting purposes in a securitisation transaction, all significant risks and benefits attached to that asset must be transferred to another entity. If this is the case, then "derecognition" will result in the assets being removed entirely from the balance sheet of the originator. If this is not the case, but the maximum risk of the originator on the assets has been capped, and the SPV and investors have "no recourse whatsoever, either explicit or implicit, to the other assets of the [originator] for losses", then a hybrid treatment known as "linked presentation" will be used. This groups the gross asset value with the risk portion that has been transferred to leave the remaining net exposure, all in a separate caption in the originator's accounts.

A linked presentation is only available to the extent that the originator has no right or obligation to repurchase the assets. Any repurchase right (e.g. the 10% clean-up call permitted by Financial Services Authority guidelines) or obligation means that the portion of the assets over which the right or obligation extends will not be deducted from the gross asset value in the accounts. The clean-up call, tax call and call and step-up embedded in most deals may be structured at the SPV level rather than the originator level in order to avoid the risk of losing FRS 5 linked presentation treatment. A linked presentation is also only available to the extent that any swap or cap provided by the originator: (i) is on market terms; (ii) is not based on rates under the control of the originator; and (iii) merely replaces existing hedges that the originator had for the asset portfolio prior to its sale. Indemnities given by the originator that allow access to all assets of the originator may prevent linked presentation treatment.

If the transferee entity is directly or indirectly controlled by the originator, and the transferee represents a source of benefits for the originator, this may lead to the transferee itself being included in the originator's consolidated accounts in a linked presentation as a "quasi-subsidiary".

Financial Reporting Exposure Draft 30 (FRED 30) was issued by the Accounting Standards Board in June 2002 in relation to the intended adoption of IAS 32 and 39 in the UK as part of convergence to IAS generally by 2005. FRED 30 recommends that the derecognition portions of IAS 39 should not be applied in the UK at present, with a view to working on a joint standard to replace both FRS 5 and IAS 39 on derecognition prior to 2005.

On 17 July 2003, the DTI announced that all UK companies would be entitled at their option to use International Accounting Standards instead of UK standards from January 2005 in both their individual accounts and their consolidated accounts. This option is over and above the requirement of the EU Regulation on International Accounting Standards, that publicly traded companies be required to use IAS in their consolidated accounts from January 2005.

See section 10.2 for more detail.

Capital treatment

Guidelines were originally published by the Bank of England (in the form of BSD/1989/1, as amended by BSD/1992/3) as to when bank assets would be considered to have been transferred off balance sheet for capital adequacy purposes following a securitisation or loan transfer by the bank as originator. These were further expanded in relation to the securitisation of revolving asset pools in notice BSD/1996/8 and a subsequent letter of 17 September 1997. On 19 January 1998, the Bank published expanded and consolidated guidelines that replaced both the bank asset and revolving asset pool guidelines, and added guidelines on credit enhancement and the provision of liquidity for securitisations, as well as guidelines on repackaging and conduit structures established by banks and on the transfer of reverse repos. These were updated and issued by the Financial Services Authority as part of their Banking Supervisory Policy Guide that came into effect on 29 June 1998.

On 31 December 1999, new guidelines were published by the Financial Services Authority, which have since been revised and updated in June 2000, June 2001 and February 2003. The guidelines are applied to UK incorporated banks acting in a primary role on a solo and consolidated basis. Where (a) a non-UK incorporated institution acts in a primary role, and (b) a UK bank in the same group acts in a secondary role, the guidelines are applied on a consolidated basis. The guidelines are not applied where both non-UK and UK institutions act only in secondary roles.

Transactions completed before 31 December 1999 are grandfathered. New pools put through structures existing before 31 December 1999 must meet the new rules.

The new guidelines have expanded significantly on the old rules, with additions such as:

- A new classification of primary roles and secondary roles (the original draft included the role of servicer as a primary role, but this was changed to a secondary role in the final version);
- Treating remote origination as direct origination;
- Changing the scope of the repackager role from packaging tradeable securities to packaging investment grade securities (with the consequence that a bank packaging non-investment grade securities which are tradeable would now be treated as an originator, and have to take a direct deduction against any second loss piece – unless the second loss piece is investment grade, in which case it will not count as credit enhancement);
- Not permitting a call and step-up structure except for mortgage deals on a case-by-case basis (the original draft of the new rules did not permit call and step-up provisions in any deal);
- Permitting the repurchase of non-performing assets at market value;
- Expressly requiring the originator to comply with FRS 5;
- Adding the use of a declaration of trust as a transfer mechanism;
- Dropping the requirement not to name enhancement providers.

The guidelines define primary roles of:

- *Originator* A transferor of an asset or package of assets, or of non-investment grade financial instruments, or a lender via an SPV ("remote origination").
- *Sponsor* A repackager of assets originated by a third party (i.e. not originated by a member of the bank's "wider accounting group" – defined in the draft of the new rules to mean a company in the group for accounting purposes, but not defined in the final version) directly (i.e. which have never appeared on the bank's balance sheet) into a conduit. Also where the bank repackages assets that are not investment grade third party financial instruments via own balance sheet, up to 10% of the conduit (in this case, the bank is regarded as an originator for that amount but not for the whole conduit). Or
- *Repackager* A seller of third-party investment grade (or where the bank can demonstrate that the assets are of similar quality) financial instruments from its balance sheet. Also where the bank sells financial instruments that are non-investment grade or where the bank has acted as originator, up to 10% of the scheme (in this case the bank is regarded as an originator for that amount but not for the whole scheme). If the credit quality of the instruments is "influenced by" that of the repackager, the repackager is treated as an originator. This last requirement could have implications for all synthetic repackagings which are not de-linked from the bank by collateral arrangements or funding, unless they can then argue for treatment akin to a sub-participation under the originator rules.

Consequently, for these purposes, assets can be divided into:

1. Own originated assets

2. Third-party assets via the bank's balance sheet
3. Third-party non-investment grade financial instruments via the bank's balance sheet
4. Third-party investment grade financial instruments via the bank's balance sheet
5. Third-party assets directly
6. Third-party non-investment grade financial instruments directly
7. Third-party investment grade financial instruments directly.

Within these:

- Deals involving 1, 2 and 3 are an originator role;
- Deals involving 5, 6 and 7 (and up to 10% of the conduit being 1, 2 or 3) are a sponsor role;
- Deals involving 4 (and up to 10% of the scheme being 3, or 1 which are securities) are a repackager role.

The guidelines also define secondary roles of:

- Servicer (the servicer must ensure that offering documentation clearly states that it will not support losses on a transaction, or it will be treated as an originator. The FSA maintains sensitivity on the level of involvement of a servicer, and may restrict a conduit sponsor or repackager from acting as servicer for more than a portion of the assets in the conduit or scheme)
- Credit enhancer
- Liquidity provider
- Underwriter or dealer
- Bridging loan provider
- Swap counterparty.

The consequences of these classifications are the primary role requirements for ensuring that assets are fully transferred away from the bank such that they are not required to be included in the bank's capital balance sheet, and also the calculation of the amount of capital to be held against any facilities provided in connection with the transaction. A bank must give the FSA reasonable advance notice of any transaction where it plans to take a primary role, to enable the FSA to have sufficient time to consider the proposal and raise concerns.

(a) *Method of transfer*   The main thrust of the guidelines is to ensure that on a transfer of assets, a "clean break" is achieved between the transferor and the assets. This entails a break in any involvement with the assets and a "moral" separation of the seller from the buyer and the assets themselves. The FSA will look at the aggregate of the different roles carried out by a bank in the transaction to determine their view of the degree of connection remaining with the transaction and the assets. Where the assets may return to the books of the bank in the future, the bank may be required to demonstrate that it has adequate measures in place (potentially including additional reporting or committed facilities) to deal with the liquidity and capital issues that could result from this. The FSA will also look at any effect of changes in the composition in the remaining book of the bank due to securitisation, and may impose limits on assets that may be securitised.

The guidelines permit transfer of assets by novation or assignment (legal or equitable) or the use of a declaration of trust or the use of a funded sub-participation. The use of other methods requires the prior approval of the FSA and a supporting legal opinion. Undrawn commitments should generally be transferred by novation (if they are transferred by assignment or sub-participation, they are treated as an exposure to the transferee rather than to the borrower).

Transfers of single assets or part of an asset are required to comply with the following guidelines:

- The transfer should not contravene the terms of the underlying assets.
- The transferor retains no interest in the principal part of the asset that has been transferred, and any further advances that are to be secured are made under a separate agreement with the borrower.
- The transferor has no right or obligation to repurchase the assets (except pursuant to: (a) a call option of the originator when the portfolio of securitised assets is less than 10% of their maximum value and the assets are still fully performing; (b) a call and step-up (this is limited to mortgage deals and will be considered on a case by case basis); (c) a breach of a warranty given at the time of sale on a matter within the control of the transferor (warranties on the future credit of the underlying borrowers are not permitted)).
- The transferor has clearly notified the transferee that it is not under an obligation to repurchase the assets.
- The transferee would be subject to the terms of any renegotiation of the assets.
- The transferor is only obliged to pay over collections on the assets as and when received, and if any such amounts are paid over before they are received, they can be recovered if not in fact received.

There are additional requirements for the transfer of packages of assets as follows:

- There must be evidence from the transferor's legal advisers that the transferor will not be liable to investors for losses.
- Auditors should be satisfied that the deal complies with FRS 5.
- The originator will be required to confirm in writing that they have evidence that their lawyers and auditors are satisfied that the FSA's requirements have been met.
- There must be a clear statement in offering documents that the originator will not support losses suffered by investors.
- Neither the originator bank nor any member of its consolidated group should own any shares or preference shares in the transferee or have direct or indirect control of the transferee.
- Neither the originator nor any member of its consolidated group may have control of the board of directors of the transferee (although they may have one director).
- The name of the transferee must not imply a connection to the transferor or any member of its consolidated group.
- A one-off provision of expenses or subordinated debt to an SPV is permitted, but a recurring payment of expenses is not. Expenses are treated as credit enhancement.
- The originator may only enter into swaps with the SPV at market rates.
- The originator may not fund the SPV.

The use of replenishment or substitution in a structure is only permissible if there is no material alteration in the asset quality of the securitised pool. An originator may only repurchase the assets: (a) for breach of warranty or (b) when the portfolio of securitised assets is less than 10% of their maximum value (whether the assets are fully performing or not). A repackager may only repurchase the assets: (a) for breach of warranty or (b) when the assets are either investment grade or defaulted financial instruments or are fully performing or defaulted non-financial instruments. Any repurchase must be at market rates (with the result that the price is likely to be nominal for defaulted assets).

(b) *Revolving pools* For revolving pools, the FSA requires a full loss-sharing between the portion of the pool funded by investors and the portion which remains funded by the originator. To ensure this, the FSA divides revolving structures into structures using a disaggregated approach (where the return to investors is based on the performance of specified receivables within the pool) and those using an aggregated approach (where the investor return is simply a percentage of total collections in the pool). For disaggregated structures, scheduled amortisation of the investor interest (in which circumstances the pool would be brought back on balance sheet at the end of the transaction) should make reasonable assumptions about the speed of amortisation. For aggregated structures, the FSA will require the originator to demonstrate that by the end of the scheduled amortisation period at least 90% of the principal and interest receivables outstanding at the start of the amortisation period could have been expected to have been repaid or declared in default. Clean-up calls are permitted when only 10% of the assets outstanding at the start of the amortisation period remain. The guidelines also set out the possible events that can lead to accelerated amortisation of the investor interest; namely, changes in the tax or legal position, failure by the originator to perform as servicer of the pool, or insolvency of the originator and/or SPV. Triggers relating to the performance of the assets are acceptable only if there is full loss-sharing between investors and the originator, and if the triggers are set at a level where the originator would feel able to reduce its new lending without damaging its reputation. The FSA will also need to be satisfied that the originator has adequate liquidity arrangements to ensure that any accelerated amortisation of the investor interest does not lead to funding difficulties for the originator.

(c) *Instalment purchase receivables* Additional requirements are put on the transfer of instalment purchase receivables for equipment or goods, due to the complex liabilities resulting from sale of defective or non-merchantable goods and due to residual maintenance liabilities on the seller. The seller is required to obtain an indemnity or insurance against product liabilities, and the buyer should carefully evaluate the potential for set-off by borrowers in relation to failure by the seller to continue to maintain assets.

(d) *Credit enhancement* In relation to credit enhancement:

- The enhancement must be clearly limited in amount and duration.
- There must be no further recourse beyond the terms of the enhancement facility itself.
- The buyer must have the ability to select someone else to provide the credit enhancement.
- The enhancement must be documented separately.
- It must be provided at the start of the transaction (credit enhancement provided

may not be increased subsequently except where provided in relation to a replenishment or substitution that does not act to subsidise earlier tranches).

- The enhancement facility should be disclosed in the offering documentation.
- The fees for the credit enhancement should not be subordinated or deferred beyond the subordination contained in the payment priorities.

If these requirements are met, the credit enhancement is classified into either "first loss" or "second loss" (second loss is enhancement that benefits from the protection of a "substantial" first loss layer that covers some multiple of historic losses, and can only be drawn after the first loss credit enhancement is exhausted).

First loss enhancement will be either:

- Directly deducted from capital for capital adequacy purposes or (if the originator so selects at the start of the transaction) weighted at the normal risk weight of the underlying assets (if provided by the originator); or
- Directly deducted from capital (if provided by a sponsor or repackager); or
- Normally weighted (if provided by an unconnected third-party bank).

Second loss enhancement will be:

- Directly deducted from capital (if provided by the originator); or
- Normally weighted (if provided by an unconnected third-party bank or if provided by a sponsor or repackager (in the case of a sponsor or repackager, where the extent of involvement of the bank is fully explained in the offering circular for the transaction and where it is made clear that the bank will not support losses beyond the level of the enhancement)).

Investment grade rated bonds are not treated as credit enhancement if the deal has sufficient other credit enhancement.

  (e) *Liquidity facilities*   In relation to liquidity facilities:

- They must be provided on an arm's-length basis.
- They must contain a provision for reducing the facility if the asset quality in the SPV deteriorates (e.g. if the remaining undrawn credit enhancement falls below the outstanding liquidity commitment).
- They should be on market terms.
- They should be clearly limited in amount and duration.
- There must be no further recourse beyond the terms of the facility itself.
- The buyer must have the ability to select someone else to provide the liquidity.
- The facility must be documented separately.
- The fees for the liquidity facility should not be subordinated or deferred beyond the subordination contained in the payment priorities.
- The facility may not be drawn for the purpose of credit enhancement.
- The facility should state clearly on what terms it may be drawn.
- It should provide for repayment of advances in a reasonable timeframe.
- Drawings should be paid to the SPV and not direct to investors.
- Drawings cannot be used to purchase assets (i.e. acquire assets into an SPV in the first place as a form of remote origination) although they can be used as a liquidity purchase mechanism for investment grade assets.

- Drawings cannot be used to cover losses.
- Repayment of the liquidity facility should not be subordinated to investors.

If these requirements are not met the facility will be treated as credit enhancement. If these requirements are met, a liquidity facility will:

- Mean that the assets will remain on balance sheet (if provided by the originator (unless designed to cover very short-term timing differences));
- Require full consolidation as a subsidiary (where provided by a sponsor or repackager whose involvement is not fully explained in the offering circular for the transaction or where it is not made clear that the bank will not support losses beyond the level of the enhancement); or
- Be normally weighted (if provided by an unconnected third-party bank or by a sponsor or repackager (in the case of a sponsor or of a repackager, where the extent of involvement of the bank is fully explained in the offering circular for the transaction and where it is made clear that the bank will not support losses beyond the level of the enhancement)).

(f) *Conduit large exposures*   A conduit sponsor is not obliged to aggregate for large exposures purposes liquidity lines feeding into its conduit, provided that the facilities are made available to different legal entities, and the sponsor can demonstrate that it has proper systems in place to monitor the assets in the conduit.

(g) *Bridge loans*   A bridge loan for a maximum of 3 months can be made, but it cannot be used for the purpose of remote origination.

(h) *Underwriting and dealing*   An originator can underwrite the issue of bonds, but it must sell 90% (the figure can be varied by the FSA) of the total bonds to third parties before the issue will be regarded as off balance sheet. Any dealing by the originator in the notes issued by the SPV must be subject to the approval of the FSA and within the limits set by them on the trading of each tranche. The originator should not be seen to support the issue, and will only be allowed to deal in investment grade level securities (dealings in non-investment grade securities will be considered to be credit enhancement). A sponsor or repackager is subject to normal capital underwriting rules, but any non-investment grade securities held at the end of the underwriting concession period will be considered to be credit enhancement (unless there is sufficient other credit enhancement in the deal). A sponsor or repackager can deal without the prior approval of the FSA, provided that there are always at least two other third-party dealers (this requirement may be waived by the FSA where the issue is small).

Credit derivatives

Guidelines on credit derivatives were first published by the FSA in 1998, and have since been revised periodically. The latest revision, effective from 1 September 2003, provides for the treatment of second to default baskets, and offers a revised treatment for first to default baskets.

Banking book   Credit derivatives are treated as either sub-participations or guarantees in the banking book in respect of the amount of exposure to which they relate (the added credit benefit of "first loss" protection is not recognised in capital terms over and above the amount of the exposure covered) depending on whether they are funded or unfunded. Credit spread products do not give any capital benefit to the buyer, and are treated as a direct exposure to the nominal amount of the reference obligation in the books of the seller. Credit derivatives with binary payouts are treated as guarantees or sub-participations to the extent of the binary payout. As general requirements for credit derivatives:

- The reference obligation must be the same as the protected asset, or at least issued by the same issuer.
- The reference obligation must rank junior to or *pari passu* with the protected asset.
- The reference obligation must cross-default to the underlying asset (the requirement for cross-default may be waived if the FSA is satisfied that the basis risk between the reference obligation and the underlying asset is minimal).
- Where the reference obligation is denominated in a different currency, the level of protection recognised will be reduced by 8% (to reflect the currency risk), and the FX exposure must be entered with other FX positions of the bank for capital purposes.
- If the credit derivative has a shorter term than the protected asset, then no protection value is recognised if the credit derivative has less than 1 year to expiry. If the credit derivative has 1 year or more to expiry, then a charge is made on the protection buyer for the residual exposure as an undrawn commitment exceeding 1 year (or, if the residual exposure is an undrawn commitment, at half the usual weight for an undrawn commitment) (thus the weighting on a 5-year drawn position protected by a 3-year credit default swap with an OECD bank would be 70% of the principal amount – 20% for the protected period plus 50% for the residual).
- Any materiality thresholds should be referred to the FSA, as they may affect the level of protection which is recognised.
- A "first to default" basket structure gives the buyer protection against the default of any one of the assets in the basket.
- Sale of a "first to default" credit derivative basket structure generates a capital charge for the protection seller equal to the addition of the respective capital charge for each asset in the basket, capped at a direct deduction from capital (although the FSA will consider disapplying this treatment if they are satisfied that the assets in the basket display a very strong degree of correlation). Under the 1 September revision, sale of a "second to default" credit derivative basket structure generates the same capital charge for the protection seller, but ignoring the single worst asset in the pool. The revision effective from 1 September 2003 provides that if the first to default or second to default basket takes the form of a credit-linked note which is rated as a qualifying debt item (i.e. investment grade), the protection sellers may instead include the basket at the weighting of the single worst asset in the pool.
- A proportionate basket structure only relieves or generates a capital charge by reference to the proportionate weighting of each asset in the basket.

In order for a protection buyer under a credit derivative to obtain protection that is recognised for capital purposes:

- The protection buyer should be seen to have transferred the credit risk (without such transfer constituting a breach of the term of the reference obligation) such that the protection seller has no recourse to the protection buyer for losses.

- The credit derivative must at the very least include "credit event" triggers relating to the reference obligation.
- For funded credit derivatives, there must also be no obligation on the protection buyer to repay any funding received under a credit derivative (except at termination of the credit derivative, or as a result of a "credit event" trigger, or for breach of warranty in relation to the reference obligations).
- The derivative is only permitted to be cancelled pursuant to an option of the protection buyer when the reference obligation is still fully performing (or in a basket structure, where the remaining uncollected value of the basket of reference obligations is less than 10% of their maximum value and the assets are still fully performing).
- In basket-funded structures, there should be no liability on the protection buyer to the protection seller or to end investors.
- The credit risk in basket structures should be transferred to an unrelated SPV entity, which should not bear a name similar to the name of the protection buyer in question.
- A one-off contribution of credit enhancement to an SPV is permitted (a recurring payment of expenses is not), although it will be directly deducted from capital.
- Swaps entered into with the SPV should not provide support for losses in the SPV.

Trading book   Credit derivatives are broken down into legs in respect of the amount of exposure to which they relate (the added credit benefit of "first loss" protection is not recognised in capital terms over and above the amount of the exposure covered). Total return swaps are treated as a long/short position in the reference obligation (carrying specific and general risks) and a short/long position in an OECD government security (carrying general risk) paying the same rate. Credit default swaps are treated as a long/short position in the reference obligation (carrying specific risk only). Premium payments may be treated as a notional position in an OECD government security, but do not normally generate a general risk requirement. Credit linked notes are treated as a long/short position in the note (carrying specific risk of the issuer and general risk) and also as a long/short position in the reference obligation (carrying specific risk only). Banks should consult with the FSA as to the appropriate treatment for credit spread products. As general requirements for credit derivatives:

- The reference obligation must be issued by the same issuer as the protected asset.
- The reference obligation must carry the same ranking in liquidation as the protection asset.
- The reference obligation must have the same currency, coupon and maturity as the protected asset (credit derivatives in a different currency than the reporting currency of the institution are subject to normal trading book FX charges).
- If the credit derivative has a shorter term than the protected asset, a forward position (i.e. an obligation to acquire the bond or other protected asset in the future) in the specific risk of the reference obligation is recorded by the protection buyer for the residual exposure.
- Any materiality thresholds should be referred to the FSA, as they may reduce the level of specific risk offset that can be recognised.

- A "first to default" basket structure allows the buyer to record a short position for any one of the assets in the basket.
- Sale of a "first to default" credit derivative basket structure creates a long position for the protection seller in each asset in the basket, capped at a direct deduction from capital (although the FSA will consider disapplying this treatment if they are satisfied that the assets in the basket display a very strong degree of correlation). Under the 1 September revision, sale of a "second to default" credit derivative basket structure generates the same long position for the protection seller, but ignoring the single worst asset in the pool. A protection seller who is acquiring a multiple-name credit-linked note that is rated as a qualifying debt item (i.e. investment grade) only records a long position in the credit-linked note itself at the specific risk weight for the note issuer.
- A proportionate basket structure only creates a long or short position by reference to the proportionate weighting of each asset in the basket.

In order for a protection buyer under a credit derivative to be able to treat the derivative as a short position for capital purposes:

- The protection buyer should be seen to have transferred the credit risk (without such transfer constituting a breach of the term of the reference obligation) such that the protection seller has no recourse to the protection buyer for losses.
- The credit derivative must at the very least include "credit event" triggers relating to the reference obligation.
- For funded credit derivatives, there must also be no obligation on the protection buyer to repay any funding received under a credit derivative (except at termination of the credit derivative, or as a result of a "credit event" trigger, or for breach of warranty in relation to the reference obligations).
- The derivative is only permitted to be cancelled pursuant to an option of the protection buyer when the reference obligation is still fully performing (or in a basket structure, where the remaining uncollected value of the basket of reference obligations is less than 10% of their maximum value and the assets are still fully performing).
- In basket-funded structures, there should be no liability on the protection buyer to the protection seller or to end investors.
- The credit risk in basket structures should be transferred to an unrelated SPV entity, which should not bear a name similar to the name of the protection buyer in question.
- A one-off contribution of credit enhancement to an SPV is permitted (a recurring payment of expenses is not), although it will be directly deducted from capital.
- Swaps entered into with the SPV should not provide support for losses in the SPV.

General capital

Banks are required to hold banking book capital equal to 8% of the risk-weighted assets in their banking book, and to hold trading book capital equal to the sum of each capital charge in their trading book (in relation to some of which the 8% ratio may be used to compute counterparty risks). The 8% ratio (the "individual ratio") may be set higher than 8% for individual institutions, to reflect their risk profile or resources. A higher "target ratio" figure is also set for each institution to act as an early warning marker of an impending capital deficiency.

Capital is required to be held by banks (both on a solo basis and via consolidation) across a group. A group for this purpose consists of a regulated entity and any entities that carry on financial activities and constitute a parent undertaking or subsidiary undertaking of the regulated entity or in which the regulated entity has a participation of 20% or more of the voting rights or capital.

(a) *Banking book versus trading book*   The banking book of a bank will consist of all its assets, except for those assets entered on the trading book. The trading book of a bank consists of: (a) its proprietary holdings of, or principal broking positions in, financial instruments (transferable securities, units in collective investment schemes, CDs/CP/other money markets instruments, financial futures, forward rate agreements, interest rate/currency/equity swaps, and options over any of the above), commodities and commodity derivatives that are held with trading intent (positions are considered to be held with trading intent if they are marked-to-market daily on a consistent basis (and if there is no market valuation, on the basis of the bank's own valuation)); (b) holdings in financial instruments, commodities and commodity derivatives taken in order to hedge trading exposures; (c) repos related to items in the trading book; (d) reverse repos which are marked-to-market daily and have daily collateral adjustments; (e) credit exposure on unsettled transactions and OTC derivatives; and (f) fees, commission, margin and interest on exchange-traded derivatives related to trading book items. There is no requirement to comply with trading book capital treatments for a book below a certain size. A bank must agree a policy statement with the FSA as to the items normally included within its trading book and its procedure for valuing positions.

(b) *Netting*   Netting is permitted in respect of on-balance-sheet items for single customer accounts and group facilities. Netting is permitted in respect of off-balance-sheet items for OTC derivatives, bond and equity forwards and repos. No netting of on-balance-sheet items against off-balance-sheet items is permitted. Netting of "add-ons" attached to off-balance-sheet items must be agreed with the FSA, following which a formula is followed to reach the relevant netted amount.

(c) *Collateral or guarantees in the banking book*   Collateral held against exposures in the banking book can be used to reduce the risk weighting of the exposure to that of the collateral. Reduction is only permitted in respect of that part of the exposure covered by the collateral. The added credit benefit of "first loss" collateral is not recognised in capital terms over and above the amount of the exposure covered.

(d) *Collateral or guarantees in the trading book*   Collateral can be held against counterparty risk in the trading book to reduce the counterparty risk weighting in the same way as for banking book assets. For trading book purposes, a collateral risk weighting is only permitted in respect of that part of the exposure covered by the collateral. The added credit benefit of "first loss" collateral is not recognised in capital terms over and above the amount of the exposure covered. Collateral is required to be marked-to-market daily and a cushion subtracted to take account of future market movements.

Permitted collateral and relevant haircut/risk weightings:

- **0% (0% risk weighting)**   Netted or cash collateralised assets or assets collateralised by OECD central government/central bank securities (where there is a daily mark-to-market of the collateral and the right to make margin calls) or assets guaranteed by an OECD central government/central bank

- **0.8% (10% risk weighting)**   Assets collateralised by OECD central government/ central bank fixed rate securities (with one year or less residual maturity) or floating rate or index-linked securities (of any maturity) (where there is no daily mark-to-market of the collateral or right to make margin calls)
- **1.6% (20% risk weighting)**   Assets collateralised by OECD central government/ central bank fixed rate securities (with more than one year residual maturity) (where there is no daily mark-to-market of the collateral or right to make margin calls) or assets guaranteed by an OECD bank or an investment firm regulated by the Capital Adequacy Directive or a similar regime.

OECD central government/central bank securities used as collateral in the trading book reduce the risk weight to 0% (rather than either 0% or 10% or 20%), as a daily mark-to-market is required for all trading book collateral in any event.

(e) *Collateral provided by way of outright transfer*   Banks that provide collateral by way of outright transfer are to hold capital against the resulting redelivery exposure on the collateral taker. Outright transfer is a method of providing collateral, but does not involve the granting of a security interest. The security provider transfers absolute title to the relevant asset to the beneficiary, who agrees to deliver equivalent assets to the security provider at the end of the relevant transaction or relationship. Outright transfer is mainly used as a form of collateral for derivative obligations, and has the advantage of avoiding possible security registration requirements for floating charges and charges over book debts, as well as allowing rehypothecation. If the collateral arrangements provide that the collateral provider has the right to call for the return of excess collateral on a daily basis, and puts in place adequate netting rights between the collateral and the collateralised exposure, then the capital charge is calculated as the excess of the mark-to-market value of the collateral given as against the collateralised exposure multiplied by the counterparty risk weight. If the collateral arrangements do not provide for the return of excess collateral and adequate netting, then the capital charge is equal to the sum of the excess of the mark-to-market value of the collateral given as against the collateralised exposure and an "add-on" figure of between 0.25% and 6% (set by reference to the residual term of the contract and the contract type (0.25% to 1.5% for interest rates, 6% for equities)) of the value of the collateral, with the aggregate figure then being multiplied by the counterparty risk weight.

(f) *Collateral taken in the form of securities*   For this form of collateral, the FSA requires that banks have legal opinions in place by 30 September 2000 as to the validity of the security interest.

(g) *Derivatives*   In addition to any trading book market risk assessments, OTC derivatives are subjected to a counterparty risk haircut by calculating the mark-to-market value of the derivative plus an "add-on" figure of between 0% and 15% (set by reference to the residual term of the contract and the contract type (0% to 1.5% for interest rates, 1% to 7.5% for FX, 6% to 10% for equities, 7% to 8% for precious metals or 10% to 15% for commodities)) of the notional principal (in total, the "credit equivalent amount"), with the aggregate figure then being multiplied by counterparty risk weight. The counterparty risk weights are between 0% and 50%. The resultant figure is then weighted by a factor of 8%. This gives rise to counterparty risk haircut charges for OTC derivatives (which arise in addition to any trading book market risk assessment) of 0% to 4% of mark-to-market and add-on.

(h) *FX* Banks are required to hold 8% of capital against their net foreign exchange position and their net gold position.

(i) *Commodities* Banks are required to hold 15% of capital against their net commodity position, together with 3% against their gross commodity position.

(j) *Settlement* Payments made free of delivery are charged to counterparty risk, on the principal amount multiplied by the counterparty risk weight and then weighted by a factor of 8%. Settlement risk is charged where a payment to be made against delivery remains unsettled 5 days or more after the due date, on an increasing percentage of either the movement in value of the asset since the due date, or the settlement price that was to have been paid on the due date (the choice of option should be approved by the FSA).

(k) *Models* FSA-approved VAR type or non-VAR type models are permitted in assessing capital requirements in respect of the FX and/or commodity position risk of a bank as well as the interest rate, equities and derivatives position risk of the bank on its trading book.

Banking book

Capital for the purpose of banking book exposures consists of Tier 1 (equity and accumulated profit reserves less goodwill and other intangible assets and less investments in non-consolidated entities engaged in financial services activities and capital issued by other banks, plus, in certain cases, subordinated debt raised through an SPV that issues preference shares, and also the new class of perpetual preferred securities approved by the Basel Committee), Upper Tier 2 (revaluation reserves, general (i.e. non-specific) loss reserves and perpetual debt) and Lower Tier 2 (subordinated debt with a minimum 5-year term – the debt is amortised for capital purposes over the last 5 years of its term). Tier 2 may only be included up to the level of the Tier 1 capital, and Lower Tier 2 only up to the level of 50% of the Tier 1 capital. Large exposures of 10% of own funds must be reported and no exposure may exceed 25% of own funds. Assets on the banking book are risk weighted as follows:

(a) *General on-balance-sheet assets* The haircut capital charges under the regime prior to the New Basel Accord coming into force are as follows:

- **0% (0% risk weighting)** Cash or claims (other than securities) on an OECD central government/central bank
- **0.8% (10% risk weighting)** Issues of OECD central government/central bank fixed rate securities (with 1 year or less residual maturity) or floating rate or index-linked securities (of any maturity)
- **1.6% (20% risk weighting)** Issues of OECD central government/central bank fixed rate securities (with more than 1 year residual maturity) or claims on an OECD bank or an investment firm regulated by the Capital Adequacy Directive or a similar regime
- **4% (50% risk weighting)** Residential mortgages (maximum 100% LTV, first ranking, either owner-occupied or rented) and residential-mortgage-backed securities (where the underlying mortgages are maximum 100% LTV, first

ranking, performing and the SPV holds no assets with more than 50% weighting)

- **8% (100% risk weighting)** Other
- **100% (1250% risk weighting; 1-for-1 deduction)** First loss enhancement provided by an originator, sponsor or repackager and second loss enhancement provided by an originator.

It should be noted that the structure of some asset-backed securities (in addition to mortgage-backed securities) permits them to carry a 20% (or other) risk weighting, where none of the underlying assets backing the securities (the receivables and any swap) carry a heavier weighting (e.g. where the underlying assets consist of claims on OECD banks or regulated investment firms).

(b) *General off-balance-sheet assets (other than derivatives)* Off-balance-sheet items other than derivatives (including guarantees, undrawn commitments, and liquidity facilities) are reported by multiplying the notional principal amount of the item by a "credit conversion factor" between 0% and 100% before multiplying by the counterparty risk weight and the 8% factor (sub-participations are reported as an exposure at the higher of the risk weighting of the underlying borrower and that of the participating bank), as follows:

- **1-for-1 deduction** Liquidity facilities that do not meet qualification requirements (for example, as to a use of a borrowing base calculation) and are therefore treated as credit enhancement in a case where there is no other first loss enhancement (assets will simply remain on balance sheet where a liquidity facility is provided by the originator and it does meet the requirements). Also, any off-balance-sheet first-loss enhancement provided by an originator, sponsor or repackager and off-balance-sheet second-loss enhancement provided by an originator
- **100%** Off-balance-sheet items that are a "direct credit substitute" (guarantees given should be reported as an exposure for the full principal amount on the party guaranteed, or on the reference entity for a credit derivative)
- **50%** An undrawn commitment with an original maturity exceeding 1 year
- **20%** Self-liquidating trade finance items
- **0%** An undrawn commitment with an original maturity of 1 year or less. The deemed beginning of the commitment for lines with a maturity of 1 year or less is 30 days after the firm offer to enter the commitment (or 60 days after the firm offer for syndicated lines). Any firm offer to extend such a line may only be made in the last 30 days (or 60 days for a syndicated line) prior to expiry of the line, or the new line and the old line will be treated as a single line with the aggregate tenor of the two lines.

(c) *Repo/stock loans* Repos and stock loan agreements do not change the underlying reporting exposure of the cash borrower/securities lender (the securities remain on the balance sheet of the lender). Reverse repos and stock borrowings are reported by the cash lender/securities borrower as a collateralised loan and given the risk weighting appropriate to the collateral (if it is collateral that is eligible for a reduced risk weighting – otherwise the risk weighting appropriate to the counterparty).

(d) *Credit derivatives* Credit derivatives are treated as either sub-participations or guarantees in the banking book in respect of the amount of exposure to which they relate (the added credit benefit of "first loss" protection is not recognised in capital terms over and above the amount of the exposure covered) depending on whether they are funded or unfunded. Credit spread products do not give any capital benefit to the buyer, and are treated as a direct exposure to the nominal amount of the reference obligation in the books of the seller. Credit derivatives with binary payouts are treated as guarantees or sub-participations to the extent of the binary payout.

Trading book

Capital for trading book exposures consists of Tier 1 and Tier 2 capital as with the banking book, but in addition banks may use Tier 3 capital (subordinated debt with a minimum 2-year maturity) against certain trading book exposures (total Tier 2 and Tier 3 capital cannot exceed Tier 1 capital and Tier 2 and Tier 3 capital set against trading book cannot exceed 200% of Tier 1 capital) of an institution. Certain elements are required to be directly deducted from capital (giving an equivalent risk weighting of 1250%). In particular, in relation to the provision of credit enhancement to an SPV in a securitisation structure where the bank is the originator of the transaction. Large exposures of 10% of own funds must be reported and no exposure may exceed 25% of own funds, although the 25% limit may be exceeded if extra capital charges are met (rising from a doubling of the haircut, up to a factor of nine increase). Capital haircuts for assets on the trading book are as follows:

(a) *Debt* Fixed income instruments are assessed for general (or position-related) market risk on matched long and short positions of the same maturity at a fraction of 0% to 12.5% of the offsetting amount without double counting (to reflect the residual maturity of the security – floating rate securities are weighted by reference to the time to the next interest determination rather than the residual maturity and will thus often fall into the 1-month or less band of 0%, the 1+ to 3-month band of 0.2% or the 3+ to 6-month band of 0.4%), which is itself weighted by a factor between 10% and 150%. Unmatched positions are assessed at a fraction of 0% to 12.5% of the principal amount, weighted by a factor of 100%. Thus, buying/selling to match a position results (at most) in a general risk haircut of 6.25% and (at best) in a reduction in capital charges of 11.25% (12.5 − 1.25). This gives rise to a general haircut ranging from 0% (short term) to a range of 0.625% to 9.375% (long term) for each half of the match (matched) or 0% to 12.5% (unmatched).

The debt securities specific (or counterparty-related) haircut as a percentage of the gross position is:

- 0% (issues of the same issuer carrying the same ranking in liquidation and the same currency, coupon and maturity where the long and short positions offset or where the exposure has been sold off under a credit default swap with the same maturity or which are issues of or collateralised by OECD central government/central bank securities);
- 0.25% for 6 months or less residual maturity "qualifying debt items";
- 1% for 6+ to 24 months residual maturity "qualifying debt items";

- 1.6% for more than 24 months residual maturity "qualifying debt items"; or
- 8% for other securities.

Qualifying debt items broadly consist of OECD public sector securities, securities issued or guaranteed by an OECD bank or an investment firm regulated by the Capital Adequacy Directive or a similar regime, securities carrying a 50% risk weighting and investment grade rated securities.

(b) *Equity*   The general haircut for equities is 8% of net position. Equities are specific risk weighted at 8% of the gross position, or 4% for equities that are highly liquid (i.e. are part of a liquid equity index) and are part of a diversified portfolio of equities.

(c) *Repos*   For repos and reverse repos, the transaction is regarded as a short (repo) or long (reverse repo) government bond position (i.e. no specific risk) to reflect the cash leg. There is no change in the treatment (or new treatment entered) for either party for the repo security. A counterparty risk haircut is assessed at 8% of the counterparty risk weight of the exposure for the relevant party (being the difference between the mark-to-market value of the collateral given as against the mark-to-market value of the collateral received). Unlike for derivatives, there is no 50% cap on risk weightings for 100% weighted counterparties. If the repo or reverse repo is inadequately documented (i.e. it does not allow both for proper netting and for the provision of variation margin), then additional "risk cushion factors" will be applied to the capital charge.

(d) *Credit derivatives*   Credit derivatives are broken down into legs in respect of the amount of exposure to which they relate (the added credit benefit of "first loss" protection is not recognised in capital terms over and above the amount of the exposure covered). Total return swaps are treated as a long/short position in the reference obligation (carrying specific and general risks) and a short/long position in an OECD government security (carrying general risk) paying the same rate. Credit default swaps are treated as a long/short position in the reference obligation (carrying specific risk only). Premium payments may be treated as a notional position in an OECD government security, but do not normally generate a general risk requirement. Credit-linked notes are treated as a long/short position in the note (carrying specific risk of the issuer and general risk) and also as a long/short position in the reference obligation (carrying specific risk only). Banks should consult with the FSA as to the appropriate treatment for credit spread products.

In addition to market risk assessments, unfunded credit derivatives such as total return swaps and credit default products (but not funded credit derivatives such as credit-linked notes) are subjected to a counterparty risk haircut by calculating the mark-to-market value of the derivative plus an "add-on" figure of between 0% and 15% (set by reference to the residual term of the contract and the contract type (0% to 1.5% for qualifying debt items), 6% to 10% for non-qualifying debt items – e.g. non-investment grade debt) of the notional principal (in total, the "credit equivalent amount"), with the aggregate figure then being multiplied by counterparty risk weight.

The counterparty risk weights are between 0% and 50%. The resultant figure is then weighted by a factor of 8%. This gives rise to counterparty risk haircut charges for unfunded credit derivatives (which arise in addition to the market risk assessment) of 0% to 4% of mark-to-market and add-on.

(e) *Derivatives*   Exchange-traded and OTC derivatives are generally broken down into their individual risk components (interest rate, equity risk, etc.) which are included in the relevant assessment of market risk requirements, as set out above. Long positions in options and warrants are generally assessed to a haircut equal to the lesser of a position in the underlying, or the market value of the instrument. Short positions in options and warrants are generally assessed to a haircut equal to a position in the underlying, but the assessment reduces by any amount that the option is out of the money. Assessments are reduced fully or partially for positions taken to hedge an underlying asset.

(f) *Underwriting*   Underwriting exposure is charged to general market risk only (debt securities) or to a limited degree of both general and specific risk (equities) until the commitment crystallises, and charges at a general and a specific level increase (or are introduced) thereafter, while the commitment remains outstanding.

Data protection/confidentiality

There is a duty on banks to keep customer information confidential. Customer information may only be disclosed in limited circumstances such as disclosure with the consent of the customer.

The Data Protection Act 1998 was brought into effect on 1 March 2000 under SI 2000/183 (Data Protection Act 1998 (Commencement) Order 2000) to comply with EU Directive 95/46 on the processing of personal data (the EU required implementation of the Directive by 25 October 1998). The act repeals the Data Protection Act 1984 (transitional provisions applied until 24 October 2001) and requires that entities ("data controllers") established in the EU or using processing equipment in the EU (e.g. a non-EU entity which has a web server recording personal data located in the EU) which control the purposes for which, and manner in which, the processing of "data" (information in automatically readable form or filed in a structured system that makes it readily accessible) that is "personal data" (data that relates to an individual and from which the individual can be identified) is carried out ensure that the eight data protection principles set out in Schedule 1 to the act are complied with (personal data is processed fairly and lawfully, data is obtained and processed only for specified purposes, data is adequate and relevant and not excessive, data is kept accurate and up-to-date, data is not kept for longer than necessary, data is processed with regard to the rights of the individual, there is adequate security protecting the data, data should not be transferred outside the European Economic Area unless the recipient territory has adequate personal data protection provisions).

Transfer of data outside the EU has caused problems for US companies seeking to buy the rights to mailing lists or information gathered within the EU, as the EU does not recognise US privacy laws as sufficient for this purpose. On 15 March 2000, the EU and the US agreed a compromise on a "safe harbour", under which US companies that sign up to oversight by regulatory authorities in the US can receive such information. Consent from the individual is required for the use of data, and there are additional requirements for the use of "sensitive personal data". Individuals are entitled to see personal data held on them and to have it deleted or corrected, to know for what purposes the personal data is being processed and to what recipients the personal data may be disclosed or to object to its use for direct marketing. The act allows individuals to bring actions to claim compensation from the data controller for any damage or distress suffered as a result of the data controller contravening the provisions of the act. Data controllers must notify the Data Protection Commissioner – known as the Information Commissioner from 30 January 2001 – that they are holding personal data. The Commissioner has 28 days to raise any concerns about a notification, during which time the data should not be processed. Failure to notify constitutes a criminal offence. The Commissioner may take action against any entity that does not comply with the eight data protection principles. There are exemptions from the act for certain human resources information, corporate finance, legal privilege and certain regulatory areas.

Consumer protection

The Consumer Credit Act 1974 governs the regulation of loans of a certain size made to consumers (individuals or partnerships), such as credit card agreements, hire purchase and conditional sale agreements and overdrafts. Loans up to £25 000 are regulated (prior to 1 May 1998 only loans for less than £15 000 were regulated) although since 20 November 2002 there are plans to increase this to loans of any size. Certain agreements are exempt from the provisions of the Act; namely loans for the purchase of a house (as opposed to second mortgages), fixed amount credits for 12 months or less (e.g. trade credit), revolving credits where debts must be discharged by a single payment (e.g. charge cards) and low cost loan agreements which are only available to a particular class of borrowers. Extortionate credit bargains are regulated under the Act even where they are exempt agreements. Persons carrying on a business of providing credit under regulated loans are required to obtain a consumer credit licence from the Office of Fair Trading, in the absence of which, loans may be unenforceable. For regulated loans where the loan is not entered into at the offices of the creditor, the consumer is given a "cooling-off" period after entering into the agreement, during which time the debtor may cancel the agreement. The period runs until 5 days after the consumer receives a notice from the creditor informing the consumer of his cancellation rights, separate from the copy of the agreement given to him on signing (for mortgages, the consumer is instead given an unsigned copy of the agreement and is then left for 7 days to consider the transaction prior to being asked to sign). The agreement must meet certain requirements as to legibility and form, including a statement of the total financing charge under the agreement and the APR; if the agreement does not meet these requirements, it will be unenforceable without a court order. Throughout the term of the agreement, the consumer retains a right to prepay the agreement, which cannot be excluded by the creditor. If the credit is used to purchase goods or services from a third-party supplier, the consumer can assert any claim he has for misrepresentation or breach of contract against the supplier against the creditor. If the consumer is in default, the creditor must serve a default notice specifying a minimum period of 7 days during which the consumer must rectify the default or pay compensation, before the creditor can terminate the contract or repossess goods. Where the consumer has paid more than one-third of the total amount payable by the consumer under a hire purchase agreement (including interest and finance charges but excluding penalties), or the creditor needs to enter premises to repossess, the creditor will need a court order for repossession.

The Unfair Contract Terms Act 1977 regulates, *inter alia*, the use of contractual clauses purporting to exclude liability of one party to the other for breach of contract or negligence. Where one party deals as consumer, no exclusion of liability for breach of contract inserted by the other party will be upheld unless it is "reasonable" (based on, *inter alia*, the bargaining strength of the parties and any inducement given to the consumer to agree to the exclusion term). In any contract, no exclusion of liability for negligence resulting in death or personal injury will be upheld, and exclusions of liability for negligence resulting in other loss or damage will only be upheld to the extent that they are "reasonable". The Unfair Terms in Consumer Contracts Regulations 1999 came into force on 1 October 1999 (replacing the Unfair Terms in Consumer Contracts Regulations 1994) and were used to implement a Directive of the EU. The Regulations apply to contracts for goods or services entered into between a business and an individual consumer, which are on a standard form or the terms of which are drafted in advance, and over the substance of which the consumer has no influence. In such a contract, any term that is "unfair" (i.e. based on the bargaining strength of the parties and any inducement given to the consumer to agree to the term, "contrary to the requirement of good faith, ... causes a significant imbalance in the parties' rights and obligations arising under the contract, to the detriment of the consumer") will not bind the consumer. Terms that are not written in "plain, intelligible language" may be considered "unfair".

Regulatory approvals

If the SPV uses the word "bank" in its name, or is considered to be taking deposits, it would need to be authorised by the Financial Services Authority as a deposit-taking entity under the provisions of the Financial Services and Markets Act 2000.

Security interests granted by the SPV (or by the originator in a secured loan transaction) may be registrable on a Form 395 under the provisions of s. 395 of the Companies Act 1985, which requires registration of security created by a UK-registered company which is security given to secure debentures, security over uncalled share capital, security which if created by an individual would be a registrable bill of sale, security over land, security over book debts, security in the form of a floating charge and security over called but unpaid share capital, ships, aircraft, goodwill and intellectual property. Registration is also required under s. 409, Companies Act 1985, for security over such assets in England and Wales where the company granting security or acquiring the assets subject to the security has an established place of business in England or Wales. In the Slavenburg case, it was held that whether a company has an established place of business in England and Wales is a question of fact, and the practice is to file a Form 395 when security is created by a non-UK company over assets situated in the UK, regardless of whether it is considered that the company actually has a place of business in England and Wales, as a safeguard.

Other issues

The categories of preferential debt set out in s. 175 of the Insolvency Act 1986 take priority over claims secured under a floating charge. These are primarily wages (to a certain limit) due in the last 4 months, PAYE and NI Contributions due in the last 12 months, VAT due in the last 6 months and occupational pension contributions. The Enterprise Act reforms this system; under s. 251, those categories of preferential debt due to the Crown (the Inland Revenue, Customs and Excise and social security) are abolished. Other preferential debts (mainly wages due in the last 4 months and occupational pension contributions) remain as preferential debts. Under s. 252, an amount prescribed by order by the Secretary of State will be ring-fenced in favour of unsecured creditors (and will not be available to holders of a floating charge to the extent that there are any such unsecured creditors).

12.51   UNITED STATES

The modern-day securitisation market began in the US and developed out of the market for mortgage-backed Ginnie Mae paper. US investment banks set up mortgage trading departments in the 1970s to deal in Ginnie Mae paper. The first private mortgage-backed securities issues for Bank of America began in 1977.

The impact of the rise of short-term interest rates in the US in October 1979 (which increased the cost of funds of the Savings and Loans – or "thrifts" – beyond their income receipts on mortgages largely bearing fixed long-term rates of interest), and the subsequent tax relief for thrifts passed in September 1981, gave a huge impetus to the market in trading of whole mortgage loans by providing that losses on the sale of mortgage assets by the thrifts could be amortised over the life of the loan and could be set against tax paid by the thrift over the previous 10 years. The debt expansion in the US over the 1980s also added to the development of the securitisation market. The first non-mortgage-backed deals were launched in 1985.

The US market is significantly larger and more liquid than other global securitisation markets. The FDIC adopted new rules on capital for securitisation by federally-insured banks on 1 January 2002, which require less capital to be held against highly rated asset-backed securities and more for lower rated securities.

Issuance of ABS product rose significantly in 2002.

The US operates a common law system. The Uniform Commercial Code (UCC), applying in the terms enacted in each state of the US, governs many aspects of the transfer of receivables.

Ring-fencing and true sale

The UCC provides at s. 9-103(3)(b) that the relevant law for determining the perfection requirements for sales of, and security interests in, receivables is that of the jurisdiction of location of the debtor, and provides for a filing system for perfection where perfection in the US is required.

Insolvent banks in the US are managed by the Federal Deposit Insurance Corporation (FDIC) (rather than under normal Bankruptcy Code provisions), which may provide guidance on the effect of different transactions. On 27 July 2000, the FDIC passed a rule that prevents receivers of a bank from repudiating securitisation contracts entered into by that bank.

S. 9 of the UCC was revised in mid-2001, with a widening of the old definition of receivables from "accounts or chattel paper" to "accounts, chattel paper, payment intangibles or promissory notes". The revised s. 9 limits the requirement for UCC filing just to the state of organisation (rather than the potential requirement for filing in several states), and widens applicability of filing to all assets, but introduces a question-mark over competing rights of priority for a particular asset.

Under s. 9-318(4) of Article 9 of the UCC, contractual prohibitions on assignment of an account are ineffective to prohibit an assignment. For "chattel paper", s. 2-210(3) of Article 2 only provides a limited protection as prohibitions will only be ineffective "unless the circumstances indicate the contrary". Chattel paper is defined in s. 9-105 of Article 9 as "a writing or writings which evidence both a monetary obligation and a security interest in or a lease of specific goods". The term "security interest" is defined for this purpose at s. 1-201(37) of Article 1 of the UCC as "an interest in personal property or fixtures which secures payment or performance of an obligation".

Undivided interest   A sale of an undivided interest in goods is considered valid to transfer a proprietary interest under the provisions of s. 2-105(4) of Article 2 of the UCC.

Recharacterisation   The main factor in determining whether a true sale is achieved is the level of recourse to the originator, relative to historical loss experience. Support in excess of the level of losses that has arisen in the past may lead to recharacterisation of the transaction as a secured loan. To avoid this, a two-tiered structure may be used, with a first transfer to a bankruptcy remote SPV (which has previously been equity capitalised to the extent of the credit support required for the transaction) at face value to achieve a true sale, and a second transfer on to the trust or other issuing entity in return for part cash payment and part subordinated notes or trust certificates.

A protective filing is usually made under Article 9 of the UCC with regard to the possibility of the transfer being a security interest.

Substantive consolidation   Substantive consolidation of an originator and an SPV may occur where the two entities are held out to creditors as constituting a single business, the assets of the entities are commingled or are not clearly segregated or where creditors dealt with the entities as a single economic unit.

Moratorium/automatic stay   Automatic stay has a wide scope, and applies under s. 362 of Chapter 3 of the Bankruptcy Code to automatically prevent enforcement of security by a creditor, and other creditor action, from the date on which a filing for bankruptcy or for Chapter 11 proceedings is made (Chapter 11 of the Bankruptcy Code provides for the rehabilitation of a company in financial difficulties). The stay persists until the bankruptcy or Chapter 11 is concluded (which can take considerable time in the case of Chapter 11). There is an exemption from the automatic stay with regard to the netting of certain forward contracts or securities contracts.

Set-off

The debtor can obtain good discharge by making payments to the originator until notice of the assignment is given to the debtor, at which point the debtor is obliged to pay to the SPV direct. The SPV will take subject to any defects in the title of the originator, and until notice is given to the debtor, the SPV is subject to any further equities (such as set-off) arising in favour of the debtor through relations between the originator and the debtor subsequent to the assignment.

Onshore SPV

Trusts have frequently been used as purchasing/issuing vehicles in the US to avoid consolidation of the SPV onto the accounting balance sheet of the originator under the now redundant substantive equity doctrine, or to avoid corporate taxation (see "Tax treatment" below). Non-US transactions being sold into the US may also use a US trust due to the preference of, or requirement for, certain US investors to invest in securities from a US transaction.

Securities laws

The US has a range of far-reaching securities laws, which are global in application, and are therefore relevant to the majority of transactions, even where taking place outside the US. The Securities Act of 1933 requires that any offering of securities on issue or resale which falls within s. 5 and is not exempted by the Securities Act or by other provisions of the Securities and Exchange Commission from registration must be preceded by a registration statement. The main exemptions on issue are for:

(a) an offer of exempt securities (e.g. commercial paper);
(b) an offering of securities falling under Rule 903 of Regulation S;
(c) a private placement under s. 4(2) of the Securities Act; or
(d) a Regulation D placement (a safe harbour under s. 4(2)).

An issue exemption could be reopened to the extent that subsequent resales are not exempt. Exemption on resale following an issue is available for:

(a) A resale of exempt securities as before;
(b) Sales under s. 4(1) by persons other than issuers, underwriters (this term being interpreted widely to include any person who purchases securities with a view to reselling them) or dealers;
(c) Sales under s. 4(3) and s. 4(4) by brokers and dealers more than 40 days after the first offering of the securities;
(d) Sales under Rule 144 (a safe harbour under s. 4(1) from possible consideration as an underwriter);
(e) Sales under "s. $4(1\frac{1}{2})$" (sales which would be a private placement but for the fact that they are not made by the issuer and are therefore outside s. 4(2));
(f) Sale under Rule 904 of Regulation S on a non-US market approved by the SEC as a DOSM; or
(g) Sale in the US under Rule 144A.

Further requirements may arise under blue sky laws or regulations. See also TEFRA under "Other tax issues" below.

The Investment Company Act of 1940 prohibits an affiliated originator from transferring financial assets to an investment company (an investment company is any issuer of securities that engages primarily in investing in securities – including any evidence of indebtedness) and requires an investment company that makes a public offer of securities in the US or makes a placement of securities in the US to be registered with the SEC.

There are exemptions for any issuer:

- whose outstanding securities (other than short-term paper) are beneficially owned by not more than 100 US persons and which is not making a public offer;
- who is engaged in the business of purchasing financial assets such as receivables that convert into cash within a definite time period where its securities are investment grade or are sold to QIBs; or
- whose securities are owned solely by qualified purchasers and which does not intend to make a public offer.

Tax treatment

Withholding tax   The US charges withholding at a rate of 30% on interest payments made offshore. This is reduced to zero by double tax treaties with the UK and various other European countries. The anti-conduit regulations (US Treasury Regulation §1.881-3) require that a borrowing by a US borrower through an intermediate lender be viewed as a pass-through of interest payments from the US borrower to the ultimate lender in certain cases, which may lead to the imposition of withholding tax where the ultimate lender cannot benefit from a tax treaty relief. The anti-conduit regulations will apply where a financing transaction for the advance of cash is undertaken pursuant to a tax avoidance plan (i.e. a plan with tax avoidance as one of its principal purposes) in such a way that US withholding tax is less than it would be disregarding the intermediate entity, and where the intermediate entity would not have participated on substantially the same terms unless the ultimate lender also participated. An intermediate level financing may be structured as a deposit of securities that cannot be sold prior to an event of default, instead of an advance of cash, to ensure that the regulations do not apply.

Profits tax   A range of securitisation trust vehicles or elections are used to eliminate corporate tax, such as:

- **Grantor trust**   A trust which the IRS will recognise as achieving fiscal transparency if it is not engaged in a profitable business and only issues a single class of trust interests and cannot vary their terms. Thus, the trust may not engage in replenishment of assets or issue multiple classes of securities (other than a subordinated tranche which pays down pro rata with the senior tranche and otherwise matches the senior tranche in its terms).
- **Owner trust**   A trust that issues multiple classes of debt that can be sequential pay, as well as an equity class. Careful structuring is required to ensure that securities sold to investors are successfully regarded as debt for tax purposes.
- **Master trust** (or credit card trust)   Used to pool receivables against which trust certificates may be issued periodically in a series of tap issues as the asset balance in the trust changes.

Two specific types of tax election have been created by statute in the US, in order to statutorily provide for fiscal transparency treatment and for the classification of specific interests as debt or equity interests:

- **REMIC** (real estate mortgage investment conduit)   A statutory form of entity (which can be any form – trust, corporation, etc.) created for the securitisation of mortgage loans. Can issue multiple tranches of securities, but cannot enter into swaps. The REMIC has fiscal transparency. Regular interests in a REMIC are classified as debt for tax purposes; residual interests are classified as equity. No gain or loss is recognised when assets are sold to a REMIC, and the tax basis of the REMIC in the assets is equal to the issue proceeds of its securities.

- **FASIT** (financial asset investment securitisation trust)   A statutory form of entity (which can be any form – trust, corporation, etc.) created for the securitisation of a wide range of debt obligations. The trust permits the replenishment of assets and the issuance of multiple classes of securities and can enter into swaps. The FASIT has fiscal transparency. Regular interests in a FASIT are classified as debt for tax purposes; residual interests are classified as equity.

In addition, the REIT (real estate investment trust) is used for real estate securitisation. The REIT is exempt from corporation tax in the US provided it meets the requirements set out in the Tax Code.

The general IRS requirement for pass-through status (e.g. for partnerships) is that the business entity in question has no more than two of the following characteristics: (a) limited liability; (b) centralised management; (c) continuous existence; and (d) free transferability of ownership interests.

In January 2003, it was proposed that the US should move to an imputation system for dividends and remove the tax charge on dividends in the hands of investors. One reason for the high levels of leverage in US companies has been seen as the preference for paying tax deductible interest, instead of non-deductible dividends which are further taxed in the hands of the investor, leaving residual value in the company for growth and reinvestment rather than losing it to the tax authorities. The change was not made, but instead, on 28 May 2003, the dividend tax rate was reduced to 15% up until tax years starting after 31 December 2008.

Other tax issues   The Tax Equity and Fiscal Responsibility Act 1982 (TEFRA) was introduced in the US to counteract tax evasion by US taxpayers on untraceable holdings of bearer securities. Securities with a maturity of 1 year or less (or 183 days or less if US-issued) are exempt from the TEFRA provisions. They require that only registered securities are issued, ownership in which can be traced by the IRS. Any issue of bearer securities world wide will be subject to adverse punitive US tax consequences unless:

(a) There are arrangements in place reasonably designed to ensure that the securities will only be sold or resold to persons who are not US persons (or to certain financial institutions who are US persons) (such as issues and resales of the securities within one of the TEFRA safe harbours – TEFRA C and TEFRA D;
(b) Interest on the securities is payable only outside the US and its possessions; and
(c) The securities and their coupons bear the TEFRA legend wording.

Accounting treatment

Financial Accounting Standard 140 issued in September 2000 to replace FAS 125 applies to transfers and servicing of financial assets that take place after 31 March 2001 (excluding some transfers committed to prior to such date – for example, further tranches of revolving transactions). The Standard applies to securitisations and to resecuritisation of existing deals. FAS 140 accords a transfer one of four treatments:

- Sale (if the requirements set out in FAS 140 are met)
- Financing (if the requirements are not met)
- Swap (for example, where loans are exchanged for notes)
- Partial sale (if the requirements of FAS 140 are met, but the originator retains servicing or one or more classes of securities issued). In this latter case, the sold assets are accorded sale treatment, and the retained assets (i.e. servicing rights to the extent that a more than adequate compensation is received for servicing, or securities) will appear on the balance sheet.

If sale treatment is accorded to a transaction, the seller is required to use "gain on sale" accounting, which involves recognition of any gain or loss on sale of assets immediately on the sale occurring. This typically leads to the originator booking an up-front profit for the excess spread on a transaction due by way of profit strip, on the basis of assumptions as to prepayment speed and interest rates. In 1998, the SEC required "gain on sale" to be applied across the board (regardless of whether it gave rise to a gain or a loss) and for assumptions used in calculating gain on sale to be clearly disclosed, following concerns arising from some originators remarking expected future values due to high prepayment rates. Some sellers have structured securitisations under FAS 140 as financings rather than sales, specifically in order to avoid gain on sale treatment. This is due to the fact that gain on sale is disliked by the equity market as it generates current accounting profit from future excess spread revenue (leading to earnings volatility if default and prepayment assumptions in the gain on sale calculation prove to be incorrect).

To qualify as a sale, the transferor must:

- Surrender control over the assets, such that they are isolated beyond the reach of the transferor, affiliates, liquidator or creditors;
- Transfer the assets to an SPV where:

  - For a QSPE (see below), noteholders have the right to pledge or exchange their notes or certificates; or
  - For other entities, the SPV itself has the right to pledge or exchange the underlying assets;

- Not retain effective control over the assets via a right and obligation to take back the assets at a certain point, or a right to take back specific assets (other than under a clean-up call where the transferor retains or subcontracts servicing, but not where the transferor sells servicing); and
- Receive cash proceeds from the sale (as opposed to a note or interest in the assets). This requirement has led to the introduction of a second onward transfer step to an issuing trust in some bank securitisations in the US, where previously a "one-step" transfer to a subsidiary in return for a note would have sufficed under FAS 125.

A Qualifying Special Purpose Entity or "QSPE" is never consolidated in the financial statements of the seller. An SPV that is not a QSPE may be consolidated with the seller (see below). To qualify as a QSPE, an SPV must:

- Be "demonstratively distinct" from the seller (i.e. where it cannot be unilaterally dissolved by the transferor or its affiliates or agents, and where at least 10% of the fair value of its beneficial interests are held by entities other than the transferor or its affiliates or agents);

- Have permitted activities that are significantly limited and specified up-front;
- Only hold passive financial assets (i.e. where no decisions other than servicing are made by the QSPE – the QSPE cannot, for example, hold controlling equity stakes), cash and investments; and
- Have limited powers to choose when to dispose of assets, such that it may only dispose of assets if required to do so as a result of an event of default outside its control, or where funds required on exercise of a put or call or predetermined maturity or liquidation date.

If the SPV is not a QSPE then it will be consolidated on the accounts of its majority owner unless it falls within Financial Accounting Standards Board Interpretation No. 46 (FIN 46) on Consolidation of Variable Interest Entities (published by the FASB on 17 January 2003, and applied from 1 February 2003 in respect of entities created after 31 January 2003, and from the first fiscal period beginning after 15 December 2003 (originally 15 June 2003) in respect of entities created before 1 February 2003). The Interpretation applies if an entity is a "Variable Interest Entity" (VIE), that is:

- Its equity is insufficient to permit the entity to finance its activities without subordinated financial support (for this purpose equity of less than 10% of total assets is considered insufficient unless the entity can demonstrate its ability to finance its activities, or it has at least as much equity as comparable entities that operate without subordinated financial support, or it can demonstrate that its equity exceeds its expected losses); or
- Its equity investors do not have votes, the obligation to absorb losses or the right to receive residual returns.

If an entity is a VIE it will be consolidated by the entity (the "Primary Beneficiary") that will absorb the majority of the expected losses of the VIE, and/or that is entitled to a majority of the VIE's expected residual return, as a result of holding "Variable Interests" in the entity. If different entities absorb the losses and receive the return, the entity which absorbs losses will consolidate. If a VIE has no Primary Beneficiary it will not be consolidated.

"Variable interests" are defined as "contractual, ownership, or other pecuniary interests in an entity that change with changes in the entity's net asset value". Variable interests can include equity and debt instruments, guarantees, put options, derivatives, servicing contracts, leases and other items. For this purpose, an entity will consider variable interests held by itself and by its related parties (which include certain de facto agents).

In addition to consolidation considerations, holders of variable interests are required to meet disclosure requirements:

- *Primary beneficiary* (as well as consolidating)   Disclose nature, purpose, size and activities of VIE, carrying amount and classification of VIE collateral, any lack of recourse by creditors of the VIE to the Primary beneficiary.
- *Holders of significant variable interests*   Disclose nature of involvement with VIE and when such involvement began, nature, purpose, size and activities of VIE, maximum exposure to loss as a result of involvement with VIE.

Capital treatment

In the US, under Regulatory Accounting Principles (RAP), any provision of credit enhancement to a transaction by the originator bank will result in the securitised assets remaining on balance sheet for capital adequacy purposes. This may be avoided by the use of a two-tiered sale structure, where the first transfer is made without credit enhancement to an SPV that has previously been equity capitalised by the originator. The second transfer then allows the SPV, a non-regulated entity, to provide the credit enhancement.

Proposals were released in February 2000 which follow the new Basel proposals in many areas. On 1 January 2002, the FDIC adopted new rules on capital for securitisation by federally-insured banks, which require less capital to be held against highly rated asset-backed securities and more for lower rated securities, as follows:

- 20% for AAA and AA (or A1/P1)
- 50% for A (or A2/P2)
- 100% for BBB (or A3/P3)
- 200% for BB
- Direct deduction for B/unrated.

In March 2000, the Federal Reserve put forward a proposal for banks to hold 50% capital against their venture capital investments, instead of 8%, although the proposal was challenged by the Office for the Comptroller of the Currency.

On 12 August 1996 and 13 June 1997, the US Federal Reserve published guidance on the capital treatment of credit derivatives.

Banking book   Credit derivatives are treated as guarantees in the banking book in respect of the amount of exposure to which they relate, but can also get credit for cash collateral where they are funded. As general requirements for credit derivatives:

- The reference obligation must be the same as the protected asset, or linked to the protected asset in documentation of the trade.
- A "first to default" basket structure gives the buyer protection against the default of the smallest and least risky risk-weighted exposure in the basket.
- Sale of a "first to default" credit derivative basket structure generates a capital charge for the protection seller equal to the most risky risk-weighted asset in the basket.
- The protection buyer should be seen to have transferred the credit risk (without such transfer constituting a breach of the term of the reference obligation) such that the protection seller has no recourse to the protection buyer for losses.

Trading book   The exposure to the reference entity is treated as a long/short specific risk position. As general requirements for credit derivatives:

- The reference obligation must be the same as the protected asset, or correlation must be demonstrated with internal models.
- A "first to default" basket structure allows the buyer to record a short position for the smallest and least risky risk-weighted asset in the basket.
- Sale of a "first to default" credit derivative basket structure creates a long position for the protection seller in the most risky risk-weighted asset in the basket.

- The protection buyer should be seen to have transferred the credit risk (without such transfer constituting a breach of the term of the reference obligation) such that the protection seller has no recourse to the protection buyer for losses.

In addition to market risk assessments, unfunded credit derivatives such as total return swaps and credit default products (but not funded credit derivatives such as credit-linked notes) are subjected to a counterparty risk haircut by calculating the mark-to-market value of the derivative plus an "add-on" percentage (which is based on either equity add-ons or commodity add-ons) of the notional principal, with the aggregate figure then being multiplied by counterparty risk weight and weighted by a factor of 8%.

Other issues

The doctrine of privity of contract is relaxed by the application of the third-party beneficiary doctrine, allowing third parties to claim rights under agreements in some cases.

Provision is made under Article 8 of the UCC for a simplification of the classification and perfection of ownership and security interests in securities held through a clearing system or custodian, where the owner's entitlement is reflected by a book entry. The ownership interest of the owner is classified under Article 8 as a bundle of rights (known as a "securities entitlement"), which includes rights against the custodian and (under s. 8-503(b)) a *pro rata* proprietary interest in the pool held by the custodian of which his account is part. Under s. 8-503(a) the securities do not form part of the custodian's insolvency estate. The custodian is obliged to take due care to obtain payment from the underlying issuer of the securities under s. 8-505(a). Under s. 9-103(d) of Article 9, the relevant law to determine the steps required for perfection of a security interest over an owner's securities entitlement is that of the law of the custodian's jurisdiction.

The Gramm–Leach–Bliley Financial Services Modernization Act of 1999 was signed on 12 November 1999 and came into effect on 12 November 2000. It is designed to remove the division of operations between commercial banks and investment banks and insurance companies under the Glass–Steagall Act and must be complied with from 1 July 2001. The Act permits securities firms, banks and insurers to diversify into each other's business, and also contains new consumer privacy protections.

The federal Riegle–Neal Interstate Banking and Branching Efficiency Act of 1994 (signed into law on 29 September 1994) relaxes previous restrictions on banking activities across state borders, and permits interstate acquisitions of banks by a bank holding company, without the opportunity for state-by-state opt-out (previously state opt-out overrode the federal provisions), and interstate bank mergers, subject to state-by-state opt-out. Interstate branching is also permitted for the first time into states where opt-in provisions are enacted.

12.52   VENEZUELA

Accounting treatment

US accounting standards are followed.

13

Terminology in the Securitisation and Derivatives Markets

An asterisk (*) indicates that the term is included in this chapter and is also of relevance to the term being defined.

ABCP   See Asset-backed commercial paper.

ABS   See Asset-backed security.

Absolute rate   A quoted Interest rate* that is expressed as a fixed figure rather than a figure connected to a particular Basis* (sense (ii)) and a set Margin* (sense (i)).

Accelerate   See Acceleration.

Acceleration   The process by which a loan or bond becomes immediately due and payable. Typically occurs as a result of an Event of default* under the conditions of the loan or bond.

Acceptance   **(i)** The signing of a Bill of exchange* by the drawee or a third party (e.g. a bank), which acts to guarantee primary payment on maturity to the holder of the bill by the acceptor (i.e. the drawee or third party). In the event of non-payment by the acceptor, the company who has drawn and transferred the bill to the holder remains liable on the bill, followed by the first endorser (i.e. the original payee), the second endorser, and so on. Cf. Confirm. A bill accepted by an Eligible bank* becomes an Eligible bank bill*.

(ii) A Bill of exchange* that is drawn under an Acceptance credit* and bears the Acceptance (see sense (i) above) of the bank issuing the acceptance credit.

Acceptance credit   A form of Letter of credit*, under which the bank undertakes to give Acceptances* (sense (i)) on Bills of exchange* issued in accordance with the terms of the acceptance credit.

Accounting period   **(i)** See Financial year, sense (i).

(ii) For UK VAT* purposes, one of four annual 3-month periods, ending on the last day in (a) June, September, December and March; (b) July, October, January and April; or (c) August, November, February and May, as allocated to a person registered for VAT as a taxable person by Customs and Excise, in relation to which to file a VAT return. The return must be filed within 1 month of the end of the related accounting period.

Accounting reference date   For UK companies, the last day in a company's Financial year* (sense (i)). A company's accounting reference date is fixed from year to year, although it is possible to change it in accordance with s. 225 Companies Act 1985*. The first accounting reference date must fall more than 6 months and less than 18 months after the company's date of incorporation.

Accounting reference period   See Financial year, sense (i).

Accounts   See Statutory accounts.

Accredited investor   For the purposes of Securities Act* regulation, and specifically Regulation D*, most institutional investors and high net worth individuals, as well as officers of the issuer in question.

Accrued interest   Interest already earned on an instrument during an interest period but not yet due for payment, which is reflected by an increase in the price of the instrument if it is sold "Dirty"* prior to the interest payment date. See also Clean.

Accumulating trust   A Discretionary trust* under which the trustees have the power of Accumulation* of income. Income and capital gains accumulated are subject to tax at the "rate applicable to trusts" (a higher rate than the basic rate or lower rate of tax) under s. 151 Finance Act* 1989 and s. 686 ICTA (income tax) and s. 5 and s. 65 TCGA (capital gains tax).

Accumulation   A power granted in the trust deed constituting certain Discretionary trusts*, enabling the trustees to accumulate trust income, thus making them Accumulating trusts* or Accumulation and maintenance settlements*. The presence of such a power means that a trust cannot be an Interest in possession trust*. Income validly accumulated is converted to and taxed as capital for UK taxation purposes (unless it is subsequently paid out in the form of income – e.g. in regular annual payments). Income may be accumulated for a maximum period of 21 years, or the life of the settlor (contrast to the Rule against perpetuities*), although an 80-year period is acceptable where the settlor is a corporate entity (provided that the use of the corporate entity is bona fide and not simply designed to circumvent the shorter accumulation period).

Accumulation and maintenance settlement   A form of Discretionary trust* under which income is accumulated in compliance with detailed provisions for the benefit of young relations of the settlor. Not subject to the usual 10-year discretionary trust inheritance tax charge on the principal amount of the trust property, although trust income and capital gains are still subject to tax at the "rate applicable to trusts" (a higher rate than the basic rate or lower rate of tax) under s. 151 Finance Act* 1989 and s. 686 ICTA (income tax) and ss. 5 and 65 TCGA (capital gains tax).

Accumulation period   In a Securitisation* transaction, a period during which principal receipts are accumulated within the deal in order to make payment of principal on a bullet tranche due to mature at the end of the accumulation period.

ACT   Advance corporation tax. Liability to pay ACT arose in respect of Distributions* until ACT was abolished from 6 April 1999. ACT was replaced with a quarterly payment system for Corporation tax* for large companies. Previously, distributions were required to be reported to the Revenue within three months of being made and payment of ACT had to be made within 14 days of an ACT assessment being raised by the Revenue on the distribution.

Actual   In relation to financial instruments, the underlying physical financial instrument, as against a Derivative* based on the instrument.

Actuarial   See Annuity.

Administration   The management of the affairs, business and property of a Registered company* (but not an association or Society*, etc.) by an Administrator* in order to protect a company that is, or is likely to become, Unable to pay its debts* and for which the court is satisfied the administration would likely achieve its survival or would allow a Voluntary arrangement* with its creditors to be effected. During administration, under s. 11 of the Insolvency Act 1986*, no Winding-up* order may be made or Administrative receiver* appointed and a Moratorium* (see also Automatic stay) prevents steps being taken to enforce security over or take proceedings against the assets of the company without the consent of the court. Appointment of an Administrative receiver* by a creditor notified of an administration petition prevents the granting of an administration order. One of the five main branches of insolvency related procedures (for the others, see Receivership, Administrative receivership, Voluntary arrangement and Liquidation). See also Insolvency Act 2000. The Enterprise Act* provides for reform to insolvency law in the UK to encourage the use of administration and voluntary procedures. The Act contains a prohibition on the ability of a creditor to appoint an administrative receiver except in certain cases, and develops more detailed provisions for the use of administration.

Under paragraphs 14–16 of Schedule 16, a holder of a qualifying floating charge is given the power to appoint an administrator selected by it on 2 business days' written notice to the holder of any previously created or prior ranking floating charges. This power may only be exercised when the relevant floating charge has become enforceable.

Under paragraphs 22–27 of Schedule 16, a company or the directors of a company are given the power to appoint an administrator selected by it or them on 5 business days' written notice to any person with the right to appoint an administrator or administrative receiver of the company. This power may only be exercised if accompanied by a statutory declaration that the company is, or is likely to become, unable to pay its debts and is not in liquidation. An administrator cannot be appointed for a company where a winding-up petition has been presented and has not yet been dismissed.

Under paragraphs 11–12 of Schedule 16, the court may make an administration order appointing an administrator on application by the company, the directors of the company or one or more creditors of the company, where the court is satisfied that the company is, or is likely to become, unable to pay its debts and that the administration is likely to achieve its purpose. The purposes of administration are set out in paragraph 3 as: rescuing the company, or failing that achieving a better result than winding-up for creditors as a whole, or failing that realising assets to make a distribution to one or more secured or preferential creditors.

An administrator may not be appointed whilst an administrative receiver is in office, unless the floating charge holder who appointed the administrative receiver consents, or the floating charge is in some way prejudiced (as set out in paragraph 37 of Schedule 16). The appointment of an administrator takes effect for an initial period of 1 year (under paragraph 76 of Schedule 16), subject to extension by the court or by consent.

Special administration regimes in relation to water and sewage undertakers, protected railway companies, air traffic services, public–private partnerships and building societies are preserved by s. 249 of the Act.

Administrative receiver   Under s. 29(2) of the Insolvency Act 1986*, a Receiver* or manager of "the whole (or substantially the whole) of a company's property" appointed by or on behalf of a creditor whose debt is secured by "a charge which, as created, was a floating charge, or such a charge and one or more other or securities" (see Floating charge). Appointed to effect an Administrative receivership*. A petition for Administration* can be blocked by the appointment of an administrative receiver. An administrative receiver does not have power to set aside Undervalues* or Preferences* (cf. Liquidator and Administrator).

The Enterprise Act* provides for reform to insolvency law in the UK to restrict administrative receivership and encourage the use of administration and voluntary procedures.

The Act contains a prohibition on the ability of a creditor to appoint an administrative receiver except in certain cases. The Act provides at s. 250 for new sections 72A to G to be inserted in the Insolvency Act 1986. New s. 72A provides that the holder of a qualifying floating charge may not appoint an administrative receiver of the company. A qualifying floating charge is defined in paragraph 14 of Schedule 16 (which is inserted as Schedule B1 of the Insolvency Act 1986) as a floating charge which expressly states that paragraph 14 applies to it, or which purports to empower the holder of the floating charge to appoint an administrator or an administrative receiver of the company, and which – either by itself, or together with other charges or security interests – is secured over "the whole or substantially the whole of the company's property".

Under s. 72A(4), the new provision restricting the appointment of an administrative receiver would apply to a floating charge created on or after a date appointed by the Secretary of State by order made by statutory instrument (effectively retaining the old rules for existing charges).

There are a series of exceptions to the new provision, which permit the appointment of an administrative receiver:

Under s. 72B and Schedule 18 (which is inserted as Schedule 2A of the Insolvency Act 1986), where there is security to a trustee/nominee/agent for holders of an instrument (or there is a third-party guarantee or security interest, or there is an arrangement involving options, futures or contracts for differences) under which a party incurs (or is expected to incur) debt of at least £50m (or currency equivalent as at the time when the arrangement is entered into) at any time during the life of the arrangement, where the arrangement involves the issue of:

(a) a debt instrument which is rated by an internationally recognised rating agency, admitted to the official list in the UK, or admitted to trading on a market established under the rules of a recognised investment exchange or on a foreign market (or is designed to be so rated, listed or traded); or

(b) a bond (construed in accordance with Article 77 of the FSMA 2000 (Regulated Activities) Order 2001) or commercial paper (which must be redeemed before its first anniversary) issued to investment professionals, high net worth individuals or sophisticated investors.

Under ss. 72C, D and E and Schedule 18, in respect of a project company (a company that holds property for the project, or has sole or principal contractual responsibility for carrying out all or part of the project (either directly or through agents), or is one of a number of companies which, together, carry out the project, or has the purpose of supplying finance to enable the project to be carried out, or is a holding company of any of these, unless in any of such cases it also performs another function that is neither related to any of these nor related to the project) for a public–private partnership project, a utility project or a project under which a party incurs (or is expected to incur) debt of at least £50m (or currency equivalent as at the time when the project begins) at any time during the life of the arrangement, where in each case a person who provides finance for the project has contractual step-in rights to assume sole or principal contractual responsibility for carrying out all or part of the project.

Under s. 72F, if the company is party to a Market contract*, or a money market contract or a related contract under Financial Markets and Insolvency (Money Market) Regulations 1995 (SI 1995/2049), or there is a money market charge or system-charge over property of the company under Financial Markets and Insolvency Regulations 1996 (SI 1996/1469), or the company is a participant in a designated system or there is a collateral security charge over property of the company under Financial Markets and Insolvency (Settlement Finality) Regulations 1999 (SI 1999/2979).

Administrative receivership   The process whereby the portion of the business of a company which has been secured in favour of a creditor or creditors is managed by an Administrative receiver* appointed pursuant to the terms of the security in order to realise the secured assets and repay the secured debt. One of the five main branches of insolvency related procedures (for the others, see Liquidation, Voluntary arrangement, Receivership and Administration). The government has restricted administrative receivership; see Enterprise Act.

Administrator   A qualified insolvency practitioner who is appointed by court order to effect an Administration*. Has power to set aside Undervalues* and Preferences*, or to apply for an order nullifying Transactions defrauding creditors*, but not to seek an order regarding Fraudulent trading*.

ADR   See American depositary receipt.

Advance   The payment of funds to a borrower by a lender under the terms of a banking Facility*. Cf. Drawdown.

Advance corporation tax   See ACT.

Advance rate   The percentage rate at which an Advance* will be made against the value of a particular asset (for example a pool of mortgages, a piece of real estate or a portfolio of bonds in a Market value CBO* structure).

Advanced pricing agreement   An agreement between a corporate multinational and a state tax authority, in which the latter agrees acceptable Transfer pricing* (sense (ii)) policies and levels for the corporate and eliminates the uncertainty of separate annual valuations from scratch. Used in, for example, the US and Australia.

Advising bank   In relation to a Documentary credit*, a bank which advises the beneficiary of a credit that the credit has been issued by the Issuing bank*. The beneficiary has no right to enforce the credit against the advising bank unless the advising bank confirms (see Confirm) the credit, or the advising bank and the issuing bank are the same entity. The advising bank should only pay on receipt of documents which conform precisely to those detailed in the credit. See also Correspondent bank and Confirming bank.

After sight bill   A Bill of exchange* payable a set number of days after it is seen by the relevant person. Acceptance* of such a bill must occur in order to fix the point at which it is deemed "seen" and thus the date of maturity.

Agencies   Securities issued by US government agencies, which, although not directly drawn against the US Treasury, are guaranteed or impliedly supported by it. The most Liquid markets* are in the securities of Ginnie Mae*, Fannie Mae* and Freddie Mac*.

Agent   A fiduciary who acts on behalf of a principal, within the scope of the authority granted by the principal. For delegation of agent powers, see Power of attorney. In a Syndicated loan* the agent is the bank which takes on the role of the administration of the loan on behalf of the Syndicate* and carries out day-to-day dealings with the borrower.

AGM   See Annual general meeting.

AIBD   Association of International Bond Dealers. Subsequently retitled as ISMA*.

AIM   See Alternative Investment Market.

All or none   A buy or sell order that is conditional upon the whole order being met on the stated terms. Also known as Fill or kill*.

All-in cost   The percentage rate per annum or Margin* (sense (i)) over a benchmark Interest rate* that a borrower pays on a financing, calculated by annualising all fees and interest costs over the life of the financing. Equivalent to the Yield* earned by the lender.

Allotment   The first placement on issue by an issuer of a share or other security to a holder. In the UK debt securities market, will be the initial Subscription* amounts.

Alternative Investment Market   The London Stock Exchange* market for Unlisted* securities, which opened on 19 June 1995. The AIM replaced the Rule 4.2* unquoted securities trading facility and the USM*, and thus has less stringent requirements than those for Listed* securities. There are no requirements as to capitalisation, length of trading record, public holdings of shares or use of a sponsor (although a nominated adviser and a nominated broker are required), but companies will be required to be Public companies* (if UK incorporated; if not they must be in a form that would permit them to make a public offer of securities under their own law) and to produce admission documentation (although not necessarily a Prospectus*) and continuing information.

Alternative option   An Option* where the holder can select one of two settlement amounts, each based on a different Actual* and a different strike price.

American depositary receipt   Or ADR. A certificate in the form of a Registered security* evidencing ownership of an underlying debt or equity issue. Similar in nature to a Global depositary receipt*, but issued to US investors rather than on a global basis. ADRs may need to comply with SEC* registration or reporting requirements.

American option   An Option* exercisable at any point over a specified period. Cf. European option.

AMEX   American Stock Exchange.

Amortisation   Repayment of the principal of a debt in periodic instalments (e.g. through the operation of a Sinking fund* or a Purchase fund* for debt securities) as opposed to a Bullet* repayment structure (see also Balloon*). With regard to different methods of calculating interest and principal on gradual amortisation of a debt, see Annuity and Rule of 78s. The annuity basis is used for debt securities.

Amortising rate swap: A swap where the buyer receives a high fixed-rate payment in exchange for taking the risk that the swap principal will amortise according to an index representing either real or synthetic interest rates.

Annual general meeting   For UK companies, an annual meeting of the Members* of the company which is required by s. 366 of the Companies Act 1985*, unless an Elective resolution* removing the requirement has been passed. An annual general meeting must under s. 369 Companies Act 1985* be called on at least 21 days' notice, unless the requisite minimum level of consents for Short notice* is obtained.

Annual return   For UK companies, an annual up-date filing on the company which is required under s. 363 Companies Act 1985*.

Announcement   See Invitation telex.

Annuity   Or Actuarial*. Method of calculating Amortisation* of the principal of a debt, carried out by assuming that all accrued interest at the Effective interest rate* is first paid out of each debt service payment, with the remainder of any debt service after payment of such accrued interest being applied to reduce principal. The remaining outstanding principal at any point can be calculated as the sum of the Net present value* of the debt service payments.

Anstaltslast   See Landesbank.

Anti-conduit regulations   US Treasury Regulation §1.881-3, which requires that a borrowing by a US borrower through an intermediate lender be viewed as a pass-through of interest payments from the US borrower to the ultimate lender in certain cases, which may lead to the imposition of withholding tax where the ultimate lender cannot benefit from a tax treaty relief. The anti-conduit regulations will apply where a financing transaction for the advance of cash is undertaken pursuant to a tax avoidance plan (i.e. a plan with tax avoidance as one of its principal purposes) in such a way that US withholding tax is less than it would be disregarding the intermediate entity, and where the intermediate entity would not have participated on substantially the same terms unless the ultimate lender also participated. An intermediate level financing may be structured as a deposit of securities which cannot be sold prior to an event of default, instead of an advance of cash, to ensure that the regulations do not apply.

Anticipatory credit   A Documentary credit* which contains a clause in red (a "red clause") authorising an advance to the seller to meet payments in advance on goods purchased for on sale to the buyer.

APR   Or annual percentage rate of charge. Percentage rate that expresses the total charge for credit, and is required to be notified to consumers entering into regulated agreements under the Consumer Credit Act 1974*. The method of calculation of an APR for an agreement is set out in the Consumer Credit (Total Charge for Credit

Agreements and Advertisements) (Amendment) Regulations 1999 (SI 1999/3177) (effective from 14 April 2000).

Arbitrage The manipulation of imperfect price Correlations* between different markets, which arise from a poor flow of information or from particular tax or regulatory regimes, in order to extract profit. An example is placing simultaneous buy and sell orders on the same security in two different markets at prices which allow an immediate Spread* (sense (i)) to the trader (relying on high volume of trading to generate a profit, as price differentials are very small). This form of arbitrage trading is seen as low risk as Positions* taken in one transaction are immediately or almost immediately Matched* in an off-setting transaction, leaving the trader Market neutral*. Another example enables access to an overseas capital market cheaply by borrowing in the local market and entering a Currency swap* or a Circus swap* with a counterparty located in the overseas market desired. Other forms of Swap* may also be used in arbitrage, the most common being a fixed to floating swap linked to a fixed rate bond issue, which may enable funds to be raised at an effective All-in cost* below LIBOR* (or the relevant benchmark for the bond), where the fixed rate receipts under the swap exceed the fixed rate payments on the bond. Favourable arbitrage opportunities for the bond issuer in this latter structure (known as Swap windows* or Spread windows*) depend on high Swap prices*/Swap spreads* relative to bond rates. Arbitrage may be Hard arbitrage* or Soft arbitrage*.

Arm's-length Generic term used to indicate that two parties are not linked or connected (see, for example, Connected persons) by mutual interests and conduct business between themselves on fair market terms. In relation to Transfer pricing* (senses (i) and (ii)), the principle that the value of any inter-company or inter-state transactions should be priced for tax calculation purposes as though the transferor and the transferee of value stood at "arm's-length", in order to tax each entity on the profits arising therein and prevent tax avoidance by shifting value to a loss-making vehicle. Cf. Unitary tax.

Arrangement fee The fee which an Arranger* charges for agreeing to undertake the setting-up of a Syndicated loan* (or other financial arrangement).

Arranger A bank which agrees to arrange a Syndicated loan* (or other financial arrangement) for a borrower, without agreeing to Underwrite* it. Cf. Lead manager.

Arrears See Delinquencies.

Article 8 See Uniform Commercial Code.

Article 9 See Uniform Commercial Code.

Articles of association The rules that govern the internal workings of a company. May be referred to as the by-laws of a company in some jurisdictions. Sample model articles for UK companies are set out in Table A*. See also Memorandum of association*.

ASEAN Association of South East Asian Nations.

Asian Development Bank A bank backed by the US government and other governments world wide, and mandated to provide financial assistance in the development of Asia.

Asian option   See Average rate option.

Asked   See Offer.

Asset allocation   The process of spreading investments among different markets, to minimise Concentration risk* or to take advantage of differing opportunities.

Asset-backed commercial paper   An Asset-backed security* issued in the form of Commercial paper*.

Asset-backed finance   Finance raised against the cash flows from, and security of, a portfolio of assets owned by the borrower by segregating the assets in a Securitisation* or Repackaging* structure.

Asset-backed security   A Security* issued under a Securitisation* or Repackaging* structure where payment is secured against a pool of assets (more often referred to as a Synthetic security* if derived from a repackaging structure or an underlying Credit default swap*). Cf. Mortgage-backed security.

Asset-based finance   Finance raised for the purchase of an asset, where either the cash flows from the purchased asset are essential to the purchaser's ability to repay the financing or where the borrower has an option to cancel its remaining indebtedness by handing the asset over to the lender, thus exposing the lender to Residual value risk*. Typically involves the exploitation of an asset, profits from which would vary depending on the owner of the asset and the locale the asset owner operates in (e.g. a ship). Cf. Project finance.

Asset finance   Any financing transaction, the purpose of which is to enable the borrower to purchase capital assets, even though the lender may not be looking to cash flows from, or security over, the asset to repay the financing.

Asset swap   A Swap* (interest rate or otherwise) that is used to convert the cash flow from a Security* (or other financial asset) into another cash flow. Often used by a financial institution to alter the underlying security's payment profile and sell the packaged cash flow to an investor, who acts as counterparty on the swap. In situations where the security is acquired by the investor, they will agree to make swap payments to the financial institution based on payments made by the underlying issuer on the underlying security, in return for payment by the financial institution to the investor of a smoothed payment stream (if the securities remain with the financial institution, the swap will simply pass some of the risk on the cash flow of the security to the investor – perhaps in a different currency from that on the underlying security for example – in return for a LIBOR-based or index-based return, as a Total return swap* or Equity swap*). The investor will be exposed to credit risk on the financial institution for the swap as well as to the underlying issuer on the underlying security, and a Repackaging* structure (where the underlying security is sold to a bankruptcy remote SPV*, and the counterparty enters into a swap with the SPV) may be used instead, allowing a reduction in the Swap price* and leaving only the debt issued by the SPV (based on the new payment flow) on the investor's balance sheet, rather than both the underlying security and the swap.

Asset value risk   See Residual value risk.

Assignment The transfer of property either by way of security or outright by way of sale. Under English law conflicts of laws principles (pursuant to Schedule 1, Article 12 of the Contracts (Applicable Law) Act 1990), the assignability or non-assignability of an intangible such as the benefit of a contract is determined by the Governing law* of the underlying contract giving rise to the intangible.

Assignment under English law can be legal or equitable:

(a) Legal assignment of a debt or chose in action is governed by the requirements of s. 136 Law of Property Act 1925, which must be complied with in order for the assignment to be legal; namely that the assignment:

(1) be in writing and signed by the assignor;
(2) be absolute (i.e. be unconditional or by way of mortgage and not merely by way of charge);
(3) covers the whole of the debt or chose in action;
(4) is notified in writing to the borrower or other obligor (notice can be given by any party and need not be given by the assignor).

A legal assignment is effective against the assignor, the debtor and third parties to transfer the full extent of the title held by the assignor. Any defenses such as Set-off* (sense (ii)) which the debtor could have raised against the assignor prior to the assignment will be effective against the assignee. The assignee can sue the debtor directly and the debtor can only obtain good discharge for payments made to the assignee.

(b) An assignment that does not meet all the s. 136 criteria is equitable in nature and no specific requirement needs to be met (e.g. the assignment need not be in writing), although an equitable assignment of an equitable chose in action must comply with the requirements of s. 53(1)(c) Law of Property Act 1925; that is, it must be in writing and signed by the assignor. An equitable assignment is effective against the assignor and third parties, but is only effective against the debtor where there is privity of contract between the debtor and the assignee. Thus in most cases, the assignee must sue the debtor in the assignor's name by joining him in proceedings (although this does not prejudice the assignee's proprietary interest in the debt, per Gibson LJ in *Three Rivers District Council v. Bank of England (1995) WLR 650*: "it is clear from the line of authorities to which I have referred that an equitable assignment creates in the equitable assignee the right to sue the debtor, subject to the procedural rule requiring the joinder of the assignor"). An equitable assignment is only effective to transfer the full extent of the title held by the assignor. Any defences that the debtor could have raised against the assignor will be effective against the assignee and the debtor can obtain good discharge by making payments to the assignor. When notice of the assignment is given from the assignee to the debtor, the debtor is obliged to pay to the assignee direct. Until such notice is given, the assignee is subject to any further equities (such as set-off rights with regard to amounts that accrue due from the assignor to the debtor prior to receipt by the debtor of the notice) arising in favour of the debtor through relations between the assignor and the debtor.

The transfer of a mortgage will automatically operate to transfer with it the debt secured by the mortgage under s. 114 Law of Property Act 1925. The burden of a contract cannot be transferred without Novation*. Cf. Declaration of trust, Negotiation, Novation, Sub-participation, Subrogation and Transfer. See also Transferable loan certificate and Transferable loan instrument. See also Future receivables and Undivided interest.

If English law governs the underlying contract (and hence an assignment of the benefit of the contract), an assignment of the benefit of the contract cannot be made where the contract contains an express prohibition on assignment. However, following the decision of the House of Lords in *Linden Gardens Trust v. Lenesta Sludge Disposals Ltd (1994) HL* that (*inter alia*) a prohibition on assignment was effective because the underlying party "wishes to ensure that he deals, and deals only, with the [assignor]", it has been argued that transfers that do not allow the assignee to deal directly with the underlying party are not prevented. This could support a Declaration of trust* by the would-be assignor over the benefit of a contract in a case where the beneficiary acting alone is not able to call for the trust to be wound up, as beneficiaries are reliant on the trustee to act and have limited direct rights with regard to the trust property. See also the case of *Don King Productions Inc. v. Warren and others (1998)*, where Lightman J in the High Court upheld a declaration of trust over the benefit of various contracts despite certain of the contracts being personal in nature and/or containing prohibitions on assignment by arguing that "a declaration of trust in favour of a third party of the benefit of obligations or the profits obtained from a contract is different in character from an assignment of the benefit of the contract to that third party" and that "whether the contract contains a provision prohibiting such a declaration of trust must be determined as a matter of construction of the contract. Such a limitation upon the freedom of the party is not lightly to be inferred and a clause prohibiting assignments is prima facie restricted to assignments of the benefit of the obligation and does not extend to declarations of trust of the benefit."

This decision was supported by the Court of Appeal, stating that "the fact that the benefit of the agreements could not be sold and were otherwise unassignable is no reason to refuse to recognise the trust which was necessary to give effect to the manifest intention of the partners", and which overruled the objection that the existence of a trust would permit the beneficiary to interfere in the underlying asset, stating that "the [beneficiary] cannot insist on rendering vicarious performance of the personal obligations arising under the contract. Rules and procedures designed to enable a beneficiary to sue in respect of a contract held in trust for him would not be applied so as to jeopardise the trust property." If the would-be assignor of a contract under which the other contracting party is in default fails, through a prohibition in the underlying contract, to effect a valid assignment, the assignee has no action against the defaulting party for damages. However, the assignor's rights in such a case were extended by the decision of the House of Lords in *Linden Gardens Trust v. Lenesta Sludge Disposals Ltd (1994) HL*. In a case where goods that are the subject matter of the contract have been transferred to a party who is also the would-be assignee of the contract rights, the case allows recovery by the assignor on behalf of the assignee where it was "in the contemplation of the parties that the proprietary interests in the goods may be transferred from one owner to another after the contract has been entered into and before the breach which causes loss or damage to the goods". The doctrine has subsequently been cited and extended in *Darlington Borough Council v. Wiltshier Northern Ltd (1995) 3 All ER*.

Contracts that are personal in nature (e.g. contracts dependent on the personal skill of the individual in question) are not assignable (although see the comments in relation to the Don King case above), although amounts accrued due under a personal contract remain assignable.

Associate   An associate of a Participator* or Director* (sense (ii)), for the purposes of the Close company* provisions, means, under ICTA, s. 417:

(a) any relative or partner of that person;
(b) the trustee or trustees of any settlement of which that person, or any relative of his (living or dead), is or was a settlor; and
(c) where that person is interested in any shares or obligations of the company that are subject to any trust or are part of the estate of a deceased person, the trustee or trustees or personal representatives concerned (as well as, if the participator is a company, any other company interested in such shares or obligations).

Associated company   For the purpose, *inter alia*, of s. 322A Companies Act 1985* (which makes voidable at the instance of the company transactions where the directors have exceeded their powers, and pursuant to which the company contracts with one of its directors or a Connected person* (sense (i)) or associated company of any of its directors), an associated company in relation to a director is, under the terms of s. 346 Companies Act 1985, a company in which the director and any Connected persons* (sense (i)) of such director have an interest in at least one-fifth of its share capital or control at least one-fifth of the voting power of its share capital.

As-you-like option   See Chooser option.

At best   A buy or sell order that is to be carried out immediately at the best price available in the market. Also known as a Market order*.

At the money   An instrument or Position* that exactly matches current market conditions. Cf. In the money, Out of the money.

ATM   **(i)** See At the money.
   (ii) Automated Teller Machine.

Authorised share capital   The aggregate Nominal value* of shares that a company's Memorandum of association* permit it to have in issue at any point in time. May be increased by an Ordinary resolution* of Members* if such power is given in the company's Articles of association* under s. 121 Companies Act 1985*.

Automatic crystallisation   Crystallisation* of a Floating charge* automatically by the terms of the relevant charging document (e.g. upon default in payment of principal or interest, or upon a prohibited form of dealing with the charged assets by the chargor), rather than upon one of the standard events of crystallisation (see Crystallisation) or following service of a Notice of crystallisation* by the chargee. Reservations have been expressed as to whether automatic crystallisation provisions are legally effective, although they are generally accepted and widely used.

Automatic stay   A stay or Moratorium* that prevents action being taken by a creditor or other claimant against a debtor in financial difficulties.

   In the UK, provisions akin to an automatic stay are extremely limited and are not really "automatic" in nature. Secured creditors are prevented from taking action to enforce security from the date of commencement of an Administration* until the administration is over. Under ss. 126 and 130(2) of the Insolvency Act 1986*, from the date on which a petition for Winding-up* of the debtor is presented, the court has a discretion to stay any pending court proceedings undertaken against the debtor. See also Insolvency Act 2000.

In the US, the automatic stay has a significantly wider scope, and applies automatically under s. 362 of Chapter 3 of the Bankruptcy Code to prevent enforcement of security by a creditor, and other creditor action, from the date on which a filing for bankruptcy or for Chapter 11* proceedings is made. The stay persists until the bankruptcy or Chapter 11 is concluded (which can take considerable time in the case of Chapter 11). There is an exemption from the automatic stay with regard to the netting of certain forward contracts or securities contracts.

Average life   See Weighted average life.

Average rate option   An Option* that generates a settlement amount calculated as the difference between the Spot* value of the Actual*, and the average value of the actual over the course of the option.

Back-to-back credit   A second Documentary credit*, opened by an Issuing bank* at the request of an applicant, who is the beneficiary under a first credit, which second credit is based on the security of the first. Undertaken to circumvent limitations of the transferability of documentary credits (see Transferable credit).

Back-to-back swap   A form of Mirror swap* that is entered into at the same time as the original swap, and is used to immediately Hedge* the Position* under the original swap. Often used as a hedge for a Securitisation* swap, due to the difficulty of accurately hedging such a swap, which will typically have variable receipts based on the level of Prepayments* on the Receivables*.

Back-up servicer   In a Securitisation* transaction, an entity that undertakes, at the start of the transaction, to act as Substitute servicer* should the appointment of the Originator* as Servicer* terminate and in the event that no other entity can be found who is willing to act as substitute servicer. The use of a back-up servicer may be required where the asset type being securitised is not widely held or serviced in the market. If there is a wide range of entities already servicing his kind of asset, there is likely to be a demand for the servicing contract if the appointment of the originator as servicer is terminated. Where the assets are unusual, or there is only a small market (or a limited number of entities) that would be capable of servicing, or willing to service, the assets, a back-up servicer may be required to commit to service the transaction by the rating agencies in order for the transaction to be rated initially. See also Cold back-up, Hot back-up and Warm back-up.

Backwardation   For Futures*, any point at which spot prices are above forward prices (i.e. an inverted market), which may be caused, for example for commodity futures, by a perceived oversupply in future supplies of the underlying. For share prices, any point at which the displayed Offer* price is lower than the Bid* price, enabling an instant profit to be made by buying at the offer price and selling at the bid. Any such reversal will be rapidly closed by Arbitrage* trading.

BACS   Bankers Automated Clearing Service. Used for bulk direct debit clearance.

Balloon   An instalment repayment structure for a Security* (sense (i)) or Facility*, where the final Redemption* of securities in the issue or the final repayment instalment of the facility is set at a greater amount than that of earlier redemptions or instalments. Cf. Bullet.

Bank   Generally, an institution that provides financial services (such as taking deposits, lending money, and underwriting securities issues) as an Intermediary* rather than simply in an advisory capacity. There are three main varieties of banks: Commercial banks*, Investment banks* (known in the UK as Merchant banks*) and Universal banks*. Subject to restrictions on Deposit-taking* under ss. 3 and 67 of the Banking Act 1987 (replaced by s. 19 FSMA* 2000) in the UK (and under s. 5 of Statutory Instrument 1992/3218 to persons authorised as a Credit institution* in an EU country). The Financial Services Authority* exerts various controls over banks in the UK, including requiring the payment of fees (see under Financial Services Authority), the payment of MLAs* to the Bank of England, and monitoring for Capital adequacy*. See also Commercial paper and Deposit-taking.

Bank bill   See Eligible bill.

Bank for International Settlements   See BIS.

Bank of England   Prior to the entry into force of the Bank of England Act 1998 on 1 June 1998, the Bank of England was the UK regulatory authority for Banks* with regard to authorisation (see under Bank), Capital adequacy*, Eligible banks*, Mandatory liquid assets* and monetary control. The Bank of England's main role is now with regard to monetary control via the level of Interest rates* prevailing in the UK economy. See Financial Services Authority with regard to the transfer of supervisory and capital adequacy regulation to the Financial Services Authority from 1 June 1998. See also UK Debt Management Office* with regard to regulation of the Gilts* market. The Bank of England commenced business on 1 January 1695 as a Joint stock company* (sense (ii)), lending deposits raised from its subscribers as loans to the government, in return for the right to issue notes against its deposits.

Banker's acceptance   See Acceptance.

Banker's draft   A form of cheque that is issued by a bank on its own account rather than on its customer's account; consequently it cannot be stopped by the customer on whose behalf it is issued. Banker's drafts cannot be issued payable to bearer (although they may be endorsed to bearer), as this would be equivalent to an issue of banknotes and is proscribed.

Bankruptcy   The formal realisation and distribution of the assets of an individual who is Unable to pay his debts* in order to repay his creditors.

Bankruptcy remote   A descriptive term for an entity that has been created and structured to prevent any party attempting its Winding-up*. Usually the SPV* used as part of a Securitisation* or Repackaging* transaction will be structured to be bankruptcy remote. The key elements of ensuring bankruptcy remoteness are limiting creditor winding-up and limiting shareholder winding-up. The steps in limiting creditor winding-up are usually:

- To establish the entity in a zero tax jurisdiction or a jurisdiction where certainty as to the amount of tax due can be achieved through a tax ruling, or to ensure that, due to matching income and expenses, the entity is tax neutral, in order to ensure that tax authorities do not attempt to wind the entity up;
- To ensure that the entity has no other claims against it which constitute Preferential debts* by ensuring it has no employees or VAT* liabilities;
- To obtain Limited recourse* and Non-petition* undertakings from all creditors of the entity relating to the transaction for which the entity was created;
- To prohibit the entity from undertaking business or incurring debts other than under the transaction in question;
- To ensure that there is no risk of Substantive consolidation* of the entity with the Originator* or any other party;
- To limit the scope of the Objects* of the company set out in its Memorandum of association* to undertaking the transaction in question; and
- As a further precautionary step, to take Security* (sense (ii)) over all the assets of the entity in favour of the transaction creditors so that any residual claims for Preferential debts* or other amounts will rank in order of Priority* after the transaction creditors in any event.

The steps in limiting shareholder winding-up are:

- To have the shares of the entity held by a trustee on Charitable trust* or on some other kind of purpose trust, which effectively removes the ability to direct winding-up from any single person except the trustee; and
- To obtain an undertaking from the trustee that, in carrying out the terms of the trust, it will not allow or cause the entity to be wound-up during the term of the transaction.

Bare trust   In the UK, a form of Interest in possession trust* where property is held by a person with no duties for the holder to perform other than to hold the legal title for the beneficiaries, or in any event where property is held absolutely for another or others as to both income and capital so that they may, collectively, on demand, require the transfer to them of the legal title in the trust property held by the trustee (*Christie v. Ovington (1873) Ch. 279*) and, in either case, with the trustee having no interest in the trust property itself (*Morgan v. Swansea Urban Authority Sanitary Authority (1878) 9 Ch. 582*). Typically arises either where a trust has effectively finished (with the beneficiary/beneficiaries holding full and unrestricted beneficial title) or where the holder is a Nominee*, giving his name to the holding of legal title in the trust property.

Bare trusts possess Fiscal transparency*: income is not chargeable to the trust under s. 151 Finance Act* 1989, as a bare trusteeship is considered by case law to be no trusteeship for these purposes and capital gains are expressly not chargeable to the trust by the provisions of s. 60 TCGA* (provided the trust meets the s. 60 definition, which was expanded on in *Anders Utkilens Rederi v Lovisa Stevedoring Co. (1985) STC 301* to state that multiple trust beneficiaries are permissible provided that their interests are concurrent (not successive) and qualitatively similar. The bare trustee may however be held liable to withhold basic rate income tax (see Withholding tax) under s. 59 ICTA*, to the extent of income received which is within Schedule D*, or under s. 21 ICTA to the extent of income received which is within Schedule A*, unless the bare trustee authorises payment of the income direct to the beneficiary, without the income entering the bare trustee's hands (under s. 76 Taxes Management Act 1970), or the income is paid only to persons within the charge to the UK corporation tax (since such persons are not liable to UK income tax under s. 6(2) ICTA and the trustee can thus resist any assessment). Fiscal transparency may be preserved where the trustee has duties to perform provided that the duties are peripheral to the beneficial ownership of the trust property (for instance instructions to a Nominee shareholder* as to how to vote shares held by him).

Barrier option A Path dependent option* where the settlement amount is affected by the movement in price of the Actual* through certain trigger levels. See Knock-in option*, Knock-out option*.

Base rate A basis rate of interest used by a financial institution to price the Interest rate* it charges for different types of loan, which loans are typically priced at a certain number of percentage points or Basis points* over base rate to reflect the particular default risk of the customer or type of loan instrument. Base rates are calculated from the cost to the bank of raising funds via deposits, with added margins to cover over-heads and target profit, and are thus influenced by the level of completion for deposits (in the medium/long term) and the cost of raising marginal funding at LIBOR* (in the short term). Base rates in many countries are set indirectly by the central bank, through its control of key interest rates used to provide Liquidity* to the market. In the UK, base rates have long been set indirectly by the Bank of England*, through its control of the Discount rate* (sense (i)) and the signals it gives to the markets through manipulation of the discount rate. The Bank of England has now been given control over monetary policy and fixing the general level of interest rates for the UK economy.

Basel Accord See Capital adequacy.

Basis (i) The amount by which the price of a Future* differs from the price of the underlying Actual*, reflecting both (a) the Cost of carry* on the future due to the time lag to delivery (being equal to the cost of carry on the underlying instrument); and (b) market expectations of shifts in rates that would effect the cost of carry calculated in (a) above. This difference, and the uncertainty surrounding it, is sometimes referred to as Basis risk* (sense (ii)).

(ii) A standard Interest rate* type (for instance LIBOR*) upon which a rate calculation under a loan, securities issue or other investment is based.

Basis point One one-hundredth of a percentage point. Abbreviated to bp*.

Basis risk (i) The Risk* of change in the Spread* (sense (ii)) between two different interest rate bases (see Basis, sense (ii)). Where income received is connected to one basis and debt servicing is connected to another, the risk of income shortfall thus arises.

(ii) See Basis, sense (i).

Basis swap A Swap* of different interest rate Basis* (sense (ii)) obligations on a notional principal amount.

BBA   British Bankers Association.

BBAIRS   British Bankers Association Interest Rate Swap agreement. Standard form master agreement for Swaps* which is designed to protect the parties to the agreement in the event of the insolvency of the other party by effecting Close-out netting*.

Bear market   A market that is moving lower or is expected to do so.

Bear spread   See Put spread.

Bearer bond   A Bond* that is a Bearer security*, e.g. a Eurobond*.

Bearer security   A Security* (sense (i)) that is payable to bearer (and is, by and large, Negotiable*), as opposed to an Order security* or a Registered security*. Eurobonds* are usually bearer securities. Company shares are registered securities in some jurisdictions (e.g. the UK, Japan and the US) and bearer securities in others (e.g. Switzerland, where shares can be either bearer or registered). In addition to ease of transfer and physical evidence of ownership, bearer securities are favoured in many jurisdictions (e.g. Germany) as the holder can retain anonymity, for tax or other purposes. Securities issues are required by the US authorities to be in registered form to allow tracing of ownership in order to protect US tax revenues. Worldwide bearer security offerings should therefore comply with the TEFRA* requirements that they are sold under "arrangements reasonably designed" to ensure that they are not sold to US persons, or risk imposition of a punitive taxation regime.

Best-of-two option   See Alternative option.

Bid   The price quoted by a buyer at which the buyer is willing to acquire an asset.

Bilateral loan   A loan from a single lender to a borrower or borrowers. Cf. Syndicated loan.

Bill   See Bill of exchange.

Bill of exchange   In the UK, defined in s. 3(1) Bills of Exchange Act 1882 as an "unconditional order in writing, addressed by one person to another, signed by the person giving it, requiring the person to whom it is addressed to pay on demand, or at a fixed or determinable future time, a sum certain in money, to, or to the order of, a specified person or to bearer". Bills of exchange are Negotiable instruments*. Bills may be After sight bills*, Time bills*, Sight bills* or on demand. On Negotiation* or other Transfer* to a recipient, they will be purchased at a discount, as they are non-interest bearing (see Discounting). Also known as a Draft* or Bill*. A Cheque* is a form of bill of exchange.

Primary liability on a bill falls on the acceptor of the bill (if the bills bears an Acceptance*), then on the drawer, the first endorser (i.e. the original payee), the second endorser, and so on.

Bills of exchange are often used in export transactions, most commonly drawn under a Documentary credit*, as part of a Payment against documents* structure, as the specification of a future date on the bill allows the buyer a period of credit (issue at a discount to Face value* (sense (i)) may also be incorporated to compensate the seller for the credit period). In such a case, the bill is accepted by the buyer at the point of delivery, in return for the receipt of shipping documents.

Bill of lading A receipt for (and document of title to) goods that are being shipped from one location to another. It can be transferred by endorsement and delivery and is evidence of the terms of the shipping contract.

Bill of sale In the UK, a bill of sale may be an absolute transfer (governed solely by the Bills of Sale Act 1878) or a transfer by way of security (governed by both the 1878 Act and the Bills of Sale Act (1878) Amendment Act 1882). A bill of sale is a document that transfers or evidences the transfer of or creates security over (and is constituted by, *inter alia*, any assignment, transfer, declaration of trust, receipt for, authority or licence to take possession of as security for a debt, or agreement conferring a right in equity or a charge or security over) "personal chattels" (articles capable of complete transfer by delivery, but excluding fixtures, securities or interests therein and choses in action). However, any document that is a transfer of goods in the ordinary course of business, or is used in the ordinary course of business as proof of possession or control of goods, or authorises the holder to transfer or receive goods, is not a bill of sale. In addition, no debenture issued by a company and secured on the company's chattels shall be a security bill of sale.

Bills of sale will only be accepted for registration if stamped (see Stamp duty). Failure to register an absolute bill of sale within 7 days of it being made means that as against trustees in bankruptcy of the estate, creditors taking under an assignment for the benefit of creditors or judgement creditors, the bill is deemed void in relation to such of the chattels as are in the possession or use or enjoyment of the grantor of the bill at the later of the expiry of the 7-day period or the date of the relevant bankruptcy petition/assignment/execution of process. Failure to register a security bill of sale within 7 days of it being made means that the bill of sale is void. Registrations must be renewed every 5 years. In addition, security bills of sale must be made in accordance with the form set out in the schedule to the 1882 Act (including a schedule of the relevant chattels), and trigger events for the seizure of chattels are limited to those set out in the 1882 Act.

BIMBO Buy-in management buy-out. An MBO* where the original managers are joined by one or more outsiders.

Binary option See Digital option.

Binomial expansion A probability expansion, which serves to determine the probability of X number of a particular event occurring (for a number of items where each of which independently has the same chance of such event occurring). Calculated using the following formula:

$$P = [(N)!/(X \cdot (N - X)!)] \cdot [\text{Prob}\% \cdot (1 - \text{Prob}\%)^{(N-X)}]$$

where   Prob% = probability of event occurring
   P = probability of X number of event occurring
   N = number of items
   X = number of particular event (i.e. between 1 and N)

Used in asset default analysis, by creating a hypothetical homogeneous pool of assets equivalent to the aggregate characteristics of the assets, where a weighted average default probability can be assigned to the assets, to determine the probability of X number of defaults occurring. This can be aggregated across all possible scenarios from

1 to N in order to calculate the total expected loss on a pool by calculating the loss severity for each scenario between 1 and N number of defaults, and weighting each loss severity by the probability of that loss occurring (i.e. the probability of that number of defaults). The sum of this calculation then gives the total expected loss.

BIS   Bank for International Settlements. An international banking institution formed in 1930 as a forum to encourage cooperation among central banks from more developed countries and to promote international financial stability. The BIS put forward Capital adequacy* proposals in July 1988 in the Basel Accord, implemented in many countries worldwide in 1992, and is currently developing new Basel Accord proposals (see Capital adequacy).

Black box   An issue of Asset-backed securities* where no disclosure, or very little disclosure, is given as to the nature of the underlying assets. Rule 23.29(a)(xii) of the Listing rules* requires that for issues of asset backed securities to be Listed* for UKLA* purposes, where the underlying assets "consist of obligations of 10 or fewer obligors or where an obligor accounts for 10% or more of the assets", the Listing particulars* must contain such information about each obligor "as ... would be required if it were itself the issuer of the securities to be listed".

Black–Scholes   See Time value.

Blue Book   See Takeover Code.

Blue sky   "Blue sky" laws and regulations refer to state-specific laws and regulations in the US which may apply to securities offered or sold in the US.

Board of directors   The Directors* of a company acting together; the chief decision-making body in the day-to-day running of a company. See Resolution.

Bond   A document evidencing a promise to pay and bearing a fixed rate of interest. Issued as a Bearer security*, a Registered security* or an Order security*. If issued in bearer or order form, may be Negotiable*. Often Listed* on a stock exchange where exemption from UK source income Withholding tax* is needed (see also Domestic bond, Eurobond and Foreign bond). Bonds are long term in nature (typically longer than 5 years to maturity). The term is often used in a generic sense to encompass FRNs* as well. Cf. Note. In the UK, may be subject to rules on Deposit-taking*.

Bonus issue   An issue of shares to existing shareholders against profits or other capital reserves in order to capitalise them into Issued share capital*. No cash or other consideration is paid by shareholders. Also known as a Scrip issue* or Capitalisation issue*. Cf. Rights issue*.

Bonus share   A share issued under a Bonus issue*.

Book debts   One of the assets over which Security* (sense (ii)) created by a company is required to be registered on a Form 395* with the Registrar of Companies*. Defined in *Independent Automatic Sales Ltd. v. Knowles and Foster [1962] 3 All ER 27* as "a debt arising in due course of a business", which "would or could in the ordinary course of such a business be entered in well kept books relating to that business".

Book runner   The bank that undertakes to assemble a Syndicate* for a Syndicated loan* or Bond* issue. Often the Lead manager*. See Running the books.

Book value   The value placed on an asset in the accounts of a business.

Borrowing base   In the context of a Liquidity facility* in a CP* funded Securitisation* structure, the borrowing base is the maximum amount that may be drawn under the facility from time to time. The borrowing base is a dynamic figure, and is designed to ensure that drawings only assist Liquidity* problems and do not provide Credit enhancement*, by being set by reference to Receivables* which are not Defaulted receivables*. Often, however, the borrowing base may be widened from this position in order to provide a full or partial Wrap* to CP investors by the liquidity bank. Any such coverage will need to be analysed carefully to ensure that it does not merit adverse treatment (e.g. as credit enhancement) under Capital adequacy* rules. The main type of borrowing base designed to give CP investors a degree of coverage that has been identified is the "look-back", and ensures full CP coverage by basing drawings against defaulted receivables as shown in the previous defaults report, on the basis of which CP was issued. Other types rely on the relative tenors of default triggers and CP maturities to ensure that no defaults can occur between CP issuance and CP redemption.

Bought deal   A method of issuing Eurobonds* whereby the Lead manager* agrees to buy the whole issue of bonds from the issuer prior to reselling them to the market.

Bourse   A Stock exchange*. For example the Paris Bourse or the Milan Bourse.

Box option   The purchase of a deeply In the money* Call option* capped by the sale of a deeply Out of the money* call option (i.e. a Call spread*) combined with the purchase of a deeply in the money Put option* capped by the sale of a deeply out of the money put option (i.e. a Put spread*). The combination results in a Matched* Position* and, as options deeply in the money behave more like Futures*, each spread should accrue value at a Money market* interest rate. This method may be used in certain jurisdictions to generate a synthetic deposit, which may be taxable as a capital gain rather than as income, thus enabling capital gains tax/income tax Arbitrage. From March 1997, such schemes are liable in the UK to Income tax* rather than Capital gains tax*.

bp   See Basis point.

Brady bond   Bonds named after Nicholas Brady, ex US Treasury Secretary, which were issued in the 1980s by governments in debt-laden developing economies as a replacement and reduction of government debt (or private sector debt assumed by the government). Issues normally offer banks bonds with a principal value at a premium over the value at which the distressed debt is trading in the secondary market, as an alternative to cash payment at the secondary market debt price. The advantage to the bank lies in whatever premium is offered plus the general reduction of debt levels in the debtor country and the increased marketability of the debt in its new form. The government may collateralise repayment of the principal on the bonds (e.g. with securities of an OECD government) to prevent their price degenerating in the secondary market, if investor confidence in the government's ability to meet its own obligations is low.

Break A lender will "break" a customer loan or debit account on notice of insolvency or (in the case of a partnership) retirement of a partner from the partnership, or on notice of second Security* being taken over the borrower's assets, in each case by Ruling-off* the account ledger, in order to defeat the application of the rule in Clayton's Case*.

Break costs Costs resulting from the "breakage" of Matched funding* status on a loan asset following a Prepayment* of all or part of the loan. Arises from the necessity to re-finance the corresponding funding liability, in order to hedge Reinvestment risk*.

Broker A party which arranges a transaction between two other parties without itself entering into the transaction itself (although some "brokers" also contract as principal in some transactions).

Building society A Society*. Building societies operate under the Building Societies Act 1986 and were regulated by the Building Societies Commission until authority for their regulation passed to the Financial Services Authority* under the Financial Services and Markets Act 2000*. They have the status of Mutuals* and their memoranda usually provide that they are owned both by their depositors and by their borrowers (who are usually mortgage borrowers). Consequently, they are subject to certain provisions and limitations that do not affect other financial institutions. As borrowers are members of the society, the society will remain obliged to deal with the membership rights of such borrowers after it has sold or securitised their mortgages, unless the securitisation is carried out by way of legal assignment (as the BSC takes the view that membership rights are linked to legal title rather than equitable interest). The BSC has expressed concern with the potential moral risk that an institution runs if it sells or securitises assets by equitable assignment or sub-participation and retains duties to members after the assets are sold (although securitisations have been carried out on this basis). Other limitations on building societies relate to mergers with non-building society entities, maximum limits on levels of wholesale funding as against total liabilities, and the use of derivatives (which can only be used to hedge exposures). The Building Societies Act 1986 was amended in May 2001 to permit building societies to use Credit derivatives* from 1 July 2001.

Bull market A market that is moving higher or is expected to do so.

Bull spread See Call spread.

Bulldog bond A Foreign bond* issued in pounds sterling.

Bullet A Security* (sense (i)) or Facility*, where the entire Principal* sum falls due on a single date. Cf. Balloon, Soft bullet.

Butterfly The purchase of a Call option* or a Put option* at a certain Strike price*, combined with the sale of two call options or put options (respectively) at a higher strike price, and the purchase of a call option or put option (respectively) at a still higher strike price. The combination achieves a maximum profit if the underlying is at the middle strike price on expiry, with the profit declining to zero on either side of the middle strike price.

Buy-in management buy-out See BIMBO.

Buy on close   A purchase effected at the Close*.

Buy on opening   A purchase effected at the Opening*.

Buyer credit   See Documentary credit.

BVI   British Virgin Islands.

By-laws   See Articles of association.

Cable   The Sterling/US Dollar FX rate*.

Cagamas Berhad   The Malaysian mortgage corporation. Sales to Cagamas are typically made with recourse to the seller bank.

Call   **(i)** An issuer's right to effect Optional redemption* of Securities* prior to Maturity* (often provided for where adverse changes arise in the taxation treatment of the securities).
   (ii) The notification to shareholders holding partly paid shares in a company of the requirement to pay an amount of the unpaid residue in respect of the relevant shares.
   (iii) See Call option.

Call and step-up   In relation to a Securitisation, a Call* (sense (i)) inserted in the securities issued that may be exercised by the SPV* at the point in time at which a Step-up* operates. Used to signal to investors that the securities are intended to be redeemed at that point in time, which gives the investor added certainty as to the Average life* of the security. Often disliked by Capital adequacy* regulators, as it increases the motivation of the originator to bring the residual deal piece back on balance sheet, regardless of the deal's performance. Cf. Clean-up call.

Call option   An Option* that gives the holder the right to buy a set amount of a specific commodity or financial instrument from the option writer at a set "strike price". May take the form of a European option* or an American option*. The value of a European call option and a European Put option* on the same financial asset at the same strike price are related (a relationship known as "put-call parity") as follows:

$$C - P = MV - K$$

where C = the call value
   P = the put value
   MV = the market value of the underlying
   K = the strike price.

The value of a call option and a put option on the same physical asset at the same strike price are related as follows:

$$C - P = MV - [K/(1 + r)^n]$$

where C = the call value
   P = the put value
   MV = the market value of the underlying
   K = the strike price
   r = the discount rate (expressed as a decimal) per compounding period
   n = the number of compounding periods.

Call spread   Or Bull spread*. The purchase of a Call option*, the potential profit on which is capped by the sale of a call option with a higher Strike price*, so that profit is only realised on the spread from the lower strike price to the higher strike price.

Call-or-put option   See Chooser option.

Callable   Securities which may be called (see Call, sense (i)) by their issuer.

Canadian Depository Service   The Clearing system* for securities in Canada.

Cap   A Derivative* contract between two parties used (for example) to hedge interest rate risk on amounts borrowed at a floating rate of interest whereby the cap purchaser, in return for a Premium* (sense (iii)), will be paid periodic payments by the cap seller equal to the excess of the interest charge at an agreed Basis* (sense (ii)) rate on a notional principal amount over an agreed "strike rate", thus assuring the purchaser that he will not have to pay more than some maximum interest rate on borrowed amounts equal to the notional principal.

Capex   Capital expenditure of a business.

Capital   (i) The long-term funding available to a company, typically considered as being any amounts contributed by Members*, accumulated profits and other reserves, and long-term finance raised from financial institutions or from subscriptions to debt Securities* issued by the company. See Equity capital; Loan capital.
(ii) Previously retained assets (as opposed to an ongoing revenue stream).

Capital adequacy   The adequacy of the amount of capital held by a bank or financial institution to cover losses arising from its assets.
  The Basel Accord of July 1988 agreed by the Basel Committee on Banking Supervision (established by the G-10* countries in 1974) established that the ratio of an institution's own capital to its risk-weighted assets should have an absolute minimum value of 8% (higher levels may be set by individual regulators or for individual institutions). Given the reduction of asset principal value by these weightings, bank capital as a percentage of actual principal value of assets tends to be less than 8%. The Basel Accord has no legal force, but is regarded as best practice and has in practice been implemented by almost all countries with international banks. Subsequent to the Basel Accord, the Basel Committee reached agreement on amendments and additions to the Accord; principally, to include an assessment of Market risk* from January 1998, and to permit the use of approved bank internal VAR* type models to set market risk capital charges. Also on 27 October 1998, the Basel Committee approved the issuance of perpetual preferred securities to qualify as Tier 1 capital (subject to a limit of 15% of total Tier 1 capital), interest on which is tax deductible. The debt can only be callable a minimum of 5 years after issue (and only with the regulator's prior approval), and must be subordinated to depositors and creditors. Coupon step-ups are permitted.
  On 3 June 1999, the Basel Committee published a Consultative Paper (CP1) on amendments to the 1988 regime, which heralded the start of a lengthy development process. On 18 January 2000 the Committee published a further consultative paper on the internal credit rating systems of banks. On 16 January 2001 the Committee issued a new Consultative Paper of their proposals (CP2) for comments by 31 May 2001, which included the foundation of the Internal Ratings Based approach. The proposals were

intended to be finalised by the end of 2001, for implementation in 2004. In June 2001 following extensive comments on the proposals, the Committee decided to issue a further proposal in early 2002, to finalise by the end of 2002 for implementation in 2005. Particular concern was voiced on the capital costs of funding SMEs (small/medium-sized enterprises) and on the operational risk charge (20% of current capital having been discussed as the appropriate level for this charge). In September 2001, following comments from ISDA and other parties, the Basel Committee announced that they would consider moving the "W" factor charge on collateral, guarantees and credit derivatives from the first "pillar" on minimum capital to a consideration of appropriate measures under the second "pillar" on supervisory review. In late 2001 papers on individual topics were issued (including a paper on operational risk in September 2001 and a working paper on securitisation in October 2001). On 5 November 2001 a press release set out potential revisions of some risk-weighting details set out in CP2 in January 2001. In December 2001 the Committee further announced the delay of issuance of further proposals into 2002.

On 10 July 2002 a new press release gave a revised timetable for implementation, with a new quantitative survey to be launched and details of new treatment for SME loans. On 1 October 2002 Quantitative Impact Study 3 (QIS3) was released, giving more detail on corporate and retail capital calculations, use of collateral to reduce capital charges, and also on weightings for securitisations. On 28 October 2002 the Basel Committee published Second Working Paper on Securitisation. On 29 April 2003 a new Consultative Paper (CP3) was published for comment by 31 July 2003. On 11 October 2003 it was announced that the final Accord would be published in June 2004. Implementation is intended for the end of 2006.

The proposals contain three "Pillars" for capital regulation:

- Minimum capital requirements;
- Supervisory review; and
- Market discipline (e.g. disclosure requirements).

Banks are required to hold banking book capital equal to 8% of the risk-weighted assets in their banking book, and to hold trading book capital equal to the sum of each capital charge in their trading book (in relation to some of which the 8% ratio may be used to compute counterparty risks).

Under CP3, for the first 2 years after implementation of the new accord at the end of 2006, banks using the IRB approach (see below) will be subject to a minimum capital floor based on the capital they would have to hold if calculated under the old accord, set at 90% of such level in 2007 and 80% in 2008.

Capital is required to be held by banking entities on a solo and consolidated basis, with the normal expectation that subsidiaries will be consolidated. CP3 tightens this basis to include holding companies that are parents of banking groups, and requires financial subsidiaries (including securities firms and unregulated entities) to be consolidated where they form part of the same group as a bank.

The EU applies the Basel Accord to Credit institutions* in Member states* through certain Directives*. EU directives applicable to credit institutions include the Own Funds Directive 89/299 (which contains a definition of capital), the Solvency Ratio Directive 89/647 (defining the risk weighting of assets and setting a minimum 8% adequacy), the Consolidated Supervision Directive 92/30 and the Large Exposures

Directive 92/121 (limiting the maximum amount of exposure to any one entity). An assessment of market risk on the trading book of credit institutions, together with an option allowing use of internal sensitivity models for derivatives exposures, was introduced in the EU by the terms of the Capital Adequacy Directive 93/6. The Capital Adequacy Directive was applied to investment firms as well as credit institutions in order to ensure that a level playing field was maintained between the two sectors. A second Capital Adequacy Directive 98/31 (known as CAD 2) was introduced in the EU in July 1998 (to be implemented across the EU by July 2000) to bring in the full terms of the January 1998 Basel amendment and to allow use of VAR type internal models across the EU. The Commission released a First Consultative Document in November 1999, and a Second Consultative Document on 5 February 2001, following the release of the Basel Committee papers in 1999 and 2001. The Second Document sought comments by the end of May 2001.

A Working Document was published on 18 November 2002. A Third Consultative Document was published on 1 July 2003 following the publication by the Basel Committee of CP3 in April 2003. The Consultative Documents and Working Document broadly approve the proposals of the Basel papers, with a few variations. Particular focus is given in the Second Consultative Document on the importance of ensuring that funding to SMEs (small/medium-sized enterprises) is not prejudiced by the application of new capital rules. Publication of a final directive on capital adequacy (CAD 3) to match the new Basel proposals is expected for the end of 2005, with member states required to implement the directive in time for the effectiveness of the Basel proposals at the end of 2006.

Banks are required to hold banking book capital equal to 8% of the risk-weighted assets in their banking book, and to hold trading book capital equal to the sum of each capital charge in their trading book (in relation to some of which the 8% ratio may be used to compute counterparty risks).

Under the Third Consultative Document, for the first 2 years after implementation of the new accord at the end of 2006, banks using the IRB approach will be subject to a minimum capital floor based on the capital they would have to hold if calculated under the old accord, set at 90% of such level in 2007 and 80% in 2008.

Capital is required to be held by credit institutions and investment firms on a solo and consolidated basis (across the group of the credit institution or investment firm and any "financial holding company"). Credit institution is defined in Article 1(1) of Directive 2000/12 of 20 March 2000 as "an undertaking whose business is to receive deposits or other repayable funds from the public and to grant credits for its own account". Investment firm is defined in Article 1(2) of Directive 93/22 of 10 May 1993 as "any legal person the regular occupation of which is the provision of investment services for third parties on a professional basis". Financial holding company is defined in Article 7(3) of the Capital Adequacy Directive 93/6.

In the UK, the capital adequacy treatment for banks (see Bank) with regard to their banking book and trading book was derived from a series of Bank of England* notices which were based on the requirements of the Basel Accord and EU Directives. The capital adequacy regulatory role of the Bank of England over banks and wholesale markets passed to the FSA in June 1998. The statements of the FSA (as set out in the Banking Supervisory Policy Guide published by the FSA, which came into effect on 29 June 1998) govern capital treatment for banks. The guide has subsequently been revised periodically. The requirements applicable to investment firms are based on notices from other UK regulators, primarily the Securities and Futures Authority. Responsibility for investment firms passes to the FSA when the Financial Services and Markets Act 2000 came into force on 30th November 2001. The second Capital Adequacy Directive to allow use of VAR type internal models across the EU was implemented in the UK by the FSA on 30 September 1998. In March 1999, the FSA approved the issuance of perpetual non-cumulative preferred securities by a "solo consolidated" SPV, the proceeds of which are on-lent to the bank and will qualify as Tier 1 capital, in a letter to the BBA. In July 1999, the Inland Revenue accepted that interest on the loan from the SPV to the bank would be tax deductible (such SPVs have subsequently been established as Jersey limited partnerships, to avoid a tax charge on the SPV resulting from the fact that payments on non-cumulative preferences shares are not deductible under UK tax rules).

On 16 July 2002, the FSA published a paper on the new Basel proposals setting out a timetable under which they would issue a consultation paper in 2003 and rules and guidance for the new regime in early 2005, to come into effect at the end of 2006. The FSA envisages allowing institutions to apply different approaches under the new Basel proposal in different areas (e.g. the IRB advanced approach in one area, and the IRB foundation approach or the standardised approach in another area).

The consultation paper was published in July 2003 as a response to the CP3 Basel paper, for comments by 14 November 2003. The FSA highlighted their views on a few areas, such as:

- Banks will be risk weighted in accordance with their own credit rating, rather than that of the country in which they are based (responding to the option, at national discretion, for a regulator to risk weight banks incorporated in its country at one category worse than the risk weight of the sovereign).
- The proposed 35% risk weight for residential mortgages in the standardised approach will be restricted by reference to the LTV of the loans; the portion of loans in excess of 75% LTV will be risk weighted at 75% (or alternatively, all residential mortgage loans of the originator will be risk weighted at 45%).
- Where firms use the IRB approach for only part of their book, then prior to moving to the IRB approach for the rest of their book they may be required to hold additional capital in respect of the rest of their book if the standardised approach gives lower capital charges than the IRB approach.
- 180 days (rather than 90 days) will be used for days past due in respect of public sector entities and retail portfolios (except for loans to SME).
- Days past due will be measured from point of billing rather than from the end of any grace period (e.g. for credit cards where, on billing, further time is given to pay).

The FSA plans to consult in mid-2004 on the text to be used in its Prudential Sourcebook to implement the Basel proposals and EU rules.

Banks are required to hold banking book capital equal to 8% of the risk-weighted assets in their banking book, and to hold trading book capital equal to the sum of each capital charge in their trading book (in relation to some of which the 8% ratio may be used to compute counterparty risks). The 8% ratio (the "individual ratio") may be set higher than 8% for individual institutions, to reflect their risk profile or resources. A higher "target ratio" figure is also set for each institution to act as an early warning marker of an impending capital deficiency.

Capital is required to be held by banks (both on a solo basis and via consolidation across a Group* (sense (vii)).

Capital allowances   Depreciation allowance for tax purposes. In the UK, no tax deduction is allowed for accounting depreciation, but instead "capital allowances" are calculated for industrial buildings (at a set rate per annum of the cost value), for plant and machinery (at a set rate per annum of the remaining unused balance of cost value; i.e. a declining balance method) and for certain other capital assets purchased. Provisions relating to capital allowances in the UK were reformed and rewritten under the Capital Allowances Act 2001.

Capital allowances may typically be claimed by the owner of the asset, and varying ownership criteria between different countries may enable allowances to be claimed simultaneously in two different countries (see Double dipping and Japanese leveraged lease). See also Finance lease and Hire purchase.

Capital gains tax   UK tax introduced on 6 April 1965 on chargeable gains accruing on the disposal (sale or gift of, or derivation of a capital sum from) a chargeable asset by a person resident or ordinarily resident in the UK (or carrying on a trade in the UK through a branch or other agency) at any point during the Tax year* in which the disposal was made. Gains are calculated by deducting from disposal proceeds (or an Arm's-length* figure where appropriate) the acquisition price, acquisition expenditure, other expenditure that relates to improvement (rather than maintenance), indexation allowance (available for assets acquired between 31 March 1982 and 5 April 1998 – assets acquired before 31 March 1982 are re-based at their market value on 31 March 1982) to compensate for inflation, the personal allowance and other reliefs. Gains are charged at Income tax* rates as the top slice of income (see also Corporation tax* for companies). Where applicable, the charge to income tax overrides the charge to capital gains tax under s. 37 TCGA*. Indexation was abolished for assets acquired after 5 April 1998, and was replaced by a system of "taper relief" which operates to reduce the rate of capital gains tax charged, for assets that have been held for longer periods, to a maximum reduction where the assets have been held for 10 years or longer. Indexation still applies to assets acquired prior to 5 April 1998, in addition to any claim for taper relief (indexation is applied first, to determine the relevant net gain on which tax is charged).

Capital indexed   A form of Index-linked security*. Capital-indexed securities offer the best inflation protection relative to the other two main types of index-linked security (Current pay* and Interest indexed*), as they are fully indexed to protect both interest and principal, and also benefit from compounding as principal receipts are left in the structure. The stated coupon is paid on an accreting principal balance (e.g. a 2% coupon when inflation is at 4% becomes 2% of a principal balance of 104). The relevant increase in the RPI for a semi-annual pay index-linked security is calculated as the increase in the RPI over the period from 8 months prior to the relevant interest payment date (or the issue date) to 2 months prior to the relevant interest payment date (or the issue date). In this way, the level of the indexation amount that will be received at the end of the interest period is known 2 months prior to commencement of the interest period. The full accreted balance is repaid to investors at maturity. Capital-indexed securities are used for government index-linked issuance in the UK and US and most other major countries.

Capital markets The longer-term (usually greater than 1 year) debt instrument markets and the equity markets. Shorter-term instruments are traded in the Money markets*.

Capital redemption reserve An Undistributable reserve* entered on the liability side of a company's balance sheet to match the Nominal value* of shares in the company purchased or redeemed (see Purchase, Redemption, Redeemable shares) by the company. Required pursuant to s. 170 Companies Act 1985* to balance the other necessary accounting entries (which will show a decrease in both Distributable reserves* and Paid-up share capital*).

Capitalisation **(i)** The addition of outstanding interest to the outstanding amount of principal drawn under a loan (leading to the charging of Compound interest*).
  (ii) The reclassification of an amount of retained profits in a company as Paid-up share capital* (usually following a Bonus issue*) or the addition of the profits to other Undistributable reserves*.

Capitalisation issue See Bonus issue.

Carriage and insurance paid to Or CIP*. Export delivery term with the same meaning as Carriage paid to*, save that the seller must also bear the cost of insuring the goods while in transit.

Carriage paid to Or CPT*. Export delivery term of general trade use and defined in INCOTERMS* meaning that the goods travel at the seller's freight expense to their destination, although risk passes to the buyer at the point of delivery to the first carrier.

Cash flow CBO See Cash flow CDO.

Cash flow CDO A CDO*, the credit analysis of which is carried out by reference to the periodic cash flows received from time to time on the underlying instruments. Cf. Synthetic CDO and Market value CDO.

Cash ratio See Mandatory liquid assets. The percentage of its Eligible liabilities* which a UK-authorised institution is obliged to deposit with the Bank of England in a non-interest-bearing account. Reduced as of 1 June 1998 to 0.15% of eligible liabilities in excess of £400m (from 0.25% as of 1 April 1998, and from 0.35% between January 1992 and 1 April 1998). A consultation paper published by the Treasury in August 2003 recommended an increase in the threshold so that cash ratio deposits would be 0.15% of eligible liabilities in excess of £500m, and provided for the Cash Ratio Deposits (Value Bands and Ratio) Order 2003 to achieve this. The Order is expected to come into force on 1 June 2004.

Catastrophe See Excess-of-loss.

CBO See Collateralised bond obligation.

CBOE See Chicago Board Options Exchange.

CBOT See Chicago Board of Trade.

CBV See Conseil des Bourses de Valeurs.

CCA See Consumer Credit Act 1974.

CCASS Central Clearing and Settlement System. The Hong Kong Clearing system* which computer settles trades on the SEHK* on an Order matching* basis and acts as a securities custodian. Securities are registered in the name of a CCASS nominee company. The system runs a Rolling settlement* basis at T + 2 from 24 September 1998 and is operated by HKSCC*.

CD See Certificate of deposit.

CDO See Collateralised debt obligation.

CDS The Canadian Depository Service*. See also Credit default swap.

Cedel See Clearstream.

Cedelbank See Clearstream.

Cedulas hipotecarias Or CH*. Spanish form of Covered bond* for mortgage debt issued under Law 2/1981 of 25 March 1981 (which updated legislation of 1869). Cf. Cedulas territoriales.

Cedulas territoriales Or CT*. Spanish form of Covered bond* for public sector debt provided for in the Financial Law (the *Ley de Medidas de Reforma del Sistema Financiero*, Law 44/2002) which was passed on 22 October 2002, and became effective on 25 November 2002. Cf. Cedulas hipotecarias.

Certainties In relation to establishment of a Trust*, the three certainties that must be satisfied in order for a trust to be validly created are: (a) certainty of intent to create a trust, (b) certainty of subject matter of the trust (cf. Undivided interest), and (c) certainty of objects or beneficiaries under the trust.

Certificate of deposit A document relating to money, in any currency, that has been deposited with the issuer or some other person, being a document which recognises an obligation to pay a stated amount to bearer or to order, with or without interest, and being a document by the delivery of which, with or without endorsement, the right to receive that stated amount, with or without interest, is transferable. May be issued only by banks or building societies, but is otherwise similar in nature to CP*. Interest may be at a fixed rate or at a floating rate (an FRCD*).

Certificate of incorporation A certificate issued on incorporation of a company, which is evidence of the date of incorporation. In the UK, issued by the Registrar of Companies* on incorporation of a Registered company*.

CFC See Controlled foreign company.

CFR See Cost and freight.

CFTC See Commodity Futures Trading Commission.

CGT See Capital gains tax.

CH   See Cedulas hipotecarias.

Chaebol   A Korean conglomerate group (such as Samsung or Hyundai).

CHAPS   Clearing House Automated Payments System. UK electronic transfer mechanism used to clear individual high-value sterling payments in Same day funds* at any point before the cut-off time (3.10 pm). Instructions are irrevocable once entered in the system. May be linked to SWIFT* to effect overseas instructions.

Chapter 11   Chapter 11 of the Bankruptcy Code in the US, which provides for the rehabilitation of a company in financial difficulties. An Automatic stay* applies from the date on which a petition for Chapter 11 is filed.

Charge   A method of taking Security* (sense (ii)) over an asset that gives a right to appropriate the asset to discharge of a debt, but does not constitute a transfer or agreement to transfer an interest in the asset (as a Mortgage* does). All charges (save a charge by way of legal mortgage over land) are equitable in nature. A charge may be a Fixed charge* or a Floating charge*. Often used to take security over goodwill, land or intellectual property, or as an alternative to a mortgage.

Charge-back   See Charge Card.

Charge Card   *Re: Charge Card Services Limited (1989) Ch.497*. A decision that a bank with whom a party has an account in credit cannot obtain Security* (sense (ii)) by means of a Charge* or Mortgage* over the account in the bank's favour (known as a "charge-back"), as the obligation to return the deposit would be effectively cancelled by the security interest pursuant to the doctrine of Merger* (sense (i)) (despite the potential lack of mutuality for insolvency Set-off* purposes in such cases). In *Morris and Others v. Agrichemicals Limited (1995)* (also known as *Re BCCI (No 8)*) the Court of Appeal held that although a charge-back does not create a proprietary interest, it is effective to create security which restricts the chargor in accordance with the wording used (e.g. Flawed asset* language). The doctrine in Charge Card was overruled by the House of Lords in the appeal of *Re BCCI (No 8) [1998] 1 BCLC 68 HL* (which joined the case of *Morris and Others v. Rayners Enterprises Incorporated* with the case of *Morris and Others v. Agrichemicals Limited*), where the court held that where a charge is used to obtain security, "there would be no merger of interests because the depositor would retain title to the deposit subject only to the bank's charge". This suggests that a mortgage (or at the very least a legal mortgage) may still be subject to the doctrine of merger.

Charge-off   Or Write-off*. In a Securitisation* (generally a trade receivables or credit card transaction), a Receivable* that is in Arrears* and has passed its due date unpaid by more than a certain threshold, or is otherwise regarded as uncollectable. For credit card transactions, an account that is 180 days past due.

Chargee   A person who is the beneficiary of Security* (sense (ii)) granted in the form of a Charge*.

Chargor   A person who grants Security* (sense (ii)) in the form of a Charge*.

Charitable trust   A form of Discretionary trust* where property is held by a trustee or trustees on trust for a general charitable purpose or purposes rather than for a specific person or persons. Often used as a part of the Bankruptcy remote* establishment of an SPV* for a Securitisation* or Repackaging* transaction, in order to establish an Orphan company* that cannot easily be subjected to Winding-up* by its shareholders. Charitable trusts are exempt from many of the standard UK Income tax* and Capital gains tax* charges.

Charter   See Memorandum of association.

Chartered company   In the UK, a now largely obsolete form of Company* that enjoys Corporate personality* as a Corporation* under royal charter or the Chartered Companies Acts of 1837 and 1884. Some (but not all) chartered companies benefit from Limited liability*.

Chattel paper   Under s. 9-105 of Article 9 of the UCC*, "a writing or writings which evidence both a monetary obligation and a security interest in or a lease of specific goods". The term "security interest" is defined for this purpose at s. 1-201(37) of Article 1 of the UCC as "an interest in personal property or fixtures which secures payment or performance of an obligation".

Cheque   A promise to pay pursuant to which the drawer directs its bank to make payment to the payee (or to the bearer of the cheque if the cheque is made payable to bearer) against the cheque being duly presented. A cheque is Negotiable* as a Bill of exchange* under the provisions of the Bills of Exchange Act 1882 and the Cheques Acts of 1957 and 1992. A cheque must be payable on demand (s. 73, Bills of Exchange Act 1882). A cheque that is crossed "account payee only" is, under the Cheques Act 1992, neither negotiable nor transferable (see Transfer).

Primary liability on a cheque falls on the drawer; the drawee (the bank) does not add its Acceptance* (sense (i)) to a cheque and is not therefore liable on the cheque (although liability may arise in relation to cheques backed by a cheque guarantee card).

Cherry-pick   In relation to a Winding-up*, refers to the actions of a Liquidator* in trying to take the best assets or rights, and leave the worst assets or the obligations, of the insolvent company. The liquidator may attempt to do this under a general power to disclaim Onerous property*, by arguing for a separation of the rights from the obligations (e.g. that they are owed under two separate agreements rather than one single agreement), or by simply disclaiming the entire agreement.

Chicago Board of Trade   US Exchange* dealing in the trading of Futures* contracts. Contracts are traded on an Open outcry* basis during trading hours, and on screens outside trading hours.

Chicago Board Options Exchange   US Exchange* dealing in the trading of Options*.

Chicago Mercantile Exchange   US Exchange* dealing in the trading of Futures* and Options* contracts. See also IMM*.

Chinese walls   Intangible barriers to the passage of information within an organisation, which are used to prevent confidential information in one area of a business passing to another area of the business, where the availability of the information may give rise to a conflict of interests. Often used in financial institutions between client advisory areas and proprietary trading areas to prevent accusations of Insider dealing* and within law firms advising two different clients in respect of the same matter. In the case of *Prince Jefri Bolkiah v. KPMG (1998) HL*, the House of Lords upheld the use of Chinese walls to prevent internal disclosure of confidential information, but only where they are part of the structure of a firm (not where they are created on an ad hoc basis). The courts can intervene to prevent the disclosure within a firm of confidential information that is relevant to a transaction in which the firm intends to become involved, where the transaction could adversely affect the interests of the party that provided the information, and there is a real risk of disclosure.

CHIPS   Clearing House Interbank Payment System. US electronic cash transfer mechanism used to clear US Dollar payments in Same day funds*.

Chooser option   An Option* that can be varied from a Call option* to a Put option* or vice versa at the discretion of the holder.

Chose in action   Intangible personal property. Often specifically used to refer to a right to payment of a sum of money that is actionable in court. Choses in action are transferable by Assignment* at law or in equity.

Chose in possession   Tangible personal property. Cf. Chose in action.

CIF   See Cost, insurance and freight.

CIP   See Carriage and insurance paid to.

Circus swap   Acronym for combined interest rate and currency swap. See under Swap. Unlike a simple Currency swap*, different interest rate bases (see Basis, sense (ii)) for periodic payments, or a fixed-rate to floating-rate swap, are used.

City Code   See Takeover Code.

Class rights   Rights (as to voting, dividends, etc.) that extend beyond those of ordinary shareholders and accrue to holders of certain shares (or to certain shareholders while they hold shares) as specified by the terms of a company's Articles of association*.

Clayton's Case   *Devaynes v. Noble; Clayton's Case (1816) 1 Mer.572.* A decision that Advances* by a lender are deemed to be repaid on a first-advanced–first-repaid basis, potentially giving a second secured lender Priority*, where the first secured lender makes further advances after receiving notice of the second lender's Security*. If, however, the first lender has made a Break* in the loan account, subsequent repayments will be applied first against advances occurring after the break. In addition, Clayton's Case will not be applied if there is evidence of a contrary intent. The decision may operate in a lender's favour to create fresh consideration where a Floating charge* is created within 12 months of a Liquidation*.

Clean   A price quoted without taking Accrued interest* into account. Cf. Dirty.

Clean-up call   In relation to a Securitisation, a Call* (sense (i)) which may be exercised by the SPV* where Amortisation* has reduced the remaining principal balance of the Asset-backed securities* outstanding below a certain threshold (often 10% of the original principal balance). Often a requirement of the originator, to enable them to wind-up a securitisation where the fixed costs of the transaction can no longer be covered by the reducing excess spread on the remaining Receivables*. Generally permitted by Capital adequacy* regulators, due to the economic costs of leaving the deal outstanding, provided that it is not used to provide credit support to the deal. Cf. Call and step-up.

Clearing house   An organisation that records transactions on a particular Exchange* or exchanges and holds Margin* (sense (ii)) posted by members and carries out Settlement* of transactions. Usually acts as a counterparty to every trade on the exchange in order to facilitate Close-out netting*.

Clearing system   An organisation through which securities may be bought and sold and Settlement* effected, with the securities deposited and immobilised with a Custodian*. Similar to a Clearing house* but not connected to a particular Exchange*, and often international in orientation. The two main Euromarkets* clearing systems are Euroclear* and Clearstream*. See also CCASS, CDS, DTC and SEGA.

Clearstream   Clearstream is the product of the 1999 merger between Cedelbank (previously known as Cedel) and Deutsche Börse Clearing AG. Since February 2002, when the 50% of the company still held by Cedel shareholders was sold to Deutsche Börse, Clearstream is 100% owned by Deutsche Börse. Clearstream is one of the two major Clearing systems* in the Euromarkets* (together with Euroclear*) and is operated from Luxembourg. Clearstream uses a Common depositary* as Custodian* for itself and Euroclear. Cash held with the Cedelbank entity (now known as Clearstream Banking, société anonyme) benefits from a 20% Capital adequacy* risk weighting under the Basel Accord regime for OECD banks.

CLO   See Collateralised loan obligation.

Close   A set period fixed by an Exchange* for the end of each session, which is used to determine the Closing price* for each asset traded on the exchange.

Close company   A UK resident company is a close company, for UK taxation purposes under ICTA, s. 414 (with the effect that certain benefits provided to Participators* in the company are treated as Distributions* to such participators for tax purposes under s. 418 ICTA), if:

(a) it is under the Control* (sense (i)) of five or fewer participators; or
(b) it is under the control of participators who are Directors*; or
(c) five or fewer participators, or participators who are directors, together possess or are entitled to acquire such rights as would, in the event of a winding-up, entitle them to receive the greater part of the assets available for distribution among participators (either with or without inclusion of any Loan creditor* rights). Participators in and directors of companies entitled to receive assets in such a notional winding-up are treated as participators in or directors of the company under consideration, but company participators are otherwise disregarded.

A company controlled by a non-close company (or where one of the participators identified above is a non-close company) is not a close company.

Close-out   The crystallisation of liabilities following the termination of Swap* and other Derivative* or FX* agreements with ongoing payment obligations, on an Event of default* or other early termination. Also sometimes used to refer to the neutralisation of a Position* and any Risk* inherent in such position to quantify any gains or losses arising therefrom, e.g. by reversing the transaction that created the original position (cf. Hedge).

Close-out netting   A form of Netting* which relies on a Close-out* following an Event of default* or other trigger event. Once all outstanding liabilities have been crystallised by the close-out mechanism, the crystallised liabilities are then reduced to a single payment obligation which is due from one party to the other party. It is argued that this reduction to a single payment obligation in fact amounts simply to a calculation of the amount due under the contract rather than a form of Set-off* and would therefore be enforced on insolvency. In any event, in the UK on insolvency mandatory set-off rules would apply under Rule 4.90 of the Insolvency Rules 1986, which would arguably have the same result.

Closing price   The range of prices recorded for transactions during the Close*.

CME   See Chicago Mercantile Exchange.

CMO   See Collateralised mortgage obligation.

CMBS   Commercial mortgage backed security. MBS* backed by commercial mortgages, or by real estate.

COB Rules   FSA* Conduct of Business Rules.

Coface   French Export credit agency*.

Cold back-up   A Back-up servicer* for a Securitisation* transaction which is not actively involved in the transaction unless and until termination of the appointment of the Originator* as Servicer*. Cf. Warm back-up and Hot back-up.

Collar   A Derivative* contract whereby the purchaser effectively purchases a Cap* and sells a Floor*, which establishes both a maximum and minimum interest "strike rate" to be paid by the purchaser on a borrowing equal to the notional principal, but for a lower Premium* (sense (iii)) than that paid on purchase of a cap alone in the same amount.

Collateral   General terminology for Security* (sense (ii)) or assets that are available to support an obligation. See also Outright transfer.

Collateralised bond obligation   Or CBO*. A bond issued against a pool of bond assets, or other securities. Referred to in a generic sense (together with the CLO*) as a CDO*.

Collateralised debt obligation   Or CDO*. A bond issued against a mixed pool of bond and loan assets. Cf. Collateralised bond obligation and Collateralised loan obligation. Can take the form of a Cash flow CDO*, a Synthetic CDO*, or a Market value CDO*.

Collateralised loan obligation   Or CLO*. A bond issued against a pool of bank loan assets. Referred to in a generic sense (together with the CBO*) as a CDO*.

Collateralised mortgage obligation   Or CMO*. A Mortgage backed security* under which the issued debt is tranched into different classes of securities to smooth the Amortisation* profile of each class arising from principal payments and Prepayments* into a more predictable format. The primary classes (e.g. A, B, and C or A1, A2 and A3) pay interest, with principal payments being made on the A-tranche until retired, then the B-tranche, and so on. The final tranche rolls-up compound interest at the stated rate until the primary tranches are retired, then pays interest and principal sums until maturity.

Collective investment scheme   An investment scheme which is defined in the Financial Services Act 1986* at s. 75(1) (repeated verbatim at s. 235(1) FSMA* 2000) as "any arrangements with respect to property of any description ... the purpose or effect of which is to enable persons ... to participate in or receive profits or income arising from the acquisition, holding, management or disposal of the property or sums paid out of such profits or income."

In addition under s. 75(2) and (3) (repeated at s. 235(2) and (3) FSMA 2000), the arrangements must not give day-to-day control over the management of the property to any participant, and must either pool the property and distributions of the scheme or must give the management of the property as a whole to the operator of the scheme.

No action may be taken to communicate an invitation or inducement to participate in a collective investment scheme in the UK, or which is capable of having an effect in the UK, unless the scheme is FSA-authorised (s. 76(1)) (repeated at s. 238(1) FSMA 2000).

The trustees of a collective investment scheme which is not an authorised Unit trust* will, if they are resident in the UK, be obliged to account for income tax on trust income at the basic rate of tax under s. 469, ICTA*.

Combination   The common law right of combination, Consolidation* (sense (i)) or Set-off* (sense (i)) of accounts is the right of a banker (and possibly a customer, if the accounts are held at the same branch – *Mutton v Peat (1900) 2 Ch.79*) to aggregate definite (i.e. non-contingent) debit and credit balances on accounts of the same nature held with him by the same customer in the same capacity, subject to express or implied agreement to the contrary. Loan accounts may on occasion be considered not to be of the same nature as current accounts. In addition, the action of terms such as a fixed maturity date in a loan or deposit agreement (as opposed to the loan/deposit being repayable on demand) may impliedly exclude combination following *Halesowen Press-work & Assemblies Ltd v. Westminster Bank Ltd (1971) 1 QB 1*. Trust accounts may not be combined with personal accounts. An agreement not to exercise rights of combination is effective to prevent combination, but only up until the Liquidation* or Bankruptcy* of the customer. As combination acts in an accounting sense to determine the amount of a single debt owing between the bank and the customer, it may therefore be available to the bank prior to, and without reference to, claims against the aggregated amounts by parties further up the order of Priorities* (sense (i)) than the bank. On this point, cf. Set-off, sense (ii).

Combination note   A Security* which has claim to two different underlying rights ranking in different point of Priority*. Generally used in CDO* transactions to combine a senior tranche and a junior tranche, in order to assist the sale of the junior tranche, as the structure is designed to create a note that is Principal protected* to a certain extent.

Comfort letter   A letter intended to provide some degree of reassurance to the addressee that the writer will provide some kind of support to a third party (typically an entity to which the addressee has lent money). The contents are generally less robust than the contents of a Letter of undertaking* and are often not intended to be legally binding.

Commercial bank   A Bank* that operates to take deposits and makes loans to corporate and personal customers, as opposed to an Investment bank*. In the US, the Glass-Steagall Act* historically prevented commercial banks from acting as investment banks by underwriting securities (leading some US banks to establish offshore investment banking subsidiaries). These structures were simplified with the reform of the Glass–Steagall Act by the Gramm–Leach–Bliley Act*. The two types of bank function can exist side by side in the UK but are typically divided between different group companies.

Commercial paper   Or CP*. A short-term unsecured debt instrument. Typically issued with a maturity of 1 year or less in the Euromarkets*, in order to achieve exemption from TEFRA* requirements for non-US paper. Generally issued for no more than 270 days in the US, in order to gain SEC* exempt status under Rule 3(a)3 (for US prime paper issued to raise working capital), and often 183 days or less, in order to gain TEFRA exemption for US paper as well. Written in large denominations and not secured or underwritten (cf. Euronotes). The BBA published new guidelines for the London CP market in 1999. Normally discounted rather than coupon-bearing (prior to 1996, coupon payments on a short-term instrument would not have been tax deductible under the Short interest* rules), the rate on CP may be quoted as a Discount rate* (sense (iii)) or as a Discount yield*. In the US, CP interest rates are often below the market Discount rate* (sense (i)), due to the high level of Reserve assets* required for banks in the US on trading Ineligible bills*, as well as Capital adequacy* costs and (historically) concerns over US banks' creditworthiness. In the UK, may be subject to rules on Deposit-taking*.

Commingling risk   The Risk* that a party that is holding receipts belonging to another party in an unsegregated Fungible* account together with its own funds becomes insolvent and the other party's funds cannot be traced (see Tracing) into the account to enable the beneficiary to claim them in priority to creditors of the insolvent party.

Commission   A fee payable to a Broker* by a client.

Commission des Opérations de Bourse   French Stock exchange* authority which monitors disclosures to be made by listed companies.

Commitment   (i) In a securities issue, the amount of the issue that a particular Underwriter* agrees to commit himself to underwrite (in the US)/subscribe to (in the UK) (prior to Syndication* to a Selling group*). Since in the UK, securities underwriting is undertaken on a joint and several basis, each of the underwriters has a commitment equal to the entire issue, if any of the institutions involved fail to take up the amount of the issue that such Manager* or selling group member has been given as an Allotment*.

(ii) In a Syndicated loan*, the amount of the facility that an Underwriter* agrees to underwrite (prior to Syndication* to Participants*) or the amount of the facility that any Manager* or participant agrees to fund, either now, or on future request for an undrawn portion (after syndication or other sell-down of commitment). In a Facility* with undrawn portions, or a Revolving facility*, the commitments of each lender thus last until the facility is fully drawn, or no longer available, respectively.

Commitment fee   A commitment fee is expressed as a percentage of any amount available for drawing but not yet drawn under the terms of a Committed facility*. Cf. Facility fee.

Committed facility   A Facility* under which the lender agrees to make the facility amount available to the borrower for an agreed period (unless an event of default occurs). Cf. Uncommitted facility and Overdraft.

Commodities Futures Trading Commission   Or CFTC. US financial markets body that regulates Futures* and Options* trading on US Exchanges*.

Commodity future   See Future.

Commodity swap   A Swap* in which the parties agree to make payments the calculation of which are linked to a commodity price.

Common Code   On application by a lead manager or paying agent, a common code identification number is allocated to a security accepted by Clearstream* or Euroclear* for clearing through their system. If the issue is a Euromarket* issue, or will be traded internationally, an ISIN* will also be given. See also CUSIP.

Common depositary   A Custodian* appointed jointly by Euroclear* and Clearstream*.

Companies Act 1985   UK statute which contains the bulk of statutory legislation for UK companies. The Act superseded other Companies Acts, notably the Companies Act 1948, certain areas of which (e.g. the 1948 Table A (see Table A)) still have an impact on certain companies. The Companies Act 1985 originated with the Joint Stock Companies Act 1844 (see Joint stock company). See also Companies Act 1989.

Companies Act 1989   UK statute that contained a large number of amending provisions to the Companies Act 1985* and the Financial Services Act 1986* and set out provisions on Set-off* (sense (ii)) of market contracts traded on an Exchange*.

Companion   A Tranche* of an ABS* securities issue that accompanies a PAC* or TAC*. For a PAC, the companion will receive Prepayments* on the underlying assets that exceed a certain level, and if prepayments fall below a certain level, principal payments are diverted from other tranches. For a TAC, the companion will simply receive Prepayments* on the underlying assets that exceed a certain level. This will reduce uncertainty as to the level of prepayments on the PAC or TAC, and enable amortisation of the PAC or TAC to move in accordance with a planned schedule.

Company   Loose generic term for a group or association of persons with a common goal, which may be a Corporation* or an Unincorporated association*. To be distinguished from a Partnership*, a Society* or a club. Most often used in the UK to mean a Registered company*, but see also Statutory company, Chartered company, Deed of settlement company, Joint stock company and Letters patent company.

Company limited by guarantee   A variety of Registered company* where the Members* enjoy Limited liability* for the debts of the company up to the value of guarantees given by members in a specific amount. Cf. Company limited by shares.

Company limited by shares   A variety of Registered company* where the Members* enjoy Limited liability* for the debts of the company up to the extent of shares held by them in the company and any amounts of share capital not paid-up by them on their shares.

Company secretary   A company officer who keeps the register of Members* and other books relating to the company.

Competition Commission   In the UK, the Commission that is responsible for examination of the effect on competition of Mergers* and Takeovers*, and replaced the Monopolies and Mergers Commission from 1 April 1999.

Composite   A security document where security is granted by more than one party.

Composition with creditors   See Voluntary arrangement.

Compound interest   Interest that is charged on any unpaid interest from a previous compounding period, as well as on principal, effectively leading to Capitalisation* (sense (i)) of the unpaid interest. The intention to calculate compound interest on an amount must be expressly stated or it will not be upheld at law.

Compound option   An Option* to buy or sell a particular option at a set rate.

Compulsory winding-up   See Liquidation.

Concentration risk   The Risk* that results from over-reliance on a single entity (for example in a debt or equity investment portfolio, or in a pool of receivables), with the result that Insolvency* or under-performance of that entity has a significant effect on the performance generated. Hedged by adequate diversification among a wide portfolio of entities whose performance is not closely correlated (see Correlation).

Condition precedent   A necessary precondition to the effectiveness at law of a contract and the obligations contained in the contract.

Condition subsequent   A condition that, if it does not occur, will generally bring a contract or a contractual obligation to an end.

Conditional sale   A sale with Retention of title*. A method of allowing a seller or financier to provide finance to a purchaser for the purchase of an asset while retaining title to the asset sold (and thus achieving protection against the asset being available to creditors generally in the insolvency of the purchaser), in a manner that is: (a) not registrable as a Bill of sale*; and (b) if the agreement is a conditional sale agreement within the meaning in the Consumer Credit Act 1974* (namely, a sale of an asset under an agreement that is a regulated agreement for the purposes of the Consumer Credit Act 1974, and where "the purchase price or part of it is payable by instalments, and the property in the goods ... is to remain in the seller ... until such conditions as to payment of instalments or otherwise as may be specified in the agreement are fulfilled"), not at risk of being overridden by a sale by the purchaser to a bona fide third party (except for a sale of a motor vehicle to a private purchaser, which may be so overridden pursuant to s. 27 Hire-Purchase Act 1964 as substituted by s. 192(3)(a) of the Consumer Credit Act 1974). Similar to a Hire purchase* in effect.

Condor   A derivative strategy similar to a Butterfly*, involving the purchase of a Call option* or a Put option* at a certain Strike price*, the sale of a call option or put option (respectively) at a higher strike price, the sale of a second call option or put option (respectively) at a still higher strike price and the purchase of a call option or put option (respectively) at a higher strike price again. The combination achieves a flat maximum profit if the underlying is between the middle two strike prices, and declines to zero on either side of this range.

Conduit   An SPV* established to issue CP*, typically to fund a series of Securitisation* or Repackaging* structures. Usually established by a financial institution as sponsor, to enable a number of different clients of the institution to sell Receivables*, leaving the institution to manage the conduit as a whole.

Confidence interval   A percentage rate used to indicate the probability of a particular scenario being the case. For example, used in data verification analysis to indicate the percentage confidence interval that the Error rate* on a particular pool of assets matches that on a sample taken from the pool (usually 95% or 99% is taken as the confidence interval to reflect 2 or 3 standard deviations).

Confirm   (i) In relation to a Documentary credit*, the express statement of a Confirming bank* that it "confirms the credit" issued by the Issuing bank*. Such confirmation gives the beneficiary of the credit an enforceable right against the confirming bank as well as (if the credit is irrevocable) against the issuing bank.

(ii) In relation to a Swap*, Future*, Option* or other derivative, the document setting out the terms of a particular transaction.

Confirming bank   In relation to a Documentary credit*, a confirming bank is an Advising bank* or Correspondent bank* which confirms (see Confirm) the credit to the beneficiary. A confirming bank that pays on a credit following presentation of the correct documentation is entitled to be reimbursed by the Issuing bank* provided that the confirm was authorised by, and effected in accordance with the terms of, the credit.

Connected persons   (i) For the purpose, *inter alia*, of s. 322A Companies Act 1985* (which makes voidable at the instance of the company transactions where the directors have exceeded their powers, and pursuant to which the company contracts with one of its directors or an Associated company* or connected person of any of its directors), a director is, under the terms of s. 346 Companies Act 1985, connected to Associated companies* (except where the context otherwise requires), the director's spouse and children, people with whom the director is in partnership and trustees of trusts where the director or associated companies of the director are beneficiaries.

(ii) For the purpose of Transfer pricing* rules (see Control, sense (ii)), persons set out at ICTA, s. 839 who are linked in such a way that transactions between them cannot be viewed as transactions at Arm's-length*, as follows:

(a) A person is connected with their spouse and with their or their spouse's relatives;
(b) A person, in the capacity of trustee of a settlement (including any trust), is connected with the settlor (if an individual), or any person connected with such a settlor, or any company that is a Close company* (or one that would be close if resident in the UK) the Participators* in which include the trustees of the settlement (or a company where Control* (sense (ii)) vests in such a close company);
(c) Except in connection with acquisitions and disposals of partnership assets pursuant to bona fide commercial arrangements, a person is connected with any person with whom he is in partnership and with any spouse or relative of any such person;

(d) A company is connected with another company if they are controlled* (Control, sense (i)) by the same person or persons, or if a person controls one company and he or persons connected with him control the other;

(e) A company is connected with another person where such person, alone or with persons connected with him, has control* (Control, sense (i)) of it;

(f) Two or more persons acting together to secure or exercise control of a company are treated in relation to that company as connected with each other and with any other person acting on their directions.

Conseil des Bourses de Valeurs   Or CBV. French regulatory body, overseeing the listing and delisting of securities.

Consolidated accounts   The collective accounting analysis required to be prepared for a Group* (sense (i)) of companies by s. 227 Companies Act 1985*, whereby Subsidiary undertakings* are consolidated into the Statutory accounts* of their Parent company* (sense (ii)). Exemptions are available for certain parent companies majority owned or wholly owned by a Parent undertaking* within the EU. In the US, FAS 140* or FIN 46* (previously, the Substantive equity* doctrine) may lead to consolidation of SPVs* in Securitisation* transactions that have Thin capitalisation* onto the accounts of the Originator*.

Consolidation   (i) See Combination.

(ii) The consolidation of a Group* (sense (i)) for accounting purposes. See Consolidated accounts.

(iii) The consolidation of a Group* (sense (vii)) for Capital adequacy* reporting purposes.

Consortium   (i) Under s. 247(9) ICTA (for the purpose of the group definition (see Group, sense (iv)) for the Group income* election), a consortium is a group of companies resident in the UK which together hold at least 75% of the shares in a subject company and where each holds at least 5% of the shares in the subject company.

(ii) Under s. 413(6) ICTA (for the purpose of the group definition (see Group, sense (vi)) for the Group relief* provisions), a consortium is a group of companies resident anywhere in the world (prior to the Finance Act 2000, such companies had to be resident in the UK) which together hold at least 75% of the shares in a subject company and where each holds at least 5% of the shares in the subject company.

Constant prepayment rate   Or CPR*. An assumed percentage rate of Prepayment* over a particular period of the principal amount due from debtors on a pool of Receivables*. Usually expressed as:

$$(p/\text{PAO}) \cdot 100$$

where p = prepayment amount per period

PAO = principal balance of receivables outstanding at start of period less scheduled principal amount over period.

Thus an unchanging CPR implies that the amount of prepayment receipts per period is falling in line with the outstanding receivables balance. Used as a basis to formulate the Weighted average life* of Asset-backed securities* issued pursuant to a Pass-through* (sense (ii)) Securitisation*, where principal receipts from debtors are passed directly to investors. See also SMM, 100% PSA, 200% PSA.

Constructive notice   The doctrine stating that a person may be considered to have notice of matters as to which he ought to have made reasonable enquiry. Cf. Deemed notice*.

Consumer Credit Act 1974   UK statute governing the regulation of loans of a certain size made to consumers (individuals or partnerships), such as credit card agreements, Hire purchase* and Conditional sale* agreements and overdrafts. Loans up to £25 000 are regulated (prior to 1 May 1998 only loans for less than £15 000 were regulated) although since 20 November 2002 there are plans to increase this to loans of any size. Certain agreements are exempt from the provisions of the Act; namely loans for the purchase of a house (as opposed to second mortgages), fixed amount credits for 12 months or less (e.g. trade credit), revolving credits where debts must be discharged by a single payment (e.g. charge cards) and low cost loan agreements which are only available to a particular class of borrowers. Extortionate credit bargains* are regulated under the Act even where they are exempt agreements. Persons carrying on a business of providing credit under regulated loans are required to obtain a consumer credit licence from the Office of Fair Trading, in the absence of which, loans may be unenforceable. For regulated loans where the loan is not entered into at the offices of the creditor, the consumer is given a "cooling-off" period after entering into the agreement, during which time the debtor may cancel the agreement. The period runs until 5 days after the consumer receives a notice from the creditor informing the consumer of his cancellation rights, separate from the copy of the agreement given to him on signing (for mortgages, the consumer is instead given an unsigned copy of the agreement and is then left for 7 days to consider the transaction prior to being asked to sign). The agreement must meet certain requirements as to legibility and form, including a statement of the total financing charge under the agreement and the APR; if the agreement does not meet these requirements, it will be unenforceable without a court order. Throughout the term of the agreement, the consumer retains a right to prepay the agreement, which cannot be excluded by the creditor. If the credit is used to purchase goods or services from a third-party supplier, the consumer can assert any claim he has for misrepresentation or breach of contract against the supplier against the creditor. If the consumer is in default, the creditor must serve a default notice specifying a minimum period of seven days during which the consumer must rectify the default or pay compensation, before the creditor can terminate the contract or repossess goods. Where the consumer has paid more than one-third of the total amount payable by the consumer under a hire purchase agreement (including interest and finance charges but excluding penalties), or the creditor needs to enter premises to repossess, the creditor will need a court order for repossession.

Consumer Credit Directive   On 11 September 2002, the EU Commission published a proposal for a directive on consumer credit to replace Directive 87/102. The new draft Directive is designed to harmonise consumer credit across the EU by preventing member states from adding to the new rules (except in certain specific areas) under Article 30. The new draft governs the regulation of "credit agreements" where credit is granted to a "consumer" (an individual acting outside his trade) by a "creditor" (an individual or legal entity granting credit in the course of business), and "surety agreements" (ancillary agreements guaranteeing the fulfilment of credit, granted by a guarantor who is a consumer). There is no minimum or maximum amount of credit under regulation. Certain agreements are exempt from the provisions of the Directive under Article 3; namely loans for the purchase or transformation of immovable property (as opposed to equity release mortgages where the proceeds are used for other purposes), hire agreements where there is no option to purchase, credit agreements where debts must be discharged by a single payment within a period not exceeding 3 months (e.g. debit cards), credit agreements granted by creditors outside their normal business activity at lower than market rates which are not offered to the public generally and certain credit agreements with investment firms (which are subject to regulation on information and advice under the investment services directive). Under Article 28, creditors and "credit intermediaries" (an individual or legal entity who acts as an intermediary in concluding credit agreements for a fee) must be registered and subject to inspection or monitoring. Credit agreements and surety agreements should be entered into on business premises under Article 5. Consumers are given a 14-day right of withdrawal from an agreement under Article 11 which runs from the date on which a copy of the agreement is transmitted to the consumer. The agreement must meet certain requirements as to form, including a statement of the "total lending rate" charged by the lender under the agreement and the "annual percentage rate of charge" or APR (which reflects the total cost of credit to the consumer). The method of calculation of the APR is set out in Annex I to the Directive. Member states are required under Article 31 to set out penalties for infringement of the requirements of the Directive. Unlike the Consumer Credit Act 1974* in the UK, the Consumer Credit Directive does not provide for liability for a creditor where the credit is used to purchase goods or services from a third-party supplier in respect of claims against the supplier, unless the supplier has acted as credit intermediary in arranging the credit (in which case the creditor is jointly and severally liable with the supplier under Article 19).

Contango   For Futures*, any point at which forward prices are above spot prices (i.e. the normal state of the market), due to the generally Negative carry* on the underlying assets, or (e.g. for commodity futures) any perceived shortage in future supplies of the underlying.

Contract grade   Those instruments delivery of which an Exchange* states to be acceptable in discharge of a matured Future*.

Contract month   The month in which a Future* matures.

Contracts for differences   Contracts for the exchange of amounts, such as a swap, future or option based on indices or interest rates (rather than delivery of a security or commodity) and which are effected exclusively by cash settlement. Unenforceable if deemed to be Gaming* or wagering contracts.

Contracts (Rights of Third Parties) Act 1999   See Privity.

Contractual subordination   The Subordination* of one debt behind another, which is achieved by contractual agreement between the subordinated creditor and the senior creditor. Cf. Structural subordination.

Control   **(i)** For the purposes of the Close company*, Controlled foreign company* and Connected persons* (sense (ii)) provisions, under s. 416 ICTA means the exercise or ability to exercise, or the entitlement to acquire, direct or indirect control over the company's affairs and includes the possession of, or the entitlement to acquire:

(a) The greater part of the share capital or issued share capital or of the voting power; or
(b) Such part of the issued share capital as would, were the whole of the company's income distributed, give the entitlement to receive the greater part of the amount so distributed; or
(c) Rights in a distribution on a winding-up or in any other circumstances to the greater part of the company's assets.

Two or more persons have control of a company if their aggregated rights satisfy the above conditions. There shall also be attributed to any person the rights and powers of any company or companies controlled by him (with or without his Associates*) or of any associate or associates of his.

(ii) For the purpose of Transfer pricing* and Connected persons* (sense (ii)) provisions, means, under s. 840 ICTA, the power of a person to secure by a shareholding or the possession of voting power (whether directly or indirectly) or under a company's Articles of association*, that the affairs of such company are conducted in accordance with the wishes of that person. In this regard, there are attributed to a person under s. 773 ICTA, the powers of any nominee on his behalf and of any Connected person* (sense (ii)) in relation to such person.

(iii) For the purposes of VAT groups (see Group, sense (iii)) under s. 43A(2) VATA*, control exists where a company is empowered by statute to control another company's activities or if it is the latter company's Holding company* (sense (ii)). An individual, or individuals, is taken to control a company if he or they, were he or they a company, would be the company's holding company as above.

Controlled foreign company   Or CFC*. For UK tax purposes, under s. 747 ICTA*, a company which is resident outside the UK and controlled (see Control, sense (i)) by corporate entities resident in the UK and is subjected in its local jurisdiction to less than 75% of the amount of tax that it would have been subjected to in the UK (as determined by performing a notional UK tax calculation). Profits of a CFC may be attributed to the parties holding interests in the CFC by the UK tax authorities whether or not such profits are in fact remitted to such parties, as the CFC may be regarded as a device for deferring UK tax.

Conversion discount   The amount of the discount of the Conversion price* of a Convertible* over the market value of the shares into which the convertible may be converted.

Conversion premium   The amount of the premium of the Conversion price* of a Convertible* over the market value of the shares into which the convertible may be converted.

Conversion price   A set share price applied to the principal of a Convertible* when determining the number of shares received on conversion of the convertible.

Convertibility risk The Risk* that exchange controls prevent an entity from converting a particular currency to another currency.

Convertibility swap A Swap* that enables a party to make payments in one currency in the local jurisdiction of that currency, and receive payments in another currency outside that jurisdiction, thus overcoming any Transfer risk* or Convertibility risk* on the first currency. Can be priced by looking at the spread difference between (a) domestic currency debt of the sovereign swapped into hard currency, and (b) hard currency debt of the sovereign.

Convertible A Bond* that may be converted, at the option of the holder or otherwise, into a holding of shares in the issuing company (or another company – typically known as an Exchangeable*). Conversion of the bond principal value occurs at a preset Conversion price* for the share (and at a preset FX rate* where the bond and the shares are denominated in different currencies), at a Conversion premium* to the current market value of the issuer's shares. Coupon rates on the bond will be lower than market level for bonds to reflect the Premium* (sense (iii)) value of the embedded conversion Option*. Typically, however, they will be higher than the Dividend* (sense (i)) on the shares, to compensate for the conversion premium charged. A Call* (sense (i)) may be inserted in a convertible to enable the issuer to force conversion if the share price reaches a certain premium over the conversion price (by the threat of redemption at a fixed value). A Put* (sense (i)) may also be inserted at a premium to par to provide investors with an all-in yield equivalent to the normal bond yield in the event that the share price remains below the conversion price. No new cash is advanced on conversion (cf. Warrant). Anti-dilution provisions are also included, to protect the investor if the issuer attempts to dilute the share price by a Bonus issue* or Rights issue*. These will typically provide for an adjustment of the conversion price in a bonus issue to reflect the new-for-old ratio (i.e. in a 4-for-1 bonus issue, the conversion price would be divided by 4 to preserve the ratio by ensuring conversion into 4 times as many shares), and an adjustment of the conversion price in a rights issue to reflect the dilution (if any) of the pre-rights issue share value arising from the discount to market (if any) at which the rights issue is priced (e.g. a rights issue of shares equal in number to 30% of the total post-rights issue number of shares, which are sold in a rights issue priced at a 20% discount to market price, should lead to a 6% dilution (30% × 20%) of the market share price, and hence a 6% reduction in the conversion price). The issuer will need to ensure that it has the proper authorities to issue new shares in the event of conversion, under s. 80 Companies Act 1985 (on authorisation of directors to allot shares) and generally in terms of its maximum permitted authorised share capital. The convertible will also need to be structured to comply with pre-emption rights arising under s. 89 Companies Act 1985. May be quoted or not; if not quoted and not issued on terms "reasonably comparable" to those on which the company's quoted securities are issued, interest is liable to reclassification as a Distribution* under s. 209(2)(e)(ii) ICTA.

Convexity A measure of the curvature, or rate of change, of the relation between yields and bond prices; in effect the rate of change of the Modified duration* as the yield varies. If yields fall, prices rise. If yields rise, prices fall. If the actual bond price exceeds the estimated price extrapolated on a straight-line basis from a small change by the use of modified duration (i.e. the price/yield relation curves above the straight line), then the bond has Positive convexity*. If the actual bond price is less than the estimated price extrapolated on a straight-line basis from a small change by the use of modified duration (i.e. the price/yield relation curves below the straight line), then the bond has Negative convexity*. Positive convexity implies that, as yields increase, the rate of fall of price gradually slows, and as yields fall, the rate of increase in price gradually increases. Mortgage bonds are negatively convex due to the effect on the bond of underlying mortgage prepayments. As yields fall, the likely increase in prepayment (through refinancing) of the underlying mortgages means that the bond principal reduces, shortening its life and decelerating its increase in value. Conversely, as yields rise, the expected life of the bond is likely to lengthen, as prepayments drop, meaning that the value drops at an accelerating rate. Similarly, a bond with a call option is likely to have negative convexity, due to the reduced likelihood of the call being exercised in a high-yield environment, and the increased likelihood of the call being exercised in a low-yield environment.

Copyright   An intellectual property right in a particular media or software work that arises automatically and entitles the author (or subsequent acquirers of the copyright) to prevent others copying the work (generally for a period of the life of the author plus 70 years in the EU under the 1993 Directive on copyright duration). Cf. Patent, Registered design, Trademark.

Corporate personality   The separate legal personality of a Corporation* from its Members* (subject to doctrines such as Piercing the veil*). Usually results in Limited liability* for members (unless the corporation has unlimited liability) and the ability for the corporation to sue and be sued in its own name. Foreign corporations established under foreign law are recognised as having corporate personality in the UK. International organisations will be recognised as enjoying corporate personality for English law purposes where they are accorded legal personality under the laws of the state where they are located *(Arab Monetary Fund v. Hashim (1991) HL 1 All ER 871)*.

Corporate services agreement   In a Securitisation* transaction, the agreement setting out the role of the Corporate services provider*.

Corporate services provider   An entity that provides corporate services for an SPV* in a Securitisation* transaction, such as the provision of independent directors, in return for a fee.

Corporate veil   The separate Corporate personality* of a Corporation*, which draws a veil over the assets of its Members*, preventing creditors from attaching members' assets, unless the members' liabilities extend beyond their shareholdings (e.g. the company is an Unlimited company*).

Corporation   An entity that has undergone Incorporation* and enjoys separate Corporate personality*, as opposed to an Unincorporated association*. For example, a Registered company*, a Statutory company* or a Chartered company*.

Corporation tax   UK tax introduced on 1 April 1964 on the taxable profits (calculated as income less expenses arising under the Income tax* Schedules*) and chargeable gains (accruing under Capital gains tax* rules) made by any company Resident* in the UK (including certain Unincorporated associations* but excluding Partnerships*) wherever they arise around the world. See Discount, Interest and Short interest in relation to the deductibility for tax purposes of these elements. Profits are calculated over an Accounting period* (sense (i)) and split between Financial years* (sense (ii)) to determine tax rates. Between April 1999 (when the ACT* regime was abolished) and April 2003, a system of quarterly payment of corporation tax was phased in for larger companies, with tax paid quarterly on expected profits on a current year basis. From 1 April 2003, corporation tax is charged at 0% on taxable profits up to £10 000, a marginal rate on profits of £10 000 to £50 000, 19% on profits of £50 000 to £300 000, a marginal rate on profits of £300 000 to £1 500 000 and 30% on profits of £1 500 000 or more. See also Group income, Group relief. See Residence in respect of branches of non-UK companies.

Correlation   A measurement of the degree to which two variables (e.g. the price of two different instruments) move in unison. Correlation falls between +1 and −1. A correlation of +1 means that on a certain percentage change in one direction of one instrument, the other instrument changes by the same amount in the same direction. A correlation of −1 means that the second instrument moves by the same percentage change, but in the opposite direction (a negative correlation).

Correlation risk   A Risk* arising from the difference between an assumed Correlation* between two or more variables (such as correlation between particular pricings or rates for securities, or correlation between default of the Reference entity* and of the credit protection provider for a Credit derivative*) and the actual correlation experienced. For example, in a Differential swap*, dealers make assumptions on the anticipated degree of correlation between changes in an interest rate and changes in an FX rate, in calculating pricing for the swap. The risk arises from the possible inaccuracies or incompleteness of such correlation assumptions.

Correspondent bank   In relation to a Documentary credit*, an Issuing bank* may use the services of another bank that regularly acts on behalf of the issuing bank (i.e. as its correspondent), and is established in the country of the beneficiary of the credit, to act as an Advising bank*.

Corridor swap   A Swap* with Amortisation* of the notional principal allowed freely within certain upper and lower limits (and not on a fixed schedule). May be used as a swap on a Securitisation* transaction, in order to provide a hedge across a range of Prepayment* scenarios, without exposing the swap counterparty to unlimited Prepayment risk*.

Cost and freight   Or CFR*. Export delivery term of general trade use and defined in INCOTERMS* meaning that costs of delivery of goods on board ship and freight costs to the named destination are borne by the seller. Costs thereafter are borne by the buyer. Risk passes to the buyer, however, when the goods are loaded (as with FOB*).

Cost, insurance and freight   Or CIF. Export delivery term of general trade use and defined in INCOTERMS* meaning that costs of delivery of goods on board ship, freight costs and minimum marine insurance costs are borne by the seller. Thereafter, costs are borne by the buyer. Risk passes to the buyer, however, when the goods are loaded (as with FOB*).

Cost of carry An annual percentage rate calculated as being the return achievable on investing an amount of cash, less the financing cost (interest, etc.) incurred in raising that amount. See Negative carry and Positive carry.

Cost-plus Basis of Transfer pricing* calculation for profits deemed earned by an administrative headquarters providing administrative services to overseas group companies, in countries such as France, Germany, Luxembourg, the Netherlands, Belgium and the UK. Profits are calculated as the cost of providing such administrative services, plus a deemed "profit" mark-up varying between 5% and 30%.

Coupon (i) The Interest rate* payable on a security expressed as a percentage of its Principal*. Coupons are often payable periodically during the course of each year.
 (ii) Part of a definitive Bond* or FRN*, which the holder presents to receive each interest payment on the instrument.

Cover A transaction which is the opposite in whole or in part to a previous transaction. Undertaken to neutralise or limit a Position*.

Covered bond A bond issued by a restricted activity institution and backed by a pool of mortgages or public sector assets under legislation which separates the pool from insolvency proceedings connected with the issuing institution. Consequently, holders of covered bonds have preferential rights to the relevant pool of assets, which are liquidated separately for the benefit of the holders of the covered bonds on insolvency of the issuer. See Cedulas hipotecarias, Cedulas territoriales, Jumbo Pfandbriefe, Obligations foncières, Pfandbriefe, Realkreditobligationer.

Covered call The sale of a Call option* on an asset that is currently held in order to generate Premium* (sense (iii)) income in a flat market where the market price of the asset is not expected to rise to the Strike price* on the call option.

Covered warrant A tradeable right which gives the holder the right to buy or sell an asset at a particular "exercise price" payable in cash on exercise at a given time (or over a given "exercise period"), issued in return for a Premium* (sense (iii)) payment, akin to that paid on issue of an Option*, resulting in an asset with Leverage* (sense (ii)). Unlike normal Warrants*, covered warrants are issued by financial institutions in respect of third-party shares or bonds, which the institution undertakes to make available on exercise of the warrant.

CP See Commercial paper.

CPMA See Cross-product master agreement.

CPR See Constant prepayment rate.

CPT See Carriage paid to.

Credit card trust See Master trust.

Credit conversion factor Percentage factor applied to the notional amount of off-balance-sheet items, in order to reduce them to a notional asset figure that can then be risk weighted for Capital adequacy* purposes.

Credit default swap   Or Default swap*. An Off-balance-sheet* (sense (i)) (i.e. un-funded) Credit derivative*. The protection buyer pays a periodic premium in return for a payout determined by occurrence of a particular Credit event* (the derivative may also specify that there should be Publicly available information* of the event, and/or that Materiality* exists).

Credit derivative   A Derivative* instrument whose payout is determined by the Credit risk* of a particular Reference entity*. Main examples are the Credit spread option*, the Credit default swap*, the Credit linked note* and the Total return swap*. In addition to general derivatives concerns as to Gaming* issues and so on, credit derivatives may be considered to constitute insurance contracts in some jurisdictions, raising further regulatory issues. Opinion in the UK is that credit derivatives do not constitute insurance contracts.

Credit enhancement   A mechanism that provides support for a debt obligation and serves to increase the likelihood that the debt obligation will be repaid. Examples that are used in Securitisation* transactions are: Reserve funds*, Overcollateralisation*, Deferred purchase price*, Wraps* from Monoline insurers* and issuance of Subordi-nated notes*, which are purchased by the Originator*. In relation to securitisations, usually subject to strict Capital adequacy* rules requiring that any credit enhancement provided by the originator be deducted from capital.

Credit equivalent amount   Notional amount calculated for derivatives exposures, equal to their mark-to-market plus a percentage "add-on", which can be risk weighted for Capital adequacy* purposes.

Credit event   In relation to a Credit default swap* or a Credit linked note*, an event with regard to the Reference entity* which triggers a payout or reduction in a payout. Common credit events are payment default by the reference entity on its debt obliga-tions, insolvency of the reference entity or restructuring of the reference entity's debt.

Credit factoring   Also known simply as Factoring* (sense (ii)) or Debt factoring*. A continuing legal relation between a business and a factor (a financial institution) whereby the factor purchases the trade Book debts* or Receivables* of the business at a discount and administers and collects them. Undertaken to provide finance and liquidity for the business. May be recourse or non-recourse. In the latter cases, it serves also to transfer the Credit risk* under the receivables.

Credit institution   Term used within the EU to set out the scope of Commercial bank* type institutions subject to regulatory and Capital adequacy* requirements. The definition is set out in Article 1 of Directive* 77/780 of 12 December 1977 as being "an undertaking whose business is to receive deposits or other repayable funds from the public and to grant credits for its own account". This definition is repeated verbatim in Statutory Instrument 1992/3218 in the UK, under s. 5 of which entities authorised as a credit institution in another EU country may carry on in the UK any of the following that they are authorised to carry on in their home state: deposit-taking activities (see Bank), Investment business*, business under the Consumer Credit Act 1974* and insurance business.

Credit-linked note   A funded Credit derivative* where the payout is determined by occurrence of a particular Credit event* (the derivative may also specify that there should be Publicly available information* of the event, and/or that Materiality* exists).

Credit rating   An alphabetical/numerical rating given by a Credit rating agency* to reflect the Credit risk* on an entity, either generally or in relation to a particular obligation; i.e. the capacity of the entity to pay interest and principal on the relevant obligation or obligations on a timely basis. See also Foreign currency rating, Local currency rating, Sovereign ceiling, Investment grade, Speculative grade, "r", Shadow rating, Unsolicited rating.

The main credit rating symbols of each of the three main agencies are set out below. Rating symbols or classifications are also given in a number of other different areas, including assessments of the financial strength of banks, the capabilities of receivables servicing companies, and so on. Certain sub-scripts can be attached to ratings to indicate their application or other warning factors to be aware of outside of pure credit risk. For example Standard & Poor's uses the following:

"r" – implies that some market or other non-credit risk exists (such as FX risk)
"m" – indicates a money market fund rating
"f" – indicates a bond fund rating
"pi" – indicates a public information rating (which is based solely on information in the public domain concerning a company such as published financial statements).

Ratings on senior secured obligations are generally one notch higher than those on senior unsecured obligations. Ratings on subordinated obligations are generally one or more notches below those on senior unsecured obligations.

(a) Standard & Poor's

Long-term debt:

AAA	extremely strong capacity for timely payment
AA	very strong capacity for timely payment
A	strong capacity but may be susceptible to adverse economic changes
BBB	adequate capacity but susceptible to adverse economic changes. Lowest investment grade rating
BB	speculative but less vulnerable to adverse conditions. Speculative grade
B	speculative and more vulnerable to adverse conditions
CCC	currently vulnerable; dependent on favourable business, financial and economic conditions
CC	currently highly vulnerable
SD, D	selective or general default.

"+" or "−" may be appended to a long-term rating to denote relative status within categories AA to CCC.

Short-term debt:

A1+	extremely strong capacity for timely payment; equivalent to AAA to A+
A1	strong capacity for timely payment; equivalent to A+ to A−

A2   satisfactory capacity for timely payment; equivalent to A to BBB
A3   adequate capacity for timely payment; equivalent to BBB to BBB−
B   speculative and vulnerable. Speculative grades; equivalent to BB+ to BB−
C   currently vulnerable and dependent on favourable business, financial and economic conditions. Speculative grades; equivalent to B+ to C.
SD, D   selective or general default.

(b) Moody's

Long-term debt:

Aaa   best quality; principal and interest are secure
Aa   high quality; margins of protection not as large
A   principal and interest adequately secure
Baa   interest and principal security appears adequate but certain protective elements may be lacking. Lowest investment grade rating; has some speculative characteristics
Ba   moderate protection of principal and interest. Speculative grade
B   small assurance of principal and interest.
Caa   poor security; present elements of danger.
Ca   highly speculative; often in default
C   extremely poor.

"1"(+), "2" (neutral) or "3"(−) may be appended to denote relative status within categories Aa to Caa.

Short-term debt:

P1   superior ability to pay; equivalent to Aaa to A3
P2   strong ability to pay; equivalent to A2 to Baa2
P3   acceptable ability to pay; equivalent to Baa2 to Baa3
Not prime equivalent to sub-investment grades.

(c) Fitch

Long-term debt:

AAA   extremely strong capacity for timely payment
AA   very strong capacity for timely payment
A   strong capacity for timely payment but may be vulnerable to changes in economic conditions
BBB   adequate capacity but more likely to be impaired by adverse economic conditions. Lowest investment grade rating
BB   possibility of credit risk developing. Speculative grade
B   significant credit risk; capacity for payment depends on favourable economic conditions
CCC   default is real possibility; capacity dependent on favourable economic conditions
CC   default appears probable
C   default is imminent

DDD   default, actual or imminent; highest potential recovery
DD   default, actual or imminent; c. 50–90% recovery
D   default, actual or imminent; likely less than 50% recovery

"+" or "−" may be appended to a long-term rating to denote relative status within categories AA to CCC.

Short-term debt:

F1+   exceptionally strong capacity for timely payment; equivalent to AAA to AA−
F1   strong capacity for timely payment; equivalent to AA− to A
F2   satisfactory capacity for timely payment; equivalent to A to BBB+
F3   adequate capacity for timely payment; equivalent to BBB to BBB−
B   minimal capacity for timely payment; vulnerable to adverse changes in economic conditions. Speculative grades; equivalent to sub-investment grades
C   default is real possibility; capacity dependent on favourable economic conditions
D   default, actual or imminent.

Credit rating agency   One of the institutions that assign Credit ratings* to debt obligations of various entities on a basis of investigation, analysis and agreement with the debt issuer. Chief international agencies are Standard & Poor's Rating Group, Moody's Investors Service and Fitch Ratings (Duff & Phelps Credit Rating Co. was acquired by Fitch in March 2000, with the result that the two agencies have combined and harmonised their criteria and rating levels).

Credit risk   The Risk* taken by a creditor that a debtor will be unable to meet its debt repayment obligations on time (reflected in its Credit rating*).

Credit spread option   An Off-balance-sheet* (sense (i)) (i.e. unfunded) Credit derivative* where the payout is determined by the degree of worsening of the spread of the relevant Reference obligation* by reference to a benchmark security.

CreditMetrics   Methodology put forward by JP Morgan in early 1997 for calculating the Value at risk* on a particular Portfolio* of instruments or Positions* due to Credit risk*, using a combination of standard deviation and historical price-mapping models. Cf. RiskMetrics and CreditRisk+.

CreditRisk+   Methodology put forward by Credit Suisse Financial Products in October 1997 for calculating the Credit risk* on a particular Portfolio* of instruments or Positions*, using volatilities of default rates. Cf. CreditMetrics.

CREPON   CREST* Nominee* company that facilitates Settlement* via CREST.

CREST   Paperless LSE* Settlement* system (allowing for securities to become Dematerialised securities*), effective in the UK from July 1996, which was brought in to replace Talisman* and operates as a Clearing house*. Settlement takes place electronically, without stock transfer forms or certificates, under the provisions of the Uncertificated Securities Regulations 1995. These regulations were replaced by the Uncertificated Securities Regulations 2001 in order to enable CREST to take on the settlement of Gilts from the Central Gilts Office. Money market instruments settled in the Central Money Markets Office will be dematerialised into "eligible debt securities" and settled in CREST from late 2003 under the provisions of the Uncertificated Securities (Amendment) (Eligible Debt Securities) Regulations 2003. CREST is operated by CRESTCo, which announced a merger with Euroclear*, the Euromarket bond clearing system, on 4 July 2002.

Cross-default   An Event of default* in relation to a borrower, issuer, swap counterparty, etc. arising as a result of a separate default in payment under certain of its (and/or its affiliates) other payment obligations.

Cross hedging   An imperfect Hedge* of a Position* carried out by a transaction on an independent underlying instrument, the price of which tends to follow that of the instrument in which the position is held.

Cross-product master agreement   Or CPMA*. A standard form of umbrella Netting* agreement released by the Bond Market Association in February 2000, which is designed to work in conjunction with existing product netting agreements such as the ISDA Master* and IFEMA*.

Cross-rate   An FX rate* that is inferred from the FX rate of each of the two relevant currencies against an independent third currency.

Crystallisation   The revocation of the licence of a company to deal with assets subject to a Floating charge* in the ordinary course of business, at which point the floating charge attaches to the assets. A crystallised floating charge ranks after Fixed charges* created prior to crystallisation in order of Priorities* (sense (i)), but before fixed charges created after crystallisation. Crystallisation can occur in accordance with the terms of the instrument creating the charge, which may provide for crystallisation to take place on the occurrence of certain events, either by notice of crystallisation served by the creditor (see Semi-automatic crystallisation), or automatically (see Automatic crystallisation). Events causing crystallisation, other than those provided for in the charging document or Debenture* (sense (i)) are: (a) the making of a winding-up order; (b) the appointment of an administrative receiver; (c) the company's ceasing to carry on business; and (d) the taking of possession by the debenture holder. In theory, there is nothing to prevent a crystallised floating charge being "decrystallised" by reintroduction of a licence to the company to deal with the assets in the ordinary course of business.

CT   See Cedulas territoriales.

Currency protected option   See Quanto option.

Currency risk   The Risk* of a loss arising from exposure to an adverse movement in FX rates*.

Currency swap   A Swap* in which the parties agree to make payment to each other in different currencies of initial principal amounts (which may or may not be physically exchanged) set by the Spot* FX rate*, and of regular fixed rate interest payments or floating rate interest payments set by reference to their swapped currencies at rates designed in the same way as discounts or premiums due on a Forward exchange agreement*. The initial principal amount is re-exchanged when the swap matures such that the swap as a whole operates in a similar fashion to a forward exchange agreement. Cf. Circus swap.

Current pay   A form of Index-linked security*. Current pay securities offer intermediate inflation protection relative to the other two main types of index-linked security (Capital indexed* and Interest indexed*), as they are fully indexed to protect both interest and principal, but do not benefit from compounding as principal indexation is paid out over the life of the security. The stated coupon is paid on an accreted principal balance, and is also increased to reflect the immediate payment of that accretion (e.g. a 2% coupon when inflation is at 4% becomes a $[(2\% \times 1.04) + 4\%]$, or 6.08% coupon). The relevant increase in the RPI for a semi-annual pay index-linked security is calculated as the increase in the RPI over the period from 8 months prior to the relevant interest payment date (or the issue date) to 2 months prior to the relevant interest payment date (or the issue date). In this way, the level of the indexation amount that will be received at the end of the interest period is known 2 months prior to commencement of the interest period. The original principal balance is repaid to investors at maturity.

Current yield   The annual return or Yield* on a security, calculated as:

$$y = (r/p) \cdot 100$$

where $y =$ the yield expressed as a percentage
$r =$ the annual coupon
$p =$ the market price of the security.

Also known as Running yield* or Interest yield*. The annualised interest yield on discounted Commercial paper* is known as Discount yield*.

CUSIP   Committee on Uniform Security Identification Procedures. A CUSIP number is a nine-digit securities identification number allocated by Standard & Poor's for use in the DTC* system. See also ISIN and Common code.

Custodian   An entity that holds a securities account for a customer identifying securities belonging to the customer. May be used as the link between a customer and a Clearing system*, where the customer is not a member of the clearing system.

Cut-off date   In a Securitisation* transaction, the date on which the principal amount of receivables outstanding is set for the purpose of determining the amount of funding to be raised.

CVA moratorium   See Insolvency Act 2000.

DAC   Detachable A Coupon. Form of senior IO*, issued as a margin percentage amount payable at the level of the senior "A" class of securities issued in a (typically) MBS* deal. The margin percentage amount is payable in respect of the declining principal balance of the relevant "A" class. Often issued with a MERC*.

DAF   See Delivered at frontier.

Data Protection Act 1984   UK statute requiring that entities that held, in computer-readable form, data that related to a living individual, and from which the individual could be identified, had to be registered with the Data Protection Registrar. Failure to register constituted a criminal offence. Data could only be used for the purposes for which the entity had specified that it would use it, and could not be disclosed in a manner that was incompatible with those purposes. Repealed by the Data Protection Act 1998* (subject to transitional provisions).

Data Protection Act 1998   UK statute that was brought into effect on 1 March 2000 under SI 2000/183 (Data Protection Act 1998 (Commencement) Order 2000) to comply with EU Directive* 95/46 on the processing of personal data (the EU required implementation of the Directive by 25 October 1998). The act repeals the Data Protection Act 1984* (transitional provisions applied until 24 October 2001) and requires that entities ("data controllers") established in the EU or using processing equipment in the EU (e.g. a non-EU entity that has a web server recording personal data located in the EU) that control the purposes for which, and manner in which, the processing of "data" (information in automatically readable form or filed in a structured system that makes it readily accessible) that is "personal data" (data that relates to an individual and from which the individual can be identified) is carried out ensure that the eight data protection principles set out in Schedule 1 to the act are complied with (personal data is processed fairly and lawfully, data is obtained and processed only for specified purposes, data is adequate and relevant and not excessive, data is kept accurate and up-to-date, data is not kept for longer than necessary, data is processed with regard to the rights of the individual, there is adequate security protecting the data, data should not be transferred outside the European Economic Area unless the recipient territory has adequate personal data protection provisions). Transfer of data outside the EU has caused problems for US companies seeking to buy the rights to mailing lists or information gathered within the EU, as the EU does not recognise US privacy laws as sufficient for this purpose. On 15 March 2000, the EU and the US agreed a compromise on a "safe harbour", under which US companies that sign up to oversight by regulatory authorities in the US can receive such information. Consent from the individual is required for the use of data, and there are additional requirements for the use of "sensitive personal data". Individuals are entitled to see personal data held on them and to have it deleted or corrected, to know for what purposes the personal data is being processed and to what recipients the personal data may be disclosed or to object to its use for direct marketing. The act allows individuals to bring actions to claim compensation from the data controller for any damage or distress suffered as a result of the data controller contravening the provisions of the act. Data controllers must notify the Data Protection Commissioner – known as the Information Commissioner from 30 January 2001 – that they are holding personal data. The Commissioner has 28 days to raise any concerns about a notification, during which time the data should not be processed. Failure to notify constitutes a criminal offence. The Commissioner may take action against any entity that does not comply with the eight data protection principles. There are exemptions from the act for certain human resources information, corporate finance, legal privilege and certain regulatory areas.

Data Protection Directive   EU Directive* 1995/46 on the processing of personal data (required to be implemented across the EU by 26 October 1998). The Directive set out certain requirements for dealing with "personal data", including the requirement that personal data should not be transferred outside the European Economic Area unless the recipient territory has adequate personal data protection provisions. Prior to 2000, this caused problems for US companies seeking to buy the rights to mailing lists or information gathered within the EU, as the EU did not recognise US privacy laws as sufficient for this purpose. On 15 March 2000, the EU and the US agreed a compromise on a "safe harbour", under which US companies that sign up to oversight by regulatory authorities in the US can receive such information. Under a Commission Decision of 15 June 2001, the EU approved the form of its standard contractual clauses for the transmission of personal data to a data controller outside the EU. On 21 December 2001, the EU decided that the transfer of data to entities in Canada subject to Canadian data protection legislation would be permitted. Under a Commission Decision of 27 December 2001, the EU approved its second form of standard contractual clauses; for the transmission of personal data to a data processor outside the EU who acts on behalf of the data controller who has sent the information.

Day order   A buy or sell order that is conditional on being met in a particular session on the stated terms. Also known as Good for the day*.

Day trading   To create and Liquidate* a Position* during the same session.

Daylight facility   A very short-term Liquidity facility* under which Advances* are required to be repaid on the same day.

DDP   See Delivered duty paid.

DDU   See Delivered duty unpaid.

Dealer   A financial instruments trader.

Dealing date   See Trade date.

Debenture   (i) An agreement which creates Security* over all assets of a company.
   (ii) Defined in Schedule 1, paragraph 2 of the Financial Services Act 1986* (repeated at Schedule 2, paragraph 12, FSMA 2000) to include an instrument "creating or acknowledging indebtedness" and constituting a Financial Services Act 1986/FSMA 2000 regulated investment. The DTI* view is that Facility agreements* are debentures within the definition in the Act. This has led to concern as to the possibility of breaching s. 47 of the Act (s. 397(1) and (2) FSMA 2000) relating to misleading statements, or of unauthorised persons committing an offence, or of entering unenforceable contracts, if the "buying" and "selling" of such agreements are considered to constitute Investment business*. Syndication* (for a Syndicated loan*) is likely to be excluded, depending on the circumstances. Sub-participation* is seen as creating a new agreement without affecting the old and is thus not regulated. Assignments* and Novations* of existing loans, however, are potentially regulated in this way.

Debt–equity scheme   Governmental financial restructuring akin to a Debt–equity swap*, which involves a government debtor taking back debt of its own that is trading at a discount in the secondary market in exchange for equity in domestic companies, at a premium to the secondary market debt value, but a discount to the debt redemption value. Used to clear debt cheaply, as well as to encourage foreign investment at times when capital is scarce.

Debt–equity swap   Agreement between a company and its creditors to write-off debts owed by the company to the creditors in return for equity interests in the company (and the dilution of the shareholdings of existing shareholders).

Debt factoring   See Credit factoring.

Debt Management Office   See UK Debt Management Office.

Debt service coverage ratio   Or DSCR*. The ratio of the amount of available periodic earnings (usually measured by EBITDA*) within a business, to the required periodic service payments on debt within the company (both to cover interest and to cover any amortisation, Sinking fund* or Defeasance* amount). See also FCF DSCR, Interest cover ratio.

Debt shelf registration   A Rule 415* Shelf registration* with the SEC* of a general form of issue prospectus and issuing company information, in relation to a potential future issue or issues of debt securities, within specified limits. Cf. Universal shelf registration and Equity shelf registration.

Debt-to-income ratio   Ratio of the annual income of a borrower to the annual debt service (principal and interest) on a mortgage or other loan. Used in credit assessment as an indication of the ability of the borrower to make payments.

Decision   A type of European Union law*. A decision of the European Court of Justice, which is (a) binding in its entirety; and (b) specific to the parties (Member states*, companies or individuals) to the case in respect of which the decision was given.

Declaration of trust   A document which declares a Trust* over certain assets. Since the case of *Don King Productions Inc. v. Warren and others (1998)* (see Assignment), the UK courts have recognised a declaration of trust as being effective to circumvent a prohibition on the assignment of receivables by arguing that "a declaration of trust in favour of a third party of the benefit of obligations or the profits obtained from a contract is different in character from an assignment of the benefit of the contract to that third party" and that "whether the contract contains a provision prohibiting such a declaration of trust must be determined as a matter of construction of the contract. Such a limitation upon the freedom of the party is not lightly to be inferred and a clause prohibiting assignments is prima facie restricted to assignments of the benefit of the obligation and does not extend to declarations of trust of the benefit." The case puts deciding weight on the intent of the parties in inserting the prohibition, and on the fact that the beneficiary of the trust cannot interfere in the trust property. This suggests that future cases will be predicated on an interpretation of the intent of the parties in creating the contract, and their specific reasons for inserting the prohibition. The most likely reason for a party to insert a prohibition on assignment would be to ensure that they can continue to deal with the person they have contracted with. Other reasons could include a desire to preserve Set-off* rights against the party they contracted with, or to ensure that the positions of the parties are not adversely affected by an assignment (for example, the possibility that Withholding tax* may be introduced to interest payments made by a borrower under a loan, if the bank lender assigns its rights in the loan to a corporate entity). The case also demonstrates, however, that the court does not consider that a trust would significantly impinge on the relations between the parties, and if it can be structured such that any considerations that could be raised by the party who inserted the prohibition are covered, the trust mechanism should prove to be robust in a wide range of scenarios. Some trusts of this nature have been structured to split the beneficial interest in the trust so that 99% of the interest is held by the SPV and 1% remains held by the originator, in order to prevent the SPV becoming the sole entitled party under the trust and seeking to wind the trust up (which could bring them into direct dealings with the other contract party). Other mechanisms can be used to achieve this purpose, however, and it is arguable that even in the absence of such mechanisms, the court may consider that such a winding-up of the trust could not be carried out by the SPV due to the intent and effect of the prohibition. Structures have generally used Security powers of attorney* given by the originator to the SPV to enable the SPV to take enforcement action where necessary in the name of the originator, in order to preserve the "fronting" nature of the originator's role. Once the trust transfer is notified to the other contract parties, set-off rights will cease to accrue (and will cease for the purposes of Rule 4.90 immediately on trust being declared), as they would with an assignment. In cases where this can be considered to be the rationale for the other party inserting the restriction, this may therefore lead to construction problems that could prevent the trust operating as intended. Given the strength of the court's decision in Don King however, it may be that even in such a case an express prohibition against trusts would be needed to prevent a trust structure working. Furthermore, set-off rights are traditionally a tool of the banking industry, and while corporates and individuals may benefit from such rights on occasion, they are unlikely to be the reason for insertion of an assignment prohibition in many cases. The declaration of trust mechanism was formally recognised by the FSA* in 1999 as an effective method of transfer in their guidelines for banks on transferring assets Off balance sheet* (sense (ii)). See Assignment, Negotiation, Novation, Sub-participation, Subrogation, Transfer.

Deed A legal document recording dealings. Necessary to effect a conveyance or transfer of land (in relation to sales or dispositions (e.g. releases, mortgages, charges or leases) of interests in land, s. 2 Law of Property (Miscellaneous Provisions) Act 1989 independently requires that any such sale or disposition is made in writing and signed by all parties thereto). Otherwise used where dealings take place with no consideration, as dealings made by deed are binding without the need for consideration. An agency where the agent is to have power to execute deeds on behalf of his principal must be made by way of deed. Similarly the donor of a Power of attorney* must execute the power by way of deed under s. 1(1) of the Powers of Attorney Act 1971. Also any document creating Security* (sense (ii)) which is to rely on the s. 101 Law of Property Act 1925 Powers of sale* and appointment of Receivers* must be a Mortgage* or a Charge* made by deed. Actions under a "specialty" (a contract under seal) carry a 12-year limitation period (rather than the usual 6-year limitation period for contracts). A party is estopped from denying the accuracy of a statement of fact made in a deed (which can render a legal effect to the recitals used in deeds). All deeds are subject to the requirements of the Law of Property (Miscellaneous Provisions) Act 1989, which requires at s. 1(2) that the document must clearly indicate that it is intended by the parties to be a deed, and must be signed by one or more parties as a deed. Deeds executed by a company formed under the Companies Act 1985* in the UK must be signed in accordance with the requirements of its Articles of association* to be effective, although other parties are entitled to rely on due execution where the deed is signed by two directors, or a director and the secretary or where the company seal is used, by s. 36A Companies Act 1985. Deeds executed by an Overseas company* should simply be executed by that company in a manner which is properly authorised by the provisions of the Foreign Companies (Execution of Documents) Regulations 1994 (Statutory Instrument 1994/950) (which requires that the deed should be "executed in any manner permitted by the laws of the territory in which the company is incorporated for the execution of documents by such a company"). Deeds executed by individuals are valid if witnessed by a witness who attests the signature. Under s. 1(1)(b) Law of Property (Miscellaneous Provisions) Act 1989, there is no longer any requirement for a seal where a deed is executed by an individual, but a seal (or a blank seal inscribed "L.S." ("*locus sigilli*")) may be added if desired. Deeds must be executed and delivered to be effective, and become effective on delivery. A deed which is a Deed poll* is enforceable by persons not parties to the deed. A deed *inter partes*, or Indenture* (sense (i)), is so enforceable, but only with regard to interests or rights in land (but see also Privity with regard to the Contracts (Rights of Third Parties) Act 1999).

Deed of covenant   Used in a Securities* issue where there is no Trust deed* (for Registered securities*) or no intention to issue definitive notes (for both Bearer securities* and registered securities). The transfer by delivery of securities that are Negotiable instruments* acts to allow the new holder to sue the issuer on the covenant to pay written on the face of the note, but instruments that are not negotiable are not transferable by mere delivery. For issues in the form of a Global note* only the holder – usually the Common depositary* or other Custodian* – has the right to sue on the note. Registered notes are in any event not negotiable in nature. Thus, in order to ensure that noteholders acquire an enforceable right against the issuer when purchasing notes, a deed of covenant is signed by the issuer by way of Deed poll*, containing a covenant to pay the notes and expressed to be in favour of the noteholders from time to time.

Deed of settlement company   In the UK, an obsolete form of Company* and Unincorporated association*. Established as a Joint stock company* combined with a deed of settlement trust.

Deed poll   A unilateral Deed*, as opposed to an Indenture* (sense (i)). A deed poll is enforceable by a person not party to the deed as an exception to the doctrine of Privity* of contract. See Deed of covenant.

Deemed notice   The doctrine stating that registration of a matter with the Registrar of Companies* is notice to the world of such matter. The doctrine is removed by s. 711A Companies Act 1985* from a date to be appointed, but with a proviso at s. 711A(2) that this does not reduce any duty to make reasonable enquiries concerning any matter (i.e. the doctrine of Constructive notice* will remain intact).

Deep discount   Securities* that bear a low (or no) interest Coupon* (sense (i)), and derive all or most of their Yield* from being issued at a substantial Discount* (sense (i)) to their Face value*. Deep discount securities falling within a UK statutory definition were, until 1996, subject to a complex and often unfavourable tax regime. This regime has now been replaced such that investors and issuers are generally subjected to tax, or permitted to recognise a tax deduction (respectively), for notional accrued interest on an accruals or Mark-to-market* basis. Cf. Zero coupon.

Default In a Securitisation*, a payment due on one of the Receivables* which is unpaid. See also Delinquency*. In a trade receivables transaction, generally used where the receivable has passed its due date by more than an upper limit used to measure Delinquencies*, and by less than an upper threshold (often 120 or 150 days) at which point it may be written-off (see Write-off).

Default probability The probability of default of an asset, generally expressed as a percentage. See also Weighted average foreclosure frequency and Expected loss.

Default risk See Credit risk. May be used specifically to refer to the risk that a Credit event* occurs under a Credit default swap*.

Default swap See Credit default swap.

Defaulted receivable See Default.

Defease See Defeasance.

Defeasance A current provision of cash collateral or other security to be set aside for the future payment of amounts due under a loan or lease. May be used to take advantage of favourable investment rates. For example, the investment of cash in a GIC* at a rate higher than the debt interest rate, so that the payment into the account can be less than the amount of the principal or aggregate rentals due, while still enabling full payment of each cash flow as and when due.

Deferred purchase price Or DPP*. A method of providing Credit enhancement* for a Securitisation* transaction, by deferring the payment to the Originator* of part of the purchase price for the Receivables*, unless and until the receivables perform to a high enough level to justify such payment. May also be used as a method of extracting Excess spread*.

Deferred share A share with subordinate rights to, for example, repayment on Liquidation*, than those that accrue to Ordinary shares*.

Deferred start option See Deferred strike option.

Deferred strike option An Option* where the holder can set the strike price at a future date.

Degrouping Loans that are regarded as not being "normal commercial loans" run the risk of being treated as equity for the purposes of corporate tax company groups (see Group, senses (ii), (iv) and (vi)), potentially resulting in the borrower being degrouped under ICTA Schedule 18, paragraph 1. See also Distribution.

Delink See Delinked.

Delinked A Securitisation* transaction where the credit risk on the notes issued is not affected by a deterioration in the creditworthiness of the Originator*. Primarily this is due to the True sale* of the assets from the originator to the SPV for the deal, but it can be due to the provision of collateral (e.g. to support a credit default swap in a Synthetic* deal).

Delinquency Or Arrears*. In a Securitisation*, a payment due on one of the Receivables* that is unpaid after expiry of any terms of payment (for example 30 day terms for a trade receivable). May be divided into buckets (e.g. 30 days arrears, 60 days arrears, 90 days arrears). See also Default and Charge-off.

Delinquent receivable See Delinquency.

Delivered at frontier Or DAF*. Export delivery term of general trade use and defined in INCOTERMS* meaning that the seller's obligations are fulfilled on delivery of goods at a named frontier; but without having taken the goods through customs at such frontier.

Delivered duty paid Or DDP*. Export delivery term of general trade use and defined in INCOTERMS* meaning that the seller's obligation is to ensure that the goods are delivered across customs frontiers to the named place of destination in the country of importation.

Delivered duty unpaid Or DDU*. Export delivery term of general trade use and defined in INCOTERMS* meaning that the seller's obligation is to ensure that the goods are delivered to the named place of destination in the country of importation without being cleared through customs.

Delivered ex quay Or DEQ*. Export delivery term of general trade use and defined in INCOTERMS* meaning that the goods remain at the seller's risk and expense until delivered onto the quay at the port of destination.

Delivered ex ship Or DES*. Export delivery term of general trade use and defined in INCOTERMS* meaning that goods remain at the seller's risk and expense until the shipment arrives at the port of destination, where the goods are made available to the buyer. Contrast FOB*.

Delivery risk See Settlement risk*.

Delta The degree of Correlation* between each unit movement in the price of an underlying asset, and the movement in the value of an Option* (or other asset) derived from such underlying asset. When an option is deeply Out of the money*, the delta will be close to 0, while when an option is At the money* the delta will be 0.5 and when an option is deeply In the money*, the delta will be close to 1 (long Positions* or short Put options* will bear a "plus" sign, short positions or long put options will bear a "minus" sign). The delta of a Future* will be 1, as will the delta of the underlying asset. Hedged by buying or selling the future or the underlying asset, or the relevant number and type of options.

Dematerialised security A Security* for which there are no certificates or paper, as opposed to an Intermediate security* or a security for which individual certificates or paper have been issued to individual investors.

Department of the Environment statement see DoE statement.

Dependent rating A dependent rating is any entity or obligation, the Credit rating* of which relates to a payment obligation necessary to ensure payment to investors in a structured transaction such as a Securitisation*, or which holds cash flow collections destined for investors. Dependent ratings for a transaction will be determined by the relevant Credit rating agencies* when analysing a transaction using the Weak link approach*.

Deposit-taking   Deposit-taking is regulated under the general prohibition in s. 19 FSMA* (replacing ss. 3 and 67 of the Banking Act 1987) and s. 5 of Statutory Instrument 1992/3218 for the EU. Prior to the FSMA, the issue of Bonds*, Commercial paper*, Medium-term notes* or other securities risked constituting deposit-taking unless it was exempt under the Banking Act 1987 (Exempt Transactions) Regulations 1997. The Regulations (and a related Bank of England notice of 17 March 1997) provided exemptions where the securities (or the guarantor of the securities) were Listed* (and, for commercial paper, where the issuer or guarantor also had at least £25m net assets, and the paper had a maximum maturity of up to 364 days). The receipt of proceeds of issue of securities outside the UK – Jersey was often used – was also used to circumvent deposit-taking provisions.

The new Financial Services and Markets Act 2000 (Regulated Activities) Order 2001 (2001/544), article 9, provides:

"(1) Subject to paragraph (2), a sum is not a deposit for the purposes of article 5 if it is received by a person as consideration for the issue by him of any investment of the kind specified by article 77 or 78.
(2) The exclusion in paragraph (1) does not apply to the receipt by a person of a sum as consideration for the issue by him of commercial paper unless –
    (a) the commercial paper is issued to persons –
        (i) whose ordinary activities involve them in acquiring, holding, managing or disposing of investments (as principal or agent) for the purposes of their businesses; or
        (ii) who it is reasonable to expect will acquire, hold, manage or dispose of investments (as principal or agent) for the purposes of their businesses; and
    (b) the redemption value of the commercial paper is not less than £100 000 (or an amount of equivalent value denominated wholly or partly in a currency other than sterling), and no part of the commercial paper may be transferred unless the redemption value of that part is not less than £100 000 (or such an equivalent amount).
(3) In paragraph (2), "commercial paper" means an investment of the kind specified by article 77 or 78 which must be redeemed before the first anniversary of the date of issue."

Depositary   An entity that holds physical certificates and securities in safe-keeping, typically for a Clearing system*.

Depositary receipt   See Global depositary receipt and American depositary receipt.

Depository Trust Company   Or DTC. US Clearing system* for bonds and other securities. DTC does not take responsibility for monitoring buyer status and as a consequence requires Rule 144A securities being cleared through DTC to be traded in PORTAL (which only permits QIBs* to trade, thus ensuring that the Rule 144A resale requirements are met) or another self-regulatory organisation system approved by the SEC for the trading of Rule 144A securities (or that certain other requirements are met, such as the bonds being investment grade).

Depth of the market   The measure of whether a market is a Liquid market*, which will determine the volatility of the market, the width of price Spreads* (sense (i)) and the ability to trade large volumes quickly.

DEQ   See Delivered ex quay.

Derecognition   Accounting terminology for the removal of an asset from the balance sheet of a company. Usually used to refer to the desired accounting Off-balance-sheet* (sense (i)) treatment that may be achieved after a Securitisation* transaction. See FRS 5, FAS 125, FAS 140, IAS 39.

Derivative   An instrument that varies in value according to a particular relationship with an Actual* such as an FX rate*, Interest rate* or Security* (sense (i)). See Future, Option, Swap, Forward, Cap, Collar, Floor, Repo, Credit derivative. Derivatives may be void in the UK if they are considered to constitute Gaming* contracts, and other jurisdictions may have similar laws against gambling. Entities that arrange or advise on derivatives business may be required to be authorised under the Financial Services Act 1986* (replaced by the FSMA* 2000). Issues as to Insider dealing* may also be relevant for derivatives relating to equities. Derivatives are typically documented on a market standard form agreement such as the ISDA Master*, IFEMA* or ICOM*, each of which provides for a form of Close-out netting*.

DES   See Delivered ex ship.

Designated nominee account   A Nominee account* in which the holding of each beneficial shareholder is separately identified, so that the name of the Nominee shareholder* appearing in the company register is accompanied by the nominee's client reference number for the particular beneficial shareholder. This method of identification is designed to ensure that the beneficial shareholder retains his shareholder benefits in relation to his holding. Cf. Pooled nominee account.

Deutsche Börse   German stock Exchange*.

Deutsche Terminbörse AG   German financial Futures* and Options* Exchange*, centred in Frankfurt and part of the Eurex* alliance, together with Soffex*.

Diff swap   See Differential swap.

Differential swap   A Swap* under which the swap writer undertakes to receive LIBOR in one currency (usually Dollars) and to pay LIBOR in another currency with that payment stream denominated in Dollars.

Digital option   Also known as a Binary option*. An Option* with a discrete or fixed payment on exercise (based on meeting or not meeting a certain criterion) rather than a continuous or variable payment (based on the degree to which the payment conditions on exercise are within the strike parameters).

Dilution   In a Securitisation* transaction, a reduction in the value of the Receivables* purchased by the SPV*, resulting from the granting by the Originator* to the relevant debtor of a discount or reduction in the payment due, or from a Set-off* by the debtor of amounts due to him from the originator (or claims he has against the originator) against the amount of the receivable.

Direct credit substitute   A direct credit substitute is a commitment for, or provision of, cash or assets that is treated for Capital adequacy* purposes as a loan or guarantee (and is therefore generally capital-weighted at 8% of the counterparty risk weight of the party whose credit risk is being taken by the provider). A direct credit substitute of a capital nature is an item that is regarded as tantamount to the provision of equity capital and is consequently directly deducted from capital for capital adequacy purposes.

Directive   A type of European Union law* that (a) is binding as to the result to be achieved; (b) is applicable only following introductory national legislation, which national legislation when enacted should be construed so as to effectively implement the Directive; and (c) can be directly enforceable, in default of implementation, if sufficiently clear and precise, but only against the defaulting Member state* or its organs or emanations (i.e. "vertical" direct effect is accepted) and not against private parties (i.e. "horizontal" direct effect is not accepted).

Director   (i) A company officer, appointed to carry out day-to-day management via operation of the Board of directors*.

(ii) For the purpose of the definition of Close company*, means, under s. 417 ICTA, any person:

(a) Who occupies the position of director (by whatever name called); or
(b) In accordance with whose directions or instructions the directors are accustomed to act (although it is thought that the Revenue will not seek to bring professional advisers, acting purely in their capacity as such, within this head); or
(c) Who is a manager of the company (or otherwise concerned in the management of the company's trade or business) and who is, either on his own or with one or more Associates*, the beneficial owner of, or able directly or indirectly to Control* (sense (i)), at least 20% of the Ordinary share capital* of the company.

Dirty   A price quoted which includes an element attributable to Accrued interest*.

Discount   (i) The amount by which the Face value* of a Security* (sense (i)) exceeds its Issue price* or current market price. Cf. Premium, sense (i). Securities issued below face value are often used in the short-term CP* market. Prior to 1996, UK tax legislation did not permit a tax deduction for Short interest*, whereas it did permit a tax deduction as a charge on income for accrued discount paid on a security.

(ii) The amount by which the Spot* value of an asset exceeds its Forward* value. Cf. Premium, sense (ii).

Discount basis   The rate of return on a non-interest-bearing security, quoted as the percentage discount of the current market price from the Face value*. Can be converted to an Interest rate* by a Discount yield* calculation.

Discount house   A Discount market* institution that undertakes Discounting* of Ineligible bills* and Eligible bills* from banks or financial institutions funded by cash short-term or call deposits. The discount houses (or other Bank of England approved entities) may engage in Re-discounting* bills that are eligible bills to the Bank of England to meet liquidity shortages.

Discount market   The Money market* for the Discounting* of Ineligible bills* and Eligible bills* to leading financial institutions (in the UK, the Discount houses*).

Discount rate   **(i)** The Interest rate* charged in the Discount market* for the Discounting* of Eligible bills* and Ineligible bills* (of a short time to maturity) to leading financial institutions (in the UK, the Discount houses*). Rates differ for eligible bills, ineligible bills and Treasury bills*. In the UK, influenced by the level of the interest rate charged by the Bank of England from time to time for Re-discounting* eligible bills from the discount houses, which latter is the rate at which the Bank of England acts as Lender of last resort* in the discount market and which forms a basis interest rate in the market.

(ii) The rate at which cash flows are discounted in a Net present value* calculation.

(iii) The rate of interest on a discount security such as Commercial paper*, calculated by deduction of the issue price from the face value of the security, expressed as a percentage of the face value and annualised. The rate may sometimes be recalculated as a Discount yield*.

Discount yield   The Yield* at a point in time on a security that is issued at a discount from Face value* (sense (i)) and is not interest bearing. Typically calculated for short-term instruments such as Commercial paper*, as:

$$y = [(f - p)/p] \cdot (d_2/d_1) \cdot 100$$

where y = the yield expressed as a percentage
f = the face value of the security
p = the market price of the security
d_1 = the number of days to maturity of the security
d_2 = the deemed number of days in the year (360 or 365).

The yield on issue will be fixed by market conditions and thus the Issue price* is in fact calculated from the yield (rather than the other way around) as follows:

$$p = f/(1 + [(d_1/d_2) \cdot (y/100)])$$

Discounted pay-off   Or DPO*. A negotiated settlement, typically undertaken by a Special servicer*, to agree settlement of amounts due in respect of a non-performing asset at a discount in return for timely payment of the discounted amount.

Discounting   The sale and purchase, via Negotiation* or other Transfer*, of Eligible bills* and Ineligible bills* at a Discount* (sense (i)) to Par* (sense (i)) to a bank or other financial institution. In the UK, discounted bills may be discounted further to the Discount houses* in the Discount market* and eligible bills may be discounted subsequently to the Bank of England (see Re-discounting).

Discretionary further advance   In relation to a Securitisation* transaction, a discretionary further advance is a Further advance* that may be made at the option of the Originator. Cf. Mandatory further advance.

Discretionary trust   A form of trust under which the trustee or trustees have a discretion as to the payment and/or a discretion as to the Accumulation* (an Accumulating trust* or Accumulation and maintenance settlement*) of the trust income, or under which the payment of income is subject to contingencies that remain unfulfilled (as opposed to an Interest in possession trust*). Subject to inheritance tax at 10-year intervals on the principal amount of the trust property where the settlor was an individual or a Close company* (or a company which, if resident in the UK, would be a close company), as well as taxation at the basic rate on trust income (under s. 151 Finance Act* 1989) and capital gains (under s. 65 TCGA) which are distributed to beneficiaries and at the "rate applicable to trusts" (a higher rate than the basic rate or lower rate of tax) on trust income (under s. 686 ICTA) and capital gains (under s. 5 TCGA) that are accumulated.

Disintermediation   The process of removal of financial Intermediaries* between a party with funds to invest and a party seeking funding. An ongoing trend that is leading to the increased use of the Capital markets* to raise finance. Disintermediation is beneficial to financial institutions due to the Capital adequacy* costs incurred on loans. Due to removal of these costs, disintermediation may also result in a reduced cost of funds for borrowers.

Distributable profits   The part of a company's annual profits and Distributable reserves* that is permitted by the Companies Act 1985* to be distributed to its shareholders.

Distributable reserves   Previous years' Distributable profits* (less accumulated losses) that have been retained as reserves rather than being distributed to members and have not been converted to Undistributable reserves* by redemption or purchase of shares, Capitalisation* (sense (ii)), etc.

Distribution   (i) For the purpose of the Companies Act 1985*, under s. 263 Companies Act 1985, any distribution of assets, whether in cash or otherwise, made by a UK company to its members, except insofar as it represents a repayment of capital on the shares, or is equal to any new consideration received by the company for the distribution. Includes Dividends*. Distributions may only be made from Distributable profits* under requirements relating to the Maintenance of capital*.

(ii) For the purposes of Corporation tax* and the deductibility of Interest* as an expense, certain payments may be treated as distributions by the Inland Revenue rather than interest payments under s. 209 ICTA* in addition to those contained within the Distribution, sense (i) definition above – typically interest on quasi-equity securities (i.e. where interest returns are linked to the company's profitability; s. 209(2)(e)(iii) ICTA) and certain Convertible* securities, interest on securities at other than an Arm's-length* rate (on the amount of the excess over a "reasonable commercial return"; s. 209(2)(d) ICTA), and interest reclassified under the Thin capitalisation* rules. Payments of interest on a quasi-equity security or convertible security made to a company which falls within the charge to UK corporation tax are, however, specifically excluded from being distributions for this purpose by the operation of s. 212 ICTA, provided that the payments do not exceed an arm's-length reasonable commercial return for use of the security principal. Distributions by a UK resident company are not charged to corporation tax, pursuant to s. 208 ICTA*. Until ACT* was abolished, distributions also rendered the company liable to pay ACT on the amount of the distribution, grossed-up to reflect the ACT payable thereon. See also Degrouping.

Dividend **(i)** A Distribution* (sense(i)) to shareholders of part of a company's Distributable profits* in relation to each shareholder's shareholding. Dividends by a UK resident company are not charged to Corporation tax*, pursuant to s. 208 ICTA*.

(ii) A payment to creditors on the Winding-up* of a company, expressed as the number of pence in the pound payable to the class of creditors in question.

DMO See UK Debt Management Office.

Documentary credit A form of Letter of credit*, which is normally subject to the Uniform Customs* rules through incorporation by reference. A documentary credit comprises an arrangement by a bank (the Issuing bank*), on behalf of a customer, for immediate or future payment by the issuing bank (or for payment or negotiation (see Negotiation credit) by one or more Nominated banks*) against presentation of Drafts* or documents to the issuing bank or its agents, for the benefit of a named beneficiary or beneficiaries. The credit may be revocable (i.e. cancellable at any time) or irrevocable. If irrevocable, the credit must be honoured by the issuing bank or any Confirming bank* (and the beneficiary will have a separate right of enforcement against each of the issuing bank and any confirming bank) unless the documents presented are incorrect or inaccurate, or there is clear evidence of fraud. Used to provide payment for goods in an export transaction. The issuing bank is substituted for the buyer as the party to make payment to the seller, which payment is to be made against presentation of the documents representing goods that have been shipped and are in transit, rather than the goods themselves. It is thus similar in concept to a Payment against documents*, but does not have the problem of credit risk on the buyer that is involved in such a procedure. The credit is referred to as a Buyer credit* where effected in reverse (i.e. where the overseas party to whom the bank pays is the buyer, enabling the buyer to pay the seller).

Documentary credits give the seller certainty of receipt of payment, subject to the solvency of the bank, and the seller's ability to provide the necessary documentation within the required period of time. If an Advising bank* is used, this also enables the seller to present documents in his own country, which overcomes another disadvantage of payment against documents. They also provide a means of financing a transaction through various intermediaries, as they are frequently transferable (see Transferable credit) or divisible into denominated parts (each of which may be transferred to a different person) and may bear a delayed payment date (thus providing a period of credit) or allow for advances to be made to the seller (see Anticipatory credit).

DoE statement A statement of the Department of the Environment in the UK, made jointly with HM Treasury in November 1989, that any transfer of residential mortgages outside of the originator's company group should not be carried out without first obtaining the consent of the borrowers to the transfer. Consent may be obtained up-front by a general consent in the mortgage application form.

Domestic bond A Bond* issued by an issuer incorporated in the country of the bond currency and offered for sale to investors in such country, on that country's public market (as opposed to a Eurobond* or a Foreign bond*).

DOSM   Designated offshore securities market for the purposes of the Regulation S* resale safe harbour under Rule 904. Includes most Western stock exchanges of any size.

Double dipping   A technique used to claim Capital allowances* twice, in two jurisdictions, through different rules relating to determining the ownership of the asset in the different jurisdictions.

Double tax treaty   An international treaty concluded between two states for the purpose of removing or mitigating potential dual taxation of profits and the potential application, via Withholding tax*, Transfer pricing* or remission of profits rules, of both national systems of taxation to receipts arising in one state which are remitted to an organisation or individual resident or domiciled in the other state. Normally includes clauses dealing with royalties, dividends, interest receipts and corporate profits. The corporate profits provisions typically deem taxable in a jurisdiction any profits arising that are attributable to a subsidiary or "permanent establishment" (e.g. a branch) operating in that jurisdiction. Such profits are thereafter not subject to profits taxation in the other jurisdiction, which may serve to mitigate tax in the context of, for instance, the US "branch profits tax" or French withholding tax on branch profits. Double tax treaties are only ever relieving provisions and cannot operate to create or increase a tax liability.

Down-and-in option   See Knock-in option.

Down-and-out option   See Knock-out option.

DPA   See Data Protection Act 1984 and Data Protection Act 1998.

DPO   See Discounted pay-off.

DPP   See Deferred purchase price.

Draft   Alternative name for a Bill of exchange*. Often used in connection with Documentary credits*.

Dragonbond   A Bond* issued by an Asian (ex-Japan) issuer that resembles a Eurobond*, in that it is sold to investors located across Asia and is denominated in a non-Asian currency.

Drawdown   A call by a borrower for the payment of funds by a lender under the terms of a banking Facility*. Cf. Advance.

Drawdown date   The date on which an Advance is paid to a borrower on a Drawdown* request.

Drawing   See Drawdown.

DSCR   See Debt service coverage ratio.

DTB   See Deutsche Terminbörse AG.

DTC   See Depository Trust Company.

DTI   Department of Trade and Industry. UK Government department responsible for the promotion of enterprise, and for business development and regulation, which is headed by the Secretary of State for Trade and Industry.

Due diligence   The analysis and investigation of a borrowing company's status and the condition of its assets and liabilities, typically carried out in relation to a new Securities* issue, Facility* or other financing. Underwriters* are potentially liable in the US in connection with offerings of securities under s. 11(a) of the Securities Act* for misstatements in SEC* registration particulars and s. 12(2) of the Securities Act and s. 10(b) of the Exchange Act* for misstatements in offering documents. Due diligence may enable an underwriter to establish a defence to a claim under s. 11(a) or s. 12(2), and provide the underwriter with reassurance that it has minimised the risk of a claim under s. 10(b).

Similarly, in the UK, as underwriters may, by virtue of their use of an offering document to promote the sale or offering of securities, be considered to have authorised the offering document as responsible persons under s. 152 Financial Services Act 1986* and may thus be liable for misstatements in its contents under s. 150 Financial Services Act 1986 (repeated at s. 79(3) and s. 90 FSMA* 2000) (with regard to Listing particulars*) or s.154A Financial Services Act 1986 (repeated at s. 86 FSMA 2000) (with regard to Prospectuses*), they may undertake extensive due diligence to seek reassurance that a claim is unlikely. See also Financial Service and Markets Act 2000.

Duration   The duration of a bond is calculated as the weighted average time to receipt of the cash flow on the bond (interest and principal) in years, where each element of the cash flow is reduced to an amount in present value terms. The duration on lower coupon bullet bonds will be closer to their maturity, whereas amortising bonds with a higher coupon will have a shorter duration. The duration of a zero coupon bond will be equal to its maturity. See also Modified duration.

Dynamic pool   In data analysis, a pool of data entries which changes over time as new entries are added to the pool.

Early amortisation event   In relation to the Revolving period* of a Securitisation*, this is a trigger which will lead to an early termination of the revolving period. This is generally an event such as a deterioration in the quality of the receivables held by the SPV* (e.g. an increase in the level of Delinquencies* or Defaults*), a drop in the level of spread earned from the receivables, a failure to generate sufficient new receivables, or the occurrence of an insolvency-related event with regard to the Originator*.

EBIT   Earnings Before Interest and Taxes. A calculation of the amount of the pre-tax revenue stream in a business net of the costs of producing that revenue, but disregarding interest service.

EBITDA   Earnings Before Interest, Taxes, Depreciation and Amortisation. A calculation of the amount of the pre-tax revenue stream in a business net of the costs of producing that revenue, but disregarding other factors in the business such as financing costs and accounting (i.e. non-cash) depreciation and amortisation of debt and goodwill.

ECB   See European Central Bank.

ECGD   Export Credit Guarantee Department. UK Export credit agency* (and government department).

ECN   (i) See Extendible commercial note.
(ii) See Electronic communication network.

ECP   See Eurocommercial paper.

ECSI   European Credit Swap Index.

ecu   (i) European currency unit. Prior to 1 January 1999, the currency used by EU institutions as a medium of exchange and unit of account – the so-called "public ecu". Interest was charged at a weighted average of the rates on constituent currencies. Converted to the Euro* from 1 January 1999.

(ii) Prior to 1 January 1999, a basket of European currencies used as a contractual currency in certain loan facilities and other agreements (the so-called "private ecu"), which was either fixed as a certain basket, or linked on an ongoing basis to EU regulations on constituent currency weightings for the "public ecu" (see (i) above) (a "closed basket" or "open basket" respectively). Interest was charged at market determined rates, independently from the weighted rate determined for the "public ecu". Converted to the Euro* from 1 January 1999, unless the parties evidence a contrary intention (which may be the case for a "closed basket" weighting).

EDGAR   Electronic Data Gathering, Analysis and Retrieval system. Electronic filing system used by the SEC* for company reporting information.

EEA   See European Economic Area.

EEIG   European Economic Interest Grouping. European service provider entity. May have Corporate personality*.

EETC   Enhanced Equipment Trust Certificate. Form of ETC*. An Asset-based finance* certificate which finances the purchase of equipment. Typically issued in multiple tranches.

Effective 51% subsidiary   See Group, sense (ii). A company is an effective 51% subsidiary of a principal company under s. 170(7) TCGA at any time if and only if:

(a) The principal company is beneficially entitled to more than 50% of any profits available for distribution to equity holders of the subsidiary; and
(b) The principal company would be beneficially entitled to more than 50% of any assets of the subsidiary available for distribution to equity holders on a winding-up.

Effective interest rate   The Discount rate* (sense (ii)) which, when applied to periodic debt service payments on an amortising (see Amortisation) loan using an Annuity* basis, means that the Net present value* of the periodic payments will be an amount equal to the principal of the loan. Cf. Flat interest rate.

EFTA   See European Free Trade Association.

EFTPOS   Electronic Funds Transfer at Point of Sale. Funds transfer via a retail outlet card terminal system.

EGM   See Extraordinary general meeting.

Either-or option   See Alternative option.

Elective regime   A simplified, deregulated administrative regime for which Private companies* may opt in whole or part through the passing of Elective resolutions*. The elements of the regime are set out in s. 379A Companies Act 1985*, and consist of elections:

(a) as to the duration of the authority of directors to issue shares under ss. 80 and 80A Companies Act 1985 (see Issued share capital);
(b) dispensing with the requirement to lay Accounts* before the Annual general meeting* under s. 252 Companies Act 1985;
(c) dispensing with the requirement to hold an annual general meeting under s. 366A Companies Act 1985;
(d) reducing the minimum consent requirement for Short notice* under ss. 369 and 378 Companies Act 1985; and/or
(e) dispensing with the requirement to appoint auditors annually under s. 386 Companies Act 1985.

Elective resolution   A resolution under s. 379A Companies Act 1985* that must be passed unanimously by those members of a private company who are entitled to vote at a General meeting* where at least 21 days' notice of the meeting and the resolution was given (unless a Written resolution* is used instead), and serves as an election for the whole or a part of the Elective regime*.

Electronic communication network   Or ECN* (sense (ii)). An electronic securities trading network that operates as an Exchange* on an Order-matching* basis, and charges a commission per trade, rather than a bid-offer spread.

Eligibility criteria   Criteria relating to the Receivables* subject of a Securitisation* transaction, which are typically set out in the Receivables sale agreement* and concern levels of Delinquencies* and Defaults* on the receivables and the currency and terms of the receivables. Breach of eligibility criteria will typically require the Originator* to repurchase the relevant receivables.

Eligible bank   A bank or other financial institution that meets minimum central bank (e.g. Bank of England) criteria on Acceptance* (sense (i)) business and market standing and appears on the list of institutions approved as eligible, enabling Bills of exchange* accepted by it to become Eligible bills*.

Eligible bill   A Bill of exchange* that bears the Acceptance* (sense (i)) of an Eligible bank* and is traded in the Discount market*. The Discount houses* or other Bank of England approved entities may engage in the Re-discounting* of eligible bills to the Bank of England. Also known as Bank bills*.

Eligible liabilities   For the purposes of MLAs* and Reserve assets*, sterling domestic deposits with an original maturity of 2 years or less held by a UK bank. See also Financial Services Authority.

EMU   See European monetary union.

Enterprise Act   The Enterprise Act in the UK received Royal Assent on 7 November 2002, and different provisions came into force at different times between June and September 2003. As well as providing for the establishment of the Office of Fair

Trading as a statutory body to take over the consumer protection responsibilities of the Director-General of Fair Trading (which was established under the Fair Trading Act 1973 and was also referred to as the Office of Fair Trading), the Act provides for various reforms of competition and merger law.

Crucially, the Act also provides for reform to insolvency law in the UK from September 2003 to encourage the use of administration and voluntary procedures. The Act contains a prohibition on the ability of a creditor to appoint an administrative receiver except in certain cases, and develops more detailed provisions for the use of administration. It has been feared that the Act would damage the prospects for the whole business and secured loan securitisation market in the UK, as it introduces the possibility that a moratorium during administration could interrupt servicing and enforcement procedures in relation to a transaction. Historically in these deals, a floating charge has been granted to creditors to permit them to appoint an administrative receiver that would block the appointment of an administrator and any moratorium that may arise as a result.

The Act provides at s. 250 for new sections 72A to G to be inserted in the Insolvency Act 1986. New s. 72A provides that the holder of a qualifying floating charge may not appoint an administrative receiver of the company. A qualifying floating charge is defined in paragraph 14 of Schedule 16 (which is inserted as Schedule B1 of the Insolvency Act 1986) as a floating charge which expressly states that paragraph 14 applies to it, or which purports to empower the holder of the floating charge to appoint an administrator or an administrative receiver of the company, and which – either by itself, or together with other charges or security interests – is secured over "the whole or substantially the whole of the company's property".

Under s. 72A(4), the new provision restricting the appointment of an administrative receiver would apply to a floating charge created on or after a date appointed by the Secretary of State by order made by statutory instrument (effectively retaining the old rules for existing charges).

There are a series of exceptions to the new provision, which permit the appointment of an administrative receiver:

Under s. 72B and Schedule 18 (which is inserted as Schedule 2A of the Insolvency Act 1986), where there is security to a trustee/nominee/agent for holders of an instrument (or there is a third-party guarantee or security interest, or there is an arrangement involving options, futures or contracts for differences) under which a party incurs (or is expected to incur) debt of at least £50m (or currency equivalent as at the time when the arrangement is entered into) at any time during the life of the arrangement, where the arrangement involves the issue of:

(a) A debt instrument that is rated by an internationally recognised rating agency, admitted to the official list in the UK, or admitted to trading on a market established under the rules of a recognised investment exchange or on a foreign market (or is designed to be so rated, listed or traded); or

(b) A bond (construed in accordance with Article 77 of the FSMA 2000 (Regulated Activities) Order 2001) or commercial paper (which must be redeemed before its first anniversary) issued to investment professionals, high net worth individuals or sophisticated investors.

Under ss. 72C, D and E and Schedule 18, in respect of a project company (a company which holds property for the project, or has sole or principal contractual responsibility for carrying out all or part of the project (either directly or through agents), or is one of a number of companies which together carry out the project, or has the purpose of supplying finance to enable the project to be carried out, or is a holding company of any of these, unless in any of such cases it also performs another function which is neither related to any of these nor related to the project) for a public–private partnership project, a utility project or a project under which a party incurs (or is expected to incur) debt of at least £50m (or currency equivalent as at the time when the project begins) at any time during the life of the arrangement, where in each case a person who provides finance for the project has contractual step-in rights to assume sole or principal contractual responsibility for carrying out all or part of the project.

Under s. 72F, if the company is party to a Market contract*, or a money market contract or a related contract under Financial Markets and Insolvency (Money Market) Regulations 1995 (SI 1995/2049), or there is a money market charge or system-charge over property of the company under Financial Markets and Insolvency Regulations 1996 (SI 1996/1469), or the company is a participant in a designated system or there is a collateral security charge over property of the company under Financial Markets and Insolvency (Settlement Finality) Regulations 1999 (SI 1999/2979).

Under paragraphs 14–16 of Schedule 16, a holder of a qualifying floating charge is given the power to appoint an administrator selected by it on 2 business days' written notice to the holder of any previously created or prior ranking floating charges. This power may only be exercised when the relevant floating charge has become enforceable.

Under paragraphs 22–27 of Schedule 16, a company or the directors of a company are given the power to appoint an administrator selected by it or them on 5 business days' written notice to any person with the right to appoint an administrator or administrative receiver of the company. This power may only be exercised if accompanied by a statutory declaration that the company is, or is likely to become, unable to pay its debts and is not in liquidation. An administrator cannot be appointed for a company where a winding-up petition has been presented and has not yet been dismissed.

Under paragraphs 11–12 of Schedule 16, the court may make an administration order appointing an administrator on application by the company, the directors of the company or one or more creditors of the company, where the court is satisfied that the company is, or is likely to become, unable to pay its debts and that the administration is likely to achieve its purpose. The purposes of administration are set out in paragraph 3 as: rescuing the company, or failing that achieving a better result than winding-up for creditors as a whole, or failing that realising assets to make a distribution to one or more secured or preferential creditors.

An administrator may not be appointed while an administrative receiver is in office, unless the floating charge holder who appointed the administrative receiver consents, or the floating charge is in some way prejudiced (as set out in paragraph 39 of Schedule 16). The appointment of an administrator takes effect for an initial period of 1 year (under paragraph 76 of Schedule 16), subject to extension by the court or by consent.

Special administration regimes in relation to water and sewage undertakers, protected railway companies, air traffic services, public–private partnerships and building societies are preserved by s. 249 of the Act.

Under s. 251, those categories of preferential debt due to the Crown (the Inland Revenue, Customs & Excise and social security – set out in paragraphs 1 to 7 of Schedule 6 to the Insolvency Act 1986) – primarily PAYE and NI Contributions due in the last 12 months and VAT due in the last 6 months – are abolished. Other preferential debts (mainly wages due in the last 4 months and occupational pension contributions) remain as preferential debts.

Under s. 252, an amount prescribed by order by the Secretary of State will be ring-fenced in favour of unsecured creditors (and will not be available to holders of a floating charge to the extent that there are any such unsecured creditors).

Enterprise value   Or EV*. The value of a business, calculated off the total asset and cash flow base of the company (before reducing the figure to the value of equity in the business by subtracting debt).

Enterprise White Paper   A White Paper published by the DTI in July 2001 which provided for the Enterprise Act*, which introduced a restriction on the right for a holder of a Floating charge* to appoint an Administrative receiver*, although it will still be permitted in relation to certain transactions.

Equity capital   That part of a company's Capital* (sense (i)) which receives a return by reference to and subject to the profitability of the company. Cf. Loan capital*.

Equity kicker   An Option* to acquire shares which may be given in favour of a debt provider in highly leveraged transactions such as MBOs*.

Equity shelf registration   A Rule 415* Shelf registration* with the SEC* relating to a future issue or issues of equity securities, within specified limits. Cf. Universal shelf registration and Debt shelf registration.

Equity swap   A form of Asset swap* in which one party agrees to make payments the calculation of which are linked to the return on an equity or are tied to an equity index, in return for a smoothed payment stream. Generally the equity payor will pay over to the equity payee any appreciation in the value of the equities, while the equity payee will pay to the equity payor any depreciation in the value of the equities. In a Total return swap*, the equity payor will also pay over any dividends paid on the equities.

ERISA   Employee Retirement Income Security Act of 1974. US statute dealing with the investment activities of pension funds.

ERM   See Exchange rate mechanism.

Error rate   A percentage rate used to indicate the number of errors in a series of data fields as against the total number of data fields. May be extrapolated in data verification analysis to calculate the percentage Confidence interval* that the error rate on a particular pool of assets matches that on a sample taken from the pool. This is usually achieved with a data-sampling process comparing tape entries against the original loan files to either a 95% or a 99% confidence interval of a particular maximum error rate (generally around 2%). Assuming that the sample does not display more than a particular number of errors (dependent on the pool/sample size, confidence interval and error rate parameters), this should establish a 95% or 99% probability respectively that the error rate across the pool as a whole does not exceed that on the sample (this assumes a log normal distribution and is based on a mean observed deviation from the norm which enables 2 and 3 standard deviations to be plotted).

ESCB   See European System of Central Banks.

ETC   Equipment Trust Certificate. Form of Asset-based finance* certificate that finances the purchase of equipment. Typically issued in a single tranche. See also EETC.

EU   See European Union.

Eurex   Futures* and Options* Exchange* founded by an alliance between the DTB* and Soffex*. Rival to the Euro-Globex* alliance.

Euribor   European Interbank Offered Rate. The Offer* rate set by the European Banking Federation for interbank loans in Euro* from a panel of 57 banks. Cf. Euro-Libor.

Euro   The single European currency, introduced for Eurozone members for non-cash transactions on 1 January 1999, with a 3-year transition until all national currency obligations were required to be redenominated in Euro on 1 January 2002. The original 12 Eurozone members were Austria, Belgium, Finland, France, Germany, Greece, Ireland, Italy, Luxembourg, the Netherlands, Portugal and Spain. The Euro is made up of 100 cents and was introduced in the participating European states at the following conversion rates: 13.7603 Austrian Schillings, 40.3399 Belgian Francs, 5.94573 Finnish Markka, 6.55957 French Francs, 1.95583 Deutschmark, 340.75 Greek Drachma, 0.787564 Irish Punt, 1936.27 Italian Lire, 40.3399 Luxembourg Francs, 2.20371 Dutch Guilders, 200.482 Portuguese Escudos and 166.386 Spanish Peseta, and at a rate of one-to-one against the ecu*. EU Regulations* provide that references in contracts to ecu will be presumed to be references to the Euro, unless there is evidence that the parties intend otherwise (as may be the case with a "closed basket" ecu definition; see ecu, sense (ii)), and that no party will have the right to unilaterally terminate a contract for frustration as a result of the introduction of the Euro, unless there is evidence that the parties intend otherwise.

Eurobond   A Bond* issued by an issuer incorporated outside the country of the bond currency and sold to investors located outside such country, on markets centred outside such country (as opposed to a Domestic bond* or a Foreign bond*). This definition applies slightly differently to Sterling bonds, as London is the principal trading centre for all Eurobonds; thus, Sterling bonds issued by a foreign issuer are regarded as Eurobonds if they are intended to be placed outside the UK. Usually Listed* on a Stock exchange*. Eurobonds are Negotiable* instruments by market custom and care should thus be taken in including any terms in the bonds that are contrary to market practice. They are typically 5 years to 30 years in tenor, issued in small denominations, and unsecured. They are generally underwritten on issue. Traded mostly on an OTC* basis through a Clearing system*. See also Floating rate notes.

Euroclear   One of the two major Clearing systems* in the Euromarkets* (together with Clearstream*). Uses a Common depositary* as Custodian* for itself and Clearstream and operates from Brussels. Morgan Guaranty Trust Company of New York, Brussels office, acted as operator of the Euroclear System under contract until 31 December 2000, when it was replaced with a newly established bank called Euroclear Bank SA, which is owned by market parties. Euroclear announced a merger with CRESTCo, the operator of the CREST* settlement system for UK equities, on 4 July 2002.

Eurocommercial paper   Commercial paper* issued in the Euromarkets*, typically in US Dollars.

EuroCreditMTS   Electronic Quote driven* trading system for issues of Covered bonds* which are AAA rated and have at least Euro 3bn outstanding. Developed by MTS* and launched in May 2000. Cf. EuroMTS.

Eurocurrency   Currency held outside its country of issue, and made available for borrowing in the Euromarkets* (e.g. Eurodollars*).

Eurodollar   See Eurocurrency.

Euro-Globex   Futures* and Options* Exchange* founded by an alliance between MATIF* and MIF (the Milan futures and options market). Rival to the Eurex* alliance.

Euro-Libor   London Interbank Offered Rate for Euro*. The Offer* rate set in the London Interbank market* for interbank loans in Euro*. Cf. Euribor.

Euromarkets   The Capital market* for Eurobonds*, and the Money market* and Facilities* market for Eurocurrency*, spread through various financial centres (chiefly London).

EuroMTS   Electronic Quote driven* trading system for European government bonds developed by MTS* in April 1999. Cf. EuroCreditMTS.

Euronext   An Exchange* founded by an alliance of the Paris, Amsterdam and Brussels stock exchanges in September 2000. Acquired LIFFE* and merged with the Portuguese stock exchange in 2002.

Euronote   A form of short-term debt instrument, similar to Commercial paper*, but issued in reliance on the terms of a Facility agreement* such as a NIF*, RUF* or MOF*, so that the securities contain more standardised terms than commercial paper. May be bid for by a Tender panel* under the terms of the facility agreement or Underwritten* by a Syndicate* under the terms of the facility agreement.

European Central Bank   A central bank institution, established on 1 June 1998, which operates monetary policy from 1 January 1999 for those of the Member states* of the EU that have adopted the Euro* as their currency, in cooperation with national central banks under the ESCB*.

European Economic Area   Free trade area preceded by the European Free Trade Association, and consisting of Iceland, Liechtenstein and Norway as well as the Member states* of the EU*.

European Free Trade Association   See European Economic Area.

European monetary union   The merging of the national currencies of certain European states into a single currency (the Euro*), which commenced on 1 January 1999 for Eurozone members by the fixing of currency conversion rates against the Euro (although no currency obligations were redenominated at such point), and by the conversion of ecu* denominated obligations into Euro at a one-to-one rate unless a contrary intention of the parties was evidenced. After a 3-year transition period, all national currency obligations were required to be redenominated in Euro from 1 January 2002. The original 12 Eurozone members were Austria, Belgium, Finland, France, Germany, Greece, Ireland, Italy, Luxembourg, the Netherlands, Portugal and Spain.

European option   An Option* exercisable only on a specified date or dates. Cf. American option.

European Securitisation Forum   Organisation formed in 1998 to promote the development of the European securitisation markets. The forum published recommended minimum periodic reporting data for ABS instruments in June 1999 to standardise data and foster transparency in the ABS trading markets.

European System of Central Banks   An association of the ECB* and the national central banks of those of the Member states* of the EU that adopt the Euro* as their currency.

European Union   Or EU*. The union pursuant to the Treaty of Rome and amendments thereto of constituent Member states* in Europe into a single harmonised market-place, designed to promote free movement of goods, services, labour and capital.

European Union law   In essence, (a) the Treaty of Rome and amendments thereto (including the Single European Act, which extensively rewrites the Treaty) which are directly applicable and enforceable by or against Member states* or private individuals or companies if capable of being so construed; and (b) legislative instruments consisting of Regulations*, Directives* and Decisions*. These instruments are proposed by the Commission and are submitted in draft to the European Parliament, Economic and Social Committee (ECOSOC) and Council for comment. They are updated and referred to the Committee of Personal Representatives (COREPER) and then to the European Parliament once more, before being finalised and sent to the Council, who vote to accept or reject them. Recommendations or Opinions given by the Council or Commission are not legally binding. A resolution was put forward in the EU Parliament in December 2002 to rename Regulations as "Laws" and to rename Directives as "Framework Laws".

Eurosterling   See Eurocurrency.

Euroyen   See Eurocurrency.

EV   See Enterprise value.

Event of default   Typically the non-payment of amounts due on a Security* (sense (i)) or loan or other agreement, the breach of other terms on which the security was issued, the loan advanced or the other agreement made or the insolvency of the borrower or counterparty. An event of default will allow a lender to cancel any outstanding Commitment* under a loan and will allow a lender, investor or counterparty to Accelerate* a loan or security or effect a Close-out* under a swap or other agreement.

Evergreen facility   A loan Facility* that has no set repayment date (or a mere nominal repayment date that is only effective on the giving of notice) but that is repayable on a set period of notice (e.g. one year) being given by the lender to the borrower.

Ex works   Or EXW*. Export delivery term of general trade use and defined in IN-COTERMS* meaning that no delivery costs or risks are to be borne by the seller. The goods are simply to be made available at the seller's factory or warehouse.

Excess spread   In a Securitisation* transaction, the interest rate earned on the Receivables*, less the transaction costs (the cost of funds of the SPV*, the SPV's expenses, and any income used to repay principal due to Charge-offs* occurring). The excess spread represents the Originator's* "profit" on the receivables, and is returned to the originator as a fee or in another tax-efficient manner.

Excess-of-loss   The top layer of insurance. Unclaimed in the vast majority of cases, but, when claimed, usually fully claimed as a result of some kind of catastrophe. Otherwise known as Catastrophe* or XOL* insurance. The London market for excess-of-loss reinsurance, known as LMX*, was the victim of heavy losses in the 1980s, due to several disasters which were compounded where Names at Lloyd's of London featured on two or more Syndicates, each of which was reinsuring the others.

Exchange   An organisation that forms (and may also regulate) a market for the trading of standardised commodities, securities or financial instruments (e.g. futures and options) or stocks and shares (see Stock exchange and Futures exchange). For example, the London Stock Exchange* or the London International Financial Futures Exchange (see LIFFE). The terms of such trades are typically largely determined by the exchange. Some exchanges use a Clearing house* to settle exchange contracts, which body will then apply its own regulations on settlement and counterparty default – e.g. the London Clearing House*, which is used by LIFFE*, the IPE* and the LME*. Typical methods applied to limit default risk across an exchange include the use of back-to-back contracts, each counterparty contracting with the exchange or clearing house, instead of directly with the other counterparty. This enables the exchange to net-out gross positions through application of Set-off* (sense (ii)) across all contracts entered into by a party, on default by such party. Exchange access may also be limited to members who contract with non-member customers on a back-to-back basis, to further facilitate mutuality of obligations for set-off purposes. Margin deposits (e.g. Initial margins*) to cover Close-out* costs may be required of members. The Companies Act 1989* allows the set-off rules of certain exchanges to take priority to UK insolvency provisions. This applies to the main London Futures exchanges*.

Exchange Act   Securities Exchange Act of 1934 (US securities statute) requiring initial registration (potentially as well as any Securities Act* registration requirements) of securities traded on US national Stock exchanges* and the trading of equity securities of a US or non-US company, where the company has more than US$ 1m total assets and has more than 500 shareholders, more than 300 of which are US resident shareholders. Ongoing reporting requirements also exist for securities' issuers which are required to be registered under this Act or the Securities Act as reporting companies, via periodic filings disclosing facts material to the market. Filings are made annually with the SEC* on Form 20-F* for non-US reporting companies, or under Rule

12g3-2(b)* for issuers supplying Home country information*. Also governs broker and dealer registrations, the monitoring of stock exchanges, Stabilisation*, Insider dealing* and anti-fraud requirements. Anti-fraud requirements under s. 10(b) allow for the SEC to prescribe rules for securities offerings, in reliance on which the SEC has formulated rules such as Rule 10b-5*.

Exchange rate   See Forex rate.

Exchange rate mechanism   An Exchange rate* system, for European currencies, which fixed the currencies within a specified band of variation against each other. The precursor to the introduction of the Euro*.

Exchangeable   A Bond* which may be converted, at the option of the holder or otherwise, into a holding of shares in a company other than the issuing company (cf. Convertible). Conversion of the bond principal value occurs at a pre-set Conversion price* for the share (and at a preset FX rate* where the bond and the shares are denominated in different currencies), at a Conversion premium* to the current market value of the relevant shares. Coupon rates on the bond will be lower than market level for bonds to reflect the Premium* (sense (iii)) value of the embedded conversion Option*. Typically, however, they will be higher than the Dividend* (sense (i)) on the shares, to compensate for the conversion premium charged. A Call* (sense (i)) may be inserted in an exchangeable to enable the issuer to force conversion if the relevant share price reaches a certain premium over the conversion price (by the threat of redemption at a fixed value). A Put* (sense (i)) may also be inserted at a premium to par to provide investors with an all-in yield equivalent to the normal bond yield in the event that the relevant share price remains below the conversion price. No new cash is advanced on conversion (cf. Warrant). Anti-dilution provisions are also included, to protect the investor if the relevant shares are diluted in value by a Bonus issue* or Rights issue*. These will typically require the issuer of the exchangeable bond to pass to the bondholders on conversion any additional bonus shares that have been received, and may involve arrangements designed to ensure that bondholders can benefit from any rights issue allocation on the relevant shares. The exchangeable may or may not be secured over the underlying shares. May be quoted or not; if not quoted and not issued on terms "reasonably comparable" to those on which the company's quoted securities are issued, interest is liable to reclassification as a Distribution* under s. 209(2)(e)(ii) ICTA.

Exercise period   See Warrant.

Exercise price   See Warrant.

Eximbank   US Export credit agency*.

Expected loss   The level of anticipated losses on an asset. Generally calculated as the product of the Default probability* and the Loss severity* for the asset and expressed as a percentage of the asset amount.

Export credit agency   An entity, or a government department, that is typically government-owned and provides unconditional payment guarantees and insurance to the banking sector as well as Buyer credits* and low-interest loans, in order to back or finance export activities by exporters in its jurisdiction. See ECGD, FEC, Eximbank and Coface.

Extendible commercial note   Or ECN* (sense (i)). A form of Commercial paper* with an initial redemption date that precedes its final maturity date. If, on the initial redemption date, there is disruption in the CP issuance market, the maturity of the notes can be extended. Designed to avoid the need for Liquidity facilities*.

Extortionate credit bargain   Under s. 138 of the Consumer Credit Act 1974*, a transaction or group of transactions which requires "the debtor ... to make payments ... which are grossly exorbitant" or which "otherwise grossly contravenes ordinary principles of fair dealing". An extortionate credit bargain may be reopened by the court, which may require repayment of amounts paid to the creditor by the debtor, or which may set aside obligations of the debtor under the transaction.

Extortionate credit transaction   Under s. 244 of the Insolvency Act 1986*, a credit transaction which "having regard to the risk accepted by the person providing the credit" requires "grossly exorbitant payments to be made ... in respect of the provision of the credit" or which otherwise grossly contravenes "ordinary principles of fair dealing". An extortionate credit transaction entered into within the period of 3 years prior to the Administration* or Liquidation* of the company may be reopened by the court, which may require repayment of amounts paid to the creditor by the debtor, or which may set aside obligations of the debtor under the transaction. The provisions relating to extortionate credit transactions closely follow those relating to Extortionate credit bargains*, save that they relate only to insolvent companies.

Extraordinary general meeting   For UK companies, any meeting of the Members* of the company that is called and is not the Annual general meeting*. In the case of a meeting called for the purpose of considering a Special resolution* or an Elective resolution* at least 21 days' notice of the meeting must be given under ss. 369 and 379A Companies Act 1985*, and for other meetings of a Limited company* at least 14 days' notice of the meeting must be given, unless in either case sufficient consents can be obtained to enable Short notice* to be given.

Extraordinary resolution   A Resolution* of the Members* of a company which, under s. 378 Companies Act 1985*, requires at least three-quarters of votes cast in favour and which must be passed at a General meeting* where sufficient notice of the meeting and resolution has been given (unless consent to Short notice* has been obtained or a Written resolution* is used).

EXW   See Ex works.

FA   See Finance Act.

Face value   Also known as Par* or Par value*. In relation to securities generally, the amount stated as being payable on the security if redeemed at its scheduled final maturity date (disregarding any element of redemption premium or accrued interest). In relation to a share, the Nominal value* of a share rather than its market value.

Facility   A service or arrangement provided by a financial institution – e.g. a Committed facility*, Uncommitted facility*, Overdraft*, Swingline facility*, Liquidity facility*, Revolving facility* etc. Typically takes the form of a borrowing arrangement or an arrangement to provide Guarantees* or Letters of credit*. Documented in a Facility agreement* or the less formal Facility letter*.

Facility agreement   An agreement to provide a Facility*. Will provide for Events of default*, warranties, indemnities and covenants as well as outlining the interest and principal structure and repayment procedures for any amounts advanced. Cf. Facility letter. See also Debenture (sense (ii)).

Facility fee   A facility fee is a fee expressed as a percentage and payable on the total amount of a Committed facility*, whether or not any part of the facility is drawn. A facility fee thus takes the place of a Commitment fee*/Margin* (sense (i)) structure and is supplemented by a margin on drawn amounts so that the combination equates to the higher margin to be found in a commitment fee/margin structure. The separation of facility fee and margin helps a bank to participate drawn amounts (see Participation) at lower cost, through holding out the low margin alone as the return for such participation.

Facility letter   A letter providing a Facility*. Less formal than a Facility agreement*.

Factor   See Pool factor and Tranche factor.

Factoring   **(i)** The entrusting of the possession of goods or the documents of title thereto to a mercantile agent (the "factor") for the purpose of sale.
   (ii) Common terminology for Credit factoring*.

Fannie Mae   See Federal National Mortgage Association.

FAS   See Free alongside ship.

FAS 77   US accounting standard which was superseded by FAS 125* on 1 January 1997.

FAS 125   In the US, Financial Accounting Standard 125 of June 1996 (effective from 1 January 1997) on the transfer of financial assets, which was superseded by FAS 140* on 1 April 2001. FAS 125 required that in order for an asset to be considered Off balance sheet* (sense (i)) of a company for accounting purposes in a Securitisation* transaction:

(a) control over the assets or effective control (e.g. through repurchase obligations, or repurchase rights when assets default) had to be surrendered by the company;
(b) the transferee had to acquire the right to pledge or exchange the assets or be a qualifying SPV (an entity which is limited to issuing securities or certificates, holding and collecting financial assets and reinvesting or distributing proceeds) whose holders obtain the right to pledge or exchange their securities or certificates; and
(c) the assets had to be transferred beyond the reach of any liquidator or creditor of the company. If this was the case, the assets were granted "derecognition" and removed from the balance sheet, to be replaced with the resulting components of the sale, including any related commitments undertaken. The standard also envisaged Gain on sale* accounting. See also FIN 46, Substantive equity.

FAS 133   In the US, Financial Accounting Standard 133 on accounting for derivatives, which was implemented for tax years beginning after 15 June 2000. FAS 133 requires companies to account fully for derivatives in a separate section in their balance sheet and mark-to-market derivative positions. Embedded derivatives in structured instruments (such as the equity option in a convertible bond) may be separated from the bond for accounting purposes unless they are sufficiently closely linked to the instrument, and instead marked-to-market as an equity derivative. The standard has generated high levels of concern in the US, as to the effect on balance sheets that will result.

FAS 140   In the US, Financial Accounting Standard 140 issued in September 2000 to replace FAS 125*, which applies to transfers and servicing of financial assets that take place after 31 March 2001 (excluding some transfers committed to prior to such date – for example, further tranches of revolving transactions). The Standard applies to securitisations and to resecuritisation of existing deals. FAS 140 accords a transfer one of four treatments:

- Sale (if the requirements set out in FAS 140 are met);
- Financing (if the requirements are not met);
- Swap (for example, where loans are exchanged for notes); or
- Partial sale (if the requirements of FAS 140 are met, but the originator retains servicing or one or more classes of securities issued). In this latter case, the sold assets are accorded sale treatment, and the retained assets (i.e. servicing rights to the extent that a more than adequate compensation is received for servicing, or securities) will appear on the balance sheet.

To qualify as a sale, the transferor must:

- Surrender control over the assets, such that they are isolated beyond the reach of the transferor, affiliates, liquidator or creditors;
- Transfer the assets to an SPV where:

  - For a QSPE (see below), noteholders have the right to pledge or exchange their notes or certificates; or
  - For other entities, the SPV itself has the right to pledge or exchange the underlying assets;

- Not retain effective control over the assets via a right and obligation to take back the assets at a certain point, or a right to take back specific assets (other than under a clean-up call where the transferor retains or subcontracts servicing, but not where the transferor sells servicing); and
- Receive cash proceeds from the sale (as opposed to a note or interest in the assets). This requirement has led to the introduction of a second onward transfer step to an issuing trust in some bank securitisations in the US, where previously a "one-step" transfer to a subsidiary in return for a note would have sufficed under FAS 125.

A Qualifying Special Purpose Entity or "QSPE" is never consolidated in the financial statements of the seller. An SPV that is not a QSPE may be consolidated with the seller (see below). To qualify as a QSPE, an SPV must:

- Be "demonstratively distinct" from the seller (i.e. where it cannot be unilaterally dissolved by the transferor or its affiliates or agents, and where at least 10% of the fair value of its beneficial interests are held by entities other than the transferor or its affiliates or agents);
- Have permitted activities which are significantly limited and specified up-front;
- Only hold passive financial assets (i.e. where no decisions other than servicing are made by the QSPE – the QSPE cannot, for example, hold controlling equity stakes), cash and investments; and
- Have limited powers to choose when to dispose of assets, such that it may only dispose of assets if required to do so as a result of an event of default outside its control, or where funds are required on exercise of a put or call or predetermined maturity or liquidation date.

If the SPV is not a QSPE then it will be consolidated on the accounts of its majority owner unless it falls within FIN 46*.

If sale treatment is accorded to a transaction, this amounts to derecognition, and the seller is required to use Gain on sale* accounting. Some sellers have structured securitisations as financings rather than sales, specifically in order to avoid gain on sale treatment. This is due to the fact that gain on sale is disliked by the equity market as it generates current accounting profit from future excess spread revenue (leading to earnings volatility if default and prepayment assumptions in the gain on sale calculation prove to be incorrect).

On 19 July 2001, the FASB issued guidance extending the ability of QSPEs to dispose of assets, by allowing servicers acting on behalf of QSPEs to buy loans out of a securitised pool at fair value without prejudicing QSPE treatment. This followed industry concerns over the ability to dispose of non-performing loans in CMBS transactions.

FASB Interpretation No. 46   Or FIN 46*. Financial Accounting Standards Board Interpretation No. 46 on Consolidation of Variable Interest Entities published by the FASB on 17 January 2003, to be applied from 1 February 2003 in respect of entities created after 31 January 2003, and from the first fiscal period beginning after 15 December 2003 (originally 15 June 2003) in respect of entities created before 1 February 2003.

The Interpretation does not apply to QSPEs*. It does apply if an entity is a "Variable Interest Entity" (VIE), that is:

- Its equity is insufficient to permit the entity to finance its activities without subordinated financial support (for this purpose equity of less than 10% of total assets is considered insufficient unless the entity can demonstrate its ability to finance its activities, or it has at least as much equity as comparable entities which operate without subordinated financial support, or it can demonstrate that its equity exceeds its expected losses); or
- Its equity investors do not have votes, the obligation to absorb losses or the right to receive residual returns.

If an entity is a VIE it will be consolidated by the entity (the "Primary Beneficiary") that will absorb the majority of the expected losses of the VIE, and/or that is entitled to a majority of the VIE's expected residual return, as a result of holding "Variable

Interests" in the entity. If different entities absorb the losses and receive the return, the entity which absorbs losses will consolidate. If a VIE has no primary beneficiary it will not be consolidated.

"Variable interests" are defined as "contractual, ownership, or other pecuniary interests in an entity that change with changes in the entity's net asset value". Variable interests can include equity and debt instruments, guarantees, put options, derivatives, servicing contracts, leases and other items. For this purpose, an entity will consider variable interests held by itself and by its related parties (which include certain de facto agents).

In addition to consolidation considerations, holders of variable interests are required to meet disclosure requirements:

- Primary beneficiary (as well as consolidating): disclose nature, purpose, size and activities of VIE, carrying amount and classification of VIE collateral, any lack of recourse by creditors of the VIE to the Primary Beneficiary
- Holders of significant variable interests: disclose nature of involvement with VIE and when such involvement began, nature, purpose, size and activities of VIE, maximum exposure to loss as a result of involvement with VIE

FASIT   Financial asset investment securitisation trust. US statutory form of entity (which can be any form – trust, corporation, etc.) created for the Securitisation* of a wide range of debt obligations. The trust permits the Replenishment* of assets and the issuance of multiple Classes* of securities and can enter into swaps. The FASIT has Fiscal transparency*. Regular interests in a FASIT are classified as debt for tax purposes; residual interests are classified as equity.

Fast-pay   With regard to Asset-backed securities*, a tranche which, although ranking at the same level of Priority* as another tranche, receives principal sequentially before such other tranche prior to enforcement following an event of default, rather than pro rata with such other tranche. Cf. Slow-pay.

FCA   See Free carrier.

FCF DSCR   See Free cash flow debt service coverage ratio.

FEC   Finnish Export Credit. Government-owned Finnish Export credit agency*. Renamed as Leonia Corporate Bank plc in May 1998. Merged with insurance company Sampo at the beginning of 2001 and renamed Sampo in April 2001.

Federal Home Loan Mortgage Corporation   Also known as FHLMC* or Freddie Mac*. A US government-sponsored agency which, like the Federal National Mortgage Association*, purchases mortgages in the secondary mortgage market and issues Mortgage-backed securities* (at a slight premium to the rates obtained by the Government National Mortgage Association*).

Federal National Mortgage Association   Also known as FNMA* or Fannie Mae*. A US government-sponsored agency mandated to purchase mortgages from mortgage lenders (to maintain availability of funds for mortgage loans in the market) and to issue Mortgage-backed securities* (rates are at a slight premium to the rates obtained by the Government National Mortgage Association*). Cf. Federal Home Loan Mortgage Corporation.

FHLMC   See Federal Home Loan Mortgage Corporation.

FIA   Futures Industry Association. Trade body operating in relation to Futures* brokers and Futures exchanges*.

Fill or kill   A buy or sell order that is conditional upon the whole order being met on the stated terms. Also known as All or none*.

FIMBRA   Financial Intermediaries, Managers and Brokers Regulatory Authority Limited. One of the self-regulating organisations (see SRO) established under the Financial Services Act 1986*. Responsible for regulating pensions advisers, life assurance advisers and unit trusts generally. Memberships were transferred to other self-regulating organisations following establishment of the PIA* in July 1994 and abolition of FIMBRA in 1995.

FIN 46   See FASB Interpretation No. 46.

Finance Act   Periodic UK taxation and budgetary statute.

Finance lease   A Lease* (sense (i)) which "transfers substantially all the risks and rewards of ownership of an asset to the lessee" (as per SSAP* no. 21 in the UK) (e.g. maintenance costs) and is used by the lessee as the economic equivalent of purchasing the asset from the lessor on credit terms, but which enables the lessor to claim Capital allowances* on acquiring the asset on behalf of the lessee, the benefit of which can be passed on to the lessee as a reduced financing charge. To classify as a lease (rather than a Hire purchase* or Conditional sale*, that would shift capital allowances to the lessee), no right is given to the lessee to purchase the asset, but instead at the end of the "primary period" of the lease (where substantive rental is charged which serves to repay the purchase price and financing costs), the asset may be sold and part of the proceeds passed to the lessee as a rent rebate, or the lease may be continued for a "secondary period" at a nominal rent. In the UK under SSAP 21, it is presumed that a lease is a finance lease "if at the inception of a lease the present value of the minimum lease payments, including any initial payment, amounts to substantially all (normally 90 per cent. or more) of the fair value of the leased asset. The present value should be calculated by using the interest rate implicit in the lease." The present value is then entered into the accounts of the lessee as a capital figure. Cf. Operating lease.

Financial assistance   Under ss. 151 and 152 of the UK Companies Act 1985* it is a criminal offence for a company or any of its Subsidiaries* (sense (iii)) to give financial assistance (whether as surety, lender or donor) directly or indirectly for the purpose of a person acquiring shares in the company or of reducing liabilities incurred in such an acquisition. There are exemptions from liability for dividend payments, or where the assistance is given in good faith in the interests of the company for some other or larger purpose than the acquisition itself. There is also an exemption for Private companies* which follow a "whitewash" procedure (whereby the directors make a statutory declaration that the company will not be Unable to pay its debts* for 12 months after giving the assistance).

Financial Collateral Directive   The EU Financial Collateral Directive (Directive 2002/47 of 6 June 2002). Member states* are required to enact the Directive through national legislation by 27 December 2003. The Directive applies to collateral arrangements over securities or cash between two entities, where at least one of them is a financial institution, and the other is not a natural person. In relation to book-entry securities, the Directive sets out conflict of laws provisions which provide that perfection of any security interest and completion of any other steps required to make the security interest effective on third parties should be carried out in accordance with the requirements of the jurisdiction where the account is held, as should any steps for enforcement of the security interest. The Directive extends the scope of the Settlement Finality Directive*.

Financial covenant   An undertaking given by a borrower (typically in a Security* or a Facility*) not to allow its total net worth, interest cover, DSCR*, Gearing*, Leverage*, liquidity ratios, turnover, or other financial indicators, to deteriorate beyond set levels.

Financial future   See Future.

Financial institution   Term defined in Article 1 of Directive* 89/646 of 15 December 1989 (the Second Coordination Directive) as an undertaking other than a Credit institution*, the principal activity of which is to engage in lending and banking services (other than taking deposits from the public).

Financial Services Act 1986   A UK statute that came into force on 29 April 1988, and was superseded and replaced by the Financial Services & Markets Act 2000*.

The Financial Services Act 1986 established offences:

(a) Under ss. 3 and 4, of engaging in "investment business" (the activities of dealing in or arranging deals in regulated investments, advising on or managing regulated investments, or establishing Collective investment schemes*) in the UK without authorisation or exemption;
(b) Under s. 47(1), of recklessly or knowingly making a misleading or false "statement, promise or forecast" to induce (or being reckless as to whether it will induce) a person to enter into an "investment agreement";
(c) Under s. 47(2), of creating a "false and misleading impression as to the market in or the price or value of any investments" to induce a person to acquire, dispose of, or exercise rights in relation to, an investment (dealings in the market for a particular undisclosed purpose (such as a bond buy-back) or disclosure of relevant information to a limited group of investors may fall foul of this provision);
(d) Under s. 56, of making "unsolicited calls" from or into the UK, during which an "investment agreement" is entered into by way of business (subject to certain exceptions for authorised parties which are provided for in regulatory codes of business, such as calling a potential investor to discuss entering into an investment on a non-private basis); and
(e) Under s. 57, of issuing, or causing to be issued, "investment advertisements" in the UK without either authorisation, exemption or approval from an authorised person (distribution of Listing particulars* or a Prospectus* is exempt from this requirement). In 1999, the Financial Services Authority* published guidelines as to its treatment of internet advertisements placed on web-sites, which indicate their belief that advertisements on websites that can be brought up on a computer in the UK can be considered to be issued in the UK. In considering whether to take enforcement action under s. 57, the Financial Services Authority will consider,

inter alia, whether the advertisements are directed to individuals in the UK or promoted in the UK via bulletin boards, whether they contain disclaimers, and the risk to UK investors arising from the website.

The penalty for these offences was imprisonment and/or an unlimited fine. Agreements entered into with a party acting in contravention of ss. 3 and 4, s. 56 or s. 57 were unenforceable by such party. Regulated investments include Shares*, Debentures* (sense (ii)), government securities, Warrants*, ADRs* and GDRs*, units in collective investment schemes, Options* (over any other regulated investment, any currency, or over gold, palladium, platinum or silver), Futures* unless entered into for commercial purposes, Contracts for differences* and long-term insurance policies.

The Act also established under s. 62 a mechanism for individuals to claim damages for breach of the 10 core rules of the Act (relating to, *inter alia*, skill and care, best market practice, conflicts of interest, custody arrangements and Capital adequacy*) or for breach of the more detailed rules of an SRO.

The Act established a hierarchical structure for authorisation and ongoing conduct of a business that was reformed under the Financial Services and Markets Act 2000.

The old structure delegated authority from HM Treasury*, via the Financial Services Authority, to various self-regulating organisations (see SRO) and recognised professional bodies (see RPB). Bodies exempted from authorisation included Recognised clearing houses*, Recognised investment exchanges*, the Bank of England*, Lloyd's of London (in relation to insurance activities) and certain other institutions, but not UK Banks*. Under s. 5 Statutory Instrument 1992/3218, entities authorised as a Credit institution* in another EU country could carry on investment business in the UK. Under s. 5 Statutory Instrument 1995/3275, persons authorised as an Investment firm* in another EU country could carry on investment business in the UK.

In relation to the regulation of finance generally, prior to the Financial Services and Markets Act 2000, regulated businesses were divided for UK regulatory purposes into deposit-taking business (see under Bank), Investment business*, wholesale market activities (exempt from the Financial Services Act 1986 under s. 43 but regulated by the Financial Services Authority* via the Grey Paper and the London Code of Conduct), loans for less than £25 000 (see under Consumer Credit Act 1974) and insurance business.

Financial Services and Markets Act 2000   Or FSMA*. In the UK, an Act that was first published in draft at the end of July 1998, and received royal assent on 14 June 2000. The FSMA came into effect at midnight on 30 November 2001 (referred to as "N2"), following delays due to consultation and lobbying periods in the City.

The Act replaces certain provisions of the Financial Services Act 1986* regime and its wholesale/retail distinction, together with certain provisions of the Banking Act 1987 and the Insurance Companies Act 1982, and establishes:

(a) Under s. 19 (comparable to ss. 3 and 4 of the Financial Services Act 1986), an offence of a person, in or from the UK in the way of business, carrying on a "regulated activity" (to be expanded by the Treasury in secondary legislation, but including the activities set out in Schedule 2 of the FSMA – dealing in investments, arranging deals in investments, deposit taking, safekeeping and administration of assets, managing investments, investment advice, establishing collective investment schemes or using computer-based systems for giving investment instructions) without authorisation or exemption (this is referred to as the "general prohibition");

(b) Under s. 21 (comparable to ss. 56 and 57 of the Financial Services Act 1986), an offence of a person, in the course of business, communicating an invitation or inducement to engage in investment activity unless that person is an authorised person or the content of the communication is approved by an authorised person. If the communication originates outside the United Kingdom, the section only applies if the communication is capable of having an effect in the United Kingdom;

(c) Under s. 118, a civil fine (which can be unlimited) for "market abuse" – behaviour in relation to qualifying investments (UK traded investments) that "is likely to be regarded by a regular user of that market ... as a failure on the part of the person or persons concerned to observe the standard of behaviour reasonably expected of a person in his or their position in relation to the market", and:

(1) is based on information not generally available to those using the market but which would be likely to be regarded by a regular user of the market as relevant when deciding the terms on which transactions in investments of the kind in question should be effected;

(2) Is likely to give a regular user of the market a false or misleading impression as to the supply of, or demand for, or as to the price or value of, investments of the kind in question; or

(3) A regular user of the market would, or would be likely to, regard as behaviour that would, or would be likely to, distort the market in investments of the kind in question. There is a defence to market abuse for people who had a reasonable belief that they were not abusing the market, or who took all reasonable precautions to avoid engaging in market abuse. The Act was amended in May 2000 to provide for the FSA to authorise a safe harbour from the market abuse offence if the relevant party has conformed to the Takeover Code* (with the FSA the ultimate arbiter on whether market abuse has occurred, but required to keep itself informed of the way in which the Takeover Panel interprets the Takeover Code);

(d) Under s. 397(1) and (2) (comparable to s. 47(1) of the Financial Services Act 1986), an offence of recklessly or knowingly making a misleading, false or deceptive "statement, promise or forecast" to induce (or being reckless as to whether it will induce) a person to enter into a "relevant agreement"; and

(e) Under s. 397(3) (comparable to s. 47(2) of the Financial Services Act 1986), an offence of creating a "false and misleading impression as to the market in or the price or value of any relevant investments" to induce a person to "acquire, dispose of, subscribe for or underwrite those investments or to refrain from doing so or to exercise, or refrain from exercising, any rights conferred by those investments" (dealings in the market for a particular undisclosed purpose (such as a bond buy-back) or disclosure of relevant information to a limited group of investors may fall foul of this provision).

The offences in (a), (b), (d) and (e) are punishable by imprisonment and/or a fine. It is also an offence to breach prohibition orders issued by the FSA (where persons are not fit and proper to carry out a regulated activity), and a civil penalty can be levied for breach of statements of principle (on the conduct of authorised persons). Agreements entered into in contravention of ss. 19 or 21 without authorisation or exemption are unenforceable by the contravening party.

Persons exempted from authorisation included Recognised clearing houses* and Recognised investment exchanges* (under s. 285) and other bodies prescribed by the Treasury (under s. 38). Authorised persons include persons who have applied for and received permission to carry on regulated activities (under the procedure and threshold conditions set out in ss. 40, 41 and Schedule 6 of the Act) and entities authorised as a Credit institution* or Investment firm* in another EU country. The Act establishes a single regulator, the Financial Services Authority*, with effect from N2, together with a first instance disciplinary tribunal, the Financial Services and Markets Tribunal (to which contested decisions of the FSA may be referred by the complainant).

Investments include Shares*, Debentures* (sense (ii)), loan stock, Bonds*, Certificates of deposit* and any other instruments creating or acknowledging a present or future indebtedness, government and public securities, Warrants* or other instruments entitling the holder to subscribe for any investment, Depositary receipts* (certificates representing securities), units in collective investment schemes, Options* to acquire or dispose of property, Futures*, Contracts for differences*, insurance contracts, participations in Lloyd's syndicates, deposits, mortgage lending (loans secured on land), and any right or interest in anything that is an investment.

Deposit-taking is regulated under the general prohibition in s. 19 FSMA (replacing ss. 3 and 67 of the Banking Act 1987) and s. 5 of Statutory Instrument 1992/3218 for the EU. Under the Financial Services Act 1986, the issue of Bonds*, Commercial paper*, Medium-term notes* or other securities risked constituting deposit-taking unless it was exempt under the Banking Act 1987 (Exempt Transactions) Regulations 1997. The receipt of proceeds of issue of securities outside the UK (e.g. Jersey) was sometimes used to circumvent deposit-taking provisions. The new Financial Services and Markets Act 2000 (Regulated Activities) Order 2001 (2001/544), Article 9, provides:

"(1) Subject to paragraph (2), a sum is not a deposit for the purposes of article 5 if it is received by a person as consideration for the issue by him of any investment of the kind specified by article 77 or 78.

(2) The exclusion in paragraph (1) does not apply to the receipt by a person of a sum as consideration for the issue by him of commercial paper unless –
(a) the commercial paper is issued to persons –
(i) whose ordinary activities involve them in acquiring, holding, managing or disposing of investments (as principal or agent) for the purposes of their businesses; or
(ii) who it is reasonable to expect will acquire, hold, manage or dispose of investments (as principal or agent) for the purposes of their businesses; and
(b) the redemption value of the commercial paper is not less than £100 000 (or an amount of equivalent value denominated wholly or partly in a currency other than sterling), and no part of the commercial paper may be transferred unless

the redemption value of that part is not less than £100 000 (or such an equivalent amount).

(3) In paragraph (2), "commercial paper" means an investment of the kind specified by article 77 or 78 which must be redeemed before the first anniversary of the date of issue."

Mortgage lending is regulated under the FSMA from "N3" on 31 October 2004. Regulated activities include lending under a regulated mortgage, advising on a regulated mortgage (advising was not originally intended to be regulated but was included from 12 December 2001) and administering (servicing or enforcing) a regulated mortgage. Regulated mortgages are mortgages where:

- The borrower is an individual;
- The mortgage is entered into on or after N3 and the borrower is in the UK at the time;
- The lender has a first charge over property in the UK;
- The property is at least 40% occupied by the borrower or his family.

Mortgage lenders will have to be authorised by the FSA. They will be subject to the rules on advertising and enforcement set out in the Mortgage Sourcebook published by the FSA, as well as minimum capital requirements (either 1% of total assets or 20% of total income, with a minimum of £100 000). The Sourcebook also sets out formalities for mortgage origination and servicing and a cooling-off period for mortgage loans other than for purchase of a property.

Mortgage securitisation SPVs are not subject to regulation for administering regulated mortgages, provided that they make use of the exemption set out in Article 62 of the Financial Services and Markets Act 2000 (Regulated Activities) Order 2001 (as interpreted in the Mortgage Sourcebook), which exempts from authorisation a non-authorised person who arranges for an authorised mortgage administrator to administer mortgages.

Regulated mortgages will not fall within the ambit of the Consumer Credit Act 1974. Other consumer credit instruments will remain regulated by the CCA 1974.

Stabilisation* provisions apply from N2 on the purchase or sale of new securities in a way designed to stabilise their price on initial distribution into the market. A new subscription should comply with FSMA conduct of business rules on stabilisation set under s. 144 FSMA (allowing use of a safe harbour under s. 397(4) FSMA), or any stabilisation activities subsequently carried out may constitute a criminal offence under s. 397(3) FSMA.

Listing requirements are set out in Part VI of the FSMA. Listing particulars are subject to disclosure on specific details as set out in the Listing rules*, as well as to an overriding duty under s. 80 FSMA to disclose all information investors would reasonably expect and require to find therein, with liability to compensate investors under s. 90 FSMA on responsible persons as specified in s. 79(3) FSMA (under regulations to be given by the Treasury) for any loss they suffer as a result of untrue or misleading statements in the particulars or the omission of relevant details. Listing particulars must be registered at Companies House under s. 83 FSMA, breach of which requirement is a criminal offence. Listing particulars may also give rise to general criminal liability under s. 397 FSMA for misleading or false statements.

The FSA will also be empowered to bring criminal actions in Money laundering* and/or Insider dealing* cases.

Financial Services Authority   Or FSA*. Prior to the renaming of the FSA in October 1997, it was called the SIB*, and had authority under the Financial Services Act 1986* to grant recognition to self-regulating organisations (see SRO) and recognised professional bodies (see RPB). Under the Financial Services and Markets Act 2000* or FSMA, the supervisory and Capital adequacy* regulatory functions of the SROs were rolled into the FSA from midnight on the 30 November 2001 (referred to as "N2"), together with the powers of the DTI* to regulate insurance companies and of the Building Societies Commission to regulate Building societies*. In addition, the supervisory and Capital adequacy* regulatory role of the Bank of England* over Banks* and wholesale markets passed to the FSA with the entry into force of the Bank of England Act 1998 on 1 June 1998, and the FSA (referred to as the UK Listing Authority or UKLA when acting in this capacity) replaced the London Stock Exchange* as listing authority from 1 May 2000, when the regulatory portion of the Yellow Book* was replaced by the new UKLA Listing Rules. The new conduct of business rules to apply to firms regulated by the FSA were subject to transitional arrangements from N2 until 30 June 2002. The new Integrated Prudential Handbook (which updates capital standards to reflect the latest market proposals, and sets out in one book the capital standards for all FSA-regulated businesses) was published in draft in June 2001. It was intended to come into effect at the same time as the new Basel capital rules and the new EU capital rules in 2004, until implementation of the Basel rules were postponed to 2005. The FSA is to regulate the investment industry generally in accordance with four main principles of: maintaining confidence in the financial system, promoting public understanding of the system, protecting consumers and reducing opportunities for criminal activity. From 1 June 1998, the FSA charges UK deposit-taking institutions a fee as a percentage of Eligible liabilities* (20% of this fee for other European Economic Area institutions with a UK branch) at a certain fraction of a basis point. The charge is also levied at one-third of such rate on non-Sterling deposits which are otherwise eligible liabilities. This charge arises in addition to the cost of holding MLAs*.

Financial Services Modernisation Act   See Gramm–Leach–Bliley Act.

Financial year   (i) Also known as an Accounting period* or Accounting reference period*. For the purpose of the preparation of Statutory accounts* in the UK, one of consecutive periods that fall between Accounting reference dates* for a company (although the directors may resolve under s. 223 Companies Act 1985* to end each financial year up to 7 days before or after the relevant accounting reference date). This sets the period for calculating accounting profits for determining taxable profits for Corporation tax* purposes, which profits are then apportioned between taxation Financial years (see sense (ii) below) to determine tax rates and bandings.

(ii) For UK Corporation tax* purposes, the period from 1 April in one year to 31 March in the following year used for the purpose of determining the appropriate rates of taxation and tax bandings for taxable profit, on apportionment of profit earned over the relevant company's Financial years (see sense (i) above) falling within such period.

Firm   (i) An organisation operating as a Partnership* rather than as a Corporation*. (ii) A loose generic term for any kind of business entity.

Firm order   An order that does not require confirmation to be sought, provided that it is carried out within the stated time limit.

First loss   In a Securitisation*, the first layer of Credit enhancement*. Defined in Financial Services Authority* guidelines as a "substantial" layer that covers some multiple of historic losses.

Fiscal agent   In a Bond* or FRN* issue, an Agent* of the issuer acting largely as principal Paying agent*. Cf. Trustee.

Fiscal transparency   An attribute of certain entities or organisations whereby tax authorities will "look through" the organisational structure to the individual members, and raise no tax assessment on the organisation, instead assessing the individual members on their respective interests in the organisation. Partnerships* generally have fiscal transparency and Bare trusts* may have, depending on the structure of the trust. Cf. Pass-through (sense (i)).

Fixed allocation percentage   Or Principal allocation percentage*. A percentage figure used in credit card Securitisation* structures after the end of the Revolving period* instead of the Floating allocation percentage* to divide principal receipts (interest receipts continue to be divided on the basis of the floating allocation percentage) between the Seller interest* and the Investor interest* – i.e the portion of the Receivables* intended to be beneficially owned by the SPV* and the portion owned by the Originator*, generally formulated as:

$$(PAO \text{ Funding Fixed}/PAO \text{ Receivables}) \cdot 100$$

where   PAO Funding Fixed = the investor principal funding remaining outstanding at the end of the revolving period
   PAO Receivables = receivables principal outstanding at the end of the previous period.

The percentage enables allocation of collections (and hence, Charge-offs*) on the receivables to continue to be made *pari passu* between investors and the originator after the end of the revolving period, when Amortisation* of the investor principal commences, while stepping-down the investor principal outstanding by a fixed amount each period.

Fixed charge   A Charge* which attaches to the charged assets immediately on creation, preventing disposal of the assets without the consent of the chargee and appropriating the assets to the satisfaction of the debt secured by the fixed charge. The degree of control residing in the chargee is a crucial factor in determining whether a so-called fixed charge is in fact fixed, or whether it is a Floating charge* (see under Floating charge for further discussion).

Fixed price re-offer   A fixed price, set in advance of a new Bond* or FRN* issue, at which subscribers to notes of the issue agree to initially re-offer the notes in the Primary placement* following the close of the issue. The fixed price re-offer system was introduced in the Eurobond* market in 1989 to secure investor support in the primary placement and to promote greater market transparency, although the system has recently come under abuse, with banks re-offering at lower prices in some cases. Once the Securities are placed, prices are freed for Secondary market* trading.

Fixed rate   An Interest rate* that is only reset at intervals of more than 1 year.

FLAP   See Floating allocation percentage.

Flat interest rate   The percentage rate applied to the original principal amount of an amortising (see Amortisation) loan over its term to determine the total amount of the financing charge. An approximate method of converting this to an Effective interest rate* over the number of compounding periods in the term of the loan in order to reflect the amortising nature of the loan is:

$$e = f \cdot [2n/(n+1)]$$

where e = the effective interest rate
f = the flat interest rate
n = the number of compounding periods.

Flawed asset   An agreement that a financial asset such as a bank account will not mature until certain specified events have occurred, thus preventing the account bank from being obliged to repay the deposit to the depositor. Often used where a bank requires some kind of control in relation to funds deposited with it until rights of Set-off* can be exercised, or where insolvency Set-off* is not applicable on the grounds of a lack of mutuality, and due to problems with normal Security* interests over such funds arising from the Charge Card* case (which has now been overruled). In *Morris and Others v. Agrichemicals Limited (1995)* (also known as *BCCI No. 8*) the Court of Appeal confirmed the effectiveness of flawed asset language as against a liquidator of the depositor in allowing the lender to retain the deposit unless and until the loan is repaid.

Floating allocation percentage   A percentage figure used in credit card Securitisation* structures to divide receipts between the Seller interest* and the Investor interest* – i.e the portion of the Receivables* intended to be beneficially owned by the SPV* and the portion owned by the Originator*, generally formulated as:

(PAO Funding/PAO Receivables) · 100

where   PAO Funding   = the investor principal funding remaining outstanding at the end of the previous period
PAO Receivables = receivables principal outstanding at the end of the previous period.

The percentage enables allocation of collections (and hence, Charge-offs*) on the receivables to be made *pari passu* between investors and the originator, with the subordinated investors who are funding part of the investor interest then suffering the first loss on the securitised portion of the pool. In partially asset-backed Future flows* transactions, the originator will typically be fully subordinated to any investor interest and take the first loss on the receivables directly. In such a case, the use of a floating allocation percentage is not necessary, with a simple order of priorities used where the investors rank above the originator in priority. Cf. Fixed allocation percentage.

Floating charge A Charge* over a class of assets that allows the Chargor* a licence to deal with the assets in the ordinary course of business until Crystallisation* of the charge, at which point the licence is revoked and the charge attaches to the assets. The classic indicators of a floating charge are set out in *Re Yorkshire Woolcombers Association Limited [1903] 2 Ch. 284*, namely that a floating charge is:

(a) a charge over a present or future class of assets;
(b) the class of assets that changes in the ordinary course of business;
(c) the class with which the chargor is to be allowed to deal.

Re Brightlife Limited [1987] Ch. 200 and *Siebe Gorman [1979] 2 Lloyd's Rep. 142* stressed that a charge described as fixed may nevertheless be floating in nature if insufficient control over the charged assets is exerted for the charge to be compatible in nature with a fixed charge. Dealing in particular with book debts, the cases stressed payment of proceeds of book debts into an account with the chargee (where, impliedly, the chargee would be able to exercise certain controls over the proceeds), or into an account over which the chargor's rights would be restricted unless and until a direction to the contrary was actively given by the chargee (as opposed to a "passive" situation where the chargor is free to deal unless and until the chargee directs otherwise), was essential to create a fixed charge.

Re New Bullas Trading Limited [1994] BCC 36 held that, where it is so specified by the contracting parties, it is possible for them to create a charge over book debts which is split in form, being fixed over the debts themselves, and floating over the proceeds realised from the collection thereof, without a lack of control over the proceeds being inconsistent with the nature of a fixed charge over the book debts themselves. That such a split charge is possible was, however, disputed in obiter dicta of Millett LJ in *Royal Trust Bank v. National Westminster Bank PLC (1996)*. It was further held by Millett LJ in *Re Cosslett (Contractors) Ltd [1997] 4 All ER 115* that: "The essence of a fixed charge is that the charge is on a particular asset or class of assets which the chargor cannot deal with free from the charge without the consent of the chargee. The question is not whether the chargor has complete freedom to carry on his business as he chooses, but whether the chargee is in control of the charged assets."

In *Agnew & Bearsley v. The Commissioner of Inland Revenue; Re Brumark Investments Ltd* (a case referred from New Zealand) on 5 June 2001, the Privy Council was asked to consider the case of a debenture drafted to give a split charge – fixed over book debts and floating over the proceeds of collection of the book debts, similar to New Bullas. The line of authority prior to New Bullas was supported (and New Bullas was overruled) by the Privy Council, where Lord Millett held that "While a debt and its proceeds are two separate assets, ... the latter are merely the traceable proceeds of the former and represent its entire value. A debt is a receivable; it is merely a right to receive payment from the debtor. Such a right cannot be enjoyed in specie; its value can be exploited only by exercising the right or by assigning it for value to a third party. ... Any attempt in the present context to separate the ownership of the debts from the ownership of their proceeds (even if conceptually possible) makes no commercial sense."

The Privy Council in Brumark further elaborated the requirements for a charge to constitute a fixed charge, with Lord Millett stating that "In deciding whether a charge is a fixed charge or a floating charge, the Court ... must construe the instrument of charge and seek to gather the intentions of the parties from the language they have used. But the object ... is not to discover whether the parties intended to create a fixed or a floating charge. It is to ascertain the nature of the rights and obligations which the parties intended to grant each other in respect of the charged assets. If their intention ... is to grant the company rights in respect of the charged assets which are inconsistent with the nature of a fixed charge, then the charge cannot be a fixed charge however they may have chosen to describe it ... The company's freedom to deal with the charged assets without the consent of the holder of the charge, which is what makes it a floating charge, is of necessity a contractual freedom ... The question is not whether the company is free to collect the uncollected debts, but whether it is free to do so for its own benefit. For this purpose it is necessary to consider what it may do with the proceeds. ... The debenture was so drafted that the company was at liberty to turn the uncollected book debts to account by its own act. Taking the relevant assets to be the uncollected book debts, the company was left in control of the process by which the charged assets were extinguished and replaced by different assets which were not the subject of a fixed charge and were at the free disposal of the company. That is inconsistent with the nature of a fixed charge."

The judgement supports the view that, as well as prohibiting transfer of the book debts, it is crucial that control be exercised in practice by the chargee over the account into which the proceeds of realisation of the book debts are paid, in order for the charge to be regarded as being fixed in nature.

A floating charge will be invalid under s. 245 of the Insolvency Act 1986* (except to the extent that fresh consideration for it is given on or after its grant – e.g. through the operation of Clayton's Case*) if granted to a person connected with the company (as defined at s. 249 of the Insolvency Act 1986) within 2 years of commencement of Liquidation*, or if granted to a person who is not so connected within 12 months of commencement of liquidation (in the latter case, only where the company was insolvent at the time of the grant or became insolvent as a result of it).

Floating rate   An Interest rate* that is reset at intervals of 1 year or less.

Floating rate note   Also known as an FRN*. A debt instrument that resembles a Bond*, but pays a floating or variable (rather than fixed) rate of interest and is often Listed* on an Exchange*.

Floor   A Derivative* contract between two parties whereby the floor purchaser, in return for a Premium* (sense (iii)), will be paid periodic payments by the floor seller equal to the deficit of the interest earned at an agreed Basis* (sense (ii)) rate on a notional principal deposit below an agreed "strike rate", thus assuring the purchaser that he will not earn less than some minimum interest rate on deposited amounts equal to the notional principal.

Floor broker   A member of an Exchange* who acts as a Broker* for other members.

Floor trader   A member of an Exchange* who trades on his own behalf or on behalf of his own clients.

Flotation   The first Public offering* of the shares in a company. Almost invariably linked to a Stock exchange* Listing* for the Shares* in a particular market. In the UK, it is an offence for a Private company* (as opposed to a Public company*) to make an offer to the public (within the meaning of ss. 81 and 59 of the Companies Act 1985*) of shares or debentures. With regard to flotation on the LSE*, see Offer for sale, Offer for subscription, Placing and Intermediaries offer (which are all methods of raising new capital for the company) and Introduction (which does not raise new capital, but allows existing securities to be listed).

FNMA   See Federal National Mortgage Association.

FOB   See Free on board.

Force majeure   A contractual clause designed to suspend or terminate a party's obligations under a contract on the occurrence of one or more events that are (a) unusual; and (b) unforeseen. Typical events include war, natural disaster or exchange control impositions. The clause is typically designed to cover events arising between signing and closing of a transaction, or where there is a long-term, ongoing relationship between the parties (e.g. a maintenance agreement).

Foreclosure   The enforcement of Security* (sense (ii)) over an asset by extinguishment of the debtor's beneficial interest (its equity of redemption), giving the creditor full and unrestricted ownership of the asset. Only available where the secured creditor has the legal title to such asset (or can require transfer of the legal title to it pursuant to a security Power of attorney*). Foreclosure is effected by applying for a court order, but the order is not often awarded as foreclosure may result in an unfair windfall for the creditor.

Foreign bond   A Bond* issued by an issuer incorporated outside the country of the bond currency but offered for sale to investors within such country, on that country's public market (or for Sterling, issued on the UK public market and intended to be placed with investors in the UK), as opposed to a Domestic bond* or a Eurobond*. Examples include the Bulldog bond*, the Yankee bond* and the Samurai bond*.

Foreign currency rating   A Credit rating* relating to the relevant entity's ability to service debt obligations in a currency other than its local currency. Typically based on an assessment of the Transfer risk* arising in the local country as well as the Credit risk* on the entity. In many cases, the foreign currency rating of an entity will be capped at the level of the foreign currency rating of its local sovereign. See also Local currency rating.

Forex   See FX.

Forex rate   See FX rate.

Form 395   In the UK, a form used for registration with the Registrar of Companies* under s. 395 of the Companies Act 1985* of Security* (sense (ii)) given to secure debentures, security over uncalled share capital, security which, if created by an individual, would be a registrable Bill of sale* (in addition, bills of sale created by an individual (absolute bills or security bills) are registrable), security over land, security over Book debts*, security in the form of a Floating charge* and security over called but unpaid share capital, ships, aircraft, goodwill or intellectual property. The form requires details of the assets over which security is given and of the debt which is secured. Often, any Negative pledge* contained in the security document is also detailed in the Form 395, in an attempt to fix third parties with Deemed notice* or Constructive notice* of the negative pledge. See also Slavenburg.

Form 20-F   Exchange Act* form requiring annual periodic reporting information from non-US companies required to be registered with the SEC*. The form is supplemented by a pricing supplement on a securities issue.

Form 6-K   Notice of material events for non-US companies reporting under the Exchange Act*.

Form 8-K   Notice of material events for US companies reporting under the Exchange Act*.

Form 10-K   Annual report form for US companies reporting under the Exchange Act*.

Form 10-Q   Quarterly report form for US companies reporting under the Exchange Act*.

Form F-1   The "long" SEC* registration form for registration under the Securities Act* of an issue of securities by a non-US issuer, running to detailed information on the terms of the issue, risk factors connected with the issue and use of the issue proceeds, distribution of the issue, the issuer and other technical disclosure details.

Form F-2   One of the "short" SEC* registration forms (together with the Form F-3*) for registration under the Securities Act* of an issue of securities by a non-US issuer, containing information on the terms of the issue. Other information is incorporated by physically appending the issuer's most recent Form 20-F*. Available where the issuer would be able to use Form F-3, or would be so able but for the minimum public capitalisation requirement.

Form F-3   One of the "short" SEC* registration forms (together with the Form F-2*) for registration under the Securities Act* of an issue of securities by a non-US issuer, containing information on the terms of the issue. Other information is given by the incorporation by reference in the Form F-3 of the issuer's most recent Form 20-F*. Since April 1994, available to issuers with a public float of US$ 75m (previously US$ 300m), and only necessitating a 12-month reporting history (previously 36 months) with at least one annual filing on Form 20-F or under Rule 12g3-2(b)*.

Form S-1   The "long" SEC* registration form for registration under the Securities Act* of an issue of securities by a US issuer.

Form S-2   One of the "short" SEC* registration forms (together with the Form S-3*) for registration under the Securities Act* of an issue of securities by a US issuer.

Form S-3   One of the "short" SEC* registration forms (together with the Form S-2*) for registration under the Securities Act* of an issue of securities by a US issuer.

Forward   A current price quotation for Settlement* on a set future date of the purchase or sale of a particular asset (as opposed to Spot*). Forwards are priced at a Discount* (sense (ii)) or Premium* (sense (ii)) to the current market price of the underlying asset, depending on the Cost of carry* on the underlying asset and market expectations of future movements in the price of the underlying asset.

Forward exchange agreement   A Derivative contract consisting of a Forward* agreement to exchange an amount of one currency for an amount of another currency on a future Value date*. As between two currencies, the forward rate will reflect the current Interest rate differential*. The currency bearing a higher interest rate will trade at a Discount* (sense (ii)) to Spot* in the forward market; the currency with the lower interest rate will trade at a Premium* (sense (ii)) to spot in the forward market.

Forward rate agreement   Also known as an FRA*. A Derivative* contract consisting of an agreement to make payment on Settlement* of an amount representing interest due on a notional principal amount, at a rate equal to the differential between an agreed interest rate on that amount set on the entry into the agreement and market interest rates on that amount as at the agreed future date for settlement of the FRA. The settlement amount is calculated as follows:

$$S = [(L - R) \cdot (D_1 \times P)]/[(D_2 \times 100) + (L \times D_1)]$$

where S = the settlement amount
L = LIBOR at the settlement date
R = the agreed contract interest rate
D_1 = the number of days from the contract date to the settlement date
D_2 = the deemed number of days in the year (360 or 365)
P = the notional principal amount.

Forward start option   See Deferred strike option.

FRA   See Forward rate agreement.

FRABBA   Forward Rate Agreement standard terms produced by the British Bankers Association.

Franked investment income   Now redundant following the abolition of ACT*, but prior to 6 April 1999, part of the ACT tax credit system. See also Franked payment*. The sum of a Distribution* received by a company and the amount of ACT paid thereon by the distributing company. Prior to 2 July 1997, a repayment of tax could be claimed by the recipient of a distribution (the right to a repayment of tax from the Inland Revenue was abolished for companies (e.g. a company exempt from Corporation tax*) from 2 July 1997, and for individuals from 6 April 1999). Otherwise the total franked investment income was available for set-off against any franked payments made by the company for the purpose of calculating ACT due from the company.

Franked payment   Now redundant following the abolition of ACT*, but prior to 6 April 1999, part of the ACT tax credit system. See also Franked investment income*. The sum of a Distribution* made by a company and the amount of ACT due thereon. The total franked payments made by a company were reduced by the total franked investment income received by that company, with ACT being paid over to the Revenue only on the resultant balance.

Fraudulent trading See s. 213 of the Insolvency Act 1986*. Any person knowingly a party to carrying on the business of the company with a view to defrauding creditors or for other fraudulent purposes is liable for fraudulent trading and can be ordered by the court to make such personal contribution to the company's assets as the court thinks proper, on the application of a Liquidator* in the course of a Liquidation*. Also a criminal offence. See also Wrongful trading.

FRCD Floating rate Certificate of deposit*.

FRED 30 Financial Reporting Exposure Draft 30. Issued by the Accounting Standards Board in June 2002 in relation to the intended adoption of IAS 32 and 39 in the UK as part of convergence to IAS generally by 2005. FRED 30 recommends that the derecognition portions of IAS 39 not be applied in the UK at present, with a view to working on a joint standard to replace both FRS 5 and IAS 39 on derecognition prior to 2005.

Freddie Mac See Federal Home Loan Mortgage Corporation.

Free alongside ship Or FAS*. Export delivery term of general trade use and defined in INCOTERMS* meaning that the goods are at the seller's risk and expense until delivered alongside a ship in the quay. Cf. FOB*.

Free carrier Or FCA*. Export delivery term with the same meaning as FOB*, save that the seller's obligations are fulfilled when the goods are delivered into the custody of the named carrier at the named point.

Free cash flow debt service coverage ratio Or FCF DSCR*. The ratio of the amount of available periodic free cash flow (usually measured by EBITDA* less Capex* and taxation) within a business, to the required periodic service payments on debt within the company (both to cover interest and to cover any amortisation, Sinking fund* or Defeasance* amount). See also DSCR, Interest cover ratio.

Free on board Or FOB*. Export delivery term of general trade use and defined in INCOTERMS* meaning that goods are at the seller's risk and expense until placed on board a ship at a named port of shipment (specifically, until the goods pass over the ship's rail). Costs and risk thereafter are borne by the buyer. Cf. FAS.

FRI See Fully repairing and insuring.

FRN See Floating rate note.

FRS 5 In the UK, Financial Reporting Standard 5 of the Accounting Standards Board on reporting the substance of transactions, which came into effect on 22 September 1994. FRS 5 requires that in order for an asset to be considered Off balance sheet* (sense (i)) of an Originator* for accounting purposes in a Securitisation* transaction, all significant risks and benefits attached to that asset must be transferred to another entity. If this is the case, then "derecognition" will result in the assets being removed entirely from the balance sheet of the originator. If this is not the case, but:

- The maximum risk of the originator on the assets has been capped; and
- The SPV and investors have "no recourse whatsoever, either explicit or implicit, to the other assets of the [originator] for losses",

then a hybrid treatment known as "linked presentation" will be used. This groups the gross asset value with the risk portion that has been transferred to leave the remaining net exposure, all in a separate caption in the originator's accounts.

A linked presentation is only available to the extent that:

- The originator has no right or obligation to repurchase the assets. Any repurchase right (e.g. the 10% Clean-up call* permitted by Financial Services Authority guidelines) or obligation means that the portion of the assets over which the right or obligation extends will not be deducted from the gross asset value in the accounts. The clean-up call, tax call and call and step-up embedded in most deals may be structured at the SPV level rather than the originator level in order to avoid the risk of losing FRS5 linked presentation treatment;

- Any swap or cap provided by the originator: (i) is on market terms; (ii) is not based on rates under the control of the originator; and (iii) merely replaces existing hedges which the originator had for the asset portfolio prior to its sale.

Indemnities given by the originator which allow access to all assets of the originator may prevent linked presentation treatment. There are different interpretations on the extent of this restriction, for example as to whether it includes an indemnity to directors of an SPV for legal liability (which is not direct support of losses on a deal, but rather other legal liabilities which could arise). Typically, this would cover any liability that the directors could incur for trading while insolvent, and if a deal has been correctly structured to be Bankruptcy remote*, a claim should never arise in practice (save possibly in a programme structure where the directors could be concerned over the incidence of ongoing expenses in the SPV).

If the transferee entity is directly or indirectly controlled by the originator, and the transferee represents a source of benefits for the originator, this may lead to the transferee itself being included in the originator's Consolidated accounts* in a linked presentation as a "quasi-subsidiary". If the transferee is also an actual Subsidiary* (sense (i)), then full consolidated accounts including the transferee will be required instead.

On 10 September 1998, the Accounting Standards Board published an amendment to FRS 5 with immediate effect to deal with the balance sheet treatment of properties (such as hospital, schools, prisons, etc.) that form part of PFI* transactions or of other similar transactions. The amendment requires that:

- Elements of the overall transaction which are capable of being separately attributed to the provision of services, rather than to the use of the property, are split out (for example, where the service element runs for a different period from the property element, has different terms and conditions or termination provisions, or can be renegotiated separately);

- If non-separable service elements remain linked to the property payments, then the amendment to FRS 5 is applied;

- If there are no remaining non-separable service elements, then SSAP 21 is applied, which treats the payments for the property as lease payments, and uses the test of who bears "substantially all the risks and rewards of ownership" to establish whether the payments create a Finance lease* or an Operating lease*. If the lease is a finance lease, then the lease payments are discounted to NPV* to create a capital figure to be entered into the accounts of the payor.

With regard to any remaining use of property payments that contain non-separable service elements (and are thus subject to the amendment to FRS 5), the amendment sets out a number of risk factors to be considered. Each of these factors should be considered where the relevant risk is significant (i.e. there is a high degree of uncertainty involved), and there is a genuine commercial possibility of the risk or scenario materialising. The factors are indicative as to whether the property appears as an asset on the balance sheet of the user (in PFI transactions, the government) or of the operator, depending on who bears the risks. The main risk factors are:

- Who bears the risk of demand for the property (a fixed payment by the user regardless of reduced or increased use of the property indicates that the user has demand risk);
- Whether the operator has access to third-party revenues to cover the property (or, for example, relies on a guaranteed minimum level of payment from the user);
- Who determines the nature of the property (or whether, for example, the operator is free to use another property to fulfill its obligations);
- Whether under-performance is penalised (in which case the property is likely to be an asset of the operator);
- Whether the operator can pass on its specific increases in costs to the purchaser (or is restricted to increasing costs in line with general indices such as the RPI);
- Who bears the risk of obsolescence; and
- Who bears residual value risk.

Other subsidies or contributions made by the user may result in on-balance-sheet items for the user related to such payments. Also, if the user has agreed to buy the property at the end of the contract term for a price other than the residual market value at that future time, the difference between the price and the expected residual value should be accrued in the accounts over the length of the contract.

FRS 17   In the UK, Financial Reporting Standard 17 of the Accounting Standards Board on accounting for retirement benefits, which replaces SSAP 24. FRS 17 requires companies to value company pension scheme assets at market value, and to value pension liabilities via projected units discounted back at a AA corporate bond yield. The transition period provided for closing balance sheet information to be given starting with accounting periods ending on or after 22 June 2001, and for the standard to be fully effective starting with accounting periods ending on or after 22 June 2003. FRS 17 has been seen as likely to generate demand for long-dated highly rated corporate bonds (as has abolition of the Minimum funding requirement*), and likely to lead to volatility in financial reporting for companies which have defined benefit (e.g. final salary) pension schemes.

FSA   See Financial Services Authority.

FSMA   See Financial Services and Markets Act 2000.

Full title guarantee   From 1 July 1995, in documentation disposing of assets or creating a Security interest* over assets under English law, the use by the owner of the words "full title guarantee" implies certain covenants as to the title which the owner has in the assets in accordance with the provisions of the Law of Property (Miscellaneous Provisions) Act 1994. These covenants are: that the owner has the right to dispose of the assets, that he is disposing of the assets free of all encumbrances, and that he will do all he reasonably can do in order to give to the other party the title he purports to give. The Act replaces the use of the phrase "as beneficial owner", which implied similar covenants for title under s. 76 of the Law of Property Act 1925. See also Limited title guarantee.

Fully repairing and insuring   or FRI*. A lease where the tenant is responsible for repairs and insurance and any moneys spent by the landlord in effecting repairs or insurance are to be reimbursed by the tenant.

Fully supported   A Conduit* where the Credit rating* of the conduit is fully dependent on the rating of the credit support provider, and there is consequently no assessment of the credit quality of the assets held in the conduit. Cf. Partially supported.

Funded risk participation   See Sub-participation.

Fungible   The quality of cash or certain other assets that they are wholly interchangeable. For example, securities of the same issue with the same terms that are kept in an account clearing system without set serial numbers being allocated to each individual customer account are effectively pooled and are fungible with each other.

Further advance   In relation to a Securitisation* transaction, the making of a further advance of cash to a Receivables* debtor, thus creating a new receivable. In some transactions, it may be intended that such advances will be purchased by the SPV* out of cash collections, as a form of Replenishment*. This may give rise to Priority* issues where the original receivable is secured (e.g. a real estate mortgage); namely can the further advance be secured under the same mortgage Security* (sense (ii)) and if so, will it achieve the same priority as the original advance, or will it be postponed behind any intervening secured creditors who have taken security over the same asset. For registered land, a further advance made by the registered proprietor of the mortgage, and for unregistered land a further advance made by the legal owner of the mortgage, may benefit from the same security, and may retain priority, if it complies with requirements as to Tacking*.

Future   A Derivative* that consists of a standardised agreement traded on a Futures exchange* for future delivery of a certain commodity (a Commodity future*) or financial instrument (such as an interest rate on a notional principal amount, an amount of currency set at a particular exchange rate or a securities index – each a Financial future*) at a set price. The value of outstanding futures is marked-to-market (see Mark-to-market) each day, with Margin calls* being made for a Variation margin* (in addition to any Initial margin* already posted) equal in value to any adverse price movement. Where favourable price movements occur, margin is released and/or cash payments made in the amount of such movement. Price movements in futures are linked to the price of the underlying commodity or instrument (the Actual*). The difference between the two prices depends on firstly, expectations of future price movements prior to maturity of the future, and secondly, the Cost of carry*; these factors together are known as the Basis* (sense (i)) for the future. Futures are therefore priced at a Discount* (sense (ii)) or Premium* (sense (ii)) to the price of the underlying, which is equal to the basis. Interest rate and securities index futures are rarely delivered and are thus settled for cash on maturity unless previously covered (see Cover). A future has Leverage* (sense (ii)) or Gearing* (sense (ii)) as an asset, since the initial investment (the initial margin) is only a fraction of the capital value of the underlying commodity or instrument. Traded on, *inter alia*, LIFFE*, MATIF*, OMLX*, the IPE*, the CBOT*, the CBOE*, the CME* and the LME*.

Future flows   A Securitisation* transaction that is partially asset-backed (i.e. where the aggregate value of currently existing receivables is a multiple of the required interest and scheduled principal Amortisation* payments for a single period, but is less than the total outstanding funding), and is therefore dependent on continued future receivables generation in order to fully repay funding. See also Future receivables*.

Future receivables   Future receivables are Receivables* that are not currently contracted for (as opposed to payments due in the future under a current contract). In the UK, it is regarded as possible to sell future receivables, per Lord Watson in *Tailby v. Official Receiver (1888) (HL)*: "an assignment for value ... has always been regarded in equity as a contract binding on the conscience of the assignor and so binding the subject-matter of the contract when it comes into existence, if it is of such a nature and so described as to be capable of being ascertained and identified." Thus, provided that "on its coming into existence, it shall answer the description in the assignment, or, in other words, that it shall be capable of being identified as the thing, or as one of the very things assigned" the contract will take effect as an agreement to assign, which will give rise to an equitable Assignment* of the receivables the moment that they come into existence, without any further act being required to be done. A Securitisation* of future receivables may be fully asset-backed (where future receivables meeting a certain description are automatically transferred when they arise, but the aggregate value of receivables, collections and Charge-offs* in existence at any one point in time matches or exceeds the outstanding funding) or may be partially asset-backed (where the aggregate value is a multiple of the required interest and scheduled principal Amortisation* payments for a single period, but is less than the total outstanding funding – also known as a Future flows* deal).

Futures contract   See Future.

Futures exchange   An Exchange* dealing primarily in Futures* and Options*.

FX   Foreign currency exchange or Forex*.

FX rate   Also known as Forex rate*. The exchange rate, or "price" or value, of one currency measured against another currency. In the long term, a floating currency will theoretically adjust to correct a balance of payments surplus or deficit. In the short term, however, it will most likely be excessively affected by speculation and be extremely volatile. Since such volatility would have a destabilising effect on international business pricing, a "managed float" is often operated by central banks, using Government reserves to support or suppress the rate towards a particular FX rate goal. Such tactics may also be used to exert political pressure on another country by buying or selling its currency. A currency may also be strengthened by raising the level of Interest rates* in the country. A falling exchange rate increases the price of imports (which may lead to imported inflation), while a rising rate may make export prices uncompetitive (leading to a decline in export sales and growth).

G-10   The "Group of Ten" countries: Belgium, Canada, France, Germany, Italy, Japan, the Netherlands, Sweden, Switzerland, the UK and the USA.

GAAP   Generally accepted accounting principles.

Gain on sale   A US accounting treatment which involves recognition of any gain or loss on sale of assets, e.g. pursuant to a Securitisation*, immediately on the sale occurring. This typically leads to the originator booking an up-front profit for the excess spread on a transaction due by way of profit strip, on the basis of assumptions as to prepayment speed and interest rates. In 1998, the SEC required "gain on sale" to be applied across the board (regardless of whether it gave rise to a gain or a loss) and for assumptions used in calculating gain on sale to be clearly disclosed, following concerns arising from some originators re-marking expected future values due to high prepayment rates. Some sellers have structured securitisations under FAS 140* as financings rather than sales, specifically in order to avoid gain on sale treatment. This is due to the fact that gain on sale is disliked by the equity market as it generates current accounting profit from future excess spread revenue (leading to earnings volatility if default and prepayment assumptions in the gain on sale calculation prove to be incorrect). See further FAS 125 and FAS 140.

Gaming   Under English law, gaming or wagering agreements are void and unenforceable (pursuant to s. 18 Gaming Act 1845 and s. 1 Gaming Act 1892), but are upheld if they fall within s. 63 of the Financial Services Act 1986* (repeated at s. 412 FSMA* 2000) (i.e. if they are regulated investments under the Act).

Gamma   The degree of movement in the Delta* of an Option* for each unit movement in the price of the underlying asset. Hedged by buying or selling options.

GDR   See Global depositary receipt.

Gearing   (i) A measurement of the relative capital indebtedness of a company, calculated by taking total interest-bearing debt (i.e. typically just capital liabilities) as a percentage of shareholders' funds (equity capital and reserves). Cf. Leverage, sense (i).
   (ii) See Leverage, sense (ii).

GEM   (i) Growth Enterprise Market. Hong Kong stock market for high-growth companies opened in 1999, where listing requirements are less strict than on the main board. Major shareholders were required to hold shares for a minimum of 2 years after listing (reduced to 6 months in March 2000, but increased again to 1 year in August 2001).
   (ii) Global Equity Market. Proposed equity Exchange* put forward in June 2000 to link Euronext*, the NYSE*, and the Tokyo, Hong Kong, Mexico, São Paolo, Australian and Toronto markets.

General meeting   A meeting of the Members* of a company. See Annual general meeting and Extraordinary general meeting.

Gensaki   Japanese Repurchase agreement* and market. See also Reverse gensaki.

Gewahrtragerhaftung   See Landesbank.

GIC   Guaranteed investment contract*.

Gilt   UK Government-backed gilt-edged security – a Bond* or FRN* issued by the UK Debt Management Office* on behalf of the Government.

Ginnie Mae   See Government National Mortgage Association.

Glass–Steagall Act   See Commercial bank and Investment bank. US statute dating from the post-depression era which governed the division of operations between commercial banks and investment banks and insurance companies. Periodic and ongoing attempts were made in the US Congress to update or relax the restrictions contained in Glass–Steagall, until it was finally reformed in the Gramm–Leach–Bliley Act*. See also Interstate banking.

Global bond   A Bond* issued for global distribution and trading via international Clearing systems* in North America, Europe and Asia and registered with the SEC* (if being publicly issued and offered to US investors). As it is likely that any attempt to make additional securities available in the US (over and above the original US portion of the offering) will be considered as an understanding that the offshore (from the US) portion of the issue may "flow back" to the US (thus potentially breaching the Regulation S* requirements for the non-US portion), global issues are generally structured to ensure that the pool of the securities in the US can only diminish (i.e. if the US portion is sold offshore) and cannot increase. In order to achieve favourable US tax treatment for registered securities, global bonds are generally issued into permanent custody arrangements in the form of a permanent global certificate that may be considered as consisting of Registered securities* for US tax purposes, with any definitive securities issued being in registered form. An alternative, where one of the main offering jurisdictions is a jurisdiction such as Germany where Bearer securities* are preferred for reasons of anonymity, is to establish a link between two clearing systems (the DTC* and the bearer-preferred jurisdiction's domestic clearing system, e.g. Clearstream*), e.g. via a bank with branches in both relevant jurisdictions. The bonds may then be held partly in each clearing system, and interchanged between the clearing systems, with the DTC holding of bonds being in registered form and the other holding of bonds being in bearer form (or registered form convertible to bearer form), an arrangement specifically approved by the IRS* under permanent custodial arrangements.

Global depositary receipt   Or GDR. A certificate in the form of a Registered security* issued by a bank depositary representing a specific investor's interest in an underlying debt or equity issue. Global depositary receipts may be traded and settled internationally without the necessity of compliance with the issuer's domestic legislation on share ownership changes. Securities regulations may still need to be met however, e.g. under SEC* registration for a NYSE* or Nasdaq* listing in the US, or LSE* listing in the UK. See also American depositary receipt.

Global note   Securities are often issued in the form of a single "global" note equal to the entire principal amount of the issue, either to save the expense of security printing definitive notes or to enable compliance with the "lock-up" requirements of the Registration S* Category 3 safe harbour or of the TEFRA D* safe harbour.

Globex   Global screen-based Futures* trading system, owned by Reuters and subscribed to by MATIF* and DTB*. Cf. Open outcry.

GmbH   Gesellschaft mit beschrankter Haftung. A German company type which combines limited liability for members and freedom to participate in management with the Fiscal transparency* of a partnership. Cf. LLC.

GNMA   See Government National Mortgage Association.

Golden share   A share created and held by the government on Privatisation* of certain companies, enabling the government to out-vote certain types of Resolution*, notably regarding Takeovers* and changes in control of the company. May last for a fixed period, or indefinitely.

Good delivery   A delivery of Securities* that are in order and are not damaged or mutilated.

Good for the day   A buy or sell order that is conditional on being met in a particular session on the stated terms. Also known as a Day order*.

Good till cancelled   An order that can be carried out at any time until it is specifically cancelled.

Good value   A payment for Securities* which is made in cleared funds.

Governing law   The law applicable to an agreement. For contracts entered into after 31 March 1991, the UK courts will apply the terms of the Rome Convention on the Law Applicable to Contractual Obligations as enacted in the Contracts (Applicable Law) Act 1990 (the Convention and the Act do not apply to obligations on negotiable instruments, company capacity, an agent's power to bind his principal, trust creation, court procedure, insurance and arbitration/jurisdiction clauses). The Act, at Schedule 1, Articles 3 and 4, upholds the parties' choice of law, applying the law of the country with which the contract is most closely connected in default of such a choice. For contracts entered into before 1 April 1991, or outside the scope of the Act, UK courts will use common law rules to uphold the parties' choice of law if the choice is legal, made in good faith and not against public policy. In default of such a choice, the UK courts will apply the law of the country with which the contract has the most real and substantial connection.

Government National Mortgage Association   Also known as GNMA* or Ginnie Mae*. A US government agency (a branch of the Department of Housing and Urban Development) that approves the issue of Mortgage backed securities* backed by the full faith and credit of the US Treasury, against the mortgages of lower-income individuals.

Gramm–Leach–Bliley Act   US act designed to remove the division of operations between commercial banks and investment banks and insurance companies under the Glass–Steagall Act*. Known in full as the Gramm–Leach–Bliley Financial Services Modernisation Act of 1999, it was signed on 12 November 1999 and came into effect on 12 November 2000, and must be complied with from 1 July 2001. The Act permits securities firms, banks and insurers to diversify into each other's business, and also contains new consumer privacy protections.

Grantor trust   A US Trust* often used for Securitisation* transactions which the IRS will recognise as achieving Fiscal transparency* if it is not engaged in a profitable business and only issues a single class of trust interests and cannot vary their terms. Thus, the trust may not engage in Replenishment* of assets or issue multiple Classes* of securities (other than a Subordinated* tranche which pays down pro rata with the senior tranche and otherwise matches the senior tranche in its terms).

Green clause   See Secured credit.

Green shoe   See Over-allotment option.

Grey market   The market for the sale and purchase of securities prior to their issue. Trades are entered into on a "when issued" basis, to be settled on closing and issue. Following the introduction of the POS Regs*, care needs to be taken to ensure that no Offer to the public* (sense (ii)) is made in the course of such trading, unless and until a Prospectus* has been published or the securities are admitted to a Listing* (sense (ii)).

Gross-up   A clause in a Facility* or Security* that requires the borrower or issuer to make increased periodic payments of interest in the event that it is required to deduct Withholding tax* from such payments, in order to ensure that the net payment received by the lender or investor is the same as it would have been had the withholding tax not been imposed.

Group   **(i)** For accounting purposes (see Consolidation, sense (ii)), a group of companies consisting of a Parent company* (sense (ii)) and its Subsidiary undertakings*.

  (ii) For Corporation tax* purposes, in relation to the capital gains treatment of transfers between members of a group under s. 171 TCGA as being made at a deemed consideration that would give rise to neither a gain nor a loss, a group of companies (which may be non-UK resident since the Finance Act 2000) consisting (under s. 170 TCGA) of:

(a) The "principal company of the group" (a company which is not a 75% Subsidiary* of another company, unless the two companies are not in the same group under (b) below or no further company could be the principal company of a group of which the company would be a member); and
(b) The principal company's 75% Subsidiaries and those subsidiaries' 75% Subsidiaries (and so on), but excluding any 75% Subsidiary which is not an Effective 51% subsidiary* of the principal company.

A company can only belong to one group, being the group which can earliest be discovered by the following tests:

(A) The group to which such company would belong if, in calculating which companies are Effective 51% subsidiaries* for the exclusion in (b) above, no account had been taken of amounts to which a principal company was entitled of profits or assets from another principal company.
(B) The group whose principal company is entitled to the greatest percentage of such company's profits available for distribution to equity holders.
(C) The group whose principal company would be entitled to the greatest percentage of such company's assets available for distribution to equity holders on a winding-up.

(D) The group whose principal company owns directly or indirectly the greatest share of such company's ordinary share capital.

A group remains the same group as long as the same company remains the principal company of the group, and if at any time the principal company of a group becomes a member of another group, the first group and the other group are regarded as the same, and the question of whether or not a company has ceased to be a member of a group is determined accordingly. If a member ceases to be regarded as a member of a group within 6 years after making an inter-group transfer, a capital gains charge will arise under ss. 178-179 TCGA.

Loans that are regarded as not being "normal commercial loans" run the risk of being treated as equity, potentially resulting in the borrower being degrouped under ICTA Schedule 18, paragraph 1.

Under the Finance Act 2000, the transfer will only be at neither a gain nor a loss if the relevant asset is and, following the transfer, remains either held by a UK resident company or situate, and used for a trade, in the UK. The Finance Act 2000 also allows for a group to elect that a disposal outside the group can be deemed to have been transferred within the group immediately prior to the disposal, such that any gain or loss resulting from the disposal outside the group can be considered to have been realised by the group company deemed transferee.

(iii) Also known as a VAT group*. For VAT purposes (see Group treatment*), under VATA, s. 43A(1), two or more bodies corporate resident in the UK are eligible to be treated as members of a group if:

(a) One of them controls (see Control, sense (iii)) each of the others;
(b) One person (whether a body corporate or an individual) controls all of them; or
(c) Two or more individuals carrying on a business in partnership control all of them.

(iv) Prior to the Finance Act 2001, for the purposes of tax on payments of dividends and interest between a paying company and a receiving company under the Group income* election under ICTA*, s. 247, a grouping of companies which are resident in the UK and where:

(a) The paying company was a 51% Subsidiary* of the other, or of a company resident in the UK of which the receiving company was also a 51% Subsidiary; or
(b) The paying company was a Trading company* (sense (i)) or Holding company* (sense (i)) which was not a 75% Subsidiary of any other company and which was owned by a Consortium* (sense (i)) the members of which included the receiving company; or
(c) (Save with regard to the payment of dividends) the receiving company was a 51% subsidiary of the paying company.

Loans that were regarded as not being "normal commercial loans" ran the risk of being treated as equity, potentially resulting in the borrower being degrouped under ICTA Schedule 18, paragraph 1. The group income regime was abolished following the introduction of the inter-company exemption from withholding tax under s. 85 Finance Act 2001, and ceased to have effect from the date on which the Act was passed.

(v) For Companies Act 1985* purposes, a group of companies consisting of a Holding company* (sense (ii)) and its Subsidiaries* (sense (iii)).

(vi) For the purposes of the transfer of trading losses made by a company to another company in the same group under the Group relief* provisions, under ICTA*, s. 413 and s. 402, a grouping of companies which are resident anywhere in the world (prior to the Finance Act 2000, such companies had to be resident in the UK) and where:

(a) One company is a 75% Subsidiary* of the other, or both are 75% subsidiaries of the same third company; or
(b) One is a member of a Consortium* (sense (ii)) and the other is a Trading company* (sense (i)) which is either owned by the consortium or is a 90% Subsidiary* of a Holding company* (sense (i)) owned by the consortium and is, in either case, not a 75% subsidiary of any other company.

Loans that are regarded as not being "normal commercial loans" run the risk of being treated as equity, potentially resulting in the borrower being degrouped under ICTA Schedule 18, paragraph 1.

(vii) For UK Capital adequacy* Consolidation* (sense (iii)) purposes, a regulated entity and any entities that carry on financial activities and constitute a Parent undertaking* or Subsidiary undertaking* of the regulated entity or in which the regulated entity has a participation of 20% or more of the voting rights or capital. The new Basel Accord proposals use a fully consolidated basis, applying to holding companies that are parents of banking groups (groups which engage predominantly in banking activities), and to each bank within the group either (a) on a sub-consolidated basis; or (b) on an individual basis with full deduction against capital of investment held in subsidiaries.

(viii) For Stamp duty* purposes in relation to intra-group transfers, see under Stamp duty.

Group income   Prior to the Finance Act 2001, for the purpose of Corporation tax* in the UK a paying company and a receiving company, could, pursuant to ICTA* s. 247 and provided that they qualified as being within the same Group* (sense (iv)), make elections relating to intra-group dividends and/or income charges. The regime was abolished following the introduction of the inter-company exemption from withholding tax under s. 85 Finance Act 2001, and ceased to have effect from the date on which the Act was passed. Previously, the effect of an election under s. 247 had been:

(a) Prior to abolition of ACT* on 6 April 1999, that Dividends* passing between such companies would not be included in Franked payments* of the paying company or Franked investment income* of the receiving company for ACT, but would constitute "group income" of the receiving company (this election is now redundant); and
(b) That payments which constituted charges on the paying company's income could be made without deduction of income tax and that ICTA s. 349 and s. 350 (dealing with deduction of tax at source) would not apply thereto.

Group relief   A Corporation tax* relief available between members of a Group (sense (vi)), which enables group companies to transfer trading (but not capital) losses from one group company to another group company (ICTA, ss. 402-403). See also Group income.

Group treatment   A VAT group (see Group, sense (iii)) is subjected to group treatment, under VATA, s. 43, with the result that any business carried on by a member of the group is treated as though carried on by the representative member of the group, and:

(a) any supply of goods or services by a member of the group to another member of the group is disregarded for VAT purposes;
(b) any other supply of goods or services by or to a group member is treated as a supply by or to the representative member; and
(c) any tax paid or payable by a group member on the acquisition of goods from another Member state* or on the importation of goods from outside the member states is treated as paid or payable by the representative member and the goods shall be treated as having been acquired or imported by the representative member.

All members of the group are jointly and severally liable for any VAT due from the representative member.

Growth Enterprise Market   See GEM.

GTC   See Good till cancelled.

Guarantee   An undertaking by one party (the Guarantor*) in favour of another party to discharge the obligations of a third party on the occurrence of certain specified events. Under English law, must be made or recorded in writing and signed by the guarantor, or it will be void under s. 4 of the Statute of Frauds 1677. Any change in the underlying debtor/creditor arrangements will void the guarantee, unless its terms specifically provide otherwise. Where there are joint and several guarantors, they must all sign in order to validate the guarantee, and termination by one joint and several guarantor terminates the entire guarantee, unless the guarantee terms provide otherwise. A pure guarantee obligation (or "guarantee of collection") is a secondary obligation, which the guarantor is only obliged to discharge if the underlying obligation is valid and in existence and has not been discharged. In order to ensure that the guarantee can be claimed against if the underlying obligation proves to be invalid, a primary Indemnity* provision (or "guarantee of payment") is often included in the guarantee document. In cases where a bank is unwilling to give a guarantee for regulatory or accounting reasons it may enter into a Standby letter of credit* instead. The payment by a guarantor to a creditor of the whole of the amount due under the guarantee on behalf of the debtor entitles the guarantor to take the benefit of rights (e.g. as to Security* (sense (ii))) held by the creditor, pro rata the guarantor's payment as against the total claim of the creditor on the debtor, under the doctrine of Subrogation*. This right may be limited by the terms and provisions of the guarantee, so that subrogation to security rights only occurs if the full amount owed by the debtor to the creditor (i.e. an amount that could exceed the amount of the guarantee) has been paid off by the guarantor.

Guarantee of collection   See Guarantee.

Guarantee of payment   See Guarantee.

Guaranteed exchange rate option   See Quanto option.

Guaranteed investment contract   A contract guaranteeing a certain minimum rate of return to the investor. Used to Hedge* Reinvestment risk*.

Guarantor   An entity or individual that agrees to grant a Guarantee* in favour of another party.

Guts   The purchase of a Call option* at a set Strike price* and the purchase of a Put option at a higher strike price.

Hague Convention   The Hague Convention on Indirectly Held Securities 2002 determines the law applicable to transactions involving securities held via an intermediary. The approach used is referred to as the Place of the Relevant Intermediary Approach (or PRIMA*). The law is at the choice of the account holder and its intermediary, subject to the proviso that the intermediary must have an office in the relevant jurisdiction. The Convention was agreed in December 2002 and presented to be ratified by the 62 members of the Hague conference.

Haircut   A fractional amount, such as a marginal increase in the amount of capital required for an institution to meet Capital adequacy* requirements, or that part of a loan written-off on reduction of the debt where the borrower is Unable to pay its debts*.

Hard arbitrage   The creation of an additional funding commitment in order to generate profit through manipulation of Arbitrage* opportunities. Cf. Soft arbitrage.

Hedge   A mechanism to reduce Risk*, which commonly takes the form of a Derivative*; often used in relation to Market risk* (e.g. to protect against changes in the value of an underlying security or commodity). The most basic example is to partially or wholly Cover* a Position* by entering into an offsetting transaction, so that any loss on one transaction will be capped at a definite figure, or will be off-set by a gain on the other transaction.

Hedge funds   An investment fund, often requiring a minimum investment of US$ 500 000 or more from high net worth individuals and/or significant sums from institutional investors, which engages in particular investment strategies (which may prove to be high risk – witness the collapse of Long-Term Capital Management in 1998 – in which case their name may be a misnomer). Often heavily leveraged by substantial borrowing. Hedge funds often adopt contrarian strategies of investing against the market tendency, and were notably active in the European Exchange Rate Mechanism crisis of September 1992, where they used their funds to short-sell particular currencies in anticipation of devaluations. Hedge funds tend to be market-leading, thus their speculations may, to an extent, become self-fulfilling prophecies. The fact that they are typically organised so as to avoid the applicability of securities laws has led to calls for regulatory controls (e.g. they are often formed as US limited partnerships with 100 or less partners, or as offshore funds with non-US investors, either of which routes enables them to avoid SEC regulation). Hedge funds may utilise automatic stop-loss procedures to liquidate a holding if the price of the investment moves against the fund by more than a minimal percentage, as a loss-limitation procedure.

Hedging   See Hedge.

HEL   See Home equity loan.

HELIBOR   Helsinki Interbank Offered Rate. Helsinki equivalent of LIBOR*.

HELOC   See Home equity line of credit.

Hell or high water   Term used to describe a payment obligation that must be met in all circumstances. May be found in Finance leases*, where the lease has the economic effect of a loan by the lessor, to ensure that the lessor is fully repaid in all circumstances.

High yield bond   See Junk bond.

Hire purchase   A bailment of an asset by way of hire, together with an option for the hirer to purchase the asset once a full set of instalment hire payments are made. A method of allowing a seller or financier to provide finance to a purchaser for the purchase of an asset while retaining title to the asset sold (and thus achieving protection against the asset being available to creditors generally in the insolvency of the purchaser), in a manner that is: (a) not registrable as a Bill of sale*; and (b) not at risk of being overridden by a sale by the purchaser to a bona fide third party (except for a sale of a motor vehicle to a private purchaser, which may be so overridden pursuant to s. 27 Hire-Purchase Act 1964 as substituted by s. 192(3)(a) of the Consumer Credit Act 1974). Any Capital allowances* available on the asset will be for the benefit of the purchaser (cf. Finance lease). Similar to a Conditional sale. See also Retention of title.

HKEx   Hong Kong Exchanges and Clearing. Merged entity resulting from the combination of the Stock Exchange of Hong Kong, the Hong Kong Futures Exchange and the Hong Kong Clearing Company on 6 March 2000.

HKFE   Hong Kong Futures Exchange. Merged with the Stock Exchange of Hong Kong into HKEx* on 6 March 2000.

HKMA   See Hong Kong Monetary Authority.

HKMC   See Hong Kong Mortgage Corporation.

HKSCC   Hong Kong Securities Clearing Co Ltd. Operator of CCASS*.

Holder   In relation to a Negotiable instrument*, the possessor of the instrument (or the payee/endorsee who is in possession if it is payable to order). Only the holder has the right to sue on the instrument. The extent of the title which rests with the holder depends on whether the holder is merely a holder or is actually a Holder for value* or Holder in due course*. A person cannot be a holder where the instrument bears a forged drawer's signature (the instrument is void *ab initio*) or a forged endorsement (only those possessing prior to the forged endorsement can be holders), or where the possessor himself is a wrongful possessor (e.g. a thief) (although in the last case, subsequent acquires may still be holders). Any person acquiring an instrument bearing a forged drawer's or endorser's signature does have the right to sue any subsequent genuine endorser, for breach of the endorser's warranty under s. 55 Bills of Exchange Act 1882 that the instrument will be paid.

Holder for value   In relation to a Negotiable instrument*, a Holder* who has given valuable consideration to obtain possession of the instrument (s. 27 Bills of Exchange Act 1882). A holder for value cannot acquire better title or rights to sue than the person who transferred the instrument to him and cannot sue the transferor, save to the extent of the value given. The holder for value can sue previous holders of the instrument, to the extent that the transferor would have been able so to do.

Holder in due course   In relation to a Negotiable instrument*, a Holder* who is a bona fide acquirer for valuable consideration, without notice of any defect in the transferor's title, of an instrument that is complete and regular on its face and not overdue (s. 29 Bills of Exchange Act 1882). A holder for due course acquires good legal title free of any defects in his transferor's title, where the instrument is transferred to him via Negotiation*.

Holding company   (i) For the purpose of the Group* (sense (iv) and sense (vi)) and Consortium* (senses (i) and (ii)) taxation provisions, under s. 247(9) and s. 413(6) ICTA, a company the business of which consists wholly or mainly in the holding of shares or securities in Trading companies* (sense (i)) which are 90% Subsidiaries*.
(ii) For Companies Act 1985 purposes under s. 736 Companies Act 1985, a company is a holding company of another company, its Subsidiary* (sense (iii)), if the holding company:
(a) Holds a majority of the voting rights in the subsidiary; or
(b) Is a member of the subsidiary and has the right to appoint or remove a majority of the subsidiary's board of directors; or
(c) Is a member of the subsidiary and controls alone, pursuant to an agreement with other shareholders or members, a majority of the voting rights in the subsidiary; or
(d) Is a holding company of a company which is itself a holding company of the subsidiary.

Home country information   Information required to be supplied by an issuer of securities on an ongoing basis to meet the Home country reporting requirements* and consisting of copies of those documents that the issuer makes available, or is required to make available to (i) holders of its securities, (ii) stock exchanges where its securities are traded and which have made such information public, or (iii) the public otherwise pursuant to its domestic laws.

Home country reporting requirement   See Rule 12g3-2(b).

Home equity loan   Or HEL*. A loan secured over the equity value present in real estate, which is taken out for a variety of purposes, such as the consolidation of existing consumer debts, to pay for college or medical bills, or for home improvement. Historically usually a second mortgage, but now increasingly consolidated into the first mortgage on the property.

Home equity line of credit   A line of credit for a Home equity loan* which is drawable over time.

Hong Kong Monetary Authority   Or HKMA. Hong Kong's de facto central bank.

Hong Kong Mortgage Corporation   Or HKMC. Hong Kong government-owned corporation mandated to purchase residential mortgages and issue Mortgage-backed securities*. Operational from late 1997.

Hot back-up   A Back-up servicer* that runs systems in parallel to the Originator* on a Securitisation* transaction, such that it can step into the role of Servicer* on termination of the appointment of the originator as servicer with minimal delay. Cf. Warm back-up and Cold back-up.

Human Rights Act 2000   UK statute that came into force on 1 October 2000.

Hypothecation   A method of taking Security* (sense (ii)) over tangible assets that are capable of physical possession (such as chattels or Negotiable instruments*), which does not consist of the security beneficiary taking possession (actual or constructive) of the relevant assets. As a species of Charge* over easily transferable assets which resembles an unperfected form of Pledge*, the security beneficiary is at risk of a subsequent transferee or security beneficiary who acquires legal title without notice of the prior security taking Priority*.

IAS   See International Accounting Standards.

IAS 27   Or International Accounting Standard* 27. IAS 27 on consolidation was published by the IASC* in April 1989 (and is effective for financial years beginning on or after 1 January 1990). The IASC issued SIC-12* (an interpretation of IAS 27 issued by the Standing Interpretations Committee) in June 1998 (effective for financial years beginning on or after 1 July 1999). The terms of IAS 1 require that financial statements under IAS meet the requirements of both the Standards and the SIC interpretations. IAS 27 requires the consolidation of all subsidiaries and of all entities controlled by a company (and the preparation of consolidated financial statements to include such subsidiaries and entities). An entity may be regarded as being controlled by a company even where the company owns little or no equity in the entity (see examples given at IAS 27.12 and see also SIC-12).

IAS 39   Or International Accounting Standard* 39. IAS 39 on derecognition was published by the IASC* in December 1998 (and is effective for financial years beginning on or after 1 January 2001). IAS 39 requires that in order for an asset to be considered Off balance sheet* (sense (i)) of a company for accounting purposes in a Securitisation* transaction control over the assets must be lost or surrendered by the company. This can be achieved where the transferee acquires the right to pledge or exchange the assets, and the transferor does not retain effective control over the assets (via a right and obligation to take back the assets at a certain point, or a right to take back the assets other than at fair market value at the time of repurchase).

If this is the case, the assets are granted "derecognition" and removed from the originator's balance sheet into the SPV, to be replaced with the resulting components of the sale at fair value, and any fair value adjustment on the sale price against the carry value of the assets. Derecognition is not available if the transferor retains substantially all the risks and benefits of the assets. There may, however, be a requirement to consolidate the SPV with the originator, under the provisions of IAS 27* and

SIC-12*. If control has not been surrendered, the transaction will be accounted for as secured borrowing. IAS 39 also deals with accounting for derivatives and hedging.

IASB   See International Accounting Standards Board.

IASC   See International Accounting Standards Committee.

ICC   International Chamber of Commerce*.

ICOM   International Currency Options Master Agreement. A standard agreement, containing terms and conditions for foreign exchange Options*, which is designed to protect the parties to the agreement in the event of the insolvency of the other party by effecting Close-out netting*.

ICTA   Income and Corporation Taxes Act 1988 (UK statute).

IET   US Interest equalisation tax on non-US securities, applied to holdings of such securities by US investors between 1963 and 1974 to reduce capital outflows from the US and rectify balance of payments problems.

IFEMA   International Foreign Exchange Master Agreement. A standard agreement, containing terms and conditions for Spot* and Forward* foreign exchange contracts, which is designed to protect the parties to the agreement in the event of the insolvency of the other party by effecting Close-out netting*.

IFRS   See International Financial Reporting Standards.

IFSC   See International Financial Services Centre.

IMF   The International Monetary Fund.

IMM   International Monetary Market. A division of the CME* which deals in the trading of certain Futures* contracts.

Implied volatility   The Volatility* of an Option* which is implied by the price (and thus the Time value*) at which the option is being traded in the market.

IMRO   Investment Management Regulatory Organisation. One of the self-regulating organisations (see SRO) established under the Financial Services Act 1986*. Responsible for regulating investment managers (both large and small) and unit trust/collective investment schemes. Its functions were rolled into the Financial Services Authority* from midnight on 30 November 2001.

In the money   An instrument or Position* that compares favourably to current market conditions and pricing. Cf. At the money, Out of the money.

Income tax   UK tax on the income less allowable expenses accruing due to a person under the income tax Schedules* ("statutory income") less any annual payments and interest deductible as charges on income ("total income") less the personal allowance and any other reliefs ("taxable income"). Taxable income is charged in rate bands (see also Corporate tax* for companies). Where applicable, the charge to income tax overrides the charge to Capital gains tax* under s. 37 TCGA*.

Incorporation   The process of formation of a Corporation that confers Corporate personality* on an entity. For Registered companies*, this occurs on the date of issue of its Certificate of incorporation*.

INCOTERMS   Standard rules for the interpretation of international trade agreements, published by the ICC*. They define the terms EXW*, FCA*, FAS*, FOB*, CFR*, CIF*, CPT*, CIP*, DAF*, DES*, DEQ*, DDU*, DDP*. Editions are regularly updated. INCOTERMS may be incorporated by reference.

Increased costs   A clause in a Facility* that requires the borrower to make payments to the lender to cover any increase in the cost to the lender of providing the facility – for example, increased capital adequacy costs, or costs of complying with new laws or regulations.

Indemnity   An undertaking by one party in favour of another party to make good any loss or damage suffered by the other party in certain circumstances. An indemnity is a primary obligation, and is not dependent on the loss having been suffered as a result of breach of a valid obligation. Cf. Guarantee.

Indenture   (i) A Deed* *inter partes* (between two or more parties) as opposed to a Deed poll*. Originally the indenture was torn, with each party keeping one part, until completion of the arrangement it related to. The term is now obsolete, indentures being referred to simply as deeds. Indentures are enforceable by persons not party to the deed, as an exception to the doctrine of Privity* of contract, but only in as far as they seek to take "an interest in land or other property, or the benefit of any condition, right of entry, covenant or agreement over or respecting land or other property" (s. 56 Law of Property Act 1925).
   (ii) See Trust indenture.

Index-linked security   Or RPI-linked security*. A security the return on which is linked to the RPI* from time to time. See Capital indexed, Current pay and Interest indexed. See also LPI-linked security.

Ineligible bill   A Bill of exchange* that bears the Acceptance* (sense (i)) of a bank and is traded in the Discount market*, but does not meet the criteria of qualification as an Eligible bill*.

Information memorandum   A document that describes a loan or other facility to be made available to a company, or gives the general terms of a programme for the issuance of Medium-term notes* or Commercial paper* (rather than the specific details of a particular offering). May constitute Listing particulars* or (in the UK) a Prospectus*. Cf. Offering circular.

Inheritance tax   UK tax, which replaced capital transfer tax from 17 March 1986, on chargeable (i.e. not within exemptions for gifts to charities, between spouses et al.) transfers of value (i.e. reductions in the value of the transferor's estate) made by an individual during his lifetime and on the value of the individual's estate on his death, as a percentage of the value involved. Transfers to individuals are potentially exempt transfers which only become chargeable, at a sliding scale of rates, if the transferor dies within 7 years of making the transfer. On each chargeable transfer, chargeable transfers are cumulated (subject to reliefs) over the previous 7 years to determine rate banding, and charged at half the normal (i.e. death) tax rates. On death, chargeable and potentially exempt transfers within 7 years before death are all cumulated (subject to reliefs) to determine rate banding, leading to the amount of tax on the included chargeable transfers being reopened, subject to a credit for tax paid.

Initial margin   The amount of the Margin* (sense (ii)) deposited by a Futures* or exchange-traded Options* trader on first entering into a future (being a fraction of the value of the underlying commodity or instrument) or certain exchange-traded options (being a fraction of the Premium* (sense (iii)). Calculated to represent the worst probable loss on the relevant position over one trading day, on the basis of historic figures. Cf. Variation margin and Maintenance margin. See also SPAN.

INS   Institutional net settlement. The Talisman* Settlement* process that was used by institutional investors, and bypassed the intermediary action of a broker.

Insider dealing   In the UK, under Part V of the Criminal Justice Act 1993, the offence by an individual of dealing or encouraging others to deal in securities on a regulated market (these are listed in the Act, and include the LSE* and LIFFE* in the UK) or via a professional intermediary (even where the dealing is not on a regulated market) while in the possession of specific or precise information relating to a security or an issuer (acquired through his job or from another known by him to be a director, shareholder or employee of the issuer of such securities) which he knows has not been made public and which would be likely to have a significant effect on the price of such securities if made public. Also the offence by him of disclosing such information to another otherwise than in the proper course of his job. The penalty for these offences is imprisonment and/or an unlimited fine.

Insolvency   The status of a company that is Unable to pay its debts*. See Insolvency Act 1986.

Insolvency Act 1986   UK statute governing proceedings for the Insolvency* or Bankruptcy* of a company or individual, respectively. See in particular Administration, Administrative receivership, Receivership, Voluntary arrangement, Winding-up, Liquidation, Transaction at an undervalue, Transactions defrauding creditors, Preference, Extortionate credit transaction, Automatic stay, Fraudulent trading, Wrongful trading, Set-off, Onerous property, Preferential debt, Floating charge. See also Insolvency Act 2000.

Insolvency Act 2000   UK statute which received Royal Assent on 30 November 2000 and came into force on 2 April 2001, except for the CVA moratorium* discussed below which came into force on 1 January 2003. The Insolvency Act 2000 makes certain amendments to the Insolvency Act 1986* with a view to promoting the rehabilitation of insolvent businesses and individuals. The main change is that the Act provides for a Moratorium* proceeding on enforcement of security to be incorporated into the existing company Voluntary arrangement* or CVA proceedings. The CVA moratorium will apply to small companies in financial difficulties while a CVA is being considered for a maximum period of 28 days (although it may be extended further for up to 2 months). The moratorium cannot be blocked by appointment of an Administrative receiver*. Small companies are companies that meet at least two of three conditions – turnover is £2.8m or less, total assets are £1.4m or less and employees number 50 or less (in accordance with s. 247 of the Companies Act 1985). These provisions were extended in August 2002 under SI 2002/1990 by the exclusion from the moratorium of companies that (a) are parties to capital market arrangements incurring debts of at least £10m and the issue of a capital market instrument, (b) are project companies in public private partnership projects, or (c) have incurred liabilities (either direct or by guarantee or indemnity) of £10m or more. The provisions are designed to follow those in the Enterprise Act* in order to exempt Securitisation* transactions from the moratorium.

Insolvency Proceedings Regulation   EU Regulation* No. 1346/2000 of 29 May 2000 on Insolvency Proceedings came into force on 31 May 2002 with direct effect in all member states except Denmark (where separate rules are expected to be enacted), and overrides domestic legislation to the extent that the two are incompatible.

The Regulation provides for the determination of the centre of a debtor's main interests (CMI) in respect of an company or individual. In respect of a company, this is presumed to be the jurisdiction of the company's registered office unless proved otherwise. The Regulation applies if the CMI is within the EU. The main proceedings in respect of a company's insolvency are to be undertaken in the CMI in respect of that company, and encompass all assets of the company save those subject to secondary proceedings. Secondary proceedings can be undertaken in any jurisdiction in which the company has an establishment, but only in respect of assets situate in that jurisdiction. Insolvency proceedings will be carried out in accordance with the *lex fori* of the jurisdiction of proceedings (Article 4(1)). The outcome of the determination of insolvency in respect of the jurisdiction of main proceedings will apply to subsequent secondary proceedings (Article 27).

The Regulation does not apply to insurance undertakings, credit institutions, investment undertakings or collective investment undertakings (Article 1(2)). The Regulation also provides for insolvency judgements to be recognised and enforceable across the EU without formalities (Article 16).

Since entry into force of the Regulation, the case of *Brac Rent-a-Car International Inc (2003) Ch* has demonstrated the potentially wide-ranging effect of the Regulation. In this case, the company was a Delaware company, but the court held that its CMI was in the UK, and upheld its application for Administration* proceedings to be opened in the UK – proceedings which, prior to the Regulation, would only have been countenanced for a UK incorporated company. This was taken further in the case of *Salvage Association (2003) Ch*, where the judge considered that an association incorporated by charter could also enter administration. In effect, neither the country of formation of the entity nor the legal form of the entity would now act as a block to UK administration proceedings. By extrapolation, the same would appear likely to be true of the application of other continental European insolvency or moratorium proceedings to UK incorporated companies that have their CMI in continental Europe.

Insolvent liquidation   The Liquidation* of a company.

Interbank market   The Money market* in which banks place and seek deposits among themselves. See LIBID and LIBOR.

Interchange   With regard to credit cards, interchange is the discount income earnt in relation to the acquisition from the relevant retailer of credit card vouchers by a "merchant acquirer" (typically the retailer's bank) at a discount to the value of the goods stated on the voucher and charged to the customer. The merchant acquirer will sell the voucher on to the relevant credit card clearing system (VISA, Mastercard, etc.) who will then sell the voucher on to the card issuing bank (the customer's bank). Each of the merchant acquirer, the clearing system and the card issuing bank will therefore acquire a portion of the interchange income.

Interest   An element earnt on a principal amount by a lender or depositor to cover financing costs, the risk of default and a profit element. Interest paid is tax deductible as (a) a trading expense or (b) a charge on income. Prior to the Finance Act* 1996, a company that was neither an Investment company* (sense (ii)) nor a Trading company* (sense (ii)) could not deduct interest payments on debt from its taxable income, pursuant to the now repealed s. 338(6) ICTA*. Under paragraph 13 of Schedule 9 to the Finance Act 1996, interest is not deductible if the related debt has a purpose "which is not amongst the business or other commercial purposes of the company". This may give rise to a desire to leave some profit in SPVs* used for Securitisation* or other transactions, in order to show commercial benefit. See also Discount and Short interest.

Interest cover ratio   The ratio of the amount of available revenue to required periodic interest service payments on debt. See also DSCR, FCF DSCR.

Interest equalisation tax   See IET.

Interest in possession trust   A form of trust under which a beneficiary or beneficiaries have an immediate entitlement to, or Vested* interest in, the income of the trust (as opposed to a Discretionary trust*). A trust where the trustees have a discretion as to the distribution of income, or the power of Accumulation* of income, cannot be an Interest in possession trust. Save with regard to Bare trusts*, interest in possession trusts are subject to taxation at the basic rate on trust income under s. 151 Finance Act* 1989 and to taxation on capital gains at the basic rate under s. 65 TCGA prior to 6 April 1998 and at the "rate applicable to trusts" (a higher rate than the basic rate or lower rate of tax) under s. 118 of the Finance Act from 6 April 1998.

Interest indexed   A form of Index-linked security*. Interest indexed securities offer the worst inflation protection relative to the other two main types of index-linked security (Capital indexed* and Current pay*), as they are only indexed to protect principal (not interest), and there is no compounding effect as principal indexation is paid out over the life of the security. The coupon for each period is increased to reflect inflation for that period on the principal amount (e.g. a 2% coupon when inflation is at 4% becomes a 6% coupon). The relevant increase in the RPI for a semi-annual pay index-linked security is calculated as the increase in the RPI over the period from 8 months prior to the relevant interest payment date (or the issue date) to 2 months prior to the relevant interest payment date (or the issue date). In this way, the level of the indexation amount that will be received at the end of the interest period is known 2 months prior to commencement of the interest period. There is no accretion of principal and the original principal balance is repaid to investors at maturity. Interest indexed securities are used for corporate index-linked issuance in the US.

Interest rate   The "price" or value of money within a country, i.e. the percentage return on an initial investment over each period. The basis level of interest rates for bank lending (from which higher rates are extrapolated for high-risk investments) is determined by the Base rate* of leading banks and, ultimately, falls within the explicit or implicit purview of the central bank, often through control over the level of Money market rates* such as the Discount rate* or over the level of the Repo rate*. Raising the level of interest rates in the economy will (theoretically) lead to an increase in savings and a fall in spending to cover increased debt repayment. This leads to a slowdown in economic growth and cuts inflation. It may also cause a rise in unemployment as firms reduce their operations due to a fall in sales and an increase in finance costs. A rise in interest rates should also attract short-term capital investment from overseas seeking to realise a greater Yield*, creating interest in, and demand for, the local currency. This causes a rise in the FX rate* and is often used as a strategy for defending an FX rate. Lowering interest rates will theoretically reverse these trends.

Interest rate swap   A single-currency Swap* in which the parties agree to make payments on different interest rate Bases* (sense (ii)), or of fixed-rate payments as against floating-rate payments, calculated by reference to the same notional principal amount.

Interest yield   See Current yield.

Intermediaries offer   One of the methods of marketing and selling LSE* Listed* securities on a Flotation*. Consists of an offer of the securities by the issuer to intermediary financial institutions, who then allocate them to their clients. Sufficiently wide distribution must be achieved to be effective: may or may not be an Offer to the public* (sense (ii)), depending on circumstance. See also Placing, Offer for sale and Offer for subscription (which are all methods of raising new capital for the company) and Introduction (which does not raise new capital, but allows existing securities to be listed).

Intermediary   An entity that borrows and on-lends money, acting as a medium between a party with funds to invest and a party seeking funding.

Intermediate security   A Security* for which some kind of certificates or paper have been issued (either in the form of a Global security* or individual certificates or paper) but which is held by an intermediary (such as a custodian), effectively creating an intervener between the rights of the individual security holder and the obligations of the issuer.

Internal rate of return   The name given to the Yield to maturity* earned on the capital investment in a financing project, calculated by discounting projected future receipts.

International Accounting Standards   Or IAS*. Standards issued by the IASC* to be adopted on an international basis. From 1 April 2001, new standards issued by the IASB* are designated as International Financial Reporting Standards*.

International Accounting Standards Board   Or IASB*. Formed from the restructuring of the International Accounting Standards Committee (IASC)* on 1 April 2001. Prepares International Financial Reporting Standards (IFRS)* for adoption on an international basis, to complement the International Accounting Standards* issued by the IASC prior to 1 April 2001.

International Accounting Standards Committee   Or IASC*. The IASC was formed in the UK in 1973 to prepare International Accounting Standards (IAS)* that could be adopted on an international basis, and published its first standard in 1975. The IASC was restructured in 1999, resulting in the formation of the International Accounting Standards Board (IASB)*, which took over from the IASC on 1 April 2001. From 1 April 2001, new reporting standards issued by the IASB are designated as International Financial Reporting Standards (IFRS)*.

International Accounting Standards Regulation   On 7 June 2002, the International Accounting Standards Regulation of the EU* was adopted, which requires at Article 4 that all EU companies that are admitted to trading on a regulated market in the EU are required to prepare their consolidated financial statements in accordance with IAS* and IFRS* for each financial year beginning on or after 1 January 2005. Member states may opt to also apply the Regulation to non-consolidated accounts and to accounts of non-listed companies, and may delay the application of the Regulation to financial years starting on or after 1 January 2007 for companies that only have debt securities listed.

International Chamber of Commerce   An international organisation that aids and assists international trade by promoting the use of universally accepted governing trade practices such as INCOTERMS*, the Uniform Customs* and the ICC Arbitration Rules.

International Finance Corporation   A private sector corporation that is an arm of the World Bank.

International Financial Reporting Standards   Or IFRS*. Accounting standards issued by the IASB* from 1 April 2001, to be adopted on an international basis. The international standards that were issued prior to 1 April 2001 are still known as International Accounting Standards*, and were issued by the IASC*.

International Financial Services Centre   A tax haven established in 1987 in the Dublin docklands to attract foreign investment and promote local employment. Harmonised into the main Irish tax system over the period from 2000 to 2003 in response to EU criticism. Companies that obtained IFSC certification from the Ministry of Finance before 31 December 1999 paid profits tax at 10% until the beginning of 2003, from which date they are subject to the harmonised Irish tax rate of 12.5% on trading income. IFSC licensed companies can also make payments of interest overseas free of Withholding tax*, and qualify for trading company status (allowing the tax deductibility of expenses against income).

Interstate banking   Banking activity across state borders within the US is subject to a regulatory regime. The federal Riegle–Neal Interstate Banking and Branching Efficiency Act of 1994 (signed into law on 29 September 1994) permits interstate acquisitions of banks by a bank holding company, without the opportunity for state-by-state opt-out (previously state opt-out overrode the federal provisions), and interstate bank mergers, subject to state-by-state opt-out. Interstate branching is also permitted for the first time, into states where opt-in provisions are enacted. See also Glass–Steagall Act and Gramm–Leach–Bliley Act.

Intrinsic value   In relation to an Option*, the amount by which the value of the underlying asset has moved beyond the option Strike price* (for American options*) or the

Net present value* of the option strike price (for European options*), creating an In the money* position.

Introduction   One of the methods of marketing and selling LSE* Listed* securities on a Flotation*. Used where a sufficient market in the company's shares already exists (e.g. due to an overseas listing), the LSE will not impose any requirements as to marketing or distribution to the public of the securities. See also Placing, Offer for sale, Offer for subscription and Intermediaries offer (which are all methods of raising new capital for the company, as opposed to the Introduction, which does not raise new capital, but allows existing securities to be listed).

Investment bank   A Bank* that advises on the structuring and underwriting of new securities issues and other financing transactions and Investment business* and on the Secondary market* distribution of securities. Often also carries out investment portfolio management. Cf. Commercial bank*. Historically known in the UK as a Merchant bank*. In the US, the Glass–Steagall Act* historically prevented investment banks acting at the same time as commercial banks (which has led to some US commercial banks setting-up offshore investment banking subsidiaries). These structures were simplified with the reform of the Glass–Steagall Act by the Gramm–Leach–Bliley Act*. The two bank functions can exist side by side in the UK, but investment banking is typically dealt with in a separate group company regulated under the Financial Services Act 1986* (now under the FSMA* 2000).

Investment business   See Financial Services Act 1986.

Investment company   (i) Status under the US Investment Company Act of 1940. The act defines an investment company as, *inter alia*, any issuer of securities that "is or holds itself out as being engaged primarily ... in the business of investing, re-investing, or trading in securities" or any issuer that "is engaged or proposes to engage in the business of investing, reinvesting, owning, holding or trading in securities, and owns or proposes to acquire investment securities having a value exceeding 40% of the value of such issuer's total assets ... on an unconsolidated basis". The definition of "securities" is wide and covers "any note ... or evidence of indebtedness".

An affiliated originator is prohibited from transferring financial assets to an investment company under s. 17(a)(2), and any investment company that makes a public offer of securities in the US is required under s. 7(d) of the Act to be registered with the SEC*. Furthermore, any investment company that makes a Placement* of securities in the US is also required to be registered pursuant to a no-action letter sent to Touche Remnant in 1987.

An exemption is available under s. 3(c)(1) for "any issuer whose outstanding securities (other than short-term paper) are beneficially owned by not more than 100 [US] persons and which is not making and does not presently propose to make a public offering of its securities". This is an ongoing requirement (and is also therefore relevant to resales), rather than simply a primary issuance requirement.

In addition, Rule 3a-7 (adopted by the SEC in 1992) provides a general exemption for any "issuer who is engaged in the business of purchasing, or otherwise acquiring, and holding eligible assets" (certain financial assets such as receivables which will "convert into cash within a definite time period"), where the securities issued off the back of the assets carry an Investment grade* credit rating or are sold to QIBs*.

An exemption is provided under s. 3(c)(7) (passed into law in 1996 and effective from April 1997) for an issuer whose securities are owned solely by Qualified purchasers* and who does not intend to make a public offering of its securities.

(ii) Status for UK taxation purposes, defined in s. 130 ICTA* as a company "whose business consists wholly or mainly in the making of investments and the principal part of whose income is derived therefrom". Prior to the Finance Act* 1996, a company that was neither an investment company nor a Trading company* (sense (ii)) could not deduct interest payments on debt from its taxable income, pursuant to the now repealed s. 338(6) ICTA (see Interest). Deductions are generally not as wide for an investment company as those given to trading companies; consequently, trading companies are often preferred when establishing an SPV* that will be subject to UK taxation as part of a Securitisation* transaction.

Investment Company Act   See Investment company, sense (i).

Investment firm   Term used within the EU to set out the scope of Investment bank* type institutions subject to regulatory and Capital adequacy* requirements. The definition is set out in Article 1 of Directive* 93/22 of 10 May 1993 as being "any legal person the regular occupation of which is the provision of investment services for third parties on a professional basis"; "investment services" are defined as execution, dealing, portfolio management or underwriting services relating to Securities*, Futures*, Forwards*, Swaps* and Options*. Only certain provisions of the Directive apply to Credit institutions*, and insurance companies and other limited classes of entity are exempted. The definition of investment firm used in the UK is set out in s. 2 Statutory Instrument 1995/3275 as "any person ... whose regular occupation or business is the provision of any one or more core investment services to third parties on a professional basis". The same definition of investment services and the same exemptions are used as under the Directive. Under s. 5 Statutory Instrument 1995/3275, persons authorised as an investment firm in another EU country may carry on in the UK any of the following which they are authorised to carry on in their home state: Investment business* or business under the Consumer Credit Act 1974*.

Investment grade   A Credit rating* for an institution, entity or securities issue at or above a certain minimum level (BBB−, or Baa3 for Moody's). Investment grade securities have increased marketability as institutions such as US commercial banks (who might otherwise be prohibited from investing) are permitted to invest in securities thus rated.

Investment manager   An exemption from consideration of a manager of investment transactions (trades in securities, FX* and some derivatives) as a UK representative (a branch or agency through which a trade is carried on in the UK) of a non-UK company. In the absence of such an exemption, the non-UK company might be subjected to Corporation tax* in the UK on the profits deriving from the trade carried on through such UK representative. In order to claim the exemption, s. 127 Finance Act* 1995 requires that the manager be carrying on a business of providing investment management services, that the investment transactions are carried out in the ordinary course of the manager's business, that the manager acts in an independent capacity (chiefly that the investment transactions carried out by the manager for the non-UK company do not exceed more than a certain percentage of the business of the investment manager), that the manager does not have a beneficial entitlement to 20% or more of the profits made via the manager, that the manager is remunerated at a rate that is not less than a customary rate for the services, and that the manager is not considered to be the UK representative of the non-UK company in respect of any other amounts.

Investment trust   A Corporation* that issues shares to investors and uses the proceeds to invest in accordance with agreed investment objectives. As a corporate entity, an investment trust is a "closed-end fund" that cannot readily increase or decrease the amount of funds under management, as can a Unit trust*. Consequently, the value of its shares varies with supply and demand and do not precisely match the Net asset value* of the investment trust, with the shares trading at a discount or premium.

Investor certificate   See Investor interest.

Investor interest   Or Investor certificate*. In a credit card Securitisation* or a Master trust* structure, the interest held by the investors in the credit card assets or other assets. The interest held is designed to remain stable despite the fluctuating balance of the receivables due to amortisation (and new draw-downs on credit card accounts). The investor interest is not senior to the Seller interest* – the two interests rank pro rata based on the Floating allocation percentage* or Fixed allocation percentage* at a point in time.

Invitation telex   A telex or fax sent to prospective Managers* of a bond issue by the Lead manager*, inviting them to underwrite the issue.

IO   Interest only. An interest Strip*. An IO will increase in value if the tenor of the security it has been stripped from lengthens, as valuation is likely to be based on an NPV* of expected cash flows over different payment scenarios (for example different Prepayment* rates if the IO is stripped from an MBS*). See also Mortgage redemption certificate.

IOFC   International Offshore Financial Centre in Labuan.

IOSCO   International Organisation of Securities Commissions.

IPAA   International Paying Agents Association. Organisation formed on 5 January 1995 to represent the interests of Paying agents* in the Euromarkets*.

IPE   International Petroleum Exchange. Trading forum for Commodity futures*, Forwards* and Options*.

IPMA   International Primary Market Association. The Eurobond* Underwriters* association. Cf. ISMA.

IPO   Initial Public Offering. The first Public offering* of the shares in a company. See Flotation.

IRR   See Internal rate of return.

IRS   The US Internal Revenue Service.

ISDA   International Swaps and Derivatives Association, Inc. (formerly known as the International Swap Dealers Association, Inc.). Derivatives market trade body that publishes standardising documentation for derivative transactions.

ISDA Master   A standard form of master agreement published by ISDA* in three forms; the 1987 form, the 1992 form and the more up to date 2002 form. The forms contain terms and conditions for Derivatives* and FX* transactions that are designed to protect the parties to the agreement in the event of the insolvency of the other party by effecting Close-out netting*.

ISIN   International Securities Identification Number. On application by a lead manager or paying agent, an ISIN is allocated to a security that is accepted by Clearstream* or Euroclear* for clearing through their system and is intended to be traded internationally. See also Common code and CUSIP.

ISMA   International Securities Market Association. The Eurobond* secondary market trade body and regulator. Cf. IPMA.

Issue   The creation of Securities* by an Issuer* for Allotment* to their initial holders in consideration of the payment of the relevant subscription price or (in relation to shares) the relevant Nominal value* and Premium* (sense (i)).

Issue price   A percentage of the Face value* of a security, which reflects the price at which such security is originally sold on issue, and from which the Managers* (sense (i)) will typically deduct their Management fee* and any Selling concession*, before passing the net proceeds on to the Issuer*. Typically varying a couple of percentage points or less from 100% for an interest-bearing security and a significantly greater percentage for Deep discount* or Zero coupon* securities. See also Re-offer price.

Issued share capital   The aggregate Nominal value* of a company's outstanding share capital from time to time. The Directors* of a company may issue new shares if authorised to do so by the company's Articles of association* or by an Ordinary resolution*, under s. 80 Companies Act 1985*. A company's issued share capital may not exceed its Authorised share capital* from time to time.

Issuer   A corporate or other entity that raises funds by issuing Securities*.

Issuing bank   In relation to a Documentary credit*, the bank that has issued the credit. It is obliged to pay on an irrevocable credit if the required documents are submitted to it, under the provisions of the UCP 500*.

ITM   See In the money.

iX   Or International exchanges. An Exchange* platform proposal announced on 3 May 2000 as a merger of Deutsche Börse* and the London Stock Exchange* in alliance with Nasdaq*. The platform was to be divided into blue chips (traded in London), hi-tech stocks (traded in Frankfurt under the Neuer Markt*) and other stocks (which will remain traded where they are currently traded). The platform intended to use the Xetra trading system to replace the SETS* trading system. The merger proposal was withdrawn on 12 September 2000.

Japanese leveraged lease   Or JLL*. A Leveraged lease* that uses a Double dipping* structure whereby both the lessor and the lessee can claim tax benefits, due to Japanese domestic legislation on the "ownership" criteria needed to claim Capital allowances*. Often combined with a Defeasance* structure. Discussions on the restructuring or removal of some of the benefits of the JLL began in 1996, resulting in legislative changes that came into effect on 1 April 1998 (applying to JLLs entered into after 1 October 1998) and require the lessor to depreciate the asset on a straight-line basis over the term of the lease, removing the economic benefit of many deals.

JLL   See Japanese leveraged lease.

Joint stock company   In the UK, a now obsolete form of Company* and Unincorporated association*, consisting of a joint account of stock used for trading. The Joint Stock Companies Act 1844 introduced incorporation by registration as a Registered company*.

Jumbo Pfandbriefe   Variety of Pfandbriefe* first issued in May 1995, designed to offer greater trading liquidity due to its size, and increased transparency due to standardisation. They are required to be listed on a German exchange, and are issued as bullet securities in bearer form (or registered form for any portion of the issue that is sold into the US). They have a minimum issue size of Euro 500m, and three market-makers are required.

Junior debt   See Subordinated debt.

Junk bond   Securities* of an issuer that has a Speculative grade* Credit rating* or no credit rating. Junk bonds fall between equity and debt in terms of their pricing basis, as their credit analysis is tied to favourable business conditions.

Kangaroo bond   A Foreign bond* issued in Australian Dollars.

Kappa   See Vega.

Kassenobligationen   Swiss MTN* issued with a 3- to 8-year maturity by a local Swiss bank. Cf. Schweizerobligationen.

Keiretsu   A Japanese corporate network, usually consisting of a bank and a group of companies in different industrial sectors, which works cooperatively.

Kerb trading   Trading that is carried out after the Close*.

KMV   A company that produces credit risk calculation services, including the equity-based valuation of credit risk by assuming that the equity value of a business represents a call option on the underlying assets of the business.

Knock-in option   A Barrier option* that only becomes operative if and when the underlying Actual* passes a certain upward or downward level.

Knock-out option   A Barrier option* that loses its effectiveness if the underlying Actual* passes a certain upward or downward level.

Kurtosis   Measure of the conformity of the tails of a standard deviation distribution to a log-normal distribution. See Value at risk.

Ladder option   A Path dependent option* that records a profit each time the underlying asset value rises above a new trigger level.

Landesbank   German public sector bank that benefits from two state guarantee mechanisms – the Gewahrtragerhaftung* (a guarantee by the public sector owners in favour of the external creditors of the Landesbank) and the Anstaltslast* (an obligation of the public sector owners in favour of the Landesbank to support the Landesbank and to enable it to meet its financial obligations). Under pressure from the EU, these state-support mechanisms will be dismantled after 18 July 2005. Until such date, both forms of guarantee will remain. After such date, only liabilities existing on or prior to 18 July 2001, and liabilities existing on or prior to 18 July 2005 which mature on or prior to 31 December 2015, will remain guaranteed. The quality of the form of the guarantee post-18 July 2005 as to timeliness of payment has been the subject of discussion among the rating agencies. Different Landesbank have proposed different structures for reorganising their businesses post-2005, and for dealing with the likely credit downgrades in the sector following removal of state guarantees and commensurate increase in funding costs. These have included a split of business into public sector (i.e. development) business and commercial business via a parent company and holding company structure, and the continuance of state guarantees on the basis of a commercial market fee. Integration of the Landesbanks with other banking entities in Germany, such as the Sparkassen savings banks, has also been discussed.

Last trading day   The last day for trading of a particular Future* or Option* prior to maturity and settlement.

LAUTRO   Life Assurance and Unit Trust Regulatory Organisation Limited. One of the self-regulating organisations (see SRO) established under the Financial Services Act 1986*. Responsible for regulating life offices, unit trust managers and friendly societies in relation to marketing activities, but see under Financial Services Authority*. Memberships were transferred to other self-regulating organisations following establishment of the PIA* in July 1994 and abolition of LAUTRO in 1995.

Law 52   Italian Law number 52 of 21 February 1991. Law 52 allows the sale of Receivables* to be made to a company set up in accordance with Law 52 (known as a Law 52 company*), without a requirement to notify the receivables debtors of the transfer in order for the transfer to be effective.

Law 52 company   See Law 52. A Law 52 company must be established with a share capital of at least Italian Lire 1bn (Euro 516,457) and must be registered to carry on a factoring business in Italy.

Law merchant   The law merchant is an area of common law consisting of "the usages of merchants and traders . . . ratified by the decisions of courts of law, which, upon such usages being proved before them, have adopted them as settled law" (*Goodwin v. Roberts 1875*). Its chief current relevance is to the determination of new categories of Negotiable instrument*. It applies to Bills of exchange*, Cheques* and Promissory notes* by section 97(2) of the Bills of Exchange Act 1882 (which essentially consolidated the prior law merchant in this area), save where expressly provided otherwise therein.

Law of Property Act 1925   UK statute dealing with rights relating to assets generally and covering, *inter alia*, the method of transfer of Choses in action* (see Assignment), the powers of secured creditors (see LPA receiver) and Tacking*.

Law of Property (Miscellaneous Provisions) Act 1989   See Deed.

Law of Property (Miscellaneous Provisions) Act 1994   See Full title guarantee.

LC See Letter of Credit.

LCH See London Clearing House.

LDC Less Developed Country.

LDMA London Discount Market Association.

Lead manager In a new Securities* issue or Syndicated loan*, the Manager* and Underwriter* who arranges the offering or Syndication* of the transaction.

Lease (i) In relation to equipment or assets, a bailment of the assets for payment that is made between the owner as lessor and the bailee as lessee. Title to the asset does not pass to the lessee (agreements that provide for title to pass are classified as Hire purchase* or Conditional sale*). See Finance lease and Operating lease.
   (ii) In relation to land, an agreement for occupation of the land that is made between the owner of the land as landlord and the would-be occupier as tenant.

Leaseback See Sale and leaseback.

Lender of last resort Role undertaken by the Bank of England in the UK Money markets* in acting as backstop Liquidity* provider (but not as credit supporter) to the market.

Leptokurtosis A fat tail on a standard deviation distribution. See Value at risk.

10b-5 Letter Issuers of securities that have a tranche sold in the US may obtain a "10b-5" from their legal counsel as reassurance that they have met the high standards of Due diligence* required by Rule 10b-5*. This is a letter from the counsel stating that they are satisfied that the issuer company has not made any misstatement in the offer documentation.

Letter of comfort See Comfort letter.

Letter of credit Or LOC. A promise by a bank to pay amounts to a beneficiary. If the letter of credit is being used for trade finance, the bank will make Payment against documents*. Such a letter of credit is referred to as a Documentary credit* and is typically governed by the incorporation by reference of the Uniform Customs* rules (variants on documentary credits are the Negotiation credit* and the Transferable credit*). If the letter of credit is being used simply as a bank Guarantee* (e.g. for repayment of a loan made to one of the bank's customers by other banks) it is referred to as a Standby letter of credit* and payment will be conditional on certain trigger events (e.g. insolvency of the borrower). Standby letters of credit may also incorporate the Uniform Customs rules by reference.

Letter of undertaking A letter issued by one company (typically a parent) to a bank or other creditor stating its approval of a loan or other financing given by such creditor to another company (typically a subsidiary), and undertaking to provide financial support to the latter company to enable it to fulfil its obligations under the financing. Legally binding. Cf. Comfort letter.

Letters patent company In the UK, a now obsolete form of Company* and Unincorporated association* originally created under the Trading Companies Act 1834.

Leverage   **(i)** A measure of the relative current and capital indebtedness of a company, calculated by taking total debt (capital and current liabilities) as a percentage of shareholders' funds (equity capital and reserves). Cf. Gearing, sense (i).

(ii) Use of an asset (such as a Future* or Option*), or Position*, which in either case relies on a contract for differences in values (rather than on the underlying value itself), or the investing of borrowed funds, in either case in order to magnify percentage returns on the amount actually paid out of own funds. Cf. Margin trading.

Leveraged buy-out   The acquisition of a business in reliance on debt financing. Often used for a Management buy-out*.

Leveraged lease   A lease mechanism often used for aircraft financing, in which the lessor finances the purchase of the aircraft through raising debt that is repaid by the rental stream from the lessee who operates the aircraft. This allows the lessor to claim 100% of the Capital allowances* for the aircraft against taxable profits, while achieving Leverage* (sense (ii)) by only investing a fraction of the price as equity in the purchase of the aircraft. See also Double dipping and Japanese leveraged lease.

LIBA   London Investment Banking Association.

LIBID   London Interbank Bid Rate. In the London Interbank market*, the Bid* rate at which the quoting bank will agree to take deposits of the quoted amount and duration from investors and depositors. Sometimes used as the base interest rate for securities issues or facilities on the grounds that it is likely to be more stable than LIBOR* in a banking crisis, as in such an event, banks approached with requests for borrowing would widen their LIBID/LIBOR spread (which is normally around 12.5 bp) to cover the increased Credit risk*. Cf. LIBOR and LIMEAN.

LIBOR   London Interbank Offered Rate. In the London Interbank market*, the Offer* rate at which the quoting bank will agree to lend funds of the quoted amount and duration to banks of the highest credit quality. LIBOR quotes from other banks represent a bank's short-term marginal cost of funds. LIBOR is normally higher than LIBID* (by around 12.5 bp) to reflect the Spread* (sense (i)) to the bank. See also LIMEAN.

Lien   A common law or possessory lien is a variety of Security* (sense (ii)) over tangible assets that are capable of physical possession, which arises by operation of common law and consists of the right to retain possession, either (a) of any and all goods or documents until all debts owed to the possessor are satisfied (a "general lien"; available to bankers (in relation to paper securities, the bankers' lien extends to a right to sell the securities in question), solicitors and factors), or (b) of goods or documents obtained in relation to a particular transaction until particular claims in relation to such transaction are satisfied (a "particular lien"; available to other creditors). A lien does not (save in certain limited cases, e.g. the bankers' lien) carry with it the right to sell the assets. A lien created by contract is more properly a form of Pledge*. A lien may also take the form of an equitable or charging lien, which arises by operation of equity and consists of a charge on certain property, such as a vendor's lien over land for the purchase money or certain maritime liens.

LIFFE   See London International Financial Futures and Options Exchange.

Lifting the veil   Also known as Piercing the veil*. Descriptive term in the UK for the courts ignoring the Corporate veil* and seeking to make members liable for liabilities of the company. Very rare and typically arises where there is evidence that the company is used to perpetrate a fraud, or where the company is used for an illegal or improper purpose. Cf. Substantive consolidation.

LIMEAN   The rate that is the average of LIBID* and LIBOR*.

Limit move   A limitation placed by a Futures exchange* on the amount by which the quoted price of any particular Future* can vary in any one session.

Limit order   A buy or sell order that is conditional on being matched at (or better than) a certain Bid* or Offer* price.

Limited company   See Limited liability company, sense (ii).

Limited liability   Often the result of the separate Corporate personality* of an entity; namely that liabilities of the entity are its sole responsibility. In the UK, applies in respect of most Statutory companies* and Registered companies*. For a Company limited by shares* this has the result that Members* are only liable to the company (or to creditors of the company on a Winding-up*) to the extent of any unpaid Premium* (sense (i)) on their shares or any part of the Nominal value* of their shares that is not yet paid up.

Limited liability company   (i) See LLC.
    (ii) A company with Limited liability* for its Members*. In the UK, most Statutory companies* and Registered companies*.

Limited partnership   In the UK, a Partnership* where one or more partners can have Limited liability*, provided one or more partners remain with unlimited liability. Any partner taking part in the management of the partnership will automatically acquire unlimited liability. Introduced by the Limited Partnerships Act 1907, which, prior to 21 December 2002, generally restricted limited partnerships to no more than 20 partners under s. 4(2), although accountants, solicitors and recognised Stock exchange* members are exempted from this requirement by s. 717 of the Companies Act 1985*. The 20 partner limit was removed by the Regulatory Reform (Removal of 20 Member Limit in Partnerships etc.) Order 2002 from the DTI* under the Regulatory Reform Act 2001 with effect from 21 December 2002.

Limited recourse   A transaction or structure where the recourse of creditors for repayment is limited to particular assets or cash flows. For example in a Securitisation* or Repackaging*, recourse is typically limited to rights against any derivative counterparty and to the underlying Receivables* or the underlying Securities* respectively.

Limited title guarantee   From 1 July 1995, in documentation disposing of assets or creating a Security interest* over assets under English law, the use by the owner of the words "limited title guarantee" implies certain covenants as to the title that the owner has in the assets in accordance with the provisions of the Law of Property (Miscellaneous Provisions) Act 1994. These covenants are: that the owner has the right to dispose of the assets, that since the last disposition of the assets for value the owner has not encumbered the assets or suffered the assets to be encumbered, and that he will do all he reasonably can do in order to give to the other party the title he purports to give. See also Full title guarantee.

Linked presentation   See FRS 5.

Liquid market   A market in a particular asset that regularly has a high volume of assets being traded and has a sufficient number of willing buyers and sellers such that the Bid*/Offer* Spread* (sense (i)) is comparatively narrow.

Liquidate   To effect a Close-out* of a Position*.

Liquidation   The Winding-up* of a company. Typically used more specifically, however to refer to the Compulsory winding-up* or Insolvent liquidation* of a company; i.e. the winding-up of a company that is Unable to pay its debts* (if necessary paying off each class of creditors in full through the order of Priorities* (sense (i)), or by paying a Dividend* (sense (ii)) to the first class of creditors reached where the proceeds realised are not sufficient to pay such class in full). Effected by appointment of a Liquidator*, following presentation to the court of a Liquidation petition*. One of the five main insolvency-related procedures (for the others, see Voluntary arrangement, Receivership, Administrative receivership and Administration).

Liquidation petition   A petition made to a court for the Liquidation* of a company under s. 124 of the Insolvency Act 1986. The petition may be made by the company itself, or by the directors of the company, or by a creditor or creditors of the company. Grounds for a petition are set out in s. 122 of the Insolvency Act 1986 and include that: the company has resolved by Special resolution to be wound-up; the number of shareholders in the company has reduced below two (unless the company is a Private company*, which is entitled to have a single shareholder); the company is Unable to pay its debts*; or the court is of the opinion that it is just and equitable that the company should be wound up.

Liquidator   A qualified insolvency practitioner appointed to effect a Liquidation*. Has power to set aside Undervalues* and Preferences* and apply for an order recognising Fraudulent trading* or nullifying Transactions defrauding creditors*.

Liquidity   For an asset, a measurement of the degree to which there is a Liquid market* in an asset, such that the asset may be monetised at any point in time with very little delay and very little risk of loss of principal or of interest penalties being incurred. Cash itself thus forms the benchmark against which the liquidity of other assets is judged. For an institution or transaction, the degree to which the institution or transaction can respond to demands for cash, by maintaining a high degree of liquid assets, or a Committed facility* such as a Liquidity facility* (which can be drawn down at very short notice).

Liquidity facility   A Facility* designed to provide the borrower with the Liquidity* to meet short-term cash requirements. Often encountered in Commercial paper* funded Securitisation* structures, in order to enable redemption of commercial paper for which a Rollover* cannot be effected due to disruption in the issuance market. Usually expressed only to be drawable against non-defaulted receivables, so as not to constitute credit enhancement (which would result in a direct deduction from capital if in a first loss position), they are, however, often intended to provide full coverage of CP that has been issued (see Borrowing base for details), and may also contain a Term out* provision. In relation to a securitisation, usually subject to specific Capital adequacy* rules if provided by the originator.

Liquidity risk   The Risk* that an asset does not have sufficient Liquidity* to enable the holder to convert it into cash quickly and without penalty or loss.

Listed   With reference to an issue of securities, means that the securities have a Listing* (sense (ii)). With reference to a company, means that the Shares* of the company have a listing.

Listing   (i) The process of gaining a Listing (see (ii) below) for Shares* or other Securities* by complying with the requirements of the relevant Listing rules*. Listing enables certain investors who would be unable to invest in unlisted securities to buy and may give the benefit of certain tax exemptions (for example, in relation to Withholding tax* in the UK, see Quoted Eurobond) or the ability to bypass currency restrictions on the currency of the country of the listing. A listing generally relates to a particular Stock exchange*, although it may simply be a regulatory process (as is the case in the UK now that the Financial Services Authority* (referred to as the UK Listing Authority or UKLA when acting in this capacity) has taken over from the London Stock Exchange* as the listing authority for the UK). Stock exchanges also have their own requirements as to which type of securities they will accept for trading on their exchange. For equity securities, this may involve requirements as to minimum market distribution levels, although for debt securities such requirements are often much reduced or waived. If the listing relates to trading on a stock exchange, it can help to ensure a Secondary market* for the security that is a Liquid market*. In relation to the first listing of equity securities in a company, see Flotation.

(ii) The actual listing itself granted pursuant to compliance with the Listing rules* in the procedure described at Listing, sense (i) above.

Listing particulars   The information that a listing authority requires to be given to investors or otherwise made available with regard to an issue (and issuer) of shares or securities in order for such authority to grant the securities a Listing* (sense (ii)). Overridden in the UK by the requirement for a Prospectus* under s. 85 FSMA* 2000 where there is an Offer to the public* (sense (ii)) prior to admission of the securities to a listing. UK listing particulars are subject to disclosure on specific details as set out in the Listing rules*, as well as to an overriding duty under s. 146 Financial Services Act 1986* (repeated at s. 80 FSMA 2000) to disclose all information investors would reasonably expect and require to find therein, with liability to compensate investors under s. 150 Financial Services Act 1986 (repeated at s. 90 FSMA 2000) on responsible persons as specified in s. 152 Financial Services Act 1986 (the issuer, its directors and any person who authorised, or is named as accepting responsibility for, the listing particulars) (repeated at s. 79(3) FSMA 2000 under regulations to be given by the Treasury) for any loss they suffer as a result of untrue or misleading statements in the particulars or the omission of relevant details. Listing particulars must be registered at Companies House under s. 149 Financial Services Act 1986 (repeated at s. 83 FSMA 2000), breach of which requirement is a criminal offence. Listing particulars may also give rise to general criminal liability under s. 47 Financial Services Act 1986 (repeated at s. 397 FSMA 2000) for misleading or false statements.

Listing Particulars Directive   In the EU, the Listing Particulars Directive (Directive 2001/34) requires that companies should be able to use a single prospectus to raise capital across the EU. The prospectus is checked by the listing authority in the home state of the issuer, and needs to be updated annually via a shelf registration. The directive also applies to the smaller companies markets across Europe (such as AIM*).

Listing rules   The rules required to be complied with in order to obtain a Listing* (sense (ii)) for an issue of securities. In relation to the UK, the rules contained in Part IV of the Financial Services Act 1986* (as replaced by Part VI of the Financial Services and Markets Act 2000*), deal with: (a) Offers to the public* (sense (ii)) of securities for which an application for listing has been made and for which publication of a Prospectus* is required; and (b) the listing of issues for which no offer to the public has been made prior to admission to listing, and for which the publication of Listing particulars* is required. In each case, the rules are expanded in the new UKLA* Listing Rules (which replaced the Yellow Book* on 1 May 2000).

LLC   The US limited liability company. A Corporation* that combines Limited liability* for members and freedom to participate in management with the Fiscal transparency* of a Partnership*. Cf. GmbH. Fiscal Pass-through* (sense (i)) status for LLCs is usually based on LLC interests being transferable only with the unanimous written consent of all members, and on the LLC being either fixed in duration (usually at 30 years) or automatically dissolved on the death, expulsion or insolvency of a member.

LME   See London Metal Exchange.

LMX   The London market for Excess-of-loss* reinsurance.

Loan capital   The part of a company's Capital* (sense (i)) that requires periodic payment of interest and/or repayment of principal regardless of the profitability of the company. Cf. Equity capital*.

Loan creditor   A loan creditor, for the purposes of the Close company* provisions, means, under s. 417 ICTA, a creditor in respect of any redeemable loan capital issued by a company or any debt incurred by a company for:

(a) Any money borrowed or capital assets acquired by the company;
(b) Any right to receive income created in favour of the company; or
(c) Any consideration the value of which to the company at the time the debt was incurred was substantially less than the amount of the debt.

A person carrying on a business of banking is not deemed to be a loan creditor in respect of any loan capital or debt issued or incurred by the company for money lent by him to the company in the ordinary course of that business.

Loan to value ratio   Or LTV*. The figure measuring the percentage of the value of an asset against which a loan or other finance has been raised.

LOC   See Letter of credit.

Local currency rating   A Credit rating* relating to the relevant entity's ability to service debt obligations in its local currency based on an assessment of the Credit risk* on the entity. See also Foreign currency rating.

Lock-up   See Regulation S, Release 4708, TEFRA D.

LOFSA   Labuan Offshore Financial Services Authority.

London Clearing House   Or LCH. A Clearing house* that deals as central counterparty for trades on four Exchanges*: IPE*, LIFFE*, LME* and OMLX*, and also acts as central counterparty for SETS* trades from 26 February 2001. On 26 June 2003 LCH announced a merger with Clearnet, the French clearing house, to form LCH.Clearnet.

London Club   The forum for rescheduling debts of a country when the debts are not issued or guaranteed by that country's government. Cf. Paris Club.

London Interbank Bid Rate   See LIBID.

London Interbank Offered Rate   See LIBOR.

London International Financial Futures and Options Exchange   Or LIFFE*. Trading Exchange* for Financial futures* and Options*. Electronic screen-based trading was introduced over time from November 1998 to replace Open outcry*, beginning with larger financial products. Acquired by Euronext* in 2002 to form Euronext.liffe.

London Metal Exchange   Or LME*. Trading Exchange* for Commodity futures*, Forwards* and Options*.

London Stock Exchange   Or LSE*. The London Stock Exchange Limited. London equity and stock trading Exchange*. Previously, securities were also traded via the USM*, which was closed in 1996, and under Rule 4.2*, which was phased out with the introduction of AIM (opened on 19 June 1995). Prior to 1 May 2000, the LSE also had regulatory authority for listing securities, and published the Yellow Book* containing Listing rules* and guidelines on pre-vetting of Prospectuses* for Unlisted* securities (used to achieve European Economic Area Mutual recognition* of the prospectus when the securities are intended to be Listed* on a non-London exchange). Regulatory authority for listing passed to the FSA* (referred to as the UK Listing Authority or UKLA when acting in this capacity) from 1 May 2000, and the Yellow Book was replaced with the new UKLA Listing Rules. In 1999, the LSE introduced shelf registration for equity securities issued within 12 months of the filing of shelf listing particulars by an issuer that has had its main shares listed for 12 months or more.

Long   A Position* characterised by the retention of ownership in an asset in reliance on an expected increase in value. Cf. Short.

Long position   See Long.

Lookback call   A Lookback option* which uses the highest price of the underlying asset to determine the settlement amount.

Lookback option   A Path dependent option* where the settlement amount reflects the highest or lowest price achieved by the underlying asset during its life. See Lookback call and Lookback put.

Lookback put   A Lookback option* which uses the lowest price of the underlying asset to determine the settlement amount.

Loss severity   The level of post-enforcement losses on a defaulted asset, generally expressed as a percentage of the asset amount. See also Weighted average loss severity and Expected loss.

LPA   See Law of Property Act 1925.

LPA receiver   A Receiver* appointed under s. 101 Law of Property Act 1925 as opposed to under a power to appoint a receiver contained in a Security* (sense (ii)) document. The section provides for appointments where the security is a Mortgage* or a Charge* made by Deed*.

LPI-linked security   Or limited price indexation linked security. A security that is similar to an Index-linked security*, but where the return is linked to a limited band of actual RPI* – typically set with a floor of 0% and a cap of 5%. Often used to match pension liabilities in the UK, as pension funds are not required by law to provide inflation-linked increases in excess of 5%, but are not permitted to decrease liabilities in deflationary environments with negative RPI. See Capital indexed, Current pay and Interest indexed.

LSE   See London Stock Exchange.

LTOM   London Traded Options Market. Trading forum for share Options*.

LTV   See Loan to value ratio.

Maintenance margin   The amount of the Margin* (sense (ii)) deposited by a Futures* or exchange-traded Options* trader on a daily basis to cover fluctuations in the value of the future or certain exchange-traded options that reduce the remaining margin deposited by the trader below a certain minimum maintenance level. Equal to the amount required to increase the margin back to the level of the Initial margin*.

Maintenance of capital   The requirement that a company should not be allowed to effect a Reduction of capital* (s. 135(1) Companies Act 1985*), Purchase* (and Redemption*) of shares or a subscription for its own shares (s. 143(1) Companies Act 1985) or other Distribution* (sense(i)) to shareholders (s. 263(1) Companies Act 1985) in a manner that prejudices the creditors of the company (who are reliant on the company's equity "cushion" as a safeguard for repayment). Generally speaking any such action should only be effected from Distributable profits* or fresh share proceeds or in accordance with specified procedures or subject to confirmation by the court. Where the net assets of a Public company* fall to half or less of its called-up share capital, the company must call an EGM* to consider the situation under s. 142 Companies Act 1985.

Making a market   See Market-making.

Management buy-in   See MBI.

Management buy-out   See MBO.

Management fee   The fee paid to the Managers* or Underwriters* for underwriting an issue of Securities*. Quoted as a percentage of the Face value* of the securities.

Management group   In a securities issue or syndicated loan, a group consisting of the Lead manager*, any co-lead managers, the Managers* and any co-managers.

Manager   In a new securities issue or Syndicated loan*, an institution that acts as Underwriter* for the transaction. The managers will on-sell their eventual Allotment* (in relation to an issue – see Selling Group) or participate portions of their Allotment* or Commitment* (in relation to a loan – see Participants).

Mandate   (i) The terms on which a bank agrees to manage a customer's account.
   (ii) The terms on which a financial institution agrees to proceed with arranging a financing transaction for a client.

Mandatory further advance   In relation to a Securitisation* transaction, a mandatory further advance is a Further advance* that the Originator is required to make by the terms of the documentation between the originator and the underlying customer. Cf. Discretionary further advance.

Mandatory liquid assets   Also known as MLAs*. These are assets that a UK financial institution is obliged to subscribe to the Bank of England and other institutions as a percentage of its Eligible liabilities*, and have historically taken three forms: Reserve assets* (intended to ensure Liquidity* in the market – removed in 1986); Special deposits*/Supplementary special deposits* (intended to act as mechanisms to control the money supply by restricting bank credit creation – removed in 1980); and Cash ratio* deposits (intended to provide income for the Bank of England and to support the Bank's role as Liquidity* supporter in the market, set at a certain fraction of a percentage of eligible liabilities in excess of a threshold). See also Financial Services Authority.

Mandatory redemption   The requirement to effect Redemption* of a Security* in certain circumstances, either in whole or in part (by lot or by a pro rata reduction of the principal amount outstanding of each security in the issue). May be effected by use of a Sinking fund*.

Manufactured housing   A sector of the US ABS market that consists of loans for the acquisition of factory-built housing that is transported to site.

Margin   (i) The Spread* (sense (ii)) over the relevant interest rate Basis* (sense (ii)) charged by a lender to a borrower on money lent, stated in Basis points* per annum. A front-end fee can be expressed as a periodic margin on a loan via:

$$m = (f \times r)/[1 - (1 + r)^{-n}]$$

where m = the margin (expressed as a percentage of the principal)
   f = the fee (expressed as a percentage of the principal)
   r = the assumed Discount rate* (sense (ii)) per compounding period
   n = the number of compounding periods.

(ii) Any Collateral* which a Futures exchange* requires from its members to support their obligations on contracts traded by them (and typically equal to or greater than the Mark-to-market* liability under the contracts from time to time) or (in relation to an Option*) as payment of the option Premium* (sense (iii)), and consisting of Initial margin*, and either Variation margin* or Maintenance margin*. Also, collateral that an entity in an OTC* Derivatives* transaction requires from its counterparty (and again typically equal to or greater than the mark-to-market value of the outstanding derivatives trades).

Margin call   A call by an Exchange* (or by a Broker* from a client who is Margin trading*) for a further Margin* (sense (ii)) amount to reflect an unfavourable fluctuation in the value of a Future* (see Variation margin*) or of another asset that has not yet been settled.

Margin trading   A form of securities investment technique, margin trading involves a credit facility given by a broker against an agreement by the investor to pay a certain percentage of the securities' price (e.g. 30%) and the pledging of the securities bought as collateral for the remainder. As a large percentage of the value of the securities bought is paid for from borrowed monies, this enables the investor to use a Leverage* technique. The return or loss on the investor's original capital is amplified by that multiple of the investor's capital that the investor has borrowed, making the technique potentially extremely profitable, even after funding costs are repaid, but also extremely high risk if the market moves against the investor (in which event the creditor – normally the broker – may make a Margin call*). Margin trading is often utilised by Hedge funds* to Leverage* (sense (ii)) annual returns. Margin trading may be used as a form of bridge finance in a Rolling settlement* system, whereby an investor who buys and then rapidly sells securities will be obliged to pay for the securities bought prior to receiving the sale proceeds (in contrast to a periodic trading account system, where all trades within the account period are settled at the same time at the end of the account period).

As margin trading allows for a boosted return on assets in much the same way as increased indebtedness in a company allows a higher return on equity, assets that are inherently forms of margin trading (e.g. Futures* and Options*) are sometimes referred to as assets with Gearing* (sense (ii)) or Leverage* (sense (ii)).

Mark to market   Or MTM. The determination of up to date market valuations for Positions* taken and assets held. The mark to market will reflect increases and decreases resulting from market movements occurring since the previous mark-to-market valuation. Generally, a mark-to-market valuation may be based on quotations from other market participants as to the price at which they would buy or sell the relevant asset, or upon an attempt to value the asset using mathematical modelling. For example, the mark-to-market value of a swap at any point in time may be calculated by determining the amount of each future payment under the swap (using implied future market rates for floating amounts), converting the payments on both sides of the swap to a common currency at the market-stated rates in the Forward* market if necessary, and discounting to Net present value* each such future payment due under the swap using the forward rate curve. Aggregating the resultant figures on each side of the swap and netting out the sides of the swap will express the swap mark-to-market value in the common currency. Alternatively, the floating leg may be valued as a payment stream equivalent to that on an FRN* (which allows a LIBOR flat leg to be valued as the final exchange amount of the floating leg plus the next interest payment, discounted for the time to the next payment date where necessary), to be netted against the NPV of the fixed leg (including the final exchange amount).

Market abuse **(i)** See Financial Services and Markets Act 2000.
(ii) See Market Abuse Directive.

Market Abuse Directive The EU* Directive on Market Abuse (Directive 2003/6 of 28 January 2003), which entered into force on 12 April 2003 and must be implemented in Member states* by 12 October 2004. The Directive covers all financial instruments admitted to trading on a regulated market within the EU and requires that each member state specify a regulator to prevent incidences of market abuse (insider dealing and market manipulation).

Market capitalisation The value of the shares in a quoted company that is traded on an Exchange*, which will fluctuate depending on the market's perception of the company's prospects, earnings potential, etc. Cf. Net worth.

Market contract See Set-off, sense (ii).

Market-if-touched order A buy or sell order that is only to be carried out when a certain Bid* or Offer* trigger price is achieved. Usually used to create a Position*. Cf. Stop order.

Market-maker An institution that quotes Bid* and Offer* prices in a range of assets and holds itself out generally as being willing to trade at those prices, as part of a Market-making* system. Thus, the firm deals as principal rather than as Broker* or other agent. LSE* market-makers, in return for putting their capital at risk, are accorded certain privileges in relation to disclosure of transactions, Stamp duty*, etc.

Market-making Also known as a Quote driven* system. The activity of one or more Market-makers* in establishing a market in an asset or range of assets. Market-making is claimed to add Liquidity* to a market, as opposed to an Order-matching* system, since the market-makers are always ready to buy and sell (albeit at a price). Market-making has traditionally been used on the LSE* (e.g. SEAQ* and SEAQ International*), whereas Tradepoint* and many US and European bourses use order-matching. Order-matching was introduced on the LSE in October 1997 with the use of SETS* for FTSE 100 stocks.

Market neutral A trading strategy in which, theoretically, little risk of loss is taken as all Positions* are either Matched* or based on aberrations from the observed market norm, where return to such norm would result in profit. Also used to refer to a position long in one asset and short in another asset of the same sector or type, such that the position is not affected by general market movements up or down in the sector, but only by the movement of the two assets relative to each other. Typically used to exploit Arbitrage* opportunities.

Market order A buy or sell order which is to be carried out immediately at the best price available in the market. Also known as an At best* order.

Market risk   The Risk* arising from the possibility of loss being suffered due to an adverse movement in market pricings. See also "r".

Market value CBO   See Market value CDO.

Market value CDO   A CDO*, the credit analysis of which is carried out by reference to the market value from time to time of the underlying instruments, and an initial Advance rate* against their value. Cf. Cash flow CDO and Synthetic CDO.

Master trust   Or Credit card trust*. A US form of Trust* used in Securitisations* to pool Receivables* against which Trust certificates* may be issued periodically in a series of Tap issues* as the asset balance in the trust changes.

In the UK, the use of master trust issuer structures has historically been hindered by tax and regulatory issues related to trusts (see Trust), leaving tap issuance via corporate issuers as the preferred structure for most deals. Trusts were generally only used for credit card transactions where the value of the interests of different parties in the assets was variable (see FLAP), or for Undivided interest* structures.

Master trust structures have been used for periodic residential mortgage securitisation issuance in the UK following the abolition of MIRAS* from 6 April 2000. The master trust structure provides for the transfer of a large pool of collateral into a trust to back multiple series of issuance, allowing the issuance of tranched soft bullet securities, including securities with legal final maturities shorter than the maturity of the assets within the pool, by diverting principal receipts from the entire pool to each bullet class in the Accumulation period* running up to its maturity. Investors are effectively backed by a revolving pool of assets due to the relatively higher levels of replenishment in such a portfolio.

Matched   A Position*, the Risk* in which is effectively neutralised by the simultaneous holding of an opposite position (e.g. a purchase matched with a sale, or the interest rate Basis* (sense (ii)) on an amount borrowed matched with that on an amount lent).

Matched funding   Funding that matches a loan asset in maturity and amount, thus removing (a) the Liquidity risk* that arises from short-term deposit liabilities backing long- or medium-term assets, and (b) the Reinvestment risk* that arises from long-term liabilities invested in short-term assets.

Materiality   In relation to a Credit default swap* or a Credit-linked note*, a threshold for deterioration in the value of the Reference obligation*, which may be inserted into the terms of the derivative to be used as a test to determine when the derivative is triggered, and to reduce the possibility of *de minimis* triggers.

MATIF   Marché à Terme International de France. French financial Futures* and Options* Exchange*, centred in Paris. Part of the Euro-Globex* alliance together with MIF*.

Maturity   The point at which a debt becomes due and payable in full. For a security, this will be the Redemption date*, assuming no early Redemption* or Purchase*.

MBI   Management buy-in. The acquisition of a business by investors who are not already managers thereof and who intend to manage the business after acquisition.

MBO   Management buy-out. The acquisition of a business by its managers, who become manager-owners thereafter. Often effected by a Leveraged buy-out*.

MBS   See Mortgage-backed security.

Medium-term note   Also known as an MTN*. Medium-term debt instruments with maturities typically ranging from 1 to 5 years. In the UK, may be subject to rules on Deposit-taking*.

Member   A Shareholder* of a company.

Member state   Each of the countries that comprise the European Union*. Since 1995, the 15 member states of the European Union have consisted of Austria, Belgium, Denmark, Finland, France, Germany, Greece, Ireland, Italy, Luxembourg, the Netherlands, Portugal, Spain, Sweden and the United Kingdom. The next wave of enlargement of new member states from 1 May 2004 consists of Cyprus, the Czech Republic, Estonia, Hungary, Latvia, Lithuania, Malta, Poland, Slovakia and Slovenia. Bulgaria and Romania are in the following wave, and Turkey is expected to be a member after that.

Memorandum of association   The rules that govern the external workings of a company through the powers and objectives set out in the Objects* clause of the memorandum. May be referred to as the charter of a company in some jurisdictions. See also Articles of association*.

MERC   Mortgage early redemption certificate. Alternate name for Mortgage redemption certificate*.

Merchant acquirer   See Interchange.

Merchant bank   An historic British term for an Investment bank*, a merchant bank specialised not in lending out its own funds but in providing various financial services such as accepting (see Acceptance) Bills*, acting as Underwriter* of new debt or equity issues, and providing advice on acquisitions, mergers, foreign exchange, and portfolio management. In origin, such banks were closely connected with the financing of trade.

Merger   (i) The doctrine that "a man cannot be the assignee of his own debt and cannot be mortgagee of property of which he is the mortgagor" (*Re George Routledge & Sons, Ltd [1904] 2 Ch 474*). The effect of such a position would be to cancel both the debt and the security. In s. 194 of the Companies Act 1985*, provision is made that with regard to the Purchase* or Redemption* by a company of its own securities, the securities are deemed not to be so cancelled unless the company's Articles of association* so provide or the company has evidenced an intent that they should be cancelled.

(ii) A joining together of two or more companies or groups into one. May arise through a Takeover*. In the UK, may be subject to scrutiny by the Competition Commission* or the European Commission. See also Takeover Code.

Mezzanine finance   High-yielding unsecured (or second charge secured) debt ranking between senior secured debt and equity in terms of Priority*. Similar to Junk bonds* in terms of its dependency on favourable market conditions to maintain its value.

MFR   See Minimum funding requirement.

Mid price   See Middle price.

Middle price   The arithmetic mean of the Bid* and Offer* prices on a security.

MIF   Milan financial Futures* and Options* Exchange*. Part of the Euro-Globex* alliance together with MATIF*.

MIG policy   Mortgage indemnity guarantee policy. See Pool policy.

Mini-max bond   A collared (see Collar) FRN* in which the maximum and minimum Coupons* are very close, so that the FRN closely resembles a fixed-rate Bond* issue.

Minimum authorised capital   A Public company* in the UK must maintain an Issued share capital* of at least £50 000 from time to time (s. 118 Companies Act 1985*), of which £12 500 or more must be paid up (s. 117 Companies Act 1985) and must maintain at least two shareholders or risk personal liability for the company's debts (s. 24 Companies Act 1985). There are no minimum share capital or shareholder requirements for a Private company* (save that an Unlimited company* should have at least two shareholders as above).

Minimum funding requirement   Or MFR. The minimum funding requirement came into effect in 1997, and required pension funds to value their future liabilities by discounting future pension payments at long Gilt* rates (or at equity rates, if the relevant pensioner was not yet receiving a pension). This led to pension funds holding large amounts of assets in gilts, and to distortions in the long-dated gilts market, with an inverted Yield curve* due to excess demand for long gilts over limited government supply. Following the Myners Report (which recommended that the MFR be scrapped), the government announced in March 2001 a long-term plan to abolish the MFR and replace it with transparency and disclosure requirements. Reform of the MFR has been seen as likely to generate demand for long-dated highly rated corporate bonds (as has the adoption of FRS 17*).

Minimum rate   In the context of Floating rate notes*, that Interest rate* below which the Coupon* may not be fixed while the issue is outstanding. The use of a minimum rate in issues is becoming less common.

Minority shareholder   Any Shareholder* who, by itself, does not have the ability to pass, or block the passing of, Resolutions* in relation to a company. See Unfair prejudice.

MIRAS   Mortgage interest relief at source. UK tax relief that was available until 6 April 2000. The relief applied under s. 369 ICTA* to individuals at up to a rate of 10% (from April 1998 – 15% prior to April 1998) on the interest paid on the first £30 000 worth of a mortgage loan used for the purchase of a residential property where the interest was paid and payable to a qualifying lender (a building society, certain other entities, or a lender approved by the Board of the Inland Revenue as a qualifying lender).

Mirror swap   A Swap* that mirrors the terms of a pre-existing swap, save that it is entered into with a different counterparty. Thus, the amounts that are being paid under the original swap match the receipts under the mirror swap, and the receipts under the original swap match the payments under the mirror swap (save that the issuing party may take a Spread* (sense (i)) between the rate charged to the new counterparty, and that passed on to the old counterparty). Used as an alternative to unwinding the original swap for a fee, where market rates have moved in favour of the mirror swap issuer (or, at a negative spread, to unwind a loss-making swap and thus cap potential liabilities). See also Back-to-back swap.

Mixer company   In relation to UK profits tax, a company set up in a country with a high tax rate and beneficial double taxation treaty provisions. The company is used to mix profits from low-tax countries and profits from high-tax countries, in order to pass them back to the UK in a manner that minimises any further UK tax liability on the profits. The March 2000 budget included measures designed to counter the use of mixer companies, although these were subsequently relaxed.

MLAs   Mandatory liquid assets*.

MOBAA   Mauritius Offshore Business Activities Authority.

Modified duration   A measure of bond volatility in response to interest rates. The modified duration of a bond is calculated as the weighted average time to receipt of the cash flow on the bond (interest and principal) in years, where each element of the cash flow is reduced to an amount in present value terms, divided by one plus the yield on the bond. The number of years of the modified duration (e.g 5, 10, etc.) is equal to the percentage change in the market value of the bond (e.g. 5%, 10%, respectively, etc.) that results from a 1% change in the yield on the bond. The measure is an approximate basis, and works for small changes in yield. For larger changes in yield, the positive Convexity* of the price/yield curve for a corporate bond means that this measure will become increasingly inaccurate. See also Duration.

Modified pro rata pay   See Pro rata pay.

MoF   Generally, the Ministry of Finance of any country. In particular, the Japanese Ministry of Finance, which regulates, *inter alia*, Eurobond* issues in Yen, Samurai bonds* and Japanese Domestic bond* issues.

MOF   Multi-option facility. A Facility agreement* designed to encompass many different types of banking arrangements such as FX* lines, Euronotes*, loan facilities, etc. Excessive competition on margins has reduced activity in this particular market.

Money laundering   In the UK under the Criminal Justice Act 1993 the offences of assisting another person to launder the proceeds of crime, failing to report suspected money laundering, disclosing to any third party information that could prejudice a money-laundering investigation, or (for an institution) failing to implement client identification and money laundering reporting procedures. The penalty for these offences is imprisonment and/or an unlimited fine. Powers are given to the FSA* to act against money laundering in authorised firms.

Money market rates   The interest rates (such as LIBOR*, LIBID* and the Discount rate* (sense (i)) charged in the various Money markets*.

Money markets   The shorter term (usually less than 1 year) debt instrument markets. The chief markets are the Discount market* and the Interbank market*, together with the CD* and CP* markets. Longer term instruments are traded in the Capital markets*.

Monoline insurer   A monoline insurer is an insurer who writes a single line of insurance; namely credit insurance. In effect, the insurer guarantees a payment obligation by writing an insurance policy to pay out if the obligation is not paid in full. Most monoline insurers are based in the US. Typically, monoline insurers carry a AAA Credit rating*, with the result that any payment obligation they guarantee (or "Wrap"*) also acquires a AAA credit rating. Monoline insurers have been widely used in Securitisation* transactions to provide a guarantee of payment obligations owed by Receivables* debtors in jurisdictions with a low Foreign currency rating* (which foreign currency rating would typically otherwise cap the rating of the payment obligation, due to the Transfer risk* associated with taking the receivables collections offshore from such a jurisdiction). Monolines are subjected to minimum requirements as to obligations they can guarantee relative to their capital base, in order to maintain their AAA ratings. This usually means that they will not guarantee any obligation that is not itself rated Investment grade*.

Monte Carlo simulation   A simulation model of multiple possible future prices and values of assets (or of possible future events such as defaults) within a Portfolio* that removes reliance on purely historic data.

Moratorium   See Administration, Automatic stay and Insolvency Act 2000. A moratorium is a suspension in payments by a debtor to creditors and/or a suspension of the legal right of creditors to take action against the debtor for non-payment.

Mortgage   A method of taking Security* (sense (ii)) over an asset that consists of a transfer or agreement to transfer the asset subject to an equity of redemption. A mortgage may be legal in nature (where the transfer is fully perfected) or equitable (where it is not). Thus, to the extent that a mortgage is taken over future assets it will be equitable unless and until the assets arise and the transfer is perfected. In many cases, the term "mortgage" is used specifically to refer to a security interest over land; in a legal sense, however, a mortgage may be used to take security (by way of assignment, for example) over diverse assets such as Choses in action*, insurance policies, registered shares and bank accounts. Cf. Charge*.

Mortgage-backed security   An Asset-backed security* where payment is secured against a pool of Mortgage* loans against land.

Mortgage bond   Form of Covered bond* backed by mortgages.

Mortgage redemption certificate   A security that receives payments equal to the amount of Prepayments* received on an underlying pool of mortgages. A mortgage redemption certificate will increase in value if the tenor of the mortgage pool shortens (i.e. inverse to the movement of an IO*), as extra prepayment penalties are received.

Mortgagee   A person who is the beneficiary of Security* (sense (ii)) granted in the form of a Mortgage*.

Mortgages trust   A form of Receivables trust* used in a mortgage Securitisation*.

Mortgagor   A person who grants Security* (sense (ii)) in the form of a Mortgage*.

Mothers   The Market for High-Growth and Emerging Stocks in Japan.

MTM   See Mark to market.

MTN   Abbreviation for Medium-term note*.

MTS   Founder of bond Exchanges* in Europe, including EuroCreditMTS* and EuroMTS*.

Multiclass issue   A debt issue with separate classes of Senior debt* and Subordinated debt*.

Mutual   An organisation established and funded by a group of members for their mutual benefit, via the provision of collective services to those same members, utilising such funding. For example a mutual insurer where members' premiums are used to insure members and pay out members' claims, or a Building society* where members' deposits are used to make loans to members for house purchase.

Mutual fund   US form of open-ended investment company. Similar to the UK Unit trust* or OEIC* and the European UCITS*.

Mutual recognition   The recognition of Listing particulars* or a Prospectus* published in one European Economic Area country as sufficient to allow Listing* (sense (i)) of the related securities in another such country, provided that "prior scrutiny" of the document in question has been carried out by a competent authority.

Naked warrant   A Warrant* issued independently of (and not attached to) an underlying Security*.

Nasdaq   National Association of Securities Dealers, Inc. automated securities quotation system. US-based electronic Exchange* for stock of US companies (often identified mostly with technology stocks), which operates on an Order-matching* basis. Cf. NYSE.

NAV   See Net asset value.

NDF   See Non-deliverable forward.

Negative carry   A Cost of carry* that is negative as funding costs exceed the return achievable on investment.

Negative control   The ability of an individual or group holding shares that carry more than 25% of the voting rights of a company to block the passing of any extraordinary or special Resolutions* at a General meeting* of the company.

Negative convexity   See Convexity.

Negative pledge   An undertaking not to create Security* interests (which may be subject to qualifications, e.g. no prior ranking security only, permissible with consent, certain security interests allowed, etc.) that may be required by an unsecured or subordinated creditor or a creditor secured by a Floating charge* to prevent later creditors obtaining prior security. May be "positive" in nature, i.e. purport to create an equal-ranking security interest over the company's assets in favour of the unsecured creditor, in the event of a subsequent security interest being created over the company's assets, or may simply require that such an equal-ranking security interest is to be created by the company. Where a subsequent security is granted, it will rank subject to the claim of the creditor who has the benefit of the negative pledge, where the second creditor has actual notice or Constructive notice* of the negative pledge. Attempts are often made to take advantage of the doctrine of constructive notice, or to rely on Deemed notice*, to give notice of a negative pledge, by registration of negative pledges together with other details of a security interest on a Form 395*. If the creditor has no notice, the usual ranking of (a) all Fixed charges* (subject to Crystallisation* of any floating charges prior to the grant of such fixed charges) then (b) all floating charges, will apply, in order of registration. Where the second creditor has notice of the negative pledge and the second charge expressly breaches the negative pledge, the first creditor may in addition have a claim in tort for the second creditor inducing the debtor into a breach of contract, should the first creditor be able to provide loss.

A similar provision is an undertaking by the company not to dispose of assets whose value exceeds a certain amount, or a certain percentage of the value of the company's total assets (either at all or without receiving market value for the disposal). A prohibition on the grant of security may prevent a Securitisation* by way of a secured loan; a prohibition on disposals may prevent a securitisation by way of True sale*.

Negotiability   See Negotiation.

Negotiable   See Negotiable instrument.

Negotiable instrument   An instrument that is Negotiable* benefits in trading from its ability to be transferred conclusively by Negotiation*. An instrument may only be negotiable where:

(a) Legal title to it may pass by simple delivery (or by endorsement and delivery) without the need to give notice to the debtor;
(b) The instrument represents a right of action in itself, entitling the holder to sue on the instrument in his own name; and
(c) The instrument does not bear a forged drawer's or endorser's signature, or indications on its face that it is not negotiable (e.g. a "not negotiable" crossing).

An instrument is only capable of being negotiable by:

(a) Statute, e.g. as a Cheque* or Bill of exchange* under s. 3(1) of the Bills of Exchange Act 1882, or as a Promissory note* under s. 83(1) of the Bills of Exchange Act 1882 (which Act was essentially a consolidation of the law merchant*);
(b) The law merchant, which can render a category of instrument negotiable by customary treatment of the instrument as negotiable in market practice.

Market practice regards only obligations to pay as negotiable, and attempts to have Bills of sale* (and other documents of title in relation to goods) recognised as negotiable have not been successful.

Bearer securities* such as Eurobonds* are by and large regarded as being negotiable, through market practice to treat them as such, though care should be taken with regard to securities that contain unusual non-standard terms that add to the basic promise to pay. Order securities* may be negotiable, but Registered securities* are non-negotiable.

Negotiation   The transfer of a Negotiable instrument*, such as a Cheque*, a Bill of exchange*, a Promissory note* or certain types of Bond*, by delivery (for an instrument payable to bearer) or signature of the transferor as endorsement together with delivery (for an instrument payable to order) which, *ipso facto*, is effective to pass the transferor's title at law without a formal assignment or any other formalities (such as registration). Furthermore, a Holder in due course* (or Holder for value* who takes via a holder in due course where the transfer to the holder in due course took place subsequent to any transfer that did not pass good title) to whom a negotiable instrument is negotiated receives good title to the instrument free and clear of any defect in the title held by the transferor (i.e. as an exception to the *nemo dat quod non habet* rule). A negotiable instrument payable to order that is transferred without endorsement does not effect a negotiation, but does pass such title as the transferor possessed, under s. 31(4) Bills of Exchange Act 1882. An instrument that bears a forged drawer's or endorser's signature is not negotiable. A transfer of an Intermediate security* may constitute a variety of negotiation or may consist of a transfer of an interest under a trust (although in the latter case it would be necessary to establish that such a transfer did not fall foul of s. 53(1)(c) of the Law Property Act 1925). Cf. Assignment, Declaration of trust, Novation, Sub-participation, Subrogation, Transfer.

Negotiation credit   A form of Documentary credit*, under the terms of which the credit may be presented to certain Nominated banks* for Negotiation* of documents or of Drafts* drawn by the beneficiary.

Net asset value   The value of a company's assets net of its liabilities and excluding assets without tangible value.

Net interest margin securities   See NIMs.

Net present value   Also known as Present value* or NPV*. The equivalent value in terms of a single lump sum payment received now, of an amount or of a series of amounts due at a point or points in time in the future. Calculated by application of a given Discount rate* (sense (ii)) (which is intended to reflect the cost to the recipient of receiving money at a future date instead of in the present) to each amount for the number of compounding periods into the future at which the amount is to be received, as follows:

$$\text{NPV} = z \cdot [1/(1+r)^n]$$

where   NPV = the net present value
   z = the amount to be received in the future
   r = the discount rate (expressed as a decimal) per compounding period
   n = the number of compounding periods.

For a series of equal amounts to be received at equal intervals going into the future, the NPV of the series is:

$$\text{NPV} = (z/r) \cdot (1 - [1/(1+r)^n])$$

where z = the amount of each equal periodic amount.
   The reverse of this process may be carried out to determine the effective Margin* (sense (i)) over the life of a deal that reflects the amount of a single up-front payment.

Where $r < 1$ (which should always be the case for r as a discount interest rate expressed as a decimal), the NPV to infinity of a series of equal static cash flows to be received into the future can be calculated as:

$$NPV = z \cdot [(1 + r)/r]$$

Net worth   See Net asset value.

Netting   Netting is the process by which payment obligations owing between two parties are aggregated to a single figure owing from one party to the other party in respect of the surplus of such former party's obligations over the latter party's obligations. Netting arrangements are typically contained within the terms of a contractual document but mandatory Set-off* provisions may override such contractual terms on insolvency of one or both parties. Since the intention is typically to limit both pre- and post-insolvency exposure, arrangements are typically structured in a manner compatible with insolvency set-off. Cf. Novation netting, Close-out netting and Settlement netting.

Neuer Markt   Segment of the Deutsche Börse* Exchange* in Germany founded in March 1997 for the trading of growth stocks (in particular tech stocks).

NIF   Note issuance facility. A Facility agreement* that provides for the issue of Euronotes*, which the facility Arranger* uses "best endeavours" to sell to the Tender panel* of banks involved. Cf. RUF.

NIMs   Net interest margin securities. US securities which repackage residual equity tranches of ABS* deals, together with other tranches such as IOs* or securities that carry the right to receive prepayment penalties.

No brainer   A transaction that is almost certain to return a profit and does not carry any major Risk*.

NOI   Net operating income.

Nominal share capital   See Issued share capital*.

Nominal value   Also known as Face value*. An arbitrary figure (often one pound sterling in the UK) attributed to a share when it is issued and will only vary on a Capitalisation* (sense (ii)) of profits or other capital restructuring, there being no link between the nominal value of a share and its market value. The nominal value of a share may be less than its issue price (the difference being Premium* (sense (i)).

Nominated bank   In relation to a Documentary credit*, a bank named in the credit as being authorised to pay or negotiate Drawings* under the credit. Unless a nominated bank gives a Confirm*, it has no obligation to pay, but if it does pay on receipt of correct documentation, it is entitled to reimbursement from the Issuing bank*.

Nominee   One holding title to property on Bare trust* for another, e.g. a Nominee shareholder*.

Nominee account   A shareholding account opened in the name of a Nominee shareholder* on behalf of a third party or third parties. Frequently used for ease of administration in Rolling settlement* systems where there is not sufficient time between dealing and Settlement* to pass share certificates backwards and forwards. May be a Pooled nominee account* or a Designated nominee account*.

Nominee shareholder   A Nominee* who has no beneficial ownership in a share or shares, but holds the legal title to them, either physically or via a Nominee account*, on Bare trust* for some other person or persons. Often used to circumvent requirements for a minimum number of shareholders for a company.

Non-callable   A Security* (sense (ii)) that does not allow the issuer to Call* (sense (i)) for Optional redemption* prior to Maturity*.

Non-conforming   In relation to a mortgage, or a pool of mortgages for a Mortgage-backed security*, credits where there are some unusual characteristics that distinguish them from Prime* mortgages – such as self-certification of income (e.g. self-employed individuals). May be used interchangeably with Sub-prime*.

Non-deliverable forward   Or NDF*. A Forward* contract relating to the FX rate* between two particular currencies that provides for settlement on a net basis in a third currency (often US dollars). Typically used where one of the underlying currencies is not freely deliverable due to capital controls or other limitations. May be subject to regulatory scrutiny in the jurisdiction of such underlying currency. May be considered to constitute Gaming* where undertaken for speculative purposes.

Non-petition   A contractual undertaking inserted in documentation relating to a transaction that uses an SPV* that is intended to be Bankruptcy remote* – e.g. a Securitisation* or Repackaging* transaction, that the entity giving the undertaking will not attempt to petition for the Winding-up* or Liquidation* of the SPV until the main transaction debt has been paid off and any related insolvency unwind period (e.g. the periods for an Undervalue* or a Preference*) has expired.

Nostro account   For a bank, the own account of such bank.

Note   Generic term for a document evidencing a promise to pay, which usually (except for FRNs*) has a shorter term than a Bond*. Typically used to refer to FRNs*, MTNs*, CP*, CDs*, Euronotes* or Promissory notes*.

Notice of crystallisation   The method of effecting Semi-automatic crystallisation*.

Novation   An agreement by all parties to an existing agreement to replace that existing agreement with a new agreement, possibly with different parties to the new agreement. The only way of effectively transferring the burden of a contract under English law. Cf. Assignment, Declaration of trust, Negotiation, Sub-participation, Subrogation, Transfer. See also Transfer certificate.

Novation netting   A form of Netting* whereby payment obligations due between two parties on the same payment date are novated and subsumed by a new single obligation equal to the amount by which the greater of the two original payment obligations exceeds the lesser. Since novation netting provisions are designed to be operative for all future payments from the moment at which the contract or contracts generating such payments are executed, this method of netting is usually effective on insolvency of either party.

NPV   See Net present value.

NYMEX   New York Mercantile Exchange.

NYSE   New York Stock Exchange, which lists larger US companies and, in particular, foreign company listings, leaving smaller US companies to be traded on the separate Nasdaq* system. The NYSE and Nasdaq are designed to accommodate the differing requirements of global and domestic share market participants, respectively.

Objects   Located in a company's Memorandum of association*, the objects clause establishes the chief objectives of the company and powers attributable to it to enable it to achieve such objectives.

Obligations foncières   Or OFs. A French variety of Covered bond* similar to the German Pfandbriefe*. They are issued under the terms of Law 99-532 of 25 June 1999 (updating and replacing the previous Act of 1852), which provides for the establishment of *sociétés de crédit foncier*, or SCFs, with the sole purpose of acquiring certain eligible mortgage assets or public sector assets and issuing OFs.

OECD   Organisation for Economic Cooperation and Development.

OEIC   Open-ended investment company. Form of collective investment vehicle modelled on the Unit trust*, but in the form of a Corporation*. Formed in the UK pursuant to 1997 regulations.

OF   See Obligations foncières.

Off balance sheet   **(i)** A transaction, such as a Swap*, a Guarantee* or a Securitisation*, the potential impact of which upon a company (e.g. on counterparty default) is not visible in the Statutory accounts* or Consolidated accounts* of the company (which show a netted-out or unfunded position not reflecting potential loss or risk on the transaction). Various accounting standards dealing with contingent liabilities, as well as standards such as FRS 5* (in the UK) or FAS 140* or FIN 46* (previously, the Substantive equity* doctrine) (in the US) may require that such a transaction is disclosed in the accounts depending on its terms.

(ii) For bank Capital adequacy* regulations, assets that have successfully been removed from the bank's regulatory capital balance sheet, and against which the bank is no longer required to post capital.

The Basel Committee published guidelines titled Asset Transfers and Securitisation in September 1992. The guidelines set out when an Originator* bank may regard assets as transferred off balance sheet for capital purposes. New guidelines are contained in the new Basel Accord proposals.

In the UK, guidelines were originally published by the Bank of England (in the form of BSD/1989/1, as amended by BSD/1992/3) as to when bank assets would be considered to have been transferred off balance sheet for capital adequacy purposes following a Securitisation* or loan transfer by the bank as Originator*. These were further expanded in relation to the securitisation of revolving asset pools in notice BSD/1996/8 and a subsequent letter of 17 September 1997. On 19 January 1998, the Bank published expanded and consolidated guidelines that replaced both the bank asset and revolving asset pool guidelines, and added guidelines on Credit enhancement* and the provision of Liquidity* for securitisations, as well as guidelines on Repackaging* and Conduit* structures established by banks and on the transfer of Reverse repos*. These were updated and issued by the Financial Services Authority* as part of their Banking Supervisory Policy Guide that came into effect on 29 June 1998. On 31 December 1999, new guidelines were published by the Financial Services Authority, which have since been revised and updated in June 2000, June 2001 and February 2003.

In the US, under RAP*, any provision of credit enhancement to a transaction by the originator bank will result in the securitised assets remaining on balance sheet for capital adequacy purposes. This may be avoided by the use of third-party credit enhancement, or by use of a two-tiered structure (see under True sale), where the first transfer is made without credit enhancement to an SPV that has previously been equity capitalised by the originator. The second transfer then allows the SPV, a non-regulated entity, to provide the credit enhancement.

Off-market   A transaction that is not effected through an Exchange*, or a pricing of a transaction that does not correspond to standard market pricing.

Offer   The price quoted by a seller at which the seller is willing to dispose of an asset.

OFFER   The Office of Electricity Regulation. UK electricity industry regulator.

Offer for sale   One of the methods of marketing and selling LSE* Listed* securities on a Flotation*. An Offer to the public* (sense (ii)) (almost always) which is Underwritten* via Subscriptions* by the Underwriters* and then on-sold to the public. May be at a fixed price, or an offer for which tenders are invited from the public as to price (in the latter case, the price for all securities is set at the level of the highest tender that would sell the issue in full). See also Placing, Offer for subscription and Intermediaries offer (which are all methods of raising new capital for the company) and Introduction (which does not raise new capital, but allows existing securities to be listed).

Offer for subscription   One of the methods of marketing and selling LSE* Listed* securities on a Flotation*. An Offer to the public* (sense (ii)) (almost always) that is not Underwritten* and relies on issuance at a Discount* (sense (i)) to fully Subscribe* the issue via direct public Subscriptions*. See also Offer for sale, Placing, Introduction and Intermediaries offer. See also Placing, Offer for sale and Intermediaries offer (which are all methods of raising new capital for the company) and Introduction (which does not raise new capital, but allows existing securities to be listed).

Offer to the public   (i) In the EU, under the terms of the Prospectus Directive*, categories of offer that are not considered as an offer to the public are contained in Article 3(2):

- Offers to qualified investors (defined in Article 2(1) as credit institutions, investment firms, insurance companies, collective investment schemes, pension funds, other financial institutions, corporates whose sole purpose is to invest in securities, supranationals, government agencies, legal entities which are not small or medium-sized enterprises (SMEs), sophisticated individual investors or SMEs who expressly ask to be treated as qualified investors);
- Offers to less than 100 persons (other than qualified investors) per member state;

- Minimum investment per investor or minimum denomination of Euro 50 000;
- Offers of less than Euro 100 000 in total over 12 months.

Small and medium-sized enterprises are defined in Article 2(1) as entities that have at least two of: less than 250 employees, total balance sheet assets of Euro 43m or less, net turnover of Euro 50m or less.

(ii) Under Schedule 11 of the FSMA* 2000 (previously, under the POS Regs*), an offer of securities to the UK public (or any section of the UK public) which does not fall within one of the exemptions contained in Schedule 11. When such an offer is made for the first time in relation to the securities in question, which offer occurs prior to admission of the securities to a Listing* (sense (ii)), a Prospectus* must be prepared under s. 85 FSMA 2000 (previously, Part IV of the Financial Services Act 1986*).

Chief exemptions are:

(a) Offers: to professionals, to no more than 50 persons, to members of a club with an interest in the use of the proceeds, to a "restricted circle" of knowledgeable investors, in connection with an underwriting, to public sector entities, in connection with a takeover or merger, which are free offerings of shares or exchange offerings of shares, to the issuing company's employees or their families, resulting from conversion of a convertible, by a charity; or
(b) Offers where the securities are: priced less than Euro 40 000 in total, acquired to the extent of at least Euro 40 000 worth by each person, denominated at Euro 40 000 or more each, building society shares, or "Euro-securities" (securities underwritten and distributed by a syndicate at least two members of which are registered in different countries, and which may only be acquired through a Credit institution*) in relation to which no advertisement (other than an advertisement of a prescribed kind) is issued in the UK.

Exemptions in (b) may not be combined with each other or with exemptions in (a) in the same offering. Exemptions in (a) may be combined with each other in the same offering.

Offering circular   A document that describes the terms of an issue of Securities* to be made by an issuer. If the securities issue is to be Listed* on a Stock exchange*, the offering circular is prepared to meet Listing particulars* requirements. For UK issues that are not to be listed, the offering circular may constitute a Prospectus* if an Offer to the public* (sense (ii)) is made. Cf. Information memorandum*.

Official receiver   A public official who may be appointed as Receiver* or Liquidator* of a company under s. 32 or s. 399 of the Insolvency Act 1986, respectively (or as a Trustee in bankruptcy* for an individual under ss. 286 and 295 of the Insolvency Act 1986).

OFTEL   Consumer "watchdog" for the UK telecommunications industry.

OM   Options Market Stockholm. Swedish financial Futures* and Options* Exchange*.

OMLX   London Securities and Derivatives Exchange. London arm of the OM* market in Sweden. Operates as an Exchange* trading financial Futures* and Options* (mostly off Swedish stocks).

Omnibus   See Composite.

On demand   A Facility* under which the lender can demand immediate repayment at any time for any reason. Always an Uncommitted facility*. An example is an Overdraft*.

Onerous contracts   See Onerous property.

Onerous property   Under s. 178 of the Insolvency Act 1986*, any "unprofitable contract" or any other asset that is "unsaleable or not readily saleable or is such that it may give rise to a liability to pay money or perform any other onerous act". A Liquidator* of a company has the power to disclaim onerous property, which terminates the rights and obligations of the company in respect of the asset or contract. The liquidator cannot terminate obligations and retain rights under the same contract, which may enable a defence against attempts by the liquidator to Cherry-pick*, if rights and obligations accrue in respect of a single agreement, such as that purported to be created for transactions under the ISDA Master* by s. 1(c) of the ISDA Master.

Open contract   A Future* that has not been Closed-out* by Settlement* on maturity or by taking a Matched* holding.

Open interest   The aggregate amount of a particular Future* in the market that has not been Closed-out* by settlement or execution of a Matched* trade. The open interest will reduce as a future nears the Contract date* and Positions* are closed-out, leaving only a small percentage to actually be delivered on the contract date.

Open order   See Good till cancelled.

Open outcry   Trading by spoken Bid* and Offer* prices and volumes given face to face on a trading floor, as opposed to a screen-based system. Now largely redundant and replaced by electronic screen-based systems, except for commodity products.

Opening   A set period fixed by an Exchange* for the beginning of each session, which is used to determine the Opening price* for each asset traded on the exchange.

Opening price   The range of prices for transactions recorded during the Opening*.

Operating lease   A Lease* (sense (i)) that does not transfer "substantially all the risks and rewards of ownership of an asset to the lessee" (as per SSAP* No. 21 in the UK). Cf. Finance lease.

Option   A Derivative* contract consisting of a right to buy (see Call Option*) or sell (see Put Option*) certain physical commodities or financial commodities (such as an interest rate, exchange rate or securities index) at a particular "strike price", which is granted in return for the payment of a Premium* (sense (iii)). Values of options comprise the Time value* and the Intrinsic value* of the option, and vary with the price, and price volatility, of the underlying Actual*, the time to maturity of the option and whether the option is In the money*, At the money* or Out of the money*. The factors influencing the value of an option are measured by the Delta*, Gamma*, Theta*, and Vega* of the option. An option deeply in the money behaves far more like a Future*: in other words the price varies with the price of the actual and the Basis* (sense (i)) applicable to the derivative. Options are assets with Leverage* (sense (ii)).

Leverage may be increased for some exchange-traded options, since on some Exchanges* such as the IPE* and LIFFE* (with regard to financial options, but not equity options) the initial investment is only a fraction of the premium on the option, the remainder being paid over the life of the option, by way of Initial margin* and Variation margin*. Premiums on OTC* options are usually paid up-front in full, as are premiums on the LME*, the OMLX* and LIFFE* (with regard to equity options and commodity options). Many options are settled by cash payment of a settlement amount, rather than by delivery of the actual. May take the form of an American option or a European option. See also Alternative option, Average rate option, Barrier option, Box option, Chooser option, Compound option, Deferred strike option, Digital option, Knock-in option, Knock-out option, Ladder option, Lockback option, Path dependent option, Quanto option. Common strategies used with options include the Covered call*, Butterfly*, Condor*, Guts*, Straddle* and Strangle*.

Option box   See Box option.

Optional redemption   The Redemption* of securities at the option of the issuer (see Call, sense (i)) or of the investor (see Put, sense (i)) prior to Maturity*.

Order driven   A stock trading system that operates on an Order-matching* basis.

Order-matching   Also known as an Order driven* system. A system of stock trading which automatically matches buy and sell orders for a share at the same price, e.g. Nasdaq* and Tradepoint*, thus reducing the Spread* (sense (i)) on the transaction. Often used in the US and mainland Europe. In opposition to Market-making* where differing Bid* and Offer* prices are quoted by each Market-maker*. Order-matching is claimed to have lower costs than market-making, since participants are not required to buy or sell at any time; the converse is a loss of Liquidity* since it can take an indefinite period of time to find a matching order and complete a transaction.

Order security   A Security* (sense (i)) that is payable to the order of a particular person. Usually encountered in the form of a Cheque*, although may be used for Notes* issued under a NIF* or for other forms of debt instrument to protect against fraud or theft. May be Negotiable*.

Ordinary resolution   A Resolution* of the Members* of a company that requires a majority of the votes cast in favour and must be passed at a General meeting* where sufficient notice of the meeting and the resolution has been given (unless consent to Short notice* has been obtained or a Written resolution* is used).

Ordinary share   The basic unmodified type of Share* issued in a company, bearing voting rights and a right to a share of profits. Cf. Preference shares.

Ordinary share capital   For tax purposes (see Director, sense (ii), 51% Subsidiary, 75% Subsidiary and 90% Subsidiary), under s. 832 ICTA, the Issued share capital* of a company, excluding shares that carry a fixed rate dividend and give no other right to share in the profits of the company.

Original margin   See Initial margin.

Originator   In a Securitisation* transaction, the entity that originates or generates the Receivables* that back the finance raised.

Orphan   See Orphan company.

Orphan company   A company that has no clearly defined Parent company* (sense (i)) or companies, usually because its shares are held on Charitable trust* or some other kind of purpose trust rather than for a certain person or persons. Often the SPV* in a Securitisation* or Repackaging* transaction will be an Orphan company*.

OSLA   Overseas Securities Lender's Agreement. A standard form of master agreement published in 1995 by the International Stock Lenders' Association. The forms contain terms and conditions for stock loan transactions that are designed to protect the parties to the agreement in the event of the insolvency of the other party by effecting Close-out netting*. A new version was published at the end of 1999.

OTC   See Over the counter.

OTM   See Out of the money.

Out of the money   An instrument or Position* that compares unfavourably to current market conditions and pricing. Cf. In the money, At the money.

Outright transfer   A method of providing Collateral* for an obligation. It does not involve the granting of a Security interest*. The security provider transfers absolute title to the relevant asset to the beneficiary, who agrees to deliver equivalent assets to the security provider at the end of the relevant transaction or relationship. Mainly used as a form of collateral for derivative obligations, as the provision of the assets as Margin* (sense (ii)) in an amount equal to the Mark-to-market* value outstanding in favour of the beneficiary helps to alleviate any concerns that the transfer is an Undervalue*. Has the advantage of avoiding possible security registration requirements for Floating charges* or charges over Book debts*, as well as allowing Rehypothecation*. May, however, be subject to Stamp duty* or other tax consequences on disposals (such as Capital gains tax*).

Over the counter   Assets that are traded Off-market* rather than on a particular Exchange*, usually because their terms are specifically tailored to a particular client. Also known as OTC.

Over-allotment option   Also known as a Green shoe*. An option granted to an Underwriter* of a Public offering* in the US, which allows the underwriter to purchase additional shares from the issuer at the public offer price, in order to cover any over-allotment by the underwriter during the distribution, thus allowing more aggressive marketing of an issue while protecting the underwriter's position.

Overcollateralisation   The provision of Collateral*, the value of that exceeds the value of the obligation that it is to be used to secure or discharge. A technique that is often used in Securitisation* transactions through a purchase of Receivables* worth more than the senior debt financing the purchase.

Overcollateralisation ratio   Or Par value test. In relation to each class of debt in a CDO*, the ratio of the par amount of the transaction collateral (certain amounts – e.g.

the par amount of defaulted securities – may be excluded, and certain other amounts – e.g the par amount of assets which are rated CCC or below – may be included at their current market value rather than their par amount) to the amount of the debt ranking at or senior to that class. Used as a trigger to divert the cash flow waterfall in order to effect amortisation of that class of debt instead of making payments on more junior classes, if the trigger is breached.

Overdraft   A Revolving facility* that is repayable On demand*.

Oversea company   Under s. 744 Companies Act 1985*, a company incorporated outside Great Britain but which has established a place of business within Great Britain. The Companies Act sets out the position of these companies as regards requirements to register UK branches with the Registry of Companies at ss. 690A to 703R.

Overseas clearing house   A Clearing house* that is recognised as a Recognised clearing house* for the purpose of exemption from FSA* regulation.

Overseas investment exchange   An Exchange* that is recognised as a Recognised investment exchange* for the purpose of exemption from regulation under the Financial Services Act 1986* (repeated under the FSMA* 2000). For example, Nasdaq*, the CME* and Globex*.

Owner trust   A US form of Trust* used in Securitisations* that issues multiple classes of debt that can be sequential pay, as well as an equity class. Careful structuring is required to ensure that securities sold to investors are successfully regarded as debt for tax purposes.

PAC   See Planned amortisation class.

PAI   See Publicly available information.

Paid-up share capital   The amount that has been paid-up by shareholders against a company's Issued share capital*.

Pantbrev   Form of Swedish mortgage.

Par   Full amount of a security's or other instrument's Face value*. In relation to shares, the Nominal value* of the share.

Par value   See Par.

Par value test   See Overcollateralisation ratio.

Parent company   (i) Loosely used to mean a Holding company* (sense (ii)).
   (ii) A Parent undertaking* that is also a company.

Parent undertaking   For accounting purposes under s. 258 Companies Act 1985* and Capital adequacy* Consolidation* (sense (iii)) purposes, an Undertaking* is a parent undertaking of another undertaking, its Subsidiary undertaking*, if:

(a) It holds a majority of the voting rights in the subsidiary undertaking; or
(b) It is a member of the subsidiary undertaking and has the right to appoint or remove a majority of its board of directors; or

(c) It has the right to exercise a dominant influence over the subsidiary undertaking through provisions in the subsidiary undertaking's Memorandum of association* or Articles of association* or in a control contract; or

(d) It is a member of the subsidiary undertaking and controls alone, pursuant to an agreement with other shareholders or members, a majority of the voting rights in the subsidiary undertaking; or

(e) It has a participating interest in the subsidiary undertaking and either actually exercises a dominant influence over the subsidiary undertaking or manages itself and the subsidiary undertaking on a unified basis; or

(f) It is a parent undertaking of an undertaking which is itself a parent undertaking of the subsidiary undertaking.

Pari passu In equal place. Typically used when speaking of the Priority* of two different debts, to indicate that they rank equally with each other.

Paris Club The forum for rescheduling debts of a country when those debts are issued or guaranteed by that country's government. Cf. London Club.

Partially supported A Conduit* where the Credit rating* of the conduit is dependent on an analysis of both the credit support provider and the credit quality of the assets held in the conduit. This kind of structure typically has a Liquidity facility* that can be used to take out CP on maturity in the event of CP market disruption, but the liquidity facility is structured so that it can only be drawn against non-defaulted assets by use of a Borrowing base*. Cf. Fully supported.

Participant In a Syndicated loan*, those members of the Syndicate* that take a Participation* from a Manager* or Underwriter*. Cf. Sub-participant.

Participation The principal amount of a Syndicated loan* that a potential Participant* will fund, or enter a Commitment* to fund (or the size of the funding or commitment held by each manager and participant or their transferees, e.g. by Transfer certificate* or TLC*, following Syndication*). Cf. Sub-participation.

Participator For the purposes of the definition of Close company*, means, under s. 417 ICTA, any person with a share in the capital or income of a company, and includes:

(a) Any person who possesses, or is entitled to acquire, share capital or voting rights;

(b) Any Loan creditor*;

(c) Any person who possesses, or is entitled to acquire, a right to receive, or to participate in, Distributions* or any amounts payable by the company (in cash or in kind) to loan creditors by way of premium on redemption; and

(d) Any person who is entitled to secure that present or future income or assets of the company will be applied directly or indirectly for his benefit.

Partnership In the UK, a form of Unincorporated association*. Under the Partnership Act 1890, defined as "the relation that subsists between persons carrying on a business in common with a view of profit". An English partnership arises when this definition is met without the need for any formalities and is regulated by the provisions of the Partnership Act 1890 unless such provisions are expressly varied or disapplied. A partnership does not have separate Corporate personality* and partners do not have

Limited liability* for partnership debts, unless the partnership is constituted as a Limited partnership* and they are one of the limited liability partners. Prior to 21 December 2002, under s. 716(1) of the Companies Act 1985*, no partnership was permitted to have more than 20 partners, although accountants, solicitors and recognised Stock exchange* members were exempted from this requirement. The 20 partner limit was removed by the Regulatory Reform (Removal of 20 Member Limit in Partnerships, etc.) Order 2002 from the DTI* under the Regulatory Reform Act 2001 with effect from 21 December 2002. The Business Names Act 1985 should be complied with on creation of a partnership, and a written partnership deed is usually executed to prevent the application of automatic Partnership Act rules on termination and operation of the partnership.

Pass-through   (i) US tax status granted by the IRS* and effectively constituting Fiscal transparency*. The general IRS requirement for pass-through status (e.g. for partnerships) is that the business entity in question has no more than two of the following characteristics: (a) Limited liability*; (b) centralised management; (c) continuous existence; and (d) free transferability of ownership interests.

(ii) An Asset-backed security* structure, typically linked to pool-based Securitisation* structures, where payments received by the Servicer* of the Receivables* are passed directly (after deduction of fees and expenses) to the end investor, thus bearing the same Amortisation* profile and fluctuations as the receipts.

Patent   An intellectual property right in a particular process or invention that is created by registration (in the UK, with the Patent Office), and entitles the owner to prevent others copying the process or invention for a certain period (20 years in the UK). Cf. Copyright, Registered design, Trademark.

Path dependent option   An Option* where the settlement amount is determined by the movement in price of the Actual* over the entire life of the option, rather than simply its value on expiry. See Average rate option, Barrier option, Ladder option, Lookback option.

Pay-in-kind   Or PIK*. A security where coupon payments are capable of being deferred and rolled-up by way of Capitalisation* (sense (i)) into the principal of the security in the event that there is insufficient cash to make payment of them, without triggering an Event of default*. Coupons may also take the form of further securities. Often a feature of mezzanine and junior note classes of Securitisation* deals, as well as Mezzanine finance* or Junk bonds*.

Pay-through   An Asset-backed security* structure that differs from a Pass-through* in that the Amortisation* profile on pay-through securities need not be directly linked to principal receipts from the pool of Receivables*. Consequently, principal can be redeemed on a scheduled basis. This smoothing of principal payments and Prepayments* sets further structural requirements for the transaction (such as use of a Defeasance* or GIC* structure to hold principal receipts, or a further degree of Overcollateralisation* or other support in the pool).

Paying agent   A bank or financial institution that acts as agent of the issuer of debt securities for the purpose of effecting interest and principal payments to investors.

Payment against documents   Payment for export goods on receipt of shipping documents. As the documents must be given to the buyer, there is a resultant delay for the seller between shipment and payment (which does not occur where Bills of exchange* are drawn by the seller under a Documentary credit* arranged by the buyer, with shipping documents given by the seller to an Advising bank* in the seller's country in return for immediate payment to the seller). The seller also bears Credit risk* (sense (i)) on the buyer (which risk may be borne by the Issuing bank* by express agreement in a documentary credit; credits may be used in conjunction with a long-dated time bill of exchange to allow a period of credit to the buyer).

PDL   See Principal deficiency ledger.

Permanent global note   A Global note* which is intended to remain in global form throughout the life of the issue.

Pfandbriefe   A German variety of Covered bond* (singular Pfandbrief, plural Pfandbriefe) that can be issued by German mortgage banks under the Mortgage Bank Act or by Landesbank under the Public Sector Pfandbriefe Act. Pfandbriefe may be backed by an eligible pool of mortgages (*Hypothekenpfandbriefe*) or by an eligible pool of public sector assets (*öffentlicher Pfandbriefe*). The two pools (mortgages and public sector assets) are segregated into separate registers or *Deckungsstock*, each of which are subject to separate insolvency proceedings from insolvency proceedings connected with the issuing institution (although the pools remain on the balance sheet of the issuing institution). Consequently, holders of Pfandbriefe have preferential rights to the relevant pool of assets supporting the Pfandbriefe, which are liquidated separately for the benefit of the Pfandbriefe holders on insolvency of the issuer, as well as a residual right as an unsecured creditor against the other assets of the issuer in the event that the asset pool is insufficient. Cf. Cedulas hipotecarias, Cedulas territoriales, Jumbo Pfandbriefe, Obligations foncières, Realkreditobligationer.

PFI   See Private finance initiative.

PIA   Personal Investment Authority. Self-regulating organisation (see SRO) established under the Financial Services Act 1986* and operative from 18 July 1994. Designed to cover the scope of, and replace, LAUTRO* and FIMBRA*, to regulate investment business carried out in the retail sector with or for the private investor. Its functions were rolled into the Financial Services Authority* from midnight on 30 November 2001.

PIBOR   Paris Interbank Offered Rate. Paris equivalent of LIBOR*. Also known as TIOP*.

Piercing the veil   See Lifting the veil.

PIK   See Pay-in-kind.

Placement   A sale of securities by arrangement to a particular institution or institutions without a general offering. See also Private placement.

Placing   One of the methods of marketing and selling LSE* Listed* securities on a Flotation* or other issue of debt or equity, but which is only allowed by the LSE on a flotation for small issues, or where market conditions are poor. Consists of a

Placement* to selected institutions. Issues such as debt stocks with limited public interest may always be placed on the LSE in any case, and this is the usual method when listing Bonds*. See also Offer for sale, Offer for subscription and Intermediaries offer (which are all methods of raising new capital for the company) and Introduction (which does not raise new capital, but allows existing securities to be listed).

Planned amortisation class   Or PAC. A Tranche* of an ABS* securities issue that is intended to amortise in accordance with a planned schedule, within certain prepayment parameters, to provide a more certain investment profile. As most ABS issues amortise on an uncertain basis as a result of the potential for Prepayments* on the underlying assets, a PAC will be accompanied by a Companion* class that will receive prepayments on the underlying assets that exceed a certain level (if prepayments fall below a certain level, principal payments are diverted from other tranches to pay the PAC). Similar to a TAC*, but due to the potential for diversion of amortisation from the companion tranche if prepayments fall below a minimum level, a PAC potentially has a shorter (and more certain) average life than a TAC.

Platykurtosis   A thin tail on a standard deviation distribution. See Value at risk.

Pledge   A method of taking Security* (sense (ii)) over tangible assets that are capable of physical possession (such as chattels or Negotiable instruments*). This consists of the delivery of actual or constructive possession in the assets (or their title documents), and is undertaken with the intent to pledge the assets. A pledge is a kind of bailment, and, as such, does not operate to transfer any legal title or ownership interest in the asset, save in the case of a negotiable instrument that is a Bearer security*, where possession constitutes the pledgee as a Holder for value* (and potentially a Holder in due course*) to the extent of the amount secured.

PO   Principal only. A principal Strip*. A PO will fall in value if the tenor of the security it has been stripped from lengthens.

Point   In relation to Futures*, a single unit of variation in price that will carry a set notional value.

Pool factor   In a Securitisation*, the percentage balance of an asset pool that is still outstanding as against its original balance outstanding. Normally expressed as a decimal fraction. See also Tranche factor.

Pool policy   Or MIG policy. An insurance policy that covers losses sustained on a pool of mortgage loans.

Pooled nominee account   A Nominee account* in which all beneficial shareholders are grouped together, so that the only name appearing on the company register is that of the Nominee shareholder*. Often used for Unit trusts* in the UK. Cf. Designated nominee account.

Pooling   US accounting treatment for a Merger*, which allows the merged company to show the combined business assets on an aggregate balance sheet without having to include goodwill on the balance sheet (which would need to be written off over time) to reflect any acquisition premium to book value.

PORTAL   A self-regulatory organisation system approved by the SEC for the trading of Rule 144A securities, and used by the NASD* for trading such securities (as well as other securities that are exempt from SEC* registration such as Reg S* and Rule 144* securities). Only QIBs* are permitted to trade in PORTAL, in order to preserve the Rule 144A resale requirements.

Portfolio   The aggregate financial asset holdings of an individual or entity.

POS Regs   See Public Offers of Securities Regulations 1995.

Position   The holding or disposal of an asset or assets, resulting in Risk* being taken on market price movements. See Long and Short.

Position trading   The holding of Long* positions as a trading method.

Positive carry   A Cost of carry* that is positive, as the return achievable on investment exceeds funding costs.

Positive convexity   See Convexity.

Postponement   See Subordination.

POT   A method of distribution of some or all of the securities in an issue that is commonly used in the US market, under which the co-managers all submit their investor orders to a central order book held by the bookrunners, who determine allocations among investors. It has been criticised by smaller market players on the basis of the disclosure of investors names and order sizes that it forces on them. The more normal Euromarket sales structure sees the lead manager allocating bonds among the managers, who then carry out allocations among their clients.

Power of attorney   A document that authorises the appointed attorney to act for the donor of the power to carry out a specific purpose (a "special power of attorney"), to act in a specified field of activity (a "general power of attorney") or to act for all purposes (a "universal power of attorney"). The power must be executed by the donor by way of deed (s. 1(1) Powers of Attorney Act 1971), and may be given as security for an obligation of the donor to the donee (a "security power of attorney"), in which case it is irrevocable and will survive bankruptcy, death, incapacity or liquidation of the donee, until the secured obligation has been discharged (s. 4 Powers of Attorney Act 1971). Otherwise, it will automatically terminate in such circumstances (unless granted as an "enduring power of attorney", in which case it will survive incapacity). In relation to fiduciaries and agents, the general rule is *delegatus non potest delegare* (i.e. the recipient of authority cannot further delegate that authority), unless express authority to subdelegate is contained in the trust deed or agency document. Even then a trustee cannot delegate a "discretion" save via a power of attorney given under s. 25 Trustee Act 1925, which lasts for a maximum period of 12 months.

Power of sale   The power to enforce Security* (sense (ii)) by selling the assets subject to the security. The power is granted by statute in s. 101 of the Law of Property Act 1925 in relation to a Mortgage* or a Charge* made by Deed*, although it is subject to limiting requirements that the power must have "arisen" within the terms of s. 101 and must be properly "exercisable" within the terms of s. 103. The power may also be contained expressly in the security document, in which case the limitations in s. 101 and s. 103 are normally removed.

Praecipium   A fee amount that may be awarded to the Lead manager* of an issue of Securities* out of the Management fee*, prior to allocating the remaining management fee among the Managers* generally.

Predator   A company attempting a Takeover* of a Target*.

Pre-emption rights   Rights granted to shareholders by the provisions of s. 89 Companies Act 1985* which require that, on any new issue of shares in a company, the shares are first offered to existing shareholders pro rata their shareholding. Pre-emption rights may be generally excluded by a Private company* (but not a Public company*) under the company's Articles of association* by s. 91 Companies Act 1985. Pre-emption rights may also be disapplied by private or public companies, if a s. 80 Companies Act 1985 authority is in place, in reliance on provisions of the company's articles of association or a Special resolution* under s. 95 Companies Act 1985. In addition, pre-emption rights may be waived by shareholders.

Preference   Under s. 239 of the Insolvency Act 1986*, where within 6 months of commencement of a Winding-up* (2 years if with a person connected to the company as defined at s. 249 of the Insolvency Act 1986), any person is a creditor of or a guarantor for a company, and the company "does anything or suffers anything to be done which ... has the effect of putting that person into a position which, in the event of the company going into insolvent Liquidation*, will be better than the position he would have been in if that thing had not been done". The company must have been insolvent at the time of the act, or have become insolvent as a result of it, and must have been influenced by a desire to prefer in doing the act (which is presumed where the preferred person is a person connected to the company).

Preference shares   Shares in a company that are accorded certain preferential rights as against Ordinary shares* in the same company, usually as regards payment of dividends (which may, for example, be at a set rate and cumulate in years when the company's profits are insufficient to pay the dividend in full). The Articles of association* contain the specific terms applying to a company's preference shares.

Preferential creditor   A creditor owed a Preferential debt*.

Preferential debt   Under s. 175 of the Insolvency Act 1986*, certain unsecured claims against a company that are set out in Schedule 6 to the Insolvency Act 1986 and are known as preferential debts will, on Winding-up* or Liquidation*, be paid in priority (see Priority) to other unsecured claims and to claims secured by Floating charges*). Primarily wages (to a certain limit) due in the last 4 months, PAYE and NI Contributions due in the last 12 months, VAT due in the last 6 months and occupational pension contributions.

The Enterprise Act* reforms the systems of preferential debts.

Under s. 251 of the Act, those categories of preferential debt due to the Crown (the Inland Revenue, Customs and Excise and social security – set out in paragraphs 1 to 7 of Schedule 6 to the Insolvency Act 1986) – primarily PAYE and NI Contributions due in the last 12 months and VAT due in the last 6 months – are abolished. Other preferential debts (mainly wages due in the last 4 months and occupational pension contributions) remain as preferential debts.

Under s. 252, an amount prescribed by order by the Secretary of State will be ring-fenced in favour of unsecured creditors (and will not be available to holders of a floating charge to the extent that there are any such unsecured creditors).

Pre-funding In a Securitisation* structure, the issuance of debt in excess of the size of the securitisation asset pool, in anticipation of further origination that will be added to the asset pool after the close of the securitisation. Proceeds of the excess initial debt raised are held in escrow (in a Pre-funding account*) and released against the origination and sale to the SPV of new assets. Pre-funding may be used to time the best point to access market rates (rather than being driven by sufficient asset build-up), or to over-issue in anticipation of increased origination rates and demand for funding when a business is undergoing rapid expansion.

Pre-funding account A bank account used in a Pre-funding* structure to hold part of the proceeds of an issue of Asset-backed securities* pending delivery by the Originator* to the SPV* of the full amount of Receivables* backing the securities.

Pre-incorporation contract Prior to Incorporation* (sense (ii)) of a company, any contract purportedly entered into by or on behalf of such company. By s. 36C Companies Act 1985*, the person making the contract on the company's behalf is personally liable on it, unless and until the fully incorporated company ratifies (see Ratification) the act of the person on its behalf and its agreement to the terms of the contract.

Premium (i) The amount by which the Issue price* or current market price of a Security* exceeds its Face value*. Cf. Discount, sense (i).

(ii) The amount by which the Forward* value of an asset exceeds its Spot* value. Cf. Discount, sense (ii).

(iii) The up-front price payable on purchase of an Option*, Cap (v), Collar* or Floor*, which is equal to the sum of the Time value* and the Intrinsic value* of the option at such point. Certain exchange-traded options do not carry an up-front premium but instead use an Initial margin* and Variation margin* structure.

Prepayment The repayment of a debt prior to its Maturity*. May be subject to penalties levied by the lender. In particular, prepayment of an obligation bearing a Fixed rate*, or prepayment of a Floating rate* obligation during an interest period, may be subject to Break costs*. Mortgages or other Receivables* forming part of a Securitisation* structure are often subject to borrower prepayment rights, which can lead to Prepayment risk*. High levels of prepayment on a pool of assets will shorten the Average life* of securities structured off the back of the assets. See also CPR, SMM, 100% PSA, 200% PSA.

Prepayment risk The Risk* of Prepayment* of a debt occurring, which can in turn give rise to Reinvestment risk*, and the risk of loss of value (if the debt prepays at par and it was trading above par). With regard to Asset-backed securities*, the likelihood of prepayments affecting an investor can be reduced by structuring the issue with various tranches which, although ranking at the same level of Priority*, are payable sequentially rather than pro rata from principal receipts (thus converting the first sequential tranche into a Fast-pay* tranche and the second sequential tranche into a

Slow-pay* tranche). May also be reduced where the Receivables* contain a Hell or high water* payment obligation, or a Spens clause*, or by the use of a GIC* to retain and reinvest receipts.

Present value   See Net present value.

PRIMA   Place of the Relevant Intermediary Approach. An approach used in The Hague Convention on Indirectly Held Securities 2002 to determine the law applicable to transactions involving securities held via an intermediary. The law is at the choice of the account holder and its intermediary, subject to the proviso that the intermediary must have an office in the relevant jurisdiction. The Convention was agreed in December 2002 and presented to be ratified by the 62 members of the Hague conference.

Primary market   The market in which Securities* are first distributed. Cf. Secondary market*.

Prime   In relation to a mortgage, or a pool of mortgages for a Mortgage-backed security*, credits that fit normal credit and underwriting guidlelines and do not have negative credit characteristics such as arrears. See also Sub-prime and Non-conforming.

Principal   The Face value* of a security, or the amount lent by a lender to a borrower.

Principal allocation percentage   See Fixed allocation percentage.

Principal deficiency ledger   Or PDL*. An accounting ledger recorded by an SPV* in a Securitisation* transaction that records losses experienced by the SPV on the underlying securitised assets (post-enforcement with regard to the underlying assets), and is used as a financial trigger and/or in the allocation of cash to different Tranches* of the deal. The PDL may subsequently be reduced by make-whole from Excess spread* on the deal.

Principal finance   Terminology for the use by a financial institution of its own balance sheet for the acquisition of assets or of an entire company, usually with the goal of arranging a Securitisation* of the assets or of any securitisable cash flows of the company (either contemporaneously with the purchase, or at a later date), in order to finance the acquisition. Cf. Warehouse.

Principal protected   A Security* where the investor has limited risk of losing the principal amount of the investment as a result of the repackaging of a higher risk investment with a lower risk investment that will repay the principal of the investment. An example is the repackaging of a junior tranche of a CDO* with a zero coupon government bond that will accrete in value to repay the principal of the investment. See also Combination note.

Priority   The order in which a company is obliged to repay its debts from particular assets. On Winding-up*, a statutory order of priorities is set, such that after the expenses of the winding-up, creditors under a Fixed charge* have priority to the extent of their Security* (save with regard to fixed charges taken after Crystallisation* of a Floating charge*, or fixed charges subject to notice of an earlier Negative pledge* clause). Among themselves, fixed creditors have priority depending on the first in time to duly register (for registrable security) or the first in time to give notice to the third party debtor (for security over Choses in action*). Other fixed creditors rank in order of taking their security, save that, for security over a Negotiable instrument*, a fixed creditor may be postponed behind a Holder in due course* or Holder for value* and that a fixed creditor with equitable security may be postponed behind a bona fide acquirer for value of a legal estate without notice. Thereafter come Preferential debts*, amounts secured by a floating charge, unsecured claims and finally distribution to the Members*. Creditors in each class normally rank *Pari passu** but this may be altered by the operation of Subordination* agreements, or by the effect of negative pledges or crystallisation of a floating charge as noted above.

Private company In the UK, those Registered companies* that have not been constituted as Public companies*. A private company in the UK may not by s. 81 Companies Act 1985* make an offer to the public (as offer to the public is defined by s. 81 rather than by the POS Regs*) or apply for a Listing* (sense (ii)) by s. 143 Financial Services Act 1986 (s. 75(3) FSMA* 2000 as expanded in the Financial Services and Markets Act 2000 (Official Listing of Securities) Regulations (SI 2001/2956) provides that bodies of a prescribed kind – including private companies – may not apply for a listing). Private companies may exclude the application of s. 89 Companies Act 1985 Pre-emption rights* under the company's Articles of association*, and may restrict the transferability of their shares.

Private finance initiative Or PFI. In the UK, the government initiative to finance public sector projects with private sector capital. The intention is to allow the private sector to raise capital to finance the completion of projects or to acquire capital assets, with the government then making payment for the provision of services with these assets by the private sector. PFI is based on the idea of using the private sector to obtain better value for money for consumers using the services provided. The risks associated with the project (such as construction and completion risks) should be borne by the party (whether private or public sector) who is able to bear them at least cost, to ensure that value for money is maintained. If possible, the transaction should be treated under FRS 5* as a payment by the government for the provision of services, rather than a borrowing by the government, although this is secondary to the fundamental objective of obtaining value for money.

Private placement **(i)** Loose terminology for any Securities* issue that is Unlisted*, or not publicised, or not syndicated (see Syndication*).

(ii) In the UK, the sale of securities without an Offer to the public* (sense (ii)), which may be made without a Prospectus*. It typically involves purchase by large institutional investors. See also Placing.

(iii) In relation to SEC* securities regulation in the US, and specifically in relation to s. 4(2) of the Securities Act*, "transactions by an issuer [of securities] not involving any public offering". Purchasers must acquire the securities for investment purposes and without a view towards distributing them in order for the issuer to claim exemption from the Securities Act registration requirements. In order for the private (i.e. non-distributed) nature of the transaction not to be open to question it is usually considered necessary to: use large note denominations, offer to a limited number of potential purchasers, offer to purchasers who are experienced investors (typically sophisticated institutions) and offer subject to resale restrictions (which are often legended on the notes); confirmation of agreement to such restrictions being obtained in a "non-distribution letter". Typically, the restrictions would only allow resales in accordance with Rule 904* of Regulation S*, Rule 144* or Rule 144A*. Regulation D*, a safe harbour under s. 4(2), is often relied on rather than s. 4(2) itself, since it is hard to monitor compliance with s. 4(2).

Privatisation   The sale of an enterprise from state ownership to private ownership. In the UK, where a former Registered company* is being privatised, the Listing* and Offer to the public* (sense (ii)) of such company on the Stock Exchange. Where a Statutory company* such as a public corporation is being privatised, a new Registered company* is usually created, in which the enterprise is vested. The shares are then offered to the public. Normally, as such privatised companies are utility monopolies, the government modifies the company's Articles of association* to include restrictions on Takeovers* or changes in control, by means such as the Golden share*. Consumer "watchdogs" are often also appointed, such as OFTEL*.

Privity   In the UK, privity of contract is the doctrine that only a party to a contract may sue on that contract (by way of contrast, the US has a third-party beneficiary doctrine, where third parties may acquire rights under a contract if they are an "intended beneficiary" rather than an "incidental beneficiary"). Also in the UK, the privity of estate that existed between a landlord and the original tenant and meant that the original tenant remained liable to the landlord regardless of any subsequent transfer of the lease (this doctrine was disapplied from 1 January 1996 where the original tenant has lawfully assigned the lease with relevant consents). In the UK, a Deed poll* is enforceable by persons not party to it as an exception to the privity of contract doctrine, and other Deeds* (i.e. Indentures*) are enforceable by persons not party in certain limited cases relating to interests or rights in land. The Contracts (Rights of Third Parties) Act 1999 came into force on 11 November 1999 and applies to contracts entered into on or after 11 May 2000 (as well as contracts entered into prior to then, if the contract expressly refers to the fact that the law applies to the contract). Certain contracts (notably negotiable instruments and some employment contracts) are excluded from the application of the law. The law gives a third party rights to enforce a term (including a protective term such as an exclusion or limitation of liability) if the contract expressly so provides or if the term confers a benefit on the third party. The law also prevents the parties to the contract from changing the contract in a way that would prejudice the third party (the court has an overriding power to amend any third party rights where the consent of the third party cannot be obtained due to difficulty with locating the third party). Obligations cannot be imposed on a third party. The law can be expressly excluded in the contract. The third party must be identified by name or class but need not be in existence.

Pro rata pay   A Securitisation* structure where amounts available for redemption of notes are applied to redeem each class of notes by the same percentage amount – e.g. in a structure with 90 Class A notes, 30 Class B notes, 15 Class C notes, where principal of 30 is to be applied, an amount of 22.2% $[30/(90 + 30 + 15)]$ of each class will be redeemed – in other words, 20 to the Class A, 6.67 to the Class B and 3.33 to the Class C. May be seen as a modified pro rata pay, with some amounts applied to junior note classes, but in a smaller percentage than that applied to more senior note classes. Cf. Sequential pay.

Programme-wide enhancement   Or PWE*. Credit enhancement used in an asset-backed Conduit* structure to support losses at a pooled programme level over and above the first loss credit enhancement used on individual deals put into the conduit.

Project finance   Finance raised for a capital investment project, where repayment is Limited recourse* to the cash flow of the project. Typically the project involves exploitation of a resource or market such as an oil field or telecommunications network, where transfer of ownership of the project from one company to another is unlikely to change the fortunes of a loss-making project. Cf. Asset-based finance*.

Promissory note   Defined by s. 83(1) Bills of Exchange Act 1882 as an "unconditional promise in writing made by one person to another, signed by the maker, engaging to pay, on demand, or at a fixed and determinable future time, a sum certain in money to, or to the order of, a specific person or to bearer". It is therefore essential that a fixed rate of interest and a fixed (or On demand*) repayment time is given. Promissory notes are Negotiable instruments*.

Property dealing company   A company where property is treated as a trading stock. Any expenses incurred in its acquisition (e.g. solicitors fees) are deductible in calculating trading income under Schedule D* Case I for the purposes of corporation tax. Stamp duty is also deductible.

Property investment company   A company where property is held on a capital account as an investment giving rise to a capital gains charge on disposal. Acquisition costs (e.g. solicitors fees) are deductible from the consideration received on disposal for the purposes of corporation tax. Stamp duty is also deductible.

Prospectus   In the UK, a document required to be prepared and published by any person who makes an Offer to the public* (sense (ii)) in relation to Securities* (sense (i)) where it is the first time that the securities being offered have been offered to the public, and the offer occurs prior to admission of the securities to a Listing* (sense (ii)), the required form and content of which is governed by Part II of the POS Regs* or Part IV of the Financial Services Act 1986* (replaced by Part VI of the FSMA* 2000). No offer to the public may be made until the prospectus is published, breach of which requirement is a criminal offence under s. 16(2) POS Regs/s. 156B(1) Financial Services Act 1986 (replaced by s. 85 FSMA 2000). Prospectuses are subject to disclosure on specific details as set out in Listing rules*, as well as to an overriding duty under s. 9 POS Regs/ s. 154A (applying s. 146) Financial Services Act 1986 (repeated at s. 86 (applying s. 80) FSMA 2000) to disclose all information investors would reasonably expect and require to find therein, with liability to compensate investors under s. 14 POS Regs/s. 154A (applying s. 150) Financial Services Act 1986 (repeated at s. 86 (applying s. 90) FSMA 2000) on responsible persons as specified in s. 154A (applying s. 152) Financial Services Act 1986 (the issuer, its directors and any person who authorised, or is named as accepting responsibility for, the prospectus) (repeated at s. 86 (applying s. 79(3)) FSMA 2000 under regulations to be given by the Treasury) for any loss they suffer as a result of untrue or misleading statements in the prospectus or the omission of relevant details. Prospectuses must be registered at Companies House under s. 4(2) POS Regs/s. 154A (applying s. 149) Financial Services Act 1986 (repeated at s. 86 (applying s. 83) FSMA 2000), breach of which requirement is a criminal offence. Prospectuses may also give rise to general criminal liability under s. 47 Financial Services Act 1986 (repeated at s. 86 (applying s. 397) FSMA 2000) for misleading or false statements.

Prospectus Directive   Discussions on the Prospectus Directive of the EU* began in May 2001, when the EU Commission set out its proposal for a directive to harmonise prospectuses across Europe. The Directive was adopted in July 2003 and is intended to be implemented in member states in 2005, with an 8-year transitional period. The Directive replaces and harmonises existing regimes for listing securities across the EU, and regulates the public offer of securities within the EU and admission to trading on an EU exchange. Delay to adoption of the Directive was due to serious concerns of financial institutions in the EU – particularly in the Eurobond market, where issues are typically listed in London or Luxembourg under developed and standardised procedures. Concern was also raised about the "one-size-fits-all" nature of the Directive, which, in its original form, could have applied the same requirements to small offers on less-regulated markets as to major IPO offerings. Following publication of the text of the Directive in September 2001, amendments were proposed through November 2001 and March 2002, and a new draft was published in June 2002. The draft was published in amended form on 9 August 2002, with a further Common Position being published on 11 March 2003 prior to adoption in July 2003. The Directive has also caused concern for non-EU issuers, as it limits the ability of EU exchanges to waive and vary disclosure requirements, potentially meaning that non-EU issuers that are listed and subject to accounting standards and disclosure requirements outside the EU could, on listing or offering securities to the public in the EU, also be required to comply with EU standards.

The Directive requires, under Article 3, delivery of a prospectus on an Offer to the public* (sense (i)) or on admission to trading, and works on the basis that the prospectus is vetted by the home authority of EU issuers (defined in Article 2(1) as the authority where the issuer has its registered office or – in respect of debt securities with a denomination of Euro 1000 or more (reduced from Euro 5000 in the March 2003 draft and from Euro 50 000 in drafts prior to November 2002) – either the state where the issuer has its registered office or the state where the securities will be admitted to trading or the state where the securities will be offered to the public, at the option of the issuer).

Issues that are exempt under Article 4(1) from the obligation to publish a prospectus on an offer to the public include:

● Securities resulting from a merger or takeover, or from conversion of a convertible; and
● Securities offered to employees.

Exemptions under Article 4(2) from the requirement to deliver a prospectus on admission to trading include:

● Small equity tap issues;
● Securities resulting from a merger or takeover, or from conversion of a convertible; and
● Securities offered to employees.

Prospectus filings may be undertaken in a single document, or via separate documents split into:

- Registration Document (a shelf document on the issuer that must be updated annually);
- Securities Note (prepared in relation to a particular issue of securities); and
- Summary Note (giving short details of the most significant items in the first two documents – the summary may have to be translated into the language of countries where offers are to be made).

The information required in a prospectus is set by reference to the type of securities (debt or equity), and also to take into account the size and activities of the company – in particular, in relation to small and medium-sized enterprises.

Proxy   (i) A representative appointed by a shareholder of a company to attend meetings and vote on behalf of that shareholder.

(ii) The appointment document by which a Proxy at sense (i) above is empowered.

100% PSA   A standardised mortgage prepayment speed which assumes a prepayment rate of 0.2% CPR*, increasing by 0.2% CPR every month until it reaches 6% CPR after 30 months, and then remaining flat at 6% CPR.

200% PSA   A standardised mortgage prepayment speed which assumes a prepayment rate of 0.4% CPR*, increasing by 0.4% CPR every month until it reaches 12% CPR after 30 months, and then remaining flat at 12% CPR.

PSA   Public Securities Association. US association which established standard mortgage prepayment speeds. See also 100% PSA, 200% PSA.

Public company   In the UK, those Registered companies* that comply with the requirements of the Companies Act 1985* (being chiefly formalistic, apart from the requirement as to Minimum authorised capital*) for establishment of public companies. A public company in the UK may, unlike a Private company*, make an offer to the public (as defined in s. 81 Companies Act 1985) or apply for a Listing* (sense (ii)). Public companies may not generally exclude the application of s. 89 Companies Act 1985 Pre-emption rights* under the company's Articles of association* as allowed for private companies* by s. 91 Companies Act 1985 (although, if a s. 80 Companies Act 1985 authority is in place, a public company may rely on their articles of association or a Special resolution* under s. 95 Companies Act 1985 in order to disapply pre-emption rights). Public companies may restrict the transferability of their shares, although if the company is Listed*, it will often be required by the relevant stock exchange to ensure free transferability.

Public offering   An offer of shares or debentures in a company to the public. In relation to the UK, see Offer to the public* (sense (ii)).

Public Offers of Securities Regulations 1995   Or POS Regs*. UK regulations replaced by Part VI of the FSMA* 2000. The POS Regs were made under the European Communities Act 1972 and were effective from 19 June 1995 to repeal Part III of the Companies Act 1985*. They were amended (with regard to the scope of some of the exemptions from being an Offer to the public* (sense (ii))) by the Public Offers of Securities (Amendment) Regulations 1999 with effect from 10 May 1999. The POS Regs required publication of a Prospectus* whenever an offer to the public was made by a person for the first time in relation to certain Securities* (sense (i)).

Publicly available information   Or PAI*. In relation to a Credit default swap* or Credit-linked note*, information that is available on a certain minimum number of specified public sources. Requirements that publicly available information exists of occurrence of a Credit event* may be inserted into the terms of the derivative as a safeguard against disputes as to the occurrence of credit events, and in some cases as a protection against Insider dealing* concerns where a party could otherwise act on non-public information.

Purchase   In a Securities* issue, the purchase of individual securities in the open market by the issuer at market price (and their subsequent cancellation). Often under-taken for debt securities through use of a Purchase fund*. Purchase of equity securities to effect Redemption* must be made out of Distributable profits*, or from the proceeds of a fresh equity issue, under requirements as to the Maintenance of capital* (unless, for Private companies* solely, the procedure under ss. 171-177 Companies Act 1985* is followed, in which case purchase may be made from capital).

Purchase fund   Arrangements made by an issuer to carry out an undertaking given in the terms and conditions of a Security* (sense (i)) that the issuer will Purchase* the security if its market price falls below a certain threshold. Cf. Sinking fund.

Put   (i) The contractual right of an investor to demand that an issuer of Securities* effect Redemption* of those of such securities as are held by the investor at some point before their Maturity*, and on given terms.
   (ii) See Put option.

Put option   An Option* that gives the holder the right to sell a set amount of a specific commodity or financial instrument to the option writer at a set "strike price". May take the form of a European option* or an American option*. The value of a European put option and a European Call option* on the same financial asset at the same strike price are related (a relationship known as "put–call parity") as follows:

$$C - P = \mathrm{MV} - K$$

where C = the call value
   P = the put value
   MV = the market value of the underlying
   K = the strike price.

The value of a put option and a call option on the same physical asset at the same strike price are related as follows:

$$C - P = \mathrm{MV} - [K/(1+r)^n]$$

where C = the call value
   P = the put value
   MV = the market value of the underlying
   K = the strike price
   r = the discount rate (expressed as a decimal) per compounding period
   n = the number of compounding periods.

Put spread   Or Bear spread*. The purchase of a Put option*, the potential profit on which is capped by the sale of a put option with a lower Strike price*, so that profit is only realised on the spread from the higher strike price to the lower strike price.

Puttable   Securities which may be Put* (sense (i)) by their holders.

PWE   See Programme-wide enhancement.

QIB   Qualified institutional buyer for the purposes of Securities Act* regulation, and specifically for the purposes of Rule 144A*. Generally speaking, an institution with over US$ 100m in assets under investment.

QSPE   See FAS 140.

QTE   Qualified technological equipment for the purposes of the US Internal Revenue Code, defined in s. 168(i)(2) of the Code as computers or peripheral equipment, high technology telephone equipment or high technology medical equipment. Advantageous depreciation rules for tax purposes have led to the development of a tax-leasing market for QTE leases by US financiers to non-US lessees.

QTE lease   See QTE.

Qualified purchaser   In relation to the s. 3(c)(7) exemption from the definition of Investment company* (sense (i)), either an individual investor with investments that equal or exceed US$ 5m in value, or a corporate investor who owns and invests on a discretionary basis an investment portfolio that equals or exceeds US$ 25m in value. Cf. QIB.

Qualifying debt item   Classification of debt instruments for Capital adequacy* purposes. Generally consists of items such as public sector securities, investment grade rated securities, securities issued by a regulated bank or securities firm.

Quanto option   An Option* in one currency where the Premium* (sense (iii)) and any settlement amount payable on maturity are payable in another currency at a set exchange rate.

Quasi-subsidiary   See FRS 5.

Quistclose trust   A constructive Trust* which, by *Barclays Bank Ltd v. Quistclose Investments Ltd (1970)*, arises where a bank receives money from a payor for a customer's account which is to be used as payment to a third-party payee for a specific purpose of which the bank either knows or has constructive notice. This prevents the money from being appropriated by the bank or the customer (or a liquidator thereof). The money is held on trust for the third-party payee, and, if this trust fails, on a resulting trust for the payor.

Quorum   In relation to General meetings* and meetings of the Board of directors* of a company, the required minimum number of attendees to constitute the meeting effective.

Quote   The price quoted by a trader as the Bid* or Offer* for an asset.

Quote driven   A stock-trading system that operates on a Market-making* basis.

Quoted Eurobond   Under s. 349(4) ICTA (inserted by s. 111 Finance Act 2000 with effect from 1 April 2001), payments of interest made on a "quoted Eurobond" may be made free of Withholding tax* charged under s. 349(2) ICTA. A "quoted eurobond" is an interest-bearing security that is Listed* on a recognised stock exchange (such as the LSE*), and is issued by a company. Prior to 1 April 2001, the quoted Eurobond rules were contained in s. 124 ICTA, and additionally required that the security be a Bearer security*, and that payments be made to a non-UK resident person or a recognised clearing system.

r   In relation to a Credit rating* on an instrument, an "r" subscript is a warning to investors that the instrument for which the rating is given carries a degree of Market risk*; e.g. because any Currency risk* attaching to the cash flows forming the basis of payments on the instrument has not been fully hedged.

Ramping   Controlling or manipulating the price of an asset on a market through ownership of most of the available quantity of such asset.

Ramp-up   In a CDO*, the acquisition of underlying assets for the deal over a period of time following the close of the transaction.

Range   The highest and lowest Bid* and Offer* at which an asset has been traded over a set period.

RAP   Regulatory accounting principles. US guidelines for determining the Capital adequacy* treatment of regulated entities. See also Off balance sheet, sense (ii).

RAROC   Risk-adjusted ROC*. Measure of the return being earned on the capital of a business, with each component of the overall figure adjusted to reflect the degree of Risk* of loss of capital associated with the generation of that return.

Ratification   The express authorisation and adoption by empowered representatives of an individual or body of an action taken previously that was not authorised by that body at the time the action was taken.

Rating   See Credit rating.

Rating agency   See Credit rating agency.

RDC   See Russian depositary certificate.

Real estate owned   Or REO*. The acquisition of auctioned real estate (usually from a court auction), typically by a Special servicer*, as part of a strategy of realising greater value for the real estate than the likely level of bid prices at the auction.

Realkreditobligationer   Danish form of Covered bond*. The issuance of *realkreditobligationer* began in the 1800s.

Receivable   An amount owing from one person to another, whether due now or at a future time. In legal terms, a Chose in action*.

Receivables sale agreement   In a Securitisation* transaction, the main agreement that provides for the sale of the Receivables* from the Originator* to the SPV*. Contains purchase price calculations and representations and warranties and Eligibility criteria* with regard to the originator and the receivables, breach of which will typically oblige the originator to repurchase the relevant assets.

Receivables trust   In relation to a Securitisation*, a Trust*, usually structured to be a Bare trust* in order to benefit from Fiscal transparency*, into which the Receivables* are transferred. Interests in the trust are accorded to the SPV*, the Originator* and any other relevant parties. Used as an efficient method of dividing up interests in a pool of receivables (particularly where the receivables balance is fluctuating), or as a tax efficient method of extracting Excess spread* from a transaction back to the originator. In mortgage transactions, may be referred to as a Mortgages trust*.

Receiver   A person appointed to realise Security* (sense (ii)). If such person is an LPA receiver (i.e. if appointed under the statutory power in s. 101, LPA*, which applies to Mortgages* or Charges* made by Deed*), he will have the powers of an LPA receiver, and if appointed under the terms of a security document, he will have the powers contained in the security document. A receiver, once appointed, manages the assets over which the security extends, collecting the income from the assets and/or selling them. Does not have power to set aside Undervalues* or Preferences* (cf. Liquidator and Administrator). See also Administrative receiver.

Receivership   The status of a company in relation to which a Receiver* has been appointed to realise assets subject to Security* (sense (ii)). One of the five main branches of insolvency-related procedure (for the others, see Voluntary arrangement, Liquidation, Administration and Administrative Receivership).

Recharacterisation   This is the risk that a transaction that is intended to be classified as a sale or outright transfer for insolvency purposes (e.g., pursuant to a Repo* or a Securitisation*), is in fact classified by the courts as a loan against Security* (sense (ii)) of some description.

In determining whether the transaction is a true sale or a secured loan, a UK court will look at whether the documentation for the transaction is a sham to conceal the true intention of the parties. If they consider it is not a sham, they will construe the documentation to determine the intent of the parties and hence the true characterisation of the transaction.

Characterisation of a transfer as a sale or as a secured loan was considered in the case of *Re George Inglefield Limited [1933] Ch 1*. The transaction was a purchase by a financing institution of goods that the company was selling on hire purchase to its customers, together with an absolute assignment by the company to the financing institution of the receivables due from the customers, with the assignment not notified to the customers. The purchase and assignment were upheld as a true sale, although Romer LJ set out three indicative criteria at pp. 27–28 which may lead to a transfer being classified as a secured loan rather than a true sale:

(a) "in a transaction of sale the vendor is not entitled to get back the subject-matter of the sale by returning to the purchaser the money that has passed between them". Cf. the equity of redemption of a mortgagor;

(b) "if the purchaser sells the subject-matter of the purchase and realises a profit, of course he has not got to account to the vendor for the profit". Cf. the duty to account of a mortgagee;

(c) "if the purchaser were to resell the purchased property at a price which was insufficient to recoup him the money that he paid to the vendor, of course he would not be entitled to recover the balance from the vendor". Cf. the repayment obligation of a mortgagor.

Hence, a right of the Originator* in a securitisation to repurchase the Receivables*, an entitlement to any profit made by the SPV* on a sale of the receivables or an obligation to compensate the SPV for a loss on sale of the receivables, could prejudice a true sale characterisation.

In the case of *Orion Finance v. Crown Financial Management [1996] 2 BCLC 78*, the court did however stress that: "no single one of these features may be determinative. The absence of any right in the transferor to recover the property transferred is inconsistent with the transaction being by way of security; but its existence may be inferred, and its presence is not conclusive. The transaction may take the form of a sale with an option to repurchase, and this is not to be equated with a right of redemption merely because the repurchase price is calculated by reference to the original sale price together with interest since the date of the sale. On the other hand, the presence of a right of recourse by the transferee against the transferor to recover a shortfall may be inconsistent with a sale; but it is not necessarily so, and its absence is not conclusive. A security may be without recourse. Moreover the nature of the property may be such that it is impossible or at least very unlikely that it will be realised at either a profit or loss. Many financing arrangements possess this feature. The fact that the transferee may have to make adjustments and payments to the transferor after the debts have been got in from the debtors does not prevent the transaction from being by way of sale."

In the Orion case the court interpreted a limited recourse hire-purchase from a financing institution by a company of computers to be sub-leased, together with an assignment of the receivables arising under the sub-lease, as a secured loan, on the basis of numerous references in the documentation to the assignment being by way of security and the fact that "there is nothing in the documentation inconsistent with the intention of the parties being to create a charge".

The court stated that: "the critical phrases are 'as security for its obligations hereunder', 'they be charged', 'such a security' and 'encumber'. The use of these phrases in this context is in my judgment only consistent with an assignment by way of security and inconsistent with an absolute assignment."

In the case of *Welsh Development Agency v. Export Finance Co Ltd [1992] BCLC 148*, the transaction consisted of a standing offer by a financing institution to purchase goods from an exporter, which the exporter would simultaneously resell (as agent) to an overseas customer of the exporter, with the financing institution an undisclosed principal, and with the financing institution retaining title to the goods until the purchase price had been paid by the customer. The court upheld the true sale characterisation, arguing that this reflected the nature of the relationship between the parties as a whole, and stating that: "if one part of the agreement purports to create a particular legal transaction, it may happen that other provisions are inconsistent with such a transaction. The task of the court is then to ascertain which is the substance, the truth, the reality ... it was plainly the intention that [the financing institution] should become entitled, as against the overseas buyers, to the rights and remedies of a seller of goods, if [the financing institution] found it necessary to exercise them. I feel unable to conclude that, in substance or in reality or in truth, the intention of the parties as derived from the terms of the written agreement was that [the financing institution] should not acquire those rights and remedies."

Recognised clearing house   A Clearing house* that is recognised for the purpose of exemption from Financial Services Act 1986* (repeated under the FSMA* 2000) regulation and for the purpose of Set-off* (sense (ii)) of Market contracts*. For example, the London Clearing House* and CREST*. Also, an Overseas clearing house* granted recognition as a recognised clearing house.

Recognised investment exchange   An Exchange* that is recognised for the purpose of exemption from Financial Services Act 1986* (repeated under the FSMA* 2000) regulation and for the purpose of Set-off* (sense (ii)) of Market contracts*. For example, LIFFE*, the LME*, the London Stock Exchange*, the IPE*, Tradepoint* and OMLX*. Also, an Overseas investment exchange* granted recognition as a recognised investment exchange.

Reconstituted bonds   Stripped bonds*, the interest and capital components of which have been bought up and repackaged as whole bonds.

Reconstruction   The transfer, under s. 132 Companies Act 1985*, of assets from a parent company to a shelf company (or other wholly-owned subsidiary) in return for shares in the subsidiary and the assumption by the subsidiary of certain of the parent's liabilities. Certain reliefs are available for this procedure, which is often used in insolvency-related circumstances. See Reorganisation, Scheme of arrangement, Voluntary arrangement.

Red clause   See Anticipatory credit.

Red herring   A preliminary Offering circular* or Information memorandum*, that is used for marketing a securities issue prior to production of the final form document. Any amendments to insert final terms must be of a minor nature, or will have to be disclosed to the Syndicate* for the issue. In the UK, care must be taken to ensure that the investment advertisement regulations under s. 57 Financial Services Act 1986* (replaced by s. 21 FSMA* 2000) are not breached in distributing such a document, as it is not exempt from the regulations in the same way that a final form version that constitutes Listing particulars* or a Prospectus* would be. It should therefore only be given to persons who are authorised persons or others to whom such advertisements may be distributed without breaching Financial Services Act 1986 (replaced by FSMA 2000) regulations.

Redeemable share   A class of shares in a company that are Callable* or Puttable* on specified terms in relation to such class contained in the Articles of association*. Subject in any event to Maintenance of capital* requirements that the shares may only be redeemed out of Distributable profits* or from the proceeds of a fresh issue of shares, and to the requirement at s.159(3) Companies Act 1985* that redeemable shares may only be redeemed if fully paid-up first.

Redemption   The payment of amounts of principal outstanding on a Security*. In relation to an equity securities issue, typically effected by Purchase* of shares in the market subject to Maintenance of capital* requirements. In relation to a debt securities issue, may be by Optional redemption*, Mandatory redemption* or Purchase*.

Redemption amount   The amount payable on a Security* (sense (i)) on Optional redemption* prior to Maturity*.

Redemption date   The stated date on which a debt security is due to be repaid, and on which payment to the holder of principal and accrued interest is to be made (assuming no early Redemption* or prior Purchase*).

Redemption yield   See Yield to maturity.

Re-discounting   The Discounting* of Eligible bills* or Treasury bills* (sense (i)) by the Discount houses* or by other Bank of England approved entities to the Bank of England acting as Lender of last resort* to finance Liquidity* shortages in the Money markets*, at a rate set by the Bank of England.

Re-domicile   The change of place of residence of a Corporation* (usually for tax purposes). In the UK, cannot be done in cases where the company is incorporated in the UK, as the company depends on UK legislation for its legal existence. If the company is incorporated outside the UK, then it can be re-domiciled for tax purposes by ensuring that its place of "central management and control" is relocated outside the UK (see also Residence).

Reduction of capital   The reduction of the value of a company's Issued share capital* either by payments to shareholders and write-down of the Nominal value* of shares (other than by way of Purchase*), cancellation of liability to pay unpaid amounts on shares or write-down of the nominal value of shares without payment. Under s. 135(1) Companies Act 1985*, may only be effected by a Special resolution* that is subject to confirmation by the court.

Reference agent   In relation to Securities* and other debts that bear a Floating rate* of interest, a bank or financial institution that sets the rate of interest payable on the debt from time to time from rates (e.g. for LIBOR*) quoted to it by a range of banks.

Reference entity   In relation to a Credit derivative*, the reference entity is the selected entity whose Credit risk* is being traded. If the credit of the reference entity worsens or a particular Credit event* occurs with respect to the reference entity, a payout may be triggered on the derivative.

Reference obligation   In relation to a Credit derivative*, a particular debt obligation of the Reference entity*. A decrease in the value of the reference obligation is used to determine the Materiality* of any Credit event* or credit worsening, and to calculate the amount of the payout on the derivative.

Reg S   See Regulation S.

Registered company   In the UK, a form of Company* that enjoys Corporate personality* as a Corporation* pursuant to registration under the provisions of the Companies Act 1985* and is subject to compliance with the requirements of the Companies Act 1985 regarding the submission of company information and accounts for registration (some of which can be avoided by small companies, by the use of Written resolutions* or by the use of the Elective regime*). May take the form of a Company limited by guarantee*, a Company limited by shares* or an Unlimited company*, and may be a Private company* or a Public company*.

Registered design   An intellectual property right in a particular pattern or design that is created by registration (in the UK, with the Design Registry), and entitles the owner to prevent others copying the pattern or design for a certain period (25 years in the UK). Cf. Copyright, Patent, Trademark.

Registered security   A Security* that is subject to registration requirements to transfer legal ownership, as opposed to a Bearer security* or an Order security*. Many jurisdictions, including the UK, require registration in a company register for the transfer of legal ownership in company shares, although the effect of this may to a certain extent be circumvented by the use of Nominee shareholders*. Bonds* may be issued in bearer form in many jurisdictions, as Eurobonds*. Publicly issued bonds (or other securities) that are offered to US investors must, however, be in registered form for US tax purposes (see TEFRA).

Registration   See Security, sense (ii) and Form 395.

Registrar of Companies   Official who supervises incorporation and administrative filings for Registered companies*, under the Companies Act 1985*.

Regulation   A type of European Union law* that is (a) binding in its entirety; (b) directly applicable in Member states* without national legislation; and (c) directly enforceable by or against (1) member states or (2) private individuals or companies (via "vertical" and "horizontal" direct effect respectively) if capable of being so construed.

Regulation D   An SEC* safe harbour within the s. 4(2) Securities Act* exemption from registration on issue for Private placements* (sense (iii)). Compliance with the Regulation D requirements ensures obtaining the issue exemption. Regulation D requires that no general solicitation or advertising of the offering occurs and that purchasers are not acquiring the securities with a view to distributing them (in order to comply with such resale restrictions, legends on the securities and "non-distribution letters" are obtained as with a private placement). Also, the issuer must reasonably believe that no more than 35 purchasers of the issue are not Accredited investors*. In addition, any such non-accredited investor purchasers must have sufficient experience to evaluate the investment (in the issuer's reasonable belief) and must have access to Exchange Act* reports (or comparable Securities Act registration information) on the issuer.

Regulation M   A regulation of the SEC* containing Rules 101 to 105, which replaced the former Rule 10b-6 and Rule 10b-7 provisions in March 1997. Regulation M is an anti-manipulation rule formulated by the SEC* under the authority given in s. 10(b) of the Exchange Act* in the US which generally prohibits bids for a purchase of securities during their distribution by an issuer, underwriter or other distributor of securities in the US, unless exempted. Designed to prevent conditioning of the market during the distribution period. Exemptions are available for securities resold to QIBs* pursuant to Rule 144A* and for Stabilisation* carried on outside the US. In addition, Regulation

M provides exemption from its provisions for certain stabilising activities by under-writers.

Regulation S   Or Reg S*. A regulation of the SEC* under the Securities Act* that was introduced in 1990 to replace Release 4708* and defined the broad scope of, and clarified previous uncertainty over, SEC registration requirements. It provides for safe harbours from the requirement to register securities, either on issue, or on resale, of the securities. An offering is considered to be made "on issue" if it is made during the distribution period; i.e. it is made by the issuer (or an affiliate) or a dis-tributor (or an affiliate) (distributors are defined as "any underwriter, dealer, or other person who participates, pursuant to a contractual arrangement, in the distribution of the securities"). The distribution period cannot end before the end of any relevant restricted period (see below), and is considered to extend indefinitely in relation to any underwriter of the issue unless and until the underwriter sells its initial allotment of securities. The safe harbours are:

(a) **Issuer Safe Harbour**   An issuer safe harbour under Rule 903 within which no registration is required. The safe harbour is not available where the securities offer is "part of a plan or scheme to avoid the registration requirements" of the Securities Act, there exists an understanding the securities will "flow back" to the US, or any dis-tributor "knows or is reckless in not knowing" that any purchaser or distributor will not meet the Regulation S general and particular requirements. To gain the Regulation S issuer safe harbour, the general requirements are that the issuer and others affiliated with an offering must:

(1) Ensure that the securities are offered in an "offshore transaction" (i.e. they are not offered to "US persons" such as US corporations, partnerships and individuals and the buy order is originated with a buyer outside the US or on the floor of a non-US exchange);
(2) Avoid "directed selling efforts" in the US (activities intended to, or that could reasonably result in, the conditioning of the US market for the securities); and
(3) Follow offering restrictions set out in the offer documentation.

The Regulation S particular requirements to gain the issuer safe harbour relate to each combination of issue and issuer within one of three categories:

• *Category 1* (issues backed by the full faith and credit of a foreign government, issues by a non-US issuer with no SUSMI* in such securities, issues directed to a single non-US country, issues pursuant to non-US employee benefit plans): no particular requirements.

• *Category 2* (issues by issuers who report under the Exchange Act* (excluding issues of equity securities by a US reporting issuer from 17 February 1998), issues of debt securities by a non-US issuer with SUSMI in such securities): a distributor must offer or sell the securities only in accordance with a registration exemption, in any sale to another distributor or dealer the purchaser must be informed that the securities are subject to these same selling restrictions, no sale within 40 days (for debt) or 1 year (for equity) of the first offer of the securities (the "restricted period") (or otherwise falling within the distribution period – see above) must be for the benefit of US person, and the securities must state that they have not been registered and may not be offered or sold in the US or to a US person save under a registration exemption.

- *Category 3* (other issues): the requirements are as for Category 2, save that in addition, during the restricted period the securities are required to be "locked-up" in the form of a Global note*, only being allowed to be released into definitives after such period and upon certification of non-US beneficial ownership, or acquisition of US beneficial ownership under a registration exemption.

Use of the Regulation S issuer safe harbour, where there is an immediate resale of the securities into the US as Seasoned securities* after the end of any issuer safe harbour restricted period, is a practice frowned upon by the SEC in their release of 27 June 1995 as potentially forming a scheme to avoid registration requirements (depending on the circumstances). In a 1997 release, the SEC mooted increasing the restricted period for equity sales to 2 years.

(b) **Resale safe harbour**   A resale safe harbour under Rule 904 (which is available whether or not the issue was Regulation S exempted) within which no registration is required for securities that are resold on a non-US market approved as a DOSM* by the SEC.

In their release of 27 June 1995, the SEC notes that attempts to "wash-off" resale restrictions (e.g. on Rule 144A* securities) by selling outside the US under Rule 904 and buying back fungible but unrestricted securities would render the replacement securities subject to the same restrictions.

Rehypothecation   The sale of a Security* (sense (i)) by a creditor to whom the security has been given as Collateral*. Only possible where the collateral document contains an express ability for the creditor to rehypothecate. Under English law, effecting rehypothecation will convert the collateral arrangements to an Outright transfer*, even where they originally took the form of a Security interest*. In the US, rehypothecation of collateral should not convert a security interest.

Reinvestment period   See Revolving period.

Reinvestment risk   The Risk* arising from Prepayment* that the recipient may suffer a loss of income if cash from the prepaid assets can only be invested at a lower rate in the current market, which may result in a Negative carry* position. The recipient may need to arrange a guaranteed rate reinvestment, such as a GIC* for such Prepayments*, or may require the payor to pay Break costs* incurred by the recipient in refinancing or maintaining its liabilities.

REIT   Real estate investment trust. US form of entity used for real estate Securitisation*. The REIT is exempt from corporation tax in the US provided it meets the requirements set out in the Tax Code.

Release   The discharge of a Security* (sense (ii)) interest by the beneficiary.

Release 4708   An SEC* release, superseded by Regulation S*, that set forth a no-action position adopted by the SEC with regard to securities offerings technically falling within s. 5 of the Securities Act*, but actually distributed outside the US to non-US nationals. Required that (a) statements be made as to non-registration of the securities and non-sale in the US or to US persons of the securities within 90 days (for debt) or 1 year (for equity) after distribution had been completed, and (b) that the securities be held "locked-up" in the form of a Global note* until completion of such period.

REMIC   Real estate mortgage investment conduit. US statutory form of entity (which can be any form – trust, corporation, etc.) created for the Securitisation* of mortgage loans. Can issue multiple tranches of securities, but cannot enter into swaps. The REMIC has Fiscal transparency*. Regular interests in a REMIC are classified as debt for tax purposes; residual interests are classified as equity. No gain or loss is recognised when assets are sold to a REMIC, and the tax basis of the REMIC in the assets is equal to the issue proceeds of its securities.

REO   See Real estate owned.

Re-offer price   The price at which securities subscribed in the Primary market* by subscribers are initially distributed in the primary market to investors. See also Fixed price re-offer and Issue price.

Reorganisation   The transfer of assets under ss. 110-111 of the Insolvency Act 1986 from a company that is undergoing voluntary Winding-up*. The transfer is made to a transferee, in return for shares in the transferee.

Repackaging   An Asset-backed finance* technique based on the transformation of certain cash flows, which typically involves the linking of a Swap* or other Derivative* to a Security* (or other financial asset), which is then sold as a package to create a Synthetic security* or Asset-backed security*. Similar to Securitisation* in many respects (including the use of a bankruptcy remote SPV* to own the underlying securities and enter into the swap), since it effectively converts one cash flow into another, more marketable, cash flow. Cf. Asset swap.

Repayment date   The stated date on which a loan is due to be repaid, and on which payment to the lender of principal and accrued interest is to be made.

Replenishment   The use of cash receipts in the SPV* in a Securitisation* transaction to purchase new Receivables*, rather than to effect Amortisation* of its funding, thus extending the Weighted average life* of the funding. Cf. Substitution.

Repo   See Repurchase agreement.

Repo rate   The Interest rate* charged in the Money markets* for Repos* of high-quality government securities that may form a Base rate* for the economy, similar to that formed by the Discount rate* (sense (i)) in some countries, as the rate reflects a money market investment instrument that is secured by high-quality collateral. Gilt repos were introduced in the UK in 1996.

Repurchase agreement   A transaction involving the current sale of securities to a counterparty, and the future obligation to repurchase equivalent securities from the same counterparty, at rates agreed in advance. Used in the Money markets* as a form of secured loan. See also Repo rate and Reverse repo.

RES   Reprise d'Entreprise par ses Salariés; French form of "employee buy-out". In other words, equivalent to an MBO* undertaken by the employees rather than by the management.

Re-securitisation   The Repackaging* of junior tranches of an existing Securitisation* issue in reliance on an increase in the seasoning of the underlying portfolio and/or a re-rating of the credit quality of the top slice of the junior tranche (for example, where the structure has sequential pay, and the junior tranche has not yet started to amortise).

Reserve assets   Assets with a high degree of Liquidity*, which a financial institution is required by its national central bank to maintain with such central bank (or other institutions), to ensure a Liquid market* in cash. Usually a percentage of local currency domestic (as opposed to Eurocurrency*) deposits, as these reflect the inherent degree of Liquidity risk* in the domestic currency system. May be interest-bearing or non-interest-bearing. Reserve assets were supplanted in the UK in 1981 by the requirement that Eligible banks* maintain certain minimum deposits (as a percentage of Eligible liabilities*) with Discount houses* in the LDMA*, which requirement was subsequently abolished in 1986. There are currently no reserve asset requirements in the UK. See also MLAs.

Reserve fund   Or Spread account*. In a Securitisation, an account used to hold back a part of the Excess spread* collected on the Receivables* (rather than releasing it to the Originator*), as a form of First loss* Credit enhancement* for the transaction.

Residence   In relation to taxation, generally a corporation is subject to income or profits taxation in the country or territory where it is resident for tax purposes (generally in relation to its worldwide income or profits). A corporation that is not resident in a country may still be subject to taxation in that country, where it has a branch in that country (typically under general principles of tax law in most countries) or a permanent establishment in that country (under the terms of most Double tax treaties* modelled on the standard OECD form of treaty). In the UK, Corporation tax* is charged on the taxable profits and chargeable gains made by any UK resident company wherever they arise around the world. Since 1988 any company that is incorporated in the UK is regarded as resident for tax purposes in the UK. Companies that are incorporated outside the UK may still be regarded as resident for tax purposes in the UK where their place of "central management and control" is in the UK. Non-resident companies are only subjected to tax on the profits of a trade carried on in the UK through a branch or agency (a "UK representative" of the company) (under s. 126 Finance Act* 1995). Brokers and Investment managers* (see ss. 126-127 Finance Act 1995) providing services in the ordinary course of business for a market remuneration are excluded from being UK representatives. Where the non-resident is located in a country with a double tax treaty with the UK, the non-resident may only be liable in respect of profits of a UK "permanent establishment" instead. See also Re-domicile.

Resident   See Residence.

Residual value risk   Or Asset value risk*. In Asset-based finance*, the Risk* that the resale value of a financed asset relinquished to a lender will be insufficient to repay the remaining financing outstanding.

Resolution   A decision of the Board of directors* or the Members* of a company reached in a duly quorate meeting. See Elective resolution, Extraordinary resolution, Ordinary resolution, Special resolution, Written resolution. Resolutions must be in the form specified by the Companies Act 1985* and other legislation. Where legislation does not specify, authority is divided between the board of directors and the members as specified in the Articles of association* of the company.

(a) **Elective resolutions** relate solely to the Elective regime* under s. 379A Companies Act 1985.

(b) **Extraordinary resolutions** are required to approve a voluntary Winding-up* under s. 84 Insolvency Act 1986.

(c) **Ordinary resolutions** are required to authorise directors to issue shares (see Issued share capital) under s. 80 Companies Act 1985, to increase Authorised share capital* where permitted by the company's Articles of association* under s. 121 Companies Act 1985, to approve a market Purchase* of the company's own shares under s. 166 Companies Act 1985, to appoint or remove a Director* of the company under ss. 292 and 303 Companies Act 1985 (although Special notice* is required, and no written resolution is permissible, for a removal), to approve a director's employment contract which extends for more than 5 years with limited termination rights under s. 319 Companies Act 1985, to approve a transaction that involves a director acquiring from (or selling to) the company non-cash assets exceeding £100 000 or 10% of the company's assets in value under s. 320 Companies Act 1985 (loan transactions with directors are generally prohibited under s. 330 Companies Act 1985) or to appoint or remove auditors under ss. 385 and 391 Companies Act 1985 (no written resolution is permissible for a removal).

(d) **Special resolutions** are required to change the name of the company under s. 28 Companies Act 1985, to change the Objects* of the company set out in its Memorandum of association* under s. 4 Companies Act 1985, to change its Articles of association* under s. 9 Companies Act 1985, to re-register a Private company* as a Public company* or vice versa under ss. 43 and 53 Companies Act 1985 respectively, to re-register an Unlimited company* as a Limited company* under s. 51 Companies Act 1985, to effect a Reduction of capital* under s. 135(1) Companies Act 1985, to effect a "whitewash" for a private company under the Financial assistance* provisions of s. 155 Companies Act 1985, to enable a Purchase* by a company of its own shares which is either Off-market* or which is a purchase made from capital by a private company under ss. 164 and 173 Companies Act 1985 respectively or to dis-apply Pre-emption rights* under s. 95 Companies Act 1985.

(e) **Written resolutions** may be used in place of any elective, extraordinary, ordinary or special resolution under s. 381A Companies Act 1985, except for resolutions as to the removal of a director or an auditor pursuant to Schedule 15A, Part I, paragraph 1 Companies Act 1985.

Retention of title   A sale of an asset subject to retention of title to the asset by the seller pending payment, undertaken in order to achieve protection against the asset being available to creditors generally in the insolvency of the purchaser, but without creating an interest that would be registrable as a Bill of sale*. Does not protect against a sale by the purchaser to a bona fide third party unless the sale constitutes a Conditional sale* within the Consumer Credit Act 1974* definition. See also Hire purchase.

Return on assets   See ROA.

Return on capital   See ROC.

Return on equity   See ROE.

Reverse gensaki   A Gensaki* that is a Reverse repo*.

Reverse mortgage   A loan made available to older homeowners against the equity value of their home. The lender will make a single lump sum advance, or regular monthly payments to the borrower, in return for a receivable that rolls up against the property value during the life of the borrower.

Reverse repo   A Repurchase agreement* described from the point of view of the party agreeing to purchase and resell securities.

Revolving facility   An Overdraft* or other Facility* where amounts repaid to the lender may subsequently be redrawn by the borrower.

Revolving period   Or Reinvestment period*. In relation to a Securitisation* transaction, that part of the life of the transaction during which Replenishment* of the Receivables* in the transaction may take place from collections received, prior to the commencement of application of collections to effect Amortisation* of the principal amount owed to investors. Usually the revolving period is set as a specific fixed period, which may terminate early on the occurrence of an Early amortisation event*.

Rights issue   An issue of additional shares undertaken to raise capital for a company (cf. Bonus issue). Current shareholders may be encouraged to invest by setting the issue price at a discount.

Risk   The chance of a loss arising due to one or more particular kinds of event. Examples of risk are Basis risk*, Commingling risk*, Concentration risk*, Convertibility risk*, Correlation risk*, Credit risk*, Currency risk*, Liquidity risk*, Market risk*, Prepayment risk*, Reinvestment risk*, Residual value risk*, Settlement risk*, Transfer risk* and volatility risk.

Risk participation   See Funded risk participation and Unfunded risk participation.

Risk reversal   The purchase of a Put* to Hedge* the Market risk* on an asset combined with the simultaneous sale of a Call* to limit the Premium* (sense (iii)) cost of the hedge.

RiskMetrics   Methodology put forward by J.P. Morgan for calculating the Value at risk* on a particular Portfolio* of instruments or Positions* due to Market risk*. Cf. CreditMetrics.

RMBS   Residential-mortgage-backed security. MBS* backed by residential mortgages.

ROA   Return on assets. Measure of the percentage return of profits of a business on its gross assets.

ROC   Return on capital. Measure of the percentage return of profits of a business on its capital (equity and long-term debt). Cf. ROE.

ROE   Return on equity. Measure of the percentage return of profits of a business on its net assets or equity. Cf. ROC.

Rolling settlement   Settlement* of securities dealings a fixed number of business days after the Trade date* so that under a 3-day system (T + 3) – as used on the London Stock Exchange* since 5 February 2001 – shares bought on Day 1 and sold on Day 3 must be paid for on Day 4, with sale proceeds being received on Day 6. CDs* and FRCDs* typically settle at T + 2. Settlement of secondary Eurobond* and FRN* trades was reduced from T + 7 to T + 3 on 1 June 1995 by ISMA*. Most government bond markets settle at T + 1 or T + 2. In many countries corporate bond trades settle at T + 3 and equities are moving to T + 3. Settlement of Brady bonds* is also now at T + 3. These reductions in settlement periods are intended to reduce Credit risk* (sense (i)) in the system. Short-term rolling settlement may necessitate Margin trading* (for instance, Euroclear* and Clearstream* offer credit facilities for settlement) and (in particular for equities) Nominee accounts*.

Rollover   The simultaneous repayment and reissue of a Security* (sense (i)). Often used with short-term securities such as CP*, in combination with a Liquidity facility* designed to allow redemption in the event that the CP markets are temporarily disrupted.

Round lot   The standard smallest trading unit for an asset.

RPB   Recognised professional body under the Financial Services Act 1986*, e.g. the Law Society, the Institute of Chartered Accountants and the actuaries' professional body. The insurance brokers' professional body is no longer recognised for this purpose. See also Financial Services Authority.

RPI   Retail price index.

RPI-linked security   Or Index-linked security*. A security the return on which is linked to the RPI* from time to time. See Capital indexed, Current pay and Interest indexed.

RTGS   Real time gross settlement. See also TARGET.

RUF   Revolving underwritten facility. A Facility agreement* that provides for the issue of Euronotes*, the sale of which is underwritten by the facility banks, thus providing the issuer with a Commitment* that lasts the length of the facility, but using funding at short-term interest rates. Cf. NIF.

Rule 4.2   London Stock Exchange* Yellow Book* rule that allowed Unlisted* securities not quoted on the USM* to be traded by dealers. Phased out following the opening of the AIM* on 19 June 1995.

Rule 10b-5   An anti-fraud provision formulated by the SEC*, under the authority given in s. 10(b) of the Exchange Act* of the US, which prohibits "the use of any means or instrumentality of interstate commerce ... to make any untrue statement of a material fact or to omit to state a material fact necessary in order to make the statements made, in the light of the circumstances under which they were made, not misleading ...", with regard to securities offering documents. The application of the rule requires the use of US "jurisdictional means". See also 10b-5 Letter*.

Rule 12g3-2(b)   An SEC* exemption from the reporting provisions to be complied with by a non-US issuer either (a) due to the number of US shareholders in the company, where the company does not wish to meet the requirements for a reporting company under the Exchange Act*, or (b) in order to meet Rule 144A* requirements, where the company does not wish to meet the Exchange Act reporting requirements or the requirement to hold information available on request. The issuer must supply, on an ongoing basis, Home country information*. The requirements of this rule are also known as the Home country reporting requirements*.

Rule 144   An SEC* safe harbour from consideration of a person as an underwriter within the meaning of s. 4(1) of the Securities Act*. Thus, a person within the safe harbour who is not an issuer or dealer can rely on the s. 4(1) resale exemption. The safe harbour allows resales after an initial 1-year holding period, and requires that resales occur in ordinary market transactions, that notice of resales is filed with the SEC, that periodic Exchange Act* reports (or comparable public information) are available on the issuer, and that the volume of resales be within certain limits (these volume limits are dropped after a 2-year holding period for sellers who are not affiliates of the issuer). Prior to April 1997 the initial holding period was 2 years and the volume limit for non-affiliates was 3 years.

Rule 144A   An SEC* securities market regulation introduced in April 1990 providing a resale exemption from registration under the Securities Act* for a securities issue (or part of an issue) that is subjected to the restriction that it may be resold solely to and among QIBs* in the Secondary market*. Rule 144A is often used immediately following a Private placement* (sense (ii)), which placement is often made to a single investment bank intending immediate resale. Rule 144A is only available in relation to a class of securities of the issuer (e.g. preferred shares, ordinary shares, debt, ADRs*, etc.), that has not already been listed on a US securities Exchange* or listed on Nasdaq*. Rule 144A is not available to an issuer unless current financial statements and statements for the 2 preceding years, together with basic information on the issuer, is available to each holder of a security, as well as to prospective investors, on request (which requirement is deemed met if the issuer is either subject to the reporting requirements of the Exchange Act*, or exempt from such requirements under Rule 12g3-2(b)* and therefore required instead to supply Home country information*).

Rule 415   SEC* rule under which Shelf registration* may be effected.

Rule 903   See Regulation S.

Rule 904   See Regulation S.

Rule against perpetuities   A rule of Trust* law, designed to limit the length of time for which property may be tied up in a trust without becoming Vested* (as to both income and capital) in an identifiable beneficiary or beneficiaries. A trust may be created to last for a maximum of 80 years (under the Perpetuities and Accumulations Act 1964, s. 1) or a "life-in-being" and 21 years (under common law), within which time the property must be fully vested for the trust to be valid. Cf. Accumulation.

Rule of 78s   Otherwise known as the sum-of-the-years-digits (which is descriptive of the method of calculation). This method of Amortisation* adds the numerical digits of each period (so that over 12 periods, the sum would be $1 + 2 + 3 + 4 + \cdots + 11 + 12$, in other words 78). The amount of each equal instalment on an Annuity* basis is first calculated. The amount of the instalment that relates to principal amortisation is then a fraction of the original loan amount equal to the number of the period divided by the total sum of the periods over the life of the deal. For example, in the fourth period of a 12-period loan, the principal amount of the instalment will be equal to 4/78ths of the loan principal. This method of amortisation will normally result in a slower amortisation schedule than that for an annuity loan. Consequently, the interest rate on a rule of 78s loan will be higher than that on a comparable annuity loan at the start of the loan, but falls during the life of the loan, so that it is lower than that on the annuity loan by the end of the loan term. As this method of amortisation allows the originator to collect more cash (absent prepayment penalties) on a loan that is prepaid during its life, it may be utilised as a disincentive to prepayment (or as a compensation measure for the originator).

Ruling-off   See Break.

Running the books   In relation to a Securities* issue or Facility*, the organisation of a Syndicate* by the Book runner*.

Running yield   See Current yield.

Russian depositary certificate   Form of Depositary receipt* representing Russian shares.

SAF   See Servicer advance facility.

Sale and leaseback   The sale of assets coupled with the lease of the assets back to the seller. Usually undertaken as a way of raising finance at a better rate than a normal loan, due to the additional credit provided by the transfer of ownership in the assets. Also serves to free up capital held in the asset.

Sallie Mae   See Student Loan Marketing Association.

Same day funds   A transfer of funds that are cleared for use on the same day (i.e. the same day is the Settlement date*). Cf. Same day value.

Same day value   A transfer of funds that are deemed credited to the payee's account on the same day, for the purposes of calculating interest payable or receivable on the account balance (i.e. the same day is the Value date*). Cf. Same day funds.

Samurai bond   A Foreign bond* issued in Japanese yen. Subject to filings in Japanese with the MoF*. Cf. Shogun bond*.

Sarbanes–Oxley Act   US act that became law on 30 July 2002 in response to the accounting frauds of 2001 and 2002. The Act creates a regulatory board to oversee auditors. The Act also sets certification requirement for accounts by the CEO and CFO, in violation of which criminal penalties may be imposed. The Act applies to any issuer that files reports with the SEC*, although foreign issuers that simply supply information under Rule 12g3-2(b) are exempted.

Savings Tax Directive   The EU Directive* on the taxation of savings income (Directive 2003/48) was eventually signed in June 2003 after 5 years of discussion. The Directive is to be implemented in Member states* by 1 January 2004, and applied from 1 January 2005. The UK and the Netherlands have agreed to ensure the adoption of the same measures in their dependent territories (the Channel Islands, Isle of Man and Caribbean dependencies).

The Directive was originally proposed by the EU Commission on 19 May 1998, as a proposal to impose a 20% withholding tax on payments of interest made from one EU state to an individual in another, in order to prevent tax evasion arising where residents of one EU state receive gross income in another member state and do not declare the income in their home state. The proposal called for each member state to choose whether to implement the 20% withholding, or to require paying institutions to report payments to the tax authorities of the EU resident's home state.

The proposal was subject to fierce opposition from Luxembourg and the UK on the grounds that it would result in a transfer of business to jurisdictions outside the EU (such as Switzerland or the US). In April 2000, proposals were put forward by the UK that information exchange be developed more fully instead of imposing withholding tax. These proposals were agreed by the EU on 20 June 2000 and were confirmed at the ECOFIN Council meeting on 26–27 November 2000, with a new proposed directive published by the Commission on 18 July 2001, that would require member states to implement information exchange. A transitional period was provided for Austria, Belgium and Luxembourg in the proposed directive, during which they would be entitled to charge a withholding tax instead of carrying out information exchange, due to concerns that information exchange requirements would breach confidentiality and bank secrecy laws.

A form of wording to insert in withholding tax gross-up provisions for new bond issues was released by IPMA* on 15 February 2001. The wording addressed the new directive by providing that issuers will not be obliged to gross-up for any withholding tax arising under the directive.

Since the 2001 proposal, discussions continued among EU members (chiefly Austria, Belgium and Luxembourg) throughout 2002 about the effect of introducing this scheme without obtaining agreement on a similar basis from other states (chiefly Switzerland, but also the US, Liechtenstein, Monaco, Andorra, San Marino). Switzerland stated that they were prepared to introduce a 35% withholding tax on EU residents' savings and to pay over 75% of amounts collected to the EU – but not to agree to information exchange (although they agreed to do so in certain limited circumstances such as cases of suspected tax fraud – but not tax evasion – in December 2002) – on the basis that Austria, Belgium and Luxembourg also impose a withholding tax at 35%.

The final version of the Directive provides for all EU states except Austria, Belgium and Luxembourg to exchange information on non-resident savings from 1 January 2005, to enable the domestic state to tax the individual properly. Paying agents or collecting agents established in the EU will be required to provide information on payments of interest made on bonds and bank deposits to individuals (not corporates) who are EU residents in another state (regardless of the location of the bond issuer or deposit bank itself). Austria, Belgium and Luxembourg would instead impose a with-holding tax of 15% from 2005 to 2007, 20% from 2008 to 2010 and 35% from 2011 (as will Switzerland), and would only move to information exchange if the EU is unan-imously satisfied that Switzerland and the US (in particular) are meeting EU informa-tion exchange requirements. Bonds issued prior to 1 March 2001 would be exempt from the provisions, and (under a further decision of the ECOFIN Council on 2 March 2001) any issues prior to 1 March 2002 that are Fungible* with bonds issued prior to 1 March 2001 would also be exempt. Bonds issued by governments or state-related entities on or after 1 March 2002, which are intended to be fungible with bonds issued prior to 1 March 2001, will result in both the original issue and the new issue being subject to the new regime. Bonds issued by corporate entities on or after 1 March 2002 will be subject to the new regime, and will not be fungible with issues prior to 1 March 2001.

SBLC   See Standby letter of credit.

Schedule   For the purposes of UK taxation of receipts, a Schedule is one of a number of particular groupings under which income is determined for the purposes of Income tax* and the income portion of Corporation tax*. A receipt that does not fall within one of the Schedules is not subject to UK income taxation, but may be subject to Capital gains tax* where it falls within the charge to taxation of gains (income tax legislation, where applicable, overrides capital gains provisions under s. 37 TCGA*). The Schedules consist of Schedule A*, Schedule B*, Schedule C*, Schedule D*, Schedule E* and Schedule F*.

Schedule A   See Schedule. Schedule A assesses: (a) receipts from property (e.g. rents and certain lease premiums), (b) arising in the current Tax year* or company Accounting period* (sense (i)) ending in the current year.

Schedule B   See Schedule. Schedule B assessed profit from woodland management and was abolished from 5 April 1998.

Schedule C   See Schedule. Schedule C assesses to withholding at the basic rate: (a) interest and dividends paid in the UK by a paying agent out of public authority or government revenue, (b) to be accounted for by the paying agent within 14 days after the end of the month in which the interest or dividend was paid.

Schedule D   See Schedule. Schedule D is divided into six "Cases":

- Case I assesses (a) profits of a trade, (b) arising in the company Accounting period* (sense (i)) or Trading account* ending in the current Tax year*;
- Case II assesses (a) profits of a profession or vocation, (b) arising in the company accounting period or trading account ending in the current tax year;
- Case III assesses (a) interest, annuities and annual payments, (b) arising in the preceding tax year or company accounting period ending in the current tax year;
- Case IV assesses (a) interest on overseas securities, (b) arising in the preceding tax year or company accounting period ending in the current tax year;
- Case V assesses (a) interest on overseas possessions, (b) arising in the preceding tax year or company accounting period ending in the current tax year;
- Case VI assesses (a) annual profit or gains not falling under any other Case above or under any other Schedule*, (b) on profits arising, or such other basis as the Commissioners direct.

Schedule E   See Schedule. Schedule E assesses: (a) emoluments of offices and employments, (b) arising in the Tax year* received.

Schedule F   See Schedule. Schedule F assesses: (a) Dividends* and other Distributions* made by UK companies, (b) save that dividends and distributions by a UK resident company are not charged to Corporation tax*, pursuant to s. 208 ICTA*, and dividends received by an individual carry a tax credit against lower rate and basic rate tax.

Scheme of arrangement   Under s. 425 of the Companies Act 1985*, a court-managed Voluntary arrangement* process.

Schuldschein   A certificate of indebtedness evidencing the terms of a Schuldschein loan, which is a form of German bilateral loan arrangement. The Schuldschein loan market is mostly used by German regional government entities and by highly rated corporates. The loans typically bear a fixed rate of interest and a bullet repayment and can be entered into over the short, medium or long term. They can be assigned by a written assignment without requiring the consent of the borrower (or by assumption of contract – a form of novation that transfers both rights and obligations), but are usually relatively illiquid. Due to the fact that they can be raised in smaller size, and that Bundesbank consent and calendar requirements are not applied to these loans, they are often used as a convenient alternative source of Deutschemark funding to Domestic bonds* or Foreign bonds*. They have also often been raised via SPVs as components of structured finance transactions.

Schweizerobligationen   Swiss Domestic bond* issued with an 8- to 15-year maturity by governmental or corporate entities. Cf. Kassenobligationen.

Scrip issue   See Bonus issue.

SDR   See Special drawing right.

SDRT   See Stamp duty reserve tax.

S.E.   See Societas Europea.

SEAQ   Stock Exchange Automated Quotation system. LSE* screen-based quotation bulletin board, which operates with Market-makers* on a Quote driven* basis. Cf. SETS, SEAQ International and SEATS plus.

SEAQ International   LSE* screen-based quotation bulletin board, using a Quote driven* basis similar to SEAQ*, but used for international equity market securities (chiefly equity securities of companies incorporated outside the UK or Ireland, and Depositary receipts* for such securities).

Seasoned securities   In the context of SEC* regulations, a Securities* issue that has been made in reliance on the Rule 903* Regulation S* safe harbour, and in relation to which the initial restricted period (or other distribution period) has ended, enabling resales within Securities Act* resale exemptions without violating the Rule 903 issuer safe harbour. The SEC, in a release of 27 June 1995, disapproved of the resale of seasoned securities into the US immediately after the end of a restricted period considering that, in certain cases, it could be considered a scheme to avoid the Securities Act registration requirements.

SEATS plus   Stock Exchange Alternative Trading Service. LSE* screen-based Order-matching* system, which also employs Quote driven* features, for trading AIM* stocks. Cf. SEAQ, SEAQ International and SETS.

SEC   The US Securities and Exchange Commission. Under s. 5 of the Securities Act*, regulates all securities issues and resales by US and foreign investors that make use of "means or instruments of transportation or communication in interstate commerce or of the mails" to sell the securities. Regulation is through registration on issue or resale of securities in compliance with requirements under the Securities Act and through registration, ongoing reporting requirements and anti-fraud requirements under the Exchange Act*. Exemption from registration requirements is available (see under Securities Act and Exchange Act). No exemption from anti-fraud requirements is available.

Second loss   In a Securitisation*, a layer of Credit enhancement* that benefits from the protection of a First loss* layer.

Secondary market   The market in which Securities* are resold after their first distribution, or loan assets are traded. Cf. Primary market*.

Secret profit   Any profit derived by a fiduciary (e.g. a trustee or agent) from utilisation of its position. Any such profit must be disclosed to the fiduciary's principal and passed on to the principal if the principal so dictates.

Secured credit   A Documentary credit* that contains a clause in green (a "green clause") authorising an advance to the seller against security to meet payments in advance on goods purchased for onsale to the buyer.

Secured creditor   A creditor whose rights carry the benefit of some variety of Security* (sense (ii)).

Secured loan   A loan with Security* (sense (ii)). A secured loan structure is often used in CMBS* or WBS* deals, as a way of obtaining True control* over the real estate owning vehicle, or the security group for the whole business deal, respectively.

Securities   See Security, sense (i).

Securities Act   Securities Act of 1933 (US securities statute) governing offerings of securities by any "means or instruments of transportation or communication in interstate commerce or of the mails" (s. 5) and consisting of requirements which are intended to compel adequate disclosure of all those facts which are material to making an informed investment decision. Any securities offering on issue or resale which falls within s. 5 and is not exempted by the Securities Act or by other SEC* provisions from registration must be preceded by a registration statement. Registration is achieved for a non-US issuer by a Form F-1*, Form F-2* or Form F-3* or by use of a Shelf registration*, which only covers one or more particular securities issues. Sections 11(a) and 12(2) provide for liability for misstatements and omissions in registration statements and in prospectuses respectively.

Exceptions from registration are available for offerings within s. 5. These are normally relied on even where there is no clear US connection, since s. 5 is so wide-ranging. The main exemptions on issue are for:

(a) An offer of exempt securities (e.g. CP* offered under s. 3(a)(3), and securities issued or guaranteed by US banks under s. 3(a)(2));
(b) A Rule 903* Regulation S* offering of securities (a safe harbour under s. 5);
(c) A Private placement* (sense (iii)) under s. 4(2); or
(d) A Regulation D* placement (a safe harbour under s. 4(2)).

Since these exemptions are often conditional on limitation of resales of the securities, an issue exemption could be reopened to the extent that subsequent resales are not exempt (or, even where such resale is within an exemption, the particular circumstances negate the necessary conditions for the issue exemption (for instance a resale under the broker/ dealer exemption might nevertheless operate to show that the purchaser intended to distribute the securities, and thus reopen a private placement issue exemption)). Exemption on resale following an issue is available for:

(a) A resale of exempt securities as before;
(b) Sales under s. 4(1) by persons other than issuers, underwriters (this term being interpreted on the facts and quite widely to include any person who purchases securities with a view to reselling them, and also any affiliates of the issuer) or dealers;
(c) Sales under s. 4(3) and s. 4(4) by brokers and dealers (including underwriters no longer acting as such) more than 40 days (or 90 days in certain cases) after the first offering of the securities;
(d) Sales under Rule 144* (a safe harbour under s. 4(1) from possible consideration as an underwriter);
(e) Sales under "s. 4($1\frac{1}{2}$)" (sales that would be a private placement but for the fact that they are not made by the issuer and are therefore outside s. 4(2));
(f) Sale under Rule 904* of Regulation S* on a non-US market approved by the SEC as a DOSM*; or
(g) Sale in the US under Rule 144A* (originally intended as a safe harbour codifying the s. 4($1\frac{1}{2}$) position, but actually differing in scope).

Further requirements may arise under Blue sky* laws or regulations. US Securities must normally take the form of Registered securities*, as opposed to Bearer securities*, for tax purposes (see TEFRA).

Securities and Exchange Commission   US financial markets regulatory body. See under SEC.

Securitisation   The process of converting cash flows arising from certain assets into a smoothed payment stream, so that Asset-backed finance* (often in the form of Asset-backed securities*) is raised which is Limited recourse* in nature to the credit of the relevant assets (typically debts or Receivables* due from a large number of third parties) rather than against the credit of the borrower or Originator* as a whole. The receivables are typically sold by the originator to another entity (often an SPV* that is Bankruptcy remote*) in order to ring-fence them against the originator's insolvency. May be undertaken as a form of credit arbitrage, whereby the higher intrinsic Credit rating* of the receivables (which is often enhanced by Overcollateralisation* of the receivables backing the financing) allows the originator to obtain cheap funding. May also be used to obtain Off-balance-sheet* (sense (i) and (ii)) treatment for the assets from the originator's accounting balance sheet and/or the originator's regulatory balance sheet for Capital adequacy* purposes. Cf. Repackaging.

Security   **(i)** Generic term for an equity or debt instrument such as a Share*, Bond* or Note*. In the UK, in relation to the POS Regs*, shares, debentures, bonds, CDs, loan stock, warrants and depositary receipts. A security may take the form of a Bearer security* or Order security* (in which case it may constitute a Negotiable instrument*) or of a Registered security*. Most securities traded in the Euromarkets* are currently issued as Intermediate securities*. It is envisaged that in the future this may develop into a market in Dematerialised securities*.

(ii) Any protection for the repayment of a debt obligation or enforcement of a contract (e.g. a Charge*, Mortgage*, Pledge* or Lien*). See also Outright transfer. Security is taken by arrangement between the security provider and the security beneficiary (which "attaches" the security to the secured assets as between the provider and the beneficiary once the assets are in existence), and by notice to the world by way of registration at a public registry (to "perfect" the security rights as against third parties and to determine Priority* among different creditors). Many forms of security created by a company that is created as a Registered company* in England and Wales may be registrable on a Form 395* under the provisions of s. 395 Companies Act 1985*, which requires registration of security given to secure debentures, security over uncalled share capital, security which, if created by an individual, would be a registrable Bill of sale* (in addition, bills of sale created by an individual (absolute bills or security bills) are registrable), security over land, security over Book debts*, security in the form of a Floating charge* and security over called but unpaid share capital, ships, aircraft, goodwill or intellectual property. In addition, such registration is required under s. 409 Companies Act 1985 for security over assets in England and Wales where the company granting security or acquiring the assets subject to the security has an established place of business in England or Wales (see Slavenburg). In the absence of registration within 21 days of the creation of the relevant security interest, it will be void as against any Liquidator*, Administrator* or creditor of the company. If the rights in question are not registrable, a subsequent beneficiary of security or transferee of rights who acquires a better title without notice of the prior security will take priority, to prevent which a legal Mortgage*, notice to any third-party debtor (when assigning Chose in action*), or a Pledge* (which may fix a subsequent beneficiary or transferee with Constructive notice* of the security) may be needed. See also Rehypothecation.

Security interest   See Security, sense (ii).

Security power of attorney   See Power of attorney.

SEGA   Swiss securities Clearing system*.

SEHK   Stock Exchange of Hong Kong. Merged with the Hong Kong Futures Exchange into HKEx* on 6 March 2000.

Seller certificate   See Seller interest.

Seller interest   Or Seller certificate*. In a credit card Securitisation* or a Master trust* structure, the interest retained by the seller in the credit card assets or other assets. The interest retained is designed to deal with the fluctuating balance of the receivables due to amortisation (and new draw-downs on credit card accounts), as the amount of the balance funded by investors is designed to stay constant. The seller interest is not subordinate to the Investor interest* – the two interests rank pro rata, based on the Floating allocation percentage* or Fixed allocation percentage* at a point in time.

Selling concession   The concession granted to the Managers*, Underwriters* and Selling group* members for purchasing and on-selling Securities* on issue. Quoted as a percentage of the Face value* of the securities.

Selling group   In relation to a Securities* issue, those dealers in a Syndicate* that simply sell-down the amount of their Allotment* without taking on the role of Underwriters* of the issue as a whole.

Selling restrictions   Covenants contained within the subscription or dealer agreement for an issue of Securities*. They are given by the subscribers or dealers to the issuer, and vice versa, and state that they will comply with applicable securities regulations (and in some cases taxation provisions and restrictions on issuance in particular currencies) in any offer or sale of the securities (such as restrictions on Public offerings* or on the issue of investment advertisements under s. 57 Financial Services Act 1986* (replaced by s. 21 FSMA* 2000) in the UK, and restrictions under Regulation S*, Rule 144A* and TEFRA* in the US). Designed to protect the parties from the risk that the actions of one party may lead to the issue as a whole being considered as a public offering (which are heavily regulated in many jurisdictions) or to be in breach of other regulations, and to compensate the issuer or the dealers for any loss or other liability that they suffer as a result.

Semi-automatic crystallisation   Crystallisation* of a Floating charge* upon Notice of crystallisation* being served by the creditor on the chargor. The notice may be served on occurrence of certain events, or at will, depending on the terms of the charging instrument.

Senior debt   Debt ranking in order of Priority* prior to Subordinated debt* for repayment purposes.

Senior notes   Senior debt* issued in the form of Notes*.

SEPON   Stock Exchange Pool Nominees. London Stock Exchange* Nominee* company that held brokers' stock and facilitated Settlement* via the now superseded Talisman* system. The Stock Exchange (Completion of Bargains) Act 1976 removed the need for share certificates to be issued for shares held by SEPON.

Sequential pay   A Securitisation* structure where amounts available for redemption of notes are applied to redeem notes in sequence of their classes – first Class A until the class is fully redeemed, then Class B, and so on. Cf. Pro rata pay.

Servicer   In a Securitisation* transaction, the entity that carries out the day-to-day collection and enforcement of the Receivables* which back the finance raised in the transaction. Almost always, the servicer will be the Originator*, in order that it can maintain its ongoing business relationship with its customers. The appointment of the originator as servicer will be expressed to terminate on insolvency of the originator, in which case a Substitute servicer* will be appointed (or a Back-up servicer* if no substitute can be found). See also Special servicer.

Servicer advance facility   A Facility* under which a Servicer* (often a Special servicer*) will agree to make cash advances to pay the expenses of collection and enforcement of a pool of assets (typically a pool of non-performing assets, where the collection costs are greater and the periodic cash flow receipts are lumpier than for performing assets), and to recover those advances from the proceeds of collection and enforcement.

Servicing agreement   In a Securitisation* transaction, the agreement that sets out the role and obligations of the Servicer* of the Receivables* and often details the allocation of cash receipts on the receivables among the parties to the transaction.

Set-off   **(i)** Alternative terminology for the Combination* or Consolidation* of accounts. Use of the term set-off in such a case has been challenged by the courts as inaccurate on occasion (see Buckley LJ in *Halesowen Presswork & Assemblies Ltd v Westminster Bank Ltd (1971) 1QB1*.

(ii) A right to aggregate obligations owed between one party and another party. A party may effect an offset in practice (although not a set-off in strict legal terms) by refusing to pay, or only part-paying, an obligation and, when sued, establishing a counter-claim (e.g. under s. 75 Consumer Credit Act 1974*). Set-off proper arises where:

(a) Prior to insolvency and pursuant to the Statutes of Set-off, the obligations in question are liquidated and have become due and payable and are owed between the parties on a mutual basis (i.e. each party is the sole beneficial owner of the obligation) (known as independent set-off);

(b) Prior to insolvency and under equitable principles, the obligations in question are closely connected (whether or not they are liquidated) and are owed between the parties on a mutual basis (i.e. each party is the sole beneficial owner of the obligation) (known as transaction set-off);

(c) Prior to insolvency and by the terms of a contract, provisions for set-off are agreed between the parties (see also Netting);

(d) On Bankruptcy* or Liquidation* of one or other party, under the terms of s. 323 Insolvency Act 1986* and Rule 4.90 of the Insolvency Rules 1986, the obligations (whether liquidated or not and whether or not future or contingent) are owed between the parties on a mutual basis (i.e. each party is the sole beneficial owner of the obligation); or

(e) Where the obligations in question arise pursuant to a "market contract" (as defined in s. 155 of the Companies Act 1989*) connected to a Recognised clearing house* or a Recognised investment exchange* (as modified by the Financial Markets and Insolvency Regulations 1998 to include OTC* contracts cleared through a recognised clearing house), in accordance with the default rules of the relevant exchange.

Set-off on insolvency may currently only occur under the statutory provisions of the Insolvency Act 1986, which permit the set-off of future or contingent liabilities, or under s. 159 of the Companies Act 1989 (relating to the default rules of exchanges as set out at (e) above). Contractual prohibitions on set-off are effective prior to insolvency, but are ousted by the Insolvency Act provisions at such point. Combination* may also be available on insolvency. As set-off involves independent obligations, the set-off of amounts may be subject to superior claims against such amounts from another party. On this point, cf. Combination. Set-off relates only to money claims, not claims for other assets.

SETS   Stock Exchange Electronic Trading Service. Screen-based Order-matching* system introduced on the LSE* in October 1997. See also SEAQ, SEAQ International and SEATS plus.

Settlement   The delivery of an asset (or the recording of electronic account holdings) against payment on the Settlement date*. For most securities transactions, a system of Rolling settlement* is used. Originally, UK share settlement used a 2- or 3-week account period, where settlement was made at the account close for all transactions within the account period. This was replaced by a 5-day rolling settlement system (T + 5*) in 1995, with paperless dealings under CREST*, and was reduced to a 3-day system (T + 3) on 5 February 2001.

Settlement date   The date on which Settlement* of a transaction (e.g. a Spot* or Forward* FX* deal or a CP* issuance) executed on the Trade date* is effected. Cf. Value date.

Settlement Finality Directive   The Settlement Finality Directive (Directive 98/26) of the EU* that was passed on 19 May 1998. The Directive states that where registered securities are provided as collateral for "securing rights and obligations potentially arising in connection with a system" (a settlement system such as Euroclear* or Clearstream*), the law governing provision of the securities as collateral will be the jurisdiction where the register is held. In some jurisdictions, the Directive is being implemented to apply also to securities held outside settlement systems, but this is not the case in the UK. The Directive also provides that rights in collateral given in connection with a system shall not be invalidated by insolvency.

Settlement netting   A form of Netting*: when payments are due between two parties on the same date, only an amount equal to the excess of the larger payment over the smaller payment is in fact made. As this is a method of simplifying settlement and reducing Settlement risk* rather than a merger or set-off of underlying obligations, settlement netting is not effective on insolvency of either party to reduce gross payment obligations to net payment obligations.

Settlement risk   The Risk* that a party will go insolvent between entering a contract and effecting Settlement* of the contract and that the counterparty will suffer a loss as a result.

SFA   Securities and Futures Authority Limited. One of the self-regulating organisations (see SRO) established under the Financial Services Act 1986*. Responsible for regulating securities and derivatives, stockbrokers, futures dealers, market makers and the capital markets. Its functions were rolled into the Financial Services Authority* from midnight on 30 November 2001.

Shadow director   Under s. 741(2) Companies Act 1985* "a person in accordance with whose directions or instructions the directors of a company are accustomed to act". A person will not be a shadow director solely by reason of advice given to the directors in a professional capacity. Shadow directors are regarded as directors for the purpose of some of the provisions of the Companies Act 1985, such as those dealing with restrictions on transactions with directors, and directors' contracts of employment.

Shadow rating   A Credit rating* that reflects the underlying rating of a particular debt obligation on the assumption that one or more Credit enhancement* mechanisms were not being used (typically, ignoring any Wrap* on the deal).

Share   A unit of the ownership of a company. A division of the company's Equity capital*.

Share capital   See Issued share capital*.

Share premium account   A liability-side balance sheet entry equal to the aggregate amount of any Premium* (sense (i)) charged on issue of a company's shares.

Shareholder   A holder of Shares* in a company. Also known as a Member*.

Shareholder's agreement   An agreement made between the shareholders of a company, typically designed to restrict certain shareholders from taking certain actions in relation to their shareholding.

Shelf-company   A newly established company, set up by an agent in anticipation of the company being used for a specific transaction or for substantive operations by a future client.

Shelf registration   A form of SEC* registration for contemplated future debt and/or equity issues under Rule 415* that are not intended to take place immediately, providing information on a securities issuer and details of the nature (debt and/or equity) and maximum aggregate amount of such issues. This registration is designed to allow an issuer to access US markets rapidly when opportunities arise, enabling one or more issues without the full registration procedure on a Form F-1*, Form F-2* or Form F-3* each time. Once the original shelf registration is effected, annual Form 20-F* reports, and a short pricing supplement for each issue are all that is required. Shelf registration was also introduced on the London Stock Exchange* in January 1999. Listed companies that file an annual statement are entitled to issue equity securities on publication of a short issue note. See Debt shelf registration, Equity shelf registration and Universal shelf allocation.

Shogun bond   A Bond* that is issued in the Japanese market and is comparable to a Foreign bond* (i.e. issued by a foreign issuer into the domestic market), but is not denominated in Yen. Cf. Samurai bond.

Short   A Position* characterised by the sale of an asset that is not owned by the seller at the time of the sale, in reliance on an expected decrease in value. Cf. Long.

Short covering   A Cover* of a Short position*.

Short interest   Interest* on a term loan that has a maximum maturity of less than 1 year. Not subject to Withholding tax* as yearly interest. Prior to 1996, short interest was only tax deductible where it qualified as (a) a trading expense (i.e. the loan is used for trading purposes) or (b) a charge on income where the lender was a UK bank or

Discount house*. This distinction was removed in the November 1995 budget. See also Discount.

Short notice   A notice of a General meeting* which, under ss. 369(4) or 378(3) Companies Act 1985*, may be given less than the number of days in advance required for such notice based on the type of meeting and type of Resolutions* to be considered at the meeting. Must be agreed to by at least 95% (by Nominal value* of shares) of the Members* (this can be reduced to 90% for a Private company* under the Elective regime*). No Special notice* can be given by way of short notice.

Short position   See Short.

SIB   Securities and Investments Board. Subsequently renamed as the Financial Services Authority*.

SIC-12   SIC-12 is an interpretation of the Standing Interpretations Committee of the IASC*, and applies to IAS 27*. SIC-12 was issued in June 1998 (and is effective for financial years beginning on or after 1 July 1999). The terms of IAS 1 require that financial statements under IAS meet the requirements of both the Standards and the SIC interpretations. SIC-12 contains guidance as to when an entity is controlled (and is consequently required to be consolidated). Control requires:

(a) Being able to direct or dominate the decision-making (or establishing an "auto-pilot" mechanism so that the entity acts in a predetermined manner) of the SPV; and

(b) Having the objective of obtaining benefits from the activities of the SPV.

SIC-12 gives scenarios which can be considered as the control of an SPV by an originator:

(a) The activities of the SPV are conducted on behalf of the originator such that the originator obtains benefits for the operation of the SPV.

(b) The originator has the decision-making powers to obtain the majority of the benefits from the SPV, or uses an "autopilot" mechanism to obtain them.

(c) The originator has the right to the majority of the benefits of the SPV and may thus be exposed to the risks of the SPV.

(d) In substance, the originator retains the majority of the ownership risks of the SPV in order to obtain benefits from the activities of the SPV.

SICAV   Société d'Investissement à Capital Variable. French form of Unit trust*.

Sight bill   A Bill of exchange* payable immediately when seen by the relevant person.

SIMEX   Singapore International Monetary Exchange. Singaporean financial Futures* and Options* Exchange*.

Single member company   A company with a single shareholder. A Private company* that is not an Unlimited company* can have a single shareholder under the Companies (Single Member Private Limited Companies) Regulations 1992.

Single month mortality   Or SMM*. An assumed percentage rate of Prepayment* over 1 month of the principal amount due from debtors on a pool of Receivables*. Expressed as:

$$(p/\text{PAO}) \cdot 100$$

where p = prepayment amount over 1 month
         PAO = principal balance of receivables outstanding at start of month less scheduled principal amount over month.

Used as a basis to formulate the CPR* of a deal. An SMM figure can be converted to a CPR figure by:

$$1 - \text{CPR} = (1 - \text{SMM})^{12}$$

See also 100% PSA, 200% PSA.

Sinking fund   Arrangements made by an issuer to carry out an undertaking given in the terms and conditions of a Security* (sense (i)) that the issuer will effect Mandatory redemption* of the security through *pro rata* reductions of the principal amount outstanding or repayment in full of certain of the securities, as selected by lot. Cf. Purchase fund.

SIV   See Structured investment vehicle.

Skew   Tilt on a standard deviation distribution curve. See Value at risk.

Slavenburg   Reference to the case of *Slavenburg's Bank NV v. Intercontinental Natural Resources Ltd [1980] 1 All ER 955*. The creation of Security* (sense (ii)) over certain assets by a company that is created as a Registered company* in England and Wales is registrable on a Form 395* under the provisions of s. 395 of the Companies Act 1985*. Registration is also required under s. 409 Companies Act 1985 for security over such assets in England and Wales where the company granting security or acquiring the assets subject to the security has an established place of business in England or Wales. In the Slavenburg case it was held that whether a company in fact has an established place of business in England and Wales is a question of fact that is separate from whether the company has complied with any resultant obligation it may have to register any place of business in England and Wales under the Companies Act 1985 (see Overseas company). Practice is to file a Form 395 when security is created by a non-UK company over assets situate in the UK, regardless of whether it is considered that the company actually has a place of business in England and Wales, as a safeguard.

SLMA   See Student Loan Marketing Association.

Slow-pay   With regard to Asset-backed securities*, a tranche which, although ranking at the same level of Priority* as another tranche, receives principal sequentially after such other tranche prior to enforcement following an event of default, rather than pro rata with such other tranche. Cf. Fast-pay.

SME   Small or medium-sized enterprise.

SMM   See Single month mortality.

Societas Europaea   Form of European company originally proposed in 1970. Developed as the subject of a Regulation* of the EU* (Regulation 2157/2001) which enters into force on 8 October 2004.

Société en commandité   Form of Limited partnership*.

Society   In the UK, a form of Unincorporated association*, although some have been incorporated by statute, e.g. Building societies* under the Building Societies Acts 1962 and 1986.

Soffex   Swiss financial Futures* and Options* Exchange*. Part of the Eurex* alliance together with the DTB*.

Soft arbitrage   The use of Arbitrage* opportunities to refinance existing funding commitments at cheaper levels. Cf. Hard arbitrage.

Soft bullet   A Security* (sense (i)) or Facility*, where most of the Principal* sum falls due on the same date. Cf. Balloon, Bullet.

Sovereign ceiling   A certain level of Credit rating* that may provide a ceiling or maximum level for ratings achievable on deals or entities subject to a particular sovereign entity. For obligations in a currency other than that of the relevant sovereign, this is typically the Foreign currency rating* of the sovereign. For deals in the sovereign's own currency, the Local currency rating* of the sovereign may act as a ceiling.

Sovereign immunity   The immunity of sovereign entities in certain jurisdictions from suit or distraint, which applies unless specifically waived.

SPAN   Standard Portfolio Analysis of Risk. A computer model designed by the CME* to calculate Initial margin*. Used by many Exchanges* world wide.

SPC   See Special purpose company.

SPE   See Special purpose entity.

Special deposits   See Mandatory liquid assets. Special deposits at the Bank of England attract interest (at a below-market rate).

Special drawing right   An SDR is a right to make drawings at the IMF* at an interest rate determined as a basket of the market rates of a number of IMF members, in order to boost foreign currency reserves used to stabilise the FX Rate* of the IMF member making the drawing. Effectively, a drawing on the IMF's own reserves. The basket composition of the SDR enables it to be used as a low-volatility basket currency.

Special notice   A form of notice of a proposed Resolution* that is required to be given for the removal of a Director* (sense (i)) under s. 303 Companies Act 1985* or in certain other cases, and for which a period of 28 days' notice is required under s. 379 Companies Act 1985.

Special-purpose company   Or SPC*. See Special-purpose vehicle.

Special-purpose entity   Or SPE*. See Special-purpose vehicle.

Special-purpose vehicle   Or SPV*. Also known as a Special-purpose company* or a Special-purpose entity*. A special-purpose vehicle is an entity established specifically to fulfill a set function or to undertake a particular transaction or transactions. If established as part of a Securitisation* or Repackaging* transaction, will usually be set up to be Bankruptcy remote* as an Orphan company* with its shares held on Charitable trust* or some other form of purpose trust, and will be used to purchase the Receivables* being securitised.

Special resolution   A Resolution* of the Members* of a company that requires at least three-quarters of votes cast in favour and must be passed at a General meeting* where at least 21 days' notice of the meeting and the resolution is given (unless consent to Short notice* has been obtained or a Written resolution* is used).

Special servicer   A Servicer* that is appointed to service a portfolio of non-performing assets, and specialises in realising value from non-performing assets by negotiating settlements (or Discounted pay-offs*) and by undertaking court auction and enforcement procedures. See also Real estate owned.

Specialty   See Deed.

Speculation   The holding of a Position* or the assumption of a Risk*, undertaken in order to generate a profit.

Speculative grade   A Credit rating* for an institution, entity or securities issue that is below a certain minimum level (BBB−, or Baa3 for Moody's).

Spens clause   A yield make-whole provision named after Lord Spens, which is often found in fixed rate bonds in the UK. The clause requires that if the bond is redeemed prior to its scheduled maturity, the issuer will be obliged to make payment on redemption of a lump sum equal to the greater of the Par* amount of the bond or the value that the bond would have if its Redemption yield* was equal to that on a gilt with a maturity matching the schedule of the bond. This calculation will serve to depress the yield on the bond to a risk-free rate below the level at which it would actually trade in the market, and consequently inflate the redemption price to a level at which the investor can reinvest the increased redemption proceeds in the gilt, and maintain the redemption yield he would have received otherwise. The formula is effectively penal, as in such a scenario the investor benefits from a improvement in the creditworthiness of his exposure at no cost.

Spot   A current price quotation for same day Settlement* (or settlement at the shortest period applicable to the market in question) of the purchase or sale of a particular asset (as opposed to Forward*). Used for FX* dealing, Drawing* under Facilities* and CP* issuance. For Eurocurrency* settlement takes 2 days; for Sterling (or the relevant domestic currency of the party) settlement is same day. Thus, proceeds of Dollar ECP* would be received 2 days after issue, while proceeds of Dollar US CP would be received as Same day funds*.

Spread   (i) The difference between the Bid* and Offer* price quoted in respect of an asset. A narrow spread indicates a Liquid market* in the product that is beneficial for traders as it means that smaller, more short-term movements in the price of an instrument on the market will raise the offer price over the old bid price, enabling a sale at a profit. Conversely, a wide spread indicates a lack of Liquidity*.

(ii) The difference between two rates of interest; e.g. between a government bond rate and LIBOR*, or between a government bond rate and an individual company's issued bond rate. A narrow, or tight, spread is beneficial for an issuer, as it indicates a high level of demand or competition for the issuer's debt and results in a lower Interest rate* for the issuer, relative to the government market benchmark rate. A wide spread indicates excessive supply of the issuer's debt, or a lack of demand for the debt among investors. Indicative of the perception in the market of the Credit risk* of the issuer.

Spread account   See Reserve fund.

Spread window   See Swap window.

SPV   See Special-purpose vehicle.

SRO   Self-regulating organisation established under the Financial Services Act 1986*. See, however, Financial Services Authority. See IMRO, PIA, SFA. See also FIMBRA, LAUTRO.

SSAP   Statement of Standard Accounting Practice. UK accounting standards.

Stabilisation   The purchase or sale of new securities in a way designed to stabilise their price on initial distribution into the market. Prior to entry into force of the FSMA* 2000 on "N2", in the UK an offer to Managers* to subscribe a new issue should specify that SIB*/IPMA* rules on stabilisation apply (allowing use of a safe harbour under s. 48(7) Financial Services Act 1986*), or any stabilisation activities subsequently carried out may constitute a criminal offence under s. 47(2) Financial Services Act 1986 on creating a false market or under Insider trading* legislation. After N2, a new subscription should comply with FSMA conduct of business rules on stabilisation set under s. 144 FSMA (allowing use of a safe harbour under s. 397(4) FSMA), or any stabilisation activities subsequently carried out may constitute a criminal offence under s. 397(3) FSMA on creating a false market or under Insider trading* legislation. See also Regulation M.

Stamp duty   UK tax that was largely abolished in the Finance Act 2003. The Finance Act 2003 provides for a new form of tax called Stamp duty land tax* to be chargeable under s. 42 on land transactions relating to UK land and provides at s. 125 for the abolition of stamp duty except in relation to stamp duty on stock or marketable securities from 1 December 2003. In particular, the new regime will remove stamp duty on the transfer of debts. See also Stamp duty reserve tax.

Stamp duty was prior to this charged at either a fixed or an *ad valorem* rate on instruments (largely, any document) which fall within one of the heads of charge, the most important being:

(a) A conveyance or transfer on sale of any property for more than £60 000, or for any amount with regard to securities (including an Assignment*, an absolute Bill of sale* or a Declaration of trust*);

(b) A limited category of agreements for such a sale – agreements for the sale of land, goods and securities are excluded (in respect of each of (a) and (b), charged at 1% – or 0.5% for securities – on the price paid; increasing to 3% (from 6 April 2000) for prices between £250 000 and £500 000, and to 4% (from 6 April 2000) for prices of more than £500 000); and

(c) A lease or agreement for a lease (charged on any premium at 1%, and on the rent at a rate of up to 2% for a lease up to 35 years in length and from there to up to 24% for a lease of more than 100 years in length).

Stamp duty on the creation and transfer of mortgages was abolished by s.64 of the Finance Act* 1971. Under s. 98 of the Finance Act 1997, stamp duty is not charged on repurchase or stock lending arrangements that meet certain conditions (including that they are arm's-length arrangements undertaken on an EEA exchange or a recognised foreign exchange). Exemptions from stamp on transfers of securities are available for Market-makers*.

In Securitisation* transactions, or other Receivables* financing transactions, documents may be executed and held outside the UK to delay triggering the stamp tax charge on the transfer of receivables until the documents are brought into the UK for enforcement against the relevant debtor (if necessary). As further protection, the sale may be carried out on an "acceptance by payment" basis, where the only written documentation for the transfer is an offer, which is then accepted by payment from the SPV* to the Originator*, without any actual stampable transfer documentation being produced (this method may be difficult to achieve for a declaration of trust route). Drawn or undrawn stamp duty reserve facilities have also been used.

Intra-group transfers have also been used (as these are exempted from stamp under the provisions of s. 42 of the Finance Act 1930), with a transfer by the Originator* to an intra-group but otherwise Bankruptcy remote* SPV*. These transfers are however threatened by provisions in the Finance Act 2000 (which came into effect on 28 July 2000), which bring the definition of group for stamp duty purposes more in line with Corporation tax* definitions, as an anti-avoidance measure. Under s. 123 Finance Act 2000, s. 42 is amended so that the group consists not just of subsidiaries in which 75% or more of the ordinary share capital is owned, but also where there is an entitlement to 75% or more of the profits; furthermore Limited recourse* debt of the SPV issued to investors may be treated as equity for the purposes of the group, potentially Degrouping* the SPV under ICTA Schedule 18, paragraph 1 and removing the s. 42 stamp duty exemption. Formal adjudication that an intra-group transfer is free of stamp is likely to be required by the rating agencies.

Intra-group transfers may also be used to repackage a sale of business assets as a sale of shares in order to reduce stamp duty. The assets are transferred to a new group company, and the shares in the company are then sold to the purchaser. To the extent that the new group company is sold with debt outstanding, the sale price for the shares (and hence the stamp duty payable) may be further reduced.

Under s. 111 of the Finance Act 2002 there is a claw back of group relief where UK property is transferred within a group, and the recipient leaves the group within 2 years, and claw back of partial relief under s. 76 Finance Act 1986 where an acquirer acquires the whole or part of the undertaking of another company in return for the issue of shares, and control of the acquirer passes to a third party within 2 years.

Duty must be paid within 30 days after the execution of the stampable instrument to avoid interest and penalties. Under s. 109 Finance Act 1999, documents executed offshore on or after 1 October 1999 and subsequently brought into the UK will be subject to interest on the duty from 30 days after execution of the document. From the Finance Act 2002, penalties for late stamping also run from 30 days after execution in relation to land (regardless of whether the documentation was executed offshore or not). Certain instruments (such as the limited range of bearer instruments that are potentially chargeable and are not exempt under Finance Act* 1986, s. 79 as loan capital – it is possible that an issue may not be exempt as loan capital where it is convertible into shares or bears an excessive or profit-linked rate of return) must be stamped on or before execution. Stampable instruments that are not stamped may not be used as evidence in legal proceedings.

Stamp duty land tax   UK tax introduced under the Finance Act 2003, which provides under s. 42 for tax to be charged on land transactions relating to UK land which are chargeable transactions, whether or not there is any instrument for the transaction (and whether or not executed in the UK). Land transactions are acquisitions of a "chargeable interest", defined in s. 48 as any estate, interest or right in or over land in the UK (thus including freehold transfers and the grant or surrender of lease), and include under s. 44 contracts or agreements for such transactions that are "substantially performed" without having been completed (i.e. where the purchaser takes possession of – including receiving or being entitled to rents or profits the whole or substantially the whole of the land, or the vendor receives a substantial amount of consideration for the land). Security interests are exempt. Land transactions are "chargeable transactions" if they are not exempt transactions (transactions with no chargeable consideration – any consideration in money or money's worth – and other transactions such as testamentary or divorce settlements) (s. 49 and Schedule 3).

Stamp duty land tax is chargeable at the same rate on the whole consideration for residential transactions at 0% for consideration up to £60 000, 1% for consideration more than £60 000 up to £250 000, 3% for consideration more than £250 000 up to £500 000 and 4% for consideration more than £500 000. Tax is chargeable at the same rate on the whole consideration for commercial transactions at 0% for consideration up to £150 000, 1% for consideration more than £150 000 up to £250 000, 3% for consideration more than £250 000 up to £500 000 and 4% for consideration more than £500 000. Sales of properties in "disadvantaged areas" will have a nil value threshold set at £150 000 for residential properties, while sales of all commercial properties in disadvantaged areas will be exempt from stamp. Identification of disadvantaged areas is based on the average income of residents in local council wards. Tax will be calculated at 1% on the NPV of future lease payments if the NPV is over £60 000 (residential) or £150 000 (commercial) (the old system taxed the grant at 2% on the first year's rent).

Land transaction returns are also required under s. 76 of the Finance Act 2003 to be delivered to the Inland Revenue in respect of "notifiable transactions" (under s. 77 and Schedule 3, land transactions that are not exempt transactions such as testamentary or divorce settlements) within 30 days of the effective date of such transaction (under s. 119, the date of completion, or when the transaction was substantially performed).

Stamp duty reserve tax   Or SDRT. UK tax charged on a written or oral agreement to transfer chargeable securities for consideration (charged at 0.5% on the price paid). Chargeable securities are defined in s. 99 Finance Act 1986 as "stock, shares or loan capital", as well as certain rights and interests in such securities. There are exemptions for stocks, share or loan capital of a foreign company (unless they are registered in a register kept in the UK) and for items exempt from stamp duty (such as exempt loan capital). Under s. 103 of the Finance Act 1997, SDRT is not charged on repurchase or stock-lending arrangements that meet certain conditions (including that they are arm's-length arrangements undertaken on an EEA exchange or a recognised foreign exchange). SDRT is payable at the end of the month following the month of the date of the agreement (or, if later, the date on which the agreement becomes unconditional). Exemptions from stamp duty reserve tax are available for Market-makers* and brokers. In addition to the main charge, there are also charges for depositary receipt schemes and clearance schemes under ss. 93 and 96 Finance Act 1986 as amended. See also Stamp duty.

Standby LC   See Standby letter of credit.

Standby letter of credit   A form of Letter of credit* that consists of an undertaking by a bank to make payment on certification of the occurrence of certain specified events, typically the failure of an underlying company to meet its obligations. It may be subject to the Uniform Customs* rules through incorporation by reference. Similar in effect to a Guarantee* or Indemnity*.

Static pool   In data analysis, a particular group of entries in a pool that are tracked through a system over time, without updating the group with new entries to the pool.

Statutory accounts   The balance sheet and profit and loss account on individual and consolidated (see Consolidated accounts) bases that a company is required to produce under s. 226 and s. 227 Companies Act 1985*.

Statutory company   In the UK, a form of Company* that enjoys Corporate personality* as a Corporation* pursuant to a special statute, such as Lloyd's of London.

Step-lock option   See Ladder option.

Step-up   An increase in the Coupon* (sense (i)) paid on a security at a particular point in its term. Often used to signal to investors that the issuer intends to redeem or refinance the security at the point at which the step-up operates. See also Call and step-up.

Stock   See Share.

Stock exchange   An Exchange* dealing primarily in Stocks* and Shares*.

Stop order   A buy or sell order that is only to be carried out when a certain Bid* or Offer* trigger price is achieved. Usually used to Close-out* a Position*. Cf. Market-if-touched order.

Straddle   The purchase (or sale) of a Call option* and a Put option* at the same Strike price*.

Strangle   The purchase (or sale) of a Put option* at a set Strike price* and purchase of a Call option* at a higher strike price.

Stress test   A model of the anticipated loss in value of an asset or Portfolio* following the occurrence of a particular significant event (e.g. a large rise in Interest rates* or change in FX rates*).

Strike price   See Option.

Strike rate   See Cap, Collar, Floor.

Stripped bonds   Bonds* created by buying regular bonds and splitting them into component parts of coupon (IOs*) and principal (POs*) payment. Also known as Strips*.

Strips   See Stripped bonds.

STRIPS   Separate Trading of Registered Interest and Principal of Securities. The UK government's programme of Strips* issuance for certain Gilts*.

Structural subordination   The Subordination* of one debt behind another, which occurs as a practical consequence of a structure rather than by contractual provisions. A typical example is a loan made to a holding company that is structurally subordinate to a loan made to its subsidiary operating company, as the claim of the holding company lender does not attach to the assets of the operating company in insolvency, but only to the residual equity of the operating company – i.e. behind that of the lender to the operating company. Cf. Contractual subordination.

Structured investment vehicle   Or SIV*. A vehicle set up to engage in Arbitrage*. A SIV will typically buy long-term paper and issue short-term paper or CP*, in order to exploit the carry available in a positive Yield curve* environment.

Student Loan Marketing Association   Also known as SLMA* or Sallie Mae*. Agency which advances loans to students in the US.

Subordinated debt   Debt that is subject to Subordination* to Senior debt* in order of Priority* of repayment. See also Mezzanine finance.

Subordinated notes   Subordinated debt* issued in the form of Notes*.

Subordination   The ranking of debts owed to one creditor behind debts owed to another creditor. Effected by contractual agreement between the subordinated creditor and the senior creditor expressing the obligations owed to the subordinated creditor to be contingent upon repayment in full of the obligations owed to the senior creditor, or by requiring the subordinated creditor to pay over to the senior creditor any amounts received by the subordinated creditor from the debtor. The latter arrangement may be reinforced by declaring that, until amounts are paid over, they are held on trust by the subordinated creditor for the senior creditor. Subordination may also be effected by contractual agreement solely between the debtor and the subordinated creditor, but this is vulnerable to variation without the consent of the senior creditor. Cf. Priority. See also Senior notes, Senior debt, Subordinated notes, Subordinated debt. See also Contractual subordination, Structural subordination.

Sub-participant   See Sub-participation.

Sub-participation   General term for an agreement between a lender and a third party (the "sub-participant") that is back-to-back to an underlying contract between the lender and a borrower and does not change or transfer the underlying contract. Sub-participation is designed to pass the risk of default by the borrower under the underlying contract to the sub-participant, who either agrees to reimburse the lender if default occurs (an "unfunded risk participation") or agrees to reimburse the lender in full for the loan up-front (a "funded risk participation"), in return for agreement by the lender to pass receipts on the loan to the sub-participant. As the sub-participant has simply a contractual right against the lender, and no right to sue the borrower, the sub-participant is at risk as an unsecured creditor in the lender's insolvency. Used to effect an economic transfer of Credit risk* and (if funded) the cost of funding the loan in the books of the lender, without losing the relationship with the borrower. Cf. Assignment, Declaration of trust, Negotiation, Novation, Subrogation, Transfer.

Sub-prime   In relation to a mortgage, or a pool of mortgages for a Mortgage-backed security*, credits where there are some negative credit characteristics that distinguish them from Prime* mortgages – such as arrears. May be used interchangeably with Non-conforming*.

Subrogation   The right of an insurer or Guarantor* to take over any rights of action of the beneficiary of the insurance or guarantee (e.g. against any party responsible for damage that led to the insurance payout or against the principal debtor) following satisfaction of all amounts due under the insurance or guarantee. Also extends to give a third party who has paid off an amount due from a debtor the rights of the creditor against the debtor (including in some cases Security* (sense (ii)) rights, e.g. where specifically agreed between the third party and the debtor or where payment is made by the third party direct to the creditor). Cf. Assignment, Declaration of trust, Negotiation, Novation, Sub-participation, Transfer.

Subscribe   The process of requesting, via Subscriptions*, the initial issue of new securities to the requester. Cf Underwriter.

Subscription agreement   An English law agreement used in an issue of Securities* that has an effect comparable to an Underwriting*. The Underwriters* agree with the issuer to Subscribe* for the issue (which is then on-sold, to investors) with liability for unsold securities arising on a joint and several basis. The New York law equivalent is the several Underwriting agreement*. Representations and warranties as to (*inter alia*) the accuracy and completeness of information contained in the Offering circular* for the issue will be required from the issuer and any guarantor. For an issue of Asset-backed securities*, any Monoline insurer* and the Originator* will also be required to make certain representations (e.g. as to their due authorisation of the transaction and as to the nature of the Receivables* backing the securities).

Subscriptions   The first orders pursuant to which a Securities* issue is sold. In the UK debt market, this will be those from the Underwriters*. In the US debt market, it will be those from the Selling group* or other buyers.

Subsidiary   **(i)** A Subsidiary undertaking*.

(ii) For tax purposes, a company that is owned to a certain percentage by another, e.g. an Effective 51% subsidiary*, a 51% Subsidiary*, a 75% Subsidiary* or a 90% Subsidiary*.

(iii) For Companies Act 1985* purposes, under s. 736 Companies Act 1985, a company is a subsidiary of another company, its Holding company* (sense (ii)), if the holding company:

(a) Holds a majority of the voting rights in the subsidiary; or

(b) Is a member of the subsidiary and has the right to appoint or remove a majority of the subsidiary's board of directors; or

(c) Is a member of the subsidiary and controls alone, pursuant to an agreement with other shareholders or members, a majority of the voting rights in the subsidiary; or

(d) Is a holding company of a company that is itself a holding company of the subsidiary.

51% Subsidiary   See Group, sense (iv). Under ICTA, s. 838, a company more than 50% of whose Ordinary share capital* is owned directly or indirectly by another body corporate.

75% Subsidiary   See Group, sense (ii), (iv) and (vi). Under s. 838 ICTA, a company not less than 75% of whose Ordinary share capital* is owned directly or indirectly by another body corporate.

90% Subsidiary   See Holding company. Under s. 838 ICTA, a company more than 90% of whose Ordinary share capital* is owned directly by another body corporate.

Subsidiary undertaking   For accounting purposes under s. 258 Companies Act 1985* and Capital adequacy* Consolidation* (sense (iii)) purposes, an Undertaking* is a subsidiary undertaking, or Subsidiary* (sense (i)) for short, of another company, its Parent undertaking*, if the parent undertaking:

(a) Holds a majority of the voting rights in the subsidiary undertaking; or

(b) Is a member of the subsidiary undertaking and has the right to appoint or remove a majority of the subsidiary's board of directors; or

(c) Has the right to exercise a dominant influence over the subsidiary undertaking through provisions in its Memorandum of association* or Articles of association* or in a control contract; or

(d) Is a member of the subsidiary undertaking and controls alone, pursuant to an agreement with other shareholders or members, a majority of the voting rights in the subsidiary undertaking; or

(e) Has a participating interest in the subsidiary undertaking and either actually exercises a dominant influence over the subsidiary undertaking or manages itself and the subsidiary undertaking on a unified basis; or

(f) Is a parent undertaking of an undertaking which is itself a parent undertaking of the subsidiary undertaking.

Substantive consolidation   US doctrine akin to, but far wider and more developed than, Lifting the veil* in the UK. Substantive consolidation will enable the courts to consolidate the assets and liabilities of two separate entities, effectively making one entity liable for the debts of the other. The doctrine looks at a wide range of factors in determining whether two entities should be consolidated, with some of the most important indications leading to consolidation being that the two entities are held out to creditors as constituting a single business, that the assets of the entities are commingled or are not clearly segregated, or that creditors dealt with the entities as a single economic unit.

Substantive equity   Now redundant US accounting consolidation issue in relation to thinly capitalised entities (see Thin capitalisation) such as an SPV*, which is replaced by the more complex guidelines provided in FAS 140* and FIN 46*. The SEC* required Consolidated accounts* to be prepared for US public companies who are Originators* under Securitisation* transactions, which consolidate entities purchasing assets from the originator whose Equity capital* is less than 3% of their total Capital* (sense (i)). Historically avoided by use of a Trust* rather than an SPV, as Trust certificates* issued by the trust were treated as equity capital for this purpose. Potential increases in the 3% level were discussed at length in 2002 and 2003 following various US accounting scandals such as Enron and WorldCom, resulting in the publication of new rules in FIN 46 and in amendments to FAS 140.

Substitute servicer   In a Securitisation* transaction, an entity appointed as Servicer* of the Receivables* in the event of the termination of the appointment of the Originator* as servicer. If no entity can be found who is willing to assume the role, any Back-up servicer* for the transaction will be appointed.

Substitution   The replacement of Receivables* held by the SPV* in a Securitisation* transaction with other receivables originated by the Originator*. This may be viewed as a form of Credit enhancement* in circumstances where substitution is used to improve the credit quality of the receivables portfolio, and may therefore prejudice accounting or capital Off-balance-sheet* (sense (i) and (ii)) treatment. The concept of Replenishment* is sometimes referred to as substitution.

Suitably rated entity   In the context of a transaction rated by a Credit rating agency*, any entity that the rating agency requires to have a minimum short-term or long-term Credit rating* equal to that awarded on the transaction, in accordance with the Weak link approach*. Typically, any entity that undertakes an obligation to pay, or holds cash amounts (requirements for a short-term or long-term credit rating depend on whether the obligation, or holding of cash, is short term or long term in nature).

Sum of the years digits   See Rule of 78s.

Supplementary special deposits   See Mandatory liquid assets. Supplementary special deposits at the Bank of England do not attract interest.

Surety   See Guarantor.

SUSMI   Substantial US Market Interest. Term used for the purposes of US securities regulations, and particularly Regulation S*, to group securities in respect of whether or not they are likely to end up being sold to US investors.

Swap   An agreement between two parties to make regular payments to each other calculated by reference to a notional principal amount. The payments are often equivalent to underlying obligations owed by each party to third parties, thereby effectively exchanging the parties' underlying obligations (subject to Credit risk* on the Mark-to-market* value of the swap at any point in time). Often used to trade and generate profit (e.g. via opportunities to Arbitrage* debt into a favourable market), or as instruments to Hedge* Risks*. Swaps may also be used to generate cheaper funding where one party has a comparative advantage in accessing fixed rate funding over floating rate funding, relative to another party. Often a lower credit will pay proportionately more than a higher credit for fixed rate funding. If the higher credit raises fixed rate funds and the lower credit raises floating rate funds, a fixed/floating swap will enable the benefit of the comparative advantage to be shared between the parties, generating cheaper funding for each. Swaps are priced off the fixed rate payment, at a stated Swap price*, or at a Swap spread* over a benchmark (e.g. Treasuries*), with the assumption of a floating rate payment at LIBOR* flat. Basis swaps* are priced at a Margin* (sense (i)) above or below one of the floating rates. See also Asset swap, Circus swap, Commodity swap, Currency swap, Equity swap, Interest rate swap and Total return swap.

Swap independent rating   In a structured finance transaction (such as a Securitisation*) that uses a Swap*, a Credit rating* granted on the financing for the transaction that does not take into consideration the possibility that the swap counterparty may default or become insolvent and that the transaction may as a consequence be exposed to Market risks* such as Currency risk* or Basis risk*. Consequently, the transaction may have a credit rating higher than that of the swap counterparty itself. To denote the commensurate risk to investors, the transaction rating may be given an "r"* sub-script to the rating.

Swap price   In a Swap* with one fixed rate obligation and one floating rate obligation, the swap price is the level of the fixed rate obligation. The swap price is quoted at two values, representing Bid* and Offer* rates for the dealer. Swap prices are determined by the level of demand to swap from fixed rate interest receipts to floating rate interest receipts (i.e. the level of demand to receive fixed rate interest as against floating rate interest). In an environment where rates are expected to rise, the level of demand is high (and consequently parties will be prepared to pay a higher fixed rate in order to receive floating rate payments), while the level of supply to receive fixed rate is correspondingly low, leading to a higher swap price. Where rates are expected to fall, there will be a low level of demand, which will equate to a tight swap price (meaning that the comparative advantage of the swap will accrue mainly to the counterparty desiring to receive floating rate). In such a case, Bond* issuers (who are typically seeking to issue fixed rate secur-ities, and hence receive fixed under the swap) will be reluctant to issue for Arbitrage* opportunities, as they have no Swap window* available, and will await a better chance to issue and swap at the best possible price. The swap yield curve trades slightly wider than the government yield curve, as it is not a "risk-free" rate, but is relatively low risk since only the market value of the swap is at risk (not the full principal amount).

Swap spread   The Spread* (sense (ii)) quoted by the dealer or bank Intermediary* of the Swap price* over a benchmark interest rate (e.g. Treasuries*). As with swap prices, quoted at two values, Bid* and Offer*.

Swap window   A positioning of Swap prices*/Swap spreads* at a high level, so as to be favourable for Arbitrage* opportunities for an issuer of fixed rate debt, due to a high level of demand for floating rate receipts arising in the swap market, for instance from a belief that rates are about to rise. Also known as a Spread window.

Swaption   An Option* to enter into a Swap* at a set rate.

SWIFT   Society for Worldwide Interbank Financial Telecommunications. A network enabling transmission of payment instructions world wide. Not a method of under-taking payment itself, which must be settled across accounts, typically in the lead financial centre of the country of the currency in question. May be interfaced with CHAPS* to allow rapid processing of sterling payment instructions.

Swingline facility   A Facility* designed to allow drawings with same-day availability of funds, typically used when switching from the US domestic markets (where Same day funds* may be obtained) to the Euromarkets* (where Spot* Settlement* is usual for currency payments) as a form of short-term bridging finance, intended to provide Liquidity* of cash flow for the beneficiary. For example used with a US CP*/ECP* programme, so that repayment of a US tranche may be effected by drawing on the swingline, with the swingline repaid from the proceeds of the Euro tranche on spot settlement two days later.

Syndicate   **(i)** In a Securities* issue, the Lead manager*, the Managers*, any other Underwriters* and any Selling group*, which Underwrite* and sell-down the securities. The syndicate for a securities issue is "broken" on completion of placement in the Primary market*.

   (ii) In a Syndicated loan*, the Lead manager*, the Managers* and the Participants* that advance funds and/or give Commitments* to advance funds in the future to the borrower.

Syndicated loan   A loan made available by more than one lender to a borrower or borrowers. Cf. Bilateral loan.

Syndication   The process of forming a Syndicate* for a Securities* issue or Syndicated loan*.

Synthetic   A Securitisation* or CDO* transaction that is backed by a Credit default swap* referencing a portfolio of assets, rather than ownership of those assets. For example, a Synthetic CDO*.

Synthetic CDO   A CDO* structured in a Synthetic* form, backed by a Credit default swap* rather than a pool of cash assets. Cf. Cash flow CDO and Market value CDO.

Synthetic security   A Security* (sense (i)) composed of a package of an underlying security and a Derivative* (often an Asset swap* or a Credit default swap*). See Repackaging.

T + 3, T + 5, etc.   Alternative name for a 3-day, 5-day, etc. Rolling settlement* system.

Table A   Standardised pro forma Articles of association* intended for use when establishing a company. The "1948 Table A" (originally appended to the Companies Act 1948) differs in structure and content from the "1985 Table A" (originally appended to the Companies Act 1985*).

TAC   See Targeted amortisation class.

Tacking   The ability to make a Further advance* under a secured loan and to be able to retain for the further advance the benefit of the Priority* of the Security* (sense (ii)) granted when the initial advance was first made, rather than being postponed behind any intervening secured creditor to the extent of the further advance. Under s. 94 Law of Property Act 1925, tacking is permitted where:

(a) An agreement to that effect is reached with the intervening creditor;
(b) The original lender had no notice of the intervening security when the further advance was made; or

(c) The original lender is under an obligation to make the further advance by the terms of the original security (whether or not notice of the intervening security has been given).

By s. 30 of the Land Registration Act 1925, a different regime applies to registered land; here, priority may only be maintained until the original lender receives (or ought to have received) notice from the registrar of the intervening security, unless there is an obligation on the original lender to make the further advance and the obligation is actually noted on the register.

Takeover   The buy-out by one company or group of the Issued share capital* of another company or group. In the UK, this may be subjected to scrutiny by the Competition Commission* or the European Commission. If the consideration is in the form of shares in the Predator* the effect may be similar to a merger. See also Takeover Code.

Takeover Code   The City Code on Takeovers and Mergers. Also known as the City Code* or Blue Book*. Contains a voluntary code on action surrounding Mergers* and Takeovers*, which is interpreted by the Takeover Panel*, and, despite being voluntary, is backed by the potential sanction of general condemnation by the market. The Takeover Code requires that merger and takeover discussions are kept confidential until such time as a public bid is put forward, to prevent excessive speculation and the potential for misleading investors. From the date on which a public bid is made (specifying the level of control that the bidder wishes to acquire), the bidder (or Predator*) has 28 days to post a public offer document (the date the offer document is posted being day T). The directors of the Target* company must respond to the offer document by T + 14. The offer can complete at any point between T + 21 and T + 60. The last offer amendment may be made by the bidder at T + 46 and the last defence at T + 39. If the bid lapses due to insufficient acceptance as against the level set by the bidder in the offer document, no further bid can be made by the bidder for 12 months. In addition to the normal rule under ss. 198–200 of the Companies Act 1985 that acquisition of more than 3% of the shares in a listed company and certain other public companies (and each subsequent 1% increase or decrease in shareholding) must be notified to the company, there are rules that acquisitions of stakes of 10% or more in a listed company from more than one person during a 7-day period that take the total stake to 15% or more are not permitted, and that any person acquiring 30% of more of a company is required to make a mandatory offer for a simple majority (more than 50%) of the shares in the company. Bids that are against the public interest may be referred by the Office of Fair Trading to the Secretary of State for Trade and Industry, who may further refer the bid to the Competition Commission*.

Takeover Directive   Proposed EU* Directive* that was to have been introduced in the EU by 2005, but was blocked by Germany in July 2001 due to concerns over the scope given to foreign predators.

Takeover Panel   The Panel on Takeovers and Mergers. See Takeover Code.

Talisman   Prior to 1996, LSE* Settlement* system that operated via receipts of share certificates and stock transfer forms at the LSE from sellers (via brokers for private investors, or directly under the INS* system) and bulk transfers of stock into SEPON*, with subsequent transfers out to buyers and certificates issued to buyers. Talisman was replaced by CREST* gradually from July 1996 and ceased operation in April 1997.

Talon   Part of a definitive Bond* or FRN* that the holder presents to receive a further batch of Coupons* (sense (ii)) relating to future interest payments on the instrument.

Tangible net worth   See Net asset value.

Tap issue   A debt or equity issue where the issuer has the ability to issue further securities if demand is sufficient or further financing is required.

Target   A company under threat of Takeover* by a Predator*.

TARGET   Trans-European Automated Real-time Gross settlement Express Transfer system. EU linkage of national RTGS* systems to create a Europe-wide gross settlement system.

Targeted amortisation class   Or TAC. A Tranche* of an ABS* securities issue that is intended to amortise at or slower than a planned schedule, by passing prepayments in excess of a certain level to a Companion* tranche, in order to provide a more certain investment profile. Similar to a PAC*, but there is no diversion of amortisation from the companion tranche if prepayments fall below a minimum level, potentially giving a TAC a longer average life than a PAC.

Tau   See Vega.

Tax sparing credit   Where a tax incentive is given in a developing country to encourage foreign investment, a tax-sparing credit may be allowed by the foreign investor's domestic tax authorities on repatriation of profits earned from the investment, so as not to negate the effect of the incentive. The profit repatriated is treated as having already been taxed by virtue of the tax-sparing credit.

Tax year   In the UK, 6 April in one year to the following 5 April.

T-Bill   See Treasury bill, sense (ii).

TCGA   Taxation of Chargeable Gains Act 1992 (UK statute).

TechMARK   The London Stock Exchange* market for companies with a market cap of at least £50m that are seeking to raise at least £20m in a Flotation*. The main market requirement for a 3-year trading history does not apply.

Ted spread   The spread between Treasuries* and LIBOR* rates.

TEFRA   Tax Equity and Fiscal Responsibility Act 1982 (US statute). TEFRA was introduced in the US to counteract tax evasion by US taxpayers on untraceable holdings of Bearer securities*. Securities with a maturity of 1 year or less (or 183 days or less if US-issued) are exempt from the TEFRA provisions. They require that only Registered securities* are issued, ownership in which can be traced by the IRS*. Any issue of bearer securities world wide will be subject to adverse US tax consequences for any issuer or purchaser of the securities who becomes subject to US taxation provisions. These adverse consequences are that purchasers of bearer securities in the Primary market* are required to register them or they will be unable to claim a loss deduction on the securities, while any gain will be taxed as income. Secondary market* purchasers are similarly treated, unless the securities are registered or held through specific financial institutions within a recognised Clearing system*. Issuers are liable to a 1% excise tax on the outstanding principal amount of the securities from year to year, cannot deduct interest payments on the securities against federal income tax and cannot claim the "portfolio interest" exemption for the purposes of US withholding tax. Issuers will be exempt from punitive tax consequences if:

(a) The arrangements in place are reasonably designed to ensure that the securities will only be sold or resold to persons who are not US persons (or to certain financial institutions who are US persons). This requirement is considered met if the issue and resale of the securities falls within one of the TEFRA safe harbours (see TEFRA C and TEFRA D) up to the point at which the securities become Seasoned securities*;
(b) Interest on the securities is payable only outside the US and its possessions; and
(c) The securities and their coupons bear the TEFRA legend* wording.

TEFRA C One of the safe harbours under the TEFRA* provisions. An issue of Bearer securities* will fall within TEFRA C if it "is issued only outside the United States and its possessions by an issuer that does not significantly engage in interstate commerce with respect to the issuance of such obligation either directly or through its agent, an underwriter, or a member of the selling group". Although there is no requirement to hold securities in global form as with the more complex TEFRA D* requirements, most issuers regard TEFRA C as being too uncertain and vaguely defined to safely rely on. In particular, it is unclear at what point interstate commerce becomes significant within the meaning of the safe harbour language. Where one of the underwriters is a US entity it is usually considered unsafe to rely on the TEFRA C safe harbour.

TEFRA D One of the safe harbours under the TEFRA* provisions. TEFRA D requires that:

(a) Neither the issuer nor any distributor shall "offer or sell the obligation during the restricted period to a person who is within the United States or its possessions or to a United States person". This restriction will be considered to have been met with regard to any distributor if the distributor covenants that "it will not offer or sell the obligation during the restricted period to a person who is within the United States or its possessions or to a United States person" and during the restricted period the distributor has in place "procedures which are reasonably designed to ensure that its employees or agents directly engaged in selling the obligation are aware that the obligation cannot be offered or sold during the restricted period to a person who is within the United States or its possessions or is a United States person".
(b) Neither the issuer or any distributor delivers the obligation in definitive form within the US or its possessions during the restricted period. To prevent the risk of this occurring, the issue is typically "locked-up" in the form of a Global note*. If an issue is intended to remain in global form as a Permanent global note*, it may be considered to be a single definitive, for which reason issues of bearer securities intended to remain in global form are typically made in the form of a Temporary

global note*, which is exchanged for a permanent global note at the end of the restricted period.

(c) On "the earlier of the date of the first actual payment of interest by the issuer on the obligation or the date delivered by the issuer of the obligation in definitive form" a certificate is provided by each holder of the obligation stating that it is not a US person.

For the purposes of TEFRA D the restricted period is the period from whichever is the earlier of the closing date or the first date on which the securities are offered, to the date 40 days after the closing date. Any subsequent offer or sale by the issuer or a distributor of an original unsold allotment or subscription will also be considered to be made during the restricted period.

TEFRA legend   The wording required to be printed on Bearer securities* and their coupons to meet TEFRA* requirements, that: "Any United States person (as defined in the United States Internal Revenue Code) who holds this obligation will be subject to limitations under the United States Income Tax Laws, including the limitations provided in Sections 165(j) and 1287(a) of the United States Internal Revenue Code."

Temporary global note   A Global note* that is intended to be exchanged for a Permanent global note* or for definitives after the end of the Regulation S* Category 3 restricted period or the TEFRA D* restricted period.

Tender panel   A group of banks that bid competitively for Euronotes* issued by a borrower under the terms of a Facility agreement* such as a NIF*.

Term loan   A loan for a set term. Repayment is instalment (see Amortisation), Bullet* or Balloon*.

Term out   In relation to a Liquidity facility*, a provision enabling the beneficiary of the facility to request an Advance* under the facility with a term equal to the tenor of the underlying transaction that the liquidity facility supports, in the event that the facility provider refuses to renew the facility at the end of its 364-day commitment period.

Texas hedge   A transaction that is not in fact a Hedge*, but is rather cumulative to the Risk* on another Position*.

Theta   Descriptive of the decay of the Time value* of an Option* over time.

Thin capitalisation   A situation where a company has very little Equity capital* relative to its Loan capital* and hence very high Gearing*. This can lead to accounting Consolidation* (sense (ii)) issues in the US under FAS 140* and FIN 46* (previously, under the Substantive equity* rules).

A high gearing may also lead tax authorities to take the view that a degree of indebtedness has been incurred that would not have been sanctioned in normal Arm's-length* financing. Consequently, the excessive gearing is viewed as an attempt to use debt rather than equity to strip profit out of a company, in order to maintain an advantageous tax position (through the tax deductions permitted on interest payments on loans, rather than being obliged to make payments, such as Dividends* or other Distributions*, out of post-tax profits). In such a case, tax authorities in many countries around the world will "reclassify" interest payments on any loans in excess of an arm's-length level as equity distributions, and tax them accordingly. See, for example, s. 209(2)(da), s. 209(8A)–(F) and s. 808A, ICTA*.

In the UK, interest payments made by any company (regardless of its gearing) that are based on an excessive interest rate (that is, exceeding an arm's-length rate) may also be reclassified as distributions, in relation to the portion of each payment which relates to the "surplus" portion of the interest rate over an arm's-length rate (see s. 209(2)(d) ICTA).

Third-party beneficiary   See Privity.

Third-party security   Security* (sense (ii)) granted in favour of a creditor by a third person in respect of liabilities of a debtor to that creditor. The creditor can only claim against the third party to the extent of the value of the assets charged, unless the security also contains a covenant by the third party to pay the full amount owed by the debtor (in which case, the third party is personally liable for the full debt over and above the value of the assets charged) (affirmed by the court in the case of *Fairmile Portfolio Management Ltd v. Davies Arnold Cooper (1998)*).

Threshold interest margin   Or TIM*. In a Securitisation* (usually a mortgage securitisation), a minimum floor set for the rate that the Originator* charges on its remaining variable rate mortgage portfolio, as this rate will continue to affect securitised variable rate mortgages unless and until the right of the originator to set the rate for the securitised pool is specifically terminated. The SPV* should not be prejudiced by the fact that, owing to the securitisation, the originator may now have different priorities when setting the mortgage rate that applies across its business. To ensure this, a TIM may be set based on the funding costs and expenses of the SPV, with which the originator will covenant to comply.

Threshold rate   See Threshold interest margin.

Thrifts   US associations, formerly known as savings and loans associations, that originate and service mortgage loans. Following the "earnings crisis" of 1979–1981, when sharp Interest rate* increases exposed the associations (which largely carried variable rate liabilities and fixed rate mortgage assets) to heavy capital losses, many thrifts no longer hold mortgage portfolios on their books but on-sell them in the secondary market to, *inter alia*, Fannie Mae* and Freddie Mac*.

Tick   A single unit of variation in price (e.g. the one hundredth of a unit movement on interest rate Futures* – also known as a Point*).

TIM   See Threshold interest margin.

Time bill   A Bill of exchange* that is not payable on demand, but only on a set future date.

Time value   In relation to an Option*, that part of the value of the option that does not derive from its Intrinsic value*. Time value is dependent on Volatility* (a higher volatility gives a higher time value) and the time to maturity of the option. The Black–Scholes mathematical model developed by Fischer Black and Myron Scholes is often used to calculate time value for European options*. Time value is most significant when the option in just In the money* or just Out of the money*. An option deeply in the money is priced more like a Future* – in other words the price is determined by the price of the underlying Actual* and the Basis* (sense (i)) applicable to the derivative.

TIOP   Taux interbancaire offert à Paris. Also known as PIBOR*.

TLC   See Transferable loan certificate.

TLI   See Transferable loan instrument.

TOGC   Transfer of a business as a going concern for VAT purposes.

Tombstone   A public advertisement of a financing issued after completion of the financing.

Total rate of return swap   Or TRORS. See Total return swap.

Total return swap   A form of Asset swap* used to convert the cash flow from a Security* (or other financial asset) into another cash flow. May be used specifically to refer to an Equity swap* where the equity payor pays over dividends to the equity payee, as well as any appreciation in the value of the equities. Also a form of hybrid off-balance-sheet* (sense (i)) (i.e. unfunded) Credit derivative* (typically under the name Total rate of return swap*), which covers a combination of credit risks and market risks.

Tracing   In the UK, money that has been misappropriated or applied in breach of prior interests may be claimed by tracing at common law or in equity. At common law money can be traced into items acquired with the money. Money cannot, however, be traced at law into a mixed fund, and money received by a bona fide purchaser for value without notice cannot be traced (in such a case, the purchaser acquires good title as money constitutes an exception from the *nemo dat quod non habet* rule). Tracing in equity follows the same principles, save that money may be traced into a mixed fund. In such a case, the party seeking to trace money will be entitled to a proportion of the remaining fund equal to the proportion in which his money was mixed with other funds. This may be disapplied in favour of the rule in Clayton's Case* where the fund is held in a bank current account, and may be disapplied in favour of the party seeking to trace and against a trustee where the trustee has merged trust money with the trustee's own funds (so that the trustee would be deemed to have spent the trustee's own money first). Despite the ability of equity to trace money into a mixed fund, equity cannot trace into an overdrawn account, since the payment of funds into such an account effectively extinguishes the asset without creating any new asset into which tracing can operate. Tracing in equity also requires that there be a fiduciary relationship between the party seeking to trace and the party who has appropriated funds. It appears, however, that this would be inferred in a wide variety of circumstances.

Trade   A transaction.

Trade date   The date of entry into a transaction, for completion on the Settlement date*. Also known as the Dealing date*.

Trademark   An intellectual property right in a particular distinguishing feature of a business (typically its name, but potentially any mark of recognition of that business, such as a sound or a design) that is created by registration (in the UK, with the Trade Mark Registry) and entitles the owner to prevent others using the mark. Registration in the UK is valid for 10 years. Cf. Copyright, Patent, Registered design.

Tradepoint   Screen-based Order driven* equity and stock Exchange* that began operation as a competitor to the LSE* in August 1995.

Trader   A party that deals either for itself or on behalf of a client in buying or selling assets, and does not typically hold the assets for an extended period.

Trading account   The annual period for which a business that is not a company prepares accounts and compiles profits.

Trading certificate   As well as a Certificate of incorporation*, a Public company* requires a trading certificate in order to begin operations. For a Private company* that re-registers as a public company, a certificate of re-registration is given instead.

Trading company   **(i)** For the purpose of the Group* (senses (iv) and (vi)) and Consortium* (senses (i) and (ii)) taxation provisions, under s. 247(9) and s. 413(6) ICTA, a company in which the business consists wholly or mainly of the carrying on of a trade or trades.

   (ii) Status for taxation purposes. Prior to the Finance Act* 1996, a company that was not either a trading company or an Investment company* (sense (ii)) could not deduct interest payments on debt from its taxable income, pursuant to the now repealed s. 338(6) ICTA (see Interest). Trading companies are generally allowed a wider range of deductible expenses than investment companies and are therefore generally preferred when forming an SPV* that will be subject to UK taxation for a Securitisation*. Indications that a company is a trading company include the entering into of repeated transactions, or the Substitution* of securitised assets.

Tranche   A part of a Securities* issue or Facility* that is separable from the remainder by its being on different terms (for example, as to currency, credit rating or interest rate).

Tranche factor   In a Securitisation*, the percentage balance of a particular tranche of securities that is still outstanding as against its original balance outstanding. Normally expressed as a decimal fraction. See also Pool factor.

Transaction at an undervalue   Under s. 238 of the Insolvency Act 1986*, where within 2 years of the commencement of a Winding-up* the company enters into any transaction with a person "for a consideration the value of which, in money or money's worth, is significantly less than the value, in money or money's worth, of the consideration provided by the company" or for no consideration (except where entered into in good faith and for the purpose of carrying on the company's business and reasonable grounds existed to believe that the transaction would be beneficial to the company). The company must have been insolvent at the time of the transaction, or have become insolvent as a result of it, except where the transaction was entered into with a person connected to the company (as defined at s. 249 of the Insolvency Act 1986).

Transactions defrauding creditors   Under ss. 423-425 of the Insolvency Act 1986*, any transaction with a person "for a consideration the value of which, in money or money's worth, is significantly less than the value, in money or money's worth, of the consideration provided", undertaken at any point in time, the purpose of which was to place assets beyond the reach of any creditor. Such a transaction may be unwound by court order at the request of a Liquidator*, a Trustee in bankruptcy*, an Administrator* or the prejudiced creditor.

Transfer   Generic term of wide and imprecise scope, covering an Assignment*, a Declaration of trust*, a Negotiation*, a Novation* and potentially any other means of passing title in property from one person to another, depending on the context. For example, a transfer by mere delivery of a Negotiable instrument* payable to order does not effect a full negotiation but does transfer the rights and title that the transferor had to the instrument (under s. 31(4) Bills of Exchange Act 1882).

Transfer certificate   A document effecting a Novation* of a transferor lender's rights and obligations under Syndicated loan* to a third party transferee. The form of certificate is signed solely by the transferor and transferee, but is founded on a clause in the Facility agreement*, whereby the borrower gives its consent in advance to any such transfer, and agrees that such a transfer will be effective to transfer both rights and obligations of the transferor. The certificate is prepared by the transferor and delivered to the Agent*. Cf. Transferable loan certificate.

Transfer pricing   **(i)** Within the UK, the substitution by the tax authorities (in computing profits for corporation tax purposes), of an Arm's-length* market value for the transaction price paid by a payor to a payee in the accounts of the payee (where the price was lower than market value), or in the accounts of the payor (where the price was higher than market value), in cases where one party is controlled (see Control, sense (ii)) by the other. The Inland Revenue proposed new rules in October 1997 through the adoption of "arm's-length provisions" generally, rather than simply an "arm's length price".

(ii) Internationally, the widely accepted concept that related parties, such as a branch and head office or subsidiary and parent company, should be deemed for tax purposes to have entered into transactions between themselves at prices that would be paid by unrelated parties (i.e. an Arm's-length* price), in order to tax profits in the state in which they arise or are earned. Relevant in particular to "management" or "administrative" expenses agreements, which may be used to repatriate profits. Fair and accurate pricing policies for transactions may be disputed at length, leading some corporates to enter into an Advanced pricing agreement* with a tax authority to achieve certainty of tax treatment. Overseas administrative headquarters may also have pricing levels fixed in advance as they are typically taxed on a Cost-plus* basis by many tax authorities eager to compete for the employment potential of such headquarters. Cf. Unitary tax.

Transfer risk   The Risk* that exchange controls or other restrictions prevent an entity from obtaining or delivering a particular currency.

Transferable credit   A Documentary credit*, the benefit of which is transferable to a third party, in whole or in part. Under the terms of the Uniform Customs* Article 48(g), they are only transferable once, in relation to each division of the credit, unless the credit specifically states otherwise. As well as being designated as transferable, the express specific consent of the transferor bank is needed for a transfer, which the bank is not obliged to give simply by virtue of having designated the credit transferable. A separate consent is still required. A transfer of a credit enables the transferee to receive payment through presenting the necessary documents. Article 49 of the Uniform Customs provides that a beneficiary may assign (see Assignment) a letter of credit whether or not it is transferable. This will, however, only operate to assign the right in the proceeds; not the right to present documents for payment.

Transferable loan certificate   A document effecting an Assignment* of an assignor lender's rights in a particular advance or advances made under a Syndicated loan* to a third-party assignee. Consent to such an assignment will be given by the borrower in advance in a clause in the Facility agreement*. The certificate is prepared by the transferor and delivered to the Agent*. Cf. Transfer certificate.

Transferable loan instrument   A debt instrument that may be issued by the borrower on the transfer of a loan by way of Transferable loan certificate* and replaces the loan that is transferred. Historically used instead of a Transferable loan certificate* (which does not use conversion to a debt instrument) in the UK to circumvent stamp duty provisions.

Transmission of shares   A change in ownership of shares, on the bankruptcy or death of a Member*, which occurs by operation of law.

Treasuries   See Treasury bill, sense (ii).

Treasury bill   (i) UK Government-backed Bill of exchange* issued by the UK Debt Management Office* on behalf of the Government in maturity bands up to 91 days.
   (ii) US Government-backed bill issued by the US Treasury at a Discount* (sense (i)) in maturities of 3 months, 6 months or 1 year.

Triple net   In the US, a lease where the tenant is obliged to pay for taxes and insurance as well as maintenance costs on the property.

TRORS   See Total rate of return swap.

True control   In relation to a Securitisation*, used to refer to a structure where True sale* is achieved without an actual sale of assets but instead, a transfer of control over the securitised assets or business to a third party (e.g. a trustee) through a security interest, trust or other device (e.g. a secured loan). The intention is to ensure that the securitisation noteholders can control the manner and timing of enforcement proceedings, and can obtain the benefit of the securitised assets in priority to other creditors.

True sale   In relation to a Securitisation* transaction, the term "true sale" is used to describe a sale of the Receivables* being securitised in a manner that ensures their isolation from the bankruptcy or insolvency of the Originator*. Under English law a sale may be by way of Assignment* (legal or equitable), by Declaration of trust* or by way of Novation*. Alternative mechanisms to a true sale that may be encountered under English law are Subrogation* of rights against the receivables debtors, Sub-participation* of rights against the debtors, or a Limited recourse* loan with Security* (sense (ii)) over the receivables (see True control). In addition, it may be necessary to transfer vehicles or other assets connected to the receivables, which may require the use of Bills of sale* or other means. Most jurisdictions have an equivalent to all or some of these methods.

Where a true sale is used, advice will be sought from legal counsel that, given certain assumptions, there is no circumstance in which a liquidator or creditor of the originator could seek to unwind the transaction and claim that the receivables are available to the general creditors of the originator, leaving the purchaser (the SPV*) to sue for return of the purchase price in the insolvency of the originator. For the alternative mechanisms to true sale, a similar analysis will need to be performed to ensure that an insolvency of the originator would not prejudice the SPV or prevent the SPV from enforcing its rights. The proviso to this is that if, as is the case with a sub-participation, the mechanism used is not one that seeks to remove the Credit risk* of the originator from the transaction, the originator's insolvency is less relevant; in such a case, the Credit rating* of the transaction will in any event be capped at the rating of the originator (unless the risk is Wrapped* by a party with a higher credit rating).

The first aspect of the analysis is the risk that the true sale or alternative mechanism used could be considered to be a Transaction at an undervalue*, a Preference*, a Transaction defrauding creditors* or could in some other way be unwound on insolvency of the originator (see various areas of possible relevance under Insolvency Act 1986). In the UK, on the basis of assumptions that the originator is acting in good faith for the purpose of carrying on its business and believes the transaction to be beneficial to it, that it is not influenced by a desire to prefer the SPV, that the purpose of the transaction was not to put assets beyond the reach of any creditor, and that the originator was not insolvent at the time of the transfer and did not become insolvent as a result of the transfer, this risk can generally be removed or limited in an acceptable fashion. Similar assumptions may remove this risk in other jurisdictions.

The second aspect of the analysis is the risk in a true sale that the sale could be recharacterised (see Recharacterisation) as a secured loan or mere contractual right of some description, such that the purchase price paid to the originator is deemed to be a loan advance, with security for the repayment of the loan given over the receivables. If this characterisation is upheld, the so-called security may be void for lack of registration or failure to comply with other requirements for security interests in the relevant jurisdictions, leaving the SPV with an unsecured claim on the originator. In the US, a protective filing is usually made under Article 9 of the UCC* with regard to the possibility of the transfer being a security interest. In the UK and certain other jurisdictions it has, however, been considered that this would act to prejudice the argument that the transfer is actually a sale rather than a secured loan, as only security interests are registrable in this way. See also Undivided interest. Where an alternative mechanism is used, such as an intentional loan with security, registrations will actually be carried out. For alternative mechanisms however, the question arises as to whether the enforcement of the security or of other claims against the receivables or the originator may be delayed or prevented by moratorium, Administration* or automatic stay proceedings (which would not affect a true sale as the receivables no longer form part of the originator's assets).

The third aspect of the analysis is whether or not there exists any risk of Substantive consolidation* of the SPV and the originator, such that the assets of the SPV could become available to creditors of the originator in the insolvency of the originator. Although important in the US, the risk of substantive consolidation is minimal in the UK (see Lifting the veil) and many other jurisdictions, and chiefly a function of fraud.

In the US, one of the main factors in determining whether a transaction is a true sale is the degree of recourse (other than recourse for breach of warranty) that is available against the originator to support losses on the receivables, such as Overcollateralisation*, provision of a Reserve fund* or the purchase of Subordinated notes*. Support in excess of the level of losses that has arisen in the past may lead to recharacterisation of the transaction as a secured loan. To avoid this, a two-tiered structure may be used, with a first transfer to a Bankruptcy remote* SPV (which has previously been equity capitalised to the extent of the credit support required for the transaction) at face value to achieve a true sale, and a second transfer on to the Trust* or other issuing entity in return for part cash payment and part subordinated notes or Trust certificates*.

Trust   A fiduciary relationship between three groups of persons – the settlor or settlors, the trustee or trustees and the beneficiary or beneficiaries – under which the settlor settles certain property on trust for the trustees to hold and administer on behalf of the beneficiaries, with the trustees holding (typically) legal or head equitable title to the trust property and the beneficiaries enjoying equitable interests in the trust property. Under English law, trusts must comply with the three Certainties* and the Rule against perpetuities* to be valid, and may be either Interest in possession trusts* or Discretionary trusts*. See also Accumulation, Accumulating trust, Accumulation and maintenance settlement, Bare trust and Charitable trust.

Trusts have often been used as the issuer in US Securitisation* structures, as Trust certificates* representing proprietary interests in the trust assets have been regarded as equity rather than debt for the purpose of the now redundant Substantive equity* doctrine, enabling the Originator* to avoid Consolidation* (sense (ii)) of the issuer onto its accounting balance sheet. In addition, trusts may enjoy Fiscal transparency* and avoid corporate taxation. Non-US transactions may also use a US trust due to the preference of, or requirement for, certain US investors to invest in securities from a US transaction. See also Master trust, FASIT, Grantor trust, Owner trust, REIT, REMIC.

In the UK, trusts may be used in Undivided interest* structures, where the value of the interests of different parties in a pool of assets is otherwise variable (see FLAP), or where periodic further issuance is intended (see Master trust). Where the trust is a Bare trust*, it may benefit from Fiscal transparency*. However, the trustee of the trust may be subjected to income tax under s. 59 ICTA (see Withholding tax). Problems may also arise in the UK with the use of a trust, due to the potential for such structures to be classified as Collective investment schemes* that would lead to limitations on the scope of offerings of securities issued by the trust and taxation of the trust on its profits (although, depending on expense deductibility, this may have little practical impact). The refusal of the Inland Revenue to allow the beneficial interest in a residential mortgage falling under the MIRAS* scheme to be split also historically hindered residential mortgage securitisation through a trust.

The use of a Declaration of trust* as a method of transferring receivables has become more popular in the UK since the 1998 Don King case (see under Assignment), and master trusts have been used for residential mortgage securitisation in the UK following the abolition of MIRAS* from 6 April 2000.

Trust certificate   A certificate evidencing the entitlement of a beneficiary of a Trust*.

Trust deed   The Deed* that constitutes the term of a Trust*. In a Securities* issue, it sets out the duties of a Trustee* for the holders of the securities and details the rights of the trustee over the trust property (i.e. the promise to pay given by the issuer and any Security* (sense (ii)) for the issue). Cf. Trust indenture.

Trust indenture   The US equivalent of a Trust deed*. Under the terms of the Trust Indenture Act of 1939, generally obligatory for public debt securities issues that are SEC* registered.

Trustee   A fiduciary who holds property settled on the terms of a Trust*, for the beneficiaries of the trust. In the UK, trustees are not themselves liable to income or corporation tax on trust receipts (save to the extent of their own interest under the trust) under s. 8(2) ICTA. Statutory powers of trustees are set out in the Trustee Act 1925, the Trustee Investment Act 1961 and the Trustee Act 2000 (which came into force on 1 February 2001, and introduces a statutory duty of care on trustees when exercising specific powers – although the duty can be contracted out of). For delegation of trustee powers, see under Power of attorney.
   In a Bond*, FRN* or other Securities* issue, a trustee will act as representative of the holders of the securities for the purposes of enforcement of security, agreeing amendments to documentation and monitoring the issuer. Cf. Fiscal agent.

Trustee in bankruptcy   In relation to the Bankruptcy* of an individual, a person appointed by creditors or the court to get in, realise and distribute the bankrupt's estate.

TVA   Taxe à la valeur ajoutée. French name for value-added tax.

UCC   See Uniform Commercial Code.

UCITS   Undertaking for collective investment in transferable securities. European form of Unit trust*. Unit trusts that are approved as a UCITS may be marketed throughout Europe.

UCP 500   See Uniform Customs.

UK Debt Management Office   The UK regulatory authority with regard to the issuance of Gilts* and the regulation of the gilts market.

UKLA   See UK Listing Autority.

UK Listing Authority   Or UKLA*. From 1 May 2000, authority for listing passed from the LSE* to the FSA* (referred to as the UK Listing Authority or UKLA when acting in this capacity), which publishes Listing Rules.

Ultra vires   **(i)** An act that a company is prohibited from undertaking by law, or is beyond the power of a company as set out in its Objects clause*.
   (ii) An action of the Board of directors* that exceeds their powers is sometimes incorrectly referred to as ultra vires. In fact, provided that the company itself has the power to perform the action, it is more technically an act of agents in excess of the authority delegated to them by their principal.

Unable to pay its debts See s. 123 of the Insolvency Act 1986. A fundamental concept in UK insolvency legislation, proof that a company is "unable to pay its debts" forms a successful grounding for a Liquidation petition* and constitutes part of the necessary grounding for an Administration order*. A company is unable to pay its debts if:

(a) A creditor to whom the company is indebted in excess of £750 serves a written demand for payment and is not paid within 3 weeks thereafter;
(b) A judgement order against the company is returned unsatisfied;
(c) It is proved that the company is unable to pay its debts as they fall due; or
(d) It is proved that the value of the company's liabilities (including its contingent and prospective liabilities) exceeds the value of its assets.

For individuals, proof that the individual is "unable to pay his debts" (using a definition at s. 268 of the Insolvency Act 1986, which is broadly similar to (a) and (b) above) is grounding for a petition for Bankruptcy*.

Unallocated shelf registration See Universal shelf registration.

Uncommitted facility A Facility* under which the lender is not obliged to advance an amount to the borrower on receipt of a Drawing* request. Once a drawing is requested and made, the cash advanced is committed, unless the facility is an Overdraft* or otherwise repayable On demand*. Cf. Committed facility*.

Undertaking For accounting purposes under s. 259 Companies Act 1985*, an undertaking is a Company*, a Partnership* or an Unincorporated association*. See Subsidiary undertaking and Parent undertaking.

Undervalue See Transaction at an undervalue.

Underwrite See Underwriting.

Underwriter (i) An entity that Underwrites* issues of Securities*. Usually the same as the Managers*, although extra institutions may also act as underwriters. In a securities issue, underwriters' liabilities are joint and several under an English law Subscription agreement* (and may thus extend beyond the amount of their Commitment*), or several under a New York law Underwriting agreement*.

(ii) An institution that Underwrites* a Syndicated loan*, and whose liabilities to take up funding or an undrawn Commitment* are several, and are thus limited to the original stated pre-Syndication* commitment.

Underwriting (i) In a Securities* issue, the undertaking by the Underwriters* to purchase any unsold securities in the issue (or, in the UK, agree to Subscribe* all the securities and take the risk of being unable to on-sell them) when they are issued, which serves to ensure that the financing will realise its full proceeds for the benefit of the issuer.

(ii) In a Syndicated loan*, the agreement, prior to Syndication* of the facility, of the Lead manager* and/or Managers* with the borrower to provide a certain level of funding and/or undrawn Commitment* for the facility, in order to ensure that the borrower will still have funding available, should insufficient Participants* be found.

Underwriting agreement   A New York law form of Subscription agreement* (which operates via true underwriting, rather than subscription and on-sale), with several liabilities for Underwriters*.

Underwriting fee   See Management fee.

Underwritten   See Underwriting.

Undistributable reserves   Company balance sheet reserves that indicate the amount of the equity investment in a company (including its Issued share capital*) and do not constitute Distributable reserves*. Assets cannot usually be distributed (see Distribution, sense (i)) from a company in a way that would reduce its assets below the value of its undistributable reserves, or while its assets remain below such level, pursuant to requirements as to Maintenance of capital*.

Undivided interest   In relation to a Securitisation* transaction, an undivided interest consists of a share, often fluctuating, of a pool of Receivables*, which share is not allocated by reference to a particular divided part of the receivables (e.g. an interest in principal collections as opposed to interest collections or VAT collections).

Under English law, an attempt by an Originator* to achieve a True sale* of an undivided interest in receivables is at risk of being regarded as a mere contractual right against the originator. In the case of *Re London Wine Company (Shippers) Ltd. (1975)*, it was held that sales of unascertained goods from a pool of goods did not operate to transfer any interest in the goods to the purchaser, either by way of equitable Assignment* or by constitution of a Trust*, due to lack of appropriation or identification of the goods in which a proprietary interest was to pass (cf. Certainties). By way of contrast, it was further held that the seller "could by appropriate words, declare himself to be a trustee of a specified proportion of [the whole pool of goods] and thus create an equitable tenancy in common between himself and the named beneficiary, so that a proprietary interest would arise in the beneficiary in an undivided share of the [pool of goods]". This distinguishes between the sale of a number of unallocated items from a pool (on the one hand) and a sale of an unallocated and undivided percentage of a pool with an express declaration of trust (on the other hand). Most English law securitisation structures attempting to fund through an undivided interest mechanism protect against the risk that no proprietary interest is transferred by a true sale of the entire interest in the receivables, with the receivables sold into a Trust* (constituted by an express Declaration of trust* over the whole of the pool), whereby the originator and investors are entitled to trust interests matching their respective shares. For example, in credit card securitisations, it is common to divide the trust assets into originator and investor shares ranking equally with each other and determined by use of a Floating allocation percentage*.

More recently, in the case of *Re Goldcorp Exchange Ltd [1994] 2 All ER 806* the Privy Council confirmed *London Wine*, when it held that it "would not be right to impose a remedial constructive trust or a restitutionary proprietary interest" in favour of purchasers of unallocated shares of a stock of bullion. In the case of *Hunter v. Moss [1994] 3 All ER 215 CA*, however, the Court of Appeal held that a person can "declare himself trustee of [a specified number of] shares in [a specific company] ... and that is effective to give a beneficial proprietary interest to the beneficiary under the trust". *London Wine* was distinguished as it dealt with passing of property in chattels rather than a declaration of trust. Academics have disputed the correctness of *Hunter v. Moss*, but the judgement in *Re Harvard Securities Ltd [1997] 2 BCLC 369* followed it in determining that an equitable assignment of an unappropriated interest in shares was effective to pass a proprietary interest to the purchaser. *London Wine* was distinguished, as it related to chattels rather than shares.

This doctrine was further developed in the Hong Kong SAR by the first instance decision in the case of *CA Pacific Securities Ltd* in December 1998. The court determined that client securities held by broker CA Pacific in a fungible CCASS* account pooled with its own securities were acquired by CA Pacific as agent for its clients as principals, and that consequently the clients did have proprietary interests in the securities despite the fungible nature of the CCASS account. This was decided on the basis of a construction of the terms of the client agreement. Furthermore, the clients had specific interests in certain of the securities in the account (rather than interests in an undivided portion of the account as tenants in common), as the client agreement clearly envisaged separate client interests rather than an interest in a changing pool with other clients. Appropriation of particular securities to a particular client was held to be unnecessary due to the nature of the securities themselves where, unlike tangible goods, the securities are fungible and segregation therefore serves no purpose. Exactly how to trace a particular interest through the pool was left undetermined.

Under New York law, a sale of an undivided interest in goods is considered valid to transfer a proprietary interest under the provisions of s. 2-105(4) of Article 2 of the Uniform Commercial Code* (see also reference to Article 8* of the Uniform Commercial Code).

Unfair Contract Terms Act 1977 UK statute that regulates, *inter alia*, the use of contractual clauses purporting to exclude liability of one party to the other for breach of contract or negligence. Where one party deals as consumer, no exclusion of liability for breach of contract inserted by the other party will be upheld unless it is "reasonable" (based on, *inter alia*, the bargaining strength of the parties and any inducement given to the consumer to agree to the exclusion term). In any contract, no exclusion of liability for negligence resulting in death or personal injury will be upheld, and exclusions of liability for negligence resulting in other loss or damage will only be upheld to the extent that they are "reasonable".

Unfair prejudice Under s. 459 of the Companies Act 1985*, any member of a company may petition the court for relief on the grounds that the company's affairs are being conducted in a manner "unfairly prejudicial" to the members or some part of the members, or that any act or omission of the company would be so prejudicial. The court is empowered to make such order for relief as it shall think fit. Typically resorted to by Minority shareholders* who lack control over the company's affairs.

Unfair Terms in Consumer Contracts Regulations 1999 UK regulations that came into force on 1 October 1999 (replacing the Unfair Terms in Consumer Contracts Regulations 1994) and were used to implement a Directive* of the EU. The Regulations apply to contracts for goods or services entered into between a business and an individual consumer, which are on a standard form or the terms of which are drafted in advance, and over the substance of which the consumer has no influence. In such a contract, any term that is "unfair" (i.e. based on the bargaining strength of the parties and any inducement given to the consumer to agree to the term, is "contrary to the requirement of good faith, ... causes a significant imbalance in the parties' rights and obligations arising under the contract, to the detriment of the consumer") will not bind the consumer. Terms that are not written in "plain, intelligible language" may be considered "unfair".

Unfunded risk participation   See Sub-participation.

Uniform Commercial Code   Or UCC*. US statutory code governing commercial law, which applies in the terms enacted in each state of the US. The UCC covers, *inter alia*, the treatment of commercial paper, letters of credit, Securities*, the sale of goods, and sales of and Security* (sense (ii)) interests over Receivables* and Chattel paper*.

The UCC provides at s. 9-103(3)(b) that the relevant law for determining the perfection requirements for sales of, and security interests in, receivables is that of the jurisdiction of location of the debtor, and provides for a filing system for perfection where perfection in the US is required. Section 9 of the UCC was revised in mid-2001, with a widening of the old definition of receivables from "accounts or chattel paper" to "accounts, chattel paper, payment intangibles or promissory notes". The revised s. 9 limits the requirement for UCC filing just to the state of organisation (rather than the potential requirement for filing in several states), and widens applicability of filing to all assets, but introduces a question-mark over competing rights of priority for a particular asset. Under s. 9-318(4) of Article 9 of the UCC, contractual prohibitions on assignment of an account are ineffective to prohibit an assignment. For "chattel paper", s. 2-210(3) of Article 2 only provides a limited protection as prohibitions will only be ineffective "unless the circumstances indicate the contrary".

Provision is made under Article 8 for a simplification of the classification and perfection of ownership and security interests in securities held through a Clearing system* or Custodian*, where the owner's entitlement is reflected by a book entry. The ownership interest of the owner is classified under Article 8 as a bundle of rights (known as a "securities entitlement") which includes rights against the custodian and (under s. 8-503(b)) a pro rata proprietary interest in the pool held by the custodian of which his account is part. Under s. 8-503(a) the securities do not form part of the custodian's insolvency estate. The custodian is obliged to take due care to obtain payment from the underlying issuer of the securities under s. 8-505(a). Under s. 9-103(d) of Article 9, the relevant law to determine the steps required for perfection of a security interest over an owner's securities entitlement is that of the law of the custodian's jurisdiction.

Uniform Customs   The International Chamber of Commerce* Uniform Customs and Practice for Documentary Credits rules (latest edition the "UCP 500" effective 1 January 1994). Normally apply to Documentary credits*. May also apply to Standby letters of credit*.

Unincorporated association   An entity that has not undergone Incorporation* and does not enjoy separate Corporate personality*. For example, a Partnership*, a Society*, a Trust*, a Joint stock company, a Deed of settlement company and a Letters patent company.

Unit trust   A Trust* fund designed as a collective investment vehicle for, in particular, small investors. Investors purchase "units", and are entitled to a portion of income and capital gains realised by the unit trust, in accordance with the provisions of the establishing Trust deed*. A "management company" undertakes the trust's day-to-day administration and operation and a "depositary" or "trustee company" holds the trust's assets and distributes proceeds of units. Units can be sold or repurchased by the management company, allowing the amount of funds under management to vary over time so that the trust is an "open-ended fund", in contrast to an Investment trust*. Equivalent forms of the UK unit trust are the UCITS* in Europe and the SICAV* in France. A UK unit trust that is approved as a UCITS may be marketed throughout Europe. See also OEIC.

Unitary tax   Taxation of foreign-owned companies or overseas branches of foreign companies in a state on an apportionment of the world-wide income of the group to which they belong, rather than by attempting to tax profits actually earned or arising in the state in question. Used in some states as an alternative to the much more widely-accepted Transfer pricing* method, using the Arm's-length* principle.

Universal bank   A Bank* that combines the functions of a Commercial bank* and an Investment bank*. See also Glass–Steagall Act and Gramm–Leach–Bliley Act.

Universal shelf registration   Also known as Unallocated shelf registration. A Rule 415* SEC* Shelf registration* under which a company can register, without needing to specify in advance whether it will issue shares, bonds or some other form of security. Since April 1994 available to those foreign (non-US) issuers who are eligible to register securities on Form F-3* (previously only available to US issuers). Cf. Debt shelf registration and Equity shelf registration.

Unlimited company   A variety of Registered company* that does not have the benefit of Limited liability* for its Members*.

Unlisted   With reference to an issue of Securities*, means that the securities are not Listed*.

Unlisted Securities Market   Until 1996, the second quoted market of the London Stock Exchange*, for securities of smaller companies not able or willing to undertake the procedure to list on the main market. Closed in 1996, when companies were required to gain a listing or use the AIM* if they intended their shares to continue to be quoted in some way.

Unsolicited rating   A Credit rating* that is given by a Credit rating agency* with regard to an entity, without having been requested by such entity, and is consequently based solely on public information (company accounts, etc.) relating to such entity.

Up-and-in option   See Knock-in option.

Up-and-out option   See Knock-out option.

USM   See Unlisted Securities Market.

Usufruct   The right to enjoy the fruits of an asset (e.g. income from the asset).

Utilisation   The making of a Drawdown* or request for an Advance* under a Facility*.

Value-added tax   See VAT.

Value at risk   Or VAR. The value at risk on an instrument, Position* or Portfolio* reflects the maximum amount that could be lost on such instrument, position or portfolio: (a) over a certain holding period; (b) at a certain confidence interval; and (c) based on a data set extracted over a certain period. Historically used to reflect loss due to market price movements (the value at risk due to Market risk*), but more recently used to reflect potential loss due to worsening credit standing of the instrument obligor or counterparty (the value at risk due to Credit risk*). In each case, models are based on trends in the value of the instrument in question, and are usually created:

(a) By a historic mapping of prices and marking different percentiles;
(b) By a standard deviation model on historical data (a covariance, Volatility* or parametric model);
(c) By a Monte Carlo simulation*; or
(d) By a Stress test* of current market conditions.

Problems cited with each of these approaches are that: (a) is time-consuming, (b) assumes a log-normal distribution without significant skew (i.e. tilt of the distribution to one side or the other) or kurtosis (i.e. the thickness of the distribution tails – thin tails are platykurtic, fat tails are leptokurtic), (c) is complex and time-consuming to calculate and (d) is arbitrary in nature. See also CreditRisk+, CreditMetrics and RiskMetrics.

Value date   The date on which value is considered to be transferred from one party to another for the purpose of calculation of interest on amounts held by the parties, regardless of whether or not the amounts represent cleared funds that may actually be withdrawn on such date. Cf. Settlement date.

VAR   See Value at risk.

VAR derivative   A Derivative* instrument whose pricing and structure is based on a transfer of VAR* from one party to another.

Variable funding note   Or VFN*. A Security* issued in undrawn form, where the issuer may subsequently request drawdown from the investor. If amounts are repaid on the security, they may subsequently be redrawn. Akin to a revolving facility in the form of a note that is transferable (provided that it may only be transferred to entities with a high enough credit rating, in order to ensure that the issuer will be able to drawdown successfully on request). Used mainly in Whole business* transactions for UK water companies, in order to provide a form of Liquidity facility*.

Variable pay term note   Or VPTN*. A note used to permit the issuance of bullet securities off the back of a pool of amortising collateral, in a similar manner to a PAC* and Companion* structure. A VPTN is issued to match the issuance of a bullet security. Amortisation payments are fully absorbed by the VPTN with the intention that the VPTN has paid down fully by the bullet maturity date. At this point a new VPTN is issued and the proceeds are used to redeem the bullet security. If the VPTN has not paid down fully by such point, the new VPTN is issued in addition to the residual outstanding under the old VPTN.

Variation margin   The amount of the Margin* (sense (ii)) deposited by a Futures* or exchange-traded Options* trader to cover fluctuations in the value of the future or certain exchange-traded options on a daily basis, calculated by a Mark to market* and being equal in amount to the fluctuation in the value of the future aggregated with any requirement to pay-down further Premium* (sense (iii)) tranches. Cf. Initial margin and Maintenance margin.

VAT   Value-added tax. EU tax introduced in the UK on 1 April 1973 on "taxable supplies" (i.e. "supplies" that are not "exempt supplies") of goods or services in the UK (or on importation into the UK) made by a taxable person (a person who is required to be registered under VATA*) in the course or furtherance of a business, as a percentage of the price of the supply. Some supplies, although still taxable, bear VAT at a reduced rate (e.g., supplies charged at 0% are zero rated). Some supplies, such as a sale of Receivables*, are exempt from VAT. Prices are deemed to be inclusive of VAT unless stated to be exclusive of VAT.

Each taxable person may recover a proportion of the VAT paid by them on supplies received (input tax) equal to the proportion of supplies made by them that are taxable supplies (including zero rated supplies, but excluding exempt supplies). Recovery is initially made against the VAT received by them on such taxable supplies (output tax) on production of valid VAT invoices that support the claim for recovery. The net surplus (or deficit) must be paid to (or will be received from) the collection authorities (Customs and Excise in the UK) within 1 month of the end of the Accounting period* (sense (ii)) to which the amount relates. See also Group treatment.

VAT group   See Group, sense (iii).

VATA   Value-added Tax Act 1994.

Vega   Or Tau or Kappa. The degree of movement in the Volatility* of an Option* for each unit movement in the price of the underlying asset.

Vested   An interest under a trust becomes vested when the size or amount of the interest can be determined with certainty (at the point at which the trustees exercise their discretion in allocation of an interest to trust assets and/or the claim to the interest is no longer contingent upon any event). The entire interest under a trust in both income and capital must vest before the end of the perpetuity period (see Rule against perpetuities) in order for the trust to be valid.

VFN   See Variable funding note.

Volatility   A measurement of the degree to which the value of an asset fluctuates over time. Commonly used in the valuation of Options*, where the figure used for volatility is the expected annualised standard deviation based on historic volatility data and/or market perceptions of likely future volatility. See also Implied volatility.

Voluntary arrangement   Under ss. 1 and 253 of the Insolvency Act 1986*, a proposal to creditors (also known as a Composition with creditors*) for the satisfaction of a company's or an individual's debts or for a scheme of arrangements of their affairs, and for the appointment of a "nominee" to oversee the implementation of the proposal. Typically undertaken in an attempt to avoid a Liquidation* or Bankruptcy*, and generally involves writing-off or re-scheduling a certain percentage of outstanding debts. One of the five main branches of insolvency-related procedures (for the others, see Liquidation, Administration, Administrative receivership and Receivership).

Vostro account   For a bank, the account of another bank.

VPTN   See Variable pay term note.

WAC   Weighted average coupon over a pool of assets.

WACC   See Weighted average cost of capital.

WAFF   See Weighted average foreclosure frequency.

WAL   See Weighted average life.

WALS   See Weighted average loss severity.

WAM   **(i)** Weighted average maturity over a pool of assets.
  (ii) Weighted average Margin* (sense (i)) over a pool of assets.

Warehouse   A bank "warehouses" a Swap*, loan or securities issue by taking it onto its own books prior to locating an appropriate counterparty or buyer for it. In a swap warehouse, the bank would back-to-back its commitments and receipts under the swap via fixed-rate investments and floating-rate funding (or, as appropriate, the reverse), prior to locating a counterparty for a Back-to-back swap*.

Warm back-up   A Back-up servicer* that receives and reviews data tapes and reports on a Securitisation* transaction periodically, but will need to establish detailed systems prior to stepping into the role of servicer on termination of the appointment of the Originator* as Servicer*. Cf. Hot back-up and Cold back-up.

Warrant   A tradeable right, issued either independently of (a Naked warrant*), or attached to, a Security* (sense (i)) (and typically issued by a company in relation to its own shares), which gives the holder the right to buy or sell an asset denominated in the same currency at a particular "exercise price" payable in cash on exercise at a given time (or over a given "exercise period"). Warrants are issued in return for a Premium* (sense (iii)) payment, akin to that paid on issue of an Option*, resulting in an asset with Leverage* (sense (ii)). See also Covered warrant.

WBS   See Whole business.

Weak link approach   An approach used by Credit rating agencies* in analysing a structured transaction. The rating agencies will examine the Credit rating* of each "link" (or Dependent rating*) in the payment chain (namely of each payment obligation which is necessary to ensure payment to investors, and of each entity holding investor cash flow collections) and will award the transaction a credit rating equal to that of the weakest "link". Consequently any entity undertaking a payment obligation, or holding cash, will need to be a Suitably rated entity*.

Weighted average cost of capital   Or WACC*. The weighted average of the cost of the debt and the cost of the equity of a business, expressed as a percentage.

Weighted average foreclosure frequency   Or WAFF*. A figure used by rating agencies to measure the weighted average level of foreclosures (i.e. enforcements) across a portfolio of receivables.

Weighted average life   Or WAL*. The weighted average of the time from issue to Redemption* of each unit of Principal* of a particular Security* (sense (i)), used to determine the effective tenor of the security and hence its pricing. An important measure for Asset-backed securities (due to the level of Prepayments* on such instruments), calculated on the basis of certain assumptions as to the Constant prepayment rate* for the Receivables*.

Weighted average loss severity   Or WALS*. A figure used by rating agencies to measure the weighted average level of post-enforcement losses on that part of a portfolio of receivables that passes into enforcement proceedings.

Whole business   Or WBS*. A Securitisation* of the general operating cash flow arising from a certain line or area of the business of the originator over the long term. The transaction does not attach to certain contractual payments over time (as is the case with a mortgage or auto loan transaction), and does not operate within a particular contractual framework (such as the customer card agreement for a credit card transaction). It also cannot be defined by means of eligibility criteria (as is the case with future flows receivables), but rather attaches to general cash flow arising from a business. They are secured over the business-generating assets of the company and are generally reserved for companies in strong competitive positions with stable cash flows.

Winding-up   The closing down of the business of a Company* and distribution of its assets first to creditors and then to Members* in accordance with the order of Priorities*. May be instigated voluntarily by the members of the company, although control will pass to creditors if the company proves to be insolvent. Usually effected by Liquidation* where the company is insolvent. Under s. 127 of the Insolvency Act 1986*, any disposition of a company's property after the commencement of its winding-up is void unless the court orders otherwise.

Withholding tax   Withholding tax is a deduction of tax at source by a payor prior to making payment to a payee, collected by assessing the payor for the tax. Grouped here with the main heads of UK withholding are, at (e) and (f) below, examples of UK Income tax* liabilities that may nevertheless operate in a similar way to withholding tax. No withholding tax is charged in the UK on the Discount* (sense (i)) on securities, or on Short interest*. Most payments under interest rate or currency Derivatives* such as Swaps* are specifically exempted from withholding tax under s. 174 Finance Act* 1995 (payments not relieved by the section would be unlikely to be regarded as interest, but might be treated as annual payments). Relief from withholding tax may be available under an applicable Double tax treaty* where the payment is being made out of the UK. Tax is principally due:

(a) Under s. 349(1) ICTA*, on UK source income that is annuities, annual payments or royalties payable from amounts that are not subject to tax (unless paid where the payor reasonably believes that the person beneficially entitled to the payment is a UK resident company, a partnership all of whose partners are UK resident companies, a non-UK resident company that is within the UK corporation tax charge on the payment in question, or a local authority or health services body or charity or one of a number of other bodies that are exempt from UK tax (under s. 349B ICTA, inserted by s. 85 Finance Act 2001 with effect from 1 April 2001 and s. 94 Finance Act 2002 with effect from October 2002)).

(b) Under s. 349(2)(a) and (b) ICTA, on UK source income that is yearly interest of money paid by a company or partnership (unless paid:

- On a loan from a bank (or originally made by a bank and assigned) where the person beneficially entitled to the interest is within the UK corporation tax charge (under s. 349(3)(a));
- On a loan from a building society (but not on loans originally made by a building society and assigned) (under s. 477A(7) ICTA);
- By a bank in the ordinary course of its business (under s. 349(3)(b));
- On a Quoted Eurobond* (under s. 349(4));
- In the ordinary course of his business by a person who is authorised for the purposes of the FSMA* and whose business consists wholly or mainly of dealing in financial instruments as principal (inserted as s. 349(3)(i) ICTA by s. 95 of the Finance Act 2002); or
- Where the payor reasonably believes that the person beneficially entitled to the payment is a UK resident company, a partnership all of whose partners are UK resident companies, a non-UK resident company that is within the UK corporation tax charge on the payment in question, or a local authority or health services body or charity or one of a number of other bodies that are exempt from UK tax (under s. 349B ICTA, inserted by s. 85 Finance Act 2001 with effect from 1 April 2001 and s. 94 Finance Act 2002 with effect from October 2002).

A bank for this purpose means a bank authorised under the FSMA (see Bank) or a European bank authorised as a Credit institution* in its home state in accordance with the reciprocal recognition provisions of Statutory Instrument 1992/3218). Following the introduction of the inter-company exemption from withholding tax under s. 85 Finance Act 2001, the Group income* election under s. 247 ICTA ceases to have effect from the date on which the Act was passed.

(c) Under s. 349(2)(c) ICTA, on UK source income that is yearly interest of money paid overseas (unless paid by a bank in the ordinary course of its business, paid on a Quoted eurobond*, or paid in the ordinary course of his business by a person who is authorised for the purposes of the FSMA* and whose business consists wholly or mainly of dealing in financial instruments as principal (inserted as s. 349(3)(i) ICTA by s. 95 of the Finance Act 2002). A bank for this purpose means a bank authorised under the FSMA (see Bank) or a European bank authorised as a Credit institution* in its home state in accordance with the reciprocal recognition provisions of Statutory Instrument 1992/3218).

(d) Under s. 349(3A) ICTA, on any dividend or interest paid on a security issued by a building society (unless paid on a qualifying certificate of deposit, on a security that is Listed* on a recognised stock exchange (such as the LSE*), or on a Quoted Eurobond*, or where the payor reasonably believes that the person beneficially entitled to the payment is a UK resident company, a partnership all of whose partners are UK resident companies, a non-UK resident company that is within the UK corporation tax charge on the payment in question, or a local authority or health services body or charity or one of a number of other bodies that are exempt from UK tax (under s. 349B ICTA, inserted by s. 85 Finance Act 2001 with effect from 1 April 2001 and s. 94 Finance Act 2002 with effect from October 2002)).

(e) Under s. 21 and s. 59 ICTA, on UK source or non-UK source income within Schedule A* (s. 21) or Schedule D* (s. 59) that a person (e.g. a trustee) receives or is entitled to and which income has not yet been brought into the charge to income tax (e.g. charged under s. 151 Finance Act* 1989 for an Interest in possession trust*, or s. 151 Finance Act 1989 and s. 686 ICTA for a Discretionary trust*), such as the income of a Bare trust* (unless (i) the persons owning the income are within the UK corporation tax charge, in which case they are not liable to UK income tax (s. 6(2), ICTA) and the trustee can resist any assessment to tax, (ii) the income is non-UK source income and the persons owning the income are non-UK residents, in which case no UK income tax liability arises, or (iii) the trustee authorises the payment of the income to be made direct from the payor to the beneficiary and notifies the Revenue accordingly, in which case the trustee is not liable under s. 76 Taxes Management Act 1970).

(f) Under s. 469 ICTA, on UK source or non-UK source income that the trustees of a Collective investment scheme*, which is not an authorised Unit trust*, receive as trust income (unless the trustees are not UK resident).

Until 1 April 2001, withholding tax was also charged under s. 118E ICTA on non-UK source income that was interest paid from an overseas entity to a UK resident via a UK collecting agent (such as a custodian) or a UK paying agent (in each case, unless paid direct to a recognised clearing system such as Euroclear*, Clearstream* or DTC* or in certain other circumstances). Under s. 111 Finance Act 2000, the paying agent and collecting agent rules were abolished with effect from 1 April 2001.

See also Savings Tax Directive.

WKN   Securities identification system used in Germany. The ISIN* system is to be used from April 2003.

Wrap   A Guarantee* or Indemnity* against a certain Risk* or risks. Typically used to refer to the guarantee by a Monoline insurer* of payments to investors in a Securitisation* transaction.

Wrapped   A Risk* or transaction that benefits from a Wrap*, such that the risk will only materialise for the beneficiaries of the wrap if the party providing the wrap defaults.

Write-off   See Charge-off.

Written resolution   A Resolution* of the Members* of a Private company* that is passed by signature of all members on the form of resolution itself under s. 381A Companies Act 1985*, without the need for a General meeting* and a vote on the resolution. A written resolution cannot be used for the removal of a director under s. 303 Companies Act 1985 or for the removal of an auditor under s. 391 Companies Act 1985, pursuant to Schedule 15A, Part I, para 1 Companies Act 1985. Written resolutions should be notified to the company's auditors and will not have effect until the earlier of: (a) the date on which the company's auditors state that they do not consider that the subject matter of the resolution needs to be considered by the company in general meeting; or (b) the date 7 days after notice of the resolution is given to the auditors if no response is received from them.

Wrongful trading   See s. 214 of the Insolvency Act 1986*. Any Director* (sense (i)) of a company in Liquidation* who, before the commencement of the liquidation, knew or ought to have concluded that there was no reasonable prospect that the company would avoid going into liquidation, and thereafter failed to take every step with a view to minimising the potential loss to the company's creditors as he ought to have taken, is liable for wrongful trading and can be ordered by the court to make such contribution (if any) to the company's assets as the court thinks proper. See also Fraudulent trading.

XOL   See Excess-of-loss.

Yankee bond   A Foreign bond* issued in US Dollars.

Year end   The last day of a company's Financial year* (sense (i)).

Year of assessment   See Tax year.

Yellow Book   The old LSE* guide that expanded on Part IV of the Financial Services Act 1986* and on the POS Regs* under the authority of s. 144 (2) Financial Services Act 1986, giving detailed Listing rules*, and giving the guidelines applied by the LSE in their optional pre-vetting of Prospectuses* for Unlisted* or non-London Listed* securities that are the subject of an Offer to the public* (sense (ii)) (used to achieve Mutual recognition* of the prospectus when the securities are intended to be Listed* on a non-London Exchange* in the European Economic Area). From 1 May 2000, authority for listing passed to the FSA* (referred to as the UK Listing Authority or UKLA when acting in this capacity), which published its own UKLA Listing Rules (largely duplicating the content of the Yellow Book).

Yield   A measure of the annual percentage return on an investment arising from the Coupon* (sense (i)) payable on the investment, and/or from any Discount* (sense (i)) or Premium* (sense (i)) that may lead to accrual or loss (respectively) of principal amounts over the life of the investment. Yields on individual securities will adjust to reflect market yields (which will in turn reflect market Interest rates*). Consequently, if market interest rates rise, the price of individual securities will fall (thus increasing their yield when principal accrual is taken into account in line with market interest rates). Current yield* only takes coupon payments into account (or discount to par in the case of Discount yield*) whereas Yield to maturity* also considers principal accrual or loss. An annualised yield figure can be separately calculated in relation to front-end fees payable to a lender (see Margin, sense (i)) and other front-end expenses of a deal.

Yield curve   A representation of the change in Yield* in a particular market from tracking an investment between short term and long term. A normal or positive yield curve slopes up as maturity increases to reflect the traditional view that investors require a greater degree of compensation if they are to lock themselves into a long-term investment, with the gradient gradually flattening over longer maturities to reflect the difficulty of calculating required investor compensation over a longer-term period. A negative or inverse yield curve slopes down as maturity increases. The angle of the slope varies according to Interest rate* expectations. Where interest rates are expected to rise in the medium to long term this will give rise to a steep positive yield curve. Conversely, expectations of falling interest rates will give rise to a flatter yield curve, or, in cases of expectations of a sharp fall, a negative yield curve (as will supply/demand imbalances – an excess of demand over supply at long maturities will lead to an increase in prices of long bonds, and hence a negative yield curve as yields are driven down).

Yield to call   The Yield to maturity* on an investment using its duration until the next Call* (sense (i)) instead of its Maturity* in the calculation.

Yield to life   The Yield to maturity* on an investment using its Average life* instead of its Maturity* in the calculation.

Yield to maturity   A measure of the Yield* on an investment to the point of its Maturity* that results from the Discount* (sense (i)) or Premium* (sense (i)) of the current market price from Face value*, and the Coupon* on the security. Calculated as being the yield which, when used as the Discount rate* (sense (ii)) to calculate the Net present value* of the future cash flows payable on the security, gives a total net present value that is equal to the current market price of the security. Also known as Redemption yield* or, in relation to a financing project, the Internal rate of return*. Calculation of yield to maturity requires a complex formula and a trial and error methodology. A simplified, approximate calculation is:

$$y = [200/(100 + p)] \cdot (r + [(100 - p)/n])$$

where y = the yield to maturity expressed as a percentage
            p = the market price of the security expressed as a percentage of its face value
            r = the coupon per compounding period
            n = the number of compounding periods until maturity.

Z-tranche   A Tranche* of an ABS issue that rolls up and accrues interest payments for an initial lockout period.

Zero coupon   Securities* that do not bear an interest Coupon* (sense (i)).

References

INVESTOR CONCERNS: INVESTOR CREDIT ANALYSIS

- Fitch *Ratings Pre-sale Report for BPV Mortgages S.r.l deal*, 20 November 2001

ASSET CLASSES

ABS: Consumer and Credit cards:

- Standard & Poor's *Auto Loan Criteria*, 1999, p. 24
- Standard & Poor's *Credit Card Criteria*, 1999, p. 12

Collateralised debt obligations:

- Standard & Poor's *Global Cash Flow and Synthetic CDO Criteria*, 21 March 2002
- Moody's *Rating Cash Flow Transactions Backed by Corporate Debt*, 7 April 1995, pp. 2–3
- Moody's *Emerging Market Collateralized Bond Obligations: An Overview*, 25 October 1996, pp. 2–3
- Fitch's *Global Rating Criteria for Collateralised Debt Obligations*, 14 July 2003

Commercial mortgage-backed securities:

- Standard & Poor's *CMBS Property Evaluation Criteria*, 1999, pp. 24 and 65–66
- Standard & Poor's *UK Commercial Real Estate Criteria*, 1997, pp. 8–14

Non-performing loans:

- Fitch *Securitizing Distressed Real Estate*, 9 April 1999, pp. 5–6

Residential mortgage-backed securities:

- Standard & Poor's *CreditWeek*, 29 March 1993, pp. 73–77
- Standard & Poor's *Revised Criteria*, 5 July 2001
- Standard & Poor's *Structured Finance Asia*, 1997, pp. 32–33
- Moody's *Approach to Rating UK Residential Mortgage-Backed Securities*, April 1998, p. 4
- Fitch *UK Mortgage Default Model*, 15 April 1996, pp. 4 and 10

Trade receivables

- Standard & Poor's *Trade Receivable Criteria*, 1999, p. 23
- Moody's *Trade Receivables Update: Concentrating on Dilution – Focus on Capital Goods and Consumer Products Receivables*, 17 January 1996, p. 1

Index

Note: Page references in **bold** refer to definitions of terms.

Index compiled by Annette Musker